PURCHASING & SUPPLY CHAIN MANAGEMENT

Analysis, Strategy, Planning and Practice

*For Ineke, Vivianne and Marijn,
who represent the most lovely and
most skilful negotiators I know . . .*

FIFTH EDITION

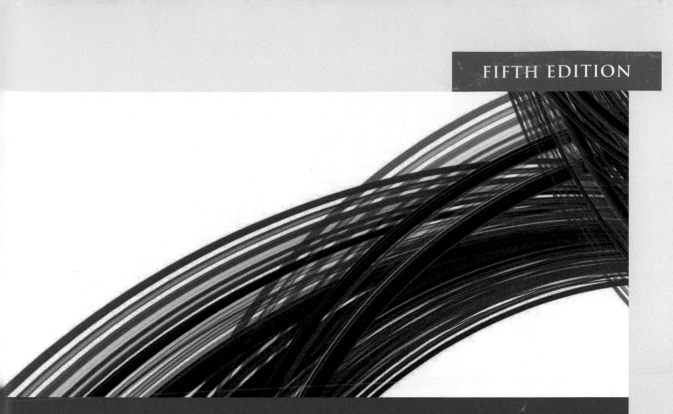

PURCHASING & SUPPLY CHAIN MANAGEMENT

Analysis, Strategy, Planning and Practice

ARJAN J. VAN WEELE Eindhoven University of Technology, The Netherlands

CENGAGE
Learning™

Australia • Brazil • Japan • Korea • Mexico • Singapore • Spain • United Kingdom • United States

CENGAGE
Learning™

Purchasing and Supply Chain Management
5th Edition
Arjan van Weele

Publishing Director: Linden Harris

Publisher: Thomas Rennie

Editorial Assistant: Jennifer Seth

Content Project Editor: Dan Benton and
Oliver Jones

Production Controller: Paul Herbert

Marketing Manager: Amanda Cheung

Typesetter: Macmillan Publishing Solutions

Cover design: Adam Renvoize

Text design: Design Deluxe

For product information and technology assistance,
contact **emea.info@cengage.com**.

For permission to use material from this text or product,
and for permission queries,
email **clsuk.permissions@cengage.com**.

The Author has asserted the right under the Copyright, Designs and
Patents Act 1988 to be identified as Author of this Work.

British Library Cataloguing-in-Publication Data
A catalogue record for this book is available from the British Library.

ISBN: 978-1-4080-1896-5

Cengage Learning EMEA
Cheriton House, North Way, Andover, Hampshire. SP10 5BE.
United Kingdom

Cengage Learning products are represented in Canada by
Nelson Education Ltd.

For your lifelong learning solutions, visit **www.cengage.co.uk**

Purchase your next print book, e-book or e-chapter at
www.ichapters.co.uk

Printed by Seng Lee Press, Singapore
1 2 3 4 5 6 7 8 9 10 – 12 11 10

BRIEF CONTENTS

CONTENTS

SECTION i

CORE CONCEPTS   1

SECTION

iii

IMPLEMENTATION 343

15 PREPARING FOR PARTNERSHIP WITH SUPPLIERS: COST APPROACHES AND TECHNIQUES

16 BUYING AND SUPPLY MANAGEMENT IN RETAIL

17 PURCHASING, CORPORATE SOCIAL RESPONSIBILITY AND ETHICS

LIST OF MEMOS

ACKNOWLEDGEMENTS

Jan Snijder, former Vice President Purchasing and Logistics DAF Trucks, Stork and former President of the Dutch Purchasing Association (NUV)

The publisher would like to thank the following academics for providing feedback that helped inform the new edition changes:

Asa Hagberg-Andersson, HANKEN, Sedish School of Economics and Business Administration

Bryan McNay, The Robert Gordon University

Ronald Salters, Fontys University of Applied Sciences

PREFACE TO THE 5TH EDITION

It is almost impossible to monitor the developments which are going on in most management disciplines nowadays. This is certainly true for the area of purchasing and supply management and was the main reason to review the text of this book.

Over the past few years purchasing and supply management has met an ever increasing interest. Not only from professional purchasing managers: the interest from general managers, financial managers and business consultants is stronger than ever before. Many professionals have become aware that purchasing in general and supplier relationships in particular represent a fantastic area for improvement. Over the past few years, the number of articles on purchasing management topics has increased as has the acceptance of purchasing and supply management as a key area for improving competitive advantage.

The business chain is as strong as its weakest link. One of the important links in the business chain is the purchasing and supply function. Many top managers are becoming increasingly aware of how much money is involved in purchasing decisions. In general, only the money related to the purchase of production materials is considered. However, in practice, large sums are also spent on investment goods, and let us not forget the purchase of all kinds of services. In many industrial companies, external costs make up more than half of the costs of goods sold! In most trading companies this figure is even higher. This implies that purchasing decision-making has a large influence on the company's financial result: one dollar saved in purchasing costs contributes directly to the company's bottom line. However, the reverse is also true. A non-professional, amateur approach to purchasing decisions can readily lead to overlooking cost-savings opportunities, which in the end may lead to a significant financial loss.

In their efforts to arrive at a sustainable competitive advantage, managers increasingly differentiate between core and non-core activities. Companies try to focus on those core activities which provide them with a competitive edge in their end-use markets. Activities which have been defined as non-core are subcontracted to suppliers. As a consequence of this development, the effect of purchasing decisions on the company's financial results is growing in many sectors.

When dealing with suppliers, sub-optimization must be prevented because it is very tempting to make price the central issue in negotiations. Strategic purchasing and supply management is more than just negotiating a deal with suppliers. It is about managing supplier relationships in such a way that suppliers actively support the company's overall business strategy and value proposition. It is about fostering a climate where suppliers are challenged to continuously improve their performance and added value added. It is about integrating suppliers in the company's overall business processes to boost productivity. It is about developing the physical and information infrastructure to enable these new ways of working.

This book aims to introduce the reader to some important principles underlying purchasing and supply management. The ideas are derived from my experience as a management consultant, trainer and academic, obtained from working with a large number of companies in Europe. Regarding its structure and presentation, the underlying idea is that this book should be both balanced, easy to read and easy to teach.

The idea of writing this book dates back a number of years. The success of the original version which appeared in Dutch in 1988, together with the many positive reactions which

I received, convinced me that a translation would be worthwhile. This version, in English, based on the many reactions which I received since the book was published, appeals to a large audience. It is used at many universities and business schools as a leading textbook in many countries. Hence, I decided to make the investment and to review it carefully again. I hope you will find even more value in using it.

Those, who are familiar with the contents of this book, will soon find out that this fifth edition cannot be used next to the fourth edition. Too many topics needed to be rewritten and updated. This is true for Chapter 2, which now discusses organizational buying behaviour, purchasing process management as well as e-procurement solutions. Compared to the previous edition, Chapters 2 and 9 have now been integrated into this chapter. Chapter 3 deals with the purchasing management process and with how procurement develops as a business function over time. Compared with the previous edition, Chapter 3 and 5 have been integrated. Chapter 4 deals with facilities buying and non-product-related buying. Chapter 5 is a totally new chapter on buying of services. Chapter 6 contains a completely revised text on public procurement, providing an update reflecting the most recent changes in European procurement law. Chapter 7 includes a combination of the content of Chapters 4 and 6 of the previous edition, discussing supply markets and market structures as well as how to set up supply market research. Chapters 8 and 9 have been updated, while Chapter 10 represents a totally new chapter on developing category sourcing strategies. The next four chapters have been moderately changed. Chapter 15 has been expanded with a discussion on how to develop collaborative supplier relationships. Chapter 16 on buying for retail companies has been updated. Chapter 17 discusses the highly important topic related to socially responsible purchasing. This chapter represents a totally new text. As a result of the review process, the number of chapters has been reduced from 19 to 17, leading to a more comprehensive and up-to-date text. Throughout, introductory cases have been replaced and updated as has been done with memos and other illustrations.

For those who teach, teaching materials and background reading materials can be found on our websites www.arjanvanweele.com and www.cengage.co.uk/vanweele5.

Writing a book is like choosing from a restaurant menu in that it is often more difficult to decide what **not to** include than what should be included. In this sense the book displays several personal choices and some subjects may not have received (sufficient) attention. In due course we would appreciate to hear from you, the reader, as to whether you agree with the selection we have made.

Realization of this book has been made possible thanks to the enthusiastic support of several people, and its contents have been enriched as a result of their critical and constructive comments. Thanks to the diligence of Tom Rennie, Jennifer Seth, Oliver Jones and Dan Benton of Cengage Learning, this book can be presented to you in its present form. I am grateful to Matthew Driver and Cosmas Georgallis for the meticulous examination of the text, for the many improvements made and for the valuable suggestions concerning the layout and design. A special word of appreciation goes to Mr Jan Snijder, former vice president Purchasing and Supply of DAF Trucks and STORK and former president of NEVI (the Dutch Purchasing Management Association), who has read the text in his meticulous manner and who provided me with so many insightful corrections and additions. It is a privilege to have known him over such a long period, both as a dear colleague and as a friend. The author extends his gratitude to Dr Wendy van der Valk for the contents of Chapter 5. Most parts were derived from her PhD dissertation 'Buyer–Seller Interaction Patterns During On Going Service Exchange', Erasmus Research Institute of Management (ERIM), RSM Erasmus University, Rotterdam, 2007 (p. 323). The author acknowledges Hein van der Horst LL.M and Mary Ann Schenk LL.M, MSc of Professional Procurement Services, Counsellors for Public Procurement for having provided the text for this Chapter. Its contents is derived from their book 'Public Procurement' (Dutch text), Sdu Publishers, The Hague, second print 2008.

Moreover, I am grateful to the many practitioners whom I have met over the past years and for whom I was happy to work as a consultant and trainer. Without exception, this work gave me the feeling that purchasing and supply management is a challenging area to work in and that it represents a business area of still unknown potential for companies. Many thanks also to my students, who always prove to be a challenging and rewarding audience to work for. I also would like to thank my colleagues at both the Institute for Purchasing and Supply Development at Eindhoven University of Technology for their support, endeavour and superb working environment. Especially, I would like to thank the Dutch Association of Purchasing Management (NEVI) in The Netherlands, who for so many years have consistently supported me in my academic teaching activities and research projects.

Finally, my wife Ineke encouraged me to (re)write this book. She knew, as no other, the sacrifices which this personal project, again, would entail for my beloved family. Ineke, Vivianne and Marijn accepted these and gave me constant moral support. It is thanks to them that I found the time and the inspiration necessary to complete this task. It is undoubtedly their book too.

Prof Dr Arjan van Weele
NEVI Chair Purchasing and Supply Management
Eindhoven University of Technology

Maarssen, The Netherlands
September, 2009

GUIDED TOUR

Learning objectives—bullet points at the start of each chapter focus on the main ideas that need to be understood.

Case studies—these appear at the start of each chapter to demonstrate the main concepts of the chapter in a real-world situation. Longer integrative case studies now also appear at the end of each section to help consolidate learning.

Introduction—this outlines the kinds of principles and issues you will meet in the chapter.

Memo—these provide interesting insights into the key issues that are being discussed in terms of a theory/concept or practical example.

SUMMARY

Summary—each chapter ends with a comprehensive summary that provides a thorough recap of the key issues in each chapter, helping you to assess your understanding and revise key content.

ASSIGNMENTS

REFERENCES

Assignments—these are provided at the end of each chapter to check understanding of the themes and issues raised in each chapter.

GLOSSARY

Key terms and glossary—key terms are highlighted and explained in full in the margins as well as at the end of the book.

REFERENCES

Further reading—comprehensive references at the end of each chapter allow you to explore the subject further, and act as a starting point for projects and assignments.

WEBSITE

About the website

Visit the *Purchasing and Supply Chain Management 5e companion* website at **www.cengage.co.uk/vanweele5 or www.cengage.co.uk** to find valuable teaching and learning material including:

For students

- Further reading an literature references to help develop your understanding of each topic in the text
- Web links to all case companies and other relevant sources of information
- Learning objectives for each chapter to support your progress and understanding
- Revision multiple choice questions

An electronic version of this textbook is available for purchase at www.ichapters.co.uk.

For lecturers

- Instructor's manual with teaching notes containing helpful hints and tips for answering questions that appear in the text
- PowerPoint slides of the key ideas and illustrations from the textbook.
- Extra case studies

All of the web material is available in a format that is compatible with virtual learning environments such as Blackboard/WebCT and Moodle. Please contact your Cengage Learning sales representative (http://edu.cengage.co.uk/contactus) should you with to use this in your teaching.

INTRODUCTION

PURCHASING AND SUPPLY MANAGEMENT ON THE MOVE

During the past years, purchasing and supply management as a discipline has changed considerably in many companies. This is reflected in the increased attention this discipline is receiving from business managers and practitioners. Considering the amount of money generally involved in the preparation and execution of purchasing and supply decisions, this is not a surprise. An effectively and efficiently operating purchasing and supply function can make an important contribution to company results. However, there is more. As a result of the implementation of improvement programmes in engineering, manufacturing and logistics management, many companies feel the need for improved relationships with suppliers. These relationships necessarily should result in lead-time reduction in new product development, and just-in-time delivery and zero defects on components. More than that, these relationships should result in a better value proposition to the company's customers. Traditionally, the purchasing department acts as the intermediary which negotiates the agreements and contracts with suppliers and supervises their compliance to the agreements. This traditional role, however, is changing rapidly as can be seen from the purchasing practices in some major, leading edge companies. Moving away from their traditional, operational roles, purchasing and supply managers are assuming more strategic roles in their organizations, focused on getting better performance from suppliers and active management of supplier relationships.

These are a few important reasons why management is becoming increasingly interested in purchasing and supply management as a business discipline.

WHY THIS BOOK?

Compared to other management disciplines, relatively little academic research has been undertaken in the area of purchasing and supply management. This explains why there is quite a gap in the development of a solid body of knowledge compared with other disciplines in business administration. As a result, it is far from simple to disseminate purchasing and supply knowledge across organizations. Most handbooks on purchasing are of American origin and date back to the 1950s. Fortunately, some new textbooks covering modern purchasing practices have become available during the last decade. Most of these, however, have been written from a truly academic background and insufficiently cover the developments which are at present taking place in the purchasing and supply practices of large, international companies. Practical descriptions of purchasing situations, which can serve as a learning vehicle and study material for students, are few. This contrasts with disciplines such as marketing, financing, organizational behaviour and other management disciplines, where many student and practitioner textbooks exist.

It is encouraging that several business schools, polytechnics and academic institutions have decided to include purchasing and supply management in their curriculum. This initiative has no chance of success, however, if there is no effective and up-to-date supportive learning and teaching material. This book aims to meet this need.

INTENDED AUDIENCE

This book is intended for those who are interested in purchasing and supply management in its broadest sense. Its contents aim to provide an in-depth discussion of purchasing and supply issues, both from a strategic and a managerial perspective. Reading this book will neither make you a buyer nor a purchasing manager. In this, the text differs from the more practitioner-oriented literature.

In particular, this book is intended for:

- polytechnic and academic students in business administration and industrial engineering who want to specialize in business strategy, operations management or supply chain management
- professional managers in trade and industry, active in purchasing or supply chain management, who are interested in opportunities for improving the effectiveness and efficiency of the purchasing and supply function in their companies
- executive students, who participate in management development programmes in the area of strategic management, operations management and supply chain management
- account managers and industrial sales representatives who in their professional capacity regularly meet with professional buyers, and who are interested in the way these buyers perform their tasks
- those who supervise purchasing staff directly or indirectly, and who come from a non-purchasing background and are interested in the latest developments in the area of purchasing.

FRAMEWORK

The book has been developed using the following principles:

- Strategic management perspective. In this book the subject of purchasing and supply management is presented as an essential link in the business system. This business system is only as strong as its weakest link. The way purchasing and supply management is executed or should be executed is presented from a strategic management perspective. This implies, for example, that attention is given to subjects such as how company objectives may influence purchasing and supply strategies and policies, how purchasing and supply strategies should support overall business strategy, how to develop these strategies, how to execute them, how to manage the purchasing process and how to monitor and manage purchasing performance.
- Practical orientation. Business administration and industrial engineering are concerned with analysing and solving practical business problems. For this reason, the various subjects are discussed from a practical point of view. This book does not aim to transform the reader into a professional buyer. The intention is to introduce the reader to the

discipline and familiarize them with the key concepts. Literature and theory are provided where we thought it needed to provide a broader perspective.

■ Scientific basis. In discussing the subject matter, repeated reference is made to existing management literature. In this way the individual reader can broaden their orientation if they so desire. When possible, views on purchasing issues are illustrated with research results from national and international specialist literature. Recent literature references have been used, as well as references from a more mature age where we felt these to be still relevant for the subject.

■ Identical structure of each chapter. Every chapter is alike in structure and encompasses:
  o the learning objectives
  o an introductory case to illustrate the practical relevance of the subject
  o an introduction, which provides a survey of the most important subjects which will be discussed in the chapter
  o a body text explaining the core concepts and techniques
  o practical illustrations and memos to emphasize and illustrate certain subjects in a chapter
  o a summary at the end of each chapter
  o assignments for classroom discussion, if desired.

STRUCTURE

The book is divided into three parts, each containing several chapters. The overall structure is presented in the figure overleaf.

Section One: Core Concepts is aimed at getting acquainted with the discipline. The key concepts and terms are presented here.

Chapter 1 focuses on the role and significance of the purchasing function for industrial and service companies. This is done by describing purchasing and supply's role in the company's value chain. Further, definitions of important terms and concepts are provided. In the remainder of the book a clear distinction will be made between the activities of the purchasing department and the purchasing function. The latter term, as we will see, has a broader meaning than the first. An active, business-driven purchasing organization can make a large contribution to innovation and quality improvement. This chapter also discusses the differences between the different kinds of products and services than can be bought. In doing so, this chapter provides a framework for the rest of the book.

Chapter 2 addresses the buying behaviour of organizations. The major differences between buying behaviour of consumers and organizations are discussed. Several stages are presented that can be observed in the decision-making process regarding purchasing and supply activities. These are illustrated by presenting a purchasing process model, in which each of the steps is briefly described. Various models of organizational buying behaviour, developed in the (industrial) marketing literature, are also presented. In this way the reader will gain insight into the complexity which characterizes many purchasing decisions in organizations. A discussion on the role and importance of e-procurement solutions, including e-auctions, completes the chapter.

The core of chapter 3 is the purchasing management process. In order to be effective, management needs to give attention to each element of the purchasing management process. This starts with defining purchasing and supply goals and objectives and strategies

FIGURE 0.1 Overview and book structure

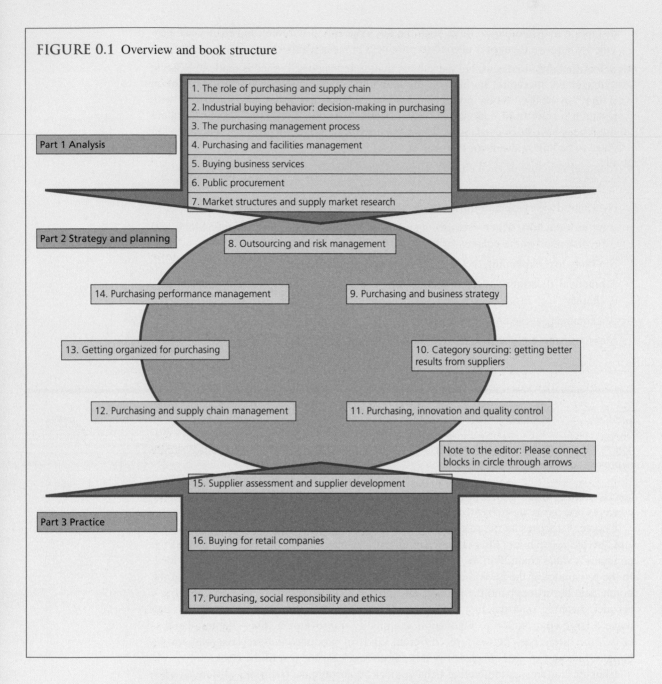

needed to realize these. Purchasing goals and objectives need to be aligned with the company goals and objectives. Purchasing strategies need to be worked out into time-phased action plans. Next, the implementation of these action plans needs to be monitored and followed up. The purchasing development model describes how purchasing and supply as a business function may develop over time. In general, six different stages of development may be identified. In this way the purchasing development model may serve as a vehicle to provide guidance for a company to professionalize procurement in the future.

Chapter 4 describes the role and position of purchasing and supply within service companies. As more companies get a better view on their non-production-related purchasing spend, they become more aware of the cost-savings potential in this area. This chapter focuses on how to professionalize purchasing in a facilities and services environment.

Chapter 5 deals with how to buy and contract for services. It will become clear what specific difficulties may arise when buying services. A classification on how to differentiate between services is provided and the implications for how to structure the purchasing process for services are discussed. Specific attention is given on how to specify for services, how to select service providers and how to contract for their services.

Chapter 6 describes the specific characteristics of public procurement, i.e. buying for governmental institutions. From this chapter it will become clear that large differences exist between buying for the government and buying for private enterprise. Governmental bodies are not free in choosing their purchasing procedures. Therefore, this chapter gives elaborate attention to the most important EC Directives on public procurement, its purchasing procedures and how to work with these.

Chapter 7 deals with the subject of markets and products. We will describe nine types of supply market structures that buyers may encounter. In doing so this part of the chapter sets the stage for our discussion on supply market research and intelligence. How to conduct purchasing market research will become clear in this chapter. Extensive attention is given to how the Internet can be used to generate purchasing market information.

Section Two: Strategy and Planning discusses in detail the elements of the purchasing management process, introduced in Chapter 3.

Purchasing's strategic role is discussed in Chapter 8. Outsourcing and risk assessment are the prime topics of this chapter. Attention is given to the growing trend towards outsourcing. Many companies decide nowadays to focus on what they can do best and those activities that provide them with a competitive edge in their end-user markets. Non-core activities are increasingly outsourced to specialist suppliers. This is, however, not without problems, as companies run the risk of becoming too dependent on their suppliers. This chapter deals with the issue of how outsourcing may be structured in a company, the underlying change processes that are required and how companies can reduce their risk profile *vis-à-vis* their suppliers.

Chapter 9 focuses on how to design effective purchasing strategies. Attention is given to the issue of how purchasing strategies can be linked to the overall business strategy of the company. Building on some strategic marketing concepts, a purchasing portfolio approach is presented on which four basic, differentiated supplier strategies are based. It will be explained, that in order to develop effective purchasing strategies, the company needs to understand its position in the supplier's customer portfolio.

Overall purchasing and supply strategies need to be worked out in specific category sourcing strategies and plans. This is the central topic of chapter 10. Here the question is addressed of how to assess cost-savings potential for different purchased categories and commodities. Key to the sourcing strategy is to select the right number of suppliers, to decide about the right type of relationship and to decide about the right type of contract that should be put in place.

The purchasing function has a complex network of relations in the company because it maintains relationships with nearly all departments within a company. The relationships with new product development, engineering and quality management on the one hand and supply chain management and logistics on the other are described in the next chapters. Chapter 11 presents the possible problems and opportunities in the relationships between purchasing and engineering, and purchasing and quality management. Special attention is given to how to improve supplier quality. Here, supplier quality assurance and supplier certification are presented as approaches which can be used in this respect. The chapter starts with a discussion of the relevance of open innovation for purchasing and supply management.

Chapter 12 describes the role of purchasing within supply chain management. After providing some key definitions, the basics of supply chain management are presented. This is achieved by providing a logistics reference model, which differentiates between several manufacturing situations (ranging from assembly to order to job shop operations). This model explains why purchasing operations within different companies and industries may be vastly different. Next, it covers a detailed discussion on materials requirements planning, just-in-time management and the required information technology.

The subject of how to organize for efficient purchasing is covered in Chapter 13. In practice a large variety of organizational structures is observed and the most important of these are discussed. There is no one best way to organize for purchasing. Specific attention is given to the issue of centralized versus decentralized purchasing in a multi-plant environment. Here different co-ordination structures are discussed through which companies try to capture purchasing synergies. Next, the issue of how to organize for efficient purchasing at the business unit level is presented. Finally, different job profiles in purchasing and supply management are discussed.

Chapter 14 concludes Section Two with a discussion on purchasing performance measurement and evaluation. The central issue here is how to measure and assess the performance of the purchasing department. Several important methods and (benchmarking) techniques are presented. The relevance of the Sarbanes–Oxley act is discussed as a platform for future procurement governance.

Section Three: Implementation deals with some special topics in purchasing and supply and a number of operational purchasing methods and techniques. Specific attention is given to supplier costing techniques, supplier development, buying for retail companies, and purchasing, ethics and sustainability.

All purchasing decisions and decisions concerning supplier selection must be based on sound business analyses. In Chapter 15 some methods and techniques which can be used to support the decisions involved are discussed. Among other things, special attention will be given to the learning curve and cost modelling. Both techniques enable the purchasing professional to get a thorough understanding of supplier costing behaviour. Such understanding is a prerequisite for developing collaborative supplier relationships.

Chapter 16 deals with buying for retail. The most important differences with the industrial purchasing function are discussed. Some modern retail concepts such as efficient consumer response (ECR), collaborative planning, forecasting and replenishment (CPFR), vendor managed inventory (VMI) and radio frequency identification (RFID) and their implications for supplier relationships are dealt with.

Chapter 17 deals with the highly important issue of how purchasing and supply professionals can contribute to sustainability or 'People, Planet, Profit'. This topic is very real today in many large companies. Buyers in Western companies have a great responsibility of buying for a better world. Besides corporate social responsibility, this chapter also deals with purchasing ethics and business integrity. Together, these three concepts create the necessary foundation for every modern purchasing supply organization.

WHAT INSTRUCTORS MATERIAL IS AVAILABLE?

Teachers and instructors, who have selected this book as the major textbook for their coursework, may use the teaching materials that are available to them through www.cengage.co.uk/vanweele5. Teaching materials consist of a teacher's manual, answers for the end of chapter discussion questions, PowerPoint presentations, literature reference lists, case studies and multiple-choice questions. This should enable them to teach their courses both in an attractive and efficient manner.

LIST OF ABBREVIATIONS

ATO: Assembly To Order
BOM: Bill Of Materials
CODP: Customer Order Decoupling Point
CPFR: Collaborative Planning, Forecasting and Replenishment
CSR: Corporate Social Responsibility
DPC: Direct Product Cost
DPP: Direct Product Profitability
ECR: Efficient Consumer Response
EOQ: Economic Order Quantity
ERP: Enterprise Resource Planning
ESI: Early Supplier Involvement
ETO: Engineer To Order (ETO). All manufacturing activities from design to assembly and even purchasing of the required materials are related to a specific customer order.
IPO: International Purchasing Office. Large companies operate IPO's at different parts of the world.
LCC   Low-Cost Country sourcing
MSS: Making and Sending to Stock
MRP I: Materials Requirements Planning
MRP II: Materials Resources Planning
MPS: Master Production Scheduling
MRO: Maintenance, Repair and Operating supplies
MTS: Make (and distribute) To Stock
MTO: Make To Order
NPR: Non-Product Related
OEM: Original Equipment Manufacturer
JIT: Just-In-Time
PR: Product Related
RFI: Request For Information
RFP: Request For Proposal
RFQ: Request for Quotation
ROI: Return on Investment
RONA: Return On Net Assets
SLA: Service Level Agreement
SQA: Supplier Quality Assurance
SRP: Socially Responsible Purchasing
TCO: Total Cost of Ownership
VMI: Vendor Managed Inventory

CORE CONCEPTS

THE ROLE OF PURCHASING IN THE VALUE CHAIN

LEARNING OBJECTIVES

After studying this chapter you should understand the following:

- The role and importance of the purchasing and supply function in the value chain.
- The difference between concepts such as ordering, buying, purchasing, procurement, sourcing, supply chain management and value chain management and how these are interrelated.
- New developments in purchasing and supply practices of organizations.
- The most important elements of the purchasing function.

INTRODUCTION

As business is becoming more and more competitive, **purchasing** and supply chain management are increasingly recognized by top managers as key business drivers. Again and again it appears that purchasing professionals and supply managers can contribute significantly not only to the company's bottom line, but also to its top line. Since most companies today spend more than half of their sales turnover on purchased parts and services, efficient and constructive relationships with suppliers are key to the company's short-term financial position and long-term competitive power.

Many companies cannot escape from exploiting the huge potential that purchasing and supply chain management represents to them today. The following case study on British Airways illustrates how companies can bring this potential to fruition. Given their need to improve their overall operating margin, BA's purchasing staff needed to generate significant cost savings. Several high-level cross-functional teams were set up in the company to deal with this task. Apart from price, these teams looked into possibilities on how to reduce supplier lead times, reduce inventory and increase quality levels. Next, they looked into opportunities to reduce the number of suppliers dramatically to a mere 2000, leading to more business per supplier and hence increasing the value of British Airways as a customer to them. More collaborative relationships needed to be established. Given the huge number of purchasing transactions, purchase orders, delivery documents and invoices, British Airways also put as a target to reduce its transaction costs in its relationship with suppliers.

Purchasing
The management of the company's external resources in such a way that the supply of all goods, services, capabilities and knowledge which are necessary for running, maintaining and managing the company's primary and support activities is secured under the most favourable conditions.

3

CASE STUDY

Suffering from heavy international competition and a growing field of small European and US-based competitors offering no frills service and cheap fares, in October 2001, British Airways decided to review its operations. The company needed to improve its operating margin dramatically to an unprecedented 10%. To get to that margin at its existing revenue rates, it determined that it would have to cut costs by $996 million.

Headcount was targeted for more than two-thirds of the cost cuts and BA unveiled plans to cut 13 000 people or 20% of its staff including members of its purchasing operations. Another area of cost reduction focused on how BA captures customers. Rather than paying high fees to travel agents and other services to book customers on BA flights, the company designed a new pricing strategy to push traffic to a self-service Web model for booking flights.

Cutting costs alone, however, was not enough. 'We realized that rather than just go through a cost-cutting exercise, we needed to fundamentally rethink the business model,' says Jonathan Counsell, head of strategy and performance at BA. Standardized procurement processes were seen as one way to transform BA's newly trimmed procurement staff of 200 to become more strategic in sourcing the airline's $6 billion annual buy, which is largely made up of fuel, user charges, in-flight products such as catering, engineering and airport services. The purchasing operations at BA are centralized; its procurement director reports directly to the CFO.

BA outlined six major goals in its procurement overhaul. First, it wanted to reduce total costs by more than $250 million. Second, it wanted to increase its online ordering to 80% of all materials and services. Next it wanted to reduce procurement **transaction costs** to $15 each. Also, the company's number of

suppliers would be reduced to 2000 and key relationships would be built with existing suppliers.

Benchmarking played an important role in inspiring BA's move to a more process-led organization. BA used several vehicles to talk with other airlines and OEMs about procurement best practices. It used its participation in the One World alliance to share best purchasing practices with other airlines. Nearly two years ago, BA established a strategic procurement forum for blue chip UK-based companies that meets monthly to share these practices.

'We saw a big difference between the best-practice companies and our practices, especially in the absence of consistent processes,' says Gavin Boswell, technology and performance manager at BA. 'We wanted to get people in our organization to agree on the processes because they had too many ways of doing things.'

In order to foster standardization, purchasing process leaders were nominated, who would report to the procurement director and who would be responsible for ensuring BA set up best practice processes.

Currently, there are five process leaders in place to identify and implement best practices in five areas: supplier relationships, strategy and performance, supplier negotiations, transactional procurement and supply chain development.

The overhaul of the procurement department at BA is getting a lot of attention throughout the company from the executive level down and across. So far, apart from significant cost savings, 40% of UK-based purchase orders are online and the supply base has been cut in half to 7000, well on its way to the goal of 2000…

Adapted from 'British Airways flies toward $996 million savings goal', *Purchasing*, 8 August 2002

Transaction costs
Transaction costs are the costs that are associated with an exchange between two parties. The level of the transaction costs depends upon three important factors: the frequency of the transaction, the level of the transaction-specific investments and the external and internal uncertainty.

New solutions, based upon web-enabled information technology, are now available to companies. In order to be able to implement these new systems company wide, British Airways needed to standardize its administrative and procurement processes.

The case study shows the new role that purchasing and supply professionals now play in organizations. First, they have a strategic role to play in terms of analysing the purchasing spend of the company, identify the key and commercial suppliers and, based upon this data, develop differentiated supplier strategies. Next, their activities are tactical in character: based upon the selected supplier strategy, purchasing professionals need to be able to standardise purchasing processes, establish effective information links with their suppliers and strive for continuous improvement of supplier performance. Finally, to fulfil their operational role, these professionals need to secure efficient material **supply** from their suppliers in time, at the right quality and quantity and at the lowest overall cost.

In this chapter, we discuss the role and importance of the purchasing function. We will take Porter's value chain as a point of departure to show that we need to differentiate between direct and indirect purchasing (Porter, 1985). Some time is spent in defining important terms and concepts and we elaborate on the role which purchasing professionals may play in cost reduction, and product and process innovation. The chapter concludes by describing some important trends and developments, which may be perceived in the purchasing strategies of companies who are leading edge in purchasing and supply chain management. In this way, this chapter sets the stage for the remaining chapters in Section One.

Supply
Supply includes at least purchasing, materials management, incoming inspection and receiving. Supply is used when relating to buying based upon total cost of ownership in a manufacturing environment.

THE ROLE OF PURCHASING IN THE VALUE CHAIN

In many business strategies the concept of **value chain management** plays a central role. Therefore this subject is elaborated on in this section. There will be an explanation of what value chain management is. When describing the role and position of the purchasing and supply function in industrial companies, the value chain of Porter (1985) is taken as a term of reference (see Figure 1.1).

The value chain in Figure 1.1 is composed of value activities and a margin, which is achieved by these activities. Value activities can be divided into physically and technically different groups of activities. Porter differentiates between **primary activities** and **support activities**. Primary activities are those which are directed at the physical transformation and handling of the final products, which the company delivers to its customers. As can be seen from Figure 1.1 distribution to the customer and providing services are parts of these primary activities. Support activities enable and support the primary activities. They can be directed at supporting one of the primary activities as well as supporting the whole primary process:

Porter differentiates between five generic categories of primary activities (1985, pp. 39–40):

Value chain management
All stakeholders belonging to the same value chain are challenged to improve the (buying) company's value proposition to its final end customers i.e. consumers.

Primary activities
Primary activities are those activities that are required to offer the company's value proposition to its customers. They consist of inbound logistics, operations, outbound logistics, marketing and sales and customer service activities.

Support activities
Those value activities that are required to support the company's primary activities. These include procurement, technology development, human resources management and facilities management (i.e. those activities aimed at maintaining the firm's infrastructure).

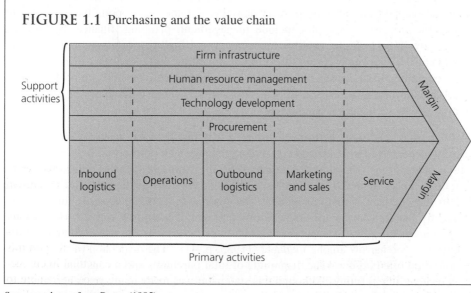

FIGURE 1.1 Purchasing and the value chain

Source: redrawn from Porter (1985)

Services
Relate to a series of more or less tangible activities, that normally take place in the inter-action between cus-tomer and supplier employees, and/or physical resources and systems, that are offered as an integrated solution to customer problems.

Procurement
Procurement includes all activities required in order to get the product from the sup-plier to its final desti-nation. It encompasses the purchasing func-tion, stores, traffic and transportation, incom-ing inspection, and quality control and assurance, allowing companies to make supplier selection decisions based on total cost of ownership (TCO), rather than price. Procurement is used when relating to buying based upon total cost of ownership in a project environment.

Raw materials
Materials which have undergone no transfor-mation or a minimal transformation, and they serve as the basis materials for a pro-duction process.

Facilities management
Relates to the manage-ment (planning, execu-tion and control), and the realization of hous-ing and accommoda-tion, the services related to these, and other means in order to enable the organiza-tion to realize its mission

- Inbound logistics. These activities are related to receiving, storing and disseminating inputs to the production process, such as inbound transportation, incoming inspection, materials handling, warehousing, inventory control, and reverse logistics.

- Operations. Activities associated with transforming inputs into the final product, such as machining, assembly, packaging, equipment maintenance, testing, printing and facil-ity operations.

- Outbound logistics. These are activities associated with collecting, storing, and physi-cally distributing the final product to customers, such as finished goods warehousing, materials handling, outbound transportation, order processing and scheduling.

- Marketing and sales. These activities relate to advertising, promotion, sales, distribution channel selection, the management of channel relations and pricing.

- Services. Activities associated with providing services to customers to enhance or maintain the value of the product, such as installation, repair and maintenance, training, parts supply and product adjustment.

Support activities are grouped into four categories:

- Procurement. Procurement relates to the function of purchasing inputs used in the firm's value chain. These may include **raw materials**, supplies, and other consumable items as well as assets such as machinery, laboratory equipment, office equipment and buildings. These examples illustrate that purchased inputs may be related to primary activities as well as support activities. This is one reason why Porter classifies procure-ment as a support activity and not as a primary activity.

- Technology development. 'Technology' has a very broad meaning in this context, since in Porter's view every activity embodies technology, be it know-how, procedures or technology embodied in process or product design. Most value activities use a technol-ogy that combines a number of different sub-technologies involving different scientific disciplines.

- Human resources management. These are all the activities directed at recruiting, hiring, training, developing and compensation of all types of personnel on the company's pay-roll, active in both primary and support activities.

- Firm infrastructure. The whole company is the customer of these activities. Infrastructure does not support one or more primary activities – rather, it supports the entire set of company processes. Examples include management, planning, finance, accounting, legal, government affairs, quality management and **facilities management**. In larger companies, which often consist of different operating units, one sees these activities divided among headquarters and the operating companies. This division of these tasks between the headquarters and the business units is often the subject of discussion, which is why it changes so frequently.

All activities need to be performed in such a way that the total value generated by the company, as perceived by its customers, is more than the sum of its costs. In Porter's terms, the total value of the company is determined by the whole of its sales value. The value chain, then, relates in fact to all activities, both inside and outside the company, that create value to the company's final customers. The margin reflects the rewards for the risks incurred by the company. Porter regards procurement as a support activity. He uses the term procurement rather than purchasing since, as he argues, the usual connotation of purchasing is too narrow among managers (1985, p. 41). 'The dispersion of the procure-ment function often obscures the magnitude of total purchases and means that many pur-chases receive little scrutiny.' Although this statement was made many years ago, it still is true for many organizations today.

Based on these observations the conclusion is that procurement should provide support to the following business activities:

- Primary activities. The procurement function should be able to meet the material requirements related to inbound and outbound logistics, and, often more importantly, related to operations. Operations may have a different structure among manufacturing companies. Usually manufacturing processes can be characterized according to the following categories.

  o Make (and distribute) to stock (MTS). Standard products are manufactured and stocked, customers are serviced from an end product inventory. Production is on dedicated machinery, often in large batches. Materials requirements planning (and therefore also planning of purchased products) is based on sales forecasts. Examples are steel plate, and most maintenance, repair and operating supplies.

  o **Make to order (MTO)**. Products are manufactured from raw material or the purchased components inventory after a customer order has been received and accepted. This is common in situations with very large or customer-specific product ranges (e.g. packaging materials) or bulk products that are very expensive to stock (e.g. insulation materials).

  o Engineer to order (ETO). All manufacturing activities from design to assembly and even purchasing of the required materials are related to a specific customer order. Production is usually on multipurpose machinery, requiring highly skilled operators, for example large customer-specific equipment and machines and vessels.

  These contrasting manufacturing situations explain why procurement activities may be radically different between companies and industries. Procurement operations for a manufacturer producing cars in large batches, controlled by a materials requirements planning system, may differ largely from those in a job-shop environment, like a shipyard, where every vessel may be new to the organization and where materials are obtained from a vast, frequently changing supplier base. Buying for primary activities will be referred to throughout this book as 'production buying', 'buying of production items' or 'purchasing **direct materials**'. Usually this area gets most of the attention from management.

- Support activities. Procurement activities may also be related to supplying products and services for the other support functions. Some examples are the buying of:

  o laboratory equipment for research and development

  o computer hardware and software for the central computer department

  o lease-cars for the sales force and senior management

  o office equipment for accounting

  o food and beverages for the catering department

  o cleaning materials for housekeeping

  o machinery and infrastructure, etc.

Again we see that the procurement function aimed at providing supplies and services for the support activities may be very different in character. Some of the purchases to be made are routine purchases (maintenance, repair and operating supplies; MRO-supplies) and may be repetitive and low in value. Other purchases may have a 'project character' and may be unique and high valued (**investment goods**, computer systems, **capital equipment**, buildings).

In general this type of purchase will be referred to as 'non production buying', 'purchasing **indirect materials**' or 'general expenses'. They may be classified into: MRO-supplies, investment goods[1] and services. The high variety of this type of purchases makes it extremely difficult to support these by one uniform computer information system or

[1]Also referred to as CAPEX (Capital Expenditure).

Make to order (MTO)
Only raw materials and components are kept in stock. Every customer order is a specific project. Examples are the manufacture of cans and basic construction materials.

Direct materials
All purchased materials and services that become part of the company's value proposition. These include raw materials, semi manufactured goods or half fabricates, components and modules (identical to BOM-materials or production materials).

Investment goods or capital equipment
Products which are not consumed immediately, but whose purchasing value is depreciated during its economic life cycle.

Indirect materials
All purchased materials and services that do not become part of the company's value proposition. May be classified into MRO-supplies, investment goods (also referred to as capital expenditure, or CAPEX) and services (identical to non-BOM-materials or non-production materials).

TABLE 1.1 Main differences between buying for primary activities and buying for support activities

Aspects	Buying for primary activities	Buying for support activities
Product assortment	Limited to large	Very large
Number of suppliers	Limited, transparent	Very large
Purchasing turnover	Very large, considerable	Limited
Number of purchase orders	Considerable	Very large
Average order size	High	Small
Control	Depends on type of production planning	Limited, forecast-related or project-related planning
Decision-making unit	Engineering, manufacturing specialists dominant	Fragmented, varies with product or service.

buying procedure. The character of this type of purchases also explains why professionalism in purchasing is usually low. This is one reason why some international companies, which have set up special programmes in this area (such as IBM, Shell, Lucent, and Philips Electronics), have reported high savings. Table 1.1 summarizes the most important differences between buying for primary and for support activities.

DEFINITION OF CONCEPTS

Purchasing function
Covers activities aimed at determining the purchasing specifications based upon 'fitness for use', selecting the best possible supplier and developing procedures and routines to be able to do so, preparing and conducting negotiations with the supplier in order to establish an agreement and to write up the legal contract, placing the order with the selected supplier or to develop efficient purchase order and handling routines, monitoring and control of the order in order to secure supply (expediting), follow up and evaluation (settling claims, keeping product and supplier files up-to-date, supplier rating and supplier ranking).

The **purchasing function** traditionally encompasses the process of buying. It involves determining the purchasing needs, selecting the supplier, arriving at a proper price, specifying terms and conditions, issuing the contract or order, and following up to ensure proper delivery and payment. In the old days it was argued that the purchasing function should obtain the proper equipment, material, supplies and services of the right quality, in the right quantity, at the right place and time, at the right price and from the right source (Aljian, 1984, p. 3). In this description, the purchasing function is regarded predominantly as an operational activity.

In practice, as well as in the literature, many terms and concepts nowadays are used in the area of purchasing. However, no agreement exists about the definition of these terms. Terms like procurement, purchasing, sourcing, and supply management are used interchangeably.

Throughout this book the definition of *purchasing* is:

'The management of the company's external resources in such a way that the supply of all goods, services, capabilities and knowledge which are necessary for running, maintaining and managing the company's primary and support activities is secured at the most favourable conditions.'

The *purchasing function* in this definition covers specifically activities aimed at:

- determining the purchasing specifications (in terms of required quality and quantities) of the goods and services that need to be bought
- selecting the best possible supplier and developing procedures and routines to be able to do this
- preparing and conducting negotiations with the supplier in order to establish an agreement and to write up the legal contract

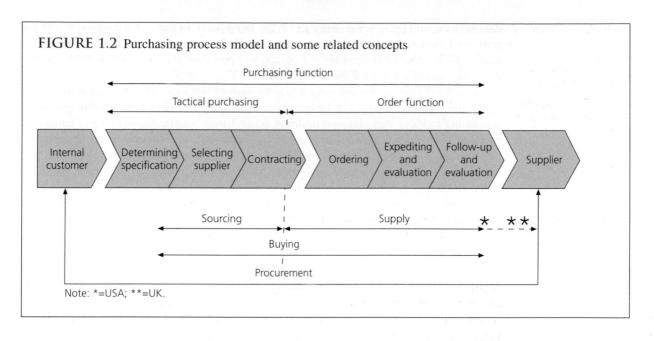

FIGURE 1.2 Purchasing process model and some related concepts

Note: *=USA; **=UK.

- placing the order with the selected supplier or to develop efficient purchase order and handling routines
- monitoring and control of the order to secure supply (**expediting**)
- follow-up and evaluation (settling claims, keeping product and supplier files up-to-date, supplier rating and supplier ranking).

Figure 1.2 schematically illustrates the main activities within the purchasing function. It shows that these activities are closely interrelated. This picture is referred to as the purchasing process model.

The purchasing function does not include the responsibility for materials requirements planning, materials scheduling, inventory management, incoming inspection and **quality** control. However, in order to be effective, purchasing operations should be closely linked and interrelated to these materials activities. In the author's opinion a purchasing manager should support each of the six activities mentioned above. However, this does not necessarily imply that all these activities should be conducted by the purchasing department, as illustrated in the following example.

A buyer who is responsible for maintenance, repair and operating supplies, is often confronted with the 'small-order problem'. Many requisitions which he receives from internal departments concern simple products of low expense. Handling these requisitions, however, is often a laborious task if that buyer is to issue a purchase order for every requisition. An alternative may be to arrange for a so-called 'catalogue' agreement with a specific supplier, for example, for the delivery of hand tools. In this arrangement he may establish the product range, which will be bought from that supplier including the list prices per product. He may agree with the supplier that the latter will provide a web-enabled catalogue to his company, enabling employees and technical staff to order directly from the supplier. Furthermore, he may negotiate a bonus from that supplier tied to the total purchasing turnover for 12 months. Next, he may communicate terms and conditions of this contract to the staff of Technical Services. Through the on-line catalogue employees of this company can order directly from the supplier, without involving the purchasing department. In this example it is the task of the buyer to develop an overall commercial agreement with the supplier and to establish an electronic catalogue and an (electronic) order routine with that supplier on

Expediting
Following up on a purchase order to make sure that the supplier is going to perform as it has confirmed through his purchase order confirmation. There are three types of expediting, i.e. routine status check, advanced status check and field expediting.

Quality
Quality refers to the total of features and characteristics of a product or service that bear on its ability to satisfy a given need (American National Standards Institute). Quality is meeting an (internal or external) customer's requirements that have been formally agreed between a customer and a supplier.

the one hand and the internal customer on the other hand. In fact, what happens is that the ordering function is delegated, in a rather controlled way, to the internal customer. In this manner it is possible to combine the purchasing power of the organization with optimal flexibility and efficiency for the internal user, i.e. Technical Services.

From the definition of purchasing it may be derived that its scope covers all activities for which the company receives an invoice from outside parties. Hence the playing ground of purchasing includes inter-company business, counter-trade arrangements, hiring of temporary personnel from outside agencies and contracting for advertising. However, many of the activities for which the company may receive invoices from suppliers may be arranged without interference from the *purchasing department* (this will be discussed later). Therefore the scope of the *purchasing function* is usually much broader than that of the purchasing department.

The term ordering refers to the placing of purchase orders with a supplier against previously arranged conditions. Furthermore, this term will be used when purchase orders are placed directly with the supplier, without questioning the supplier's conditions and without sufficient supplier market testing. Call-off orders fall into this category as well as telephone orders for products bought from a supplier catalogue. Ordering is considered to be a part of the purchasing process. In fact it relates to the last three steps of the purchasing process. The use of the term 'tactical purchasing' refers to the first three steps.

It is difficult to find a description of *buying* in management literature. It differs from purchasing in the sense that it does not encompass the first step of the purchasing process. This is in line with the practice of trading and retail companies (e.g. department stores), where this term is most often applied. Here, discussions about the specifications of products to be purchased are more limited than for industrial companies, since in many cases the supplier decides these. Buying therefore relates to the commercial activity of soliciting competitive bids from a limited number of suppliers, and negotiating a final contract with the lowest bidder. Several negotiation rounds may be required before closing a final deal.

Purchasing differs from buying and ordering in one important aspect: while specifications may be a given in the situation of ordering and buying, these are challenged when it comes to purchasing. In that case a discussion may start about the degree to which the specifications are really fit for purpose. Features, which are not necessary for meeting the function which the product needs to fulfil, are skipped. This often leads to a situation where an (expensive) supplier branded product is replaced by an identical product from a less known supplier.

As seen from Figure 1.2 *procurement* is a somewhat broader term. It includes all activities required in order to get the product from the supplier to its final destination. It encompasses the purchasing function, stores, traffic and transportation, incoming inspection, and quality control and assurance. Many firms also consider environmental issues (as they are related to materials) as a part of procurement (see also Memo 1.1). This task has become more important in recent years, with the increasing impact of environmental issues. Procurement is based on the **total cost of ownership**. When buying a copier it may be more important to look at the price per copy (based upon all costs associated), rather than the purchase price of the copier itself.

Another term often used in the materials area is *supply*. This is somewhat more difficult to grasp, because it appears that there are differences in connotation between North America and Europe. In America 'supply' covers the stores function of internally consumed items such as office supplies and cleaning materials. However, in the United Kingdom and Europe, the term supply seems to have a broader meaning, which includes at least purchasing, stores and receiving. The governmental sector also uses this broader interpretation. Supply is used when relating to buying based upon total cost of ownership in a manufacturing environment. Procurement is related to buying based upon TCO in a project driven manufacturing environment (like the construction industry, or the ship building industry).

A term which has become increasingly popular in the materials area is ***sourcing***. This activity relates to developing the most appropriate supplier strategy for a certain commodity or product **category**. A **sourcing strategy** describes how many suppliers the company

---

Total cost of ownership (TCO)
Relates to the total costs that the company will incur over the lifetime of the product that is purchased.

Sourcing
Finding, selecting, contracting and managing the best possible source of supply on a worldwide basis.

Category
A group of products which can be substituted for one another by a consumer; examples include cereals, bakery, household products, body care and so on.

Sourcing strategy
Identifies for a certain category from how many suppliers to buy, what type of relationship to pursue, contract duration, type of contract to negotiate for, and whether to source locally, regionally or globally.

favours for that commodity or category, what type of relationship to pursue (arm's length or **partner**ship) and what type of contract to negotiate for (one year to multi-year). It is all about finding the best possible supplier for the company on a worldwide basis.

Purchasing management refers to all activities necessary to manage supplier relationships in such a way that their activities are aligned with the company's overall business strategies and interests. It is focused on structuring and continuously improving purchasing processes within the organization and between the organization and its suppliers. Purchasing management, hence, has an internal aspect and an external aspect. The idea behind purchasing management is that if suppliers are not managed by their customers, customer relationships will be managed by the suppliers. Given the widespread acceptance of marketing management, customer relationship and account management in business, suppliers usually are in a favourable position. Given the cross-functional nature of purchasing management and its wider playing ground it is also referred to in this text as *supplier resource management.*

Purchasing management is related to *supply chain management.* The latter concept can be described as the management of all activities, information, knowledge and financial resources associated with the flow and transformation of goods and services up from the raw materials suppliers, component suppliers and other suppliers in such a way that the expectations of the end users of the company are being met or surpassed. Supply chain management differs from purchasing in that it also encompasses all logistics activities. Moreover it entails the management of relationships not only with first tier suppliers but also with lower tier suppliers. An example is Ford who urges its suppliers of exhaust-systems to use one steel contract. Both Ford and suppliers are buying steel; by combining the contract value all parties involved can benefit from better conditions. *Value chain management*, finally, builds on the former concept. Here the idea is that suppliers are challenged to improve the (buying) company's value proposition to its customers. Usually the suppliers work closely together with the (buying) company's technical and marketing staff to reduce the product's overall costs, add new designs or features to the product which are attractive for the end customer and that make the product sell better. An example here is Microsoft's X-Box, which was originally developed by Microsoft, but which actually is produced by Flextronics. Flextronics is crucial for the success of the X-Box in that it is determining the X-Box's cost price and hence, the consumer price of the product (Carbone, 2002).

Partner
A (supplier) partner is defined as a firm with whom your company has an ongoing buyer–seller relationship, involving a commitment over an extended period, a mutual sharing of information and a sharing of risks and rewards resulting from the relationship.

Purchasing management
Relates to all activities necessary to manage supplier relationships in such a way that their activities are aligned with the company's overall business strategies and interests.

Request for information (RFI)
Suppliers are invited to submit general information that may help them to qualify for a potential tender.

MEMO 1.1   SUPPLIER RELATIONSHIPS AT VOLVO

VOLVO CORE VALUES

Before applying to be a Volvo Supplier you should understand and agree on Volvo's core values expressed as follows:

Quality is our mindset. We provide products and services that can be trusted. In all aspects of our business, from product development and manufacturing to delivery and customer support, the focus is on the customers' needs and expectations.

Safety relates to the use of our products in society. We strive to minimize the risks and consequences of accidents and to improve safety and work conditions for the drivers and vehicle operators.

Environmental Care expresses our commitment to improve energy and resource efficiency and to reduce emissions in all aspects of our business, with a special focus on the use of our products in society.

VOLVO SOURCING PROCESS

Enter the competition to become a Volvo supplier.

Request for information (RFI). The Supplier is invited to answer to a Request For Information collecting general data about his company and its products or services.

▶

Evaluation. Volvo evaluates the RFI answers in order to set up a list of potential candidates to receive request for quotation.

Request for quotation (RFQ). Suppliers are invited to quote on Volvo parts based on a package of specifications and drawings.

Selection. After evaluating the RFQ answers and the supplier's profile (according to Volvo evaluation citeria), Sourcing Committees decide on the Supplier(s) to be awarded.

OUR REQUIREMENTS

Strategy

- Global partners, but supplying locally, including local content markets
- Considering Volvo as a preferred customer when giving access to innovation
- Transparency in terms of cost and strategy.

Development

- Complete system suppliers where it adds value
- Technical skills/innovation skills
- Resident engineers when required.

Relationship

- Long-term relationship
- Pro-active in reducing cost and improving performance (proposing new features).

Quality

- Highest quality standards
- Good management of your lower tier suppliers (low cost countries).

Supplier evaluation. Volvo Group uses the Supplier Evaluation Model (SEM) to evaluate its potential and current suppliers. The SEM is implemented during our selection process.

Environment. Environmental care is a corporate value for the Volvo Group. Already in the mission statement, we state that 'we use our expertise to create transport-related hard and soft products of superior quality, safety and environmental care'. Suppliers should actively contribute to reduce the environmental impact of present and future products. They should be committed to reduce the environmental impact of our manufacturing operations.

(Source: www.volvo.com)

IMPORTANCE OF PURCHASING TO BUSINESS

Request for quotation (RFQ)
Suppliers are invited to submit a detailed bid which meets the requirements as laid down in the request for quotation against the lowest possible price (identical to request for tender).

DuPont analysis
Financial diagnostic tool to calculate the company's return on investment based upon sales margin and capital turnover ratio. Used to assess the effect of a 2% purchasing saving on the company's return on investment (ROI).

An analysis of the cost structure of manufacturing companies immediately shows the importance of purchasing to organizations. In general the largest part of the cost of goods sold (COGS) or sales revenues appears to be taken up by purchased materials and services. Figure 1.3 shows that the average purchasing value in relation to cost of goods sold is approximately 50%. If the other business costs, which have an important purchasing component, are added to the purchasing value, the total amounts to approximately 68%.

Through the DuPont chart (Figure 1.4), the effects of purchasing savings on the company's return on investment can be illustrated. Figure 1.4 shows how a 2% saving on purchasing related expenditure for a company (in this case Heineken) may lead to an improvement of the return on net assets (RONA) of 9%. Of course, the reverse is valid also: due to a lack of a well defined purchasing policy and a lack of structure in the purchasing (decision making) process, the resulting lack of control on purchasing costs may lead to an unforeseen financial loss.

The **DuPont analysis** shows that purchasing contributes to improving the company's RONA in three ways:

- Through reduction of all direct materials costs. This will immediately lead to an improvement of the company's sales margin, which in turn will affect RONA in a positive manner. A number of measures may lead to lower direct materials costs such

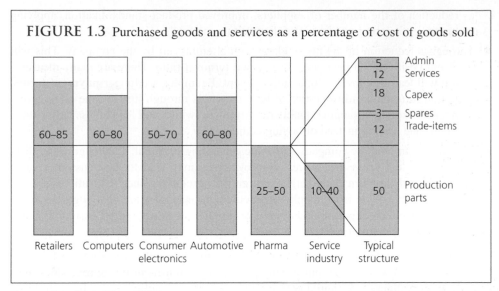

FIGURE 1.3 Purchased goods and services as a percentage of cost of goods sold

Source: adapted from Kluge (1996)

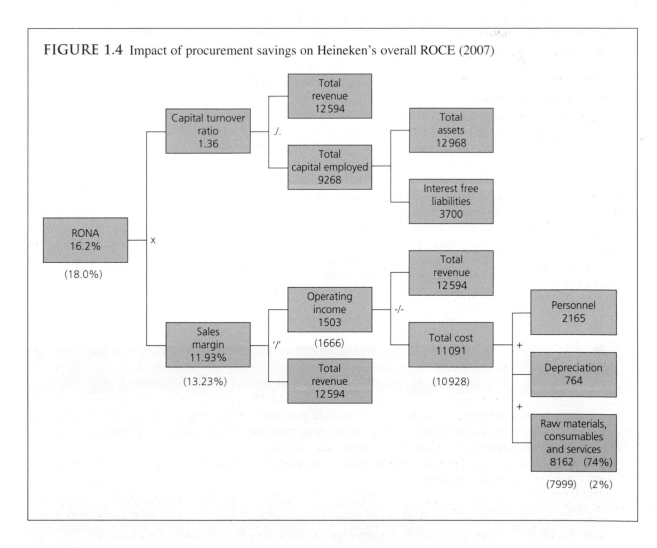

FIGURE 1.4 Impact of procurement savings on Heineken's overall ROCE (2007)

as reduction of the number of suppliers, improved product standardization, applying competitive tendering and looking for substitute materials.

- Through a reduction of the net working capital employed by the company. This will work out positively on the company's capital turnover ratio. There are many measures which will lead to a lower capital employment. Examples are longer **payment terms**, reduction of (pipeline) inventories of base materials through just-in-time (JIT) agreements with suppliers, supplier quality improvement (which will lead to less buffer stock required) and leasing instead of buying equipment.

- Through improving the company's revenue generating potential. Challenging suppliers for new product ideas and process improvements may lead to new customer value propositions that in turn lead to higher margin new products. Since innovations in many industries today come from suppliers, procurement managers are challenged to mobilize their suppliers' expertise and to involve supplier technical experts early in the new product development process.

Payment terms
Payment terms relate to what, how and when the buyer will pay for the products and services delivered by the supplier.

It can be concluded that purchasing policies fundamentally contribute to business success in several ways. First, purchasing policies can significantly improve sales margins through realizing substantial cost savings. A dollar saved in purchasing is a dollar added to the bottom line. Second, through better quality and logistics arrangements with suppliers, purchasing can contribute to a reduction of working capital and, hence, the company's cash position. Third, suppliers may contribute significantly, when addressed properly, to the company's innovation processes. However, as companies become more dependent on their suppliers the strategic value of purchasing lies in developing a world-class supplier base which is more competitive than that of the company's main competitors. Looking for the most competitive suppliers worldwide and developing effective relationships with them should therefore be one of the most important concerns of any purchasing manager. As has been demonstrated, even small improvements in the relationship with suppliers may have a significant impact on the company's return on net assets.

The conclusion we can draw from this discussion is that as the purchasing to sales ratio increases for a specific company, purchasing decisions will have a more profound impact on the company's returns. The same goes for the capital turnover ratio. A higher ratio will lead to a greater leverage of savings on direct materials costs. It is therefore important that companies keep track of their purchasing expenditure. Next, they need to manage their relationships with suppliers in a professional way. In order to do that, detailed management information is required. Obtaining detailed purchasing spend information is in most large companies, however, quite a challenge. Memo 1.2 provides some guidelines on how to proceed.

MEMO 1.2   SPEND MANAGEMENT: THE FOUNDATION FOR EVERY PURCHASING STRATEGY

According to a survey, which was conducted by Purchasing Magazine in the United States in 2004, 71% of large American companies today have developed formal sourcing programs. Of the respondents, 24% reported to have such sourcing programs underway. The most important objectives of sourcing programs are cost-reduction, standardization, and preventing reinvention of the wheel in supplier contract

negotiations, generating supply market knowledge and reducing supplier logistics lead times.

Surprisingly enough, the most difficult part of developing sourcing strategies appears to be the collection of detailed spend management information: in many cases these large companies do not have a clue of what they purchase internationally. Financial and accounting departments simply are not equipped to provide this type of information. Large conglomerates cannot, without significant efforts, assess what they have purchased at a certain supplier, what money they have spent on the acquisition of certain materials and services. In many cases this type of information needs to be obtained through contacting the suppliers . . . A large problem concerns the absence of a corporate-wide, uniform article coding system, which can be used to classify purchasing expenditure.

For this reason spend management has become a prime issue. International consultants and IT providers (like SAP, Oracle, Peoplesoft and I2), today provide specific software applications to chart purchasing expenditure in detail. Usually, the purchasing spend is presented through a so-called 'spend cube' (see Figure 1.5). This spend cube allows us to allocate purchasing expenditure from three different angles, i.e. purchasing segments or categories, suppliers and internal budget holders or departments. In this way the purchasing spend cube is an indispensable tool for developing specific purchasing and supplier strategies.

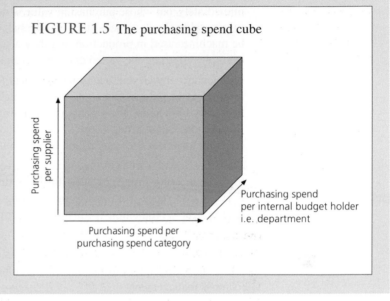

FIGURE 1.5 The purchasing spend cube

CLASSIFICATION OF PURCHASING GOODS

The purchasing process may concern a large variety of goods and, of course, services. In general, purchased materials and services can be grouped into the following categories:

- Raw materials. Raw materials are materials which have undergone no transformation or a minimal transformation, and they serve as the basis materials for a production process. We may differentiate between physical raw materials, such as iron ore, copper ore, coal, and natural raw materials, such as grains, soya and coffee.

- Supplementary materials. These are materials which are not absorbed physically in the end product; they are used or consumed during the production process. Examples of this type of product are lubricating oil, cooling water, polishing materials, welding electrodes and industrial gases.

- Semi-manufactured products. These products have already been processed once or more, and they will be processed further at a later stage. They are physically present in the end product. Examples are steel plate, rolled wire and plastic foils.

- Components. Components are manufactured goods which will not undergo additional physical changes, but which will be incorporated in a system with which there is a functional relationship by joining it with other components. They are built into an end product. Examples are lamp units, batteries, engine parts, electronic parts and transmissions. A distinction can be made between specific, customized components and standard components. Specific, customized components are produced according to design or specification of the customer, whereas standard components are produced according to specification of the supplier or an industry norm.

- Finished products or trade items. These encompass all products which are purchased to be sold, after negligible added value, either together with other finished products or manufactured products. Examples of this product category are accessories which are supplied by car manufacturers, such as navigation systems, car stereo systems and alloy wheels and tyres. The manufacturer does not produce these products, but obtains them from specialized suppliers. Commercial products and articles sold by department stores are also in this category.

- Investment goods or capital equipment. These are the products which are not consumed immediately, but whose purchasing value is depreciated during its economic life cycle. In general the book value is stated on the balance sheet annually. Investment goods can be machines used in production, but they also include computers and buildings. These examples illustrate the varied character of this category of goods.

- Maintenance, repair and operating materials (MRO items). These products, sometimes referred to as indirect materials or consumable items, represent materials, which are necessary for keeping the organization running in general, and for the support activities in particular. These products are often supplied from stock; examples are office supplies, cleaning materials and copy paper, but also maintenance materials and spare parts.

- Services. Services are activities which are executed by third parties (suppliers, contractors, engineering firms), or other business units of the company, on a contract basis. Services can range from providing cleaning services and hiring temporary labour to having a new production facility for a chemical company designed by a specialized engineering firm (a contractor).

Having defined the most important categories of purchased goods and services we now turn to a short description of major new developments going on in the area of purchasing and supply management.

NEW DEVELOPMENTS IN PURCHASING

Many companies are now confronted with diminishing growth opportunities, which results in a situation where an increase in turnover can only be realized at the expense of the competition and only with a great deal of effort. This leads to increased pressure on sales prices and consequently on cost prices and margins, which causes two developments. On the one hand it has resulted in shifts of power between purchasing and selling parties in many markets. Due to the fact that in many cases the market has changed from a seller's-market to a buyer's-market, the role of the buyer is now more dominant than a number of years ago. On the other hand the increasing pressure on sales prices and margins has resulted in an increased pressure on direct materials-related costs. Because the purchasing prices determine the sales prices in the industrial sector to a large extent, the company will be constantly on the lookout for opportunities to keep these prices as low as possible. As a result of both developments, the purchasing and supply strategies of industrial companies have undergone major changes. Several examples of these changes are presented below:

Global sourcing
Proactively integrating and co-ordinating common items and materials, processes, designs, technologies and suppliers across worldwide purchasing, engineering and operating locations.

- Leveraged purchasing and supply strategies. In companies with several manufacturing plants, important purchasing advantages can be realized by combining common purchasing requirements. A trend towards leveraged or co-ordinated purchasing strategies is apparent in many large, European companies, across national borders. Traditionally this was already common for raw materials, which most of the time were contracted at a corporate level. At present, however, a similar approach is used for the purchase of computer hardware and software, capital goods and components.

- Global sourcing. As the companies' competitive position is directly related to the competitiveness of its supply base, companies have adopted a global scope towards sourcing issues. Components are increasingly sourced from foreign, low cost countries, a reason why large manufacturing organisations have set up International Purchasing Offices (IPO's) in different regions of the world. Purchasing professionals, hence, are forced to adopt an international scope towards their supply markets. Supplier benchmarking, being able to deal with different cultures effectively, being able to negotiate in different languages have become prerequisites for today's purchasing professional.

- Supplier integration. Modern information technology enables companies to improve their materials planning and supply systems, internally but also in their relationships with suppliers. Information technology significantly improves productivity within materials activities. An integrated approach of materials management requires close co-operation between production planning, inventory control, quality inspection and purchasing. To achieve successful integration, system standardization is a prerequisite. Next, suppliers should be seamlessly integrated within these applications. Hence, the capability of a supplier to link up to the buyer's manufacturing and planning systems becomes of a much higher concern in order to be able to apply concepts like total quality control, quick response logistics and just in time scheduling successfully (see Memo 1.3 for an example of UPS and Dell).

- Early supplier involvement in new product development. As more and more innovations in industry come from suppliers, getting them involved early in the new product development process becomes an issue of prime concern. In many industries both the rapid development of technology and the cost related to developing new products force large organisations to work more closely with their suppliers. In doing so purchasing professionals need to alter their traditional ways of working and relationships with suppliers. It should be decided at an early stage what part of the development process will be done in house and what part will be delegated to suppliers. Being able to work in cross-functional development teams and a sound technical background also become important prerequisites. Purchasing professionals should be able to solve the issue of how to reward innovative suppliers for their contributions and ideas on new product development. Gain and risk sharing agreements replace the traditional price negotiations and agreements, enabling a more intensive and long-term relationship with these suppliers.

Early supplier involvement (ESI)
Situation where the supplier is involved by the buyer in an early stage of the new product development process.

- Reciprocity agreements. Companies operating on the international markets are often obliged to compensate (part of) their sales turnover by counter-purchase obligations. The opening up of the Eastern European bloc and some Southeast Asian countries has made counter-trade an actual issue. Buying from these countries may even open up interesting sales opportunities. Purchasing becomes increasingly involved in fulfilling such obligations.

- Corporate Social Responsibility and business integrity. Environmental problems in many European countries become more and more prevalent. National governments have become stricter in their regulations on this point. In Germany, for instance, strict regulations on industrial and consumer packaging recently came into force. In due course all superfluous packaging needs to be avoided (e.g. blister packaging and the box-packaging of toothpaste); aluminium cans are charged and need to be recollected. Manufacturers of packaging will increasingly be held responsible for its disposal after use. This is one reason why Volkswagen constructed its latest Golf (the Rabbit in North America) in such a way that the different parts and components can be easily disassembled and reprocessed at the end of the car's lifespan. Volkswagen has even founded its own rework facilities for this purpose. Apart from environmental issues there is a growing pressure from the public that products should be clean, and come from countries with free trade. Child labour has become an issue of particular concern, implying that purchasing professionals should secure that the products that they buy come from sources of high integrity. These issues pose new and important challenges to purchasing.

Corporate social responsibility
How to contribute to a better world, a better environment and better labour conditions. The idea is to develop business solutions in such a way that requirements of the current world population are met without doing harm to the needs of future generations. Companies need to balance the interests of customers, employees, the environment and its shareholders, i.e. serving the needs of 'People, Planet, Profit'.

Memo 1.3 provides an illustration of some of the challenges that lie ahead for purchasing professionals and supply chain managers.

MEMO 1.3   WHAT'S AHEAD?

As supply chain strategies mature, a major part of a business will involve managing the external value supply chain. Important will be the need to manage costs strategically at all levels of the supply chain. Supply managers will find they are doing more business with outside suppliers than inside ones. They will be working much more with Tier 1 and Tier 2 suppliers to take costs out of products. They will require ongoing development, cost reduction, and innovation on a collaborative basis among all participants in the supply chain.

Many supply chain managers will be deeply involved in building e-sourcing and supply portfolios. Many will be forced to make more informed decisions about whether to use industry-sponsored consortia, build private exchanges, or use markets. Many will need sophisticated assortments of e-sourcing, supply, and collaboration tools. They will need to do more in the way of building value-chain models to understand both product and logistics costs as well as technology. They will need to decide where research, development, and design will occur in the value chain.

Supply chain leaders over the next five years will also need to decide the extent to which their companies create unique designs or standardize, and at what levels in the product or service they do these things. Creating entirely unique designs risks creation of production difficulties and/or features that don't mean anything to customers. The ideal will be to standardize – at the right level – and make unique only what is important to the customer. Most companies have a long way to go in making this work on a consistent basis.

Source: R.M. Monczka and J.P. Morgan, *Purchasing*, 6 June, 2002, pp. 26-28

It can be appreciated from this discussion that purchasing and supply represents a business area which is being confronted with many changes and challenges. Most of the problems, however, require intensive interaction, communication and co-operation with other disciplines in the organization. Purchasing and supply is developing increasingly as a business function which cuts across other disciplines. Managing the purchasing and supply function requires a thorough understanding of the purchasing processes that take place within the organization. Only then can these challenges be dealt with effectively.

SUMMARY

Supply chain management
The management of all activities, information, knowledge and financial resources associated with the flow and transformation of goods and services up from the raw materials suppliers, component suppliers and other suppliers in such a way that the expectations of the end users of the company are met or surpassed.

Globalisation of trade, the fast development of information technology and ever increasing consumer demands are changing the international competitive landscape. As a result, companies are changing their business processes. Positioning the company at the right place within the value chain has become a prime concern for top managers. For this reason companies started to rethink their core and non-core activities. With their core activities companies try to develop and offer a distinctive value proposition to their targeted customers. Non-core activities are increasingly outsourced to specialist suppliers. This has put purchasing and supply management in the spotlight. Given the high purchasing to sales turnover ratio which can be observed nowadays in many companies, purchasing and **supply chain management** has developed into one of the key business drivers. Its main purpose is to develop a competitive, world-class supply base for the company. In order to be able to do so companies need to adopt a process orientation rather than a functional orientation towards purchasing issues.

Purchasing encompasses everything for which the company receives an invoice. Based upon this broad scope of purchasing we have differentiated between direct and indirect purchasing. Both are important activity domains within purchasing, though each has a different logic due to their different characteristics. Traditionally direct purchasing has received the most attention. However, this picture is rapidly changing.

Although developed some years ago, Porter's **Value Chain** is still a useful concept for explaining the role which the purchasing function has for many companies. Contrary to Porter's opinion, we have stressed the strategic importance of purchasing to organizations. We have explained our view by using the DuPont model. This enables the purchasing manager to demonstrate the sensitivity of his company's financial results to purchasing savings. As we have seen, the leverage effect of purchasing can be enormous, depending on its purchasing-to-sales ratio and its capital turnover ratio. Purchasing and supply chain management can contribute in several ways, both in a quantitative and qualitative way, to improve the company's bottom line. It can also help to improve the company's top line.

In shaping their purchasing and supply chain strategies, companies can use different connotations and definitions related to the scope of purchasing, ranging from ordering, buying and purchasing to procurement, sourcing, supply (chain) management and value chain management. As the activity goes through each of these definitions the scope of purchasing broadens as well as its impact to the business. New challenges lying ahead will change the scope and role of purchasing within organisations. The most important ones are the need to develop leveraged purchasing and supply strategies, global sourcing, integration of suppliers in both materials and new product development processes, reciprocal arrangements, and socially responsible purchasing. Without doubt these challenges will put purchasing and supply chain management more in the spotlight in many organizations.

Value Chain
Composed of value activities and a margin which is achieved by these activities. Value activities can be divided into primary activities and support activities. The margin represents the value that customers want to pay extra for the company's efforts compared with the costs that were required for these.

ASSIGNMENTS

1.1 Take the annual report of an industrial company. Calculate the purchasing value in relation to the turnover. Calculate the effect of a 2 and 5% saving on the purchasing value.
   Do the same for a 2 and 5% increase in the purchasing value *ceteris paribus*. Describe the elements in the DuPont chart (Figure 1.4) that are affected by purchasing policy directly or indirectly.

1.2 What would you consider to be purchasing's added value to a company? Mention at least three areas where purchasing can contribute. What would you consider to be purchasing's core and non-core activities?

1.3 What are the major differences between purchasing, procurement, sourcing and supply management? Would you consider the purchasing function to be part of supply chain management or would you favour the reverse? Discuss.

1.4 What are the major differences between the activities of the purchasing function and the activities conducted by the purchasing department? Do you think it is important to differentiate between these two concepts? Why?

1.5 The chapter describes a number of new developments in purchasing and also addresses the aim for total quality control in companies. Describe the major consequences of total quality control on the purchasing function in general and on the relationships with suppliers in particular.

REFERENCES

Aljian, G.W. (1984) *Purchasing Handbook*, New York: McGraw-Hill.
Carbone, J. (2002) 'Outsourcing the Xbox', *Purchasing*, 15 August.
Porter, M.E. (1985) *Competitive Advantage*, New York: The Free Press.

INDUSTRIAL BUYING BEHAVIOUR: DECISION-MAKING IN PURCHASING

LEARNING OBJECTIVES

After studying this chapter you should understand the following:

- The major differences between organizational and consumer buying behaviour.
- The key elements of the purchasing process.
- The various roles in a buying decision-making unit.
- The involvement of the purchasing department in the acquisition of various goods.
- How to model organizational buying behaviour and network-theory.

INTRODUCTION

The following case study outlines one part of a complex decision-making process related to an important purchase. Decision-making processes concerning the purchase of products or services that are still to be developed, are generally characterized by a high degree of complexity and uncertainty. For this reason the decision-making in such situations usually involves many disciplines and departments in the organization. In this car-lease company it involved the management, the systems manager, the marketing department, the sales department, and the internal controlling department. In addition, the external consultant and the suppliers involved exerted considerable influence. So, various disciplines and stakeholders are involved, with varying interests and different views and opinions about what should be done. Circumstances such as these often make the purchasing decision-making process complex and obscure. When ill structured, these processes can easily end up in frustration, considerable loss of time and **budget** overruns. Hence, a major question is how decision-making processes in purchasing can be structured in such a way that all parties involved arrive at solutions which are satisfactory to them.

In this chapter different models that are available to answer this question will be explained, starting with the main differences between organizational and consumer buying behaviour. Next, the purchasing process will be described in more detail. Finally, some sources from business marketing theory on how organizational buying behaviour can be modelled and analysed are described. The chapter ends with a discussion on e-procurement solutions.

Budget
A budget serves as a vehicle for delegating activities and responsibilities to lower management levels in the organization.

CASE STUDY BUYING COMPUTER SYSTEMS IN A CAR LEASING COMPANY

The management of a car leasing company has requested its business systems manager to prepare a proposal for further automation of all activities related to customer order handling. This management decision is in line with the intention to increase the efficiency of the sales back office: in the future, more administrative work must be done with fewer people. Therefore, an IT solution has been designed allowing customers to deal directly with a lot of queries and administrative matters. The management already has its eye on a particular IT-system: contact has been made with a software supplier, who has references from the automobile branch. Documentation has been requested and the systems manager is asked to give his opinion. The systems manager thinks that the management's ideas on further computerization of administrative sales tasks is best elaborated in close co-operation with the future users of the system. A project group is installed, consisting of employees from the internal sales department, the field sales organization, the internal control department and an external consultant. The working group's course is plotted. It immediately becomes clear during the first meetings that there is no apparent fit between the intended software system and the organization's present ways of working. When asked, the supplier states that this is usually the case: the current operating procedures will have to be adjusted here and there. However, before going ahead, the systems manager decides to get information from other suppliers. It appears that adjustments in the sales organizations are necessary no matter what software system management decides to implement. There is no system readily available on the market that corresponds exactly with the organization's present and future needs. The working group decides to invite another software company to help determine whether the organization will have to develop its own system. The question is what type of software will qualify. The systems department at headquarters is asked about their experience with software companies. Several names are provided, and it is decided to approach four companies. After talking to these four suppliers, the group decides to go ahead with one selected supplier for the time being.

The supplier in question proposes to start with a thorough analysis of the information needs of the company. Only then can the system requirements be defined. Supervision of these first steps will cost money, of course! A €150 000 quote is submitted and accepted. All this has taken three months.

The activities turn out to be more complex than expected. They also turn out to take much more time than anticipated: it has taken four months to describe the system requirements. Analysis of available software systems is then commenced. This reveals that one system will do, but that a considerable amount of 'application engineering' will be necessary. The software company can be of help in this too. A quotation is solicited: it amounts to €650 000. The systems manager has the strong impression that this price is far too high and again wants to invite competitive quotations from other software companies. However, the management is opposed: the current supplier is well-informed about the organization's problems. A new supplier would have to start all over, and that would cost too much money and time . . .

ORGANIZATIONAL BUYING BEHAVIOUR: BASIC CHARACTERISTICS

Buying processes *Includes determining the purchasing needs, selecting the supplier, arriving at a proper price, specifying terms and conditions, issuing the contract or order, and following up to ensure proper delivery and payment.*

It is tempting to take the literature on consumer buying behaviour as a frame of reference for studying **buying processes** in organizations. However, it soon becomes clear that these theories have only limited value in this regard. There appear to be major differences between consumer marketing on the one hand and industrial or business-to-business marketing on the other. The industrial marketer has to deal with companies, governmental organizations or institutions, who need the purchased product to feed, support and maintain their primary and supporting processes. In consumer marketing, however, the marketer faces individuals who strive for an immediate satisfaction of their needs. Table 2.1 summarizes the major differences between both types of marketing.

The following are a few important characteristics of industrial markets:

- Professional purchasing. Usually, professional buyers are involved in purchasing decision-making and purchase operations. Because of their education, experience and responsibilities, buyers usually are experienced and well-informed counterparts in discussions with industrial sales people and account managers.

- **Derived demand**. Most companies sell to other companies. Few manufacturing companies deliver directly to the end user. For this reason developments in industrial markets are often related to changes which occur in the end-user markets.

- Inelastic, fluctuating demand. Due to complex decision-making, the price-elasticity in industrial markets is frequently lower than for consumer products.

- Geographical concentration. Many industrial markets are geographically concentrated (unlike consumer markets, which are geographically dispersed). The European chemical industry, for example, is concentrated in the Ruhr area in Germany, the automobile industry in southern Germany, France and northern Italy. The microchip industry is concentrated in Silicon Valley in the United States.

- Large order quantities and large amounts of money involved. Business-to-business transactions often involve large quantities of goods and services and, therefore, large sums of money.

- Limited number of customers. The customer market of industrial suppliers often consists of only a few companies. In Europe, the automotive industry—if limited to the producers—is made up of approximately six major independent manufacturers. Manufacturers of fast moving consumer products are confronted with only a handful of supermarket chains in most European countries. Therefore, only a limited number of buyers determine the success of a new product.

Derived demand
Most companies sell to other companies. Few manufacturing companies deliver directly to the end user. For this reason developments in industrial markets are often influenced by changes which occur in the end-user markets.

TABLE 2.1 Main differences between industrial and consumer markets

Aspect	Industrial market	Consumer market
Buying objective	Enable production	Personal need satisfaction
Buying motive	Mainly rational	Also emotional
Purchasing function	Professional buying, predominantly men	Consumers, mainly women
Decision-making	Many persons involved, much discussion	Often impulsive, without consulting others
Characteristics	Negotiations, intense interaction	Often without negotiation, little interaction
Product and market knowledge	Large	Limited
Order size	Often large	Mostly small
Demand	Derived demand, may fluctuate strongly	Autonomous demand, relatively stable
Price elasticity	Rather inelastic	Rather elastic
Number of customers	Mostly limited	Very large
Spread of customers	Sometimes large geographic concentration	Large geographical spread

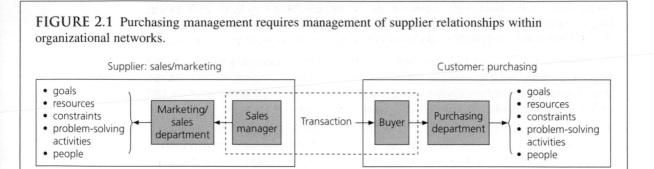

FIGURE 2.1 Purchasing management requires management of supplier relationships within organizational networks.

A major difference between the consumer sector and the industrial sector is related to the interaction and (mutual) interdependency between buyer and seller. Unlike the consumer sector, business-to-business markets are often characterized by long-lasting relationships between the buying and the selling parties. As a consequence, business-to-business marketers must regard their markets as a network of relationships. Their marketing strategies are aimed at extending, investing in and continuously maintaining these networks. In other words, business-to-business marketing, and professional purchasing, require active management of relationships within complex organizational networks (see Figure 2.1).

MODELS OF INDUSTRIAL BUYING BEHAVIOUR

In Chapter 1, we introduced the purchasing process and its different stages. We will now address the variables that affect the course or the outcomes of this process. We, therefore, will distinguish between: (1) variables that affect the buying process and (2) variables that affect buying behaviour.

Variables that affect the buying process

Products, routine
These products produce few technical or commercial problems from a purchasing point of view. They usually have a small value per item and there are many alternative suppliers.

Products, bottleneck
These items represent a relatively limited value in terms of money but they are vulnerable with regard to their supply. They can only be obtained from one supplier.

- Characteristics of the product. Decisions about the purchase of raw materials differ from, for example, those for the purchase of spare parts. The differences stem from the financial importance (and therefore the influence on the cost price of the end product) of both types of goods, their technical complexity and the supply risk involved. In practice, many differences in the way the buying process develops can be traced to specific product characteristics. Technical specialists (designers, engineers, technical/maintenance department, etc.) usually make decisions about the purchase of technically complex products. Decisions concerning the purchase of standard-grade, high-volume products (such as raw materials and commodities) are made primarily by financial managers or top management. Purchase decisions about **routine products** are generally left to the lower echelons of the organization.

- Strategic importance of the purchase. The higher the importance of the purchase to the company, the more involved general management will be in the purchase decision. The strategic importance is not merely determined by the amounts of money or the investment involved in the purchase. For example, low-cost **bottleneck** items can sometimes show significant risk in terms of availability and supply, and often turn out to be a direct threat to the continuity of production. For this reason they are of prime interest to top management. Other examples of key purchase decisions are contracting for licenses or development contracts.

- Sums of money involved in the purchases. As the amounts of money involved increase, management's role in the purchase decision will grow. This is why management is often directly involved in negotiations about important raw materials and investment goods.

- Characteristics of the purchasing market. The approach towards suppliers varies depending on the organization's freedom of choice in terms of purchasing. In a monopolist or oligopolistic market, negotiations with suppliers will be far more complex and difficult than in markets characterized by free competition. The management of the company will therefore be more interested in the former.

- Degree of risk related to the purchase. As the risk related to the purchase decision is higher, more disciplines will be involved in the process. The case study at the beginning of this chapter illustrates this situation. The risk attached to the purchase decision decreases and the lead-time of the process diminishes as the organization has more experience with the purchase of a particular product or a particular supplier.

- Role of the purchasing department in the organization. The tasks, responsibilities and competences of the purchasing department vary between organizations. Purchasing departments in large companies usually operate more professionally than those in smaller ones, and very small companies usually dispense with having a specialist explicitly in charge of the purchasing task. The internal structure of the organization generally governs the way in which the purchasing decisions are made.

- Degree to which the purchase product affects existing routines in the organization. The decision-making will be more complex, take more time and require the involvement of more disciplines as the products that are to be purchased require adjustments in the internal organization or necessitate education and training. This situation occurs, for example, when implementing new computer systems and new manufacturing technology.

Lehman and O'Shaughnessy (1974) provide an interesting elaboration of the second-to-last aspect. These authors distinguish four categories of products, based on the potential post-purchase problems: (1) routine products, (2) products that require instruction, (3) products whose adequate technical functioning in the organization is uncertain and (4) products that can result in problems in the internal organization. As more adaptation within the organization is required, more disciplines will be involved in the buying decision, and the decision-making process will be more complex.

According to Fisher (1970) the purchasing decision-making process is primarily determined by two aspects: product complexity and commercial uncertainty. If these two aspects are combined, statements can be made about what disciplines will be involved in the decision-making process (see Figure 2.2).

Variables that affect the buying decision

Here we adopt the ideas developed by Webster and Wind (1972). These authors distinguish between 'task' variables and 'non-task' variables. They define **task variables** as those variables that are related to the tasks, responsibilities and competences assigned by the organization to the person involved in the purchase decision. The engineer's main focus will be on the design, construction and technical aspects of the purchase product. A materials planner will focus mainly on logistic aspects, such as minimum order quantities, packing requirements and delivery times. Every specialist will want a say in the discussion from their own perspective and interests.

The **non-task variables** are related to the professional's personality. People differ in terms of personality, for example, the degree to which they either accept or avoid risks, their ambitions, how much they avoid or confront personal conflicts with suppliers.

Task variables
Are those variables that are related to the tasks, responsibilities and competences assigned by the organization to the persons involved in the purchase decision-making process.

Non-task variables
Variables that are related to the personalities of the persons involved in the purchase decision-making process.

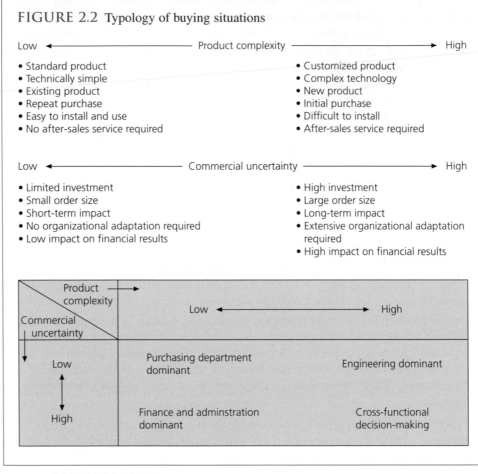

FIGURE 2.2 Typology of buying situations

Low ← Product complexity → High

- Standard product
- Technically simple
- Existing product
- Repeat purchase
- Easy to install and use
- No after-sales service required

- Customized product
- Complex technology
- New product
- Initial purchase
- Difficult to install
- After-sales service required

Low ← Commercial uncertainty → High

- Limited investment
- Small order size
- Short-term impact
- No organizational adaptation required
- Low impact on financial results

- High investment
- Large order size
- Long-term impact
- Extensive organizational adaptation required
- High impact on financial results

Product complexity →
Commercial uncertainty ↓

Low ← → High

	Low	High
Low	Purchasing department dominant	Engineering dominant
High	Finance and adminstration dominant	Cross-functional decision-making

Source: adapted from Fisher (1970)

According to Webster and Wind (1972), task and non-task variables can be identified not only on the level of the individual, but also on a departmental level, at the level of the organization, and the level of the company and its environment. For example, the group culture in a purchasing department may focus on strengthening its own position within the organization, which may lead to boundary problems with other disciplines and suboptimal decisions. Another example: when the culture in an organization is highly informal, this will prevent a successful introduction of formal purchasing procedures. As an illustration of how the relationships between a company and its environment may affect relationships with suppliers, the organization's implicit objective might be to avoid introducing environmentally sensitive products to the market. As a result this company may impose requirements on its suppliers to formally comply with environmental legislation. Depicts Webster and Wind's model.

This description clearly shows that Webster and Wind attach a great significance to the influence of psychological, social, organizational and environmental factors on the buying process. They place purchasing decision processes in a larger context, suggesting that purchasing processes can only be understood if the researcher takes these factors into consideration. This perspective is also shared by Sheth (1973) and provides an understanding of the large differences which exist between organizations in the field of organizational buying behaviour.

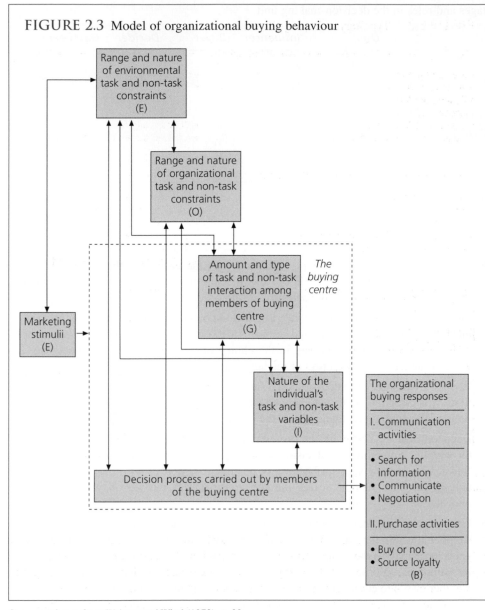

FIGURE 2.3 Model of organizational buying behaviour

Source: redrawn from Webster and Wind (1972), p. 30

Decision-making unit (DMU)
DMU relates to all those individuals and groups who partici-pate in the purchasing decision-making proc-ess, who share some common goals and the risks arising from the decisions (identical to buying centre).

Buying centre
Relates to all those individuals and groups who participate in the purchasing decision-making process, who share some common goals and the risks arising from the deci-sions (identical to decision-making unit).

On the basis of observations from a number of purchasing practices we feel that the importance of social, psychological and emotional factors on purchasing decision-making can hardly be overstated. There have been many examples where rational purchasing decision-making was blurred and obstructed by the fact that deeply felt emotions and per-sonal preferences were insufficiently recognized. Remarkably, these aspects of purchasing decision-making have gained only little interest from researchers up to now.

Collectively, the relevant literature makes it clear that organizational purchasing processes are very complex, always involving more than one person, i.e. group decision-making. The literature refers to this group as the **decision-making unit** (DMU). Webster and Wind (1972) speak of the **'buying centre',** which they define as 'all those individuals and groups who participate in the purchasing decision-making process, who share some common goals and the risks arising from the decisions'. Within the DMU various roles can be distinguished:

TABLE 2.2 Decision stages and roles in the decision-making unit

	User	Influencer	Buyer	Decider	Gatekeeper
Identification of need	X	X			
Establishing specifications and scheduling the purchase	X	X	X	X	
Identifying buying alternatives	X	X	X		X
Evaluating alternative buying actions	X	X	X		
Selecting the suppliers	X	X	X	X	

Source: Webster and Wind (1972)

- Users. These are the people who will work with the product, either on an individual basis or in a group context. It is obvious that the user has an important say when it concerns the specification and selection of the product.
- Influencers. The influencers are able to affect the outcome of the purchasing process by means of solicited or unsolicited advice. In the construction business, for example, architects have an important say in the choice of materials. Software specialists can exert influence on the selection of the hardware supplier (and vice versa).
- Buyers. Buyers are not necessarily the same individuals as the users. In large organizations, it is often the buyer who negotiates with the supplier about the terms and conditions of the contract and who places the order.
- Decision-makers. These are the professionals who actually determine the selection of the supplier. Sometimes the decision-maker is a designer who writes their specifications 'towards' a specific supplier because of positive experiences with this supplier's products in the past. In other cases the decision-maker is the person who controls the budget.
- Gatekeepers. Gatekeepers are the people who control the flow of information from the supplier towards the other members of the DMU (and vice versa). In some cases the gatekeeper may be the technical director's secretary who screens contacts with (particular) suppliers. In other cases the buyer is the gatekeeper, who has the power to decide whether or not to circulate specific supplier documentation within the organization.

Table 2.2 relates these roles to the various phases of the purchasing process. It can be seen that the importance of individual roles can differ, depending on which phase the purchasing process is in.

THE PURCHASING PROCESS

In Chapter 1, some purchasing terms and definitions were given. In this chapter, we will expand on the purchasing process model described, based on Figure 2.4. The purchasing process model shows how the different purchasing activities are interrelated. Some of the important aspects of this model are now emphasized and explained:

- Leading with business needs. Business needs and requirements are the input for the purchasing process model. These needs and requirements may be defined in a more general

FIGURE 2.4 Purchasing process approach: managing interfaces

	Define specification	Select supplier	Contract agreement	Ordering	Expediting	Evaluation
P&S Role	• Get specification	• Assure adequate supplier selection	• Prepare contract	• Establish order routine	• Establish expediting routine	• Assess supplier
Elements	• Functional specification • Technical changes • Bring supplier-knowledge to engineering	• Prequalification of suppliers • Request for quotation	• Contracting expertise • Negotiating expertise	• Develop order routines • Order handling	• Expediting • 'Trouble-shooting'	• Supplier evaluation • Supplier rating
Documents	• Functional specification • Norm/spec control	• Supplier selection proposal	• Contract	• Order	• Exception report • Due date listings • Invoices	• Preferred supplier list • Supplier ranking scheme

way, or in a very detailed manner. A manufacturer of high-tech modules may decide to enter the aerospace business to obtain work with a higher value added and a better margin. Since technical requirements are very high in this market, the company may need to invest in high precision milling machines. Next, the capacity and **technical specifications** of these milling machines should be determined in order to be able to contact the right vendors of this equipment. Having contacted several suppliers, the precise specifications for the milling machines are determined and the **supplier selection** process can be started. This is just an illustration of how changing business needs may trigger a purchasing process.

- Process approach. Throughout this book purchasing and supply issues will be considered from a process perspective. The various steps in the process model are closely connected. The quality of the **output** of the preceding steps determines to a large extent the quality of the output of the subsequent steps. Deficiencies in one step will lead to problems in the next steps. As an example, quality problems related to purchased materials often become visible at the end of the purchasing process in terms of rejected deliveries (step 5). In practice, however, poor quality of incoming materials can frequently be traced to incorrect or incomplete specifications (step 1), or to an incorrect sourcing decision in that a supplier has been selected who cannot deliver against required specifications (step 2). Also the contract may have been incomplete in that it did not provide for any **penalty clauses** as a result of poor quality on delivery (step 3).

- Defining the interfaces. The purchasing process model implies that in order to get a full grip on buying operations, the output of each phase is clearly defined. Preferably it should be possible to trace and track every activity in the purchasing process. Every consecutive step should only be started when a decision has been made on the previous step. Therefore, it is recommended that the result of each step is documented in the form of a 'go–no-go' document. This will help to structure and formalize the purchasing process. The correct process is usually explained in the company's purchasing procedures, which are laid down in a purchasing manual. When such procedures are absent, this usually results in highly unstructured purchasing decision-making processes and operational problems.

Technical specification
Describes the technical properties and characteristics of the product as well as the activities to be performed by the supplier.

Supplier selection
Supplier selection relates to all activities, which are required to select the best possible supplier and includes determining on the method of subcontracting, preliminary qualification of suppliers and drawing up the 'bidders' list', preparation of the request for quotation and analysis of the bids received and selection of the supplier.

Output
Relates to the functionality of the service instead of the activity itself.

- Determining responsibilities. The author considers purchasing to be a cross-functional responsibility. As indicated before, the purchasing process is not limited to the purchasing department. Many levels in the organization are usually involved. This demands adequate communication and co-operation among the disciplines involved. The tasks, responsibilities and authority of each department should be indicated in each phase, to prevent misunderstandings and role conflicts. For example, when deciding on specifications of technical components, engineering departments often have the sole authority. Engineering departments, however, are in most cases not responsible for the supply of base materials at the manufacturing stage. What often happens is that engineers, after careful selection, decide to integrate supplier and brand-specific **components** in their final designs leaving the buyer with a monopolist supplier. The author suggests that decisions on specifications of purchased materials and supplier selection are considered as a joint activity between engineers and buyers. Wynstra (1998) presented an interesting framework which may serve as a reference to structure collaboration on product development between engineering, purchasing and suppliers. We will come back to this subject in Chapter 11.

- Combining different skills, different types of knowledge and expertise. The first three steps, called the initial or tactical purchasing function, are primarily of a technical–commercial nature. The remaining three steps, referred to as the **ordering** function, are of a more logistics–administrative nature. A key problem in many companies is how to combine the different types of knowledge, skills and expertise in such a way that all parties involved arrive at an optimal solution for the company. It would be almost impossible to combine all these elements in one person, which is why we see an increasing tendency towards specialization in purchasing jobs, while at the same time cross-functional co-operation between different disciplines is growing.

The added value of the professional buyer primarily lies in his ability to act as a facilitator for the entire purchasing and supply cycle. This includes, among other things:

- identifying new, potential suppliers and business partners for the company's changing business needs

- being involved in new product development projects and investment projects at an early stage, based on proven expertise

- supporting internal customers in defining purchasing specifications in an objective and unequivocal manner

- preparing a list of approved suppliers in co-operation with the internal customer, and after that drawing up requests for quotations and preparing their evaluation together with the user, as well as selecting a supplier by mutual agreement.

- preparing and carrying out the contract negotiations as well as drawing up and reviewing the terms and conditions of the contract

- setting up requisitioning and ordering routines in such a way that the users (if possible and so desired) can place orders themselves, within the terms and conditions established with the suppliers, resulting in full contract compliance

- in case orders cannot be placed by users themselves, taking care of order handling, i.e., handling internal requisitions; placing orders at suppliers and maintaining and monitoring order and supplier files

- expediting (arranging) or following up outstanding orders to secure on-time delivery and monitoring outstanding financial obligations

- following up and evaluating, in terms of settling claims, evaluating supplier performance and maintaining and keeping up-to-date the relevant supplier documentation.

The cause of delivery problems of purchased materials is often related to late requisitioning by other departments (often due to time pressure). In practice this leads not only to a higher price being paid (as a result of extra work, speed of delivery, buying from stock-keeping wholesalers), but also in many cases to higher organizational costs and operational problems (the delivered materials do not comply with the specifications, many partial deliveries, postponed delivery of critical parts). The presented purchasing model may help managers to structure their purchasing decision-making processes and the operational processes involved. The results will not only pay off in terms of lower prices paid for materials and services, but certainly also in lower organizational costs and a higher productivity.

There are relatively few situations in which all of the steps in the purchasing process are passed through. This only happens in the case of a first-time purchase of a product or service. In practice, most purchasing transactions involve more or less **straight rebuys**. In general, three types of purchasing situations are distinguished (Robinson *et al.*, 1967; see Brand, 1968 for the first studies on this subject):

- The **new-task situation**. This situation occurs when the organization decides to buy a completely new product, supplied by an unknown supplier. This type of transaction is characterized by a high degree of uncertainty and high risk in that the specifications of the product still have to be mapped. The decision-making process is characterized by extensive problem solving and becomes protracted because various disciplines, distributed across various hierarchical levels in the organization, will probably assert their influence. The new-task situation occurs, for example, in the acquisition of capital goods and the purchase of new components, which must be produced to the organization's specifications (see Figure 2.5). The case study of the car-lease company at the beginning of this chapter also falls into this category. Another example of a new task situation is buying components for a newly developed product.

- The **modified rebuy**. This is when the organization wants to purchase a new product from a known supplier, or an existing product from a new supplier, and usually occurs when there is some dissatisfaction about the current supplier, or when better alternatives for existing products have become available. This situation is more certain than the new-task situation because the relevant criteria on how to value the functionality of the product or service or how to select the supplier are more or less known. The purchasing process focuses in particular on the last four steps of the model and decision-making is characterized by limited problem solving.

- The straight rebuy. This is the most common situation and entails the acquisition of a known product from a known supplier. Uncertainty regarding the outcome of the transaction is low because the terms and conditions of the contract are known and are periodically re-established in negotiations with the supplier. In the case of regularly recurring (repetitive) deliveries of identical goods, blanket orders or annual agreements are used that cover the main terms and conditions. Ordering takes place through call-off orders, often placed directly by the user department through advanced **e-procurement solutions**. This benefits both the speed and efficiency of the transaction (for buyer as well as supplier). In this situation the purchasing process only covers the final three steps of the model. Straight rebuy situations relate to all kinds of routine items and consumable items, such as office supplies, fixing materials, cleaning materials, catering products. These may also relate to bulk products, such as raw materials, that are negotiated once a year and then ordered weekly for production. After negotiations with the seller about the contract, orders should be placed directly by the users without interference from the purchasing department. As will be explained later, Internet technology and especially e-commerce provide interesting solutions for efficient order handling in this area (see below).

This typology of buying situations explains why the degree of uncertainty and risk that buyers may deal with strongly depends on the type of purchasing situation. This is reflected in

Straight rebuy
Relates to the acquisition of a known product from a known supplier (identical to routine buy).

New-task situation
Situation when the organization decides to buy a completely new product, supplied by an unknown supplier.

Modified rebuy
Relates to a situation when the organization wants to purchase a new product from a known supplier, or an existing product from a new supplier.

E-procurement solutions
Relate to all web-enabled solutions aimed at supporting the purchasing process and all electronic data exchange that is needed for efficient transaction processing. E-procurement solutions can be divided into three types, i.e. electronic marketplaces, electronic auctions (e-auctions) and electronic catalogues and order and payment solutions (order to pay solutions).

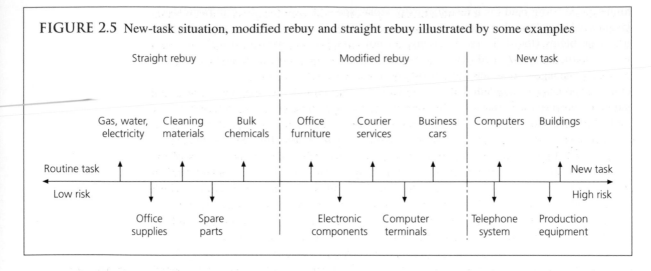

FIGURE 2.5 New-task situation, modified rebuy and straight rebuy illustrated by some examples

the way the decision-making process evolves. The higher the sums of money involved and the higher the technical complexity, the higher the perceived risk will be, and more functions and persons will become involved in the decision-making. The involvement of these persons as well as their role, will vary at each step of the purchasing process model. In light of the interdisciplinary nature of many purchasing decisions, it is essential that the decision-making process is well organized. Many problems regarding purchasing decision-making and supplier relationships are caused by a lack of organization within the DMU.

THE SPECIFICATION PHASE

Functional specification
Describes the functionality which the product must have for the user.

Outsourcing
Outsourcing means that the company divests itself of the resources to fulfil a particular activity to another company, to focus more effectively on its own competence. The difference with subcontracting is the divestment of assets, infrastructure, people and competencies.

During this initial stage of the purchasing process, the purchasing requirements are determined and the company is also faced with the 'make-or-buy' question. It has to determine which products or activities will be produced i.e. performed by the company itself, and which products or activities will be contracted out. In what follows only the contracting-out issue will be discussed (see also Chapter 8 on this topic). The process of assessing 'make versus buy' actually starts when the company decides about its future business plan. It may, for instance, decide to enter new markets or it may decide to develop new products. Next, the resources that are required to realize the business plan need to be identified. Then it may become clear that in order to be able to develop the intended new products, new equipment (e.g. testing equipment) will be required to enable testing of the physical characteristics of the prototypes. As an alternative the company might consider subcontracting the testing activity to an outside supplier. In case the company decides to buy the new testing equipment, the purchasing process starts with defining the capacity and requirements of the testing equipment that will be bought. This exercise may require different steps, which may have a different level of detail. In general, purchasing managers differentiate between **functional specifications** and technical specifications.

A functional specification describes the functionality which the product must have for the user.[1] For example, when **outsourcing** greenkeeping a buyer may state in its contract with the gardener that he is expected to mow a lawn once every week, using personnel with a specific educational background and using a Honda low-noise, high-performance mower.

[1]In this book, the term 'user' is employed in a broader sense. It can refer to the person who actually uses the product that is to be bought, but it can also refer to the person who has to make the financial decision about the purchase, who allocates the budget.

Alternatively, the contract might state that the gardener will keep the grass at a maximum of one inch, whilst keeping noise below a certain number of decibels during execution. The difference will be clear: in the first situation the gardener will probably mow the lawn every week (also during winter), since that is what has been agreed with the customer. In the second situation the gardener will only mow the grass when needed.

The advantages of working with functional specifications will be clear. Firstly, potential suppliers are given the best possible opportunity to apply their expertise. Secondly, new technologies can be used, technologies that the buyer is not familiar with, but the supplier is. Thirdly, it creates one standard, against which all supplier proposals can be evaluated.

A technical specification describes the technical properties and characteristics of the product as well as the activities to be performed by the supplier. Usually these technical specifications are laid down in detailed technical drawings and activity schedules which can be used to monitor the supplier's activities in detail. This way of working by the contractor can easily lead to over-specification, where the user imposes requirements on both product and supplier which easily lead to higher cost but no better functionality.

Both functional and technical specification are part of a wider concept, which is referred to as the **purchase order specification**. This document (usually a set of documents) comprises the following:

■ quality specifications, describing how the product should be delivered (with or without a quality certificate) and what technical norms and standards the product should meet

■ the logistics specifications, indicating the quantities needed, the place and time of delivery and the physical conditions to be respected

■ a maintenance specification, describing how the product will be maintained and serviced by the supplier (and whether or not spare parts need to be supplied in the future)

■ legal and environmental requirements, determining that both product and production process should be in compliance with health, safety and environmental legislation

■ a target budget, which indicates within what financial constraints the solution to be provided by the prospective supplier should be found.

Purchase (order) specification
Relates to all specifications needed to select the right supplier including quality specifications, logistics specifications, maintenance specifications, legal and environmental requirements and a target budget.

In the purchase of construction work and civil projects, the purchase order specifications are usually recorded in a scope-of-work description.

The user or budget holder is responsible for specifying the purchasing order requirements and the buyer's task is to ensure that the specification is drawn up in objective, supplier-neutral terms. Several manufacturing companies have regulated this responsibility in so-called sign-off procedures. Before a specification is released to a supplier, it must have the formal approval of purchasing or the (potential) suppliers. The purpose of this procedure is to prevent misunderstandings in the consecutive stages of the purchasing process. In this way the costs of so-called 'technical or spec changes' are reduced. Experience has shown that this type of preparation will result in a considerable reduction of the project's total engineering lead time.

Technical changes that occur during the project must be dealt with in accordance with the change order procedures. The buyer's job is to ensure that the supplier's work is conducted according to the last specifications sent. Suppliers should ideally confirm each approved change, preferably in writing. Sound configuration management can prevent many problems!

SUPPLIER SELECTION AND SUPPLIER ASSESSMENT

After the purchasing requirements have been defined and translated in functional or technical specifications, the buyer can start the supply market research. In practice these steps are intertwined. When drawing up the technical specifications, the practical feasibility and the costs are estimated. The selection of basic technologies—through which the product design will have to be realized—is frequently made with the names of a few suppliers in mind. In practice, the step of 'selection' contains a number of separate steps: (1) determining the method of subcontracting, (2) preliminary qualification of suppliers and drawing up the 'bidders' list', (3) preparation of the request for quotation and analysis of the bids received and (4) selection of the supplier. Each of these activities is briefly described below.

The first issue to be dealt with in supplier selection is whether to opt for turnkey or partial subcontracting.[2] In the case of turnkey subcontracting the responsibility for the execution of the entire assignment (often including design activities) is placed with the supplier. In the case of partial subcontracting the assignment is divided into parts which are contracted out separately, often to various suppliers. Co-ordination rests with the buyer. Partial subcontracting usually results in savings, but obviously has some important drawbacks. Table 2.3 lists the advantages and disadvantages of both types of subcontracting.

Principal
Provides the assignment to the supplier or service provider. Principal is equivalent to customer or buyer.

A major point against partial subcontracting is that the **principal** must be sure that the separate contracts are attuned to one another. In this case, full responsibility for the continuity of the whole of the project activities rests with the buyer. If the buyer fails, it is clear that the expected cost advantage will not materialize, and considerable additional costs will result.

A second issue to be considered at this stage is whether the work will be awarded on a fixed-price, lump sum or a cost-reimbursable basis.[3]

When work is executed on the basis of a fixed-price contract, the principal orders the supplier to perform the required activities at a fixed price, and to have the work completed by a predetermined date. The advantages of this method are that the principal knows its exact financial position. Moreover, after completion of the work there is no need for settlements because all risks are carried by the supplier. A final advantage is that the firm has certainty about the completion date.

As the price is fixed, it is in the supplier's interest to execute the work as efficiently as possible. The fixed price is an incentive to complete the work, or deliver the goods, as quickly as possible within the agreed term. A major disadvantage of this method is that it is difficult to get insight into the supplier's cost breakdown if the principal lacks expertise;

TABLE 2.3 Advantages and disadvantages of turnkey and partial subcontracting

	Advantages	Disadvantages
Turnkey subcontracting	Limited interference by principal during project execution	No insight in cost/price structure of project
	No experience in similar projects required from principal	Limited influence only on materials used (quality and quantities)
	Limited efforts from principal required	
Partial subcontracting	Better insight in cost/price structure of project by principal	In-depth knowledge and experience from principal required
	Better grip on suppliers and materials used	Much time and effort required for project coordination and monitoring
	Lower overall project costs in general	Risk that communication problems may delay project activities

[2]The term 'subcontracting' is used here. Alternative terms used in the literature for the same activity are 'outsourcing' (see Chapter 7) and 'contracting out'.
[3]Also referred to in the literature as 'time and materials' contract.

this problem can be avoided by requesting quotations from more than one supplier. Another disadvantage of this manner of contracting is that it requires a thorough preparation, and hence, time—the question is whether there is enough time to prepare a detailed specification and have a formal bidding procedure. Finally, one does not know in advance which supplier will turn out to be the best.

In the case of a cost-reimbursable contract the nature and scope of the activities to be performed are not established in advance. The principal orders the supplier to perform the required activities at a predetermined hourly rate, sometimes in combination with a prearranged percentage to cover the overhead costs. Settlement follows after completion of the activities based on the supplier's day reports (stating the hours worked) and (if relevant) the materials that have been consumed. An advantage of this method is that the principal obtains an exact picture of the cost structure of the work. The principal is free in its choice of suppliers; the principal knows the supplier in advance. Naturally, there are also some disadvantages related to this type of contracting. Firstly, there is no predetermined fixed price, so the buyer is not quite sure about the financial consequences. Also, there is no incentive to work faster, as the supplier is reimbursed for every hour worked; every setback is charged to the principal; and the buyer has no certainty about the completion date.

An additional disadvantage of this method is that the principal is not forced to specify exactly what is required. Frequently this specification is left to the supplier for the sake of convenience. Due to the uncertainty of the final cost, many buyers avoid working with cost-reimbursable contracts. Some only use them in the case of specific, minor maintenance/repair activities, for which the financial risks are relatively clear. Cost-reimbursable contracts are not without problems and several points have to be discussed with the supplier in advance (see Figure 2.6). The decision in favour of either fixed-price or cost-reimbursable contracts is determined by a number of factors, such as:

- Comprehensiveness of the specification. The availability of extensive specifications is a crucial prerequisite of lump sum contracting. Absence of specifications makes a fair comparison of the various quotations impossible.

- Available time. Does the principal have enough time for a **tender** procedure and price negotiations or should the work be started immediately?

- Technical expertise. If the work requires specialized knowledge and skills, which are not present at the client organization, a cost-reimbursable contract is often preferred.

- Knowledge of the industry. The degree to which the principal knows the methods and price arrangements that apply in that particular industry.

Tender
Situation where a buyer asks for bids from different suppliers, creating a level playing field (identical to competitive bidding).

FIGURE 2.6 Aspects to be considered when contracting on a cost-reimbursable basis

- Wages and salaries
- Percentage for general expense
- Profit percentage/mark-up
- Reporting procedures for hours worked and consumption of materials
- Costs of tooling and special equipment
- Costs related to coordinating the work of third parties
- Agreement on cost estimates for extra work
- Agreement on what to be supplied by principal
- Agreement on what facilities (telephone, electricity, housing) to be provided by principal/contractor
- Key personnel to be assigned on the job by contractor
- Arrangement of required licences and permits from local authorities
- Selection of sub-suppliers of contractors.

In summary, the first step in the stage of supplier selection consists of determining whether to opt for partial or turnkey contracting out. Second, it should be decided whether execution will take place by means of fixed-price or a cost-reimbursable agreement.

A third type of contract which is often used in the subcontracting world and which should be mentioned here is the unit-rate contract. These contracts determine the cost per activity for standardized and routine work. Petrochemical companies, for example, annually negotiate unit rates for simple installation and maintenance activities, which are subcontracted to suppliers (for instance unit rate per metre of piping that is installed, or **unit rate** per square metre of ground floor which is cleaned). Unit rate contracts are used for activities which are standardized but which are difficult to estimate in terms of volume and time.

The selected contracting method determines to a great extent how the next steps of the buying process will evolve. For that reason, these decisions must be made together with the user or budget holder. However, the buyer presents the different contracting methods deemed possible and outlines the considerations that may influence the decision.

The selection of a supplier is one of the most important steps in the purchasing process and several activities precede this decision. Activities start with summarizing the prequalification requirements, based on the purchase order specification, that the suppliers who are going to be approached for a quotation will have to meet. Next, the initial bidders' list (so-called **bidders' long list**) that indicates which suppliers may probably do the job, is assembled. Usually, those suppliers with an excellent vendor rating score, which represents excellent past performance, will be put on the initial bidders' list. Next, to each of these long listed suppliers a request for information (RFI) will be sent. These suppliers are contacted to provide references of prior projects and previous experience and other information that will help them qualify for the order. At this stage it may be necessary to conduct a supplier visit or audit in order to get a precise idea of the supplier's capabilities. Large companies generally work with 'approved vendors lists' in order to select the suppliers for the long list. The long list of suppliers is then reduced to a supplier short list. Based upon the information that was gathered the most promising suppliers are selected. These short-listed suppliers will be contacted through a request for quotation (RFQ). At this stage suppliers are invited to submit a bid which meets the requirements as laid down in the request for quotation. The idea behind this is that suppliers should submit their bids in such a way that they can be compared by the buyer. An important aspect of their bids is the price that they will offer to the prospective buyer.

These activities are commonly referred to as the tendering process. Tenders can be formal or informal and can be open or closed. An open tender is a tender without prequalification of suppliers. A closed tender is limited to a small number of suppliers who have been carefully preselected.

Sometimes there is not a sufficient number of approved suppliers available. Then, new suppliers need to be found through thorough supply market research (see Chapter 7). For important contracts new suppliers are first scrutinized and screened before any bids will be solicited from them.

It is common practice to identify three to five prospective suppliers, from whom quotations will be solicited. These suppliers make up the **bidders' short list**. If circumstances give cause to revise the invitation to bid, then all of the competing suppliers should be given the opportunity to respond to this revision.

After receipt of the quotations, the purchasing department will make a preliminary technical and commercial evaluation, during which all relevant aspects are acknowledged. The technical, logistic, quality, financial and legal aspects need to be weighed. Of course, prices are compared but at this stage most buyers will prefer to look at total cost of ownership (TCO), i.e. the total costs that the company will incur over the lifetime of the product. To be able to do this detailed cost information must be provided by suppliers. Rather than

Contract, unit rate
Rates are agreed for regular, routine activities, the size of which cannot be anticipated. Rates are defined per square metre of paintwork, metre of cable to be installed, etc. Payments are made based upon the actual number of units produced during the completion of the work.

Bidders' long list
Includes those suppliers that meet the buyer's prequalification criteria and that will be requested to submit a first proposal.

Bidders' short list
Includes those suppliers that meet the buyer's pre-qualification criteria and who will be requested to submit a detailed bid.

looking for individual car sales prices, lease rates may be used, which reflect much better the total costs to be expected for a car during its contract period. Ranking schemes may be used with a different degree of sophistication in order to facilitate the process of evaluating the supplier bids. These schemes are employed jointly by users and buyers involved. Usually this step ends with a supplier selection proposal, which consists of: (1) a decision to select a certain supplier, (2) the underlying ranking schemes and (3) the underlying quotations which have been considered.

For strategic and critical suppliers, the next step is to carry out a risk analysis for critical suppliers and purchase parts. During this step potential risks related to a particular choice of supplier are investigated. An example is presented in Memo 2.1.

MEMO 2.1   RISK ANALYSIS BY THE MINISTRY OF DEFENCE

If a supplier does not fulfill his obligations in the realization of complex and extensive projects, this can lead to considerable damages or loss for a military organization. To limit the risk of problems as much as possible, the Ministries of Defence of several European countries sometimes carry out an analysis of the risks related to doing business with suppliers for strategic projects. In general, three categories of risks are distinguished:

1 Technical risk regarding the suitability/professionalism of the management, the means of production, the skills, tools and testing equipment of the company in question for the manufacture of the required goods and services, which must meet the agreed requirements and must be delivered within the agreed term.

2 Quality risk with regard to the quality management of the company in general and the quality control system of the project in question in particular.

3 Financial risk related to the degree in which the company is considered to function soundly and effectively for the duration of the project. Of importance in this respect are: financial condition, investment elasticity and a solid financial condition in the near future.

In large and technologically complex projects the risks can be so large that additional measures and arrangements are required. These measures should consist of at least periodical preventive audits aimed at assessing the technical capacity and quality control (the so-called 'preaward survey'), to be conducted by the military; and the financial status of the company in question, to be conducted by the accounting department. This latter analysis concerns the actual and the anticipated results of the company activities (such as turnover and company results) and ratio analysis of several financial parameters (such as liquidity and solvency).

Ultimately one supplier will be selected with whom the delivery of the product (or service) will be negotiated. In some cases the assignment may be given to two or more suppliers (when dual or **multiple sourcing** is the preferred sourcing strategy). The suppliers who are not selected are informed about the reasons for rejecting their proposals.

Sourcing, multiple
Situation in which a company within a certain category buys from more than one supplier.

NEGOTIATION AND CONTRACTING

After the supplier has been selected, a contract will have to be drawn up. Depending on the industry, the contract may refer to specific additional terms and conditions.

The technical contents of the purchase agreement naturally depend on the product or project that is to be purchased. Specific commercial and legal terms and conditions will vary per contract, differences being caused by, for example, purchasing policy, company culture, market situation or product characteristics. This limits the use of standard purchase contracts. The next section discusses several important aspects of the purchase agreement.

Prices and terms of delivery

Competitive bidding
Situation where a buyer asks for bids from different suppliers, creating a level playing field (identical to tender).

In general the buyer should insist on a fixed price, arrived at through **competitive bidding** or negotiation, which is acceptable to both principal and supplier. Financial obligations should be defined unequivocally. Ideally the supplier should be willing to accept all risks, in so far as these are not excluded contractually. A fixed price is definitely preferred from the perspective of cost control or budget management.

In practice, different price arrangements are used in purchase agreements:

- Fixed price plus incentive fee. This type of contract is designed to motivate suppliers by means of rewards to execute the work above the agreed standard. The incentives do not have to relate to immediately visible **cost reductions**, which are realized by the supplier. They can also relate to earlier delivery, a better delivery reliability or a better quality performance than agreed.

Cost reductions
Purchasing cost reductions are sustainable in character. These may be the result from a change of specification, a change of supplier or omitting an unnecessary product quality requirement

- Cost-plus contract. This type of contract may have different forms: cost-plus with a percentage fee, cost-reimbursable plus a fixed fee, and cost-plus with a guaranteed maximum. In practice this type of contract often turns out to be more expensive for the buyer than other types of contracts. Cost-plus contracts are used in situations where the work cannot be specified adequately, or when a fixed price constitutes too big a risk for both the supplier and the buyer.

- Cost-reimbursable contracts. This type of contract is usually based on fixed hourly rates for labour and equipment. However, without a bonus or penalty clause these contracts provide little incentive to minimize labour hours or costs. The buyer should therefore always make sure that:
  o the supplier keeps a sound cost administration, so that inspection is possible
  o a maximum price is recorded in the contract
  o this amount may only be exceeded after written agreement has been obtained from the buyer
  o the costs which are to be reimbursed are made payable to the supplier on a well-specified invoice.

Escalation clause
Price is linked to a price adjustment formula (index), which is based on external factors such as material costs or changes in labour costs.

- Agreement with price-adjustment (**escalation clauses**). This type of contract is used mainly for agreements with a long-term delivery, or when very specific, market-sensitive materials are processed. The price is linked to a price adjustment formula (index), which is based on **external factors** such as material costs or changes in labour costs.

External factors
Are those which determine the degree of availability of a certain product and which cannot be influenced by individual companies.

When buying equipment, it is recommended to record optional prices for future deliveries of spare parts, and, when appropriate, service rates. Finally, when buying from foreign suppliers, currency risks need to be dealt with. This is quite a challenge for international contractors that operate in the offshore business. The time that elapses between the date of winning the order and the date of completion of the project may easily be a few years. During that period currency exchange rates may change significantly. There are several ways to deal with this. One way is to contract for the materials and services in the same currency as the company will be paid in by its customer. Another way is to work with currency exchange change clauses in the contract, which define how the company will be compensated by its customer in case a currency exchange rate changes. Hedging of currency risk is another option, but this usually is open for contracts with a shorter completion time (less than a year).

Terms of payment

When capital goods or installations are purchased, it is common practice that payment takes place in several terms, partly because the supplier will have to make large investments to be able to produce the desired product. If this method of payment is used, account should be taken of the influence of the payment terms on the final price. Attention should also be paid to covering the currency risk related to paying for goods that have not yet been delivered.

In general, the preferred method of payment is based on the supplier's performance (performance bond). For instance: payment of 20% of the total sum when 25% of the work is completed. The last 5 or 10% of the payment is held back until the client is absolutely sure that the equipment operates exactly as it should or in the case of a service, that the supplier's work has been up to the customer's satisfaction.

Advance payments should preferably be covered by a bank guarantee in which the supplier agrees to fulfil his obligations. Such a bank guarantee completely covers the prepaid sum and is valid for the period of delivery of the part to which the bank guarantee relates. If appropriate, a concern guarantee from the holding company (which is often less expensive) will suffice.

Subsequently, attention should be paid to drawing up an agreement providing specifically for the transfer of ownership.

Penalty clauses and warranty conditions

According to the general purchase conditions of several large companies, suppliers must guarantee with respect to the delivered goods that they are of good quality and completely in accordance with the agreed requirements, specifications, conditions, drawings, samples, etc. and that they are suitable for their intended purpose. Furthermore, the supplier needs to guarantee that the goods will be completely new and free of defects, that new materials of good and suitable quality will be used for the manufacture of these goods and that first-rate technical and expert personnel will be used.

An important clause in the contract is to agree on what legal system the contract will be subject to. Usually, the supplier will select the legal rules that apply for the country in which the supplier is domiciled. These may be different from the country where the buyer is located. Whatever system is chosen, it should be arranged that the purchased goods, or the uses of them, do not contain any risk regarding the health or security of persons, property and environment.

Agreements will also have to be made with the supplier about the performance of the goods to be delivered. In the case of acquisition of investment goods a performance guarantee can be agreed upon, for example by agreeing that a particular production unit will produce 10 tons of end product of a certain quality per day. If the agreed performance is not met, one should first discuss corrective measures. If these also turn out to be inadequate then the resulting costs are to be recovered from the supplier. This procedure must be agreed upon in the terms and conditions of the contract. Penalty clauses do not, therefore, provide a solution for problems occurring at the stage of execution or delivery; at most they can limit the resulting damages afterwards.

In some circumstances, a penalty clause is not effective. This may be the case if, for example, performance of equipment, that is bought, is found to be more than 5% under the agreed performance standard. In such a case, the buyer must have the right to refuse the product or equipment in question. Another example is when a supplier does not meet local legal requirements. Then, the supplier must be able to reject the delivery. Also in this case, a penalty clause will not be effective.

It is also important that the period during which the supplier is liable for the reliability and adequate functioning of the delivered goods in the specified circumstances is recorded in the contract. In general a period of 12 months is included as the warranty period in the terms and conditions of the agreement. The agreement should also state when the warranty comes into effect; this can be the date that the goods are put into service, or it can be the delivery date.

One special aspect in the case of investment goods is the systems responsibility; it is common to demand from the supplier that measures are taken to maintain the delivered product during its economic or technical lifespan. Maintenance and spare parts must be available during this period. This is why manufacturers of trucks are required to maintain their vehicles, sometimes for a period of more than 20 years!

Other arrangements

In many companies the issues described above will be recorded in the general purchase conditions. Other subjects that can be addressed in these regulations include insurance and safety regulations, transfer of rights and obligations, contracting out to third parties and specific terms of delivery.

In general, buyers should strive for a situation in which they can prescribe the company's terms of purchase. In practice, however, a supplier will frequently accept an order only on his own sales conditions. If the supplier does not explicitly reject the terms of purchase in his **order confirmation**, the terms of purchase are still valid (from a legal point of view). If he does reject them, however, then there is basically no consensus and therefore no purchase agreement. In this type of situation, additional negotiations will be necessary. This tug-of-war about terms of sale and purchase is sometimes referred to as the 'battle of forms'.

Naturally, attempts have been made in international trade to standardize much-used trade terms. The Incoterms are an example. The main standard terms and conditions are discussed in Memo 2.2.

Purchase order confirmation
A document that is used by the supplier in which they agree to perform according to the buyer's purchase order.

MEMO 2.2   THE INCOTERMS 1990

Incoterms is short for international commerce terms. These terms relate to several important standard conditions in connection with the delivery and transportation of, and risk attached to, goods. The Incoterms have been carefully defined: it has been established how each condition must be interpreted. Using the Incoterms may prevent misunderstandings between supplier and buyer.

The Incoterms were first published in 1936 and they have been adapted regularly since. The newest version, Incoterms 2000, distinguishes the following standard conditions:

EXW	Ex Works
FCA	Free Carrier
FAS	Free Alongside Ship
FOB	Free On Board
CPT	Carriage Paid To
CIP	Carriage and Insurance Paid To
CFR	Cost and Freight
CIF	Cost, Insurance, Freight
DAF	Delivered at Frontier
DES	Delivered Ex Ship
DEQ	Delivered Ex Quay
DDU	Delivered Duty Unpaid
DDP	Delivered Duty Paid

Each Incoterm arranges the distribution of the costs (transportation, insurance) and the risk (in case of loss and damage) of the physical delivery. In addition, the Incoterms regulate which documents should be provided by the supplier, or that the supplier must help the buyer in this, and who is to pay the costs of these documents. Incoterms do not regulate the legal delivery, the legal transfer of title. This is arranged in the legal system that applies to the purchase agreement.

An Incoterm only applies if both parties have reached an agreement about it and the contract will then refer to the Incoterm in question. Incoterms are not part of permissive or imperative law and parties are free to agree to deviations from an Incoterm. This is risky, however, because adding a word or even a single letter to an Incoterm may lead a judge (especially a foreign judge) to a different interpretation than was intended by the buyer.

The 13 Incoterms 2000 can be organized according to:

- type of transportation
- type of agreement.

Table 2.4 reflects the resulting classification of Incoterms. This classification, as well as their meaning, will be briefly explained, but for a complete explanation see the *Guide to Incoterms,* 2000 edition, published by the International Chamber of Commerce.

The first classification is a very rough one: sea carriage versus 'other' methods of transportation; traditionally, the Incoterms have played an important role in sea carriage. The classification into types of contract determine to a high degree where the physical delivery from supplier to buyer takes place. Four types of contracts can be distinguished:

- departure
- main carriage unpaid

TABLE 2.4 Incoterms 2000 classification

Transportation method		Type of contract		
	Departure	Main carriage unpaid	Main carriage paid	Arrival
Sea carriage	EXW	FOB	CIF	DES
		FAS	CFR	DEQ
Other transportation	EXW	FCA	CPT	DAF
			CIP	DDU
				DDP

- main carriage paid
- arrival.

The first group consists exclusively of the Incoterm EXW (Ex Works). In the case of EXW the buyer is responsible for arranging and settling everything. The supplier only makes the goods available for the buyer, who has to collect these from the factory or warehouse.

In the second group of Incoterms the buyer arranges most of the physical delivery. In the case of sea carriage, the supplier delivers the goods to the quay (FAS) or on board (FOB). Then the ship can leave at the expense and risk of the buyer. The Incoterm FCA rests on the same principle: the supplier has met his obligations as soon as the goods have been transferred to a transporter at the agreed location. In this situation also the supplier carries the costs and responsibility up until the moment that the goods are delivered.

Characteristic of the third group is that the supplier takes responsibility for most of the transport. In the case of sea carriage the supplier will bring the goods into a harbor in the buyer's country. In the case of CIF the supplier pays the costs of loading, transportation and the transport insurance. The risk is transferred to the buyer (as it is in the case of FOB) when the goods have passed the ship's rail. Incoterm CFR is a variation on CIF in which the buyer carries the risk of transportation. It is of course wise to cover this risk by means of transport insurance. The same difference (who carries the risk?) applies to CIP and CPT. In the case of CIP the supplier carries the risk and pays for transportation to the agreed location of transfer; in the case of CPT the buyer carries the transportation risk. Within the fourth group of Incoterms, arrival, the most extreme Incoterms are DDU and DDP. DDP is the exact opposite of EXW in that the supplier brings the goods to the buyer's 'front door'. The same goes for DDU, except that the buyer pays the import duties. Less extreme is delivery to a ship (DES), to the quay (DEQ) or to the border (DAF). There are now two versions of the Incoterm DEQ: duty paid and duty unpaid. This difference is important in view of import duties. Figure 2.7 shows where the supplier is supposed to deliver under the various Incoterms.

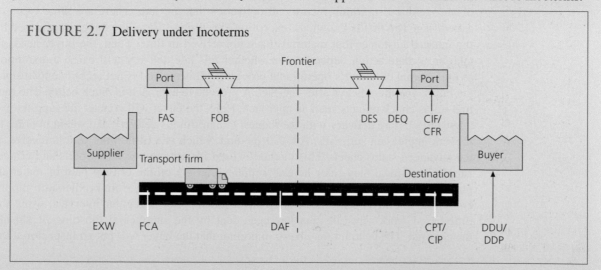

FIGURE 2.7 Delivery under Incoterms

THE ORDERING PROCESS AND EXPEDITING

Routine buy
Relates to the acquisi-
tion of a known prod-
uct from a known sup-
plier (identical to
straight rebuy).

After the terms and conditions of the contract have been agreed and recorded, the order can be placed. In some cases the contract in fact is the purchase order. In other cases, for example in case of a **routine buying** situation, buyers will negotiate a call-off agreement, covering the materials and products needed for a longer period (one year or even longer). Next, purchase orders are placed against this agreement. In those cases contracting and ordering are separate activities.

A purchase order usually is initiated (electronically) through a purchase order requisition or a materials requisition. For production and inventory items this requisition is generated through the materials requirements planning systems through the matching of the materials volume needed for production for a given period and the available (pipeline) inventories. When inventories seem to get lower than their minimum acceptable levels, the MRP-system generates a signal to the purchasing department by means of a detailed materials or purchase order requisition. Most advanced (integrated) materials planning software packages enable the transfer of this requisition to a purchase order electronically. In other cases, purchase requisitions must be initiated manually by filling in purchase requisition forms, which, after approval by the budget holder, are forwarded to the purchasing department.

When ordering from a supplier, it is very important to be specific about the information and instructions to the supplier. Generally, a purchase order will include the following entities: an order number, a concise description of the product, unit price, number of units required, expected delivery time or date, delivery address and invoicing address. A purchase order may contain several order lines, that describe different products that must be delivered. All of these data need to be reflected on the delivery documents and invoice, sent by the supplier in order to facilitate (electronic) matching.

Usually the supplier is requested to send in a confirmation for each purchase order received. Together, the purchase order, the supplier's delivery documents and invoices form the basis for the buyer's vendor rating system (see Chapter 14 for a more detailed discussion of this subject).

If all of these preparatory activities have been executed adequately, there will be less work in the ordering and order handling stages. In practice, however, things often work out differently, and considerable efforts are required from the buyer during the phase of ordering and expediting to make sure that suppliers live up to their agreements. Expediting, therefore, demands a lot of the buyer's attention and is often conducted on the basis of an overdue list, which records all deliveries that are late. There are three types of expediting. The first is known as 'exception expediting'. Here, the buyer is informed by the internal customer that materials have not arrived in time. Then, the buyer needs to take immediate action depending on whether this late delivery will cause a disruption of the internal customer's operational processes. This method is not recommended since the buyer operates always after-the-fact. A preventive approach is much better. The routine status check reflects such an approach. Here, the buyer will contact the supplier just a few days before delivery with the request to confirm his delivery date again in order to prevent unpleasant surprises. Another method, which is a little more time intensive, is the advanced status check. This method is used for critical purchased parts and critical suppliers. Critical may refer here to supplies that are on the critical path of materials planning, or to materials with tight quality tolerances coming from problematic suppliers. Here, the buyer will check progress at the supplier at regular intervals, using the time-based work schedule that has been sent by the supplier at the time of closing the contract. The contract may be so important that the buyer will put an inspector at the supplier's production site. This is known as 'field expediting'. It is limited to very costly and high-risk contracts.

When the products or equipment are delivered they will have to be checked to ensure that they meet the specified requirements. Acceptance of equipment often consists of a number of steps: (1) an **acceptance test** at the supplier's site before shipment, (2) an acceptance test at the user's site after delivery and (3) an acceptance test when the equipment is put into operation for the first time. Depending on the size and technical complexity there may be more than one acceptance test at the supplier's site during the production of the equipment.

The business world is far from ideal. Notwithstanding good contracts and purchase orders, things may go wrong at delivery: delivery times may not be respected by the supplier, quality problems may occur with purchased materials, suppliers may charge more for their products than allowed. Therefore it is very important that the company has a reporting system for all the problems which may occur. Quality and delivery problems should be reported daily to the buyer through a supplier complaint reporting procedure. These problems should be immediately communicated to the supplier in order to prevent a recurrence in the future. In other chapters in this book this matter will be discussed in more detail (see Chapters 11 and 12).

Acceptance test
This is a technical test performed at either the supplier's site, the buyer's site or both, to check whether the equipment that is bought by the buyer meets their functional and technical requirements.

FOLLOW-UP AND EVALUATION OF THE BUYING PROCESS

The buyer's role continues even after the new product has been taken into production, or the new installation has been put into operation. Warranty claims and penalty clauses need to be settled. Excess and minor work needs to be administered and arranged. Purchasing and supplier files need to be updated and archived. Supplier and project evaluations need to be finalized and filed.

With regard to excess work, it is important to establish that this must be reported to the principal in advance, and that the principal must give permission first. Extra work must always be reported to the purchasing manager so that the purchase costs remain clear. This fosters efficient administrative processing of the invoices that are submitted later on by the supplier.

In the case of investment goods, maintenance activities will become necessary after a while. At that time it becomes clear whether the supplier can substantiate promises about service, maintenance and the supply of spare parts.

Experiences with individual suppliers should be documented carefully. It is recommended that buyers keep track of the supplier's quality and delivery record, competitiveness and innovativeness since these data can lead to an adjustment of the so-called vendor rating (see Chapter 14). It is important to have a thorough and up-to-date record of the actual capabilities of each supplier. Reporting this kind of information, both to management and the supplier's management, is one major source of added value contributed by the buyer. That concludes the cycle, because this information can be used in a subsequent purchasing cycle to assemble the bidders' short list for future projects and contracts. In this way the company learns to work with suppliers with proven capabilities. When companies learn to work this way, this usually results in a significant reduction of the supplier base. Companies, then, will gradually concentrate more business among the suppliers who, based on their excellent vendor rating scores, have proven to be their best.

E-PROCUREMENT

Electronic marketplace

Is a marketplace on the Internet where, with the support of Internet technology, transactions between business-to-business partners can be made.

Auction, electronic (e-auction)

Electronic auction (e-auction) is a tool used by the buyer to invite suppliers to bid simultaneously based on a predetermined purchasing specification using web technology.

E-procurement solutions, here, are defined as all web enabled solutions aimed at supporting the purchasing process and all electronic data exchange that is needed for efficient transaction processing. E-procurement solutions basically can be divided into three types: **electronic marketplaces,** electronic auctions (e-auctions) and electronic catalogue, order and payment solutions (order to pay solutions). Each of these solutions is described below.

An electronic marketplace is a marketplace on the Internet where, with the support of Internet technology, transactions between business-to-business partners can be made. Electronic marketplaces simplify the process of searching and finding suitable suppliers. Purchasing professionals are allowed to go beyond traditional supplier markets to find new suppliers. Important marketplaces are, amongst others, www.wwre.com for retailers, www.foodtrader.com for food producers, www.chemconnect.com for chemical companies, www.areoxchange.com for the aerospace industry and www.covisint.com for the automotive industry. Marketplaces that particularly serve the interests of consumers are www.ebay.com and www.marktplaats.com (Dutch).

Among the e-procurement solutions **electronic auctions** are the most popular. They are not new to most businesses. Most of us will be familiar with antique auctions, that are conducted by famous market makers Christie's and Sotheby's. Also for most agricultural products, like wheat and soybeans, international trade exchanges exist where buyers and sellers daily meet for their transactions. Other examples are flowers and vegetables, which are traditionally traded through public auctions. An important characteristic of auctions is that the price is made by bringing supply and demand together in a transparent way. Web technology today allows these auctions to be conducted virtually. Electronic auctions can have different forms. We make a distinction here between:

Request for proposal (RFP)

Suppliers are invited to submit a first proposal prior to the buyer's invitation to tender which meets the requirements as laid down in the request for quotation.

- Open RFI/RFP. In this case, potential suppliers are requested by the buyer to qualify before the actual auction will take place. The buyer will assure that the supplier will meet certain basic qualifications. Suppliers are requested to provide important background information, like their financial status and customer references, their product range and information covering their expertise and experience. The buyer obtains this information through a so-called request for information (RFI), that is sent to the supplier through the web. Next, the buyer can send a **request for proposal** (RFP) to the supplier to get a first idea about his competitiveness. After an evaluation of their initial proposals, it is decided which suppliers will be invited for the actual auction.

- Reversed auction. In this type of auction (see Figure 2.8) the buyer sets a starting price that the supplier needs to meet in order to get access to the auction. Visible in the auction is also the target price that the buyer wants to reach as a minimum. If this target price is not reached, the auction will not be awarded. During the auction suppliers can follow the price mechanism. How this information is presented towards the supplier can be decided by the buyer, who can decide to show the actual prices as they are offered by the suppliers, but can also decide to show them only their ranking. Next, the buyer may decide to show only the price difference between the actual supplier price and the best price. The supplier may perceive at any time the number of 'clicks' required to meet the best price proposal. Buyers can also each determine that suppliers need to come up with a proposal every five or ten minutes to assure sufficient activity during the auction and to prevent 'bird watching'. Suppliers that do not provide bids every ten minutes are to be eliminated from the auction.

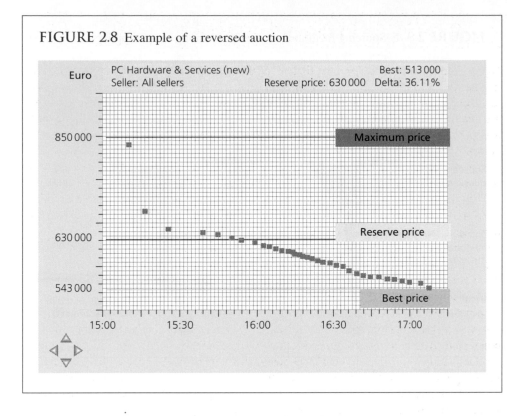

FIGURE 2.8 Example of a reversed auction

- **Forward auction**. This auction is used to sell products. Different buyers need to offer their bids to the seller. Also in this case the auction manager can decide about a target sales price at the beginning of the auction. The seller can decide about the same aspects as the buyer in the case of a **reverse auction**, on how to manage their auction.

For obvious reasons, the reverse auction is the most popular among buyers. In some cases, however, the forward auction is used by buyers. For example, in the case of selling surplus materials, inventories and machines, that otherwise would be scrapped.

Auctions cannot be applied in all situations. Markets as well as products should meet a number of conditions. It is essential that a high volume is committed. This is necessary to ensure that the savings that result from the auction will outweigh the investments in terms of time and money. There should be sufficient competition among suppliers. There should be a level playing field to allow suppliers to compete under equal conditions. The buyer should be sufficiently interesting for the supplier to prepare for the auction. Apart from these conditions, the specifications that are communicated to the suppliers should be very clear and not subject to change. The buyer should support the supplier in getting sufficiently acquainted with the auction software and methodology. These are just a few concerns that an auction manager needs to consider when conducting an e-auction.

An important advantage of electronic auctions is the considerable savings that can be generated. In practice the savings can vary between 5 and 40%. The savings are possible through the meticulous preparation that is required from the buyer. All departments and specialists involved with the purchase need to be aligned. Another reason for these savings is the fact that an e-auction essentially causes suppliers to compete against each other. The

Auction, forward
An e-auction which is used by suppliers to enforce bidding among a number of prospective buyers based on a starting price that is increased during the auction.

Auction, reverse
An e-auction which is used by buyers to enforce competitive bidding among a limited number of prequalified suppliers based on a starting price that is lowered during the auction.

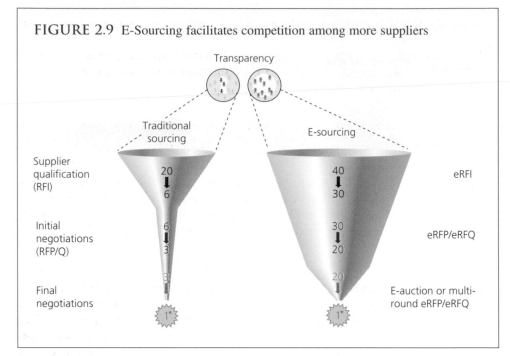

FIGURE 2.9 E-Sourcing facilitates competition among more suppliers

Source: adapted from IBX, Sweden

buyer is able to create more competition among a larger sample of suppliers than he is able to do in face-to-face negotiations (see Figure 2.9). Preparing for an e-auction, however, will take time and this is considered by some managers to be an important disadvantage. Of course, most suppliers do not like this type of electronic buying since the price pressure that is generated by electronic auctions generally reduces their margins. They do not like to be put on a level playing field. Of course, e-auctions cost time and money. The benefits should clearly outweigh the investment. Therefore, e-auctions are used for products and services that are bought at large volumes (such as leverage items and routine items, see Chapter 9).

Electronic catalogues and ordering systems Are used for more efficient order handling, improved logistics and improved and better-controlled payments. May be integrated with the company's ERP-system.

The third type of e-procurement solutions is **electronic catalogues and ordering systems.** Electronic catalogues offer buyers greater opportunities for more efficient order handling, improved logistics and improved and better controlled payments. The information technology that is available today allows companies to manage impressive amounts of transactions without any human interference. Cisco, the global leader in routers and other Internet technology, may serves as an example. By the year 2000, this company had already reported that 55% of its orders, coming from over 34 000 customers, representing an order volume of $4 billion, were managed without any Cisco interference. Besides considerable savings on transaction costs, the introduction of this type of e-procurement solution allows for a considerable reduction of customer order lead times. Through this technology Cisco was able to reduce customer order lead time from 6 to 8 weeks to less than 3 weeks. Handling costs per order may be reduced from €100 to mere tens of cents.

By using electronic catalogue systems more purchasing transactions can be brought under contract, as a result of which the percentage of maverick buying[4] can be reduced

---

[4]Maverick buying relates to the percentage of purchases made beyond existing corporate purchasing agreements.

considerably. This is another reason why this type of solution may result in a considerable purchasing saving.

Introducing this type of procurement solutions, however, requires considerable sophistication and expertise. Generally, with regard to electronic transaction processing, many companies still have a long way to go.

MAJOR BOTTLENECKS AND PROBLEMS

The purchasing process model that has been presented in this chapter is a construct, an abstraction from reality. In the real world organizational purchasing processes deviate from this model. Observation of numerous companies and institutions over many years has demonstrated that the purchasing process can be obstructed by the following situations:

- Supplier or brand specifications. Specifications are worked out in detail by the user, i.e. a technical specialist, and written for one specific supplier. The use of a particular brand or supplier specification seriously limits the buyer's commercial latitude (in terms of negotiations) with the supplier, who in most cases is well aware of the selection of his product. Only recognizing the technical expertise of a supplier, may easily lead to situations where the supplier selected cannot meet the capacity and logistics requirements of the company:

- Inadequate supplier selection. Selecting a supplier is one of the most important decisions in the purchasing process, particularly if the products delivered require many years of maintenance and service (as in the case of many investment goods). Failure to check the supplier's (bank) references can produce very unpleasant surprises such as unexpected bankruptcy, inability to meet quality requirements or unwillingness to keep up to warranty obligations.

- Personal relationships. Purchase orders are placed with suppliers with whom the user has a friendly relationship; this is one reason why long relationships between organizations may exist. As a result such suppliers may not be as competitive as the internal customers think they are.

- Lack of good contractual arrangements. Contracts, when available, are stated in general terms, they are not complete and have not passed legal scrutiny, and a clear description of the product or supplier requirements may be missing. Another problem may be, that the contract is drafted by the supplier using its own legal terms and conditions.

- Too much emphasis on price. Especially when buying capital equipment buying decisions need to be based upon total cost of ownership (TCO) rather than price only. Many equipment manufacturers (e.g. computer printers) have adopted a sales strategy where they charge a fairly low price for their equipment. However, their warranties and service contracts require the customer to source spare parts and all maintenance services from the original equipment manufacturer (OEM). In order to handle this type of purchase effectively, buyers need to base their decisions on TCO models in which the initial purchase of the equipment is balanced against the lifecycle costs of the equipment.

- Poor administrative processes. In some cases the supplier may have actually made the delivery, and now the purchasing department is requested by the user to produce a purchase order with a purchase order number to be issued to the supplier so that payment can be made. Another administrative problem may be that invoices are paid without proper matching with the original purchase order and delivery document. Putting a sound administrative system in place could lead to significant savings (see Memo 2.3).

- Delivery problems. At the stage of delivery, problems occur: suppliers deliver too late, deliveries are not complete, products are damaged or do not meet quality requirements, packaging is unsound, and information labels cannot be read by bar code systems. The reason for these problems usually can be traced back to unclear specifications or a careless supplier selection. Another reason may be that suppliers are not systematically evaluated, as a result of which troublesome suppliers stay on board and delivery problems occur time after time.

To prevent these problems, companies need clear rules and guidelines with regard to procurement governance. A professional administrative organization should be in place. In dealing with payments of invoices, a basic principle should be that invoices without a purchase order number will not get paid. Another principle could be that, from a certain financial value, the organization commits itself to issuing three competitive bids before awarding a contract to a supplier. A third principle could be that the organization decides that a formal contract is needed before engaging in a formal relationship with a supplier and making any purchase order.

Budget authority
Allows a manager to spend money and resources of the company for company purposes.

This set of rules and guidelines should be communicated to the supplier community with the names of the persons who will have procurement authority. Procurement authority needs to be differentiated from **budget authority**. When these rules and guidelines are in place, companies will not only benefit from fewer delivery problems but will also get much better value for the money that they spend. However, as we will see further in this book, in practice it is far from simple to put these procurement governance in place.

SUMMARY

This chapter describes how organizational buying behaviour can be studied and analysed. The conclusion is that the buying behaviour of organizations differs significantly from consumer buying behaviour. Industrial companies, governmental organizations and institutions buy goods and services to feed, support and maintain their primary and supportive processes, while consumers purchase products to immediately satisfy their needs. The value of the models that have been developed for explaining consumer buying behaviour is therefore, in the author's opinion, limited when studying industrial buying processes.

Several theoretical models in the field of **industrial buying behaviour** were discussed in this chapter. A distinction can be made between the models that view the purchasing process exclusively from an organizational perspective, and the models that regard the buying process as an interaction between two or more parties. Both types of models have their value: they explain why it is often so difficult for an outsider to fathom organizational purchasing processes and why they are often so hard to organize.

Although organizational purchasing processes may vary to a great extent, each purchasing process evolves according to similar stages. In this chapter the purchasing process model has been explained. The essence of this model is that effective purchasing decision-making requires a cross-functional approach. The key issue is to direct and guide the efforts of the various organizational parties involved in such a way, that an optimal result is achieved for the organization. The professional buyer can make a major contribution here. Not all phases of the purchasing process are passed through in all cases. Three types of buying situations can be distinguished: the new-task situation, the modified rebuy and the straight rebuy. The composition of the decision-making unit (DMU) will be different for each of these situations.

In this chapter the position of the purchasing department was discussed. In general, the purchasing department's involvement is highest when it concerns the purchase of routine items. Its role is more limited when it concerns investment goods. It has furthermore been demonstrated that purchasing's involvement is highest during the operational stages of the purchasing process; purchasing's involvement is relatively low in the early stages of product development (when specifications are determined and materials selected). Theory runs ahead of practice here.

The purchasing process model offers organizations a tool for structuring their purchasing processes. Ideally, each stage of the purchasing process should result in some kind of a decision document. These documents are as follows: the purchase order specification, the supplier selection proposal, the purchasing contract, the purchase order, the delivery document, the invoice and the vendor rating. Using these documents allows for effective tracing and tracking of all aspects of the purchasing process. However, using this type of tracing and tracking requires the effort of many stakeholders in the organization. It may also lead to longer lead times. Of course an efficient purchasing administrative organization and system should be in place.

E-procurement solutions offer the purchasing professional today many opportunities to deal with most of the problems that are related to the management of purchasing processes. Electronic marketplaces provide for a fast and efficient scanning of supplier markets and supply market opportunities. Electronic auctions may facilitate a more transparent pricing mechanism among competing suppliers, resulting in considerable purchasing savings. Electronic catalogues and order-to-pay solutions will contribute to more efficient transaction processing at a lower cost, whilst at the same time reducing maverick buying. Whatever procurement solution the company goes for, they should match the internal operational processes and match the IT infrastructure that is present within the company.

Industrial buying behaviour
Set of internal and external variables and model that explain how organizations make buying decisions.

ASSIGNMENTS

2.1 To what extent is the purchasing process model in your opinion complete? What would you like to add or change?

2.2 What is meant by 'procurement governance' and what does it take a company to put a proper 'procurement governance' in place?

2.3 What would it take a procurement manager of a manufacturer of consumer electronics, based upon the purchasing process model, to arrive at zero defects deliveries to the internal customer?

2.4 As a buyer for a do-it-yourself chain you import hand-tooling equipment from China. You desperately want to have these tools before the spring in your supermarkets. What Incoterms would you choose for your purchasing contract with the Chinese supplier and why?

2.5 What is the value of a procurement auctions for a buyer? When would you go for an e-auction? Provide arguments for and against.

REFERENCES

Brand, G. (1968) *How British Industry Buys*, London: Hutchinson.

Fisher, L. (1970) *Industrial Marketing: an Analytical Approach to Planning and Execution*, 2nd edn, London: Business Book.

Lehman, D.R. and O'Shaughnessy, J. (1974) 'Different industrial products', *Journal of Marketing*, April: 36–42.

Robinson, P.J., Faris, Ch. W. and Wind, Y. (1967) *Industrial Buying and Creative Marketing*, Boston: Allyn & Bacon.

Sheth, J.N. (1973) 'A model of industrial buyer behaviour', *Journal of Marketing*, October:50–54.

Webster, F.E. and Wind, Y. (1972) *Organizational Buying Behaviour*, Englewood Cliffs, NJ: Prentice-Hall.

Wynstra, J.Y.F. (1998) Purchasing Involvement in Product Development, PhD dissertation, Eindhoven University of Technology.

THE PURCHASING MANAGEMENT PROCESS

LEARNING OBJECTIVES

After studying this chapter you should understand the following:

- The major tasks and responsibilities of purchasing.
- The basic principles on which purchasing policy can be based.
- The major policy areas in purchasing.
- How purchasing may develop over time as a business function.

INTRODUCTION

Procter & Gamble, as discussed in the following case study, is not the only multinational company that went through a massive transition in its purchasing and supply operations and strategies. As large retailers have intensified their struggle for a larger share of the consumer's wallet, they have put increasing pressure on their manufacturers and suppliers. Cost control and new product innovation are, therefore, key to the consumer goods manufacturers. As a result these manufacturers have put the spotlight on their purchasing and supply operations. Procter & Gamble have set an example that is followed by many others.

When discussing how to professionalize purchasing and supply operations, we observe major differences among organizations and industries. Tasks, responsibilities and the degree of authority, assigned to the purchasing department, differ greatly, even among companies which are operating in the same industry. The objective of this chapter is to systematically answer the question of what it takes to professionalize purchasing as a key business driver, building on the concepts presented in the previous chapters. This chapter describes the basic principles underlying modern purchasing and supply management, and the key elements of the **purchasing management** process. The chapter ends with a discussion on how purchasing and supply management may develop as a business function over time.

Purchasing management
Relates to all activities necessary to manage supplier relationships in such a way that their activities are aligned with the company's overall business strategies and interests.

CASE STUDY P&G IS KING OF COLLABORATION

If only William Procter and James Gamble could see the company they started now! In 1837, when the brothers-in-law began making soaps and candles, their supply base was limited to nearby meat-packing plants in the general vicinity of Cincinnati, where they sourced lard and beef tallow.

Today, that supply base stretches across the globe, and the $83.5-billion company sources thousands of chemicals, polymers, packaging and other materials for some 300 products – ranging from prescription-medication Actonel to Zest hair and body wash. Procter & Gamble (P&G) today is, according to many analysts, the largest consumer-products company in the world. And among its hallmarks is a dedication to continuing the kind of collaboration that brought its founders together. Now, of course, there are many more parties to collaborate with...

Some 90 000 suppliers provide the raw materials used by the company's 150 manufacturing plants worldwide, and supply P&G a separate suite of already-manufactured finished products. It's one of the largest supply bases in the world. And, the number is down from 100 000 three years ago. The company plans to knock it down further, to 70 000 in the next two years, even while adding new suppliers where appropriate. Of the total, 400 suppliers qualify as key partners and get about a quarter of P&G's spend.

Managing collaborative relationships with such a large and dispersed supply base is a gargantuan chore, especially since, by corporate design, much of the innovation behind P&G's products comes from outside the company, including the supply base. But P&G's Global Purchases organization has excelled in that management. And for its success, as well as its accomplishments in delivering both value and significant savings to the corporation, *Purchasing* has awarded the company its Medal of Professional Excellence.

The 1700-strong Global Purchases group, led by Vice President Richard A. Hughes, includes 1400 buyers and managers. It's a globally focused, center-led organization that covers nearly 100% of P&G's $48 billion outside spend. Excluded from its mandate are taxes, contributions and mergers/acquisitions.

Here is the basic organizational structure:

- Global Purchases has strategic sourcing groups located in six regional centers (Cincinnati; Geneva, Switzerland; Frankfurt, Germany; Guangzhou, China; Singapore and Caracas, Venezuela.). The staff uses software from SAP as the backbone of its spend-management efforts. It also uses Combinenet and Upside software.

- There is one purchasing leader for each category of spend who speaks for and represents all of P&G's business units for that category or industry. Among the spend categories: chemicals; packaging; logistics; shared services such as **MRO**, IT, consulting and facilities management; and marketing.

- Additionally, many of those category leaders represent the Global Purchases organization on business-unit leadership teams, providing a single point of contact for the business-unit presidents. 'That matrix allows us to stay in touch with our businesses and leverage scale and knowledge across the company,' says Hughes.

- Buyers also are part of the company's Global Business Services organization, leading supplier management and spend for outside services, such as consulting and professional services, facilities management, employee services and IT support.

- Of the 90 000 suppliers, 15 000 are in the marketing arena, a core competency for P&G as it is for many consumer-products companies. Those 15 000 include advertising agencies and other marketing-services-related suppliers around the world.

- About 600 other suppliers provide the **finished products** to P&G, like the Mr. Clean Magic Eraser and Swiffer product lines. They actually make the final products in their own plants under the guidance of purchasing and operation staff in P&G's external supplies and global devices organization...

Rising energy costs have drained budgets. Those same costs, among other economic factors, have pushed up the costs of the raw materials P&G and other companies need to historic highs. But recovering those costs through higher prices to customers can be a losing strategy. 'With consumer spending dropping, you can't price yourself out of reach,' says Harrison. That leads to unprecedented emphasis on cost-improvement strategies. 'P&G has done great cost reduction work over the last couple of years,' he says... Since 1995 the organization has delivered more than $1 billion per year in savings. In 2007, the figure was $2 billion. Results like that have helped the company post healthy financial results...

Source: *Purchasing, November, 9th, 2008*

PRIMARY TASKS AND RESPONSIBILITIES

Based on the framework of concepts developed earlier, the following tasks responsibilities are considered to be core to the purchasing function in any organization. In each organization purchasing and supply managers have to take care of the following:

- Secure timely and undisturbed availability of purchased goods and services, both in the short and long term. This relates to purchasing's *supply task*. The materials and services which are to be purchased, must become available in line with the requirements of purchasing's internal customers. Purchasing's primary task is, therefore, that of securing supply from reliable suppliers of a consistent quality at reasonable (total) cost. Effective and efficient supply is mandatory. If this task is not executed effectively, the buyer and the purchasing department will lose their credibility. The internal customers, such as marketing, engineering, manufacturing and technical maintenance, will then bypass the purchasing department and start doing purchasing on their own. Effective purchasing therefore requires an explicit supply orientation.

- Control and reduction of all purchasing-related spend. This relates to purchasing's *spend management task*. Having secured supply, purchasing needs to make sure that goods and services are supplied at the lowest total cost of ownership (TCO) or best value. TCO consists of two major elements: direct materials cost and all (indirect) costs related to the logistics and handling of these materials (costs related to transport, incoming inspection, materials handling, inventory, administration, and scrap, etc.). Buyers should attempt to reduce indirect costs by reducing the 'buffers or 'waste' that may be built into the company's materials process or supply chain (e.g., safety stocks, incoming inspection, quality inspection, field expediting). Best value relates to the best value the company can acquire against the money spent. Of course, a major task is to make sure that materials and services are bought at fair and **competitive prices** from the best suppliers that can be found. Whatever purchasing decision is made, however, it requires a sound balancing of cost versus risk and value aspects. In view of the fact that on average 60% of the production value of industrial companies consists of purchased products, it is obvious that purchasing's contribution on this aspect is a major one.[1]

- Reduction of the company's risk exposure in relation to its supply markets. This relates to purchasing's *risk management task*. If possible, the company should avoid becoming too dependent on just a few suppliers. Both in terms of supply and technology. 'Captive' sales situations must be prevented or reduced and it is important to have access to reliable suppliers because high quality and punctual delivery are often more important than price. In order to minimize its technological and supply risks in the long term, the company's management preferably should aim to spread its purchasing requirements among different suppliers. Memo 3.1 illustrates what might happen if a company reduces its supply base too much. Today, purchasing managers should contribute to Corporate Social Responsibility (CSR) to make sure that the company's supply chains operate according to agreed rules and guidelines in the area of human rights, and local labour laws and environmental laws.

- Contribution to product and process innovation. This relates to purchasing's *development task*. Suppliers are often a source of new products and production technologies. In many industries technological developments take place at such a rate that even large enterprises, such as Philips Electronics and IBM, are unable to generate all the investments needed to keep up with technology development in every area. In some cases this leads to partnerships with suppliers in the research and development field.

Maintenance, repair and operating materials (MRO items)
These products, sometimes referred to as indirect materials or consumable items, represent materials, which are necessary for keeping the organization running in general, and for the support activities in particular.

Finished products
These encompass all products which are purchased to be sold, after negligible added value, either together with other finished products or manufactured products (identical to trade items).

Pricing, competitive
The price paid for a product is based upon competitive tendering among a number of preselected suppliers. E-auctions or other formal tendering vehicles may be used.

---

[1]See also Chapter 1 on purchasing's impact on the company's return on net assets (DuPont analysis).

MEMO 3.1   STEEL SHORTAGES AT NISSAN

One of the most competitive arenas in business is the relationship between automotive companies and their steel suppliers. Since steel makes up an important part of a car's cost price, and since many steel suppliers exist in the global marketplace, buyers of automotive companies are relentlessly looking for opportunities to reduce steel prices and costs. In its endeavor to pay competitive prices for steel, Nissan in Japan decided in 2004 to reduce its number of steel suppliers to just two companies: Nippon Steel and JFE Steel. By allocating its huge volume to just two suppliers, the company was able to realize considerable price reductions.

The markets for commodities like steel are characterized by supply and demand. Since the relationship between supply and demand may vary over time, the negotiation position between market parties is subject to change. Buyers' markets, where automotive manufacturers are in the lead, may change into times where supply is scarce and where, conversely, steel suppliers are in the lead. Experienced steel buyers are aware of this business cycle with its downturns and upswings. As an automotive manufacturer, you have to be careful not to upset steel suppliers in an economic downturn, since this may backfire in times when suppliers are in the lead and when you are in desperate need of certain steel volumes.

This became painfully clear to Nissan in late 2004 when, despite being Japan's second-biggest carmaker, it needed to suspend operations at three of its four domestic plants. Earlier, in September that year, Nissan introduced a series of new automotive models in Japan which, of course, required higher steel volumes. Demand for new models, including the Tiida compact car and Fuga sedan, was high and started to outstrip the company's projections. As a result Nissan sought more steel from its suppliers – Nippon Steel and JFE Steel – however both were at that time operating at full capacity to meet booming demand at home and in China and were unable to comply to Nissan's requests for delivery. Steel prices had also been rising due to tight raw material supplies and the surge in demand from the Chinese economy. Given the less attractive prices which would be paid by Nissan, both companies were not willing to change their capacity commitments at the cost of losing other more profitable customers. As a result Nissan had to skip production of over 25.000 vehicles in the next year.

The Smart Car, which was developed by Daimler-Chrysler in co-operation with Swatch company is one example; another is the development of high-precision wafer steppers (for the manufacture of microchips) by ASM Lithography in The Netherlands with Carl Zeiss, manufacturer of high-tech lenses, from Germany.

The company's image is partly determined by what it communicates to its customer markets and the financial community. It is certainly also influenced by what it communicates to its suppliers. A fair and open attitude towards suppliers can help the company position itself as an attractive business partner. Buyers must make sure that the company actually meets its contractual obligations towards suppliers. It is therefore important that purchasing operates according to a minimum set of purchasing procedures which describe how orders are placed, who is authorized to make purchasing decisions and how the purchasing process is structured. The ways of working should be described preferably in purchasing procedures, which are simple to use and easy to communicate. Examples of such procedures are the simple rule that no invoice will be paid to suppliers unless it has a purchase order number. Or, another example: that all purchases beyond a certain amount of money (for instance, €5000) need to be covered by at least three quotations from suppliers. Of increasing importance are codes of conduct on how to deal with supplier relationships, on what is allowed when accepting gifts and other fringe benefits from suppliers. As co-collaboration with suppliers becomes more intensive the need for this kind of formal procedures grows.[2] The importance of a clear and professional communication on the company's purchasing policies is increasingly being recognized by larger companies (see Memo 3.2). Most of them have developed over time brochures and sophisticated

[2]See also Chapter 17 on 'rules of conduct' and 'purchasing ethics'.

MEMO 3.2 THE CHANGING PURCHASING AGENDA: MANAGING COST, RISK AND VALUE

During the past years the traditional agenda of the purchasing manager has changed dramatically. For many years purchasing managers had only one important priority: cost reduction. Buyers have been very creative in this area. Electronic auctions were used to create maximum competition in supply markets and to play off suppliers against each other. In many companies the number of suppliers has been drastically reduced as the result of a supply base reduction programme. The objective was to go for the lowest possible price at much lower transaction costs. Local suppliers were replaced with suppliers from low-cost countries. However, as a consequence of these actions the dependency on suppliers increased. Global sourcing contributed to an increasing complexity of international supply chains, causing many disruptions in the supply of materials. The traditional strong price orientation in purchasing deteriorated the margins of smaller suppliers, which were taken over by large powerful companies. As a consequence the concentration of large companies in many industries increased and the number of players decreased. Global sourcing gave rise to discussions with regard to sustainability and ethical questions were raised about child labour and exploiting people in low-cost countries. Some large Western companies, among them Mattel, manufacturer of Barbie dolls and other toys, suffered from bad news in September 2007 in the financial press because of using suppliers who clearly violated product safety regulations. Obviously, reducing suppliers and pursuing global sourcing gave rise to important supply risks. Supply risks that should be made visible and transparent today. As a consequence risk management in supply-chain management has become an increasingly important topic. This is not all. Suppliers in many industries represent an important source of innovation. Therefore, it has become strategically important to involve suppliers early in the company's new product development processes. Suppliers today are requested to contribute to a large part of the new product development budget. As a vehicle so-called 'gain and risk sharing agreements' are used. In these agreements the supplier future income is partially determined by the success of the customer's new products in its end markets. In this kind of collaboration the traditional, arm's length buyer–supplier relationship gradually evolves into a longer term strategic partnership, i.e. strategic alliance. In this new type of supply chain collaboration discussions focus much more on growth and revenue generation, than on pressing the supplier for the lowest possible cost per unit. Figure 3.1 summarizes this idea. The figure indicates that many topics have been added to the traditional purchasing agenda. Increasingly, purchasing managers need to balance cost and risk factors against value aspects.

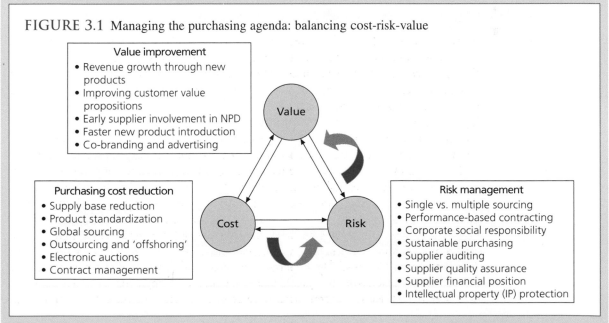

FIGURE 3.1 Managing the purchasing agenda: balancing cost-risk-value

purchasing Internet solutions to explain their policies both internally and externally. It is part of the purchasing manager's responsibility to communicate how the company wants to act in the relationship with its suppliers.

A clear purchasing process model, as presented in Chapter 2, may help purchasing manages to organize for these important purchasing tasks and responsibilities. Preferably, the purchasing process needs to be structured in a number of steps. This is necessary to create uniformity in the way purchasing managers operate, internally as well as externally. The purchasing procedure and policies need to cover all stages of the purchasing process model. It should be based on a clear sequencing of the different purchasing activities, so that a description can be made of the roles and responsibilities between all disciplines involved in a particular purchase. Figure 3.2 illustrates how Chevron has structured its purchasing process worldwide. It is the purchasing managers task to explain how purchasing processes are structured in the organization. Many companies use attractive purchasing intranet solutions for this purpose, which provide access to all employees. The objective in all cases is to show how the company deals with important purchasing decisions and what role the company's purchasing professionals fulfil in this process. Based upon this purchasing process model, purchasing procedures are worked out in detail by means of a purchasing manual. This manual provides the rules and guidelines on how to operate with purchasing decision-making processes and how to deal with supplier relationships in detail. Hence, such a manual is the basis for the periodic internal audit. The purchasing manual is a essential part of the company's governance and control structure. Figure 3.3 provides an example of a simple purchasing procedure.

Purchasing authority
Allows a manager to legally bind their company to an external partner.

It is important to decide on who in the organization has **purchasing authority**. Here, a distinction needs to be made between budget authority and procurement authority. Only when a manager has purchasing authority is he or she entitled to engage in a contractual relationship between the organization and a third party. As a consequence, a contract needs to be signed by at least two parties in the company, i.e. the budget holder and the

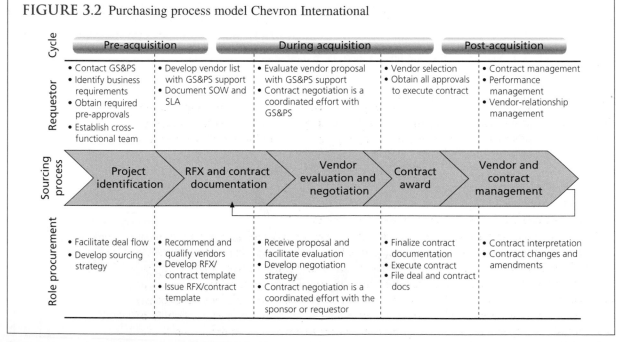

FIGURE 3.2 Purchasing process model Chevron International

Source: www.purchasing.com

FIGURE 3.3 Purchasing procedure (example)

STANDARD PURCHASE PROCEDURE

Choose the best companies (according to their reputation, references, quality of service, competitiveness, motivation and dynamism)

 I. Send an offer of collaboration to those different companies on the same day, enclosing the specifications and projecting the final reply date, in a strictly confidential letter.

 II. Reject the offers delivered after the deadline.

 III. Proceed with an opening session of the letters, in the presence of:
   • the financial management
   • the purchase management
   • the management concerned with the purchase.

 IV. Jointly countersign the offers, send a copy of these to those concerned.

 V. Draw up a comparative table of costs.

 VI. Proceed with a consistency check of offers on a technical level.

 VII. Check the debit–equity ratio of the companies.

 VIII. Preselect the two best proposals, according to quality and costs.

 IX. Check the references.

 X. Draw up an assessment grid of recent realizations.

 XI. Compare costs and renegotiate item by item.

 XII. Recommend a final choice (favouring quality, price, security).

 XIII. Maintain contact with the other supplier, to avoid any monopolies.

 XIV. Draft the contract with our legal department (payment methods, penalties for lateness, etc....).

 XV. Write to the companies not chosen to notify them of our refusal.

 XVI. Regularly sound out the competition.

 XVII. Preserve our partners' long-term motivations.

Source: Claire Cortez, Purchasing Manager, Brasseries Heineken, 1998

purchasing professional. It is important to apply separate roles here. The budget holder signs off allocation of the budget. The purchasing manager's signature indicates that the purchase was made in accordance with the company's overall purchasing rules and guidelines. Next, a clear division of roles should be made when it comes to payment of the invoices. There should be a separation of roles between the person who actually orders a certain product, the person who checks up on inspection at delivery, and the person who decides about the actual payment. The reason for this is to prevent fraud. Therefore, these activities can never be accomplished by the same person.

The relevance of this simple structure becomes clear if one keeps an eye on the news. Regularly, the international press reports on irregularities that have occurred in the way a company spent its money. Some years ago, at a major university in one of the European countries, an administrative clerk from the finance and administration department was sentenced for fraud. For about 5 years this person had sent the university invoices from a small company that he had set up. Invoices were small and in the range of a couple of thousand of euros per month. Over a period of 5 years this person was able to cash over €250 000, for services that they never provided. All invoices were signed off by themselves. The auditors found no formal agreement when they stumbled on this case. Nor did they find any procedures that would stipulate how the university would go about checking on and paying invoices. Obviously, some basic rules about how to allocate responsibilities and authorities with regard to the operational purchasing process were violated heavily within this university.

As mentioned earlier, it is important that invoices that are sent to the company by suppliers reflect the company's purchase order number. Invoices that do not have such a number will not get paid. In this way the company keeps control of its massive purchasing spend.

Of course, it is not necessary that all purchasing processes are structured in the same way. Whether a purchasing decision needs to be aligned exactly according to the company's agreed purchasing policies and procedures will be decided by the strategic importance that it represents to the company. Small transactions and orders need to be managed and dealt with fast and efficiently and without any bureaucracy. For small orders, it will not be practical to ask for different proposals from suppliers. The savings will probably not outweigh the costs. This is different for large purchase orders and strategic purchasing decisions. Therefore, every company needs to decide at what financial threshold the purchasing process model needs to be applied. In all cases, our purchasing process model needs to be translated into a pragmatic and sound purchasing procedure.

It is not only important to have clear rules and guidelines to manage the internal process of purchasing. Rules and guidelines are also necessary to orchestrate the many and often complex relationships with suppliers. Such rules and guidelines are needed because the financial interests in the relationship with suppliers can be very high. The purchasing policy and the way in which it is executed clearly affect the reputation of the company to its external world. Through a businesslike but fair attitude the organization is able to position itself as an attractive and reliable business partner to suppliers. Rules and guidelines are needed, related to the acceptance of business gifts, invitations for study trips, seminars, conferences, dinners, etc. Purchasing professionals need to ensure that contractual arrangements made with suppliers are never violated by unethical behaviour by company managers, or that these managers end up in situations in which the company is compromised. Therefore, such rules and guidelines need to be communicated effectively to the supplier community.

Purchasing professionals need to support the company's business managers in realizing their business objectives and goals. Buyers should therefore spend a substantial part of their time in contact with internal users, such as marketing, operations, product development and engineering. Bureaucracy ('this order must be placed according to our purchasing procedures') and too strong an emphasis on price aspects ('let's see what discount we can get'), which many buyers are accused of in practice, are incompatible with a true business orientation. Experience shows that internal users will only consider costs when they are convinced the buyer will ensure timely delivery or availability at the quality they want. Those aspects should be of primary concern to them (see Memo 3.3).

MEMO 3.3   VALUE VERSUS PRICE

It is unwise to pay too much, as it is unwise to pay too little. When you pay too much, you lose a little money, thats all. When you pay too little, you sometimes lose everything, because the thing you bought was incapable of doing the things you bought it to do. The common law of business balance prohibits paying a little and getting a lot. If you deal with the lowest bidder, it is well to add something for the risk you run. And if you do that, you will have enough to pay for something better.

Source: anonymous

The various purchasing tasks cannot necessarily be applied collectively, and in certain situations they can even be contradictory and conflicting. **Single sourcing** is often pursued on the intent to reduce materials costs – by placing all purchasing requirements with one supplier it is often possible to substantially negotiate better conditions. However, this policy certainly has its price in that it will lead to increased supply risk or dependency on one supplier. Balancing the pros and cons of this particular problem exceeds the authority of a buyer. This is one reason why strategic supplier decisions need to be made by (top) management.

The idea that buyers can indeed make significant contributions to product and process innovation implies high demands on buyers' technical competences and personal qualities. Collaboration with engineering and research and development on the one hand, and the purchasing department on the other hand, is in practice often troublesome. Engineers and developers do not believe that buyers can make a significant contribution to their work because buyers often lack the required technical background and have insufficient affinity with product development and design, and specific engineering problems. In those cases the purchasing department's professional staff should be upgraded to bring its technical expertise in line with the level of professionalism, which is present in the surrounding business areas. Another approach is, as we will see later in this book, to put the responsibility to deploy purchasing policies and procedures to the technical specialists and line managers. This is one way to overcome the often (seemingly) conflicting interests between purchasing professionals and their internal customers.

Sourcing, single
Situation in which a company within a certain category with clear intent buys from just one supplier.

PROFESSIONALIZING PURCHASING: A FEW PRINCIPLES

This section describes the major principles of purchasing policies. Preferably, purchasing policies should be based on a sound business orientation, reflect a cross-functional approach and be directed at improving the company's bottom and top-line.

Business alignment

Developing a purchasing and supply strategy requires a thorough understanding of the company's overall business policy. What end-user markets is the company targeting and what are the major developments going on in those markets? What competition is the company suffering from and what leeway does the company have in setting its own pricing policies? To what extent can materials price increases be passed on to the final customer or is this impossible? What changes are happening in the company's product, operations and information technologies? What investments are made by the company in terms of new products and technology and what products will be taken out of the market for the years to come? Understanding these kinds of questions is important since it will determine how purchasing and supply strategies will need to support the company in meeting its goals and objectives.

Center Parcs is a well-known company operating resort parks in many European countries. In the early 1990s this company decided to centralize most of its procurement activities, which until then resided predominantly at the individual parks with resort managers.

A spend analysis showed that the majority of expenditure was with just a few key suppliers. It also appeared from the analysis that Center Parcs was a major customer to each of these key suppliers. Prior to starting contract negotiations with each of these suppliers (among them important beer and beverage companies, a major construction firm, the retailer that operated the supermarkets at the resorts), the business team that was assigned with the task to set up the centralized procurement department decided to bring all key suppliers together in a meeting. In that meeting the business team pointed out that, in fact both Center Parcs and these key suppliers had one common interest: to make sure that all cottages and bungalows were fully booked. Next, all suppliers were invited to come up with ideas on what they would do to improve the number of client reservations in the Center Parcs resorts. They were invited to present their business case formally in the next meeting with the business team. When the initial confusion about this invitation disappeared, most of the suppliers proved to be very creative. Through specific advertising campaigns allowing consumers to enjoy rebates at a Center Parcs stay, promoting Center Parcs to their employees and giving them special offers, and holding parts of their training programmes and executive meetings at the resorts, these suppliers were able to generate thousands of additional bookings. This generated much better occupancy rates, and, hence, much better business for Center Parcs and its suppliers.

Integrated, cross-functional approach

Purchasing performance
The extent to which the purchasing function is able to realize its predetermined goals at the sacrifice of a minimum of the company's resources, i.e. costs.

Purchasing decisions cannot be made in isolation, and should not be aimed only at optimization of **purchasing performance**. Purchasing decisions should be made taking into account the effects of these decisions on the other business activities (such as operations management, marketing and sales, logistics and transportation). Therefore, purchasing decisions need to be based on optimizing total cost of ownership or creating the maximum value for the company's purchasing spend, rather than going for the lowest price. When buying a new packaging line, for instance, it is important to consider not only the initial investment, but also the costs which will be incurred in the future for buying packaging materials, spare parts and technical services. Moreover, unplanned downtime of the equipment against a predetermined level needs to be agreed by the supplier during the packaging lines' technical and economic lifespan. The selling of equipment by a supplier is one thing; servicing that same equipment satisfactorily over a large number of years by that same supplier is often something different. This example illustrates the complexity of this type of purchase and the different kinds of decisions that need to be made. Careful decision-making in those circumstances will require an integrated, cross-functional and team-based approach among all the affected business disciplines. Purchasing and supply strategies can only be developed effectively in close co-operation with all disciplines and (top) managers involved. Purchasing managers should adopt a leading role in orchestrating the activities of all players. This is an important aspect of purchasing process management.

The acquisition of a small computer printer Serves as an example of why buying at the lowest total cost may be better than going for the lowest price. These printers are offered in many European countries at very affordable prices. Why manufacturers are doing this becomes clear when the consumer needs to buy a toner cartridges for the first time. It then becomes apparent that just one cartridge will account for about 25–30% of the printer's purchase price. Obviously, the consumer will need to buy many of these cartridges over the lifetime of the printer. In this case the buyer would do much better to consider the price per page printed during the lifetime of the printer rather than just looking at the printer's initial purchase price. Examples illustrating this phenomenon are abundant. They include cars, for which buyers would be better off looking at leasing rates rather than prices offered by dealers, and packaging machines, for which it might be advisable to investigate the cost price per unit handled rather than equipment acquisition costs.

Performance driven

We do not share the view that purchasing should only operate as a service function, which should work on behalf of and comply with its customers' requirements without asking too many questions. We would rather see that purchasing engages in a healthy debate with its internal customers. Rather than just accepting to buy a branded product, the buyer should inform him or herself about the functionality that is looked for by the internal customer. What is it precisely that the customer needs the product for? What is it specifically that he or she is after? Getting a basic idea about the customer's real needs, enables the buyer to generate alternatives in close collaboration with the internal customer. Then, in many cases product and supplier solutions will develop that probably much better suit the needs of the internal customer, even at a lower cost. Through their activities buyers should make the company more cost aware. They should consistently look for improving the price/value ratio of the goods and services bought by the company. They should relentlessly seek to improve supplier performance. To accomplish this, purchasing should be able to suggest alternatives to existing product designs, materials or components to be used and challenge current suppliers. They should be constantly on the outlook for new promising suppliers. Experience with companies in which purchasing is recognized as a business driven activity shows that this function contributes to a permanent reduction of materials and supply chain costs, whilst stimulating collaboration and innovation from suppliers at the same time.

An example that may serve here is a European fruit juice supplier and its overambitious marketing department. Once, an energetic marketing manager had stipulated that the company should be consistent in communicating its brands Europe-wide. In all cases the quality and the superior taste of the company's products should be emphasized in all of its advertisements, brochures and its packaging materials (juice containers as well as outer boxes). For a number of years this company used very colourful boxes for shipping its products to retailers and food services companies. Compared to the normal grey, carton boxes, these full colour outer boxes did cost a fortune. When asked how many people, i.e. customers, would have contact with these boxes and when the cost per contact was calculated, the idea of using these colourful boxes was quickly rejected. Today, the company just works with plain, grey boxes, leaving them with a saving on packaging materials of over 50%. This example shows how a performance driven orientation in purchasing decision-making can contribute to the company's top line, i.e. sales turnover, and a better result for all parties involved.

PURCHASING MANAGEMENT PROCESS

It has been argued that purchasing policies and strategies should be based on the company's overall (financial) objectives and product/market strategies. A company that operates in a highly competitive end-user market (e.g. the automotive industry) will undoubtedly have a strong focus on cost reduction and innovation. Hence, its purchasing and supply strategies should reflect those aspects and the purchasing activities will be directed through detailed materials budgets and well-prepared cost reduction projects. Constantly looking for new and more competitive sources of supply on an international basis (global sourcing) will be part of these projects. As an example, Volkswagen AG, since 1993 has pursued an aggressive sourcing strategy for its components. Having sourced traditionally from German suppliers, its flamboyant purchasing director Ignacio Lopez changed its sourcing strategy into one based upon global sourcing. Volkswagen's international purchasing offices nowadays invite quotations from suppliers worldwide, which are compared by an executive board which convenes weekly at Wolfsburg. As a result Volkswagen reported significant materials cost savings. Important savings (up to 20% of initial materials costs) were reported during 1994–1995. After these years, however, severe delivery and quality problems occurred: most suppliers were not capable (or willing) to keep up with Volkswagen's growing materials volumes. In order to meet Volkswagen's strict cost reduction targets suppliers started to compromise quality. This led to many disruptions in production. Too strong a focus on cost, will gradually drive out quality. Today, Volkswagen's sourcing strategies are much more balanced.

A high-tech company operating in a niche market where it sells unique products, however, will have other concerns in the area of purchasing and supply strategy. Early supplier involvement, securing proprietary knowledge, reducing time to market, development lead time and development cost, will be of prime interest to the top management. Of course, apart from that the purchasing and supply function needs to secure flawless delivery of components and materials. Innovation and supply come first; next price and cost aspects are considered. Philips Medical Systems, manufacturer of advanced medical equipment, may serve as an example here. This company has gone to great lengths to involve purchasing and suppliers at an early stage of development. Suppliers are primarily selected on their technological capabilities and invited to take an active role during the development stage. After development, suppliers are requested to submit quotations, which, in most cases, are very competitive due to the fact that the supplier has gone through its **learning curve** earlier than its competitors. Also, ASM-Lithography, a manufacturer of high-tech wafer steppers in The Netherlands, is practising this approach in its supplier relationships. This company needs to be innovative in its approach to suppliers since the technology that it produces will be out of date within 18 months.

Learning curve
The learning curve was originally developed in the American aircraft industry. It was discovered that the cost price per airplane decreased at a fixed percentage as experience, i.e. the cumulative production volume of a particular type of aircraft, doubled.

Purchasing and supply strategies and operations, therefore, need to be aligned with the company's overall product/market strategies in a dynamic way. To achieve this, purchasing managers need to consistently adapt their purchasing management processes. The purchasing management process consists of several elements. Much can be learned about these from the literature available on marketing management (e.g. Kotler, 1997). There are some striking similarities between marketing and purchasing:

- The primary focus of both activities is on the exchange of values between two or more parties, resulting in the buy/sell transaction.
- Both activities are externally oriented, i.e. aimed at outside parties.
- Neither activity can be executed adequately without a thorough knowledge of markets, competition, prices, costs, technology and products.
- As a result of the amounts of money involved, both activities have a great impact on the company's bottom and top line.

Analogous to marketing management, the following successive elements are identified in managing purchasing and supply: (1) purchasing and supply (market) research, (2) determining purchasing and supply objectives, (3) determining purchasing and supply strategy, (4) action planning, (5) implementation, (6) control and evaluation. Each of these activities

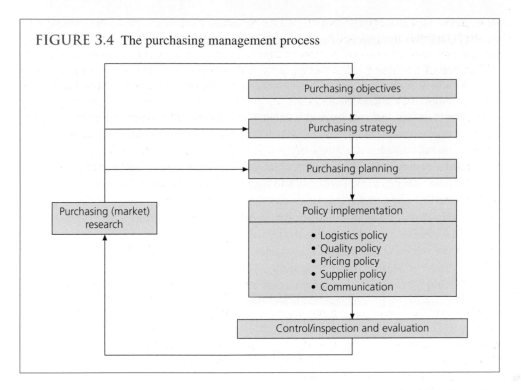

FIGURE 3.4 The purchasing management process

is part of the purchasing management process (see Figure 3.4). A more detailed description of each of these activities follows in the paragraphs below.

Purchasing and supply (market) research

Supply market research can be defined as the systematic gathering, classification and analysis of data considering all relevant factors that influence the procurement of goods and services for the purpose of meeting present and future company requirements.

Purchasing (market) research is used first of all to support purchasing policies and decision-making. It must generate data and alternatives on which the buyer or management can make better purchasing decisions. Purchasing research may have both an external and an internal focus. Examples of the former are supplier studies, supply market studies and materials cost and price analyses. Examples of the latter are analysis of the company's total purchasing spend, its purchasing portfolio and analysis of the costs that may be related to holding inventory and the **quality costs** of incoming materials.

A detailed description of the role and significance of **purchasing market research** is included in Chapter 7.

Purchasing and supply objectives, strategy and planning

Based upon the company's overall objectives, purchasing objectives will relate to cost-reduction, reduction of the supplier base, improving product quality, lead time reduction and so on. Through these objectives the company directs, manages and controls its purchasing activities and relationships with suppliers. In line with these purchasing and supply objectives purchasing management can focus on different areas for action (see Figure 3.5).

Important decisions need to be made in terms of supplier strategies. How many suppliers are needed per product category? For what product categories are we going to reduce or increase the number of suppliers? Are we going to pursue a relationship based upon partnership or one based upon competitive bidding? For what products do we need to source globally and for what products do we need to find local suppliers? These and other aspects are covered in the commodity sourcing strategy document.

Quality costs
Relate to three types of costs, i.e. prevention costs (the costs of preventing errors) and assessment costs (the costs related to the timely recognition of errors) and correction costs (the costs that result from correcting mistakes).

Purchasing market research
The systematic gathering, classification and analysis of data considering all relevant factors that influence the procurement of goods and services for the purpose of meeting present and future company requirements.

FIGURE 3.5 Examples of areas for action in purchasing

Sourcing policy – determining dependency on suppliers and designing plans to reduce this dependency.

Direct versus indirect buying – determining the (possible) cost benefits of buying from importers and distributors, or buying directly from the manufacturer.

Make-or-buy analysis – analysis of savings opportunities by eliminating particular production activities and buying the required products from third parties; buy-or-lease may be considered as an alternative.

Integration between purchasing and other functional areas – plans aimed at removing interface problems between purchasing and materials management, purchasing and engineering and between purchasing and financial administration or treasury.

Setting up a purchasing information and control system – analysis of purchasing's information needs and design of an automation plan; possibilities of linking this system with existing information systems in other functional areas.

Centralized or decentralized purchasing – balancing cost benefits and strategic considerations related to a centralized or decentralized organization of purchasing.

Standardization – determining possibilities to achieve standardization in order to reduce product and supplier variety; balancing savings and risks.

Implementation of purchasing policy

Important areas to consider when implementing purchasing and supply policy are supply, product and supplier quality, materials costs and prices, supplier policy and communication policy (see Table 3.1):

- Supply. Supply is aimed at the optimization of both the order to pay process and the incoming materials flow. Purchasing order processing entails handling of purchasing requisitions, purchase orders and expediting, as well as the development of efficient,

TABLE 3.1 Aspects of purchasing policy

Tools	Aspects
Supply policy	Purchasing order processing
	Materials and supply planning
Product and supplier quality policy	Early involvement in development
	Improving suppliers' quality performance
Materials cost policy	Control of materials costs and prices
	Reduction of materials costs and prices
Supplier policy	Sourcing policy
	Improvement of supplier performance
Communication policy	Internal contacts
	External contacts

computer-supported routines with regards to payment. Materials and supply planning relates to issuing materials delivery schedules to suppliers, reducing supplier lead times, troubleshooting in case of delivery problems, reducing (pipeline) inventories, and monitoring supplier delivery performance.

- Product and supplier quality. Central to this aspect are the materials specifications. Two important subjects of concern here are purchasing's early involvement in design and product development and improving product and supplier quality performance. Activities which may contribute to both areas are:
  - standardization of materials – by striving for simplification or standardization of product specifications, the buyer may reduce product variety resulting in both cost reduction and a lesser supplier dependence at the same time
  - a purchasing policy focused on the life cycle of the end products – there is not much point in investigating material cost and quality improvements used in products which will be eliminated shortly
  - specific quality improvements – negotiating targets on improving reject rates, reducing incoming inspection, and negotiating quality agreements with suppliers
  - agreeing on and gradually extending permanent warranty conditions that are to be provided by the supplier
  - initiating special programmes in the field of value analysis to simplify product design or reduce product costs.

- Materials cost policy. The objective of materials cost policy is twofold. The first is to obtain control of materials cost and prices in such a way that suppliers are unable to pass on unjustified price increases to the company. Changes in the supplier's raw and base materials should be adequately reflected in its selling prices. This is true not only when the business cycle goes up, but also when the business cycle goes down. A second objective is to systematically reduce the supplier's materials cost through joint, well-prepared action plans. In order to be successful a thorough knowledge of the supplier's pricing policies and cost structure is required. In this context, understanding and knowledge of **market structures** and of the sensitivity of the supplier's selling price to market and cost factors is necessary. It should be decided for what products to build detailed cost-models, for what products to monitor underlying cost factors, and for what products to develop detailed materials budget estimates.

- Supplier policy. The supplier policy is focused on the systematic management of the company's supplier base. First, decisions need to be made for what commodities to pursue a multiple sourcing strategy, to go for single sourcing or a partnership relationship. Suppliers who actually perform best should be rewarded with more business in the future. Targets and possible projects for future co-operation should be determined carefully. Relationships with suppliers who consistently fail to meet the company's expectations should be terminated. However, such decisions need to be made based on detailed data on how the supplier performed in the past and be implemented carefully.

- Communication policy. The company's purchasing policies need to be communicated both internally and to suppliers. Increasingly, companies use their intranet for the former. At this time many companies employ their own purchasing website (see Memo 3.4) in order to communicate their future materials requirements and ways of working with their suppliers. The next step is that preferred suppliers have access to the customer's intranet through which internal users can order directly from them through their electronic catalogues. The facilities to communicate both internally and externally for buyers have considerably improved over the past years. Most companies at this time are only at the beginning of discovering the vast opportunities in purchasing and supply that the new electronic media offer.

Market structure
Is defined in this book as the total set of conditions in which a company sells its products, with special attention to the number of parties in the market and the nature of the product being traded.

MEMO 3.4   REVERSE MARKETING AT SONY

The Internet site of Sony (see Figure 3.6) provides an interesting example of how large manufacturers communicate with their suppliers nowadays. New suppliers are explicitly invited to study Sony's purchasing policy, structure and pre-qualification procedure. In fact, Sony uses the Internet as a marketing instrument to inform suppliers about their current procurement vision and strategy. Through this website future 'partners' (as Sony like to refer to suppliers who are capable of meeting all Sony requirements) can subscribe and inform themselves about what it takes to become a prospective Sony supplier.

Also other progressive manufacturers have a purchasing website on the Internet. Usually the following information is communicated to their supplier communities:

- description of company policy, strategy and structure
- vision on procurement and supplier relationships

- what it takes to qualify as a prospective supplier
- structure of the procurement organization
- list of persons that may be contacted
- invitation to submit quotations for certain products or services
- description of the supplier quality assurance program
- general procurement conditions and compliance to laws and regulations
- recent press information that may be relevant for suppliers.

Contrary to some years ago, most parts of these sites are now confidential and only open to suppliers who are part of the company's established supplier community. Many sites now provide facilities for buyers to closely monitor the incoming materials flows from suppliers.

FIGURE 3.6 Sony global procurement and purchasing

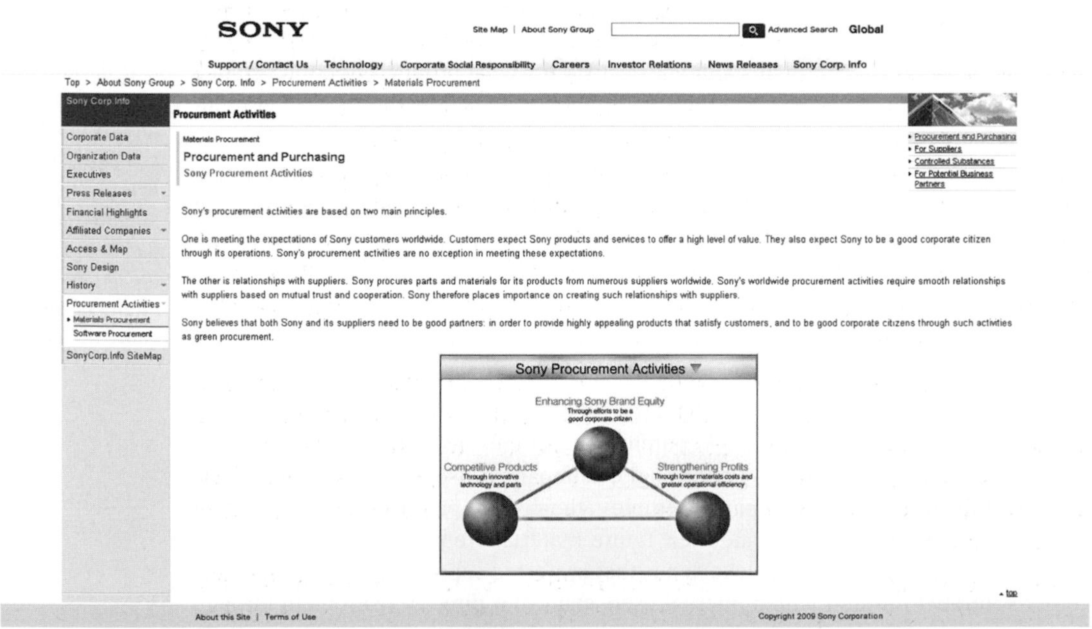

Control and evaluation

Purchasing management must see to it that both results and activities that have been planned are realized within the available financial resources. To this end the actual performance, obtained through purchasing activities, must be periodically checked against the purchasing plans. In most cases reports are required about the savings and costs reductions realized through (cross-functional) purchasing activities. Furthermore, the performance of suppliers should be checked periodically through vendor performance reports. These subjects need to be reported to management through a consistent procedure so that management is able to assess overall purchasing performance.

As Figure 3.4 shows, the purchasing management process is in fact a closed loop. If one of the elements gets insufficient attention, the effect will be that activities will get out of control. When objectives and concrete targets are absent, this will lead to a situation in which purchasing activities will lack clear guidance. When objectives and targets have not been translated into detailed action plans, this will lead to a lack of understanding of who is responsible for doing what. The absence of a management reporting structure is often a prime reason why managers do not understand what purchasing has contributed to the company's bottom line. In many companies, elements of this purchasing management process are ill structured. This is one of the reasons why purchasing in those companies has little professionalism. Most problems related to purchasing and supply management, therefore, are problems of management rather than that they are related to the purchasing area itself.

HOW PURCHASING AND SUPPLY MANAGEMENT DEVELOPS OVER TIME

Purchasing structures in large companies nowadays are very different from those structures in place during the 1970s or 1980s, and they will, beyond doubt, be different in the future. Two decades ago concepts like purchasing portfolio management, total cost of ownership, supplier partnerships, early supplier involvement and cross-functional buying teams were not known. Since then many new strategic and organizational concepts in the field of purchasing and supply chain management have been developed. The professional development of the purchasing function in organizations can be analysed from different angles or aspects. Over the past years many authors have suggested conceptual models on this subject. Most authors assume a stage-wise or step-wise development of purchasing and supply management within organizations with the following characteristics:

- Integrated final stage. Most authors assume the existence of a final stage of excellence towards which all improvement efforts should be directed. Almost all models show a final phase where purchasing is integrated in the major lines of business. At this stage line management is actively involved in purchasing strategies and tactics. Also at this stage, it is assumed, purchasing processes are organized around multi-disciplinary, team-based structures.

- Purchasing's organizational status. Most models point out that purchasing initially reports rather low in the organizational hierarchy. Next there may be some degree of centralization, which in a business unit structure will turn to some form of co-ordinated purchasing (where responsibility for executing purchasing policy resides within the individual business units).

- Supplier management. The development of supplier management is another similarity in the different development models. In the first stage, supplier management seems to be reactive ('opportunity driven'). In the next phase, it becomes more proactive ('supplier performance improvement'), and in the last phase it becomes relationship management ('partnership').

- Supplier relationships. Most authors assume that, as purchasing moves through the different stages of development, relationships with suppliers will change, starting with a purchasing department handling many suppliers at 'arm's length'. In the next stage, purchasing has reduced its number of suppliers considerably so that closer relationships with a smaller number of (preferred) suppliers are able to develop.

Major drivers, which influence how purchasing and supply management will develop over time, are considered to be:

- Business context. It is generally assumed that the more competitive the business context and the more mature the technology in the industry, in which the company is operating, the higher the pressure on purchasing to contribute to the bottom line will be.

- Company strategy. The more explicit the company is about the goals and objectives it wants to realize and the more formalized the planning process, the greater the chance that purchasing issues are integrated into the overall company strategy.

- Systems development. Modern information and communication technologies are considered to be important enablers for the implementation of modern purchasing and supply management concepts.

- Top management commitment. This relates to the degree to which top management shows active interest in, and is actively involved in, purchasing strategy and supply issues.

- Functional leadership. This relates to the personality of the purchasing manager, his management style and prominence.

The approach that has been described by Keough (1993) is one of the most interesting. It is very detailed. This author identifies five stages of development and he assumes a direct causal relationship between the industry a company is in and the stage of development in purchasing. For the remainder of this chapter this model is taken as the point of departure. The author has tried, however, to integrate and combine some valuable insights from other contributors in order to arrive at an integrated purchasing developmental model.

Based upon these general parameters the following six-stage purchasing developmental model has been identified (see Figure 3.7)

Stage 1 'Transaction orientation: serve the factory'

In this first stage the primary task of purchasing is to find appropriate suppliers and ensure that the company's operations processes do not run out of raw materials and supplied components. There is no explicit purchasing strategy in place. Formulation of purchasing goals is very rudimentary and intuitive. The value added of the purchasing function is considered to be securing availability of the right materials and goods for production. The organizational structure can be characterized by a decentralized sub-department at business unit level, reporting mostly to a production or logistics manager. The purchasing function is strongly orientated on operational and administrative activities. Non-production buying is predominantly done by users themselves, and is considered by purchasing as of secondary importance. There is very little knowledge of what is exactly the total purchasing

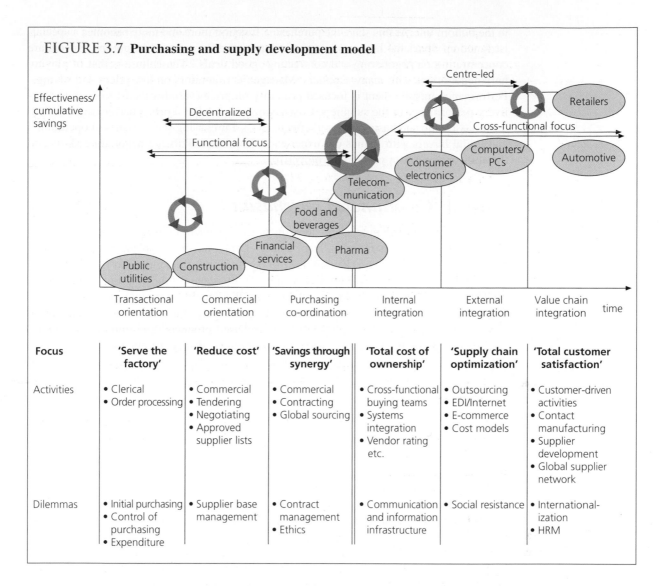

FIGURE 3.7 **Purchasing and supply development model**

Focus	'Serve the factory'	'Reduce cost'	'Savings through synergy'	'Total cost of ownership'	'Supply chain optimization'	'Total customer satisfaction'
Activities	• Clerical • Order processing	• Commercial • Tendering • Negotiating • Approved supplier lists	• Commercial • Contracting • Global sourcing	• Cross-functional buying teams • Systems integration • Vendor rating etc.	• Outsourcing • EDI/Internet • E-commerce • Cost models	• Customer-driven activities • Contact manufacturing • Supplier development • Global supplier network
Dilemmas	• Initial purchasing • Control of purchasing • Expenditure	• Supplier base management	• Contract management • Ethics	• Communication and information infrastructure	• Social resistance	• International-ization • HRM

spend of the company. The culture is 'reactive'. Management is based on complaints. No complaints means purchasing does a good job. The information systems, if in place already, are developed by purchasing and very much administratively oriented. The purchasing staff consists usually of operational and administrative buyers, strongly supply-task oriented, and with little professional education to do the job.

Stage 2 'Commercial orientation: lowest unit price'

At this stage a proactive type of purchasing manager is recruited who can negotiate credibly with suppliers for lower prices. Striving for the lowest unit cost requires some independence from functions like product development, engineering and manufacturing. As a result purchasing, while reporting to a senior executive, has more autonomy at lower organizational levels. Purchasing strategy at this stage is characterized by a sharp focus on low prices. The purchasing function has its own department at business unit level, reporting directly to the business unit manager, who is interested in the savings purchasing adds

Purchasing and supply development model
This model identifies six stages of development over time, indicating how purchasing and supply may develop in terms of professionalism within a company. These six stages are: transaction orientation, commercial orientation, co-ordination orientation, internal integration, external integration and value chain integration.

to the bottom line. At this stage the purchasing function more and more becomes a specialist function. Specialist buyers are organized around different product groups. Buyers are concentrating on negotiating and contracting 'good deals'. The culture is that of playing hard negotiations with many suppliers. Management monitors on low prices and savings. Performance measurement is focused primarily on price (variance), cost savings and delivery performance of the suppliers. Cost savings are used as a prime performance indicator for assessing purchasing's overall effectiveness. Purchasing staff consists of operational and initial buyers with 'hands on' experience. Important skills are negotiating skills and the ability to make supplier price comparisons.

Stage 3 'Co-ordinated purchasing'

Led by a strong central purchasing department to implement uniform buying policies and systems, the emphasis here lies on cross unit co-ordination and compliance with nationally negotiated contracts. This stage may lead to purchasing bureaucracy and lack of responsiveness from the decentralized business units. At this stage for the first time there is some kind of strategy formulation, aimed at capturing the benefits from internal co-ordination and synergy. Apart from price and costs, the purchasing function is seen as having an important influence on the quality level of purchased products. The importance of non-production buying becomes recognized by purchasing. Slowly the purchasing function is getting some attention from top management. However, the rest of the organization is still not convinced of the value adding potential of the purchasing function. Supplier management is a central issue at this stage and is characterized by looking for synergy by bundling purchasing power of the different business units and developing differentiated supplier strategies based upon portfolio-analysis techniques. The organizational structure of the purchasing function is a centralized purchasing department at corporate level that is responsible for purchasing policy. Formalization of the purchasing process and procedures is at full speed. The purchasing organization is (still) strongly product oriented. The focus is on improving communication between the central purchasing unit and the decentralized business units. There is a clear intention to foster collaboration among business units. Computerized information systems are in place now, but still not linked to each other. The stand-alone databases are linked among the business units, but not yet fully integrated. Purchasing staff have a specific purchasing background and training and there are a large number of different purchasing jobs in place. Training is aimed at developing analytical skills, total quality management and communication skills.

Stage 4 'Internal integration: cross-functional purchasing'

At this stage the emphasis is on cross-functional problem solving with the objective of reducing total life cycle cost and not just the unit cost of purchased components. These cross-functional efforts often include involving key suppliers as joint problem solvers, which implies a move from confrontational to more partnership sourcing. Until this stage the purchasing function was very much functionally oriented, and trying to organize the company around the purchasing function. At this stage purchasing is becoming more process-oriented, trying to organize the purchasing function around the internal customers. There is serious attention for non-production purchasing. The strategic importance of the purchasing function comes to full recognition, and purchasing is involved in strategic issues like core/non-core questions and make-or-buy decisions. The structure is 'centre-led'. Operational buying disappears in the line, i.e. is integrated with materials planning or scheduling or line planning thanks to the introduction of advanced electronic catalogues and order-to-pay systems. The culture is characterized by team-based management, illustrated by the many cross-functional buying teams that are now in place. Improvement actions are aimed at integrating and harmonizing the purchasing processes over the different business units. At this stage the focus is still internal, but process oriented. Information systems are integrated with that of other departments/functions and divisions, but not yet with those of the most important suppliers. **Purchasing performance measurement** is done in the form of internal customer satisfaction surveys and benchmarking. However, a strong focus on realizing hard and soft purchasing cost savings remains. People involved in the purchasing process have a broad business perspective and a high educational level. Skills looked for at this stage are strong team-building abilities and strong communication skills.

Stage 5 'External integration: supply-chain management'

This stage is characterized by an explicit outsourcing strategy combined with extra attention to collaborate with supply chain partners on product development and preproduction planning. The purchasing function concentrates on creating maximum leverage of the company's external resources. Suppliers are actively involved in new product development and process improvement and often reside within the company. Non-production buying is fully supported or executed by the purchasing function. Users order themselves against corporate contracts through advanced, web enabled catalogue systems to which some major suppliers have been hooked up. This is especially true for the non-production area. Purchasing works hard to make things simple for their internal customers, by using systems contracting, purchasing cards, electronic business and catalogues or EDI. Supplier management becomes supply chain management at this stage. Companies invest a lot to really involve supply partners in different business processes, instead of just buying goods and services from them as efficiently and effectively as possible. Responsibility for initial purchasing resides with cross-functional teams (inter-divisional and inter-organizational) and is no longer executed by a separate department. There are **residential engineering** teams, and improvement teams with members from different disciplines, divisions and organizations (suppliers). Integration with other disciplines, divisions and especially suppliers is at full speed, to enable integrated supply chain management. The management style is business and performance driven, though supportive and coaching at the same time. The culture is characterized by participation and consensus style decision-making. Important skills are knowledge of TCO principles, being able to build detailed cost models, strategic supply chain management, and general managerial and leadership abilities. Information systems are not only integrated internally, but also with those of the partner suppliers.

Stage 6 'Value chain orientation'

The 'purchasing' strategy in this stage will be based on the recognition that most important for success is delivering value to the end customer. To satisfy the needs in end-customer markets, subcontractors seek support among their suppliers. Suppliers are consistently challenged to support the company's product/market strategies and to actively participate in product development. The goal is to design the most efficient and effective value chain possible to serve the end-customer. Apart from contributions to the bottom line, suppliers are now challenged to also contribute to the company's top line, i.e. to create additional sales revenue through new business development. Purchasing strategy is evaporated in the total business strategy. The orientation is both stream upwards as well as downwards. In fact the traditional marketing and purchasing functions are integrated, and have become 'virtual' in the company. The functioning is based on a shared vision carried by all

Purchasing performance measurement
Four dimensions are suggested on which measurement and evaluation of purchasing activities can be based: (1) a price/cost dimension, (2) a product/quality dimension, (3) a logistics dimension and (4) an organizational dimension.

Residential engineering
Situation where engineers from the supplier on a more or less permanent basis are co-located at the buyer's organization, in order to work on design or manufacturing problems which appear during the successive stages of development. Residential engineering also relates to a situation where a large OEM has placed its own engineering specialists at the supplier's premises in order to resolve a variety of technical problems.

organizational members. The culture is entrepreneurial. Information systems are integrated as much as possible.

Although this model may seem rather straightforward, some critical remarks must be directed towards it. It must be noted that the model has never been tested by thorough academic research. It is important to question and test the validity and reliability of this model. Is the process of development in purchasing a rational process, as the model suggests, or rather an irrational one? Does purchasing development really take place as a process of continuous change or is it in reality characterized more by step-changes and discontinuity? What change strategies underlie purchasing development processes in organizations? Do all organizations follow the stages identified or can some stages be skipped? To what extent are purchasing managers the most decisive actors in the process of purchasing development? Or are they rather receptive in general and are the real change agents coming from other disciplines?

Questions that are often raised are: How much time does it take to go through the different stages of the model? And, is it possible to skip some stages in the model? The answer is not easy to find. As experience shows companies will move faster through the learning curve as their need for cash is more urgent and as they put more resources into the process of change.

More research is warranted in order to use this model as a term of reference for guiding purchasing and supply's organizational and professional development.

SOME OBSERVATIONS FROM PRACTICE

So far, we have described the most important elements of the purchasing management process. As we have seen, it is important to create a closed loop between the different process elements. If such a closed loop is not present, purchasing activities may suffer from a lack of control. Purchasing managers can pursue different purchasing policies to realize their objectives. The purchasing objectives should be aligned with the overall corporate strategies in order to prevent sub-optimization. In our experience it is very difficult to create such alignment and to create a systematic and consistent approach to purchasing processes and purchasing decision-making. A few examples may serve as an example here.

In practice, many echelons in the company are taking responsibility for and heavily involved in purchasing decision-making. Product specification and supplier selection decisions are made without giving sufficient attention to contractual and commercial aspects. Orders are placed at suppliers without a proper prequalification procedure. Later it may appear that the suppliers that have been selected are not able to meet the commitments made and the expectations that were communicated. This may be especially true when contracting for investment goods, in which the involvement of professional purchasing staff may be low.

Purchasing responsibilities and tasks are in many cases ill defined. Purchasing procedures, if present at all, are limited to administrative matters like the routing of requisitions and order forms and purchasing authorization. Clear targets and objectives for the purchasing function are not in place. Where targets and objectives are present for other business areas, in many cases these are still missing for purchasing. As a result, the actual performance in the area of purchasing can be barely measured or monitored based on a regular management reporting.

However, during the past years significant progress can be observed. Purchasing automation has improved and freed up the buyers from administrative and operational duties.

The will to invest in procurement has increased. Increasingly, purchasing is considered to be an investment rather than a cost. As a result professional buyers with a higher educational background and more relevant business experience are recruited. Purchasing has become more integrated with other business domains, such as operations management and supply chain management. The increasing popularity of supply chain management is just an example of this. In many leading companies purchasing professionals become more and more involved in new product development processes and new business development. Many companies have now put Chief Procurement Officers (CPOs) in place, who bring in extensive operational line management experience, to lead their procurement transformation process. These are all clear signs of a growing acceptance of purchasing in business. However, there is still a lot to be done.

SUMMARY

In summary, the argument is that most companies have a large potential for professionalizing purchasing management. A systematic approach of the purchasing policy can help make this potential visible and accessible.

The tasks, responsibilities and authority of the purchasing function must be established first: securing availability of required materials and services at consistent quality from reliable suppliers is the prime task and responsibility for purchasing. However, activities should not be exclusively limited to this. Purchasing and supply management has more to do. Purchasing and supply management should also strive for continuously improving the price/value ratio in the relationship with suppliers. Materials price control and cost reduction are therefore important policy areas. At the same time the risk exposure, in terms of the company's dependence on suppliers, should be minimized. Furthermore, buyers should be alert to technological innovations that take place in their supplier markets, which may be beneficial to the company.

Professional purchasing requires effective communication both internally and externally. Purchasing procedures and policies should be approved by top management and communicated to the internal users. Simple brochures and leaflets, which explain how purchasing prefers to work with suppliers and what may be expected in terms of professional support may be helpful. The new electronic media also provide new and vast opportunities in this respect.

Managing purchasing implies that all elements of the purchasing management process are defined. Purchasing objectives need to be derived from the overall company strategies and should support these. They need to be translated into detailed sourcing strategies and action plans, indicating what performance will be targeted in terms of cost reduction, supplier quality improvement, improving supplier logistics performance and internal efficiency. Finally, purchasing management should provide for periodical, detailed management reporting.

Putting these elements of the purchasing management process in place takes time, however. This explains why differences exist in purchasing operations between companies, even if they operate in the same type of industry. The purchasing development model, which has been presented in this chapter, provides a picture of the stages companies may go through when they want to develop purchasing professionalism. However, this model should be used carefully, for all stages may not be relevant for all types of commodities, companies and industries, as some authors may want us to believe.

ASSIGNMENTS

3.1 In this chapter five major tasks and responsibilities have been described which can be attributed to purchasing and supply management. What are these? It has been argued that these five tasks and responsibilities should not necessarily be in line with each other. Provide at least four situations where two or more of these tasks and responsibilities may be conflicting. How would you solve these conflicts?

3.2 Why would communications both internally and to suppliers be so important for effective purchasing? Who would you see as the most important 'competitor' of a buyer? How would you prevent 'back-door selling' from a supplier's representative?

3.3 A reporting structure has been presented as an essential part of the purchasing management process. If you were a purchasing manager, what would you report to your superiors on a monthly basis? Would you report the same thing to your production and logistics manager? Discuss.

3.4 This chapter discussed a six-stage purchasing development. It suggests that as purchasing as a discipline in companies moves from one stage to another, purchasing managers need to prepare for resistance from the organization. What kind of problems and/or resistance may purchasing managers expect when companies move from stage 1 to stage 2, from stage 2 to stage 3 and so on?

3.5 Management has requested you to develop a cost-down programme for your organization related to non-production buying. What would such a cost-down program look like? What structure would you give to it? How would you execute it? Describe and present.

REFERENCES

Keough, M. (1993) 'Buying your way to the top', *McKinsey Quarterly*, 3: 41–62.

Kotler, P. (1997) *Marketing Management: Analysis, Planning, Implementation and Control*, 9th edn, Upper Saddle River: Prentice-Hall.

PURCHASING AND FACILITIES MANAGEMENT

LEARNING OBJECTIVES

After studying this chapter you should understand the following:

- The role and position of purchasing in a facilities environment.

- Key success variables for purchasing in a facilities environment.

- Measures aimed at improving the effectiveness of purchasing in a facilities environment.

- How to classify services that are contracted by organisations.

- What it takes to buy indirect products and services.

INTRODUCTION

Earlier chapters have demonstrated that purchasing, as a management discipline in industrial companies, has developed strongly over the last few years. Due to increased international competition, industrial companies in particular have given first priority to issues such as cost reduction, quality improvement and cycle time reduction in their relationships with suppliers. At the same time many top managers have focused on reinforcing their company's core activities. Non-core activities have increasingly been put to the block with decisions to outsource these to specialized suppliers. The purchasing department has played an important role in initiating and implementing these management policies.

Companies in the service sector have lagged behind in this development. Here, purchasing activities traditionally have an operational character and are limited to placing orders, expediting and invoice handling. The situation in most companies is reflected by the case study on the next page: purchasing operations are scattered throughout the organization due to the absence of a professional purchasing department.

However, this picture is gradually changing. Due to the fact that service companies are much less tied to strict technical specifications, purchasing's cost savings potential is significant. As in the case study, however, many service companies face the problem of how to improve purchasing professionalism. Managers often try to translate successful purchasing practices, as applied in the industrial sector, to their own organization. However, this is not without problems. This chapter discusses some of these problems, which, for the

CASE STUDY PURCHASING POLICY IN A LARGE INSURANCE COMPANY

Four years ago the management of a large European insurance company decided to drastically change its purchasing operations. As these activities were scattered throughout the company, internal control on purchasing spend was non-existent. Since managers did not give much attention to purchasing decisions, most employees had a large degree of freedom in dealing with suppliers. In some cases, it appeared that this freedom was used for personal advantage. Apart from fringe benefits (such as fairly large gifts at Christmas and luxury study trips paid for by suppliers) a few employees appeared to have received fairly large amounts of money in their personal bank accounts as a reward for the business that they awarded to some suppliers. Since the credibility of the company was at stake and company morale was affected, the board of management had to take immediate action. The staff concerned were fired and management started to consider how best to prevent these problems in the future. The ensuing discussion resulted in the decision to centralize all purchasing activities in a single department. A purchasing manager was appointed from outside the company and was given a free hand to organize this department. The assignment was simple: see to it that all purchases are made through the department. All departmental managers within the organization were informed about this decision by sending them copies of the new purchasing charter, signed by the president of the board. The purchasing manager and his colleagues set to work.

Three years later the purchasing manager assessed his position. After careful analysis it appeared that only 25% of the total purchasing spend of the company went through his department! This was a disappointment – according to the purchasing manager it should have been much higher. However, during the past three years he had found achieving credibility for his department was an extremely difficult matter. Most budget holders and other managers responsible for purchasing decisions seemed not to be very cost conscious; neither were they disciplined in the way they arrived at their decisions. Most had pursued their existing relationships with suppliers, without involving or even consulting the purchasing department. At best the purchasing department was asked to deal with administrative matters, after supplier selection had been made. This seemed particularly true for all kinds of services that were bought. The large ICT organization, for example, contracted annually, for large sums of money, various IT specialists. The marketing organization negotiated agreements with advertising agencies in their own manner and appeared very sensitive to interference from the purchasing department. Car leasing agreements were dealt with by Finance and Administration, given the financial nature of this type of contracts. And the HRM departments made their own deals on temporary labour and training. The board itself seemed not to be aware of the money that was spent on accountants, fiscal and legal specialists and management consultants; these professional services were in almost every case decided upon on a very personal basis by one of the board members. . . .

This situation was very unsatisfactory to the purchasing manager since he felt that this company context prevented him from doing a professional job. He decided that top management should now be informed of the problem – departmental managers should adhere more strictly to company policies and procedures and the board should see to it that they actually did. He planned to write a detailed memorandum on this in order to point out the responsibilities of top management in this matter . . .

most part, stem from the fundamental differences between the purchasing function in the industrial sector and in the service sector. First, however, it is necessary to be aware of the most important trends and developments within the service sector in Western economies. Also of importance is understanding how the trend towards facilities management affects purchasing operations in service organizations. Next, the key success factors underlying successful purchasing in service companies will be discussed. Building on these, measures which may lead to more effective purchasing operations in service companies are described. Next, we will discuss how to proceed when buying and contracting for indirect goods and services. Our description will reveal that in buying indirect goods and services personal relationships and trust play an important role. Which is why the user is always heavily involved, if not leading, in the purchasing process.

PURCHASING AND FACILITIES MANAGEMENT

The most important characteristic of service companies is the absence of a physical transformation, i.e. a manufacturing process. Also, a clear and well-defined relationship between input, throughput and output is frequently absent.

Looking at the cost structure of service companies it is clear that the larger part of costs is related to labour. In general these companies represent a large value added component. As a result, in contrast to industrial and retail organizations, the purchasing-to-sales turnover ratio is comparatively low. This may run from less than 10% for an accounting firm, to 30–40% for a large banking organization, or even 50% for an international airline company. This implies that purchasing savings, although impressive amounts of money may be at stake here, have a limited effect on the return on assets (RONA) of service companies. When discussing competitive strategy, top management in service organizations will understandably spend most of their time on value added and people-related issues and activities. In general they will spend little time and effort on the support activities, among which is purchasing.

However, although the relative purchasing spend may be rather low, the products and services on which the company's money is spent show a large diversity. This is illustrated by Figure 4.1. Using Porter's value chain concept it is clear that almost all purchasing activities are aimed at the other support activities (see Chapter 1). Purchasing for the primary process is almost absent, since service companies by definition do not have a production process in

---

FIGURE 4.1 Major categories of non-product-related expenditure

Buildings, installation and infrastructure

- Real estate
- Restructuring and renewal
- Maintenance
- Technical installations
- Security systems
- Office furniture
- System walls
- Kitchens and canteens
- Temporary buildings

Housekeeping

- Energy
- Catering
- Cleaning and sanitary services
- Greenkeeping
- Removal services
- Security
- Garbage removal
- Clothing
- Technical support materials

Temporary labour

- Hiring of temporary personnel
- Interim managers
- Consultants
- IT programmers, analysts and project managers

Services

- Transport services
- Cars and transport vehicles
- Travel
- Accommodation
- Training and education
- Search and recruitment services
- Market research
- Marketing and promotion
- Media
- Events
- Factoring
- Professional services

IT and telematics

- Mainframes, hardware- and software
- Midrange systems
- PCs
- Peripherals
- Data communication networks
- Telephone switching equipment
- Infrastructure
- IT projects
- Outsourcing
- Information services

Office supplies and printing

- Copying
- Office equipment
- Office supplies
- Paper
- Packaging materials
- Printing
- Representation
- Books and subscriptions

Source: adapted from Rietveld (1995), pp. 138–40

which inputs are physically transformed to outputs. This is an important difference from industrial companies, where buying for primary activities represents the bulk of purchasing expenditure. It explains why managers in service companies reveal so little interest in the purchasing operations of their company – they consider it primarily as a support activity.

The competitive scene for the service sector is gradually changing from a traditional, local national arena to a truly international arena. As a result, service companies strive to improve their services to the end user whilst reducing operational costs. In some cases service companies have tried to establish international networks through mergers and acquisitions and joint ventures with overseas companies. This trend can be observed for example in the airline, banking, IT and insurance industries. As a result, large companies have become larger and more powerful. This development has affected their purchasing operations in several ways.

- Increased outsourcing of support activities. Focus on core activities often leads to the decision to put non-core activities to the market test. This was the prime reason for contracting out transportation and distribution by a major international bank. As a result the bank personnel involved were hired by the transportation company on a five-year fixed contract. Other activities which are often outsourced as a result of this exercise include security, catering, cleaning services, mail-room activities, maintenance activities, print and photocopying and garden and greenkeeping services.

- Integration of support activities in a facility management organization. In order to reduce costs and to improve the quality level of support activities, more companies have adopted a facilities management concept (see Memo 4.1) in which these activities are brought under one managerial responsibility. This development is not without relevance for purchasing. Firstly, it often implies that the purchasing manager is to report to the facilities manager. Secondly, it often leads to more purchases going through the purchasing organization, because this organizational concept facilitates the co-operation between purchasing and the other support functions.

- Increased scale of operations. As a result of the growth, which some service companies have experienced, opportunities to set up a specialized purchasing department have increased. This is especially true for companies which have merged with other organizations. These mergers often result in an impressive non-product related purchasing spend which, because of the amount of money involved, warrant treatment by professional buyers. This has encouraged companies to set up a professional purchasing department.

MEMO 4.1   FACILITIES MANAGEMENT

Facilities relate to all the physical conditions that enable an organization to conduct its primary activities. This includes the buildings, technical installations, equipment, and their related services, but excludes human resources management (HRM) and all manufacturing equipment. Facilities management can therefore be described as the management (planning, execution and control), and the realization of housing and accommodation, the services related to these, and other means in order to enable the organization to realize its mission. It includes activities such as building and technical maintenance, security, catering, travel, reception, transportation and distribution, and warehousing. Traditionally, one would find these activities scattered throughout the organization. Within a facilities management concept these activities are brought under one organizational responsibility. Adoption of the concept often leads to a more professional view on each of these activities. Most large companies are aware of the amount of money related to these activities. Moreover, the management of these activities consumes a lot of management's time and energy. The task of facilities managers is to provide their services at a competitive cost and quality level. When these conditions cannot be met, a decision to contract out this activity to outside suppliers is likely to be made. The trend towards facilities management explains, among other things, the rapid growth of some of these industries during the cost years (e.g. catering, transportation, courier services, security, etc.).

Major service companies nowadays are actively pursuing opportunities to improve their competitive edge. As a result they are looking for ways to reduce labour and operational costs, while improving the quality of their services to their customers. These efforts, clearly, have consequences for purchasing. The trend towards outsourcing means that service companies have a lot to gain from a professional purchasing organization, which can take care of defining purchasing requirements, supplier selection, negotiation and contract management. By adopting a facilities management concept support activities are much better integrated and managed, providing purchasing departments with the chance to work more closely with 'big spenders' within the service organization. Finally, since the scale of operations of many service organizations has increased through mergers and acquisitions, opportunities for a more professional approach to purchasing have improved considerably.

Given the nature of service companies and their comparatively low purchasing-to-sales ratio, cost considerations are not prime to internal customers, i.e. departments. They often feel it is more important for suppliers to deliver on time and in the right quantity, rather than to obtain the lowest purchasing price. Given the specialized nature of buying facilities and other indirect goods and services (information technology, software, marketing services) the user and the budget holder play a dominant role in purchasing decision-making (developing specifications, supplier selection, negotiation), leaving administrative matters, at best, to the purchasing department. This situation develops when purchasing does not possess sufficient knowledge in the appropriate specialist areas to enable it to act as a valuable partner to the internal customers. As a result, strong relationships can and will develop between internal users and suppliers, which are very difficult to change. The purchasing department therefore concentrates on what is left, the general, routine and low-cost items, which are ordered through fixed order routines from traditional sources of supply.

These considerations suggest that in most service companies an impressive potential for improvement in purchasing probably exists. Indeed, a professional approach to purchasing, as experience with several of these companies has shown, can result in savings of between 5 and 20%. At the same time, however, it will be clear that improving purchasing professionalism is a far from simple matter. Because of the relatively low purchasing spend, top management will often fail to provide sufficient support to purchasing procedures and policies, and buyers will get recognition particularly by providing a superior service to their internal departments. Purchasing managers operating in a service company should therefore be service driven rather than cost driven.

TOWARDS MORE EFFECTIVE PURCHASING IN A FACILITIES ENVIRONMENT

Previously we argued that major differences exist between buying for production purposes and buying for support activities. In particular, effective purchasing in a facilities environment requires that buyers are sympathetic to the needs and requirements of their internal customers. In practice, however, a gap exists between how internal customers perceive the role of the purchasing department, and how this department sees its role. This is illustrated in Figure 4.2.

Most managers of other departments will point to the following success factors for their purchasing department. They will favour easy access (both by telephone and personally), a fast reaction to questions and problems, prompt delivery of goods and services ordered, short delivery times, consistent quality of goods delivered, and immediate feedback in case of (unforeseen) delivery problems. Provided that buyers are able to meet these requirements, users are willing to allow purchasing to take a more pro-active role in the purchasing process.

The purchasing department will emphasize, however, other aspects in the relationship with the internal customer, such as low price, savings, good contracts, alternative sources of supply and clear specifications. It is clear that when the expectations of both the purchasing

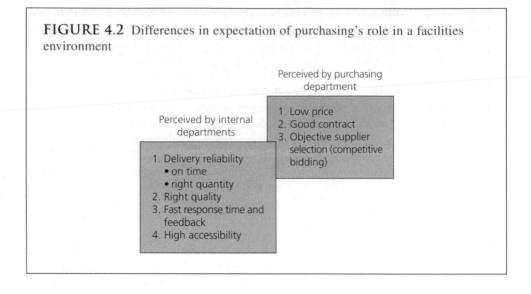

FIGURE 4.2 Differences in expectation of purchasing's role in a facilities environment

Perceived by purchasing department

1. Low price
2. Good contract
3. Objective supplier selection (competitive bidding)

Perceived by internal departments

1. Delivery reliability
   • on time
   • right quantity
2. Right quality
3. Fast response time and feedback
4. High accessibility

department and the internal users differ with regard to the role of the purchasing department, this may lead to significant boundary problems and friction between the parties involved. In those cases most internal departments will prefer to deal with the purchasing process themselves, simply to avoid these problems when they can.

When improving purchasing professionalism, a prime concern, therefore, should be how to improve the customer orientation of the purchasing department. In order to do this the following approach may be useful:

1   Analyse and document internal customer/product category combinations step-by-step. Based upon the purchasing spend cube (see Chapter 1), the idea here is to find out the total purchasing spend per department. This purchasing spend should be analysed per product category and per supplier. This sounds simple but is often a time-consuming matter, since many organizations do not keep account of these data in a systematic way. Next, what part of a specific department's purchasing spend is contracted through the purchasing department should be assessed. In this way the internal market share of the purchasing department, both for specific departments and product categories, can be established (see Table 4.1).

2   Assess internal customer satisfaction. Each department should be visited to find out how they experience the service rendered by the purchasing department. The attitude here is: 'You are OK, but how are we?' This is easier said than done, since when this investigation is conducted by employees of the purchasing department they will immediately explain or defend themselves against every criticism they encounter. At least one additional objective interviewer is therefore essential in this kind of investigation, the purpose of which is to find out what bottlenecks exist in the relationship between other departments and the purchasing department. These need to be documented and thoroughly analysed. Next, ideas should be developed on how to solve these bottlenecks.

3   Target setting. Based on the information gathered in the previous step, targets now can be set with regard to increasing the market share of the purchasing department in each of the cells. It often appears that although tremendous potential for improvement does exist in some cells (for example contracting for software for the IT department), this potential cannot be captured due to a lack of specific expertise within the purchasing department in this area. It should then be decided whether to build up expertise first, in order to increase market share in this area.

This step should result in a detailed action plan for the purchasing department, indicating:

- in what customer/product category combinations the purchasing department will maintain or reinforce its position, i.e. market share
- the actions which will be necessary to make this happen
- the results which can be expected from these actions (in terms of savings, lead time reduction, supply base reduction, etc).

4 **Cross-functional buying teams** and organizational structure. Since it will be impossible for any purchasing department to build up sufficient expertise on every product that is purchased by the company, a cross-functional team approach will be crucial for success. Specialists from user departments who work with suppliers and buyers should be put together in cross-functional buying teams in order to develop specific sourcing and commodity strategies and plans. These teams could be supervised by a purchasing specialist, but this will not always be necessary. In any case, they should report directly to the manager in charge or the board of directors. Apart from a team structure, an appropriate organization structure should be decided upon for the purchasing department. This subject will be covered in the next section.

Cross-functional buying teams
Specialists from user departments and buyers are put together in teams to develop specific sourcing and commodity strategies and plans.

5 Develop sourcing strategies. Each buying team should develop its supply strategies and commodity plans. Chapter 10 may serve as a guideline here. Using a detailed analysis based upon the purchasing product portfolio, each team can decide on the most favourable sourcing strategy for the future. Most likely, depending on the position of the company vis-a-vis its suppliers, different sourcing strategies will emerge. Each

TABLE 4.1 Customer/product category matrix

Internal department → ↓ Product group	Computer department	Technical maintenance	Distribution department	Etc.	Total volume
Computer hardware/software	A _____ B _____ C _____ D _____	Etc.			
Computer supplies	Etc.				
Office equipment					
Office furniture					
Office supplies					
Temporary labour					
Services					
Etc.					
Total volume					

Notes: A = Total purchasing volume; B = Purchasing expenditure through purchasing department; C = Market share purchasing department; D = Expected future total purchasing volume (↗ → ↘)

sourcing plan will provide a detailed action plan, which is presented to purchasing and senior management for approval.

6 Implementation. At this stage the sourcing plans which have been developed and approved, are executed. This requires close and careful monitoring by purchasing and general management. Results are to be measured in terms of:

- purchasing's market share per department as a measure of how satisfactorily the purchasing department performs in the eyes of internal customers

- operational measures such as:
  - savings generated as a result of the actions conducted towards suppliers
  - purchasing customer satisfaction expressed by some form of index based upon a standardized survey, to be conducted periodically
  - purchasing administrative lead time expressing the responsiveness of purchasing to internal customer needs.

- progress against other targets, as described in the sourcing plans.

Figure 4.3 provides some practical suggestions with regard to actions which can be taken in order to improve facilities buying.

FIGURE 4.3 Some suggestions for improving facilities buying

Improvement measures aimed at improving the purchasing–internal customer interface:

- joint efforts aimed at reducing product variety through standardization
- joint efforts at supplier reduction (doing more with less) through:
  - establishing well-defined procedures for supplier selection
  - introducing preferred supplier lists
  - introducing tender boards, sourcing committees, and/or cross-functional category teams for key commodities.
- improve accessibility and customer orientation of purchasing department through:
  - improvement of telephone facilities
  - effective help-desk
  - improving social skills through training
  - purchasing intranet
  - improve purchasing systems and procedures.

Internal measures aimed to improve purchasing processes and operations:

- improving product and market knowledge
- improving purchasing process management
- simplify order to pay processes for customers
- introduce electronic catalogues for routine items
- introduce electronic order to pay solutions to internal customers
- simplify authorization procedures
- simplify invoice handling and approval procedures.

This approach cannot be applied to facilities buying only. The area of indirect, i.e. non-production, buying is increasingly being acknowledged as an area where substantial savings can be made. For this reason, many large companies have initiated corporate programmes in this sector. Philips Electronics started an initiative in 1996 with the aim to reduce purchasing expenditure by 12% on in this area. Philips' example was followed by many other international companies. Today, most of these companies have corporate wide programs in place to reduce cost related to indirect materials and services. Memo 4.2 explains how Intel has structured its approach towards this important spend area.

MEMO 4.2   INTEL GOES GLOBAL WITH INDIRECT BUYING STRATEGY

High-tech giant Intel is successfully leveraging a single global sourcing process across its entire indirect materials spend. The internally developed five-step process emphasizes the use of source teams, which are made up of representatives of the company's various global business units. Within the five steps are such activities as a documented sourcing plan, Internet negotiations and e-catalogues, and formal supplier business reviews. In 2 years, the global indirect materials organization (IDM) has used the five-step process to source 95% of the company's indirect goods and services buy. It has helped to reduce costs by 10%.

Perhaps more importantly, 'the five-step sourcing process has provided a standard framework and common language to Intel's Corporate Purchasing global commodity management team,' says Roger Whittier, co-director of corporate purchasing at Intel in Santa Clara, California. 'It has clearly accelerated global sourcing of indirect materials.'

Intel's indirect buy consists of spending for construction, travel, professional services, marketing services, logistics, IT and facilities services, and makes up 60% of the company's annual procurement spend. Until 2002, Intel had been mainly sourcing indirect goods and services by region. Purchasing professionals in three regions – USA, Europe, and Asia – did not work closely with their internal customers in the business units or exchange best practices. It was clear the IDM organization was not fully leveraging the company's global buying power.

At the same time, Intel was becoming more global. More of the company's revenues were starting to come from regions other than the USA and the separate business units were becoming increasingly global in nature. Spending on indirect goods and services was growing faster than spending on direct materials – 25% faster from 1997 to 2002 – and maverick or off-contract spending was growing in step.

The IDM organization conducted some extensive benchmarking activities and learned that more world-class sourcing organizations were working hand in hand with their internal customers at company business units, aggregating spend volumes worldwide, consolidating purchasing activities, and documenting global strategy.

To reach world class, the IDM organization first had to overcome several daunting challenges. The first involved the company's organizational structure. In 2002, purchasing professionals in each geographic region reported to management in their respective region. Intel left this decentralized organization in place in the new plan, only now the purchasers also report functionally to a centralized global sourcing team. While a sourcing specialist for IT in Europe now reports to European management, his or her functional responsibilities align to a global IT sourcing team.

A second challenge: there was minimal spend data available on the indirect buy. Intel had been using several purchasing systems around the world making it hard for the IDM organization to gather information on its annual spending on indirect materials. Today, the company has one ERP system that tracks more than 90% of the spend worldwide.

The five-step sourcing process is not new. Intel's materials management organization has long used it and the IDM organization has always been involved in such activities as market research, working with the business units, negotiating with suppliers and managing costs. The difference is that the purchasing professionals in each region now have a framework for sourcing indirect goods and services. 'We have a consistent process across the globe, and we don't miss a step,' says Ghiya.

Step one: Collect and analyze internal data. At this step, the IDM organization identifies internal stakeholders and puts together a global sourcing team to purchase similar goods and services in all regions. In addition to representatives of business units from each region, the team also includes a member of the company's finance organization. All are equal members.

The global source team collects, analyzes and validates internal requirements. Using one ERP system worldwide helps the source teams to track and analyze spending.

Step two: Converge internal and supplier market data. Next, the global source team identifies the supply base, and benchmarks with other companies and market research firms. For individuals serving on the global source teams, Intel provides formal training in market intelligence as well as supplier management, documenting the strategic sourcing plan, the five-step process, global diversity and global reporting.

Step three: Develop sourcing strategy. Now, the global source team documents its strategic sourcing plan (SSP)—the heart of the process. In putting together the strategy, the team carefully considers

such components as technology, quality, availability, cost and fulfillment. The SSP may include setting up and conducting an e-auction for negotiations with suppliers or creating and managing an e-catalogue. Typically the SSP is for 1 to 3 years. To date, IDM has documented SSPs for 48 goods and services, covering more than 95% of spending.

Step four: Execute strategy and implementation plan. In this step, the global source team qualifies and selects suppliers and develops a negotiation strategy. The action plan laid out in SSP is executed at this step.

Step five: Manage supplier relationship. The final step closes the loop. The source team continues to collect market intelligence to determine if they need to make any changes to the sourcing strategy. They establish supplier expectations, and monitor performance through audits, score cards and business reviews.

Source: Purchasing, 4th July 2005

In discussing the optimal structure for a purchasing department within a service company the question is posed as to what principle to use. The basic dilemma is how to secure an effective internal customer orientation in combination with sufficient in-depth expertise and knowledge of products/services and supply markets. The structure most often encountered is that based on product characteristics: each buyer is responsible for managing a specific product category, i.e. spend category. Interface problems with internal customers are solved by assigning one senior purchasing staff member as the account manager for a specific customer department. On a daily basis the employees of a customer department can deal with any of the purchasing specialists. However, policy matters and specific problems are discussed with the account manager. They act as an intermediary between the customer and the purchasing department. Figure 4.4 provides an illustration of a purchasing department of a large international bank. Here the buying groups are formed around commodities, i.e. product categories. However, routine operations are separated from these groups by means of a special help desk and order group. This group focuses on answering routine questions from internal customers and placing small orders directly for them. Large orders are transmitted to the appropriate buying groups. Office and computer supplies have been covered by annual agreements with a limited number of suppliers; internal users directly place call-off orders with these suppliers for the materials they need. All products, and the terms and conditions, are available through an attractive electronic catalogue, which is developed and kept up to date by the 'systems, research and catalogue-group'. In this way the organization is able to free up considerable time, traditionally spent on administrative matters by the professional buyers, while at the same time reducing order cycle time for the internal users.

So far, we have discussed the relationship between purchasing and facilities management. As we have seen, introducing facilities management has enabled purchasing to become more professional. It has also allowed the facilities buyer to become a valuable specialist function. Many similarities exist between facilities buying and buying other,

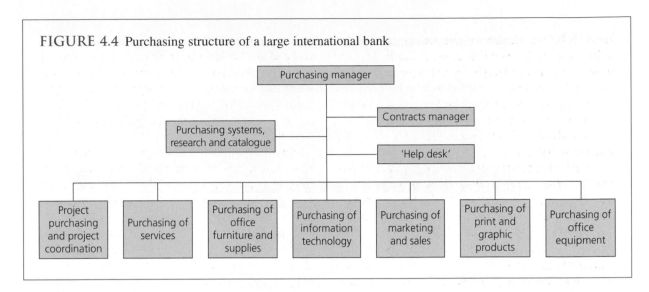

FIGURE 4.4 Purchasing structure of a large international bank

indirect goods and services. Therefore, we extend our discussion to this important spend area in the next section.

BUYING INDIRECT GOODS AND SERVICES

Facility goods and services are part of indirect sourcing. Indirect sourcing includes the buying of all goods and services that are required for those activities that do not belong to the company's primary processes. In general, a distinction is made between: (1) the buying of general goods and services, (2) the buying and purchasing of investment goods, and (3) the buying of trade items. This classification rests on where purchased materials and services are being used by the company.

Another classification is based upon the character of purchased goods and services. Here, a distinction is made between: (1) information technology, (2) marketing and communication, (3) professional services, (4) human resource management, (5) facility management, (6) transport and logistics and (7) technical maintenance. This classification is the foundation, as has been explained earlier, for the so-called **category tree**, i.e. the detailed classification of all goods and services that are being bought by the company. Within this classification all goods and services have a unique part number that is used to analyse the company's purchasing spend data and consumption and usage pattern. A purchase article coding system can easily include several tens of thousands of items.

Category tree
Product classification based upon product or supply market characteristics. Basis for category sourcing strategies.

For many companies the indirect spend is higher than the direct purchasing spend. On average the ratio is 50:50 (Carter *et al.*, 2003). The reason for this is the high level of outsourcing that many companies have practised in this area. In many companies IT has been outsourced to India, catering has been outsourced to contract caterers, and part of HR services are our outsourced to temps providers.

Compared to the direct purchasing spend, the product variety and hence logistics complexity related to managing indirect purchasing spend is enormous (see Figure 4.5). Making this huge purchasing expenditure transparent may result in significant purchasing savings. However, in practice, creating this transparency is very troublesome. Depending on the degree of automation, putting together a purchasing spend cube will take a company many months.

Creating transparency is an important condition in order to get better control over the purchase of indirect goods and services. So, the question here concerns how to

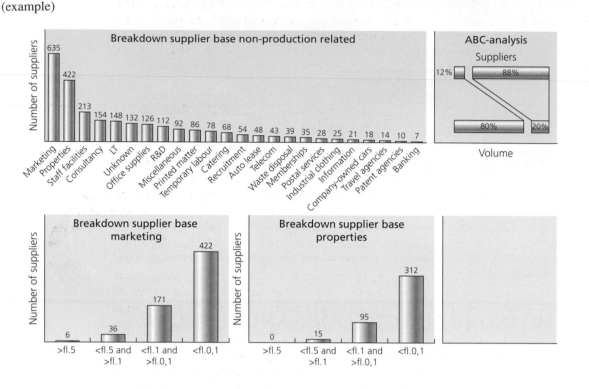

FIGURE 4.5 Breakdown purchasing spend and supplier base non-production related goods and services (example)

professionalize indirect buying of goods and services and how to realize the existing cost savings potential. The answer to these questions lies in the approach presented earlier. Also, Chapter 10 may serve as a guideline here. We conclude this section with some specific observations.

Part of the cost savings potential related to indirect spend can be obtained through analysing the exact consumption patterns of these goods and services. It will appear that many of these products have a consumption pattern that increases towards the end of the year. In order to prevent a cutting of their departmental budgets, managers may try to catch up at the end of the year by spending their budgets to the full. This 'end of year fever' is visible in many budget-driven organizations. Goods and articles are being purchased or ordered without a specific need or necessity. Examples are office supplies, laptops, office furniture, travel. Suppliers, which operate in these types of industries, easily make 60% of their annual sales turnover in the last 3 months of the year. Of course, the solution to this problem could be just not to purchase. Based on the budget principle, however, the budget holder will lose part of the future budget. Saving on this budget will not make the budget holder particularly popular as a manager among the staff. Sometimes, however, the circumstances necessitate engagement in this type of measure. Other measures to save on indirect goods and services are less orthodox: product standardization, supply base reduction, reviewing current contracts and agreements, reducing transaction costs, and outsourcing the purchase of small items and contracts may often generate impressive cost savings.

In general, the operational transaction costs related to indirect goods and services are considerable. For this reason many companies have implemented electronic procurement solutions. When these kinds of solutions are in place a logical next step for larger companies is to put all support activities together in a shared service centre. This shared service centre includes the processing of small orders and invoices. To reduce this kind of operational costs even further large companies have decided to outsource the entire shared service centre to low-cost country providers. For example, Philips Electronics initially set up a shared service centre in Lodz, Poland. This shared service centre has now been outsourced to a low-cost country provider.

SUMMARY

Service companies represent a growing share of economic activity in most European countries. Purchasing represents, in general, a low share of the service company's overall cost. Compared with industrial companies, purchasing savings therefore have a lower effect on the company's return on net assets. Moreover, purchasing expenditure is related to a large variety of activities, and is scattered throughout the organization. One result is that the purchasing function is far less visible to management than in industrial companies, which is why the development of purchasing management in service companies has lagged behind. This picture is gradually changing, for three reasons: (1) the tendency nowadays to outsource support activities, (2) the trend towards facilities management and (3) the increased scale of operations of many service organizations. These developments have in general increased the need for a professional purchasing approach. As a result many service companies have built up separate purchasing departments within their organization.

Developing a professional purchasing approach in service organizations is a far from simple matter. An important reason for this is that top management frequently fails to support and control purchasing procedures. This explains the freedom exercised by departmental managers when purchasing activities are involved. Professional purchasing decision-making requires considerable specialist knowledge, which is often not available from within the purchasing department. In those cases the purchasing department has little value to add to its internal customers.

From this we concluded that buyers, in order to be effective, should be primarily service driven, rather than cost driven. In order to be able to structure the buying process a team-based approach was recommended in which the user and product specialists play a major role. A strong customer orientation and cross-functional teamwork are prerequisites for the success of any purchasing department in this kind of organization. In order to professionalize purchasing in a facilities environment we presented a six-step approach: (1) analyse and document internal product/customer combinations in order to assess present and future market share, (2) assess internal customer satisfaction in order to discover bottlenecks and problems in the relationship with internal departments, (3) set targets for improving internal service levels, (4) decide on what organizational structure will be most appropriate, (5) develop specific sourcing strategies for each department and product category and (6) implement and monitor progress.

Facility goods and services are part of indirect sourcing. Indirect sourcing includes the buying of all goods and services that are required for those activities that do not belong to the company's primary processes. A classification of this type of purchases can be based on destination or product characteristics. Due to a complete lack of transparency, these types of purchases present a considerable cost savings potential. This potential can only be captured by using a systematic purchasing approach with professional purchasing process management principles and active involvement of the internal user. For this reason large companies have embarked on corporate, worldwide programs aimed at professionalizing indirect sourcing.

ASSIGNMENTS

4.1　Why is professionalizing purchasing in service companies so much more difficult than in industrial companies? Give five reasons.

4.2　What specific problems are related to buying services? State five problems.

4.3　What does it take for a purchasing manager to professionalize the process of indirect sourcing in a service company?

4.4　What explains the large cost savings potential with regard to indirect sourcing?

4.5　What benefits would a company enjoy from implementing the procurement solutions in indirect sourcing?

REFERENCE

Carter, P., Beall, S., Rosetti, C., Leduc, E. (2003) *Indirect Spend, Critical Issues Report*, Tempe, AZ: CAPS Research.

BUYING BUSINESS SERVICES

Having read this chapter readers should have learned about the following subjects:

- The increasing importance of buying of services.

- The differences between buying services and buying goods.

- Different views on buying services and the implications for the purchasing process.

- The importance of stakeholder management for buying services.

- Specific areas of attention in specifying services, and selecting and contracting service providers.

- The importance of professional contract management.

INTRODUCTION

Some people may think that companies operating in the service sector compared to those operating in industrial sectors are lagging behind when it comes to the development of purchasing as a business function. Recognizing the purchasing development model (see Chapter 3) the purchase function within manufacturing firms seems to be more advanced. The purchasing function at service providers usually is in one of the first stages of the purchasing development model. However, a number of service companies have made significant progress in achieving **purchasing excellence**. During the past years many large service providers nominated a Chief Procurement Officer (CPO) to head up their (global) procurement operations. Given the increasing popularity of outsourcing and offshoring in this sector, service companies have become aware of the necessity to put professional purchasing and contract management in place. Today, companies are increasingly buying services instead of goods. Traditionally, transportation companies would buy trucks from a truck manufacturer's dealership and would negotiate an attractive acquisition price. Today these transportation companies seek integrated transportation solutions by negotiating the best all-in rate per kilometer. In such deals the truck manufacturer guarantees a flawless transportation capacity from A to B to its customers during the contract period.

Purchasing excellence, model
Explains how to professionalize purchasing, making use of two types of processes, i.e. strategic management processes and enabling processes.

CASE STUDY BUYING MARKETING SERVICES AT A EUROPEAN TELECOM PROVIDER

Some years ago a European telecom provider decided to investigate its massive purchasing spend related to marketing and promotions. A young assistant controller was given the assignment to investigate the company's purchasing spend and the extent to which purchasing processes with regard to this category were in control. His findings were surprising. The company appeared to do business with a mere 921 suppliers. Among the suppliers were marketing and advertising agencies, market research and media agencies, printing companies supplying all promotion materials and brochures, suppliers of sales promotion items and all kinds of larger and smaller consulting companies. The company did not seem to select its suppliers in a methodical manner. Many suppliers had already been supplying the company for a long period of time, which had resulted in the development of strong personal relationships. Contracts were not always present and if they were, they were not up to date. When comparing supplier invoices with contract prices and rates, many deviations were identified, all of which were disadvantageous to the telecom provider. With a few suppliers, the relationship was highly problematic. Relationships with advertising agencies were under pressure. Briefings to these agencies were revised regularly, in one case even 17 times before the first proof for a commercial was produced. End of year bonuses, if agreed, were paid to the company without proper verification whether the amounts paid were right. When

asked, the marketing professionals responded that they were simply too busy to spend time on this.

Many assignments were provided to suppliers by telephone, fax or by e-mail and not properly administered. The marketing director had no idea of the financial obligations that were incurred by the company towards its suppliers. Over 20 000 invoices needed to be processed each year and this number was growing fast. The reason was the tedious handling of invoices by the company. Making payment often took on average more than 3 months lead time. Since the standard payment terms of suppliers were not respected, suppliers sent many interest notes. These added to the administrative burden of the company. Not surprisingly, the transaction costs were enormous, without anyone in the telecom company knowing. When analyzing payment lead times, the long times could be explained by the fact that every invoice needed to be authorized by the departmental managers involved before it could be paid. In one case an invoice had to wait for 6 months before proper authorization was provided by the manager, who appeared to be abroad frequently. Based upon his analysis, the assistant controller had the feeling that the company paid far too much for the services that were provided by the suppliers. His idea was that a professional purchasing approach could pay off handsomely if the purchasing and transaction processes within the marketing department were managed more effectively.

Costs for services and maintenance of the truck are included in the transport rates. Manufacturers of copying machines operate in a similar way. Buyers of this type of equipment no longer want to arrange deals on the acquisition price of the copy machines. They rather negotiate a price per copy or print. In the price per copy, all costs including the maintenance and services costs during the lifetime of the contract are supposed to be covered. Of course, the manufacturer or supplier also needs to guarantee a predefined service level. In this situation the buyer also wants to contract for the lowest total cost of ownership for the equipment to be delivered by the supplier.

Services are not only purchased by service providers. Manufacturing companies increasingly buy services. Think about Philips Electronics that has outsourced the entire production of its CD, DVD and MP3-players. Traditionally, most purchased services were related to non-product related areas, such as cleaning services and subcontracted catering. However, today companies may buy services that are a fundamental part of the value proposition to their customers. An example is the buying of cleaning services by railway companies. When cleaning the train coaches, the cleaning company clearly influences the traveller's perception of the quality of the service provided by the railway company.

Buying professional services is not without problems. The introductory case at the beginning of this chapter is illustrative of what may happen when buying marketing services. In many cases the services buyer has to deal with a wide range of internal customers, which are spread out over the entire organization, each having their own wishes and preferences. In general, it is not simple to translate all wishes into a specification that is clear and fully accepted by every internal stakeholder. Because demand is highly dispersed throughout the organization, it is difficult to get an idea of the volume of service expenditures, to identify the actual users and decision makers, and to find out with which service providers the company does business.

This chapter deals with the specific characteristics of buying professional services. Firstly, a definition of business services is provided, as well as a view on how to deal with buying services. Differences between buying services and goods will become clear, as well as the consequences this may have for the purchasing (decision-making) process.

THE INCREASING IMPORTANCE OF SERVICES

The share of services in the company's purchasing portfolio has gradually been on the rise. In Chapter 1, we argued that the purchasing to sales ratio for industrial companies may range between 60 and 80%. For service companies the purchasing to sales ratio usually amounts to 10–50%. For service providers the largest part of their total cost is related to personnel. Think about the consultants working for consulting companies or the cleaning staff employed by cleaning services companies. Traditionally, most services purchased were related to the supporting processes of the company (see Chapter 1). Examples of this type of service are car leasing, salary administration and office automation. However, nowadays, services are increasingly contracted from outside providers that make up an important part of the company's value proposition to its customers. An example is the contracting of services from external research laboratories and contract research organizations (CROs) by pharmaceutical companies. Suppliers involved clearly affect the service delivery of these manufacturers and, hence, the market success of the product and service solutions for their end-user markets. Another example is a large international bank that has outsourced the management of its electronic banking systems and electronic payment systems to an outside IT provider.

Traditionally, when buying services, personal relationships were deemed more important than cost considerations. This is primarily due to the fact that services are actually produced in close collaboration and interaction between the buyer and the seller. As a consequence, internal users and budget holders have a dominant role in overall purchasing decision-making, e.g. preparing the scope of work, supplier selection, contracting and negotiation. Understandably, the purchasing organization will only be included in the process for the handling of administrative matters. Such a situation can easily occur when the purchasing department has insufficient knowledge to act as a qualified business partner to the internal customer. In such a situation strong bonds may develop between internal users and the external suppliers involved, which appear difficult to change. As a result the services buyer will be forced into an administrative role. In such situations, however, the purchasing cost savings potential may be highly significant. As practitioners and researchers have demonstrated, a professional purchasing approach for services can result in considerable savings. Stradford and Tiura (2003) have demonstrated that for services these savings can range from 10 to 29%. However, in some cases cost savings may be of no particular concern. In the situation where the supplier's services are part of the company's customer value proposition, the discussion should focus primarily on how to challenge the supplier to improve their added value to the final customer. It is here where professional services buying can come into play as well.

The previous discussion explains why improving the professionalism of services buying is far from simple. Different authors have demonstrated that purchasing professionals think that buying services is more difficult than buying goods (Jackson *et al.*, 1995). Other researchers found that managers have just the opposite view, which is why rather inexperienced purchasing staff are often lumbered with this task (Smeltzer and Ogden, 2002).

Nevertheless, professional services-buying is rising on the corporate agenda. Patel (2005) interviewed 30 chief executive officers (CEOs) of large companies and found out that 70% were worried about how professional services like consultancy, legal services, financial services and marketing services were contracted in their respective companies. These CEOs were also of the opinion that CPOs and their purchasing departments could and should make the difference with regard to contracting for business services. They expressed having high expectations of the contributions made by these professionals. They considered providing superior services and support to internal customers by purchasing professionals to be mandatory. Buyers of services therefore need to be more service driven than cost driven in comparison with their colleagues who buy predominantly goods. Schiele (2005) and Schiele and McCue (2006) therefore introduced the concept of 'meaningful involvement'. They argue that purchasing involvement is not always necessary or desirable. Intervention by a purchasing professional should always be meaningful to the internal customer.

DIFFERENCES BETWEEN GOODS AND SERVICES

The differences between buying services and goods are many. These differences are due to the special characteristics of services: going through the different stages of the purchasing process is more difficult for services than for goods.

To understand this, it is necessary to define services. Here, we follow Grönroos (2000) who defines services as 'a process consisting of a series of more or less tangible activities, that normally take place in the interaction between customer and supplier employees, or physical resources and systems, that are offered as an integrated solution to customer problems'.

This definition shows that services can be offered in combination with tangible goods. Examples are investment goods that suppliers provide in combination with a service contract for maintenance during the economic lifetime of the equipment. Another example is painters that are going to paint your house and provide for their own paints and brushes. According to the definition, services are offered as a response to a customer need. Sometimes the need for a specific service is very clear, as may be the case in the situation of a truck driver who needs immediate assistance for repairing his flat tyre. Sometimes, however, both the problem and the solution are not precisely clear. In these cases, the problem needs to be correctly defined first, for example by conducting a provisional study before a supplier can be approached for a solution. An example of this is the financial manager who seeks an accounting firm to put together the annual report. In this case the dividing line between the customer organization and the accounting firm requires clarification. What information is available to the customer? Which part of the auditing process can be done by the customer? How detailed should the accountant's audit be? When should the annual report be finished? In this case, a concise definition study should be conducted related to these questions before the accounting firm can provide a suitable offer to its customer.

Services are produced in close interaction between customer and supplier. Providing services requires human interaction. Such interaction requires that employees from both sides know and respect each other. It generally takes time to develop a constructive relationship. Many aspects play a role in developing effective business-to-business relationships. Perceptions of the expertise and knowledge that is present with both parties, economical and commercial aspects and technical aspects, and also personal elements like emotions, personal feelings and personal preferences may support or interfere in business-to-business relationships. This is one of the reasons why it is so difficult for a buyer to interfere in a relationship that has grown over time between the internal employees and the employees of the supplier. It will be clear that nobody will like a newcomer to interfere in what parties consider to be their process and their relationship.

In the literature, services are differentiated from goods through four basic characteristics: intangibility, perishability, heterogeneity and simultaneity. The first characteristic relates to the fact that services cannot be touched. Services relate to the performance of a previously defined activity that is conducted in close collaboration with the customer. The problem here is the demarcation of what activity is seen as the prime responsibility of the supplier, and that of the customer. Since services are intangible they cannot be produced on stock. Therefore the availability of capacity is and should be a major subject in discussions with the supplier. A free chair in an aeroplane loses its value at the moment of departure of the plane. Supplier expertise and resources should be available at the right time in order to meet the service needs of a customer. That is not simple in situations where the future demand of the customer cannot be predicted. As an example, in the **service level agreement** for copiers the buyer states that the supplier will be on-site within two hours of having been informed about a failure of the equipment. In such a situation the customer does not pay only for the hours spent on repair activities, but also for the capacity that the supplier needs to have available to be able to react quickly to customer calls for immediate service.

Heterogeneity implies that every service is unique. Since services involve people and every person is unique, service exchanges cannot be standardized. Services relate to the exchange of knowledge, expertise and capacity that are embedded in human beings. Therefore the actual exchange will be different depending on the individuals a buyer deals with. This explains why it is so difficult to produce services at a consistent quality (Ellram, et al., 2004).

Simultaneity, relates to the fact that services are produced and consumed at the same time. This happens in a continuous interaction between employees of the customer and of the supplier. We will discuss this matter in more detail in section 5.4. Table 5.1 summarizes

Service level agreement (SLA)
A service level agreement describes the performance, which needs to be delivered by the supplier. Key performance indicators (in terms of cost, service and quality levels) are agreed by both parties. Payment to suppliers is based upon specific rates plus a bonus or minus based upon actual performance versus targeted performance.

TABLE 5.1 Differences between goods and services

Pure services offering	Pure product offering
100%	100%
Services	Product
Intangible	Tangible
Heterogeneous	Homogeneous
Production, distribution and consumption are simultaneous processes	Production and distribution are separated from consumption
More difficult to demonstrate (not available)	Can be demonstrated before moment of purchase
Cannot be transported	Can be transported
Is an activity or a process	Is a physical entity
Is produced in interaction between buyer and seller	Is produced in a specialized remote facility
Customers participate in production process	Customers in general do not participate in the production process
Cannot be stored	Can be stored
Property cannot be physically transferred	Property is physically passed on to new owner

these four characteristics and some other important aspects of services. This table shows that service propositions may vary from almost 100% tangible goods to services without any tangible element. This continuum can be used to categorize services depending on the degree of tangibility.

The position of a service on this continuum has a large impact on how to manage the purchasing process of services. The most important implications are discussed in sections 5.5 and 5.6.

TOWARDS A CLASSIFICATION OF SERVICES

Purchasing portfolio, approach (identical to Kraljic portfolio)
Portfolio consisting of four quadrants (i.e. leverage products, strategic products, routine products and bottleneck products) based upon two criteria: financial impact and supply risk. Serves to develop four differentiated supplier strategies.

For a first classification of services the **purchasing portfolio approach** (see Chapter 9) can be used. However, a more popular way to classify services is the one based upon their physical characteristics. Axelsson and Wynstra (2002) proposed a classification of services in line with the one suggested by the OECD in 1999. In this classification a distinction is made between:

- Facility services like cleaning services, contract catering, security and buildings maintenance.
- Financial services like banking services, leasing, salary administration, insurance, accounting services, tax consultancy services.
- Information and communication technology services like computer help desk services, call centre services, telecommunications services and software development and implementation.
- Operational services like management consultancy, environmental consultancy, legal services, risk management services.
- Research and development and technical services, like technical maintenance, repair and support services, development and engineering services.
- Transportation and distribution services like warehousing, value-added logistics, transport services.
- Human resource services like training, recruitment and hiring temporary personnel.
- Marketing services like sales support, reselling, advertising, sales agency services, website design and call centre services.

This classification is, in principle, based upon the functional environment in which the service is consumed. It can be used to explain what specialists will be involved in purchasing decision-making.

Apart from this classification, other classifications of business services are available (see for an overview Cook *et al.*, 1999). The classification by Fitzsimmons *et al.* (1998) is based on who the service, that is to be purchased, will be aimed at (e.g. people, a process, or property such as equipment or facilities) and on how important the service is for the company itself. These dimensions, however, neither explain what functional disciplines should be involved in the services purchasing decision, nor which management levels need to be involved. For critical services, involvement of higher management is more likely than for less critical services.

Another popular classification is the one proposed by Silvestro *et al.* (1992). These authors identify three different services, i.e. professional services, service shop and mass services. These three categories vary in terms of the contact intensity, i.e. the degree to which humans are required to provide the service, the degree of customer specificity of the service, and the number of customers that can on average be served on a single day.

Of course, fewer customers can be served by providers of professional services than by those of mass services. Silvestro *et al.* (1992) argue that every type of service process requires a different strategy, different management and a different performance measuring system.

Jackson and Cooper (1988) differentiate between services that make up part of the company's customer value proposition, services that actually are consumed in the process of servicing these customers, and services that are consumed within the organization. Wynstra *et al.* (2006) build on this classification and for the first group of services make a further distinction between services that are passed on to the customer, and services that are reworked before passing these on to the customer. An example of the first category is luggage handling at Schiphol Airport Amsterdam, which is contracted for by, for example, Air France-KLM. This service is directly provided by the handling agent to Air France-KLM's customers without any interference of Air France-KLM. An example of the second category is the weather forecast that is is reworked by Air France-KLM and integrated into a flight plan for its pilots. Wynstra *et al.* (2006) argue that the way in which a service is classified determines how the customer and supplier should interact after the contract has been closed. This is relevant to define and decide what functional disciplines need to be involved in the continuous balancing of supply and demand of services, what capabilities will be needed from both sides, what kind of relation-specific investments need to be made, and what key issues need to be addressed in the dialogue between customer and supplier.

We conclude that there are many ways to classify services. One classification is not necessarily better than the other. It is important to realize, that the way in which companies classify services will affect purchasing decision-making and will also influence the operational phase that follows after contract closure. Of course the way in which services are being purchased depends strongly on the company's business strategy, the way the company is organized and the type of internal customer to whom the services are

---

MEMO 5.1   A CLASSIFICATION OF SERVICES BASED ON THE ACTUAL USE BY THE CUSTOMER ORGANIZATION

Van der Valk (2007) has focused on the question of how customers and suppliers should collaborate during the lifetime of the service contract to accomplish successful business-to-business service exchange. She elaborated on the classification proposed by Wynstra *et al.* (2006) and identified four basic services types:

1 Component services, that are passed on unaltered to the final customers of the buying organization (e.g. luggage handling at the airport for an airline company).

2 Semi-manufactured services, that are being integrated into the buying organization's value proposition to its customers (e.g. in-flight catering services contracted for by an airline).

3 Instrumental services, that are used by the buying organization to change their primary processes (i.e. management consultancy to professionalize the airline's operational processes).

4 Consumption services, that are used in different support processes within the buying organization (e.g. cleaning services for offices of the same airline company).

For each of these four types of services Van der Valk identified different interaction patterns between the buying organization and the service provider. The way in which services actually were used by the buying organization appeared to be a useful way to segment services.

delivered. Hence, companies should choose what classification fits their objectives best. Also, the composition of the decision-making unit for services will depend on the criticality of the service. Due to the larger uncertainty, critical services will by definition have more stakeholders involved than non-critical services.

THE INITIAL PURCHASING PROCESS FOR SERVICES

We will discuss three important stages of the initial purchasing process, i.e. specifying, selecting and contracting services.

Specifying: defining the scope of work for service providers

Prior to the actual supplier selection decision it is often difficult to determine what the service provider exactly should accomplish. Axelsson and Wynstra (2002) argue that the scope of work for service providers can be specified in three different ways:

- **Specification of the inputs that will be used by the service provider.** In this situation the contract is aimed at describing the resources and capacities that will be used by the service provider to produce the required services. An example here is the HR manager who is looking for temporary labour for seasonal activities. The temporary labour agency will probably send the HR manager some curricula vitae of available people. Next the HR manager will make his choice based upon the information provided and some additional interviews. The contract is about making people available to the customer at a predetermined time period and at a predetermined rate. The contract states very little about what performance needs to be delivered by the persons that are actually hired.

- **Specification of the throughputs, or the processes that need to be in place in order to produce the requested service.** Based upon a general description of the work that needs to be accomplished both parties agree on the activities that will be performed by the service provider. This is common practice when contracting for civil projects or buildings. Apart from the price, parties need to agree on a detailed project planning that contains a reasonable estimate of the number of employee hours taken and the materials that will be used for the project. The project planning includes a time-based milestone planning for the project including the payments that will be made over time. The contract states very little about the functionality that the house being built needs to have for the principal.

- **Specification of the outputs (or outcome) that need to be generated by the supplier.** Here, the buyer is explicit in terms of the results that need to be accomplished and delivered by the service provider. Axelsson and Wynstra (2002) make a distinction between output and outcome. Output relates to the functionality of the service instead of the activity itself. An example is a service contract for a technical installation. The contract can stipulate the maximum acceptable unplanned downtime as a percentage of the total operational time ('uptime') of a specific machine. The supplier, then, is responsible for maintaining a preventive maintenance scheme so that the unplanned downtime target is not exceeded. Although the customer will be interested in the details of the maintenance scheme, he is likely more interested in the equipment's actual output. This output is monitored based on a number of key performance indicators that have been agreed upon. The functionality of the service is emphasized, i.e. keeping the machine running instead of focusing on how well the maintenance activities were conducted by the supplier. **Service level agreements** (SLAs) are an illustration of this way of specifying services. Outcome relates to the economic value that is generated by the provider for the customer. To stick to the previous example, fewer failures will lead to a higher productivity and availability of machines, which will result in larger profits to the buying organization.

Service level agreements
The functionality of the service is emphasized, i.e. keeping the machine running instead, rather than focusing on how well the maintenance activities were conducted by the supplier.

In many cases it is not easy to assess the total costs incurred when contracting for a specific service. Part of defining the service specifications is also that both customer and supplier agree on who will be responsible and accountable for what part of the expected output or outcome. If the quality of the service does not meet the expectations of the buyer, the buyer probably will hold the supplier responsible. However, a probable explanation for this might be a lack of communication and information or insufficient preparations and instructions from the side of the buying organization. It is therefore necessary to be explicit about the expectations, roles and responsibilities of both parties to a fair degree of detail. A detailed project planning, with clear milestones that need to be accomplished within a certain timeframe by both buyer and seller therefore needs to be part of the pre-contractual discussions.

The question is of course when should a buyer opt for an input specification, when for a throughput specification and when an output specification should be preferred. Preferably, the buyer should always strive for an output or outcome specification. The reason for this is that it allows the supplier more degrees of freedom to select the work methods that will suit him best and to organize the work in the best possible way. All of this should work out positively in terms of pricing, but also in terms of quality and flexibility. Moreover, the supplier is requested to put down a certain performance, which is relevant when the buying organization seeks a performance-based contract. In general, performance-based contracts are largely preferred over contracts in which the supplier only commits to perform certain activities. Hence, the way in which the service is specified (input, throughput, output) is also decisive for the type of contract that can be used.

We could conclude that output/outcome specifications should always be preferred over input or throughput specifications. This, however, is too easy a statement. From a purchasing point of view, it is always very important to check whether a service provider is capable of delivering the required output or outcome. Think, for example, of Nedtrain, a specialist in train and railway maintenance, operating in The Netherlands.

For many years Nedtrain was very explicit in its relationships with cleaning companies on how to clean the trains' coaches and what cleaning materials to use. Recently the company started to explore whether it could use output specifications for its discussion with suppliers rather than input specifications. The company engaged in a discussion with its suppliers to have them commit to a certain level of traveller satisfaction. In this case the supplier was willing to face the challenge. However, in many cases it is doubtful whether suppliers are willing to work this way. One argument against this way of working is that traveller satisfaction with regard to the cleaning activities is dependent on many factors. Factors like the general condition of the train, a chair that is worn out, the delay that the traveller has experienced, bad weather conditions can all negatively affect customer satisfaction and the customer's perception of the train interior. These kinds of externalities are difficult to influence for the supplier, which may prevent provision of a consistent service quality. In general, the more difficult it is to specify the outcome and output of the service, the more difficult it is to arrange for a performance-based contract.

FIGURE 5.1 Methods for specifying business services

Input specification →	Throughput specification →	Output specification →	Outcome specification
Focus on resources and capabilities of the supplier	Focus on supplier processes needed to produce the service	Focus on the functionality or the performance of the service	Focus on the economic value for the customer to be generated by the service

Source: Adapted from Wynstra and Axelsson, 2002, p. 144

Selecting service providers

If the scope of a specific service cannot be defined, it will be difficult to define what qualifications a future supplier should be able to meet. The more intangible the service is, the more time the buyer will spend on prequalifying and pre-selecting the future service provider. In those cases buyers need to check supplier references and experiences of other customers thoroughly as well as the reputation of the supplier. The preliminary prequalification will cover an assessment of the organization of the provider, its operational processes, its expertise and capacity, the quality of the staff and the management involved. In case of an input specification the buyer will probably be interested in certain certificates that can be handed over by the supplier. In the case of an output or outcome specification the buyer will be much more interested in positive references provided by key customers. As discussed before, the buyer will ensure that the supplier has sufficient capacity available at the moment the service needs to be provided. This is important for instance when contracting for call centre services. Here, it is important to ensure sufficient capacity, both in terms of quality and quantity, and the equipment to be used as well as other resources that are needed to deliver the required service. By providing the supplier with the right information and instructions, the buyer may positively influence productivity and performance. As a result, the buyer can influence the operational costs of the supplier and hence the prices and the rates that are being charged.

Contracting for services

When buying goods, it is fairly simple to assess what contractually has been agreed upon. It also is fairly easy to assess whether the supplier has lived up to the agreement. When both parties agree about the quality and quantity of the goods delivered, payment may follow. When buying services, however, it is often not so clear when the contracted performance has been delivered by the service provider. The key question here being: when is the service delivered exactly in line with the expectations of the customer? What will happen if an architect delivers a design that meets the technical criteria of the customer, but which does not match with the customer's personal taste? In such a case the contract probably will not give the answer, unless it contains clauses that cover such a situation. In reality, it is almost impossible to formulate clauses that deal with all possible problems and misunderstandings that may arise with service contracts.

When the service is to be delivered within the physical premises of the buying company, sufficient workspace and office space should be provided to the service provider's technical staff. In many cases these employees need to get access to the company's internal

---

FIGURE 5.2 Some suggestions for contracting services

- Specify the performance to be delivered by the supplier instead of the activities to be conducted.
- Describe when and where the service needs to be provided.
- Describe who would benefit from the service and in what way.
- Check reputation, expertise and qualifications of the supplier.
- Request the CVs of key personnel and make sure that personnel are available during the period in which service needs to be delivered.
- Analyse how the service process will be organized and check the quality system and training policy of the service provider, discuss potential threats and weaknesses and most important risks.
- Invite potential service providers to present a business case which is based on the scope of work.
- Check the cultural fit between your company and the company of the service provider.
- Aim for a performance-based contract, a service level agreement which includes critical performance indicators as well as a detailed work plan and time schedule.
- Agree on financial, personnel, technical and information resources to be made available by the buying organization.
- Prepare for detailed inspection and quality procedures.
- Discuss and agree on procedures for dispute resolution.
- Agree on performance-based payment schedules.
- Agree on an effective communication structure and make working arrangements.

---

information and administrative systems. A service contract, here, should cover the special arrangements that need to be made by the principal.

At the contractual stage, it is important to agree on what criteria will be used to assess the quality of the service provided by the service provider. Both parties need to agree on specific key performance indicators. These indicators are, as we have discussed earlier, a key component of SLAs. If the supplier meets the agreed service levels, immediate payment will follow. In case the supplier is not able to reach the targeted service levels, they will get paid less. In order to make such a contract work, the buyer needs to periodically report on the supplier's performance (or have the supplier do that).

THE POST-CONTRACTUAL STAGE

Having agreed on the contract, the most important stage in the purchasing process is yet to follow. At this stage the buying organization and the service provider should actively collaborate to establish a successful service delivery. The interaction between buying organization and service provider is continuous in nature, as in the situation where internal activities have been outsourced to an outside service provider and in which service provider staff actually reside within the buying organization (e.g. security services, catering services, cleaning services).

Here, it becomes clear how successful the previous purchasing activities actually have been. In reality, many problems emerge at this stage. It is not uncommon that during the contracting stage a lot of discussion takes place about what service to provide, how to organize for it, how to pay for it, etc. Apparently, the way in which the services should be executed received less attention than it should have in the initial stages of the purchasing process. An example is a company that has outsourced its IT services. The IT help desk is now operated by new staff that needs to get acquainted with the internal organization. The new staff may, based upon their company's standard instructions, be more strict and formal in responding to internal customer demands than in the old situation, leading to more paperwork and frustration among internal employees. How the help desk actually operates becomes clear at this stage. Outsourcing this type of process is not the same as 'we do not have to work on it anymore'. Although the supervision of the activity resides with the contractor, it is still the customer that needs to manage the relationship. This requires different competencies and capabilities from the staff involved on the side of the buying organization. In general, it is wise to differentiate between the person who supervises the quality of services provided by the service provider and the person who monitors the follow-up of the contractor of arrangements made with the service provider.

During the implementation stage it may appear that key performance indicators and bonus/incentive arrangements work out in the wrong way. In the IT contract specific clauses may have been agreed upon about the uptime of the servers; however, nothing has been said about internal customer satisfaction related to help desk functions. As may be expected, supplier behaviour is highly influenced by the key performance indicators that have been contractually agreed. Probably, the help desk will immediately cut their support as soon as the server is causing difficulties. Again, the buying organization needs to anticipate this type of problem at an early stage in discussions with a future service provider. It means having a clear and detailed picture of how the service, in reality, will be conducted.

Creating an effective link between the initial purchasing process and the operational stages of the contract is therefore extremely important. It means that operational staff members in the company are consulted at an early stage about how activities actually take place.

From the very beginning, a relationship develops between the service provider and the customer organization. This relationship may be more or less intensive, be based on a higher or lower degree of integration between parties, be more or less critical for the parties involved, and so forth. The relationship will develop at multiple levels between the organizations involved: at the operational level between the individuals or teams that are involved in actual service delivery, but also at the management level, where the relationship and contractual arrangements will be periodically reviewed. Until now, little has been known about how these types of relationships develop over time, what their interrelationships are and what aspects essentially determine long-term success in service relationships.

INVOLVEMENT OF PURCHASING IN CONTRACTING FOR SERVICES

From what we have discussed above, it will be clear that, in general, there is much room for professionalizing services contracting. The first question in many companies today is, what services are contracted where, by whom and against what price? In order to obtain this information, the services buyer needs to team up with the internal customer. Traditionally buyers are involved in buying business travel, print services, and courier services. As most of these services are of low importance, buyer involvement is high. This is different when buying highly important or critical services, such as marketing services and ICT.

Here, the company experts play a very important role. These types of services are not contracted for by the purchasing department, but by the respective functional departments. Internal experts may have long-term experiences with service providers, leading to excellent interpersonal relationships. Since the most important players are known to each other, new business is awarded to a small inner circle of suppliers. In most cases internal experts value these supplier relationships very much and hold the opinion that the value added by a supplier cannot be stated in objective terms. Too much of a price focus will work out negatively on the relationship with the supplier and, hence, on the quality of the service provided. This is why professional buyers usually are requested for their support, if any, only when the contract is about to be put together and signed.

In general, when these kinds of tight interpersonal relationships between internal customer and supplier exist, it will be difficult for any buyer to interfere. Since the buyer has no relationship with the supplier, they will stress objectivity as well as the fact that the performance of the supplier involved does not need to be 'top of the bill'. Also the buyer will probably stress a fair price, cost savings potential, clear contractual agreements, alternative suppliers and clear performance specifications. The internal customer, however, may feel that the supplier's loyalty, flexibility and quality cannot be expressed in a few simple indicators. How to, in such a situation, team up as a buyer with an internal customer is situation specific and depends to a large extent on the personality and experience of the buyer. Until now no standard approaches to this challenge has been found. The best thing a buyer can do is to provide for superior transparency in terms of the purchasing spend that is related to services, the number of service providers the company works with, and the actual quality provided by the providers involved. This information will enable them to engage in a more factual discussion with the internal customer. In any case, the buyer cannot go faster than the internal customer will allow.

If the expectations and the ways of working between the purchasing department and other departments are not aligned, competence problems and friction between the parties involved will be the result. In these cases, internal departments will prefer to deal directly with the supplier.

Therefore purchasing and the internal customers need to be aligned on the role and importance of professional supplier management. An important objective may be to seek control and good governance in all supplier relationships. Another objective can be to get superior value provided by service suppliers for the money spent. A buyer who consistently acts in the interests of all its internal customers will create credibility, allowing earlier involvement in the services buying process. The recommendations in Chapter 4 for creating a better customer orientation and purchasing, also apply here. Improving customer service and creating active involvement of the customer in the buying process are essential elements for professionalizing services buying.

SUMMARY

Services represent a growing share of economic activities in most European countries. Services also represent a growing share in the purchasing spend of organizations, both in industry and government. Traditionally, services buying was limited to contracting for facility services. Today, many service providers directly affect the buying firm's value proposition to its end markets. As a result, these service providers are crucial for the buying company's customer performance. This is why buying services is a key domain in purchasing management.

Professionalizing services buying is far from simple. Many companies have difficulty in getting to grips with this services expenditure. This is due to the fact that most of the service expenditures are spread throughout the company. Another problem is that services are highly differentiated in nature and highly diverse. As a result it is not easy to create a good overview of what is spent by the company on what kind of services and by whom.

Buying services requires specific expertise and close collaboration with internal experts in the company. Usually, the internal customer is much more knowledgeable about the service that needs to be bought than the buyer. Moreover, the internal customer has strong personal relationships with the service provider, since most **services** require close collaboration between the parties involved. In such a situation the buyer is perceived to add little value to the internal customer. However, the buyer needs to represent the strategic and commercial interests of the company and may be more factual and objective in dealing with supplier relationships. This is why the relationship between the internal customer and the purchasing department is controversial, which may lead to both challenges and opportunities for suppliers involved. In getting a better grip on services, buyers need to be primarily 'service driven' rather than 'cost driven'. In the services arena buyers need to be more facilitating and supportive in the purchasing process, rather than taking a lead position.

Buying services in a professional way represents significant challenges. First, deciding on the specification of services may take much more time than when specifying for goods. Here, buyers may choose to specify services based on inputs, throughputs, or outputs/ outcome. Inputs relate to the resources needed to produce the service, whereas throughputs relate to the activities needed to produce the service. As we have seen in this chapter, a specification based on output or outcome is preferred since it requires the supplier to tailor his value proposition to his specific expertise and capabilities. Moreover, this type of specifying allows for using service-level agreements in the relationship with the service provider. Second, since the quality of the service provided may be embedded in unique human expertise and capabilities, it is much more difficult to decide on objective selection criteria. This is also why, especially for knowledge intensive services, suppliers are sometimes very hard to compare.

When contracting for services, specific arrangements need to be made relating to the expected performance, price and what to do in case the service provision fails. Using service-level agreements stimulates internal customers to express the results that they expect from the services that are contracted for. Key performance indicators can be used to check predefined service levels and, hence, may provide for an objective reporting of actual supplier performance. In general, these critical performance indicators lead to a better understanding by the members of the decision-making unit on one hand and by the service provider on the other hand. They facilitate discussions on how to improve service levels. They also allow the application of penalties and incentives in contracts to stimulate service providers to perform better.

ASSIGNMENTS

5.1   Traditionally services and goods differ in four aspects. What are these aspects and what is the relevance of each to the services buyer?

5.2   Three ways to specify services have been described in this chapter. Could you apply each of these three types to contracting for cleaning services (offices)? And to contracting purchasing consultancy services?

5.3   Buying marketing services is usually done by the marketing department. You are recruited as a marketing services buyer. You reside within the purchasing department. How would you proceed to professionalize the buying of all marketing services?

REFERENCES

Axelsson, B. and Wynstra, J.Y.F. (2002) *Buying Business Services*, Chichester: John Wiley and Sons.

Cook, D.P., Goh, C.H. and Chung, C.H. (1999) 'Service typologies: a state of the art survey', *Production and Operations Management*, 8(3):318–38.

Ellram, L.M., Tate, W.L. and Billington, C. (2004) 'Understanding and managing the services supply chain', *Journal of Supply Chain Management*, 40(4):17–32.

Fitzsimmons, J.A., Noh, J. and Thies, E. (1998) 'Purchasing business services', *Journal of Business and Industrial Marketing*, 13(4/5):370–80.

Grönroos, C. (2000) *Service Management and Marketing: A Customer Relationship Management Approach*, 2nd edn, Chichester: John Wiley & Sons Ltd.

Jackson, R.W. and Cooper, P.D (1988) 'Unique aspects of marketing industrial services', *Industrial Marketing Management*, 17:111–18.

Jackson, R.W., Neidell, L.A. and Lunsford, D.A. (1995) 'An empirical investigation of the differences in goods and services as perceived by organisational buyers', *Industrial Marketing Management*, 24: 99–108.

Patel, R. (2005) 'Walking a tightrope', *CPO Agenda*, 1(3):44–49.

Schiele, J. (2005) 'Meaningful involvement of municipal purchasing departments in the procurement of consulting services: case studies from Ontario, Canada', *Journal of Purchasing & Supply Management*, 11(1):14–27.

Schiele, J. and McCue, C. (2006) 'Professional service acquisition in public sector procurement: A conceptual model of meaningful involvement', *International Journal of Operations & Production Management*, 26(3):300–25.

Silvestro, R., Fitzgerald, L., Johnston, R. and Voss, C. (1992) 'Towards a classification of service processes', *International Journal of Service Industry Management*, 3(3):62–75.

Smeltzer, L.R. and Ogden, J.A. (2002) 'Purchasing professionals' perceived differences between purchasing materials and purchasing services', *Journal of Supply Chain Management*, 38(1):54–70.

Stradford, D. and Tiura, D. (2003) 'Keeping the savings you thought you were getting in services sourcing', paper given at 88th Annual International Supply Management Conference Proceedings, ISM, Tempe, AZ.

Van der Valk, W. (2007) 'Buyer–seller interaction during ongoing service exchange'. Doctoral Dissertation, Erasmus Research Institute of Management, RSM Erasmus University, Rotterdam. Promoters: Prof. Dr. J.Y.F. Wynstra (RSM Erasmus University) and Prof. Dr. B. Axelsson (Stockholm School of Economics).

Wynstra, F., Axelsson, B. and Van der Valk, W. (2006) 'An application-based classification to understand buyer–supplier interaction in business services', *International Journal of Service Industry Management*, 5(17):474–96.

PUBLIC PROCUREMENT

LEARNING OBJECTIVES

After reading this chapter, the reader should have an understanding of the following subjects:

- The principles which are at the basis of public procurement and tendering.
- The specific characteristics of public procurement policy.
- The content and scope of the European Public Procurement Directives.
- The content and all of the six purchasing procedures for public procurement.
- The specific problems that may occur when executing these purchasing procedures.

INTRODUCTION

For many suppliers, service providers and construction firms the government is one of the most important customers. In some sectors public institutions and public utilities may, in fact, have the position of a monopolist (see Chapter 7). Demand for weapon systems and tanks are limited to the Ministry of Defense. Demand for water purification installations is limited to water control companies, which are often owned by government. Tendering for civil infrastructure, such as roads, bridges and tunnels, is in large part also limited to the transport ministries and municipalities in many countries. The total volume of the market for governmental contracts in all European Commission (EC) countries is considerable. In 2002 the EC estimated this volume at 16.3% of the gross domestic product (GDP), representing a contract value of about €1500 billion (European Commission, 2004). This figure excludes the GDP of the 12 member states that have entered the European Union (EU) since 1995. See Memo 6.1.

Representing 16.3% of GDP, governmental institutions play a crucial role in developing the internal market within the EU. The idea behind the European Treaty is to create one European market without trade barriers, based upon a liberal market mechanism, so that free exchange of goods, persons, services and capital can be accomplished.

CASE STUDY WHAT IS GOOD PROCUREMENT?

Good procurement means getting value for money – that is, buying a product that is fit for purpose, taking account of the whole-life cost. A good procurement process should also be delivered efficiently, to limit the time and expense for the parties involved. Successful procurement is good for the public, good for the taxpayer, and good for businesses supplying government.

While there is no single method that will guarantee the delivery of those objectives for all procurements, the following general principles set out the key steps to successful procurement in most cases. A procuring authority should:

- be clear on the objectives of the procurement from the outset
- be aware of external factors that will impact on the procurement such as the policy environment or planning issues
- communicate those objectives to potential suppliers at an early stage, to gauge the market's ability to deliver and explore a range of possible solutions
- consider using an output or outcome based specification, to give suppliers – who naturally know more about their business than potential buyers – more scope to provide innovative solutions to solve the underlying problem the procurement is designed to deal with, rather than

deciding what the precise solution should be at the outset

- follow a competitive, efficient, fair and transparent procurement process, and communicate to potential suppliers at the outset what that process will be. This will give suppliers greater certainty about the costs and benefits to them of submitting a bid, which should encourage effective competition. As all suppliers have the same knowledge going into the process, and will be assessed in the same way, the successful bidder can be chosen purely on its ability to provide the best solution
- be clear about affordability – the resources available to spend on the particular good or service. The procurer has to select on the basis of whole-life value for money, but in setting budgets for individual projects departments also need to make decisions about relative policy priorities and needs. If more is spent on one project than originally allocated, that will mean less is available for other priorities. Conversely, if savings are achieved, then these can be redeployed into frontline services
- establish effective contract management processes and resources in good time to drive excellent supplier performance throughout the contract.

Source: Transforming government procurement HM Treasury (UK); January 2007

THE NATURE OF PUBLIC PROCUREMENT

The purchasing policy of the classical government (the State, regional or local authorities, bodies governed by public law, associations formed by one or more of such authorities or bodies governed by public law) has some specific characteristics. These characteristics do not specifically apply to the public utilities sector (public transport, water control, energy supply and ports authorities). Therefore, for this sector an enlightened regime exists.

An important characteristic of public procurement policy is its public accountability. This holds that companies may sue the government for not being compliant with the public procurement directives. Therefore a prime consideration in executing procurement decisions is their legitimacy. Since governmental institutions can be sued publicly, the legitimacy of procurement decisions often overrides their efficacy, i.e. efficiency. This explains why contracting authorities are primarily procedure driven rather than result or

The EU consists of the following member countries (with their year of entry to the EU): Belgium 1951, Bulgaria 2007, Cyprus 2004, Denmark 1973, Germany 1951, Estonia 2004, Finland 1995, France 1951, Greece 1981, Hungary 2004, Ireland 1973, Italy 1951, Latvia 2004, Lithuania 2004, Luxembourg 1951, Malta 2004, The Netherlands 1951, Austria 1995, Poland 2004, Portugal 1986, Romania 2007, Slovenia 2004, Slovakia 2004, Spain 1986, Czech Republic 2004, UK 1973, and Sweden 1995. The total population is 480 million.

A compartmentalized market of government contracts, where national governments favour their national and local suppliers, is in conflict with the realization of one common European market. For this reason the EU introduced strict procurement directives, which prescribe, to a fair level of detail, how governmental institutions and municipalities should buy. The basic idea behind these directives is that the massive EU market should be accessible for all suppliers within the EC.

Four major principles underlie each of these procurement directives. These are: non-discrimination, equality, transparency and proportionality. When applying the procurement directives, governmental institutions should comply with these four principles.

The principle of non-discrimination should safeguard that the market for government contracts is accessible to every supplier, whatever the nationality and country. For this reason, it is not allowed to prescribe that a company should be located, for instance, in The Netherlands, or should have done business previously with the Dutch government. Neither is it allowed to require a specific product name or brand. The only discriminating requirement that is permitted, is that suppliers should be able to speak and write in the language where the contracting authority is established, if this is considered to be necessary for a successful completion of the contract.

The principle of equality is related to the previous principle. It stipulates that all competitors that compete for the same government contracts should be dealt with in a similar way and that they should be provided with the same information at the same time. In this manner the procurement directives try to create 'one level playing field' for every supplier.

The principle of transparency forces governmental institutions and public utilities to publish those contracts, the value of which exceeds certain financial thresholds, in the *Tender Electronic Daily* (TED), the EU database that keeps record of all European tenders. This principle also holds, in case there is a clear interest from suppliers in the other member states, that even the smaller contracts, which do not meet the financial thresholds, and the so-called B-services, are communicated to the European business community. In these cases public institutions may use their websites or may place specific advertisements in European newspapers.

The principle of transparency holds that the public institution communicates in advance what procurement procedure will be used, what requirements will be imposed on the supplier and how the contract will be awarded among competing suppliers. In general these procedures also prescribe that suppliers are informed of the reasons for not being selected.

The principle of proportionality states that the requirements and conditions that are imposed on the future supplier are reasonable. This means that they should be in balance with the scope and volume of the contract. These four principles underlying public procurement are the backbone of what will follow in this chapter.

An important concept that will be used in this chapter is the concept of the contracting authority. The contracting authority is in general a public institution or public utility that is subjected to the EU procurement directives.

performance driven. EU procurement law prescribes how purchases should be made and contracts should be awarded.

A second characteristic is that governmental activities are not subjected to the rules of free markets. They are funded by the tax income provided by taxpayers, whereas private enterprises primarily get their income from customers and markets. Commercial incentives are almost totally absent in public institutions, and, hence, there is no drive to create the best value for taxpayers' money. Other, political objectives may underlie public procurement decision-making. For a small municipality, it may be important to promote local employability by placing orders for construction or installation work to local suppliers. For another municipality it may be important to foster sustainability by buying products and services against a higher price, but which do not do any damage to the environment. A large city may want to buy coffee from developing countries to show its commitment to create a better world for poor farmers in those countries. These examples illustrate that political objectives may override economic objectives of buying goods and services against the lowest possible price.

A third characteristic, that is specific for the central government, is related to how finances are managed within the government. In some countries, e.g. The Netherlands, ministries need to spend the budget within the year in which it is allocated to them. Available budgets need to be spent in that specific year. If a contracting authority, by spending the money more wisely, is able to save money, it will lose that money to the central government. This explains why at the end of the year so many public institutions issue extra contracts and work to providers and suppliers. They just want to make sure that the total budget is going to be spent. In the case of the budget being left at the end of the year, this may work out detrimental to the contracting authority, since the central government will then award a lower budget for the next year. Another aspect of public finance is that budgets for investments and budgets for exploitation are separated. As a consequence a contracting authority may decide to buy investment goods without considering the cost that will be incurred over the lifetime of that investment, since the exploitation cost will be paid from a different budget, which usually resides under a different department. This explains why introducing procurement decision-making based upon total cost of ownership is so troublesome for the government. To overcome these negative effects, some countries have introduced an integrated budgeting system which allows public institutions to use purchasing savings over a period of time and which also allows purchasing decision-making to be based on total cost of ownership considerations. However, in most countries progress is slow.

Public accountability, the absence of commercial incentives and the budget system are prime reasons for the slow development of procurement as a discipline within the government. In many public institutions procurement professionals reside low in the organization and have little visibility to their top management. Technical experts, legal specialists and policymakers usually dominate purchasing decision-making.

The European procurement directives have obviously put public procurement more on the forefront. As a result political leaders and governmental managers have become more interested in how to structure and execute the procurement function within their organizations. The procurement function can be compared with the tactical purchasing function, which was discussed earlier, in Chapter 1. However, the major difference is that legal

MEMO 6.2   PUBLIC TENDERING

Public tendering includes supply market research, developing a sourcing strategy based on a detailed specification for the delivery of goods and services or construction, selecting the right procurement procedure, preparing the tendering documents, which will include the technical requirements, supplier selection and award criteria, contractual conditions, as well as evaluating supplier data and supplier bids, contracting, writing up the final version of the contract, and follow-up of the tender procedure.

specialists within the public procurement function are much more dominant than in the private sector. Tendering is far more subject to legal and procedural complexities than in the private sector.

Tendering is a crucial part of the public procurement function. It may be surrounded by all kinds of specific legal rules and complexities. This is less true for public utilities, which increasingly are subjected to the laws of supply and demand. For this sector, there are far more similarities with how the private sector makes its purchases.

PUBLIC PROCUREMENT LAW

Public procurement law is based upon the body of international, European law, national laws and directives and jurisprudence. Public procurement law prescribes in a formal way, how to go about government contracts, i.e. how to deal with suppliers and how to award public contracts. The objective of procurement law is to make the European market for government assignments accessible to all providers and suppliers regardless of their nationality. Over the years, it became clear that national governments violated these principles when awarding contracts to suppliers. In most cases, they kept on protecting national interests by placing contracts with local and national suppliers. For this reason, during the early 1970s, the first European Directives for Public Procurement were introduced. Initially, specific directives were made for 'Works' and 'Supplies'.[1] In the early 1990s the directives related to 'Services' and 'Public Utilities' followed.

These four European Procurement Directives were replaced in 2004 by two major European Procurement Directives: 2004/17, related to the public utilities sector, and 2004/18, related to the classical government. Important reasons to replace the four original directives were their lack of consistency and their lack of pragmatism. The new directives now allow for the application of longer-term **framework agreements**, a central purchasing body, and electronic auctions.

Many European countries have since 2004 brought these European procurement directives into force in national legislation. European procurement directives and national legislation provided the legal framework, upon which national contracting authorities should act. However, apart from these laws and directives, contracting authorities in the EU member states also have to comply with the regulations resulting from the Agreement on Government Procurement (GPA), that was agreed upon within GATT (General Agreement on Tariffs and Trade), now the WTO (World Trade Organization). The following countries participate in the GPA: EU, Aruba (The Netherlands), Canada, Hong Kong, Japan, Iceland, Israel, Liechtenstein, New Zealand, Norway, Singapore, USA, South Korea and Switzerland.

Suppliers from these countries have free access to the large market of central governmental contracts in the areas of construction, products and services. A consequence of GPA is, that countries need to acknowledge lower financial threshold levels for the central government (the State) (€133 000.00 instead of € 206 000.00).

In summary, the government needs to acknowledge complex legislation when making purchasing decisions. A thorough understanding of international and European procurement law is necessary in order to prevent problems in the relationship with suppliers. Suppliers should be dealt with in a fair way, respecting the four principles of non-discrimination, equality, transparency and proportionality. Procedural mistakes may easily cause delays in project execution and may unnecessarily result in supplier claims being brought before court.

Public procurement, law

Public procurement law prescribes in a formal way how to go about government contracts i.e. how to deal with suppliers and how to award public contracts. Major constituents of public procurement law are the European Public Procurement Directives 2004/17 for the public utilities sector and 2004/18 for the classical government.

Framework agreement

A framework agreement is an agreement between one or more contracting entities and one or more suppliers, the purpose of which is to establish the terms governing contracts to be awarded during a given period, in particular with regard to price and, where appropriate, the quantities envisaged.

[1]European Public Procurement Directive on 'Works' originates from 26th July 1971 and the European Public Procurement Directive on 'Supplies' originates from 21st December 1976.

SCOPE OF THE EUROPEAN DIRECTIVES ON PUBLIC PROCUREMENT

Scope

Public procurement, scope
The European directives apply to all governmental institutions, including the State, regional or local authorities and bodies governed by public law.

With regards to the **scope** of the European Directives for public procurement we need to differentiate between to whom the directives apply and what contracts need to be tendered according to these directives.

In general the European directives apply to all governmental institutions, including the State, regional or local authorities and bodies governed by public law. The latter may include specific research organizations, universities, academic hospitals, educational institutions police authorities, new town development corporations and museums and water control. These examples illustrate the wide range of institutions to which the European Directives may apply. In the remainder of this chapter these institutions will be referred to as 'contracting authorities'.

The European Directives for public procurement of 2004 introduced a new contracting authority: the central purchasing bodies. These are organizations that are instituted by member contracting authorities to obtain benefits from human collaborations (see Chapter 13). Central purchasing bodies also need to comply with this legislation.

The Procurement Directives define 'supply, works and service contracts' as contracts for pecuniary interest concluded in writing between one or more of the contracting entities and one or more contractors, suppliers, or service providers. This definition has two important elements. First, the agreement must be in writing. Secondly, the agreement must stipulate an exchange of value between parties. To be more precise: one party needs to supply goods and services, for which the other party is willing to pay. A formal agreement does not need to imply a large, complex contract. It can also relate to a purchase order, which has been sent by e-mail. Or, it may simply relate to an invoice that has been accepted by the customer for payment.

The exchange of value between parties assumes that both parties have rights and obligations. The one party needs to deliver, whereas the other party needs to pay. Payment does not necessarily have to happen in terms of money. Payment can also be made through exchange of a special permit or could simply relate to exchange of goods (barter). For example, a real estate company acquires land from a city against the promise that it will develop the area and will build a new city hall for the city council free of charge. Hence, the European procurement directives apply to any contract for which a customer wants to pay with a return that can be put in monetary terms. As discussed before, the contract may relate to works, goods and services.

'Works contracts' are contracts with the objective of either the execution, or both the design and execution. A work means the outcome of building or civil engineering work taken as a whole which is sufficient in itself to fulfil an economic or technical function.

In practice, contracts for the delivery of a ship, acoustic installations for a theatre, or pumps for a water purification installation have mistakenly been defined as a work: these are examples of goods deliveries. This is why the appendices of the European directives on public procurement have been included. These appendices describe exactly what needs to be considered as a work. In case of doubt, the contracting authorities can find the exact answer here.

Goods relate to physical products like computers, office furniture, helicopters, trucks, etc. However, goods also relate to leasing and rental contracts of these physical products. If a public institution decides to lease its car fleet, this is considered to be a goods delivery and not a service. This is also true when a vessel is being rented. Additional services, such as installation services when acquiring a new telephone centre, may be part of the goods delivery. This is important when it comes to assessing the total value of the contract involved.

Services are in fact a rest category. Services relate to assignments, which can neither be considered a work nor a good. In reality, the differentiation between a good and a service is very hard to make. Standard software is to be considered a goods delivery; however, developing a customized software solution is considered to be a service. In this case, the way in which tendering takes place will not make any difference. However, when contracting for catering, differences may occur. Prefabricated meals and delivery of drinks, whether supplied by a vending machine or not, are considered to be a good. But, meals prepared in the kitchen of an on-site canteen, are considered as a service. This is an example of a so-called B-service. Therefore, contracting for this kind of service needs to be performed following specific rules and guidelines.

The European directives for public procurement differentiate between A and B services. A-services are fully subject to European legislation. For B-services an enlightened regime exists. Enlightened, since the **public procurement procedures** do not fully apply. However, in all cases these services need to be acquired recognizing the earlier mentioned general public **procurement principles**. In case there is a clear interest from suppliers from other member states, there should be a certain degree of publicity of the contract. Examples of be B-services are, amongst others, catering services, rail transport, transport by vessel, temporary labour, legal support services, healthcare and education.

Framework agreements

The classical governmental organizations have the possibility of implementing framework agreements. A framework agreement is an agreement between one or more contracting entities and one or more suppliers, the purpose of which is to establish the terms governing contracts to be awarded during a given period, in particular with regard to price and, where appropriate, the quantities envisaged. These terms and conditions are related to a description of the characteristics of the goods and services to be supplied, the quality of the goods and services to be supplied, special delivery guarantees, payment and delivery conditions and price escalation clauses. The framework agreements are used to deal with representative supplies in an efficient manner. When a contracting authority is confronted with repetitive purchases, such as when buying office supplies, it may contract for a framework agreement with a distributor outlining the general conditions. Different departments may then call off against this framework agreement, placing their purchase orders directly at the distributor, whilst referring to the framework agreement.

For the classical governmental organizations there are restrictions to entering a framework agreement. A contracting authority may enter a framework agreement with one or more suppliers. In the latter there should be minimum of three tenders. In the case of three or more suppliers there is the possibility of a 'mini-competition'. The other restriction is that the maximum duration for framework agreements is four years.

Some people think that supply or service contracts (not being framework agreements) may not go beyond this time period. However, when entering a maintenance and operations contract for an ICT system, the actual contract duration may take many more years. The high investment costs to be incurred by the contracts may justify in such a case a longer contract period.

Excluded assignments

As for every legislation, the European Directives on public procurement arrange for exceptions. Exceptions may fall into two categories: there are contracts for which the European regime is not applicable and there are contracts for which special arrangements are made.

Public procurement, procedures
Public procurement procedures relate to the procedures that public institutions need to adhere to when making purchasing decisions. Different procedures are: (1) open procedure, (2) restricted procedure, (3) competitive dialogue, (4) negotiated procedure with prior publication of a contract notice, (5) negotiated procedure without prior publication of a contract notice and (6) design contest.

Public procurement, principles
Four major principles underlie each of these procurement directives. These are nondiscrimination, equality, transparency and proportionality.

The first category is referred to as excluded contracts. The second category is referred to as negotiable European contracts. The latter category will be discussed in more detail below ('Notices and public procurement procedures').

The following governmental contracts are not subject to the European directives:

- The acquisition and rental of existing immovable property, unless it concerns the rental or acquisition of a building which has been specifically (technically) designed for the contracting authority.

- Contracts for the Ministry of Defence, such as the acquisition of aeroplanes, fighters, ammunition, weapons and such like. Contracts related to non-military activities such as the acquisition of car leasing, computers or contract catering, are subject to European procurement law.

- Secret assignments or assignments aimed at protecting state security. Such may be the case when soliciting services for placing telephone tabs to monitor criminal activity. In such cases these services need not to be tended according to European procurement procedures.

- Contracts that are placed as the outcome of international treaties and arrangements, and for which other international procurement procedures apply. Such may be the case when buying for projects organized by the World Bank or at the World Health Organization (WHO).

- **Intra-public assignments.** These are assignments that are placed by one contracting authority at another contracting authority. In such a case the service to be provided should be unique and based on published law, regulation or administrative provision, which is compatible with the EC Treaty. The latter means that the intra-public contract should not obstruct normal market behaviour. It is therefore not possible for a city to summon a contract for rubbish collection from another governmental special service company in this area without soliciting bids from other private companies.

Public procurement, threshold values
Threshold values represent the purchasing volumes beyond which public institutions are obliged to follow European legislation when making their purchase decisions. There are different threshold values for work, supplies and services.

Threshold values

The European procurement regime only applies to contracts that meet certain **threshold values.** Table 6.1 provides an overview of the threshold values involved. The structural values, which are put here excluding VAT, are updated every two years.

TABLE 6.1 Threshold values European Directives on public procurement

Classical government	Threshold values
Works	€ 5 150 000
Goods: Central government	€ 133 000
Goods: Local contracting authorities	€ 206 000
Services: Central government	€ 133 000
Services: Local contracting authorities	€ 206 000
Public utilities	
Works	€ 5 150 000
Goods	€ 412 000
Services	€ 412 000

The reason for the lower threshold values for central government is the fact that contracts also need to comply with the regulations as stipulated by the GPA, as we have shown earlier ('Public procurement law'). When estimating the value of a contract, all costs need to be recognized that will be incurred during the execution of the building assignment, the delivery contract or the service contract including all supportive activities (options). For example, when contracting for a new telephone installation, the contracting authority, besides the acquisition cost of the installation itself, needs to recognize all costs related to the acquisition of the handsets and other accessories. It is not allowed to cut the total assignment in more pieces to work around the European procurement procedures. It is forbidden to split a larger assignment into a few smaller ones, just for this purpose. There is, however, one exception to this rule. It is allowed to split a larger assignment into smaller, coherent lots. When buying office and computer supplies, for example, the contracting authority may split the contract into one for office supplies, and one for computer supplies, allowing prospective suppliers to bid on the total contract, or to bid on each individual lot. This arrangement is also relevant for construction contracts. It is allowed, for instance, to take the contract for installation work out of the total contract and to solicit bids from competing installation firms, just for this part of the work. However, when doing so, the contract value of the lot should be less than €1 000 000. Next, the total value of the lots, which are separated from the total contract, should not exceed 20% of the total contract value. When tendering for a contract for railway maintenance by a European railway authority, with an estimated value of €50 million, the value of all lots together may not exceed €10 million, whereas each separate subcontract should not exceed the value of €1 million. These examples relate to tendering for works. In the case of tendering for goods and services similar arrangements apply. Again, the value of individual lots may not exceed 20% of the total contract value. However, the individual lot value may not exceed €80 000.

NOTICES AND PUBLIC PROCUREMENT PROCEDURES

Notice

A European tender starts with a formal notice. A notice is in fact an advertisement through which the contracting authority invites interested parties to submit a proposal. The notices states the characteristics, the specific requirements related to the assignment and the qualification criteria that prospective providers should meet. The notice is sent to the database of the EC: TED. The electronic forms, i.e. templates for the notice to be made can be found at www.simap.eu.int.

Most European procedures differentiate between three types of notices: the prior information notice, contract notice and the contract award notice.

With the prior information notice, the contracting authority can reduce the legal minimum terms[2], i.e. time span (see later under 'Public procurement procedures'). To be able to do so, the prior information notice should be placed at least 52 calendar days before the formal notice and should not be older than 12 months. The prior information notice also has another advantage: prospective suppliers and providers will be informed early about the intended tender, so that they can prepare properly. This may be relevant for large construction projects, where market parties need to develop some kind of combination or joint venture in order to be able to submit their bids. The joint effort may lead to

---

[2]Terms are used in this paragraph to denote 'time span', i.e. 'lead time'.

Public procurement,
design contest
*The design contest is a
procedure that is used
to obtain a plan or a
design based on com-
petition among expert
parties. The design is
to be judged by a
professional jury.*

Public procurement,
open procedure
*The open procedure
implies that every
market party within
the EU should be able
to subscribe to a gov-
ernmental tender.*

Public procurement,
restricted procedure.
*This procedure
acknowledges two dis-
tinct stages: the stage
of selecting suppliers
that are interested, and
the stage in which the
preselected suppliers
are invited for tender.
This procedure is also
referred to as the
procedure with
preselection.*

Public procurement,
negotiation procedure
*Here, the contracting
authority can negotiate
face-to-face with mar-
ket parties about the
contents, execution
and costs related to
the contract. The nego-
tiation procedure can
be used with or
without (pre)-
announcement.*

a much better position for the contracting authority. A prior information notice is not compulsory.

The contract notice of the intended tender describes the project in general terms, necessary for prospective suppliers to decide whether the contract will be of interest. The contract notice of the tender on TED is compulsory for all contracts that exceed the threshold values (see 'Scope of the European Directives on Public Procurement', above). This requirement does not apply to the so-called excluded contracts that we discussed earlier, the so-called B-services and the special cases with negotiated procedure without prior publication of a contract notice.

When the contracting authority has awarded the contract to a specific supplier, it needs to inform market parties within 40 days (public utilities within two months) through a contract award notice. This requirement also relates to contracts that have been obtained through the negotiated procedure and for all B-services.

European procurement procedures

Of all the arrangements, the European procurement procedures have raised the most discussion. A European procurement procedure is defined here as 'the total set of rules and regulations that are aimed at selecting the best supplier for the best product against the best conditions, recognizing European laws and regulations'. The European Directives on public procurement include the following procedures:

- Open procedure
- Restricted procedure
- Competitive dialogue
- Negotiated procedure with prior publication of a contract notice
- Negotiated procedure without prior publication of a contract notice
- **Design contest.**

In general, governmental institutions have a free choice between the **open procedure**, **restricted procedure** and the design contest. The competitive dialogue and both the negotiated procedures can only be applied in very specific situations, as we will discuss later. Public utilities have the greatest freedom. They only need to be careful when applying the **negotiation procedure** without prior publication of a contract notice. For this sector the competitive dialogue does not apply.

Open procedure

The idea underlying the open procedure is that every market party within the EU should be able to subscribe to a governmental tender. The maximum term for submitting bids is 52 calendar days, starting with the day that the notice has been made public. In the case of a prior information notice being previously published, this term may be reduced to 22–36 days. When sending all tender forms electronically to interested market parties, the contracting authority may further reduce the maximum term by seven days. If all tender documents (including technical information and drawings) are sent electronically, the maximum term may be reduced by a further five days. When communicating electronically, the contracting authority, may therefore reduce the maximum term for suppliers to react by 12 days, leaving them with a minimum term to react of just 15 days. Of course, contacting authorities are reluctant to reduce the reaction time for suppliers by too much. The risk will be that too few bids are obtained and that bids will be badly prepared. This will serve nobody's interest.

Restricted procedure

Although the name of this procedure suggests otherwise, each EU supplier may compete for contracts that are tendered through this procedure. This procedure is different from the previous in the fact that the tender process is split into two distinct stages: the stage of selecting suppliers that are interested, and the stage in which the preselected suppliers are invited for tender. Therefore, a better name might have been the preselection procedure. However, in this chapter we stick with the original name. When discussing this subject we will differentiate between the traditional government and public utilities.

For governmental institutions the minimum term for the notice amounts to 37 days, to be calculated from the day that the notice has been sent to TED. The contracting authority invites the selected companies to express their interest for tender. The minimum number of market parties to be selected needs to be at least five, matching the prequalification criteria that have been published by the contracting authority.

For submitting their bids, the contracting authority needs to provide 40 days at least to the preselected suppliers, again to be calculated from the day that the invitation to bid has been published. When a prior information notice has been made, this term can be reduced to just 36 days.

As in the case of the public procedure, the contracting authority can reduce the term for submitting the actual bids by 5 days, when submitting all tender documents electronically to interested market parties. However, the minimum term should not be shorter than 22 days.

In cases where urgency renders the time limits impracticable (not to be confused with extreme urgency), the contracting authority may go for a shorter reaction time. The time for prequalification of suppliers may then be only 15 days, whereas the time needed to solicit bids from the preselected suppliers may be reduced to a mere 10 days. The urgency may, however, never be due to circumstances related to the contracting authority itself. The urgency may be that, after awarding a contract to a specific supplier, the supplier cannot deliver. In such cases, the contracting authority may go for a second, speedier tender process. Whatever the reason, the contracting authority should mention the background for reducing the reaction times in its notice. Urgency is only acknowledged in case of the non-public procedure. The public procedure does not have any specific arrangements for this.

The terms for public utilities are as follows. For the stage of preselecting suppliers, the term of 37 days may be reduced to 22 days minimum. For the tender stage, the minimum term is 37 days. However, in consultation with market parties this term may be reduced. In case contracting authority and market parties do not come to an arrangement, the legal minimum term will amount at least to 24 days.

Competitive dialogue

Competitive dialogue is a special procedure, which may be applied by governmental institutions in specific circumstances and for very complex projects. It is not relevant for the public utilities sector. A project is considered to be very complex if a contracting authority is not able to come up with a detailed specification and when the legal and financial terms and conditions of the project cannot be defined. In such cases competitive dialogue may be used. The procedure is as follows. First, just like the restricted procedure, a preselection of qualified market parties is made. This should result in at least three parties being interested and qualified for the assignment. Next, these parties are consulted for the solutions that best fit the functional specifications that have been submitted by the contracting authority. The dialogue ends when the contracting authority has selected the best possible solution that was presented by one of the market parties. Next, the contracting authority will put a detailed specification together and the market parties, that were solicited earlier, are invited for their detailed bids. The contracting authority evaluates the bids on the basis of the most economical offer (rather than price only). Just like the open and restricted procedures it is strictly forbidden to negotiate on the final arrangements.

The minimum term for prequalification of market parties amounts to 37 days. This term may be reduced to 30 days if the notice is made electronically. For obtaining the bids and final offers, no minimum terms are mentioned in the European regulations.

Negotiation procedure

The negotiation procedure can only be followed in special circumstances. Here, the contracting authority can negotiate face-to-face with market parties about the contents, execution, and costs related to the contract. The negotiation procedure can be used with or without (prior) announcement.

The negotiation procedure with prior publication of a contract notice starts with a pre-selection of interested and qualified market parties. The term for this is 37 days minimum. Again this term may be reduced by seven days if all documentation is sent electronically. In situations of urgency, the selection may be reduced to 15 days or 10 days when the notice is made electronically. For obtaining bids from suppliers no minimum terms are stipulated in the directives. These only state that the term should be reasonable for suppliers to prepare for their bids.

For the public utility sector only minimum terms apply for the selection stage. This term needs to be 20 days minimum. In case the notice is made electronically, this period may be reduced to 15 days. Also here, no minimum term is stated for soliciting the bids from the suppliers involved.

The negotiation procedure with a contract notice can be applied by contracting authorities only in very specific cases. The four most important cases are:

- When, in case of a public or non-public procedure or competitive dialogue, irregular bids by suppliers have been obtained. This may apply, for example, to situations in which suppliers obtrusively have made price agreements between each other.

- When the bids that have been solicited are in fact unacceptable. This may be the case when the prices that have been offered are way off the available budget or when the offers that have been made simply do not meet the minimal requirements.

- In very specific cases where the cost related to executing the assignment cannot be estimated in whatever way due to unforeseen circumstances. This may be the case when restoration of historical buildings or old paintings is needed. In such cases the contracting authority may engage in face-to-face discussions with the limited number of experts that is available.

- When it is impossible to specify the work to be conducted and the product to be delivered at a fair level of detail. This may apply to specific research assignments or when consulting support is needed for a major personnel restructuring.

These limitations do not apply to the public utilities sector.

As the name already suggests, the negotiation procedure without a contract notice does not need to be published. The contracting authority may approach suppliers independently to obtain their ideas and bids. Situations, where this very special procedure may be used, are, among others:

- The contracting authority did not receive any bids, or the bids received were totally unsuitable.

- Only one specific supplier was available, due to technical or artistic reasons, or due to exclusive rights that may relate to the product or service to be acquired. In such cases the contracting authority needs to demonstrate and prove that only one supplier was available and that only one way working was possible.

- Extreme urgency due to unforeseen circumstances that cannot be ascribed to the contracting authority. Examples here are the acquisition of goods needed in case of war or natural disasters (such as a wildfire or a flood).
- In the case of additional delivery of goods and services, that could not have been foreseen in the original contract, but which due to unforeseen circumstances are necessary.

Also for both negotiation procedures the general principles apply that were discussed in the Introduction. In all cases the contracting authority should publish through TED which party was awarded the contract.

In case the contracting authority decides to go for the competitive dialogue or the negotiation procedure, it should indicate such a decision in the procurement dossier.

Design contest

The design contest is a procedure that is used to obtain a plan or a design based on competition between expert parties. The design is to be judged by a professional jury and market parties may be rewarded in terms of a monetary value or otherwise. The design contest is used for architectural work, but also for the design of complex ICT architectures. It may also be used for procurement projects that require a high degree of innovation. Contracting authorities are free on how to orchestrate a design contest. It is not necessary to explain why a design contest was deemed necessary. There are no specific terms i.e. lead times that one needs to consider.

PROCUREMENT PROCESS

Defining specifications

As was discussed earlier in Chapter 2, a specification is a description of what the contracting authority intends to buy. Specifications are important since they are the input for the consecutive stages of our purchasing process model. This observation is very relevant when tendering for governmental contracts. It will appear, that specifications not only will be decisive for what supplier qualification criteria to use, and what contract award criteria to use, these will also determine the actual contract to be agreed upon with the supplier. One of the principles to be met during a European purchasing procedure is the principle of proportionality. This means that the specifications and conditions should be in line with the nature of the assignment.

When defining specifications, contracting authorities should comply with the principle of non-discrimination. Specifications should be defined in such a way that free trade is not impeded. Besides brand specifications, national norms and standards belong to the most popular barriers in interstate trade. The technical requirements for building a new school in Wingles, France may serve as an example. These requirements made reference to specific classifications, norms and standards of French contractors associations, which were hardly accessible for foreign construction firms. When brought to court, the judge was of the opinion that these classifications and standards were so discouraging to foreign companies, that these could be considered as discriminatory and a major barrier to free trade, which was in conflict with the European Treaty.

Therefore, it will not come as a surprise that brand and supplier-specific specifications are forbidden. These are only allowed if the contracting authority is not capable of describing specifications in supplier neutral terms. In that case a brand name may be used if and only if 'or equal' is added. When buying computers, referring to 'using Intel processors or equal' is not sufficient. In 2004 and 2006 the EC started an investigation into the practice of the compulsory prescription of a certain clock speed, referring to Intel processors. The investigation has not been closed.

Also the principle of equality is of great importance. The contracting authority should recognize that if some companies have been involved early in the preparation of the tender process, this could have resulted in a competitive advantage. This is because these companies could have acquired crucial knowledge and insight with regards to the intent and expectations of the contracting authority. In such cases these suppliers need to be excluded from the tender process. There is, however, no general rule on this. Contracting authorities need to consider this aspect case by case.

Supplier selection

Having defined the tender specifications, the next stage begins: the stage of supplier selection. Selection criteria are the requirements that the contracting authority will use to select all preselected suppliers. At this stage the question is, which suppliers will qualify in principle for a successful completion of the assignment? Award criteria are used to evaluate the detailed supplier proposals. How is the preselected supplier going to execute the assignment and at what cost? Mixing up supplier selection criteria and award criteria is a frequently made error in public procurement practice and, hence, the basis of many cases that have been brought to court.

Memo 6.3 illustrates that selection criteria relate to the quality of the supplier organization and do not relate to the quality of the performance to be delivered. What selection criteria to use, is described extensively in the European procurement directives. The procedures for the public utility sector, however, are far less explicit. This sector, when selecting suppliers, needs to comply only with the principles of non-discrimination, equality, transparency and proportionality.

For governmental institutions selection criteria can be divided into two distinct categories: exclusion criteria and suitability criteria.

Exclusion criteria relate to the personal situation of suppliers and are further divided into compulsory and voluntary exclusion criteria. Compulsory exclusion criteria may relate to fraud with EU money, corruption, laundry of black money, being a member of a criminal organization, etc. In case a company or a private person has been fined for such an act, the contracting authority *should* exclude that party from any future business.

MEMO 6.3   SELECTION AND AWARD CRITERIA

When publishing its announcement for a tender related to a special investigation, the Greek municipality of Alexandroupolis communicated the following award criteria: demonstrable experience, personnel capacity, expertise of the research agency, capacity available to conduct the investigation at a predetermined time interval, academic reputation of the agency. The European Court decided that criteria that are not aimed at assessing the most economical offer, but in essence are aimed at assessing the supplier's potential for a successful completion of the assignment, cannot be used as award criteria.

Source: Lianakis Case C-532/06 January 24th, 2008

In case of voluntary exclusion criteria, a supplier *can* be excluded when these criteria have been communicated at an early stage. Such criteria are amongst others:

- The party involved is facing severe financial problems or even bankruptcy.
- The party involved has violated ethical or professional codes of conduct.
- The party involved has in the past made severe mistakes and has made false statements in public.
- The party involved has not paid its taxes and Social Securities.

Parties, which have not been excluded, are evaluated using suitability criteria. These criteria relate to financial and economic standing and technical or professional ability (proven performance). Based upon these criteria, the contracting authority needs to assess whether the party involved will be sufficiently qualified to execute the assignment. Suitability criteria can be divided into absolute and relative suitability criteria. The absolute suitability criteria are also referred to as minimal ('knockout') requirements. If a supplier is not able to demonstrate specific expertise and experience in a certain area which is crucial for the completion of the assignment, this may lead to a decision to exclude it. When using the public procedure only minimal requirements can be used. In the case of the restricted procedure, the contracting authority may also use other voluntary requirements, also referred to as qualitative selection criteria, in order to bring down the number of future suppliers to five (restricted procedure) or three (competitive dialogue, negotiation procedure with notice). When doing so, the method through which suppliers will be evaluated needs to be objective and needs to be communicated to the parties involved in advance. Again, in all cases the criteria to be used should be non-discriminatory, transparent, equal and proportional. One may not stipulate for instance that a company needs to be located within a radius of a certain number of kilometres from its prospective customer. So, requirements imposed on the supplier should be in line and in balance with the nature and scope of the assignment.

Suppliers, which were not selected, are to be informed about the reasons for decline. In case a supplier requests more detailed information, the contracting authority needs to deliver this information within 15 days. In this way the contracting authority needs to adhere to the principle of transparency.

Soliciting bids and awarding contracts

The final stages of the tender process are evaluating the bids received, the initial award of the bid, informing non-selected parties about refusal and, finally, awarding the contract to the supplier selected. In general, all contractors will receive all tender documents at the same time, including the technical requirements, selection and award criteria, the invitation to bid (request for quotation; RFQ), and a draft agreement.

MEMO 6.4 DISPROPORTIONALITY

During the early 1990s two municipalities in an EU member state tendered jointly for collecting rubbish from about 28 000 addresses. As a minimal requirement it was communicated that the rubbish collector selected should demonstrate that it had conducted similar assignments from municipalities over 40 000 inhabitants. The court decided such a minimal requirement as disproportional. The defence of the municipalities that during the coming years the number of addresses would be extended to 30 000–40 000 was considered by the court not to be valid.

When evaluating the bids received, the contracting authority may choose between the lowest price and the most economically advantageous bid (best economic offer). Going for the lowest price, other aspects will not be considered. Of course, all bids received will be checked on compliance with all technical and quality requirements. Suppliers that will not meet the knockout criteria will be removed from the list immediately. The decision process in this case is fairly simple. Discussions about quality, delivery times, services, etc. will not take place.

Going for the lowest price is practical in case of contracting straightforward commodities, where price may be the only decisive criterion. Such may be the case when buying electricity, gas or other natural commodities. As soon as products and services become more customized, using the criterion of best economic offer will be the preferred way to act.

During the process of supplier selection and soliciting the best offers from suppliers, the contracting authority may decide to use electronic auctions. When doing so, all parties that are invited need to be fully informed and prepared to participate. In advance, they need to be informed about how the contracting authority will award the contract. It also should be clear from the outset how market parties can check on their relative position to the best offer during the course of the auction. The contract may be awarded both on lowest price and best economic offer.

When going for the best economic offer, other aspects than price will play a dominant role. These aspects may include quality, technical merit, aesthetics, functional or environmental characteristics, running costs, cost-effectiveness, total cost of ownership, customer service, technical support, date of delivery or period of completion and execution. However, the contracting authority may also use other criteria, as far as they relate directly to the actual performance, product or service to be delivered and as long as they have been communicated widely in advance. This list of criteria already shows that not all criteria need to be objective. If subjective criteria, such as aesthetic characteristics, are used, it should be explained how these will be assessed. Otherwise the contracting authority may be vulnerable if the case is brought to court. All of the criteria (including the weighting factors that will be used) need to be communicated, and cannot be changed during the tender process. It will not come as a surprise that most of the jurisprudence on public procurement is related to the criteria and weight factors that have been used, their legitimacy and the changes that have been made in the process.

As discussed before, the contracting authority needs to communicate, in its initial announcement, but in more detail in the tender documents, how bids will be evaluated. More specifically, it needs to indicate whether it will award a contract based on lowest price or best economic offer. Next, it needs to communicate the criteria and weighting factors that will be used. The assessment grid needs to be supplied to each of the suppliers. As a consequence, the assessment grid cannot be changed during the tender process. Doing so, will put the contracting authority in a difficult position when its case is brought to court.

In reality, this procedure creates considerable problems and challenges to government institutions. Procurement processes and their outcome are, by definition, sometimes hard to predict. In the course of the action it may appear that other aspects need to be considered than previously envisaged. The buyer may come to the conclusion that the assessment grid needs to be changed. In such a case, it does not have any other option but to stop the procedure and start a new one. This is one of the great disadvantages of the current European procurement legislation.

After the evaluation round, the supplier to which the contract is awarded should be made known to the public. The procedure is as follows. The buyer informs in writing, by letter and by e-mail or by fax, all suppliers that have been declined of the decision. In this letter it is explained why the contract has been awarded to the winning tenderer. Next, the buyer stipulates that the contracting authority will execute the contract, only after the 15 days (the Alcatel period) have expired in which the non-winning tenderers may object to the decision. The winning tenderer at the same time receives a letter indicating that the contract will be awarded to them, provided that no formal objections or claims by all other parties are received, and provided that both parties come to a final agreement.

Earlier in this chapter ('Scope of the European Directives on Public Procurement' and 'Notices and public procurement procedures') we discussed the obligation of the buyer to inform market parties about a decision to award the contract to a certain tenderer. In all cases the motivation should be fact-based. When a supplier, who has been declined, asks for more detailed information, the buyer should deliver this information within 15 days of having received the formal request. The buyer informs the supplier of the results and benefits that were obtained. Such a motivation may be omitted, when more detailed information may not be in the interest of the public, or when it may damage the commercial interests of the winning supplier. To avoid unnecessary friction, it is generally recommended to organize a so-called 'lost bid' meeting. Here the buyer may explain its decision and may answer specific supplier questions.

When all parties involved have signed contracts, the contracting authority needs to publish the winning offer within 48 days of the decision (for public utilities two months) using TED. This announcement states to whom the contract was awarded and against what price. Again, the buyer may refrain from the latter in case such information may damage the commercial interests of the contracting authority. For complex contracts, where, apart from the major investment services purchased during the lifetime of the investment, it will hardly be possible to mention the full cost involved. This announcement is also compulsory for contracts awarded using the negotiation procedure without notice and for all B-services.

Finally, the European directives on public procurement also prescribe that all documentation related to the tender is archived. This archive needs to contain contact data of the contracting authority, the characteristics, volume and nature of the assignment, the procedure that has been followed, names of all preselected suppliers, i.e. all suppliers that have been invited to bid, the buyer motivations, special circumstances and, if the contract was not awarded, the reason for this.

IMPLICATIONS FOR PUBLIC PROCUREMENT

In general, the European directives on public procurement have met great resistance, as much in the public procurement community, as in the circle of government managers and politicians. This resistance is caused by relentless complaints concerning the complexity of directives themselves, their lack of flexibility, the terms that need to be adhered to for publication and answering questions, the fact that the directives do not stimulate supply chain collaboration and innovation sufficiently, and the complex (project) administration that is required for the application of these directives.

Many of the challenges and concerns relate to the fact that governmental institutions have not professionalized their procurement organization, systems and staff. A successful implementation of European procurement legislation requires purchasing procedures that are highly structured and a professional organization, where procurement tasks, authorities and responsibilities are clearly defined and communicated to all departments and stakeholders involved. This is what political and government leaders have neglected to do. The core of this problem lies in the management culture that is prevailing in many governmental institutions. Decision-making on important purchases is of a highly political nature. Procurement decision-making in the government suffers from a lack of rationality and a fact-based mentality. As we have seen earlier, the budget culture within governmental institutions stimulates overspending of budgets, rather than going for purchasing savings or

TABLE 6.2 Compliance rates in 2002 and 2004 for all governmental sectors in the Netherlands

Sector	Purchasing volume			Number of projects		
	2002	2004	Increase		2004	Increase
Ministries	80–90%	80–90%	0–10%	50–60%	70–80%	10–20%
Cities and municipalities	30–40%	40–50%	10–20%	0–10%	20–30%	10–20%
Provinces	40–50%	70–80%	30–40%	20–30%	40–50%	10–20%
Water control authorities	40–50%	50–60%	10–20%	10–20%	20–30%	10–20%
Academic hospitals	20–30%	50–60%	30–40%	20–30%	50–60%	30–40%
Polytechnic institutes	10–20%	30–40%	10–20%	0–10%	10–20%	10–20%
Universities	40–50%	50–60%	10–20%	20–30%	40–50%	20–30%
Museums	0–10%	0–10%	0–10%	10–20%	10–20%	0–10%
Police districts	30–40%	40–50%	10–20%	20–30%	40–50%	20–30%

Source: Ibid Significant (2004)

creating best value for taxpayers' money. This subject has a low priority on the political and managerial agenda. The following example comes from The Netherlands. In 2002 only 12% of the governmental procurement contracts that were subject to European tendering were actually being contracted following the EU procurement directives.[3] Table 6.2 gives a comparison of the outcome of the compliance rates in 2002 and 2004 in this country. Although a slight improvement can be observed, the performance of the government is far below standard.

Since it concerns a lack of compliance with formal European and national legislation, the governmental institutions could, in principle, be sued for damage claims and in some European countries even for committing criminal acts. It is clear that the compliance on implementing these procurement directives is insufficient and that the government is not effective in terms of its control measures. In reality, very little action is taken to correct the situation. The situation for the member states is not very different.

Other member states within the EU suffer from similar problems. Greece, Spain and the UK have the highest compliance rates with 46, 24 and 21%, respectively. At the other end of the spectrum we find Germany and Luxembourg with 7.2 and 13.3% respectively. The Netherlands obtained a meagre 8.9% in this research (Ibid IP/04/149: Report on the functioning of public procurement markets in the EU: benefits from the application of EU directives and challenges for the future, January 2004). The research indicated that implementation of the European procurement directives creates significant benefits: as a result of this member states reported price reductions up to 30% (Ibid Significant (2004), Compliance Reports of Public Procurement, Ministry of Economic Affairs, The Netherlands). This high percentage is the result of a much broader, in many cases much more international, competitive bidding. As a consequence, the EC decided to update and modernize the European procurement directives in 2004.

The most important criticism is that the European directives on public procurement have been developed without a clear eye on the present structure and position of the

[3]See Significant (2004), Compliance Reports of Public Procurement, Ministry of Economic Affairs, The Netherlands. This 12% accounted for 35% of the total tender volume.

procurement function within governmental institutions. In itself, the European directives make a lot of sense. However, the government in many European countries is not capable of handling them appropriately. The objectives that are at the basis of the European procurement legislation cannot be realized by legislation alone. More effort is needed for this. The directives foster, in a rather artificial way, the governmental buyer to more professional behaviour. However, if politicians rely on legislation only, the result will be a lot of confusion. An impressive control apparatus will be needed to secure compliance. Implementing the rather complex procedures requires a wide acceptance by the procurement and government community. Large investments in communication and training programs will be necessary to create such an acceptance. The procurement function within the government needs to be considerably strengthened. The same holds for the often weak administrative organization that should be improved to monitor and report on the implementation of the European procurement directives. There is still a lot of work to be done.

SUMMARY

Procurement within the government concerns a lot of money. On average, the EU member states spend about 16.3% of their gross domestic product (GDP) on buying goods, services and projects. This large sum of money (estimate in 2002 at over €1500 billion annually) is spent on a wide variety of products, services and works by an even wider variety of institutions.

One of the purposes for which the EU was founded was to create free cross-border trade between its member states. As we have seen the EU Treaty has a significant implication for governmental procurement. Governmental procurement differentiates from procurement by private enterprise in that it primarily serves political objectives and plans. Political ambitions in reality conflict with the intent to spend taxpayer's money as wisely as possible. Because of political ambitions, governmental institutions prefer to do business with local and national suppliers. The budget culture within the government does not stimulate effective spending aimed at achieving purchasing cost savings, where possible, or striving for the best price value relationship. The European directives for public procurement try to harmonize procurement policies among European member states. The most important principles underlying these directives are non-discrimination, equality, transparency and proportionality. These principles have been worked out into two important European procurement directives: one covering procurement for governmental institutions and another covering procurement for public utilities. Over the years the member states have translated these directives into national legislation. These together create a set of rules and guidelines that contracting authorities need to follow in their dealings with external suppliers and service providers. As we have seen these rules and regulations are stricter for classical governmental institutions than for public utilities, which enjoy more degrees of freedom.

As a result of the general EU principles, it is not allowed to use brand or specific supplier specifications since such practices may impede free trade and free competition among market parties. The transparency principle holds that contracting authorities are able to explain their supplier selection decisions. As a consequence the criteria and weight factors used to assess suppliers and their bids, need to be clear and communicated early in the process.

Another major characteristic of the EU procurement procedures is, that contracting authorities need to respect certain financial thresholds, which determine whether the European procurement procedures should be followed. These threshold values are different when contracting for works, goods and services and are different for the central and local government. In fact, governmental institutions can choose from six different document procedures: (1) the open procedure, (2) restricted procedure, (3) the competitive dialogue, (4) the negotiation procedure with notice, (5) the negotiation procedure without notice, (6) the design contest. Each of these procedures has strict requirements in terms of whether or not market parties should be notified before a invitation for tender is made public, whether or not market parties will be preselected, how to solicit bids from competing suppliers, how to evaluate the bids obtained from suppliers, how to award the contract and how to notify the suppliers that have been declined, how to explain the supplier choice that has been made. Given the lead times that are prescribed in the procedures proper and effective project management is a must. It is almost impossible to make changes after the procedures have been put into motion. Most of the jurisprudence and claims from suppliers are related to infringements with this general rule as well as violations with regards to the basic principles underlying the directives. Applying these directives requires a professional procurement organization, which, in general, is absent in many countries. In the area of public procurement there is still a lot of work to be done.

ASSIGNMENTS

6.1 Why do governmental institutions often have a preference for dealing with local or national suppliers? Provide and discuss some recent examples from the press.

6.2 Describe the most important principles underlying the EU Treaty. In what manner do the EU procurement directives contribute to the EU Treaty?

6.3 What procurement procedures are available to governmental institutions in Europe? Describe each procedure and indicate when and for whom it would be applicable by using the web links that are provided in this chapter.

6.4 A Police organization in one of the EU member states wants to tender for a new car-leasing contract. The police organization is subject to EU procurement law. Which procedure would you recommend? Prepare for a detailed project planning based on this procedure.

6.5 When buying copying equipment for a small city, which criteria would you use: (1) lowest price or (2) best economic offer? Why?

REFERENCES

European Commission (2004) *A Report on the Functioning of Public Procurement Markets in the EU: Benefits from the Application of EU Directives and Challenges for the Future*, 3 February, Brussels: European Commission.

Significant (2004) Compliance Reports of Public Procurement, Ministry of Economic Affairs, The Netherlands.

MARKET STRUCTURES AND SUPPLY MARKET RESEARCH

LEARNING OBJECTIVES

After studying this chapter you should understand the following:

- The different supply market structures that purchasing managers may encounter.
- How supply market structures may affect purchasing strategies.
- The role and importance of supply market research in the purchasing management process.
- The most important characteristics and types of supply market research.
- How to organize and conduct supply market research.
- How purchasing managers can use the Internet for supply market research.

INTRODUCTION

Today, the Internet is an indispensable tool for buyers when investigating supplier markets. A wide variety of product and supplier databases is available, providing links between supplier directories and providers of financial and supply market information. Through this and the rapidly improving search facilities business-to-business markets have become much more transparent. The Internet provides consumers and professional buyers with tools which facilitate product selection, tendering, ordering, shipment and payment. Through these tools the productivity of many purchasing departments has increased, whilst at the same time the quality of purchasing decision-making has improved.

This chapter covers the subject of purchasing and **supply market research**. A major objective of supply market research is to support sound decision-making. Just as for other types of research, supply market research has to identify and analyse the risks related to important purchasing decisions. Purchasing market research will not reduce the risks related to decision-making. However, it makes these risks more visible and transparent.

Some authors make a distinction between purchasing research and supply market research. Purchasing research refers to subjects concerning the internal organization (such as analysing the purchasing spend, transaction costs, individual buyer productivity, and internal efficiency). Supply market research refers to the external suppliers' market. It includes analyses of macro-economic developments in supplier countries, analyses of supply

Supply market research
Defined as the systematic gathering, classification and analysis of data considering all relevant factors that influence the procurement of goods and services for the purpose of meeting present and future company requirements.

125

CASE STUDY SUPPLY MARKET RESEARCH THROUGH THE INTERNET

Using the Internet to locate and evaluate suppliers just got easier. Finding a supplier and determining its adequacy, often two separate endeavours, can now be combined into one 'Net-based chore'. Renowned business information company Dun & Bradstreet has teamed with SupplyBase, a San Francisco-based web-directory firm, to offer online supplier directories that include detailed information on supplier performance and manufacturing capacity.

According to *Purchasing*'s [Purchasing Magazine (www.purchasing.com)] recent Internet-usage survey researching potential suppliers is the number-one reason buyers log on to the Internet. Chris Golec, vice president of marketing at SupplyBase, noticed a similar trend. 'Manufacturers were looking for reliable third-party information to differentiate suppliers based on performance, risk and other business factors,' says Golec.

Dave Otterness, director of supplier management for Flextronics International, an electronics contract manufacturer, has used the D&B/SupplyBase directories. 'It is difficult to determine if a supplier's information is accurately portrayed on the Internet, or if the company has sufficient expertise to handle high-volume projects,' says Otterness. 'Integrating D&B's supplier-evaluation tools with SupplyBase's industry-capability information will reduce business risk and increase sourcing productivity.'

Finding and assessing a supplier on one of these sites is quite a seamless process. For example, a buyer in search of recycled plastic materials might have an experience like this: from a list of five supplier categories, the buyer chooses 'materials', and then from a menu of more specific industries, 'recycled plastics'. The buyer can choose to narrow the search by geography and the next screen contains relevant suppliers. By clicking on one of the suppliers, the buyer comes to a profile page containing a brief company profile, product showcase, RFQ option, and contact information. Included prominently on this page is the supplier's standard D&B D-U-N-S number, hyperlinked to D&B's information store on that company.

According to Chris Golec, once the buyer has identified a prospective supplier, detailed D&B reports, including the supplier evaluation report (SER) and the supplier performance review (SPR), are available for purchase. The SER measures the financial stability of a supplier and quantifies the risk of doing business with them. The SPR determines how well a supplier performs in key areas, like quality, tech support and delivery, relative to the industry average.

Source: *Purchasing* (1998)

and demand of important raw materials and components, and the financial assessment of individual suppliers. In this chapter the focus will be on supply market research only; it will show what areas and aspects to consider. Also, some research techniques that can be used will be discussed. At this point we will present the possibilities and opportunities related to using the Internet for this purpose. Finally, the subject of how to organize for supply market research will be discussed.

MARKETS AND MARKET STRUCTURES

External structure
External structure consists of a number of links (companies, institutions) that are connected via markets.

The patterns of relationships between supplier and buyer are primarily determined by the underlying pattern of the goods and service deliveries, the **external structure** (Figure 7.1). The external structure consists of a number of links (companies, institutions) that are connected via markets. Within the external structure, **industrial branches** and **industrial columns** can be distinguished.

An industrial branch is defined as the horizontal relationship of organizations that experience each other as effective competitors (for example, the leather and footwear industry, the electronics industry).

An industrial column is defined as a series of companies (links) in which the consecutive stages of production of an economic product take place, i.e. from primary producer to consumer. A more popular term to denote this phenomenon is supply chain. We will use both terms here interchangeably.

Depending on the number of stages one can speak of a short or a long industry column, i.e. supply chain. Depending on the location of the link in the industry column, the materials-flow between successive links can take the following forms (see Figure 7.2):

- Diverging materials flow. The finished product of one link is the main or sole input for the next production stages of various other industry columns. This applies to industries which process raw materials.

- Linear materials flow. The finished product of one link is the main or sole input for the subsequent link.

- Converging materials flow. Various finished products of links of various industry columns are the input for the next link. This situation is found in companies with assembly-oriented production.

Diverging materials flows are usually found at the beginning of an industry column. Converging materials flows are found at the end of an industry column.

External factors are those which determine the degree of availability of a certain product and which cannot be influenced by individual companies. Examples are:

- the number of customers or buyers in a market
- the number of suppliers
- the market structure (transparency, pricing method)
- the stock situation of the product in question
- speed of technological innovation.

External factors are relevant because they determine the market structure. Market structure is defined in this book as the total set of conditions in which a company sells its products, with special attention to the number of parties in the market and the nature of the product being traded. Central to this definition are, therefore:

- the number of suppliers
- the number of buyers
- the degree of product differentiation.

The market is the total of supply and demand. Sometimes this refers to a physical market, where buyers and sellers actually meet, but in general abstract markets are dealt with. Economic theory uses a number of constructs to explain the relationship between the variables mentioned and market price. It distinguishes between various market structures both on the supply side and the demand side, which in reality do not exist in their pure form.

Supply side

Four types of market structures are usually distinguished on the supply side:

- **Pure competition.** Characteristic of this market structure is that neither the supplier nor the buyer can influence the price of the product. Thus, the price is a given one for all parties involved. Furthermore it is assumed that in this market structure complete information is available. In other words, there is a high degree of market transparency. In addition, the product is homogeneous and fully replaceable by substitutes. Examples of this market type are commodities markets for natural products such as wheat, cocoa, coffee and soybeans and for metals such as iron, copper and aluminium. Most auctions (flowers, vegetables) resemble this situation.

Industrial branch
Is defined as the horizontal relationship of organizations that experience each other as effective competitors (for example, the leather and footwear industry and the electronics industry).

Industrial column
Is defined as a series of companies (links) in which the consecutive stages of production of an economic product take place – from primary producer to consumer (identical to Supply Chain).

Pure competition
Characteristic of this market structure is that neither the supplier nor the buyer can influence the price of the product.

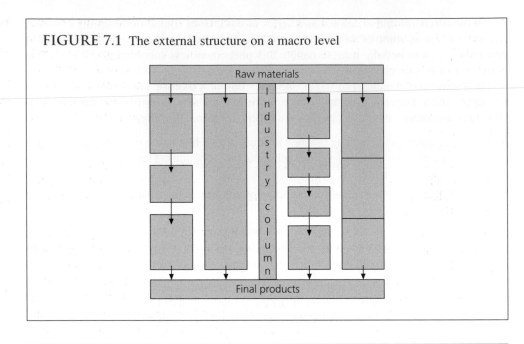

FIGURE 7.1 The external structure on a macro level

Raw materials

Industry column

Final products

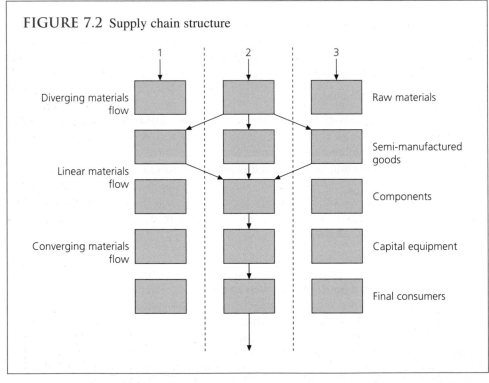

FIGURE 7.2 Supply chain structure

1   2   3

Diverging materials flow — Raw materials

— Semi-manufactured goods

Linear materials flow — Components

Converging materials flow — Capital equipment

— Final consumers

- **Monopolistic competition.** This market structure is similar to many actual markets and is characterized by a high degree of product differentiation. Each supplier tries to make its product stand out in order to create a **monopoly** situation for itself. This situation is favourable for the supplier because it provides it with some room to manipulate prices, within a given bandwidth. There is no direct pressure on its prices from competitors' offers. Examples are the markets for cigarettes, detergents, hi-fi equipment and other durable consumer goods.

- **Oligopoly.** An oligopoly is a market type characterized by a limited number of suppliers and a limited product differentiation. Moreover, it is very difficult to get a foothold in the market, due to some important entry barriers. The suppliers are familiar with each other's market behaviour. An oligopoly can have various forms (see Figure 7.3). Depending on the situation, the market price can be set by a market- or price-leader, or arranged through some form of price arrangements (**cartels**). Also, it may happen that the players in the market cannot combine to pursue cut-throat competition.

  When there are few suppliers, but a differentiated or heterogeneous product, this is referred to as a heterogeneous oligopoly. As soon as there are more suppliers in such a situation, the preferred term is monopolistic competition. Examples are found primarily in the industrial sector: the markets for forklift trucks, chemicals, semi-manufactured goods, flavourings, etc.

- Monopoly. A monopoly is characterized by the presence of only one supplier of the product in question. Substitutes are (virtually) absent. This enables the monopolist to pursue his own pricing policy. Natural monopolies exist when the entire supply of raw materials or a particular manufacturing process is owned by just one producer or manufacturer, excluding others by means of contracts or patents (e.g. oil concessions, diamonds). Government monopolies exist when based on special licences which are required from the government or when based on state law. Examples are postal services, railways and some public utilities (water supply, gas, etc.).

The big advantage of a monopoly, to the supplier, is that it enables the supplier to dictate the price and other conditions to the market. Naturally this dictat has its limits in so far as the buyer is not obliged to purchase the product. Purchasing practice shows many situations which resemble monopolies. For example, an original equipment manufacturer's (OEM) clause in the service contract stipulates that only original spare parts are to be used under penalty of lapse of the warranty conditions. Another example is a situation where the purchase requisitions only mention a product's brand name and a specific supplier name. Engineering departments may limit choice among suppliers by allowing only one particular technology for some purchasing component.

Through its marketing and communications policy the supplier's account manager tries to influence the customer's preferences. The buyer needs to be attentive to these matters and should continuously reflect whether the perceived differences in value of the product that is offered by the supplier outweighs the price difference and the risk of a larger dependency.

Monopoly
Is characterized by the presence of only one supplier of the product in question.

Oligopoly
An oligopoly is a market type characterized by a limited number of suppliers and a limited product differentiation.

Cartel
Price can be set by a market or price-leader, or arranged through some form of price arrangements (cartels).

FIGURE 7.3 Examples of the oligopolistic market structure

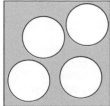 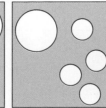 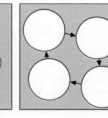 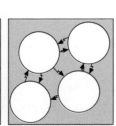

At price P1 and quantity Q1, all capacity is used: *price stability*

There is a *price leader* and this is accepted

Price agreeements are reached

At price P1 and quantity Q1, one party operates below cost price and starts a *price offensive*

Demand side

In general, three types of market structure on the demand side can be distinguished:

- Pure competition. The description given above also applies here.
- **Oligopsony**. This is the oligopoly situation in reverse: there are only a few buyers and a large number of suppliers. The (frequently large) buyers are aware of one another's behaviour and in this way collectively occupy a power position through the usually smaller suppliers. One example of this market structure is the automobile industry in its capacity of buyer of **semi-manufactured products** and components. Other examples are agricultural co-operatives or buying consortia which can be found in numerous branches. These organizations in fact co-ordinate the buying volumes of their members through usually much larger suppliers.
- **Monopsony**. In this situation there is only one buyer of the product versus a large number of suppliers. In reality this is a very rare situation. Examples are the sugar industry, dairy industry, the railways (as buyer of locomotives and trains), ministries of defence (weaponry) and public utilities in some countries (gas, electricity, water supply).

Oligopsony
This is the oligopoly situation in reverse: there are only a few buyers and a large number of suppliers.

Semi-manufactured products
These products have already been processed once or more, and they will be processed further at a later stage.

Monopsony
In this situation there is only one buyer of the product versus a large number of suppliers.

The supply and demand situations described above can be placed in a matrix and the result is shown in Figure 7.4. Depending on the number of suppliers in the market and their positions relative to those of immediate competitors, the buyer's position can be dominant, equal or subordinate to the opposite party. To assess one's position of power it is important to take into account one's position relative to the opposition. An airline company like SAS may be one of the few buyers of turbo-jet engines but, compared to a company the size of

FIGURE 7.4 Typology of market structures

Number of suppliers \ Number of buyers	One	Few	Many
One	Bilateral monopoly, 'captive market' (spare parts)	Limited supply-side monopoly (fuel pumps)	Supply-side monopoly (gas, water, electricity)
Few	Limited demand-side monopoly (telephone exchanges, trains	Bilateral oligopoly (chemical semi-manufacturers)	Supply-side oligopoly (copiers, computers)
Many	Demand-side monopoly (weapons systems, ammunition)	Demand-side oligopoly suppliers (components automobile industry)	Polypolistic competition (office supplies)

= demand-side stronger than supply-side
= Demand and supply more or less in balance
= Supply-side stronger than demand-side

General Electric, SAS's negotiating position is minor. To take another example, DAF Trucks only has a minor power position compared with ZF, the largest European supplier of gearboxes. DAF Trucks orders add up to tens of millions of euros annually but, compared with Daimler, DAF Trucks is only a small player to ZF. One of the reasons to become part of Paccar in 1996 was to benefit from a leveraged negotiation position in its dealings with large, international suppliers.

When developing a purchasing policy, the purchasing manager should reflect on the following questions:

- Which types of markets are we dealing with in relation to product X; how many (potential) suppliers are in the market, from whom we could, in principle, obtain this product?

- What reactions will placing an order of volume Y and price Z with one supplier generate from the other suppliers?

- What is the degree of differentiation for a particular product in the supplier market; which alternatives or substitutes are available?

- What is our company's market share for product P in the supply market and who are our competitors with regard to this product? Who else is buying this product?

- What is likely to happen in the short and the long term with regard to the supply of product Q and what effect will the expected developments have on price levels and product availability?

Knowledge of market structures is important to the buyer because these determine to a large extent the desired sourcing strategy and the negotiating strategies that will be pursued.

SUPPLY MARKET RESEARCH: DEFINITION

Supply market research can be defined as the systematic gathering, classification and analysis of data considering all relevant factors that influence the procurement of goods and services for the purpose of meeting present and future company requirements.

Some aspects of this definition warrant further explanation. Supply market research can relate to research which is conducted at regular intervals, such as monitoring market prices of strategic commodities. However, it may also be conducted on a project basis. Examples of this type of research are developing a detailed cost model for a strategic commodity, auditing suppliers on compliance with CSR-principles (see Chapter 17) or conducting a specific country study against the background of global sourcing initiatives.

Supply market research can be qualitative or quantitative in character. Qualitative research is based on gathering views or opinions on trends and developments going on in a specific industrial sector. Usually this type of research is based upon interviews with industry experts. Quantitative research is based on numerical data possibly derived from general statistics and other public sources. For example, what is the market share of a specific supplier? How do supply and demand develop over time? How can supply and demand patterns be clarified by other macro-economic indicators? Other examples are cost-breakdown analyses which explain whether the price charged by a given supplier is fair or not. Most supply market research covers both aspects. Supplier benchmark studies are examples of both quantitative and qualitative research.

Supply market research can focus on short-term as well as long-term issues. Concentration of supply markets and materials shortages, which are to be expected, in certain industries may require that the company covers its materials needs for a longer period and may foster long-term relationships with suppliers. Short-term supply market analysis may be required when a major supplier is unexpectedly suffering from production problems or goes bankrupt, and an alternative supplier needs to be found quickly.

As demonstrated in Chapter 3, purchasing market research is a key element of the purchasing management process. Its major benefit is that the data gathered through it may serve as a thorough and objective basis for key purchasing decisions.

Subjects of purchasing market research

It will be clear by now that purchasing market research covers a wide variety of subjects. In general three main areas of investigation can be identified:

- Materials, goods and services. This kind of research aims at realizing purchasing savings or at reducing supply chain and transaction costs. It can also aim at reducing the supply risks incurred by the firm by searching for alternative supply sources.

- Suppliers. Supplier-related research is concerned with analysing the relationship with a specific supplier. Questions to be addressed here include, for example, 'Will the supplier continue to be able to satisfy both future technical, quality and logistical requirements and still remain competitive?'

- Systems and procedures. A good purchasing information system is of great importance to all buyers and efforts should be directed constantly at improving the availability of management information. Information and communications technology offers great possibilities for this, but it has to be guided on the basis of buyers' needs. In connection with this, supply research can also focus on how to simplify and harmonize administrative procedures in the relationship between buyers, their internal customers and their suppliers.

Another distinction is the one between macro-, meso- and microeconomic research (see Figure 7.5):

Macroeconomic research
This refers to the general economic and business environment. It focuses on factors that can influence the future balance between supply and demand.

Mesoeconomic research
Research which focuses on specific sectors of industry.

- **Macroeconomic research.** This refers to the general economic and business environment. It focuses on factors that can influence the future balance between supply and demand. Examples of these factors are developments in unemployment or employment in a country, labour costs, inflation, consumer price index, order position.

- **Mesoeconomic research.** This focuses on specific sectors of industry and at this level a lot of information is often available at central statistical offices and industrial agencies, established in many countries. They have specific information on profitability of the sector, technological developments, labour cost, direct versus indirect cost, capacity utilization, order position, energy consumption, etc.

- Microeconomic research. This focuses on assessing strengths and weaknesses of individual suppliers and products. Examples are financial audits of suppliers, quality audits as part of a supplier certification programme, supplier cost analyses, supplier sustainability audits, etc. The objective here is to get a thorough understanding of the supplier's specific capabilities and its long-term market position.

A well-known economic indicator is the Purchasing Managers Index (PMI). This index is published monthly for different countries and is derived from the contracted volumes issued by purchasing professionals in that specific month. In the USA this index is published by the Institute of Supply Management (ISM). Besides the contracted purchasing volumes, the PMI report provides detailed insight into actual sales and purchase price levels, inventory positions, supply lead times, and the employment within the companies concerned. An index higher than 50 indicates a growth of economic activity. A score lower than 50 demonstrates a declining economic activity. In the USA and UK the PMI has developed into one of the leading economic indicators. Figure 7.6 provides a picture of the PMI for Europe during the period 1996–2008. For buyers the PMI is an indispensable tool. They can subscribe to it through their local professional association.

FIGURE 7.5 Three areas of purchasing market research

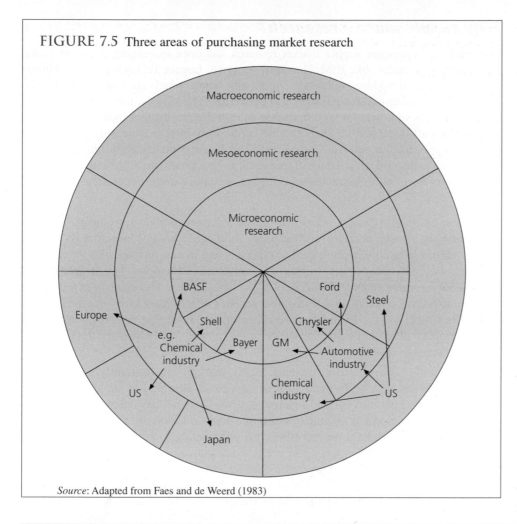

Source: Adapted from Faes and de Weerd (1983)

FIGURE 7.6 Eurozone Purchasing Managers' Index 1996–2008

Why supply market research?

The need for systematic supply market research has been increasing in recent years. Many large companies, like IBM, Honda of America, Lucent Technologies and Philips Electronics have introduced corporate commodity teams which are responsible for the world-wide sourcing of strategic parts and materials. Relentlessly, these teams look for the best-in-class suppliers for their materials and service needs. Originally supported by specialized staff departments, the corporate commodity buyers increasingly commit to conduct supply market research themselves. The Internet increasingly provides better and more up to date information on supply markets in a faster and more convenient way. What factors have led to a greater need for active supply market research? The major ones are:

- Continuing technological developments. As was seen earlier, every company, whether operating in industry or trade, in order to stay competitive has to concentrate on product innovation and quality improvement. When investing in new technologies the question arises: should we develop new technologies ourselves or should we buy them? Strained financial resources often lead managers to the latter option. The make-or-buy decision demands a lot of research, as does the final supplier selection decision once the decision has been made to buy. Buyers have to refresh their knowledge constantly about new technological developments which are going on in their supply markets, through product and supplier research.

- Supply market dynamics. International supply markets are constantly on the move. Price levels may change from an all time high to an all time low in just a couple of months, influencing the company's margin directly. Demand may dramatically change – demand can be extremely volatile (for example demand for oil and steel was skyrocketing early in 2008 whilst at the end of the year plummeting to an all time low, all of this within 1 year) affecting supply and price levels immediately. Buyers, then, have to anticipate likely changes in a product's demand and supply situation and thus develop a better understanding of the price dynamics of their commodities. Next, export facilities can suddenly be limited because of changes in political arrangements between countries, suppliers can disappear as a result of bankruptcy, suppliers may be acquired by a competitor with several consequences for the price level and continuity of supply. Changes in Western society. The relatively high wages level in Western Europe has led to changes in the suppliers' market. An example is the change in textile supply for most European retailers, who years ago shifted from local to European suppliers and to the Far East due to much lower wages. The same trend applies to many industrial products (varying from television glass to car tires). For a lot of products, industrial production has shifted from Western countries to the Far East (especially to China) or the developing countries and this development probably will continue.

- Monetary developments. The ever-increasing volatility of some major currencies poses new problems to buyers, who operate internationally. High inflation in some countries, large governmental budget deficits, rapidly changing currency exchange rates may require immediate action from buyers in terms of a reallocation of their materials requirements.

- Offset obligations and changes in tax regimes. When companies export to some countries (e.g. development countries), they need to offset part of their sales volume through buying local merchandise and products. Governments do so in order to stimulate local economic activity. In such cases the buyer needs to investigate what products or components could be purchased. This requires a lot of desk research; sometimes visits need to be made to the prospective country. Changes in tax regimes may also be the reason for extensive supply market research. The European Union may impose extra import taxes on products coming from a certain country or region (this happened a few years ago for the import of textiles from China), which may be the reason for the buyer to look for other countries and suppliers from which to get products.

These are some of the factors which underline the importance of systematic purchasing market research.

HOW TO STRUCTURE PURCHASING MARKET RESEARCH

Figure 7.7 shows the most important steps to be made, when conducting purchasing market research. These are in more detail:

1. **Determine objectives.** What exactly is the problem to be solved? What information is desired? How accurate does the information have to be? These questions are not a problem if the buyer carries out the research itself. If, however, the research is delegated to others a good briefing is of great importance, in order to generate useful information.

FIGURE 7.7 How to structure purchasing market research: a stepwise approach

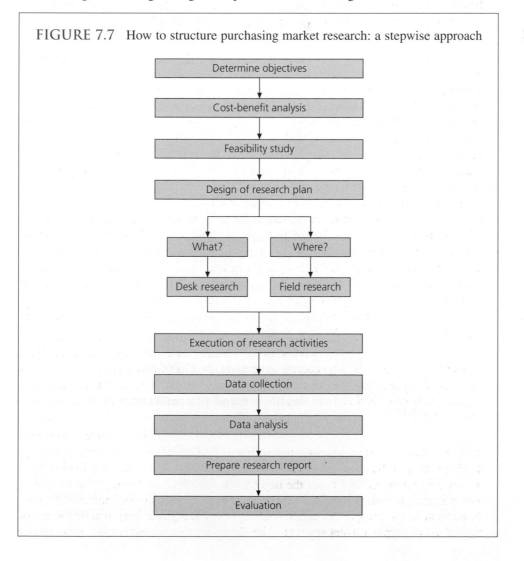

MEMO 7.1   ELECTRONIC SOURCES OF SUPPLY MARKET INFORMATION

There are about 1000 e-marketplaces for businesses in the world today, but only a handful have the participation of the world's biggest companies and handle large trading volumes. Below are some of the most important e-marketplaces are listed per industry.

Automotive

Covisint (www.covisint.com)
Established in February 2000, Covisint provides a platform for OEMs (original equipment manufacturers) and automotive suppliers to trade with some of the worlds major automotive companies.

SupplyOn (www.supplyon.com)
Established in mid 2000 by leading companies within the automotive supply industry (e.g. Bosch, Continental, INA and ZF along with SAP as a technology partner). At the end of 2001, Siemens VDO also joined the company.

Aviation

Aeroxchange (www.aeroxchange.com)
Was founded on 1st of October 2000 by 13 airlines. 19 additional airlines have since joined the founding group. Among the founding airlines are Air Canada, Air New Zealand, Cathay Pacific, FedEx, KLM, Lufthansa, SAS and Singapore Airlines. The e-marketplace is focused on streamlining the buying and selling process of products such as airframes, avionics, engine components, maintenance services as well as airline-specific goods and services.

B2B-Aero.com (www.b2b-aero.com)
Founded in Feb. 2000 . . . the e-marketplaces' mission is to connect airlines, OEMs and aviation repair facilities to streamline the overhaul and repair business using the Internet.

Exostar (www.exostar.com)
Founded by Bae Systems, Boeing, Lockheed Martin Group, Raytheon Co and Rolls Royce. The e-marketplace is an electronic business service provider built for the aerospace and defense industry.

Building and construction

BravoSolution (www.bravosolution.com)
Founded in July 2000 by Italcementi Group one of the most important cement producers and distributors in Italy.

Edilportale (www.edilportale.com)
On-line from March 2001, Edilportale was founded by Italian private investors and venture capitalists. The e-marketplace offers a good industry directory and it is rich in news, industry laws and events.

CTSpace (www.ctspace.com)
Although not strictly an e-marketplace, Citadon provides a web-based software application for project collaboration, document access, sharing and business process automation for the global engineering and construction industry. Its members are some of the worlds major EPC (Engineer, Procure, and Construct) companies including Alcoa, Bechtel Corp., Fluor Daniel, Marriott, Halliburton, GE Power Systems, and Kvaerner Oilfield Products.

Chemicals

Elemica (www.elemica.com)
Founded in August 2000 by 22 of the worlds biggest chemical companies including: BASF, Bayer, BP, Dow, DuPont, Mitsubishi Chemical Corporation, Mitsui Chemicals, Rhodia, Rohm and Haas, Shell Chemicals, Sumitomo Chemical, & Royal Vopak.

ChemConnect (www.chemconnect.com)
Founded in 1995, ChemConnect is a global trading hub for chemical products such as: petrochemicals, industrial chemicals, plastics and polymers, pharmaceutical inputs, fine and speciality chemicals, industrial gases and agrochemicals.

Food and beverages

1Sync (www.transora.com)
Transora's investors include more than 50 of the world's largest Consumer Packaged Goods manufacturers including PepsiCo, Coca-Cola, Mars, Kellogg's, Danone, Procter & Gamble, Unilever NV, Quaker Oats and Heineken. Operating in seven languages Transora has interoperability projects underway with CPGmarket and GlobalNetXchange (GNX).

Healthcare and pharmaceutical

Global Healthcare Exchange (www.ghx.com) GHX was founded in March 2000 for hospitals, manufacturers and wholesalers. Products traded include medical and healthcare equipment, products and services and pharmaceuticals. Members include Siemens, 3M Medical, Arrow International, Bayer Diagnostics, Boston Scientific Corp. and GE Medical Systems.

Retail and consumer goods
WorldWideRetailExchange
(/www.worldwideretailexchange.org/)
WWRE was founded in March 2000 for retailers and suppliers in the food, general merchandise, textile/home, and drugstore sectors. Members include: Edeka, Tengelmann Group, Rewe, K Mart, Target, Marks & Spencer, Tesco, Seibu Dept Stores, Jusco, and others.

Transportation and logistics
TransCore (www.transcore.com)
TransCore's freight exchange, Powered by DAT Services, is an e-marketplace for the matching of freight shippers with carriers. With installations in 37 countries and 1800 employees Transcore handles over 2.5 million transactions monthly. The e-marketplace is based in Beaverton, USA and was established in 2000.

Are we talking about a global market review or is an extensive analysis required of the suppliers' financial and market positions? When does the answer have to be available? These aspects should be covered in a concise briefing.

2. Cost–benefit analysis. What will be the costs of the research? How many work hours are required for the research? Will the value of the obtained information outweigh the expense?

3. Feasibility study. What information is already available within the company? What information is available from publications and statistics? There may be more information readily available than originally expected. A good (computer-based) documentation service can be invaluable. On many issues international electronic databases exist (see Memo 7.1) and specialized agencies may conduct market and product studies at limited costs. If a public database cannot be found directly, it is worthwhile asking for such a survey at services such as university libraries or electronic information services. The next research step should only be taken once it is confirmed that the required information is unavailable in the form of publications or statistics.

4. Design of a research plan. Specific action is sometimes needed to obtain information, as, for example, in the case of auditing a specific supplier. Another example is an investigation to analyse possibilities for a 'catalogue buying' contract – a situation in which the buyer looks for opportunities to transfer a coherent assortment of products (e.g. fasteners, computer supplies) from many suppliers to only one supplier. In addition to desk research, interviews with buyers and suppliers will be required, followed by field research. It is important to prepare well for such research through a detailed project plan.

5. Execution of research activities. In the execution stage it is important to follow the project plan prepared earlier. Decision-making is often dependent on a certain amount of information being available. Excuses for delays in research activity cannot be accepted – potential problems should have been anticipated while designing the time plan and estimating the workload.

6. Preparing research report and evaluation. When the research is finished a report has to be prepared – this has to contain the assignment, as well as the obtained results. Did the buyer get an answer to his questions? Is the report drawn up in a comprehensive manner? What assumptions underlie the obtained results? These are issues that require attention in the report; finally, what is the opinion on the research after it has been carried out? Have the method and the result been satisfactory? These questions have to be considered to prevent mistakes being repeated in the future.

In the case of purchasing market research it is common to differentiate between desk research and field research. Desk research is the gathering, analysis and interpretation of data that serve the research assignment, but which have already been gathered by others. In purchasing, this type of research is used the most. Large companies in most cases have a special documentation service that continuously gathers general and market-specific technical information. Much of this information is published and made available to buyers nowadays through a special purchasing intranet (see Memo 7.2).

Field research is the gathering, analysis and interpretation of information that cannot be obtained by means of desk research. It tries to track down new information; visits to industrial exhibitions and suppliers are examples of field research methods.

Not every research project will follow the phases described above exactly. The available time usually places restrictions on research design and each project will require its own approach so that a standard method is hard to provide.

MEMO 7.2   PURCHASING INTRANET DAF TRUCKS

DAF Trucks, the leading truck manufacturer located in The Netherlands, was acquired in 1996 by Paccar, a leading manufacturer in the US. Important brands of Paccar are Peterbilt and Kenworth. One of the reasons for Paccar to acquire DAF Trucks was to realize a strong foothold in the European truck market. Another reason was to create significant global leverage in purchasing and supply. Today buyers at DAF Trucks work with an advanced purchasing information system, which supports them in their strategic and operational activities (see Figure 7.8).

FIGURE 7.8 Example of DAF Trucks' purchasing information system

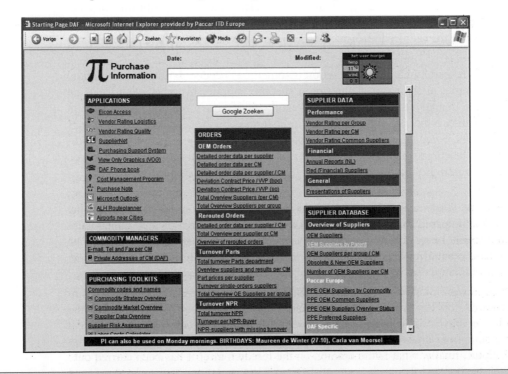

A differentiation can be made between:

- The different applications that buyers can use for their tactical activities. Here you will find vendor rating information, corporate purchasing information (standard presentations and contract templates), travel information, access to DAF Trucks' Supplier Net

- Contact list and contact information for all DAF Trucks and Paccar commodity managers enabling them to communicate quickly and efficiently worldwide

- Purchasing toolkit including templates for developing commodity plans and conducting supply market surveys, supplier risk assessment tools, a labour costs calculator, a fixed costs calculator (see below)

- Detailed order information related to OEM orders, rerouted orders, parts, non-product-related purchases

- Detailed supplier data related to supplier performance, financial data with regard to suppliers and general supplier information.

- Supplier database providing all kinds of information with regard to DAF Trucks' suppliers.

Notable are the labour costs calculator and the fixed costs calculator. The first allows the buyer to quickly calculate the extra cost that is incurred when he changes from a local supplier to a foreign supplier. The calculator compensates for higher transportation costs, pipeline inventory, risk of late delivery, etc. The fixed cost calculator allows the buyer to calculate the effect, based upon the percentage of fixed cost in the cost price of a specific part, of a higher order volume. When the buyer is going to order a higher volume this tool calculates the net effect on the supplier's sales price. Purchasing and supply market research are prime tasks for the buyers and commodity managers of DAF Trucks. Among other things they keep a sharp eye on the supply chain structure and developments of DAF's main competitors.

PURCHASING MARKET RESEARCH AND INFORMATION TECHNOLOGY

At the beginning of this chapter it was illustrated how Internet technology may be used to conduct purchasing market research. Currently, companies are discovering the many ways in which this new technology may support their purchasing operations and strategies. The following examples further illustrate this point:

- Company's like Saint Gobain, the French conglomerate which is active in a wide range of products ranging from glass manufacturing to insulation and construction materials, have installed a worldwide purchasing Intranet enabling exchange of product, supplier and contract information among all sites and operating companies. Other manufacturing companies, ranging from automotive and computer industry to the beverage and food industry, have built similar systems based on Microsoft Outlook software.

- Data-suppliers like Yellow Pages, ABC, Kompass and Wer Liefert Was now have available through their websites vast supplier bases covering supplier addresses in all major EC-countries enabling buyers to conduct market surveys in a very short time. For commodities, long lists of potential suppliers may be developed in just a few minutes. Supplier information (with regard to product assortment, references, financial stability) may be asked for through extensive database searches and directly through e-mail from the supplier. Requests for quotations may be submitted through simple, computer-supported ordering systems or directly through e-mailing the supplier concerned.

- Some companies use their purchasing website to attract new suppliers for certain commodities. Suppliers are requested to react for components which are short of supply or for which new suppliers are wanted. Suppliers may act through filling in the SQA-questionnaire and sending it through e-mail directly to the purchasing department of the prospective customer. In this way the Internet is actively being used for 'reversed marketing'.

- Companies like FedEx, DHL Worldwide Express and UPS provide linkages through the Internet which enable companies to keep track of their deliveries. Some of these sites enable cost breakdowns per port of destination enabling buyers to find their most competitive source of supply for shipment and transportation.

- Although electronic payment is still troublesome, developments are moving fast in this area. In the consumer goods business some companies have posted impressive turnover figures and financial results (such as Amazon and Dell). It is expected that electronic commerce and payment will grow rapidly in the years to come.

Other examples can be added to this list. Memo 7.3 summarizes how the Internet may be used in the purchasing area nowadays. It will be clear from this list that the electronification of purchasing is developing very quickly. New IT-supported tools have become available, and are accessible not only to buyers. The same tools will also be available to all other disciplines in the company (who in general are computer-wise and much better equipped than their counterparts in the purchasing organization), which will call for a sometimes drastic review and reorientation of the traditional role of the purchasing function in companies.

MEMO 7.3   INTERNET AND INTRANET APPLICATIONS IN PURCHASING SUPPLY MARKET RESEARCH

The Internet may provide buyers with different kinds of information related to each step of the purchasing process:

- Purchasing market research and supplier selection. Examples are Wer Liefert Was, Yellow Pages, Industrynet, all of which may be used to find (new) suppliers.

- Getting the right product specifications. Product descriptions may be derived from a Purchasing Extranet.

- Checking supplier references. Supplier financial and performance references may be checked from Dun & Bradstreet.

- Sending requests for proposal. This may be done through e-mail directly to the supplier or through the websites of supplier data-providers.

- Bid information is exposed through specialized intermediaries such as BidCast or Tender Daily.

- Virtual auctions. Free Markets Online, Ariba, Procuri provide software and services to organize auctions among suppliers for individual

buyers. Some large retailers (such as Wehkamp in The Netherlands) have daily auctions for merchandise on sale.

- Reversed marketing. Some large contractors and manufacturers (such as NASA and Sony) have a special purchasing website on which they expose products for which they seek new suppliers. Initial screening is done through filling out a detailed questionnaire.

- Commodity buying. Some major commodities can now be traced online through the Internet enabling buyers to manage their commodity buyers from hour to hour and enabling them to buy at the right moment.

- Shipment tracking. FedEx, DHL Worldwide Express and UPS have extensive websites with which rates may be asked for express freight and shipments and deliveries may be tracked and traced.

- Electronic payment. Payment may be tied to credit cards or special purchasing cards, enabling paperless invoice handling.

SUMMARY

The ever-increasing turbulence in global supply markets makes supply market research a crucial activity. Supply market research is required in order to keep informed about changes going on in technology, supplier markets, competition and supplier relationships. It is also necessary to assess the competitiveness of the current supply base against best in class suppliers and to keep track of changes in currency rates, to name just a few.

To be able to purchase effectively, the buyer must have a sound knowledge of the supply-markets in which it operates and of the products it buys. Supply market structures determine the buyer's tactics – its attitude towards a monopolist will differ greatly from the attitude it adopts when dealing with an oligopoly situation. When deciding on its tactics the buyer will take into account the demand side and the supply side of a specific market. At the supply side of the market four market structures can be found, including pure competition, monopolistic competition, oligopoly and monopoly. At the demand side of the market three different market structures can be found, including pure competition, oligopsony and monopsony. A sound analysis of the buyers' power position requires a thorough analysis of the supply market from both demand and supply perspective.

In setting up research a stepwise approach is recommended. First, the objectives of the research should be clearly formulated. What questions should be answered by this activity? Will the value of the information to be gathered probably outweigh the costs? What information is already known about the subject? In most cases desk research will be sufficient. In some specific cases field research and surveys may be necessary, although these will add to the costs of the activity and its lead time. Finally, the results should be presented in a concise report.

As discussed, the Internet provides ample opportunities to buyers to conduct purchasing market surveys. For some commodities and services, information may be found covering all parts of the purchasing process, just by using Internet technology. And these opportunities and facilities expand every day! Therefore it is very important for buyers to keep informed about this medium, since it will make supply markets more transparent than ever before. This is not only true for macro-economic research, but also for sector studies and individual supplier studies. The fact that as a result of the Internet many supply markets have become very transparent, is the reason for their increasing turbulence.

ASSIGNMENTS

7.1   Your purchasing manager has requested you as a buyer to develop a commodity strategy for the product group that you are responsible for (stamped, steel components). In your commodity plan you should come up with a future sourcing plan. What information would you need in developing a sourcing plan for your commodity group?

7.2. Investigate the websites of some large data suppliers such as Wer Liefert Was, Yellow Pages, Kompass, etc. What kinds of functionality do these data suppliers provide to the buyer today? How do these suppliers support the purchasing process model that was described in Chapter 2?

7.3   A distinction is made between macro-, meso- and microeconomic research. Name some sources of information to be consulted in each of these types of purchasing market research.

7.4   You are working for a larger supplier in the automotive industry. Your purchasing manager has requested you to investigate whether it is worthwhile to participate as a member in Covisint. What kinds of solutions does Covisint offer to the medium sized automotive supplier today? Would you recommend your purchasing manager to take part in this important electronic, automotive marketplace?

7.5   Internet technology is open to everyone. Not only to buyers, but also to users and budget holders within organizations. Today, every employee is able to buy from the Internet without interference of a buyer. What would you consider to be the most important threats and opportunities from buying through the Internet? What recommendations would you make to companies in order to benefit from modern web-enabled buying opportunities?

INTEGRATIVE CASE 7.1

SPECIAL MECHANICS LTD.

BY A.RJAN VAN WEELE

Introduction

'Here we go again,' Jeremy Clark, purchasing manager for Special Mechanics Ltd. in Doncaster, UK, lamented, 'production planning has once again gone too far and now we can clean up their mess. I really don't know how we are going to get out of this one.' He spoke these words to his project buyer, Cheryl Sturrock, who listened closely to what her boss was saying.

The two colleagues were discussing a problem, which was dropped in their laps by the production manager the day before. Production planning had made far-reaching promises concerning the purchase of a high-precision milling machine. The core of the problem was that the milling machine would probably not be delivered on time, but also that the machine which would be delivered was not the version ordered. The supplier, Lodex Ltd. from Northern Ireland, had already sent a confirmation of

order. The prospects were unpleasant to say the least, and now Phillip Samuelson, the production manager, had raised the affair with the purchasing department to see what could be done.

Special Mechanics Ltd.

Special Mechanics Ltd is a company domiciled in England, which specialises in high-quality metal works. The company has an outstanding reputation in the areas of machining and high-precision lathe work. The original company was started by the Peterson brothers in 1919. After a prosperous growth, the family sold the company to a Swiss multinational in the late 1960s. This multinational left the organization structure intact: the company retained its English management and management culture. It is governed as a separate profit centre. Every year management must realize a pre-determined profit. Not counting a few exceptions, the company has been reasonably successful in this respect up to now.

The company has a turnover of approximately £45 million, and a work force of 380 employees. Major customers are engineering factories, the car

This case describes the problems surrounding a purchasing process concerning capital goods. The case was constructed on the basis of various practical situations we encountered. Special Mechanics Ltd. is a fictitious high-quality metal works company; any similarities to existing companies are purely coincidental.

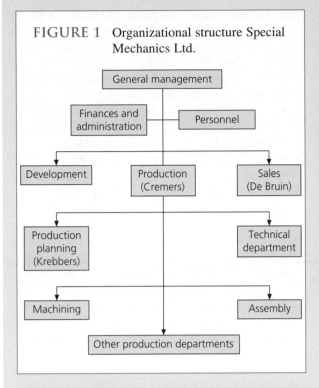

FIGURE 1   Organizational structure Special Mechanics Ltd.

industry and the aircraft industry. In the early 1970s a sales programme was drawn up, aimed at obtaining foreign orders. This program was reasonably successful: approximately 25% of the turnover was now realized through foreign clients. For the past years the company obtained orders from a few West European companies active in space systems. These customers were highly appreciated by 'Special Mechanics' because they were known for their high quality demands, which made them a very good reference for obtaining other orders.

The organizational structure of Special Mechanics Ltd. is shown in Figure 1. Not visible in the Figure is that purchasing, as a staff function, reports to the production manager (Samuelson).

The order from Ariane

One of the most important potential customers in the space sector was the Ariane consortium. In the past Special Mechanics had already wanted to do several projects for them; the company was of the opinion that Ariane was looking to extend their supplier file and that Special Mechanics Ltd. had caught their eye. Special Mechanics felt strongly that they were being 'tested'.

Early May 2007, the sales director, Grant Humphreys, was invited by Ariane to come to France for the purpose of exchanging views about future possibilities. This meeting was not without results, because in several follow-up meetings, after substantial negotiations, a £4.2 million order for high-precision lathe work on space panels was obtained. This news so delighted the general management that a celebration was organized for the entire personnel one Friday afternoon.

The delivery date was set for May 2009, which gave Special Mechanics ample opportunity to prepare for the production activities. However, after consultation with production planning, it soon became obvious that the available machinery was inadequate: it would not be capable of executing the necessary machining operations with the required precision. This rather late observation caused production planning to submit an investment proposal for the purchase of a specialised milling machine.

Although management had some reservations concerning this request (why was this not foreseen?), they approved the proposal. The company wanted to focus on high-quality machining even more in the future, so that this proposal matched with company policy.

Further developments

After the proposal was approved, the departments of Development and Production planning (see Figure 1) were asked to provide a functional specification for the milling machine to be purchased. In general this is not an easy task, because in addition to the requirements concerning the lathe work the machine must be able to execute, it must take into account the requirements of the Technical department.

Maintenance requirements are one important aspect. Furthermore, this kind of high-quality equipment demands a conditioned area, where the climate (temperature, humidity) can be regulated. A project team was installed, chaired by Samuelson, head of Production planning. In addition representatives from the Technical department, the Development department, the Machining department and the Financial/Administrative department were part of the team.

To obtain a clear picture of the market, several industrial exhibitions were visited at home and abroad during the period August 2007 to February

2008. These visits yielded few new perspectives; the eligible suppliers were already known through previous contacts. The problem in meetings with prospective suppliers was the absence of a detailed specification; this still wasn't completed. In the meantime, Samuelson made several visits to Fimec Ltd. in Amsterdam, a company specialising in the sale of machining equipment. Fimec Ltd. represented among others the Northern Ireland producer Lodex (a company Samuelson was quite taken with). Lodex saw no problems in meeting the wishes of Special Mechanics Ltd.

Problems

On May 25 2008 the sales director, Humphreys, was summoned to France. The space project, for which Special Mechanics was to machine the space panels, had been moved up. The panels must be delivered not in May 2009, but in February of that year. The sales director was aware of the state of affairs concerning the purchase of the milling machine. Nevertheless, he gave in to Ariane's wishes, because he might lose this important order if he didn't.

These developments caused considerable commotion in the project team; quick action must be taken now. Early March, later Samuelson invited Fimec Ltd. to submit a quotation; the decision was made to go ahead with Fimec, provided the quotation was within the budget applied for. Fimec was requested to react within two weeks.

The purchasing manager, Clark, received a copy of the request for quotation. This caused him to contact Samuelson, who informed him about the current state of affairs. Clark was indignant about not being told earlier what happened. Because he has a lot of other things to attend to, he promises to return to the matter at a later stage.

Fimec reacts quickly; a quotation is on the table within ten days. It names a final price of £650 000, provided the decision to purchase is made before the end of April. After that date a price increase was possible as a result of the changing rate of the Pound Sterling. The equipment could be inspected in Northern Ireland, at the Lodex premises.

The project team loses no time; early April two men immediately fly in to Belfast and from there they went directly to Lodex. On the face of it, the milling machine they have available seems to meet

the demands made by Special Mechanics; a final decision could not be made, however, because the complete specification Production planning was preparing, was not finished yet.

Fimec's Sales manager, John Jaspers, inquires at the end of April whether Special Mechanics is interested. They must make up their minds quickly, because another customer will be there to inspect the machine the next day, so he informs them casually. Samuelson tells Jaspers that he is very interested and asks him not to sell the machine to anyone else.

Back home, the project team reports to Samuelson. He introduces a new element into the discussion: he has been informed by contacts that the machine they inspected the day before, was originally intended for another customer of Lodex! According to his information, Lodex made an all-out effort to realize the modifications on time; the previous 'customer' decided against the purchase because the machine was not up to his quality specifications!

Sameulson is in for another surprise. The next day he finds on his desk a letter from Fimec Ltd., containing the following extract:

'We hereby confirm your purchase of a milling machine type Lodex 1002 AA, at the price offered by us on April 28th of £650,000 ...' and ... conditions of delivery to be agreed upon ...'

That was not the intention! During the meeting following these surprises, the production manager promises to raise the affair with the Purchasing department.

Communication with Lodex Ltd.

Clark and Sturrock decide to write a letter to Fimec Ltd., informing them they feel they have no obligations whatsoever. Nothing has been signed, so there is no legal ground for a purchasing contract. Furthermore, Special Mechanics immediately contacts Lodex Ltd. in Northern Ireland by telephone. A meeting is arranged for the next day to inspect the milling machine. Clark and Sturrock will be met at the airport by the Lodex' Sales manager.

The meeting which follows quickly reveals a common interest to reach an agreement. Lodex Ltd. admits that the machine in question was originally intended for another customer; and yes, it does concern a modified specimen! Every day the machine just sits there means loss of interest. Clark is aware of the importance of the machine for his company. If Special Mechanics wants to be able to execute the order for space panels, the machine must be operating by July. He doesn't have the time to go looking for another supplier.

The negotiations proceed successfully, for Special Mechanics, that is: Clark and Sturrock are able to talk Lodex into lowering the price by £150 000 – the weak spot in Lodex' position is that they have a cash-flow problem. They are willing to accept this price reduction, provided Special Mechanics agrees to make a 50% downpayment when the purchasing contract is signed.

When they depart, Clark and Sturrock urge Lodex to deliver the machine as soon as possible. Leaving behind the purchasing conditions, both buyers embark on the journey home.

On May, 15th, a Lodex delegation comes to Special Mechanics and the purchasing contract is signed. Delivery will take place before 1st July.

Modifications in the agreements

Early June, Clark at Production planning receives an extended report containing the functional specification of the milling machine. The report is a thorough piece of work: it contains a technical description of over 40 pages.

Reading the report, Clark stumbles across a numerically controlled measuring device, which must be built into the machine. Nobody has mentioned this before! Upon inquiry it is learned that advanced measuring and regulating equipment is required to check the very precise tolerances the machine will have to work with. This has been agreed with the customer of the space panels.

Clark forwards the specification to Lodex Ltd. These added demands meet with problems; Lodex is only willing to take care of these extra provisions if the price is adapted. In addition they state that these developments will prolong the term of delivery by at least four weeks. The planned date of delivery is set for July 26th; Special Mechanics will pay an additional £30 000 upfront for the extra provisions.

Early July Clark travels to Northern Ireland once more to see if everything is going as planned;

it turns out they have hardly started! The explanation given is that the testing of the measuring and regulating equipment (which is in fact very advanced) has taken longer than expected. The Sales manager informs Clark that Special Mechanics shouldn't count on delivery before the end of August. He thinks the first week of October is feasible . . .

Questions

1 Describe what you see as major problems in this case.

2 Define the buying situation using the classification of Faris and Wind. Describe the most important problems related to the purchasing process using the purchasing process model.

3 How would you prevent similar problems in future? What would you recommend to Special Mechanics' management?

4 If you were the acting purchasing manager, what actions would you take to ensure that Special Mechanics would be able to meet its deadline to Ariane?

As a presentation team you are asked to set out your findings in a punchy and well-designed PowerPoint presentation. You are also asked to summarise the results in the form of a concise paper (maximum 8–10 pages, not including appendices).

When making your proposals, make use of the theory described in chapters 1, 2 and 3. You should also add at least two articles (not more than 5-years-old) from scientific trade literature, with a link to the problem described in this case.

The other teams are asked to prepare a paper of 4–5 papers based on the problem definition. You must at least include the content of chapters 1, 2 and 3 in your paper.

The way in which you link scientific insights to practical solutions is an important point of assessment for your paper and presentation.

It is possible that not all answers can be found in this book. In that case, you will have to rely on your own creativity. Or better still: you are expected to consult scientific literature with a link to the relevant subject. Include at least two recent articles from international scientific journals, not older than 5 years.

TECHNIX: MATERIAL SUPPLY PROBLEMS IN OFFSHORE DREDGING IN RIO . . .

BY ARJAN VAN WEELE

Introduction

'What a mess,' Hans Willems, director of Technix BV, sighed while he was reading the message that just came in on the fax machine. The fax stated a damages claim for the total sum of €2.1 million from one of Technix's most important clients: NedWorks. Willems stared at the short message on the paper for a long time. The telephone conversation he had had two days ago with Jan van Daal, purchase manager at NedWorks, regarding a quality problem with parts delivered by Technix BV, did not go well at the time.

'We've been on good terms with NedWorks for at least 10 years and now this happens,' he said with disbelief. Hans Willems was surprised about NedWorks' strong reaction. The claim for damages concerned an order delivered by Technix last year and – this was the message he received – the products did not comply with the standards for the dredging project in Brazil, which NedWorks had been carrying out for some time. Before getting into action, Willems decided to list all the points first.

Technix BV

Since 1993, Willems has been the director of Technix BV, a medium-sized trading company, active in high quality technical components for the building industry and the offshore market. The turnover for 2006 was €19.5 million. The company was located in Hendrik Ido Ambacht in the Netherlands, close to the international contractors, most of which were situated in the Rotterdam Europoort. The company has 25 employees. Technix obtains its goods from a large number of manufacturers mostly located abroad. For many of these manufacturers, Technix holds an exclusive agency contract. Based upon such a contract, Technix sells the manufacturer's components to its clients. In many cases, the delivery is not made by Technix, but directly by the manufacturer represented by Technix. Technix's most important clients are active in the offshore and dredging sector and the international construction industry. Throughout the years, Technix has acquired a reputation as a reliable business partner. This can be concluded, among other things, from the long-standing relationships Technix has with its numerous clients.

Technix–NedWorks relationship

One of Technix's largest customers is NedWorks BV, established in Rotterdam, The Netherlands. NedWorks is a renowned, international dredging company, operating all over the world. The relationship between NedWorks and Technix began more than ten years ago. In 1998, Technix was already the supplier of parts for NedWorks' dredging machines and cutters, adapters and cutter teeth in particular. These parts are needed for carrying out dredging works. A cutter suction dredge sucks up the soil/rock cut loose by the cutter and pushes it away via pipelines. The cutter has adapters welded to a number of arms/wings, which serve as a setting for interchangeable teeth. Obviously, recognizing the often harsh operating conditions, the amount of teeth used is many fold compared with the number of adapters (see appendix 1).

The cutters, adapters and cutter teeth were originally manufactured by the American Machine Company (AMC) and currently, Technix is the only distributor of these products in the Benelux. In 2003, AMC closed down, but the production was taken over by Kilkenny Tools & Machines (KTM), established in Kentucky, USA. Technix considered KTM to be a worthy successor and continued business

This case describes contractual and material supply problems in an international offshore dredging project. The case is extracted from several company practices. Any resemblance with reality is based on coincidence. The case study is written for educational purposes only. The names of any persons and companies named within are fictitious, as are any numbers mentioned in this case.

with this manufacturer. KTM decided soon to produce the cutters itself, but to outsource the production of adapters and teeth to a specialist supplier in India. Technix did not communicate this so-called subcontracting to its clients.

Until 2005, NedWorks did not have general conditions of purchase. The involved goods had been bought at Technix at the time and the delivery was made directly from the manufacturer to the site where NedWorks was operational in the world, without any interference of Technix. Until 2008, Technix acted as an exclusive distributor for KTM.

In 2005, a new purchasing manager came on board at NedWorks. In order to get organized, he sent its general purchase conditions to Technix (see appendix 2) for approval. Furthermore, he requested Technix to fax a copy of all orders that Technix placed with KTM. Third, from that moment on he instructed Technix to send all shipment documents for the goods to be delivered directly to NedWorks.

Technix–NedWorks relationship in a historical perspective

In over 10 years, only two problems occurred regarding the usability of the components delivered by Technix. In both cases it concerned adapters and cutter teeth that appeared not to have the required quality. These quality problems were often attributed to the extreme conditions in which cutters, adapters and cutter teeth had to operate. Interesting detail: from Technix's very first delivered order to NedWorks in 1998, the cutter broke during use in Portsmouth. Defective cutter teeth lead to a too large wear of the cutter itself, consequently making the cutter fail after a few weeks. In that instance, AMC and Technix reimbursed all costs related to the adapters and cutter teeth, but attributed the breaking during use to the way of working. NedWorks accepted this at the time. Apart from some minor problems, during 2003, a second, bigger problem occurred. The problem surfaced at a dredging project in Bahrain in the Persian Gulf, where the rocky bed appeared to be very hard. Technix' supplied adapters could not handle the tough rock bed and broke continuously. The problems were solved in close consultation: Technix replaced the cutter teeth and adapters that were initially shipped, again at its own expense. In this case, indirect damages or consequential damages were again not claimed by NedWorks.

In the beginning of this decade, NedWorks hardly dredged in hard soil, so no considerable problems occurred.

Solutions to problem cases in the past

In all cases, the above mentioned problems have been solved through close consultation between Technix and NedWorks. Examples of arrangements taken by Technix at the time:

- direct consultation with regard to possible replacement of the involved sets of parts
- direct replacement of components that did not comply with the specifications
- consultation on causes and possible preventive measures in order to avoid recurrence in the future.

In none of the above-mentioned cases has NedWorks claimed against Technix for direct damages or consequential damages. This was in line with normal practices. In the dredging or contractor industry, claims regarding consequential damages for this type of product are exceptional.

The project in Rio de Janeiro

Early 2005, NedWorks landed a major contract for the deepening of Rio de Janeiro's harbour and the connecting entrance channel. In 2000, NedWorks had already widened the channel during a previous assignment.

Rio de Janeiro's harbour is a popular mooring place for cruise ships, but the larger cruise ships could not reach Rio's harbour at that time. NedWorks was contracted to deepen the channel to the ocean and a part of the harbour basin. Late 2005, they started the project. The entrance channel had to be deepened to 14 metres over a total length of 1000 metres.

The execution of this project suffered from substantial delay. This was caused partly by the hard rock bed the contractors encountered. Before commencing the work on their initial proposal, NedWorks had conducted a number of soil tests and test drillings in order to determine the hardness of the ground. Notwithstanding, halfway down the entrance channel (July 2006), NedWorks dredging staff to their surprise stumbled upon hard rock formations. This caused, understandably, problems with the adapters and the cutter teeth, that wore out at excessive speed. Another major problem was that

▶

during that period, the crew had to struggle with heavy seas: because the wind came from the wrong side, ocean water was pushed up forming heavy seas in the channel area. Dredging in such conditions is impossible. This problem deteriorated, when the floating pipeline between the suction dredge and the shore took some hard knocks. The shore connection could not withstand the protracted force of the ocean. There was no alternative but to anchor all machinery down and wait for better weather. And for better times, for NedWorks reckoned with the project bearing a severe financial loss due to these problems . . .

Technix had not been notified of these extreme circumstances beforehand, and Willems did not get informed of this situation until, by coincidence, he was reading NedWorks' monthly company newspaper, NeWs Worldwide, including an article about the project in Rio.

Material problems with the adapters and cutter teeth

The adapters and cutter teeth used by NedWorks at the start of the activities in Rio originated from batches delivered by KTM in December 2005 and early 2006. Some parts from these batches were used at the harbour entrance and also on another major dredging project in Brazil, carried out by NedWorks. The 'inferior' quality only came to light during activities at the entrance channel, during the second stage of the Rio project.

When investigating the causes of the problems during that time, NedWorks started to suspect that something was wrong with the cutter teeth. After a phone call to Rotterdam, the project manager commissioned Profile Testing, a specialist technical consultancy, on 15th August 2006 to test the adapters and teeth. Profile Testing pointed out that the tested parts did not meet the standard technical specifications. However, NedWorks neglected to inform Technix or KTM about these findings.

On 15th September 2006, NedWorks informed Technix of the problems that were encountered. From that moment on, Technix and KTM have done all in their power to limit the damages for NedWorks as much as possible by sending supreme, heavy-duty adapters and cutter teeth to the Rio site. This was done so as not to put the excellent business relationship with NedWorks in danger. The problem

was, however, that it would take a month to get these parts delivered to the right spot. The reason for this was that the new cutter teeth needed to be subject to a special heating treatment by a specialist subcontractor in order to harden them for heavy-duty work. This urged NedWorks to get surplus spare parts from other jobsites to the Rio project with speed delivery. Nedworks considered it fair that these extra materials and logistics costs were to be incurred by its suppliers.

At the end of September 2006, NedWorks held Technix liable for the incurred damages attributed to the poor quality of the delivered products. The claim represents a total sum of €1 162 739.85 (see Table 1).

TABLE 1 Damages incurred in Rio project with NedWork 345 as a result of poor quality cutter teeth and adapters.

Costs as a result of used poor quality teeth and adapters:	€248 000.00
Costs as a result of extra reparations for welding broken adapters:	€262 620.00
Transport costs incurred by supplying durable teeth and adapters:	€345 245.00
Idleness costs NedWorks 345 due to reparation stagnation:	€1 128 300.00
Subtotal:	€1 984 165.00
9% General costs:	€ 178 574.85
Total:	**€2 162 739.85**

Further developments

In spite of NedWorks' claim, Technix continued to supply to NedWorks. NedWorks' project manager in Brazil, Jack Nijsen, personally requested Willems to do so. In this way, the consequential damages of idleness of the cutter were limited to a minimum. Additionally, in order to decrease its dependency on Technix, NedWorks' purchase manager started to contact another supplier for the delivery of adapters and cutter teeth.

Starting 1st August, NedWorks did not send Technix any more written orders as they had previously. Despite repeated requests for formal purchase orders from Technix. Technix kept taking orders from NedWorks by telephone and continued supplying. Technix did not receive any additional complaints from NedWorks concerning the quality of the supplied goods or other delivery problems.

Starting late September, NedWorks stops paying for the parts delivered by Technix. A few months later, the total of Technix's outstanding invoices at NedWorks amounted to about €880 000.00. These invoices related to shipments that were accepted by NedWorks project management staff. That is, none of the shipments that were made had been rejected by NedWorks.

When Willems asked why his shipments were not being paid for, the NedWorks purchasing manager answered that payment would be suspended until the claim was paid by Technix.

Hans Willems was peering out of the window. The dark clouds hanging over Rotterdam resembled how he felt. KTM had to be paid soon for the components that they had shipped to the Rio site. If he could not solve the issue, larger interests were at stake. It was likely that KTM would see a good reason to break up the lucrative distribution agreement that Technix had had for so many years. Although Technix' financial position was healthy, this would change dramatically when they paid the claim. However, when no payments were made by NedWorks, there was little doubt that the bank would cut their credit limits and loans. He did not like the game that NedWorks purchasing manager was playing with him. What would he need to do to change the situation for the better?

Assignment

Imagine Technix calls upon you as an external consultant to solve this issue with NedWorks. Based on the above situation:

1. Would you feel NedWorks' purchasing manager has a strong case? Why? Why not?

2. Which solution would you suggest, respecting the interests of both parties?

3. How could these problems have been prevented?

APPENDIX 1

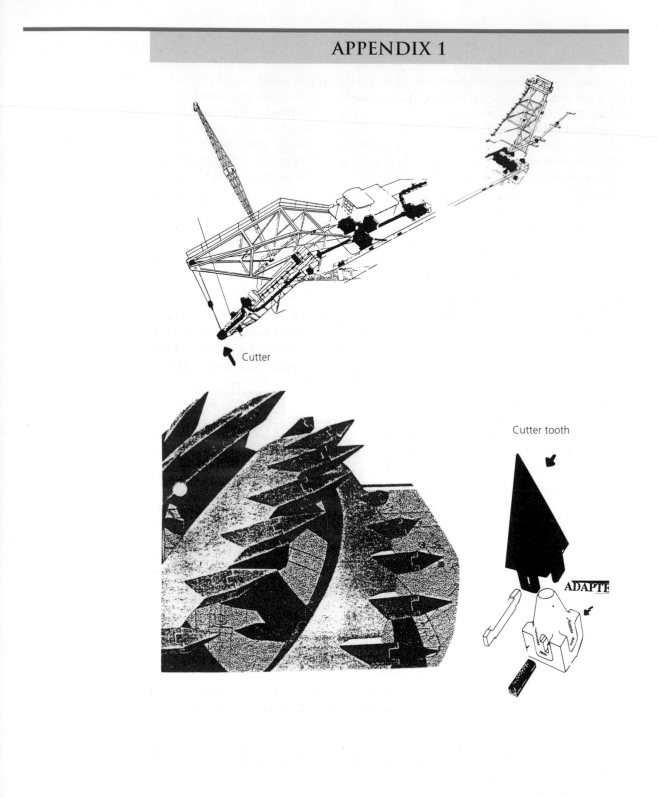

Cutter

Cutter tooth

ADAPTE

APPENDIX 2

General Conditions of Purchase
NedWorks BV

Article 1

The following definitions shall apply:

Buyer: NedWorks or one of its subsidiary companies.

Seller: The natural or legal person with whom the contract to supply goods has been concluded.

The goods: The object and/or services in the widest sense of the word as are specified in the order.

The order: The written instruction (in accordance with the present general conditions of purchase) from the buyer for the supply of goods.

The contract: The order, as such is deemed to have been accepted by the seller in conformity with article 2 hereof.

Article 2 Acceptance of the order

The order shall be deemed to have been accepted by seller at the moment of receipt of the order by seller. In the case where the goods have explicitly been offered 'without obligation' by seller the order shall be deemed to have been accepted by seller at the moment of receipt of the order by seller, unless seller has within 5 working days after receipt of the order notified buyer in writing that he does not accept the order.

Article 3 The contract

The contract shall be subject to no conditions other than those mentioned in the order to which the present general conditions of purchase apply. In the event of contradictions between the order and the present general conditions of purchase, the provisions in the order shall take precedence over the present general conditions of purchase.

Article 4 Information forming part of the contract

Drawings, calculations, models and all other documentation and/or information in connection with the contract and made available by buyer or as the case may be specially produced for buyer by seller shall remain the property of buyer or as the case may be become the property of buyer as at the moment when they have been produced for buyer's benefit in conformity with the contract. The foregoing also means that such documents must not be made available by seller to third parties or given to them for perusal. After execution of the contract they must be returned or as the case may be sent to buyer forthwith.

Article 5 Price

The price (prices) mentioned in the order is (are) fixed and irrevocable.

Article 6 Delivery time

1. Seller shall deliver the goods on the date laid down in the order. A contractual delivery period shall commence on the date on which the order is dated, except where explicitly agreed otherwise.

2. As soon as seller knows or expects that it will not be possible to deliver the goods on time, he shall without delay notify buyer thereof in writing, whilst mentioning the circumstances which are the cause thereof.

Article 7 Penalty

In the event of exceeding the agreed instalment(s) or date(s) of delivery, seller shall be liable to pay a penalty as is laid down in the order. The aforesaid penalty shall be applicable without prejudice to buyer's right to cancel the contract and/or to claim compensation by virtue of article 12 thereof.

Article 8 Delivery and transfer of ownership

1. Each delivery shall be made c.i.f. at the place of destination mentioned in the order.

2. The ownership of and risk for the goods shall transfer to buyer at the moment of delivery (at the place of destination). However, the provisions of article 10.3, article 12 and article 16.2 hereof shall remain in full force and effect.

Article 9 Quality
As regards their quantity, specification and quality the goods shall:

a. be in conformity with what is stated in the contract.

b. be of sound materials and good construction

c. be identical in all respects to the sample(s), model(s) or specification(s) which have been made available or furnished by seller and/or buyer. Specification shall be taken to mean the (technical) description of the goods as is included in the order, to which reference is made in the order or, failing such, that which is customary between the parties or is otherwise general practice.

d. be capable of providing the performance as defined in the order.

Article 10 Inspection and testing

1. Subject to the provisions of paragraphs 2 and 3 of the present article and subject to seller's obligation to carry out the necessary inspections himself buyer shall have the right to examine and test the goods during processing, manufacture or storage and hence prior to delivery, for which purpose seller shall provide the necessary facilities.

2. Regardless of whether buyer has made use of his right as described in the first paragraph of the present article, seller shall remain liable in full for the correct performance of the contract.

3. If, upon inspection and/or testing by buyer after delivery, it is found that the goods are wholly or partially not in accordance with the contract or do not in some other way comply with the standards set for such goods, buyer shall send to seller a notice of rejection. As from the day on which such notice is dated, the risk for the rejected goods shall pass to seller.

4. Unless explicitly agreed otherwise, seller shall during the construction period cause the required drawings, calculations and specifications to be sent in triplicate to buyer for his approval before a start is made on the building, manufacture or ordering of the relevant part. Approval from buyer shall not release seller from his liability for the soundness of the design and execution. Buyer shall return the approved drawings within 14 days after receipt.

5. Seller is obliged to carry out or to cause to be carried out all trials that have been agreed or otherwise necessary and the results of these shall be handed over to buyer. Upon being so requested seller is obliged to furnish authenticated certificates of trial.

Article 11 (hidden) effects
Seller is liable for all direct and indirect damage with the exception of consequential losses which buyer suffers as a result of (hidden) effects in the goods supplied and seller shall indemnity buyer against such damage.

Article 12 Non-fulfilment

1. If it should be found at any time that seller will not be able or has not been able to fulfil in good time or property all or part of his obligation arising from the contract, as well as in the event of seller's bankruptcy, suspension of payment of his debts, or discontinuation or liquidation of his business, buyer shall have the right to cancel all or part of the contract

without further summons and notice of default or legal proceedings being required for such purpose, and to claim compensation of costs, losses and interest. All claims which buyer may have against seller or which he acquires at a later date shall, in the event of cancellation of the present contract, be payable on demand forthwith and in full. The aforesaid right to cancel the contract, shall be without prejudice to buyer's right to demand full or partial performance together with compensation for costs, losses and interest.

2. If and as soon as buyer has cancelled the contract in full or in part, he shall have the right to return all or part of the goods to the seller for the latter's account and risk, on the understanding that buyer shall have the right to retain possession of such goods as security for the repayment of any purchase moneys already paid by buyer and for the reimbursement of any damage suffered or still to be suffered by buyer as a result of the non-fulfilment. Seller hereby declares that he will in such case pledge such goods in such manner to buyer, which pledging buyer hereby declares to accept.

3. Solely where the non fulfilment is or will be a consequence of circumstances beyond seller's control shall seller not be obliged to compensate the costs, losses and interest as referred above, provided that seller has notified buyer in writing without delay as soon as they know that circumstances have occurred, are occurring or will occur as a result of which seller has not been able to, cannot, or will not be able to fulfil its obligations in accordance with the contract.

Article 13 Guarantee

1. Seller guarantees that the goods are of good and sound workmanship and that they will comply, inter alia, with the requirements set forth in article 9 of the present general conditions of purchase. This guarantee shall be valid at least for a period of six (6) months after the putting into operation, within six (6) months after delivery, for a period of twelve (12) months after delivery of the goods, except where materials or goods delivered to seller under the contract have a longer guarantee period or where a longer guarantee period is specified in the order, in which case such longer guarantee period shall be applicable.

2. Without prejudice to what is provided elsewhere in the present general conditions of purchase, buyer may, in the case where any defect is observed in what has been delivered within the guarantee period as referred to in article 13.1 hereof, replace or repair the defective goods without delay and at a time and place to be determined by buyer. All costs involved in such replacement or repair shall be for seller's account.

Article 14 Sub-contracting

1. Without buyer's written permission, seller is not entitled to transfer the contract or any part thereof to third parties or to cause it to be performed by third parties or to contract out the agreed work to third parties, except where such relates to raw materials and/or parts of subordinate importance. The above shall not apply to that part of the delivery whose manufacturer is mentioned by name in the order or in the accompanying specification.

2. Seller shall at all times be fully liable, also in the case mentioned in article 14.1 hereof, for the performance of the contract and for damage caused in connection with such performance by him, by his personnel or by third parties.

3. Seller shall indemnify buyer against all claims by third parties in respect of or in connection with the contract.

Article 15 Material made available by buyer

1. Materials made available by buyer to seller shall remain the full property of buyer. Seller is obliged to use such materials solely for buyer's benefit and in accordance with the contract.

2. If within two working days after receipt of the materials supplied by buyer seller has not made a complaint to buyer with regard to such materials, the materials shall be deemed to have been made available to seller without defects in conformity with the contract.

Article 16 Postponement of delivery and storage

1. If buyer is unable for whatever reason to accept delivery of the goods on the agreed date, seller shall adequately store the goods or cause them to be stored and shall take measures to prevent a deterioration in their quality and/or any other damage.

2. As departure from the provisions relating at the moment of the transfer of ownership, the ownership of the stored goods shall in the case referred to in article 16.1 hereof, be transferred to buyer at the moment when seller has given notice that the goods are ready for delivery to buyer, transfer of ownership. Seller shall from that moment on retain possession of the goods on buyer's behalf; the goods must have been marked and individually, specified by seller as being buyer's property. During storage the goods shall remain for seller's risk. Seller shall take out adequate insurance for such goods. The costs of such insurance shall be reimbursed by buyer.

Article 17 Statutory requirements

Seller guarantees that the design, the composition, the construction and the quality of goods comply in all respects with all relevant requirements laid down in regard thereof in the legislation and/or in other government regulations relating thereto which may be in effect at the time of the delivery. All damage and costs resulting from non-compliance with the aforesaid requirements shall be for seller's account.

Article 18 Patents, etc.

1. Buyer shall hold the non-exclusive licence(s) in respect of any patent rights and/or other industrial property rights relating to the goods. Such licence(s) shall comprise:

   a. the authority to use the relevant patented and/or otherwise protected goods in buyer's own business and in that of his subsidiary companies, which shall include repairing and/or causing the repair of such goods;

   b. the authority to supply such goods, whether or not forming part of other goods, to third parties.

   The payment for such licence(s) is included in the price.

2. Seller shall indemnify buyer in full against all costs, damage and interest which may result from any infringement or alleged infringement of patents, licences, copyrights, registered drawings or design, trademark or trade name, relating to the goods supplied, yet on the understanding that such indemnification shall not apply if and in so far as the alleged infringement relates to a design, drawing or model of buyer which seller is copying for the purpose for which is was made available to them by the buyer.

3. If any proceedings should be instituted against buyer by virtue of the present article, he shall notify seller thereof forthwith and shall send the relevant information. Seller shall then ensure, by means of an amicable settlement or juridical proceedings, that buyer may have the goods at his free and unrestricted disposal. All costs relating thereto (including any payments made to third parties for the use of such industrial property rights) shall be for the seller's account. Except where they have the seller's permission, buyer shall refrain from undertaking any action with regard to the proceedings which have been instituted, unless seller fails to conduct the negotiations and/or court cases in an energetic manner, in which case buyer shall have the right to conduct or as the case may be to conclude the negotiations and/or court proceedings as they see fit for and on behalf of seller and for the latter's account. Seller shall be fully bound by the outcome of such negotiations and/or legal proceedings which have been conducted and/or concluded by buyer.

Article 19 Payment

If seller has complied with all obligations arising from the contract, seller shall invoice buyer to the agreed price, after which buyer shall make payment within forty (40) days after receipt of the relevant invoice. Buyer is entitled to set any payments, costs, damages and/or interest which are or will be payable by seller to buyer against any payment(s) due to seller.

Article 20 Applicable law and jurisdiction

Unless explicitly agreed otherwise, the contract shall be subject to the law of The Netherlands. All disputes which may arise from or in connection with the contract shall, unless an appeal is made to a higher court, be adjudicated solely by the competent court of Rotterdam.

APPENDIX 3

Specification damages sustained in Rio project with NedWork 345 resulting from poor-quality cutter teeth and adapters.

1. *Acquired and used cutter teeth and adapters of inferior quality:*

2960 Cutter-teeth type A-7654 at € 61,82	=	€ 183 000.00
313 Adapters type B-4780 at € 207,67	=	€ 65 000.00
Total:		€ 248 000.00

2. *Costs resulting from extra repairs for welding broken adapters. From week 34 up to and including week 50, 18 extra welders were employed for this.*

Weekly costs:	
18 Welders at € 545,00	€ 9 800.00
Local tax	€ 1 100.00
2 Helpers at € 320,00	€ 640.00
Fuel	€ 700.00
Electrodes	€ 2 350.00
Total: € 14 590.00 per 18 weeks	€ 262 620.00

3. *Transport costs incurred by supplying durable teeth and adapters:*

a. 3500 Teeth ex-Bahrain

Air cargo (Pre/AIR/0065-Sept 2006)	€ 216 370.00
Road transport	€ 2 100.00

b. 150 Adapters ex-South NedWork

Air cargo (Pre/ AIR/0087.1-Sept 2006)	€ 33 000.00

c. 40 Adapters ex-stock air cargo

(Pre/AIR/009-Sept 2006)	€ 10 225.00

d. 2 Cutters ex-Damman

Air cargo (Fre/AIR/0045-Sept 2006)	€ 20 500.00
Road transport Damman	€ 3 200.00
Road/ocean transport Miami-Rio	€ 9 500.00

e. Return of 2 cutters to Damman

Land/sea transport Rio/Miami (Oct. 2006)	€ 9 500.00
Sea transport Miami/Damman	€ 20 500.00
Road transport Damman/site	€ 3 200.00

   f. Return of 3500 teeth to Bahrain still to be carried out:

Sea transport	€ 13 450.00
Road transport	€ 2 250.00

   g. Return of 150 adapters to South NedWork

Still to be carried out	€ <u>1 450.00</u>
Total:	€ 345 245.00

4. *Idling costs NedWork 345 resulting directly from delivery of inferior quality cutter teeth and adapters.*

   Weekly costs:

NedWork 345	€ 234 250.00
Aiding equipment	€ 34 625.00
Floating pipeline	€ 16 250.00
Land pipeline	€ 8 750.00
Site overheads	€ <u>28 500.00</u>
	€ 322 375.00

   Idling time 3.5 weeks, therefore

Total: 3.5 weeks × € 322 375.00	€ 1 128 300.00

Subtotal	€ 1 984 165.00
9% General costs	€ 178 574.85
Total	€ 2 162 739.85

STRATEGY AND PLANNING

OUTSOURCING AND RISK MANAGEMENT

INTRODUCTION

This case on the following page explains what can happen to firms that act too fast in the area of outsourcing. Identifying and deciding between core and non-core activities within a firm is one matter; bringing this concept into practice is another. Companies must realize that when complex activities such as IT are outsourced to an outside specialist based upon a single source agreement, the risk profile of the company will change dramatically. It appears, therefore, that decision-making exclusively based upon economical and financial considerations may lead to disappointment. Later, at the stage of implementation, the perceived and expected savings and economies are often more than outweighed by the price the company has to pay for its total dependence on the partner that was selected. Such situations cannot be quickly improved.

The objective of this chapter is threefold. First, to determine whether and under what circumstances outsourcing is a successful business strategy. Second, to determine what the critical success factors of outsourcing are on a strategic, tactical and operational level. And finally, to identify the most important risks related to outsourcing decisions and how these can be managed. In this chapter, first the concept of outsourcing will be introduced by presenting the factors behind the growth of outsourcing as a business strategy and the different activities that can be outsourced. Then, in the next part the different definitions and concepts of outsourcing are presented, followed by the rationales for outsourcing. Finally, the risks related to outsourcing are discussed.

CASE STUDY OUTSOURCING OF IT . . .

The telecom market in many European countries has been a playing field of fierce competition over the past decade. Traditional, state owned telecom companies have been privatized and new players have entered the field. The period of unprecedented growth for mobile phones in many European markets has come to an end; as new technologies and applications have become more mature, value propositions have become more alike among the different providers, enabling consumers and businesses to shop around for the most attractive prices and rates. This is facilitated by the Internet, where consumers have better access to benchmark information, enabling them to go for the best rates and deals. This has put significant pressure on the fat margins of the providers, who as a result are desperately seeking for opportunities to slash costs. Moreover, most of them are seeking for opportunities to improve their cash position due to their careless decisions in the recent past to win government initiated tenders to obtain new technology licenses (such as UMTS and GPRS). The participation in these tenders, requiring billions of euros, has consumed most of the cash of these players.

Against this background a major telecom player in Europe looked for drastic measures to both reduce its operational cost dramatically and improve its cash position. After a careful selection of projects it decided to outsource all of its IT-activities and call centres. The outsourcing deal for IT, which was closed some years ago with one of the large IT-providers encompassed the sale and lease back of all hardware, peripherals and other IT-infrastructure and all software. The IT-provider, which was selected after a competitive tender, also had to take over most of the company's IT-staff. The future relationship was based upon a thorough long-term, service-level agreement, which consisted of a detailed description of the activities to be performed by the IT-provider, and the costs and rates that could be incurred. Of course the agreement described the impressive sum of money to be paid to the Telecom company. It was agreed that rates and fees would be paid to the IT-provider based upon a limited number of critical key performance indicators (KPIs), which would be monitored and discussed on a monthly basis between the parties involved. For this an impressive communication structure was built up at both organisations, involving several working groups, technical committees and steering platforms.

After two years it became clear to the telecom Account Team that things had not worked out as intended. First of all, the IT-provider was dissatisfied about the sums that were paid; in hindsight, since prices of hardware and software had gone down significantly, the IT provider thought it had paid far too much when buying the hardware and software. In order to secure its margin and recoup part of the investment it started to cut costs in its services to the telecom company. By putting inexperienced, lower paid staff on crucial service functions (such as help desks) the service level to the telecom's internal staff developed to a surprisingly low level, leading to all kinds of disruptions in simple, but crucial operational processes. Next, although the contract stipulated the use of leading edge technology and although investment schedules were agreed upon, the IT-provider postponed investments in new solutions. Furthermore, there was a constant debate about extra allowances, rates and fees to be incurred by the IT provider. The final development was that the IT provider warned that if bills were not paid by the telecom provider in time, this would lead to disruptions or even temporary stoppage of services. This all led to a situation where internal staff constantly started to challenge the outsourcing decision that was made. Most of the staff felt that the IT-provider was not up to its tasks and wanted to in-source most of the IT-activities again . . .

OUTSOURCING AS A BUSINESS CONCEPT

In an attempt to enhance their competitiveness, organizations are increasingly turning to outsourcing. Not only are changes in the business environment drivers of the rise in outsourcing as a business strategy, also new management concepts such as business process re-engineering, organizational restructuring, benchmarking, alliance management and **lean management** have stimulated the trend.

The Outsourcing Institute reported in 2000 that outsourcing in the United States had become a standard business practice across small and large companies in just about every industry. From 1996 onwards, outsourcing has grown at a tremendous rate. Outsourcing expenditures in 2000 in the US were around $340 billion and were expected to grow at a growth rate of 15%.

This trend is not only visible in the USA but in Europe and Asia as well, where the market for outsourcing has grown at a rate of double digits. The reason for this growth is that companies view outsourcing as a way to achieve strategic goals, reduce costs, improve customer satisfaction and provide other efficiency and effectiveness improvements. This makes outsourcing a mandatory business strategy for companies to compete in today's competitive market environment. In general, outsourcing is viewed as one of many approaches to maintain or develop competitive advantage. (Quinn and Hilmer, 1994; Gilley and Rasheed, 2000).

The types of activities that are outsourced have evolved over time. Starting out with *activities* more and more entire business *functions* are being outsourced. In 2005, Monczka *et al.* (2005) conducted a large-scale survey of outsourcing practices in the United States. They concluded that companies pursued outsourcing broadly in many activities. Outsourcing was particularly conducted for information technology, distribution/fulfilment, legal/regulatory, manufacturing/operations, engineering/detailed design and call centres (see Figure 8.1).

As outsourcing for many firms is not just a trend, but more and more a viable business strategy, the questions on how to successfully engage in outsourcing and how to stay successful in an outsourcing relationships are very important. These, therefore, are addressed next.

Lean management
A philosophy that focuses on the elimination of waste in all forms and the efficient flow of materials and information throughout the value chain to obtain faster customer response, higher quality and lower costs.

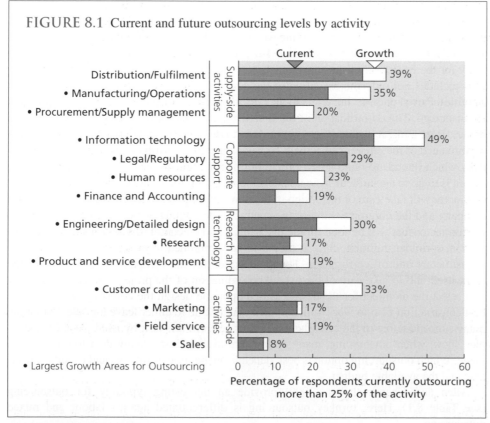

FIGURE 8.1 Current and future outsourcing levels by activity

Percentage of respondents currently outsourcing more than 25% of the activity

Source: Monczka *et al.*, 2005, p. 21

DEFINITIONS AND CONCEPTS

Definitions on outsourcing are abundant. In general, outsourcing can be described as the transfer of activities that were previously conducted in-house, to a third party. Ellram and Billington (2001) see outsourcing primarily as 'the transfer of the production of goods or services that had been performed internally to an external party.' A wider definition is reported by NEVI (2000): 'Outsourcing means that the company divests itself of the resources to fulfil a particular activity to another company, to focus more effectively on its own competence. The difference with subcontracting is the divestment of assets, infrastructure, people and competencies.' We favour the definition as provided by Axelsson and Wynstra (2002), who define outsourcing as: 'The decision and subsequent transfer process by which activities that constitute a function, that earlier have been carried out within the company, are instead purchased from an external supplier.' Major characteristics of outsourcing are: (1) that activities that initially were performed in-house are transferred to an external party, (2) that assets, knowledge and, in some cases, people go over to that external party, (3) that there will be an extended relationship between the parties involved over a longer period of time, (4) that in transferring the activity to the external party the buyer is exposed to both a cost and risk profile, both of which are new to the companies involved.

Outsourcing may come in different forms. Companies may decide to go for a nearby or distant solution. **Offshoring** relates to the commissioning of work to a provider in a low-cost country. In many cases offshoring is concerned with outsourcing of (IT) services. Other terms, which are used are 'nearshoring' and 'onshoring'. Nearshoring concerns outsourcing of activities to nearby low-cost countries. Onshoring concerns outsourcing of activities to providers which are operating in the same country as the customer organization.

Now that the basic definitions of outsourcing have been discussed, two additional types of outsourcing can be presented. In line with Chapter 2, we differentiate here between turnkey (integral) and **partial outsourcing. Turnkey outsourcing** applies when the responsibility for the execution of the entire function (or activities) lies with the external provider. This includes not only the execution of the activities, but also the co-ordination of these activities. Partial outsourcing refers to the case in which only a part of an integrated function is outsourced. The co-ordination of the function and activities still lies with the client (the buyer). Here a major problem is of course how to demarcate the responsibility for the final performance of the outsourced activity between the parties involved. An example is a company which intends to build a new office. In principle, the company has two options. One option is to go to a contractor who will develop and build the office turnkey. In this case the contractor will take care of the design of the new building, the selection of the construction company and the commissioning of the contract. The contractor may even arrange for the subcontractor that will be used for the mechanical and electrical installations (heating, ventilation, sprinkler, lighting, etc.). It may also be summoned to provide the office with all infrastructure and office furniture. The other option for the company is to do most of the work itself and to take care of the overall co-ordination of the project. Here, the company will select the architect for the design. Based upon the design the company will select the best construction firm to work with and then may decide to either leave the selection of the many subcontractors to the construction firm or perform this task by itself. As these examples show, when outsourcing, many options are available and many decision need to be made. Which outsourcing option is best, depends on the time, resources and expertise available and the available budget.

Allen and Chandrashekar (2000) provide an interesting typology for outsourcing (see Table 8.1). Here, turnkey outsourcing is differentiated against labour and mixed outsourcing.

Offshoring
Offshoring relates to the commissioning of work, which was previously done in-house, to a provider in a low-cost country. In many cases, offshoring is concerned with outsourcing of services.

Outsourcing, partial
Partial outsourcing refers to the case in which only a part of an integrated function is outsourced. The co-ordination of the function and activities still lies with the client (the buyer).

Outsourcing, turnkey
Turnkey outsourcing applies when the responsibility for the execution of the entire outsourced function (or set of outsourced activities) lies with the external provider. This includes not only the execution of the activities, but also the co-ordination of these activities.

TABLE 8.1 Forms of outsourcing services

	Labour outsourcing	Mixed outsourcing	Complete outsourcing
Contractor provides ...	■ Some employees	Some or all of the following: ■ Employees ■ Materials ■ Process and Systems ■ Technology and Equipment ■ Facilities ■ Management/Supervision	■ Employees ■ Materials ■ Process and Systems ■ Technology and Equipment ■ Facilities ■ Management/Supervision
Host firm provides ...	■ Some employees ■ Materials ■ Process and Systems ■ Technology and Equipment ■ Facilities ■ Management/Supervision	Some or all of the following: ■ Employees ■ Materials ■ Process and Systems ■ Technology and Equipment ■ Facilities ■ Management/Supervision	■ Programme management

Source: Chandrashekar 2000, p. 26

This categorization is about the same as the two types of outsourcing that we identified, because 'labour outsourcing' essentially can be considered as a specific form of partial outsourcing.

Table 8.2 gives an overview of the advantages and disadvantages of the two types of outsourcing.

TABLE 8.2 Partial versus turnkey outsourcing

	Advantages	Disadvantages
Turnkey outsourcing	Buyer has minimal responsibility for outsourced processes	The buyer has limited influence on the determination of the price and little insight in cost structure of provider
	Buyer doesn't need to have experience with similar projects	The buyer has limited influence on the staff, technology and materials used and their quality
	The project generally goes smoothly for the buyer	Large dependence of buyer on provider resulting in high commercial, technical and performance risks
Partial outsourcing	The buyer has more influence on prices, rates and costs	The buyer is required to have knowledge of the separate parts of the outsourced function/activities
	The buyer has more influence on the staff, technology and materials used and their quality	The buyer is required to have the organizational capacities to co-ordinate and integrate the outsourced function/activities
	Specific advantages can result in cost reductions	Communication and co-ordination problems between parties involved can be a cause of delay and disappointment

Two important dimensions of outsourcing are the decision to outsource and the transfer of the function being outsourced. Both are usually highly complex processes in organizations. A company that opts for outsourcing can decide whether it prefers partial or turnkey outsourcing, based on the advantages and disadvantages each type has.

RATIONALES FOR OUTSOURCING

Research shows that there are different reasons for firms to engage in outsourcing. Due to the development of outsourcing as a business strategy, these reasons may range from just tactical to more strategic.

Tactical reasons are to reduce control costs and operating costs, to free up internal resources, to receive an important cash infusion, to improve performance and to be able to manage functions that are out of control. Strategic reasons may be to improve company focus, to gain access to world class capabilities, get access to resources that are not available internally, to accelerate reengineering benefits, improve customer satisfaction, increase flexibility and share risks.

As Figure 8.2 shows, cost and focus seem among managers in the USA the primary drivers of outsourcing, with more than 80% of the companies indicating that cost reduction (operating cost and capital investment) and the need to focus on the core business led them to outsource activities.

All these reasons underlie one overall objective: to improve the overall performance of the outsourcing firm and increasing revenues by enhancing the company's value propositions to its customers.

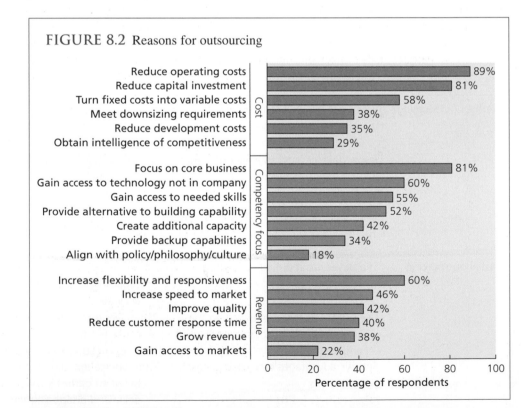

FIGURE 8.2 Reasons for outsourcing

Source: Monczka *et al.*, 2005, p. 22

Next, the considerations underlying outsourcing may be either capacity related or expertise related. When the company has not enough capacity to perform the requested service it can opt for outsourcing. This type of outsourcing is defined as 'capacity outsourcing'. When the expertise to perform the activity at the required quality level or for an acceptable cost level is no longer present, the company can also opt for outsourcing. This type of outsourcing is referred to as 'specialist outsourcing'.

Deciding about outsourcing is a delicate matter. It is not a purchasing affair. When should companies decide to go for outsourcing and when would they be better off keeping activities in-house? Here, the outsourcing matrix can provide purchasing managers with some guidelines (see Figure 8.3; Savelkoul, 2008). Figure 8.3 shows that the decision to outsource is dependent on two variables, i.e. the strategic importance of a specific competence to the company and the level of competitiveness relative to suppliers. Based upon these variables companies can choose between four options. Clearly, when a company has a high level of competence relative to external providers and, at the same time, the competence involved actually differentiates the company from its competitors, outsourcing is not an option. Hence, the company would go for an in-house solution. Outsourcing of activities should clearly be considered if the company scores low at both variables. When a specific activity is not strategic but the company has a fair competence in it, it should continue to keep this activity in house as long as it can perform at a competitive level. In the last case, when an activity is strategic for the company, but its competence is relatively low, it should seek long-term collaboration or partnerships. As an example may serve the alliances that large electronic manufacturers have established with key component suppliers (like IBM with Intel).

Apparently, as the case at the beginning of this chapter illustrates, there are risks and disadvantages associated with outsourcing. These may relate to loss of control, loss of critical skills and knowledge, loss of intellectual property, loss of security, service quality drops, increase in cost and loss of innovative capability. As a company moves some or a larger part of its assets to a specialist service provider, it must realize that its risk profile will dramatically change. In general, its ways of working with the external provider will need to be much more disciplined and organized than when working with internal departments. Working with internal departments allows, in general, for much more flexibility than working with an external partner, who will often refer to the contractual agreements

FIGURE 8.3 The outsourcing matrix

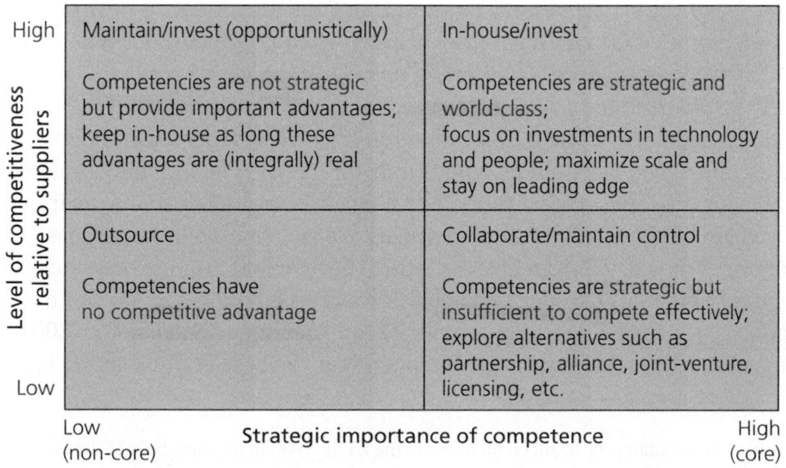

Source: Savelkoul, 2008

TABLE 8.3 Advantages and disadvantages of outsourcing

Advantages	Disadvantages
Freeing up of cash: investments can be concentrated on core activities	Increased dependence on suppliers
Optimal usage of knowledge, equipment and experience of third party	Continuous follow-up and monitoring of the supplier relationship is necessary
Increased flexibility: fluctuations in the workload can more easily be absorbed	Risks of communication and organizational problems during the transfer of activities to a third party
Outsourcing leads to easier and more focussed primary processes in the organization	Risk of leakage of confidential information
Input through an independent party's point of view which reduces the risks of introvert short-sightedness in the organization	Depending on balance of power between parties: inability to execute contractual performance incentives and penalties
	Risk of losing essential strategic knowledge

made when special requests are made by the customer or when the customer wants to initiate changes in its requirements. One of the most important challenges in dealing with outsourcing is how to deal with the change in the balance of power that usually turns in the favour of the service provider. We will discuss this aspect later in this chapter.

Table 8.3 provides a general picture of the advantages and disadvantages of outsourcing.

Success of outsourcing as a business strategy

It is difficult to be able to determine the success of outsourcing as a business strategy, because the external factors in the before and after situations may have significantly changed. Determining the success of outsourcing in terms of cost savings is not an easy task, because often it is almost impossible to determine the costs of the function/activity before it was outsourced due to all kinds of hidden costs that are involved. When outsourcing has been selected as a favourable business strategy due to different reasons other than obtaining cost savings, it is even more difficult to assess the success of outsourcing in an objective manner. This is probably one of the reasons that in the literature not much evidence can be found on the success or failure rate of outsourcing as a business strategy. Another reason might be the fact that outsourcing is often poorly evaluated so that data is just not available. Since academic research is scarce on the actual results of outsourcing decision-making, we need to turn to the research that has been conducted by some international research agencies. Lyons (2001) reported that '76% of the outsourcers rate their outsourcing as either good or extremely good value for money. The rest thinks that the value is average. Nobody considers it to be poor. The IT sector is least likely to rate their outsourcing as good value'.[1] Gartner (2003) reported that: 'Satisfaction with the business benefits from outsourcing contracts fell from 86% in 2001 to 50% in 2002 among board-level executives in Western Europe . . . European companies wasted €6 billion due to poor deal structures and poorly managed relationships with IT outsourcing companies in 2002 . . .',[2] During that period, Michael Corbett (2002) reports that 'The use of outsourcing is growing

[1]As reported from a survey among 71 financial directors in the FTSE 1000 in the industries IT, finance, engineering, logistics/distribution and business consultancies.
[2]Press release from Gartner, Inc, a research and advisory firm on its annual Outsourcing and IT services summit in London.

stronger . . . Satisfaction with service providers is strong but there are some concerns. Only 60% of executives are satisfied with their outsourcing initiatives and only 11% of the executives are very satisfied . . . '.[3] Monczka *et al.* (2005) reported that 9–31% of the companies reported that outsourcing initiatives were falling short of their expectations and goals. Obviously, the success of outsourcing as reported by the various researchers varies enormously. Despite these mixed results, both in the USA and in Europe outsourcing as a business strategy and as a market continues to grow at a fast rate.

THE OUTSOURCING PROCESS

This paragraph describes the basics of the **outsourcing process**. First, the outsourcing process and its importance is introduced. Then the three different phases of the outsourcing process will be discussed and the factors that contribute to their success. In the next paragraph the critical success factors derived from the discussion on the outsourcing process and other literature will be presented.

Outsourcing process
The outsourcing process can be structured around essentially three distinct phases: a strategic phase (why, what, who?), a transition phase (how?) and an operation phase (how to manage?).

The outsourcing process can be structured around different elements. Most authors would agree that essentially three distinct phases can be identified: a strategic phase (why, what, who?), a transition phase (how?) and an operation phase (how to manage?). Based upon these phases, Momme and Hvolby (2002) present a framework that identifies six generic steps of outsourcing that provide guidance to the outsourcing process (Figure 8.4).

Strategic phase

During the strategic phase three essential questions have to be answered by a firm. The first question relates to the objective of the firm with regard to its intent to outsource a certain activity. The next question that has to be answered is what activities are considered for outsourcing. The final question is what qualifications a supplier should be able to meet in order to qualify as a potential future partner for providing the activity concerned.

Companies may have, as we have seen earlier, many motives for outsourcing. Whatever the reason, the decision to outsource should support and enable the company's overall strategy. As we have seen earlier, motives that are cited most are: (1) focus on core competence, (2) focus on cost efficiency/effectiveness and (3) focus on service (Brandes *et al.*, 1997). This implies that the strategy of the outsourcing company should be aligned with these three motives and that the outsourced activities should contribute to this strategy.

The second question relates to *what* should be outsourced. In other words: which activities or which function are candidates for outsourcing? In the literature two important

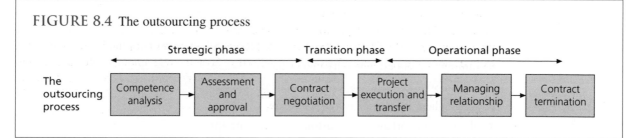

FIGURE 8.4 The outsourcing process

Source: Adapted from Momme *et al.*, 2002, p. 71

[3]Data from the 1999 Outsourcing Trends Study. The data from this study reflect the opinions of a variety of private and public sector executives, industry experts, and a small number of non-US managers.

***Transaction cost
approach***

*The transaction cost
approach is based on
the idea of finding a
governance structure
to arrive at the lowest
cost possible for each
transaction and com-
paring whether to
perform an activity
internally or out-
source the activity in
the market.*

approaches are used to answer this question, i.e. the **transaction cost approach** and the core-competence approach.

The transaction cost approach is based on the idea of finding a governance structure aimed at arriving at the lowest cost possible of each transaction that is made comparing whether to perform an activity internally or outsource the activity in the market. Williamson (1983, 1985) is one of the founders of the transaction costs theory. He defines transaction costs as the costs that are associated with an exchange between two parties. The assumption underlying the transaction costs approach is that an exchange with an external party is based on a contract. The (potential) costs associated with establishing, monitoring and enforcing the contract as well as the costs associated with managing the relationship with the external party are all considered to be part of the transaction costs as well as the costs associated with the transaction itself. Therefore, all of these costs should be taken into account when deciding between make or buy options.

The level of the transaction costs depends upon three important factors (Ellram and Billington, 2001). These factors are the frequency of the transaction, the level of the transaction-specific investments and the external and internal uncertainty. The frequency of the transaction is an important factor because the more frequent exchanges occur between partners, the higher the total costs that are involved. The level of the transaction-specific investments also determines the level of transaction costs, because transaction specific investments are investments that are more or less unique to a specific buyer–supplier relationship. Examples are investments in specific supplier tooling (such as moulds and dies) by a large automotive manufacturer and the change costs involved when choosing a new accountant (internal staff needs to get accustomed to the new accountant, the new accountant needs to be thoroughly briefed to get acquainted with the company, etc.). These examples show that investments are made in assets as well as in human capital. Obviously the higher these investments are, the higher the transaction costs will be. The last factor that determines the transaction costs is the external and internal uncertainty. Uncertainty is a normal parameter in the decision-making process. It can be defined as the inability to predict contingencies that may occur (Williamson, 1983). The higher these uncertainties, the more slack a supplier wants to have in presenting his proposal and rates and the more difficult it will be to make a fixed price or lump sum contract that deals with all uncertainties beforehand. Therefore, the higher the level of uncertainty, the higher the transaction costs will be.

***Core competence,
approach***

*The core competence
approach is based on
the assumption that, in
order to create a sus-
tainable competitive
advantage, a company
should concentrate its
resources on a set of
core competencies
where it can achieve
definable pre-eminence
and provide a unique
value for the customer.
Therefore, it should
outsource all other
activities.*

The other approach on which an outsourcing decision can be based is the **core competence approach**. This theory is based, among others, on the work of Quinn and Hilmer (1994). The core competence approach is based on the assumption that, in order to create a sustainable competitive advantage, a company should 'concentrate its resources on a set of core competencies where it can achieve definable pre-eminence and provide a unique value for customers . . . [hence, it should] strategically outsource all other activities' (Quinn and Hilmer, 1994, p. 43). The important question to be answered here is: what are the firm's core competencies? Quinn and Hilmer (1994) suggest that characteristics of core competencies are:

- skills or knowledge sets, not products or functions
- flexible, long-term platforms that are capable of adaptation or evolution
- limited in number: generally two or three
- unique sources of leverage in the value chain
- areas where the company can dominate
- elements important to the customer in the long run.
- embedded in the organization's systems.

The competencies that satisfy these requirements are the core competencies of the firm and provide the firm its long-term competitive advantage. These competencies must be closely protected and are not to be outsourced. All other activities should be procured from the market if these markets were totally reliable and efficient. Besides core versus non-core competences, Arnold (2000) differentiates between four types of activities:

- company core activities: activities that are necessarily connected with a company's existence
- close-core activities: the activities that are directly related to the core activities
- core distinct activities: the supporting activities
- disposable activities: activities with general availability.

Arnold suggests that the outsourcing decision framework based upon the work from Quinn and Hilmer (1994) needs adjustment. He proposes a general framework for outsourcing decisions, that is based upon both the transaction cost theory and the core competence approach (Figure 8.5). This framework may serve as a vehicle to practitioners when answering the *what*

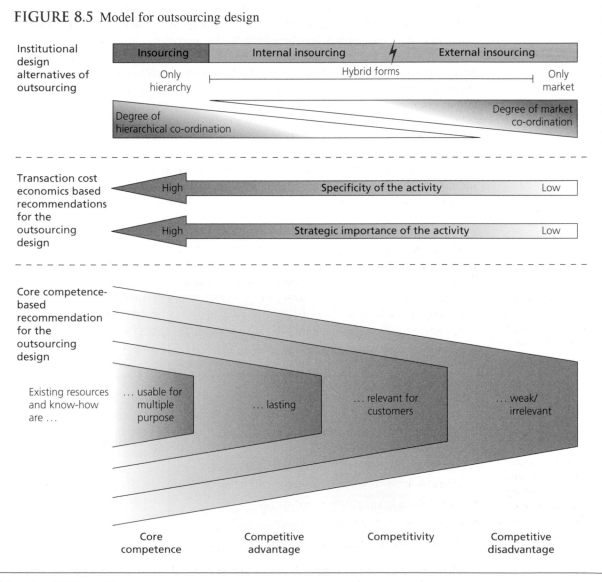

FIGURE 8.5 Model for outsourcing design

Source: Arnold, 2000, p. 26

question. The functions or activities that are candidates for outsourcing are those that can be found in the right part of the model, i.e. the functions or activities that have low transaction costs and that are non-core for the existence of the firm.

The final question to be discussed is that of to whom the function should be outsourced. After the decision to outsource has been made, it is essential that the right supplier is chosen. A supplier has to be selected that has the necessary technical and managerial capabilities to deliver the expected and required level of performance. Also the supplier should be able to understand and be committed to these requirements.

The supplier selection process is key to the success of the buyer–supplier relationship Companies that make extensive use of supplier selection and monitoring practices in supplier partnerships seem to be more successful then the companies that don't make use of these practices (Ittner *et al.*, 1999). An adequate supplier selection model seems crucial for a successful outsourcing decision.

Momme and Hvolby (2002) present a four-phase model (Figure 8.6). This model provides some guidance on how to identify, evaluate and select outsourcing candidates and therefore is an appropriate tool to use in the strategic phase (see Figure 8.5, phases 1 and 2). It also gives a brief guidance for the transition (phases 2 and 3) and the operational phase (phase 4), but needs to be elaborated for that purpose.

Also Axelsson and Wynstra (2002) emphasizes the importance of the supplier selection process and provides some important aspects to consider, such as supplier market structure, supplier capabilities, supplier improvement capacity, strategic fit, conditions for collaboration and others.

The transition phase

After the strategic phase in which the outsourced activities and supplier have been identified, the transition phase starts. The transition phase consists of the contract negotiation and the project execution and transfer (see Figure 8.3). The most important

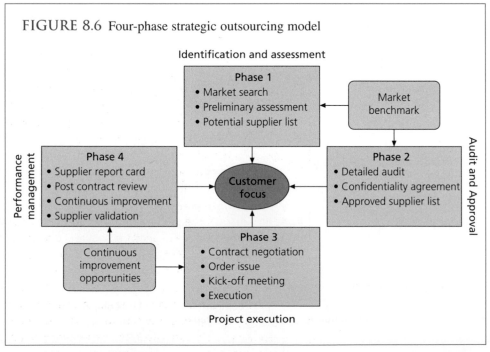

FIGURE 8.6 Four-phase strategic outsourcing model

Source: Momme *et al.*, 2002, p. 191

issue in the contract negotiations is the contract itself. Also it is important to keep in mind that the contract negotiation in an outsourcing agreement is often the start of a long-term relationship, so not only the contractual issues should be dealt with but the people issues and the importance of a sound and cooperative relationship should be covered as well.

The contract is the legal basis for the relationship and is therefore the key document in the outsourcing process. It allows both organizations to maximize the rewards of the relationship, while minimizing the risk. This makes the outsourcing contract a key success factor for the establishment of a strategic outsourcing relationship (Deckelman, 1998). The contract and the type of contract should reflect the business plan (the goal of the cooperation) the two parties have and should be reasonable to both parties.

There are different types of contracts. The type chosen depends on the characteristics and the scope of the contract and the function or activities that are outsourced. NEVI (2000) suggests eight types of contracts (Table 8.4). A service level agreement (SLA) is a special type of contract. An SLA defines the required (minimum) service that the supplier has to provide. The SLA should have the following features: (1) reflect the overall business goals, (2) be objective, (3) be measurable and (4) be comparable against pre-established criteria. The SLA should be a living document and be able to change when business conditions or client requirements change. Also the contract should specify the required actions if the service levels are not achieved.

Contract, lump sum
Contract is based upon a fixed price (per period) for executing the project or a certain activity.

Contract, reimbursable
Contract in which the buyer agrees to pay the supplier all materials costs and employee hours against predetermined hourly rates and margin for services rendered (identical to time and materials contracts).

TABLE 8.4 Types of contract

Lump sum turnkey	Contract is based upon a fixed price (per period) for executing the project or a certain activity
Reimbursable turnkey (In some cases also referred to as 'time and materials contract')	In this situation the provider is compensated for all costs that he incurs for executing the project or a certain activity
Semi-lump-sum turnkey	Part of the work is compensated for on a fixed price basis; the other part is compensated on a reimbursable basis
Lump sum fixed price	The supplier agrees to complete the work against a fixed price based upon a predefined, detailed scope of work. Everything that is not included in the scope of work is settled between parties on an ad-hoc basis
Cost reimbursable	The supplier agrees to complete the work on an open book, open cost basis, based upon a general scope of work. There is no sharing of savings
Guaranteed maximum contract	The same as a cost reimbursable contract, only the outsourcer pays to a certain agreed maximum. The extra costs are for the supplier
Share the savings/loss (target price contract)	The services are paid for on a reimbursable basis. When the contract costs are higher or lower than the original budget (target price), the difference is shared between parties on a pre-agreed basis
Unit rate	Rates are agreed for regular, routine activities, the size of which cannot be anticipated. Rates are defined per square metre of paintwork, metre of cable to be installed, etc. Payments are made based upon the actual number of units produced during the completion of the work
Service level agreement (SLA)	An SLA describes the performance, which needs to be delivered by the supplier. Key performance indicators (in terms of cost, service and quality levels) are agreed by both parties. Payment to suppliers is based upon specific rates plus a bonus or minus based upon actual performance versus targeted performance

As said before, the type of contract has a great impact on the success of the joint operations. One of the key issues in the contract phase is whether to use incentives and penalties in a contract. The idea of using incentives and penalties in a contract is generally supported and seen as a critical success factor for the output of an outsourcing agreement. Incentives enable the provider to work as a partner and enable the partners to work together towards joint goals. They also enable both parties to profit from successful achievement of the goals. Incentives motivate the service provider to perform beyond targets. The use of incentives, however, is only possible when both parties agree on the goals of in the contract, the level of service that has to be provided and the performance measurement system.

The type of contract and the use of incentives is just one of the many issues to be discussed in the contract negotiations. There are many other 'ingredients' in an outsourcing agreement. They include the following:

- Scope of services. The description of the services that will be provided.

- Term of the agreement. The duration of the contract, this depends on the objective of the outsourcer. Usually short-term contracts are favoured.

- Rates, fees, incentives. The pricing and fee structure should be clear to both parties.

- Termination plan. When the relationship is terminated, it should be executed in a fair and equitable manner, without resulting in disruption of service. Also items such as ownership of data, intellectual property and so on should be agreed upon on forehand.

- Conflict resolution. It is very important to manage the relationship in such a way that conflicts are resolved in a cooperative manner. In the contract an informal conflict resolution method can be arranged. But also the formal dispute resolution method should be arranged.

- Communication. A communication plan is a key document of the contract. It should contain guidelines on reporting, staff communication, periodic meetings, etc.

- Management and control. The parties should develop procedures for managing and performing the services. This part of the contract can contain many different subjects, such as a manual for day-to-day operations, guidelines for subcontractors, the supplier's obligation to work with customer's technical standards, etc. Also this document should contain a section on how changes in the contract should be handled. Also the mandate, the degree to which the supplier is empowered, of the supplier should be defined.

- Other. A contract can contain many more items than discussed above. These include: warranty, confidentiality, audit rights, transfer of assets, escalation clauses, etc.

After the contract is signed and all the issues in the preceding phases have been dealt with, the outsourced function has to be transferred to the supplier. The key activities in this phase are establishing the basis for supplier integration, defining the workflow interfaces and adapting the organization to the transfer of activities to the supplier.

The outsourcing transition can be a very complex event. The transfer should be conducted using project management principles. This approach includes the assignment of a dedicated project manager by both the customer and the service provider. The project transition manager should in fact manage all phases of the implementation and would act as the centre point of contact. Furthermore, they would see to the preparation of a sound transition plan. This plan is a document that identifies the steps that must be made to accomplish a successful transition. Also a project timeline needs to be set up, with designated milestones that need to be formally signed off. The last phase before going live is a test phase in which the supplier's organization is tested against the contract requirements. Obviously an important task for the outsourcing company is to provide training and support for the supplier's staff if necessary.

The operational phase

After the transition phase has been completed successfully, the operational phase of the outsourcing process starts. This operational phase consists of two processes: (1) managing the relationship and (2) contract termination.

Managing the buyer–supplier relationship management is one of the, if not *the*, critical stage in the outsourcing relationship. Achieving the goal of the outsourcing relationship is impossible without close co-operation between the parties involved. When the relationship is not properly managed, the conditions for close cooperation will not be present and the outcome of the outsourcing relationship will be far from optimal. In an article from Greco (1997, p. 54), a director of strategic resources of a large brewery is quoted, 'the true value of outsourcing comes after the relationship has had time to develop and additional synergies have emerged. Creating a sustaining, long term relationship with a supplier is exciting; it's where the win-win is really beginning to show.'

Many researchers have published on the characteristics of a successful buyer–supplier relationship. The top five of these include the factors trust, flexibility, team approach, shared objectives and open communication. In a study on a sales environment between manufacturers' and their customers McQuiston (2001) identifies a conceptual model for building and maintaining the relationship between business partners. The author identifies six core values as being critical to the success of these relationships. These six core values are supported by four supporting factors. The parameters in this conceptual model seem to be consistent with other outsourcing literature. The factors found by McQuiston to be core to a successful outsourcing relationship are presented in Table 8.5.

Successful outsourcing relationships are performance driven. The performance of the service provider should be measured against the agreed service level on a regular basis and be benchmarked against the performance of other providers in the same business when possible. Both the buyer and the supplier are responsible for this process. But in an outsourcing relationship it has to be clear which party is responsible for what. A common mistake made by a buyer is not only to feel and act responsibly for the measurement process, but also to feel and act responsibly for the execution of the contract. Successful outsourcing requires a shift in mindset from the buying organization. The contract manager, the person responsible for the relationship, should manage paper rather than people. However, he should be careful not to be too detailed in prescribing the supplier what is needed. Quinn (1999) gives the following opinion: 'A primary reason for outsourcing is to leverage the supplier's greater skills, knowledge basis, investments and processes. If the buyer specifies the job in detail, it will kill innovation and violate the real advantage.' So, the buyer must explain *what* it is they want, in terms of services and results, but leave it to the supplier to determine *how* these results are achieved.

The contract review process should be a recurring process in which the outsourcing organization assesses the alternatives to prolonging the relationship with the outsourcing provider. These alternatives are either to replace the current supplier with a new supplier,

TABLE 8.5 Core values and supporting factors of an outsourcing relationship

Core values	Supporting factors
Shared goals and objectives	Developing a personal relationship
Mutual dependence	Having professional respect
Open lines for communication	Investment of effort by top management
Concern for the other's profitability	Commitment to continuous improvement
Mutual commitment to customer satisfaction	
Trust	

obviously based on proper research or bringing the activity or function in-house again. This is only a viable option when the knowledge and capacity in the organization has not gone and when the business context has changed so much, that the decision to outsource this function apparently has to be reviewed.

RISK ASSESSMENT

Based upon the above it will be clear that managing outsourcing relationships goes far beyond dealing with traditional buyer–seller relationships. Due to the fact that both parties engage in a long-term relationship many aspects need to be taken into consideration. This is particularly true for those outsourcing relationships in which the parties involved have no history or have not built up experience (see also Chapter 2 on organizational buying behaviour). In those cases companies will try to cover for all kinds of risks and uncertainties that they perceive to be associated with their future relationship. In such cases, where trust and interpersonal relationships are not present, parties will arrange for dealing with these risks and uncertainties by detailed contracts. Of course, the discussions and dealings on these contracts (and the many contract clauses involved) will require a lot of stamina and energy from the executives that are involved. When legal specialists (lawyers) enter the scene too early, it will appear that negotiations and discussions get lost due to the fact that the letter of the text of the contract becomes more important than the intention with which it was initiated.

Based upon our experience, we feel that outsourcing contracts are associated with the following kinds of risks:

Risk, technical
This kind of risk is related to the extent to which the provider is able to provide the desired functionality and performance.

- *Technical risks.* This kind of risk is related to the extent to which the provider is able to provide the desired functionality and performance. The degree of risk is related to the question of whether the actual performance to be delivered by the provider can be stated in objective terms. Outsourcing contracts should be preferably based upon an output or outcome specification rather than on an input or process specification (see Chapter 5). Technical risk is related to the question of how to maintain crucial knowledge in the company over the time that is needed to manage the outsourced activity effectively, how to secure that the supplier will apply leading edge technology and solutions, how to make sure that supplier staff is capable and remains capable of doing its job.

Risk, commercial
Commercial risk is related to the uncertainty with regard to the price we will pay and the costs that we will incur when having outsourced our activities to the supplier.

- *Commercial risks.* Commercial risk is related to the uncertainty with regard to the price we will pay and the costs that we will incur when having outsourced our activities to the supplier. Covering this type of risk requires an in-depth knowledge of the cost structure of the activities that are conducted by the supplier, the key cost drivers and the underlying cost parameters. Commercial risk also relates to the extra cost and allowances we have to pay when the supplier needs to deviate from the agreed scope of work (allowance for extra work or paying less for less work). Commercial risks can be reduced by using incentives and penalties for above average or below average performance. A final aspect relates to IP (intellectual property): how to prevent sensitive information from leaving the company uncontrolled or, even worse, gets known to our most important competitors. Therefore a confidentiality agreement will be a necessary part of the outsourcing contract.

- *Contractual risks.* Does the contract describe in sufficient detail the performance that is expected from the supplier? Do the performance indicators that have been defined sufficiently cover what needs to be accomplished by the supplier? Have sufficient arrangements been made should (1) the scope of work or (2) the resources that have been agreed upon to be used by the supplier changed? Should things go wrong, can the penalties actually be enforced in the relationship with the supplier, without destroying the relationship or without putting the service delivery by the supplier in immediate danger? Did we make sufficient arrangements for dealing with subcontracting issues? These are aspects that need to be considered when assessing the contractual risks.

■ *Performance risks*. These risks relate to the chance that the supplier is not capable of doing the job it was hired for. Does the supplier have sufficient capacity and flexibility to meet our fluctuating requirements? Do we have sufficient capacity and information to trace and track the supplier's operational processes? What if the supplier is not able to meet the agreed targets on service levels, quality and cost?

Risk, performance
These risks relate to the chance that the supplier is not capable of doing the job it was hired for.

The risks that are described here are related to the change of the balance of power between the contractor and the provider. As a result of outsourcing, the contractor becomes much more dependent, and usually for a long period of time, on the provider, who after the initial period (when people, assets and knowledge have gone over to them) may find themselves in a more powerful position. In deciding about outsourcing, therefore, this dependency and the associated risks need to be carefully balanced against the anticipated cost savings.

Before coming to an agreement with an outsourcing partner, a careful risk analysis must be made. After the objectives and the deliverables of the services to be provided by the provider have been defined, it is useful to analyse all factors that may impede the realization of the agreement and deliverables. These risk factors should be assessed on the basis of two criteria: (1) the negative impact on the company's financial performance or operations, and (2) the likelihood with which the risk factor probably would occur. Based on these two criteria, a risk assessment matrix can be developed (see Figure 8.7), that allows the development of specific risk mitigation strategies and activities per risk factor. Of course, most efforts should be concentrated on those risk factors that would represent both a high negative impact on the company's performance and that could occur with high probability.

Risk, matrix
Risks are assessed based on two criteria, i.e. (1) the negative impact on the company's financial performance or operations and (2) the likelihood with which the risk factor probably would occur.

As business-to-business relationships may change over time and the business scene may change rapidly, this analysis and the resulting fall back scenarios should be regularly reviewed and discussed. In this way unpleasant surprises in the relationship with the service provider may be prevented.

FIGURE 8.7 **Risk matrix:** systematic analysis of risk factors

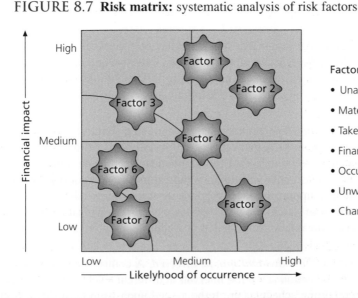

Factors:

• Unavailability of qualified staff

• Materials shortages

• Takeover of provider by competitor

• Financial problems at provider

• Occurrence of unforeseen disputes

• Unwillingness of provider to invest in new technology

• Change of key management positions

Many authors over time have pointed out, that in dealing with these risks, detailed contracts will not solve the problem. Many times the importance of trust and partnership in the relationship are stressed. Developing trust and an atmosphere of partnership, however, is easier said than done. It is our observation that the level of trust seems to be conversely related to the size and complexity of the contract: the more suspicious parties are, the higher the need for an all encompassing, legal contract. The more mature the relationship between the parties, the less the need to put everything in writing. Therefore, we feel (in line with Chapter 2) that the best chances for successful outsourcing relationships are predominantly present between parties that have already been dealing with each other for a long time in other business areas or activities. The less familiar buyer and seller are, the more they should refrain from complex outsourcing deals. In the next chapter we will see that having historical bonds and a good personal relationship are necessary, but not sufficient conditions for making partnership in general and outsourcing in particular a success. Rather, a careful strategic positioning and a sound balance of power between the parties seem to be just as important.

CRITICAL SUCCESS FACTORS OF OUTSOURCING

At the end of this chapter we provide an overview of the most important critical success factors that should be considered prior to engaging in an outsourcing relationship with an external provider. Here, we have take the ideas that originally were suggested by the Outsourcing Institute (www.theoutsourcinginstitute.com) as a point of departure for our discussion. This Institute considers the following factors as critical for success in outsourcing:

- *Understanding company goals and objectives.* The motive to start with an outsourcing process has to be in line with the overall business strategy. When a company has decided to outsource part of its manufacturing, since it considered this activity as non core to its business, it should not reconsider this decision when going through an economic recession.

- *A strategic vision and plan.* Outsourcing should not be conducted to solve just an operational problem, e.g. solving people issues and capacity problems related to IT. The activity or function that is a candidate for outsourcing should be assessed thoroughly and the potential benefits, risks and resistance to be met from the internal organization should be analysed beforehand.

- *Selecting the right vendor.* An exhaustive supplier selection process is recommended. The future provider should be selected on the basis of a cohesive and consistent set of criteria related to the supplier's technical and managerial capabilities, as well as the extent to which future visions and strategies and culture aspects at different levels of the organization are shared.

- *A properly structured contract.* The contract that is negotiated should be fair for both parties, the basis of it being an SLA that reflects the overall goals of the relationship. Preferably the performance to be delivered by the provider need to be translated in a limited set of objective, measurable performance indicators that are comparable over time. The contract should support the idea of going for a long-term relationship. The goal of the contract therefore should not be a win–lose, but a win–win situation. In the contract all the aspects of the relationship such as procedures, communication, termination, etc. should be arranged.

- *Open communication with the individual groups involved.* A communication structure would require frequent interaction at regular intervals at different levels of the organisations involved. Also reporting schedules are to be agreed upon from both sides. Both parties could agree on joint training programs in order to make everyone aware of the new environment and new ways of running the processes involved.

- *Ongoing management of the relationship.* Performance incentives should be considered in order to motivate the supplier to meet and exceed expectations. Contract management is vital to the success of the outsourcing agreement.

- *Senior executive support and involvement.* Since outsourcing usually relates to complex decision-making, large sums of money and a long-term commitment from the company, top management support is crucial for making it happen.

- *Careful attention to personnel issues.* Outsourcing will affect the ways of working and routines of all people involved. Jobs will change or even disappear. New tasks will emerge. It is therefore important that staff is informed and prepared timely on what management expects from them. Management of people issues therefore is crucial.

One of the most important factors for the success of outsourcing is also the way the company is strategically positioned vis-à-vis its future provider. It is our view that the company should have strategic control over its provider. When the company becomes totally dependent on the provider, the outsourcing relationship may backfire: it may show, that when people, assets and knowledge has been transferred to the provider, the provider will after some time engage in discussions on raising prices and rates (often by a considerable percentage). The provider actually may engage in slowing down its services to its customer in order to enforce concessions from its customer. Therefore the essence of making sound outsourcing decisions lies in a careful analysis of the expected cost economies and operational benefits against the change in risk profile and provider dependency. In the next chapter we will introduce a portfolio method which can be used to assess these risks and dependencies.

SUMMARY

This chapter has shown that outsourcing as a business strategy has become very popular in many industries, not only in the USA but also in Europe and Asia. From the type of activities that are outsourced it can be derived that the interest in outsourcing as a business strategy is growing, because, apart from individual activities, business functions are being outsourced. Based upon its popularity, it might be concluded that outsourcing is a successful business strategy. However, as we have seen in this chapter, it is difficult to determine the real success of outsourcing. There are many reasons for a company to go for outsourcing. Most companies start outsourcing to benefit from cost advantages and to create more focus. Based upon studies by consultants in this field outsourcing leads to mixed results, which is why we feel it should be approached with great caution and care.

Outsourcing relates to a strategy whereby a company decides to move an activity, that was conducted in-house, to an outside provider. An important characteristic is that, when doing so, it transfers important resources (in terms of assets, knowledge, people) to its future service provider. As a result outsourcing decision-making is surrounded with great uncertainty and complexity. Offshoring is a similar strategy to outsourcing. However, it usually relates to services and a situation in which the provider is located in a low-cost country.

Although it is difficult to determine the success of outsourcing, it is still possible to determine the factors that can influence the outcome of outsourcing. A careful outsourcing process is crucial for its success. This process consists, as we have seen, of three important phases, i.e. the strategic, transition and operational phases. In the strategic phase the outsourcing decision and supplier selection process are key issues to be dealt with. In the transition phase, deciding on the proper type of contract and negotiating the final contract are key elements. During the operational phase getting superior service delivery and management of the relationship are key issues. From these three phases the most important overall success factors have been identified.

As we have argued, it is important to align the outsourcing strategy with overall corporate strategy. At this stage expectations and objectives to be met by the outsourcing project need to be defined in detail. First, the issue of what activities should be considered, core to the company, need to be addressed. Next, potential cost savings through outsourcing non-core activities or business functions should be validated using a transaction cost analysis approach. Then, a project proposal can be prepared outlining what activities should be outsourced and what performance should be expected from an external provider. Based upon this information the supply market should be thoroughly analysed in order to be able to find the partner that best meets all qualifications. Apart from technical competences, the vision and strategy, management style, and organisational culture should fit with those of the outsourced company. Since trust is an important element, providers should be favoured with whom the company has already a relationship. The basis of the future relationship consists of a detailed service level agreement in which the most important key performance indicators are defined, and which are used to validate and monitor actual supplier performance. Penalties and incentives may be part of this contract to stimulate the supplier to exceed expectations. It is the role of the contract manager to monitor progress based upon this contract and to regularly review whether actual performance levels are met by the supplier. In this way they should support the project manager, who primarily deals with operational and people issues.

As a result of outsourcing, the traditional balance of power between the outsourcing company and its provider changes dramatically. The customer will become much more dependent on its provider, which is why a careful risk assessment should be part of the preparation. We have differentiated between technical risk, commercial risk, contract risk and performance risks, which are all affected when entering into a complex outsourcing relationship. These analyses should result in a picture of how dependent and vulnerable the company will be vis-à-vis its future partner. This picture could be made using the risk assessment matrix that was presented in this chapter. In all cases the company should avoid a too large dependency and vulnerability, which is why outsourcing should be avoided in some cases.

ASSIGNMENTS

8.1   In business many terms are used to describe purchasing and contracting activities. What would you consider to be the most important differences between purchasing, subcontracting and outsourcing? Discuss.

8.2   Looking at the case study before the Introduction of this chapter: what went wrong at the telecom company? What would the telecom company need to do in order to get more control over its provider?

8.3   What would you consider to be the most important elements of an outsourcing contract? Provide at least 15 items that you would need to arrange for apart from the usual contract terms and conditions (such as price, delivery, quality).

8.4   When outsourcing an activity that was conducted in house to another firm what kind of resistance would you likely meet and what would be the consequences for organizing this kind of event? What would you consider to be the role of the buyer i.e. contract manager?

8.5   As a result of outsourcing, the outsourcing company would become more dependent on the supplier. What could a company do in order not to become too dependent on a specific supplier? What would you recommend to the outsourcing company to be able to exert some degree of control over its supplier?

REFERENCES

Allen, S., Chandrashekar, A. (2000) 'Outsourcing services: the contract is just the beginning', *Business Horizon,* March–April: 25–33.

Arnold, U. (2000) 'New dimensions of outsourcing: a combination of transaction cost economics and the core competence concept', *European Journal of Purchasing & Supply Management,* 6:23–9.

Axelsson, B., Wynstra, F. (2002) *Buying Business Services*, New York: John Wiley & Sons.

Brandes, H., *et.al.*, 1997 Outsourcing – success or failure? European Journal of Purchasing & Supply Management, 3(2):63–75.

Deckelman, B. (1998) 'Strategic outsourcing: the contractual perspective', *Outsourcing Journal,* May: http://www.outsourcing-journal.com/may1998-legal.html

Ellram, L., Billington, C. (2001) Purchasing leverage considerations in the outsourcing decision, *European Journal of Purchasing & Supply Management,* 7:15–22.

Gartner, Inc. (2003). 'Gardner Says Outsourcing Grows in Declining European IT Services Market', Press release 28th of April 2003, Egham, UK.

Gilley, K.M., Rasheed, A. (2000) 'Making more by doing less: An analysis of outsourcing and its effect on firm performance', *Journal of Management,* 26(4): 763–90.

Greco, J. (1997) 'Outsourcing: the new partnership', *Journal of Business Strategy,* (July–August):48–54.

Ittner, C.D., *et al.* (1999) 'Supplier selection, monitoring practices and firm performance', *Journal of Accounting and Public Policy,* 18:253–81.

Lyons, T. (2001) Outsourcing survey 2001, www.tarlolyons.com

McQuiston, D.H., (2001) 'A conceptual model for building and maintaining relationships between manufacturers' representatives and their principals', *Industrial Marketing Management,* 30:165–81.

Michael F. Corbett & Associates, Ltd. (2002) Highlights from the 1999 Outsourcing Trends Study.

Momme, J., Hvolby, HH. (2002). An outsourcing framework: action research in the heavy industry sector, *European Journal of Purchasing and Supply Management,* 8:185–96.

Monczka, R.M., Carter, J.R., Markham, W.J., *et al.* (2005) *Outsourcing Strategically for Sustainable Competitive Advantage*, Tempe, AZ: Center for Advanced Research Studies.

NEVI (2000) *Working Group Outsourcing,* CD-ROM.

Quinn, J.B. (1999). 'Strategic outsourcing: leveraging knowledge capabilities', *Sloan Management Review,* (Summer): 9–21.

Quinn, J.B., Hilmer, F.G. (1994) 'Strategic outsourcing', *Sloan Management Review* 36 (Summer): 43–55.

Savelkoul, R. (2008) 'Creating value in the 21st century, public lecture', Eindhoven University of Technology, 25th February.

The Outsourcing Institute (2000) 'Effectively managing the outsourcing relation', www.outsourcing.com

Williamson, O.E. (1983) *Markets and Hierarchies: Analysis and Antitrust Implications: a Study in the Economics of Internal Organization*, London: Collier MacMillan.

Williamson, O.E. (1985) *The Economic Institutions of Capitalism*, New York: Free Press.

PURCHASING AND BUSINESS STRATEGY

LEARNING OBJECTIVES

After studying this chapter you should understand the following:

- The changing international business context and how companies strategically respond.
- The increasing strategic role of the purchasing function.
- How purchasing can support the company's overall competitive strategy.
- How to develop a differentiated purchasing and supplier strategy.

INTRODUCTION

Increasingly, suppliers are being acknowledged as important sources for competitive advantage. This chapter discusses the strategic role that purchasing and supply management may represent to manufacturing and service companies and how to develop differentiated supplier strategies to support the company's overall product/market and business strategies.

PURCHASING AND COMPETITIVE STRATEGY

Over the past decades the competitive situation of West European industry has changed dramatically. European manufacturers experience far more competition from countries that were not considered as major producers until some years ago (e.g. Korea, Hong Kong, Singapore, Thailand, Taiwan and China). Industry in Western Europe seems to be under-represented in the areas of new technologies and emerging new industries (e.g. the computer industry, telecommunications, computer chips). Looking at most industrial sectors in Europe it seems that many industries are at the stage of market saturation or decline (see Memo 9.1).

As a result of this situation, the long-term strategy of many companies nowadays focuses on 'selective growth', i.e. a combination of enhancing the core activity and new

CASE STUDY INTEGRATED SUPPLY CHAIN MANAGEMENT HAS BECOME A WAY OF LIFE AT CESSNA AIRCRAFT

As recently as 1997, the aircraft manufacturer had little strategic supply chain process. Relationships with suppliers were adversarial (except in engines and avionics) and it showed: contract prices rose 3% per year, incoming quality was running at 50 000 parts per million (ppm) and on-time delivery was 65%. Buyers spent their time placing purchase orders and expediting orders.

While Cessna was successful at producing and marketing business jets (it had 50% of the market), shareholder and customer expectations were rising. Management realized that if it wanted to maintain the company's leadership position, Cessna would have to shift gears. Charles B. Johnson, president and chief operating officer, recalls, 'As our supply chain processes house the majority of our cost, it was necessary to create a more strategically aligned supply chain that yielded the most competitive quality, delivery, flexibility and value.' His strategy: transform a tactical materials department into an enterprise-wide supply chain process.

The man for the job was Michael R. Katzorke, senior vice president, supply chain management, a seasoned purchasing veteran who had worked for such companies as AlliedSignal and Honeywell. Under his leadership, the supply chain management organization at Cessna has created a long-range strategic plan and cross-functional commodity teams that have worked to rationalize the company's supplier base; developed a tool called Maturity Path Development that aligns supplier strategy with that of Cessna's; revamped the company's sales, inventory and operations plan (SIOP) improving performance to customer expectations and reducing inventory turns; implemented use of Malcolm Baldrige National Quality award criteria and Six Sigma quality tools to drive improvement in supplier performance and introduced a value analysis/value engineering process that encourages supplier involvement in removing cost from the supply chain.

Katzorke and the supply chain management team have involved the company and its suppliers in supporting Cessna's corporate 'high five' objectives of total customer satisfaction, world quality standard for aviation, breakthrough operating performance, top 10 company to work for and superior financial results.

In the past 5 years, these activities have yielded such outstanding improved business results as:

- 86% improvement in supply chain quality
- 28% improvement in material availability
- 113% improvement in production inventory turns
- significant cost take-out in the supply chain through a strategic supply chain management process integrated into Cessna's overall business plan
- 62% reduction in production suppliers from the transition of phase-out to growth suppliers.

'These achievements have translated directly into improved customer satisfaction and improved financial results for the shareholder,' says Johnson. Aircraft quality is significantly improved. Defects resulting from supplier quality issues are down, reducing the number of production test reflights. Parts availability – which 5 years ago was about 65% to schedule – is consistently at 99%, while inventory turns continue to improve.

Cessna concluded 2002 with the highest revenues ($3.2 billion) in its 75-year history. While the aircraft manufacturer is experiencing some challenges related to the economy in 2003, it still introduced two new aircraft (Citation Mustang and Citation CJ3) late last year to ensure future growth.

'Perhaps the biggest achievement of Katzorke and his team,' says Johnson, 'has been the engagement of the organization in the Cessna supply chain transformation process from a transactional purchasing organization to an integrated full supply chain process.'

For these reasons Cessna Aircraft Co. is the 2003 recipient of *Purchasing* magazine's Medal of Professional Excellence.

Source: *Purchasing*, September 4th, 2003, pp. 25–35

business development and innovation. One consequence of this strategy is that companies consistently outsource those activities that are not considered to belong to their 'core business' (see Chapter 8).

In general, the following reasons may underlie this trend:

- Increased outsourcing and subcontracting, as a result of make-or-buy studies. Based on internal and external cost price studies, carried out in the context of a so-called 'competitive benchmarking programme', a manufacturer of office equipment discovered that particular manufacturing activities could not be carried out competitively any longer. The internal manufacturing costs appeared to be much higher than the costs of external suppliers. This prompted the manufacturer to start a 'make-or-buy' programme. As a result the company decided to focus its manufacturing on a higher level of assembly. At present, modular components are being sourced from a limited number of preferred suppliers. The company focuses on design, assembly, marketing and sales, and most component manufacturing has ceased. The same trend is observed in other companies. For example, a manufacturer of electronic appliances decided to standardize its production technology and to focus on large series production in the near future. As a result specialized activities such as stamping, lathe work and plastic moulding were contracted out to external suppliers.

- Buying of finished products instead of components. Due to the high labour costs level in some European countries, it is hard for some enterprises to compete. For example, Western Europe is expensive for the clothing and apparel industry to operate in. This industry is experiencing heavy competition from 'low-wage countries' and as a result there has been a dramatic shift of production capacity to low-cost countries. Large retailers buy the raw materials, which are then sent together with the design to 'low-wage countries', where the end products are made.

- Turnkey delivery. Manufacturers of specialized optical instruments often have to supply their products including sophisticated measuring devices. As a rule these costly devices need to be purchased by the manufacturers from specialized suppliers. To cite another example: manufacturers of industrial fencing need to deliver their products' turnkey (at the buyer's request), which means that they have to take care of all installations including safety and surveillance equipment (camera's, keyless entry systems). These relatively expensive products also need to be obtained from specialist suppliers. As a result the purchasing share for these manufacturing companies in the project cost has increased considerably.

- Technological development. In some industries the technology develops at such a pace that even large manufacturers cannot afford the investments needed to keep up. Take for example the computer manufacturers who obtain their microprocessors from specialized suppliers, or the manufacturer of compressors who has to rely on specialized foundries to be able to benefit from new developments in casting technology. Other examples are manufacturers of mobile phones and PDAs, who use a multitude of technologies coming from a wide array of specialist suppliers.

In summary, the ever-changing competitive situation in many Western European industries requires that management of many manufacturers focus on their core activities. Specialist activities outside the scope of these core activities are increasingly farmed out. As a consequence, purchasing's share in the cost price of many end products is steeply rising. Hence, purchasing decisions will have an even greater influence on the company's financial result. That is why management has become increasingly aware of the purchasing function. The consequences of these developments for integrating purchasing in the company business strategy will now be discussed.

MEMO 9.1   HOW INDUSTRY LIFE CYCLES AFFECT THE ROLE OF PURCHASING AND SUPPLY MANAGEMENT

The competitive situation of West European industry has changed dramatically over the past two decades.

As a result of improved transportation, the rapid progress in information technology and the increased *globalization* of markets, competition (from the Far East in particular) has increased. This competition is manifest in both conventional and new products, and their associated technologies.

Looking at the industrial structure of most European countries, a relatively large number of industries are in the phase of saturation or decline. There are relatively few European companies with a strong position in new, emerging industries, i.e. industries that are in the introduction or growth phase (see Figure 9.1). Most industrial activity (and employment opportunities!) in Europe seem to be situated in the latter two stages of the industry life cycle.

There are apparent differences in competitive strategy depending on the stage in the industry life cycle.

In the stages of introduction and growth, companies obtain a market position through research and development, product development, the introduction of new models and varieties and improvement of existing products. Research and development and, of course,

marketing, aimed at tailoring products and services to the requirements of specific market segments and target groups, are key success variables here. In the stages of saturation and decline, however, the company can only maintain or reinforce its market position if it is able to sell end products (of basically the same quality and service level) at very competitive prices.

Technology in these stages is mature and not subject to significant changes. In other words, during these stages of the industry life cycle measures aimed at cost reduction, quality improvement and lead time reduction play a major role in maintaining or reinforcing the market position. Contracting out non-core activities to specialized suppliers can serve all these objectives. This explains the rising purchasing-to-sales ratio of many industrial enterprises, including Xerox, Electrolux, Philips Electronics, DAF Trucks, Alcatel, Volvo, over the past few years. This in turn results in an increased awareness among top-management of the strategic value of the purchasing function. This Memo also demonstrates the lasting nature of this interest, since no major changes in favour of European companies are expected in the international competitive situation over the next few years.

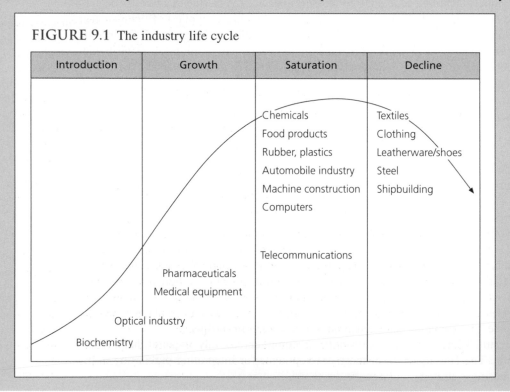

FIGURE 9.1 The industry life cycle

Introduction	Growth	Saturation	Decline
		Chemicals	Textiles
		Food products	Clothing
		Rubber, plastics	Leatherware/shoes
		Automobile industry	Steel
		Machine construction	Shipbuilding
		Computers	
		Telecommunications	
	Pharmaceuticals		
	Medical equipment		
	Optical industry		
Biochemistry			

COST LEADERSHIP AND DIFFERENTIATION: CONSEQUENCES FOR MANUFACTURING AND PURCHASING STRATEGY

Every company's goal is to develop a distinctive, sustainable competitive advantage. Only then will the company be able to guarantee its long-term survival. For many years the question of how to obtain such a position has received a lot of attention in the literature. One of the most interesting books on this subject is still the classic written by Porter (1980): *Competitive Strategy*. According to this author, there are three basic strategies that can lead to a distinguishing market position:

- **Cost leadership**. The main focus of this strategy is to continually work at reducing the cost price of the end product. If a company succeeds in marketing products at a lower cost price than its competitors, it will achieve a satisfactory return. Companies that employ this strategy usually have a strong financial-economic orientation, expressed in meticulous budgeting and reporting procedures and strict control of overheads. This type of strategy is usually only successful if a large market share can be obtained. This makes it possible to manufacture in large volumes, on streamlined production lines, with specialized production equipment.

    This strategy must also pay attention to aspects such as quality and service, but costs come first. Its application is illustrated by some automobile manufacturers (General Motors, Chrysler, Ford), a few computer manufacturers (manufacturers of PC-clones) and some manufacturers of domestic appliances.

- **Differentiation**. This strategy aims at marketing products which are perceived by the customer as being unique. Product individuality can be in the design (Swatch watches), the logo (Lacoste), the technology (Apple), service (American Express) and many other dimensions. Combinations are also possible; in addition to a high-quality technical product, most truck manufacturers have an after-sales service organization that can supply parts within 24 hours all across Europe. In this way these manufacturers anticipate and respond to the problem of downtime which is experienced by every hauler: every hour the truck does not run costs a lot of money! A differentiation strategy aims at creating customer loyalty and brand preference, thereby reducing the importance of price.

- **Focus strategy**. This strategy aims to serve a specific, clearly defined group of customers in an optimal way. Examples are to be found primarily in the industrial sector (relatively small paper finishing companies that concentrate on finishing the products supplied by printers), or in transportation (some haulers are equipped specifically for the transportation of clothing, furniture or computers). A focus strategy means that the company studies the activities of the customer group, becomes familiar with their operational requirements, and provides specific solutions.

The importance of Porter's (1980) classification is that the company will have to make a clear choice between these strategic alternatives. The consequence of not making a choice is that the company will be unable to build up a sustainable competitive advantage in the end-user markets. This will probably result in a mediocre return accompanied by a small market share!

This reasoning seems simple, but applying it in practice is something else. Many entrepreneurs have a hard time in making a choice. They frequently want everything at the same time – very high quality and high customer service at the lowest price!

Limiting ourselves to the first two strategies, in Porter's view a company cannot realize both simultaneously because the necessary infrastructure in terms of technology, organization and company culture is different for each of the strategies.

strategy, cost leadership
The main focus of this strategy is to continually work at reducing the cost price of the end product. If a company succeeds in marketing products at a lower cost price than its competitors, it will achieve a satisfactory return.

strategy, differentiation
This strategy aims at marketing products which are perceived by the customer as being unique. Product individuality can be in the design (Swatch watches), the logo (Lacoste), the technology (Apple), service (American Express) and many other dimensions.

strategy, focus
This strategy aims to serve a specific, clearly-defined group of customers in an optimal way. A focus strategy means that the company studies the activities of the customer group, becomes familiar with their operational requirements and provides specific solutions.

A company that strives for cost leadership will emphasize cost reduction. Since inventories raise costs, they are kept as low as possible; investments in automation are analysed with regard to their efficiency; strict budget systems and budget reports prevent cost overruns. The production tasks are prepared in detail and, to run as efficiently as possible, breakdowns in production must be prevented at all times. Because everything has been prepared so thoroughly and high-quality technical production equipment is used, there is no reliance on improvization or human creativity. Production managers are judged on the capacity utilization of their machines and changes in production planning are not really acceptable, because they would result in production loss and therefore increased costs. Production companies that strive for cost leadership are usually large, integrated companies that take advantage of effects of scale through vertical integration (textile industry, food products industry, producers of insulation materials).

The company that applies a differentiation strategy operates in a completely different way and there is much less attention to costs (although they are not ignored). A company that wants to respond flexibly to customer requirements is constantly searching for opportunities to reduce internal lead times.

Production utilization may vary over time, which means that personnel must be able to perform different tasks. Flexibility, a high level of education, and a strong identification with the company are important here. Budgeting can be less detailed since it is known that capacity planning is never fully realized.

A company that wants to differentiate in the area of technology must invest continuously in its people and machines. A well-equipped development and design function guarantees a steady stream of innovative products and the quality of the end product.

In practice, elements of both cost leadership and differentiation will often be found. However, the descriptions demonstrate that the choice between them has far-reaching consequences for the design of the production strategy and the organizational structure. It goes without saying that the consequences for the production organization will have to be translated in terms of purchasing and supplier strategy. Cost leadership and differentiation require totally different types of supplier networks and therefore different purchasing and supplier strategies.

In the case of cost leadership, price and costs are central in the negotiations with the supplier. An important criterion for supplier selection is not so much delivery time, but delivery reliability. Regular failure by the supplier to comply with delivery requirements results in production failures, which in turn may result in high costs. Rejection of incoming materials should be prevented for the same reason. Therefore, these suppliers need to deliver right on time all the time and deliver flawless quality.

In the case of differentiation the emphasis is much more on collaboration and co-operation with the supplier. Suppliers will be involved in new product development, process and product improvement, lead time reduction and activities that allow for better flexibility. It is important that there is a direct relationship between the technical experts from the supplier and the company's product development experts and engineering staff, which is why a central purchasing department can have a disruptive effect in this type of company. The buyer is more or less the intermediary between the technical specialists and the supplier market and therefore needs to have a sound technical background.

LEAN MANUFACTURING

Porter's ideas on competitive strategy have influenced management thinking for a long time. Over the years his basic beliefs about competitive strategy have been put to the test by some major Japanese and US manufacturers, who seem to have been able to combine the elements of a low-cost strategy with the advantages of a differentiation strategy. The core concept through which they are able to do this seems to lie in what has been designated as lean management. This concept originated first in an extensive study on the automotive industry, conducted by the Massachusetts Institute of Technology (MIT) during the early 1990s (Womack *et al.* 1990). Lean management is a philosophy concerning how to run a manufacturing organization. It covers all aspects of the business system in general, including design, and manufacturing and supply management in particular. Fundamental to lean management is that:

> *it transfers the maximum number of tasks and responsibilities to those workers actually adding value to the car on the line, and it has in place a system for detecting defects that quickly traces every problem, once discovered, to its ultimate cause.*

> (Womack *et al.* 1990, p. 99).

Important features of lean management are the teamwork among line workers, who are trained in a variety of skills to conduct different jobs within their working group. These not only relate to manufacturing tasks; workers are also trained to do simple machine repairs, quality checks, housekeeping and materials ordering. Next, lean management uses simple, but comprehensive information display systems that make it possible for everyone in the plant to respond quickly to problems and understand the plant's overall situation. Furthermore, in lean management there is a total commitment to quality improvement on the shop floor. Workers are encouraged to think and act positively on how to improve the effectiveness of their work, whereas their supervisors need to provide active support to bring these ideas to reality. It will not come as a surprise that the lean management concept has been inspired by Japanese manufacturing practices.

Japanese manufacturers spend considerable time and effort on the design of new products. First, the manager in charge of new product development has far greater authority to make decisions than a Western counterpart. Second, product and process engineering are integrated responsibility areas. Third, the engineering manager decides on who to involve in the engineering team and for what period. These are significant differences compared with how engineering projects are organized in Western manufacturing companies.

The most important differences are apparent, however, in the way that Japanese manufacturers manage their supply chain (see also Lamming 1993):

- The average supply base is much smaller than for Western manufacturers. Most Japanese manufacturers are dependent for a large part of their business on their suppliers and the power balance is definitely to the manufacturer's advantage. As a result OEMs have organized their suppliers into regional supplier associations which meet several times per year in order to learn about the future product/market plans of their customers.

- Most Japanese OEMs have a 'layered' supplier structure, which is often three or more tiers deep (see also Chapter 12 for more background information on this subject). Assemblies and subassemblies (such as seats, engines and gearboxes) are assigned to first-tier suppliers ('main suppliers'), who in turn rely on a team of second-tier suppliers for specialist components, and so forth.

- Suppliers are usually involved in new product development at a very early stage. It is not uncommon for Japanese OEMs to delegate half of the engineering hours to their first-tier suppliers. Engineers from the manufacturer and the supplier may work full time at each other's premises when solving technical problems or working out improvements.

- Suppliers are confronted with well-defined targets in terms of quality improvement, lead-time reduction and cost reduction and are, by means of a simple though effective grading and performance measurement system, fully informed as to whether they meet their cost, quality and delivery performance targets.

Since the principles of lean management extend to marketing, design, manufacturing and supply management, Japanese manufacturing companies have been able to obtain impressive results, which has put them in terms of productivity at a safe distance from their foreign competitors. Supply and supplier management is definitely one of the cornerstones of their success. Most impressions on lean management are related to the (Japanese) automotive industry and we have to be careful about generalizing. However, for this type of manufacturing environment, the ideas of Porter clearly need to be refined. As Japanese producers have demonstrated it is indeed possible to combine high variety output with low cost, provided that the right infrastructure and drivers are in place.

In previous sections the influence of the corporate strategy on the purchasing and supplier strategies has been discussed. It has become clear that the contents of the purchasing strategy depend on whether the company in question pursues a cost leadership strategy, a differentiation strategy or lean management. The next section shows how to integrate purchasing into business strategy.

INTEGRATING PURCHASING INTO BUSINESS STRATEGY

In designing their overall business strategy top management will have to make explicit decisions about the company's positioning as regards its three major stakeholders. The following stakeholders constitute what we would call the '**strategic triangle**'.

Strategic triangle
Explains how a company positions itself against its three main stakeholders, i.e. customers, competitors and suppliers.

■ Primary customer groups or target groups. This touches upon the issue of market positioning and segmentation. Products and services will have to be tailored increasingly to the needs of more differentiated customer target groups, which requires specific product/ market strategies. This subject is not elaborated here but can be studied in the specialized marketing literature, for example Kotler and Keller (2006).

■ Major competitors. Companies must not only be able to respond to customer needs; they also need to respond in such a way that they achieve a so-called 'distinctive, sustainable competitive advantage'. This may explain why customers are turning to the company, instead of its competitors. As we have argued earlier, a competitive advantage may be derived from a superior cost position (Asian car manufacturers), a superior brand image (many top consumer brands), superior product quality (Rolls Royce), superior logistics performance and customer service (DHL, UPS, FedEx). To guarantee that customers will turn to the company, they must be able to clearly differentiate the company's products and services from the offerings of their direct competitors. In order to be able to do so, continuous benchmarking of the company's overall performance is required against that of direct competitors and those companies who are considered to be best-in-class in a specific activity.

■ Major suppliers. Developments within the supplier markets necessitate continuous review of the company's core activities. Management will have to ask itself continuously to what extent core and non-core activities (both production activities and support services) are carried out competitively. If the conclusion is that current (production) activities cannot be carried out competitively in the long run, it will be necessary to investigate subcontracting options or possible partnerships with suppliers. One example is a European automobile manufacturer who transfers the design and production of compressor valves for the automatic gearboxes of a new generation of cars to a specialized supplier. With financial support from the buyer, this supplier has built a factory to enable just-in-time deliveries based on call-off orders. Both parties are completely dependent on each other for the supply of this type of components; the relationship has developed from an adversarial, arm's length relationship into a long-term partnership relationship. Other examples in the automotive industry are manufacturers who contract out the complete design to design studio's like Pininfarina and Giugiaro. At the same time the manufacturing of small series, niche models are contracted out to specialist producers like Karmann in Germany.

The conclusion from the above is that the ultimate competitive position of a company is thus a result of: (a) the company's positioning relative to its major customers, (b) its sustainable, distinctive advantage compared with direct and indirect competitors and (c) its positioning versus its major suppliers and its supply chain strategies. Some authors have added a fourth group of stakeholders, namely employees. As more and more companies see knowledge and human capital as key success factors for their organization, the Strategic Triangle may develop into a Strategic Square in the future.

The Strategic Triangle is depicted in Figure 9.2. For many years customer-driven marketing strategies have become the cornerstone of the business strategies of large enterprises. For example, Philips Electronics, at the beginning of this decade, changed its technology focus into a customer focus through its highly successful campaign 'Sense and Simplicity'. Today, competitive benchmarking has also become a standard practice at many large companies. As may be observed from the retail industry where retailers keep a sharp eye daily on the pricing behaviour of their competitors. Increasingly, large companies have started to systematically benchmark the performance of their internal, key processes against those of specialist suppliers. This may explain the growing interest currently seen in global sourcing, supply chain management and supplier strategy.

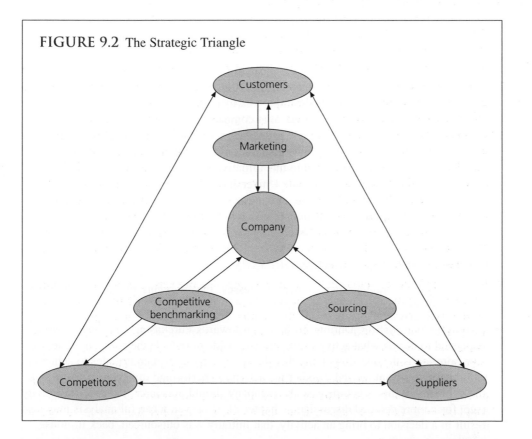

FIGURE 9.2 The Strategic Triangle

In shaping the relationship with suppliers three elements play a major role. The first is 'costs'. Large companies are looking increasingly for suppliers who can produce at minimum total cost of ownership. In trying to find the most competitive sources of supply most manufacturers have adopted a global sourcing approach at the expense of their traditionally 'nationally' oriented sourcing strategies. The second element is superior customer service. At the same time manufacturers are looking for suppliers who can support their manufacturing, operations, logistics and just-in-time programmes. Some authors (for example, Fisher, 1997) have demonstrated that in structuring their supply chain and supplier strategies, manufacturers need to differentiate between functional products (commodities) and innovative products ('specialities'). Functional products have a rather predictable demand and have a rather long life cycle, whereas demand for innovative products can barely be predicted due to their short life cycle. Managing supply chains for the latter requires a highly structured, local supplier network. Due to the fact that customer demand can be predicted much better for functional products, supply chains need to be less responsive. Hence, global sourcing for this type of product is an option.

In many cases manufacturers develop and sell a mix of both functional and innovative products. Therefore, they need to manage different supply chains and supplier networks at the same time. This obviously explains why most companies have adopted both a local and a global approach in their dealings and relationships with suppliers.

TOWARDS PURCHASING EXCELLENCE

In the previous paragraphs the relationship between business strategy and purchasing and supply management has been described. As companies pursue different types of business strategies, the role of purchasing will be different. It has been argued that purchasing strategies definitely need to be linked to overall business strategies. The following paragraphs describe how purchasing and supply strategies can be designed and what steps can be helpful in formulating them.

In doing so the author is following the ideas of Monczka and Trent (1991, 1992), who have published extensively on this subject. Based at Michigan State University Monczka launched a Global Procurement and Supply Chain Benchmarking Initiative in the early 1990s. The idea behind this initiative was that companies participating in it would be able to compare their purchasing and supply processes, to exchange experiences and to learn from 'best-practices'. A number of large manufacturing companies (such as Shell, Philips, Motorola and Coca-Cola) subscribed to this initiative and, for a number of years, worked with the researchers from Michigan State University to leverage their purchasing and supply strategies. The outcome of the programme was the idea that companies, when pursuing Purchasing Excellence, need to pay attention to two kinds of processes: strategic management processes (see Figure 9.3) and enabling processes (see Figure 9.4).

Strategic management processes

With regard to the strategic management processes, the following processes need to be defined, conceptualized and implemented:

■ Insourcing/outsourcing. During the first step towards Purchasing Excellence, companies need to decide what activities to perform inside or outside the company. The decisive criterion is the question of whether the activity concerned contributes to achieving a competitive advantage and whether the activity is performed in a competitive way by the company. If this is not the case the company should outsource that specific activity (see, for a more detailed discussiant, Chapter 8). However, a careful analysis may also result in a decision to bring an activity, that initially was outsourced, back in-house.

FIGURE 9.3 Towards purchasing excellence: strategic management processes

Source: R.M. Monczka as quoted by Purspective www.purspective.com

- Develop commodity strategies. At this stage the company needs to develop a clear and detailed picture of its purchasing spend. On what commodities do we spend the most money? And on what suppliers? How many suppliers do we have per commodity and are we happy about the outcome of this analysis? Commodity is used here in its broadest sense since it may relate to raw materials, technical and high-tech components and standard, off-the-shelf products. A commodity strategy should then be developed. Such a strategy provides guidelines on whether or not to pursue product standardization and reduce product variety, whether or not to reduce the number of suppliers, what type of relationship should be developed, etc. Of course the strategy for each commodity should be in line with and support the company's overall business strategy. It should be absolutely clear what benefits should be expected when the commodity strategy is implemented. Therefore a commodity plan maps out who will be responsible for each activity, supported by a detailed timeframe and how progress will be monitored.

- Establish and leverage world class supply base management. Supply base management is part of every commodity strategy. Supply base management covers how many suppliers will be dealt with for a certain commodity, what conditions and qualifications the best-in-class suppliers should meet and how the best suppliers will be selected. At this stage suppliers are investigated and benchmarked and, often, submitted to a detailed audit. The idea here is to increase business with those suppliers who perform best and to foster that these suppliers are going to work for the corporation on a worldwide basis.

- Develop and manage supplier relationships. In order to do so suppliers need to be grouped into distinctive categories. Philips Electronics may serve as an example here, as a company which differentiates between:
  - Commercial suppliers: these suppliers just need to deliver the goods and services according to the agreed terms.
  - Preferred suppliers: mutual objectives and improvement programmes are developed and agreed by both parties. The preferred status is reciprocal.

o Supplier partners: these suppliers work intensely with Philips to develop new technologies, products and business opportunities. Usually, it concerns a limited number of suppliers, who are considered to be crucial in supporting Philips' overall business strategies and core-technologies.

As will be seen later, developing partnerships is a very difficult issue and takes a long time between parties to develop. In general a major step forward is reached when suppliers no longer suspect that their customer is simply trying to find out and cut back their profit margins:

■ Integration of suppliers in product development. Having carefully selected the best-in-class suppliers, companies next should focus their efforts on building constructive relationships with suppliers in the area of new product development. This implies that technical experts from the suppliers will become part of the research and development teams and other project teams and vice versa. Often both parties are confronted with difficulties in collaborating effectively together, which relate to differences in working methods, management style and culture. This subject will be discussed in more depth in Chapter 11.

■ Supplier integration into the order fulfilment process. Motorola is one of the few companies which integrates suppliers into their Customer Focus Teams. The idea behind this is that manufacturer and supplier in the end have one mutual objective which is to satisfy the final consumer as best as they can. Joint teams work on issues like how to increase responsiveness and customer service, how to improve asset utilization, how to reduce pipeline inventories in the supply chain and how to improve communications and transaction flexibility by applying modern ICT.

Supplier development Characteristic for this type of programme is that the buying company shares the benefits gained from all supplier improvement activities that are generated from its suppliers, rather than taking it all itself.

■ **Supplier development** and quality management. At this stage suppliers are challenged actively to provide new ideas for improvement. These ideas may relate to product design, manufacturing technology and other business processes. Ideas and suggestions from suppliers are carefully considered and action is taken to implement them. Suggestions from suppliers are no longer considered as criticism but as sources for innovation and improvement. Motorola refers to this process as the 'Open Kimono' approach. This is the reason why it often asks its suppliers to value Motorola as a customer to work for. As experience has shown, adopting such a practice is not without risk. If suppliers feel that ideas are not taken seriously or good ideas simply are not being implemented, they will no longer support this type of programme.

■ Strategic cost management. This concept includes the identification of all costs, cost drivers and strategies aimed at reducing or eliminating costs throughout the supply chain (see Chapter 15 for more details on these subjects). Developing cost models and value stream mapping are important concepts and vehicles at this stage. The idea behind this is that both parties (or clusters of suppliers) work jointly with the end customer to realize cost savings. Obviously, this will only work when each party may share some benefits of this exercise. Otherwise, this will lead to a clear lack of motivation for such initiatives in the future.

Through this eight-step process some leading-edge manufacturers have actually been able to integrate suppliers into their business processes. Based upon experience we in general support the approach as suggested by Monczka. However, one of the questions is to what extent for each type of products and for each commodity every stage of this model needs to be followed. The more strategic a product is, the more energy and investments a company may be willing to make. Therefore, for many products and suppliers it will not be necessary to go through the full cycle.

Enabling processes

Besides giving attention to these management processes, purchasing managers also need to recognize six enabling processes following the view of Monczka (see Figure 9.4). These processes can be described as follows:

- Establish globally integrated and aligned purchasing and supply chain strategies and plans. Earlier we argued that purchasing and supply strategies should support the overall business strategies of the company. Strategic priorities should be reflected in the incumbent purchasing strategies and plans. This is not always easy in the case of multinational companies. For strategic commodities it should be avoided that every business unit creates its own priorities and individual supply plans. It is important that rules and guidelines are available on how to develop and implement such plans. Therefore, the templates to be used as well as how to structure the process of decision-making should be outlined top-down.

- Develop organization and teaming strategies. Our view is that professional purchasing is all about cross-functional teamwork. Purchasing strategies and plans need to be developed in close collaboration with all stakeholders concerned, and the strategies and plans need to be communicated and shared. In general, training and education are mandatory in order to change the often traditional view on purchasing, that is prevalent in companies. In case the company wants to work with cross-functional, cross business procurement teams, these teams need to be thoroughly briefed and prepared for their important tasks and responsibilities.

- Deploying globalization. International companies that market and sell their products and solutions in worldwide markets need to pursue an international and global approach towards their sourcing strategies. This is also true for smaller and medium-sized companies, who increasingly find attractive sources of supply in low-cost countries. However, global sourcing requires a good feel for the culture of the countries the company does business with, a fair amount of knowledge of the legal requirements locally, as well as a fair understanding of the local language. It will appear that the interpretation of what has contractually been agreed will be different among the cultures that one is dealing with.

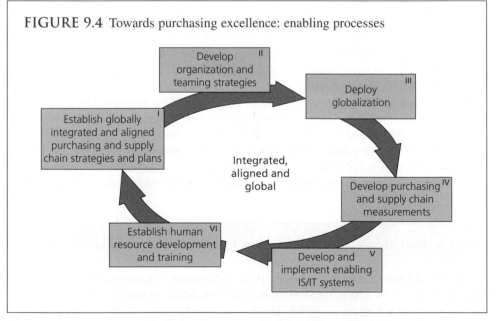

FIGURE 9.4 Towards purchasing excellence: enabling processes

Source: R.M. Monczka as quoted by Purspective www.purspective.com

- Develop purchasing and supply chain measurements. This process is aimed at developing and setting up periodic reports to the management based on a limited number of well-chosen key performance indicators. These indicators, in general, will relate to cost savings that have been realized, supplier performance, lead-time reduction, inventory reduction, reduction of capital employed, payment terms. In the purchasing reporting actual results will be compared against previously established goals and targets. In international companies some uniformity in reporting is mandatory to be able to allow for sufficient comparison among business units and purchasing units. Such reporting allows for effective management of purchasing as well as supplier performance.

- Develop and implement enabling IS/IT systems. To be able to produce effective purchasing management information, investments in advanced IT systems are necessary. Purchasing information systems should be seamlessly integrated with incumbent ERP systems. These purchasing information systems should include specific procurement solutions aimed at simplifying order to pay transactions through electronic ordering and payment. This is one of the reasons why large companies have initiated worldwide standardization of procurement processes (such as Shell with its international Streamline project that was initiated in 2007).

- Establish human resource development and training. A company is as good as the people that work for it. HRM is aimed at defining the right competence profiles for the purchasing positions involved, recruitment, and training and development of the employees meeting these profiles. Next, HRM is aimed at conducting performance appraisals, defining a proper salary and remuneration policy, and providing an attractive career path for those professionals who have proven to be suitable for the job. As purchasing grows more mature in organizations, the competence profiles need to be changed and adapted. As a consequence, change is a constant factor in modern procurement organizations.

Together these six processes create the enabling processes. The essence of the differentiation between strategic management and enabling processes is that both need to be conducted in parallel in a company, if that company wants to create a sustainable performance. If the company only invests in strategic management processes, the internal organizational structure and the lack of systems and competent staff will impede a sustainable implementation. If the company only invests in enabling processes, it will suffer from a lack of sufficient payback. Since resources for these kinds of investments are usually scarce, the purchasing manager will need to be selective about where it puts its money in. In all cases, it is recommended to simultaneously invest in part of the strategic management processes and some of the enabling processes.

These processes will be described in more detail in the next chapters. Outsourcing as a phenomenon has already been discussed in Chapter 8. In Chapter 1, we discussed how basic spend data could be collected and presented. In the next part we will describe how a company can design differentiated supplier strategies. The purchasing portfolio that will be presented, is a major vehicle for this. This discussion will be followed by Chapter 10, where we provide more details on how commodity strategies in purchasing may be developed.

PURCHASING PORTFOLIO ANALYSIS: PRINCIPLES

When designing commodity strategies, the portfolio approach originally suggested by Kraljic (1983) in his classic article in *Harvard Business Review*, is recommended. Fundamental to his approach is the idea that, since suppliers represent a different interest to the company, purchasing managers need to develop differentiated strategies towards their supply markets.

Key in developing purchasing and supply strategies is the issue of influencing the balance of power between the company and its key suppliers. In the author's view the balance of power should preferably be in favour of the buyer. If the situation is the reverse, the buying company may suffer from being too dependent on a specific supplier, who may be able to pass on his requirements and conditions to his customers. Obviously, when a company is too dependent on a supplier, something should be done to change this situation. In developing effective supplier strategies, the following questions may be helpful:

- Does the present purchasing strategy support our business strategy and does it meet our long-term requirements? Are opportunities for benefiting from synergies between divisions/business units fully exploited, for example by joint contracting for common materials requirements?

- What is the balance of power between our company and our major suppliers? For which products/materials does the company have a dominant position on the supply market and for which products/materials is the company dependent on one single supplier?

- Are the **strategic products** and services sourced from the best-in-class suppliers? To what extent have the purchasing requirements and volumes been evenly spread over several suppliers and geographic regions?

- What percentage of our purchasing requirements is covered by long-term contracts? What percentage is covered by spot-market transactions or short-term contracts?

- To what extent are internal operations benchmarked against those of specialist suppliers?

- What difficulties or interruptions in supply can be expected in the near future and how can these problems influence the profit and growth objectives of our company?

- What opportunities exist for collaboration with suppliers with regard to product development, quality improvement, lead-time reduction and cost reduction? Are these opportunities sufficiently being used?

Products, strategic
These are high-tech, high-volume products, which are often supplied at customer specification.

An analysis of the company's purchasing spend per category and its supplier base in general will show that the 20–80 rule applies: 20% of the products and suppliers will represent about 80% of purchasing turnover. This analysis is a first step in identifying the company's strategic commodities and suppliers. It also reveals the often huge number of small expense items and small suppliers, who in general are responsible for 80% of the company's internal handling costs. After this step the analysis can be refined using **Kraljic's** (1983) purchasing product portfolio-approach. In this approach the purchasing turnover and the supplier base are analysed on the basis of two variables:

Kraljic portfolio
See 'purchasing portfolio'.

- Purchasing's impact on the bottom line to the company. The profit impact of a given supply item is measured against criteria such as cost of materials, total costs, volume purchased, percentage of total purchase cost, or impact on product quality or business growth. The higher the volume or amount of money involved, the higher the financial impact of purchasing on the bottom line.

- The supply risk. This is measured against criteria such as short-term and long-term product availability, number of potential suppliers available, cost of changing a supplier, supply market structure, geographic distance, inventory risks and available substitutes. Sourcing a product from just one supplier without an alternative source of supply, in general will represent a high supply risk. Supply risk is low when a (standard) product can be sourced from many suppliers, and switching costs are low.

For reasons of simplicity many purchasing managers use the number of potential suppliers as a main criterion to assess the supply risk of a certain commodity. In reality, many criteria need to be considered in order to develop a fair idea about this aspect (see Table 9.1).

TABLE 9.1 Criteria purchasing portfolio

Impact on company's bottom line	Supply risk
■ Volume compared to total purchasing volume	■ Branded product versus standardized product
■ Products share in overall cost price	■ Patent i.e. licensed products
■ Products contribution to total company margin	■ Availability of substitutes
■ Cost savings potential through:	■ Specific quality and logistics requirements (JIT)
○ competitive bidding	■ Degree to which suppliers are prescribed by our company's customers
○ volume agreements	■ Supplier's share in buyer's purchasing volume
■ Price elasticity	■ Buyer's share in supplier sales turnover
■ Rebate and bonus scheme	■ Market structure: free competition edition versus monopoly
	■ Market situation: buyer's versus supplier's market
	■ Supplier production capacity utilization
	■ Supplier's financial position
	■ Supplier's switching costs

Combination of these variables yields a two-dimensional matrix with four quadrants. These represent the product groups or suppliers, each offering different interests to the company (see Figure 9.6):

■ Strategic products. These are high-tech, high-volume products, which are often supplied at customer specification. Only one source of supply is available, which cannot be changed in the short term without incurring considerable costs. Usually this type of product represents a high share in the cost price of the company's end product. Examples are engines and gearboxes for automobile manufacturers, turbines for the chemical industry and bottling equipment for breweries. Other examples are company wide computer systems (ERP systems) and telephone and communication equipment. Communication and interaction between customer and supplier are usually intensive, and, as they relate to different aspects of the relationship, complex. Looking at the balance of power between the parties involved one can differentiate between three different sub-segments:

○ Buyer-dominated segment. Here requirements are in fact imposed on the supplier by the buyer/manufacturer. Although some of these manufacturers have developed partnership programmes for their suppliers, suppliers will experience the relationship as rather one-sided. This situation is common in the automotive industry. The relationship between supplier and contractor is not a balanced one. The manufacturers dictate their demands to the suppliers, who just have to meet their requirements.

○ Supplier-dominated segment. Here the situation is different. Through its technology and carefully designed marketing strategies the supplier actually has the customer 'locked in' a relationship. This is often the case in business information technology industry, where IT providers have made their customers totally dependent on them in terms of supply of hardware, software and services (SAP, Oracle, Microsoft). Customers buy their hardware and software from one single supplier, only to find out that the same supplier charges enormously for these. Usually the performance guarantee

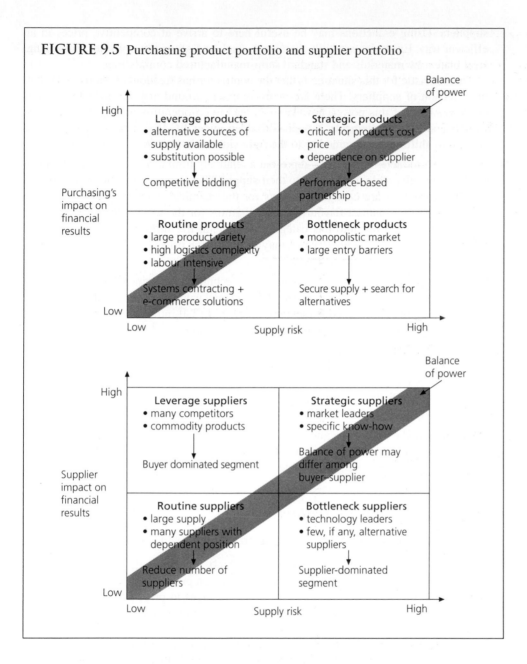

FIGURE 9.5 Purchasing product portfolio and supplier portfolio

is only valid if all products and services are bought from that same supplier. The customer has little leeway in general; it can only accept the conditions imposed by the supplier. Outsourcing may easily lead to this type of situation.

○ **Balanced relationship.** In this situation neither of the two parties dominates the other. They have a mutual interest in keeping the relationship stable. In this situation a 'partnership relationship' may develop over time.

■ **Leverage products.** In general these are the products that can be obtained from various suppliers at standard quality grades. They represent a relatively large share of the end product's cost price and are bought at large volumes. A small change in price has a relatively strong effect on the cost price of the end product. This is the reason why the buyer exerts aggressive sourcing and tendering among a small sample of prequalified

Products, leverage
In general, these are the products that can be obtained from various suppliers at standard quality grades. They represent a relatively large share of the end product's cost price and are bought at large volumes.

suppliers. Using e-auctions may be useful here to arrive at competitive prices in an efficient way. Examples are bulk chemicals, steel, and aluminium profiles, packaging, steel plate, raw materials and standard semi-manufactured commodities.

Characteristic for this situation is that the contractor has freedom of choice regarding his selection of suppliers. There are many suppliers around and the 'switching costs' are low. Abuse of this power, however, can lead to co-operation among the suppliers. Cartels and price agreements, though forbidden under EC-law, may develop in these situations, shifting the commodity to the right side of the matrix.

- Bottleneck products. These items represent a relatively limited value in terms of money but they are vulnerable with regard to their supply. They can only be obtained from one supplier. Examples are catalytic products for the chemical industry, pigments for the paint industry and natural flavourings and vitamins for the food industry. Spare parts for equipment also fall into this category. In general the supplier is dominant in the relationship with the customer, which may result in high prices, long delivery time, bad service and severe cost consequences.

- Routine products. These products produce few technical or commercial problems from a purchasing point of view. They usually have a small value per item and there are many alternative suppliers. In practice most inventory items fall into this category. Examples are cleaning materials, office supplies, maintenance supplies, fasteners, etc.

The problem with this group of products is that the costs of handling are higher than the value of the products itself. Usually, 80% of the time and energy of purchasing is used for these products: a reason why purchasing is often seen as an administrative job. The purchasing of these routine products should be organized efficiently, in order to spare time for the other, more interesting products.

Depending on the product segment of the portfolio, the supply strategy will differ. The emphasis should lie with the strategic and leverage products. Work related to routine products has to be limited as much as possible.

Four basic supplier strategies

For every segment of the portfolio a different strategy is possible. The strategies are:

- Performance-based partnership. Strategic products together with the leverage products make up 80% of total turnover. Minor changes in price levels will have an immediate impact on the end product's costs so that changes in price and costs, as well as the developments in the supplier market, must be monitored closely. At the same time, the supply risks are high, since the company is very dependent on one supplier. These arguments justify a centralized or co-ordinated purchasing approach. Depending on the relative power position of the different parties involved, the purchasing policy for strategic products will be aimed at partnership or collaboration. The goal is to create mutual participation based on pre-planned and mutually agreed cost and operational improvement targets. A relationship based on 'open costing' is preferred. With the suppliers, efficiency programmes are developed to achieve cost reduction, quality improvement, process improvement, and improved product development. Such co-operation can in the end lead to the fading of borders between the different companies.

An essential aspect of this partnership strategy is the thorough selection of the supplier. Early in the development, the market is scanned for the 'best-in-class' suppliers. These suppliers are screened on their references, financial stability, their present and future research and development potential, production capacities, their logistics and their **quality systems**, and of course their research and development and engineering capabilities.

- Competitive bidding. For leverage products a purchasing policy based on the principle of competitive bidding or tendering will be pursued. Since the suppliers and products are basically interchangeable, there will be, as a rule, no long-term supply contracts. Long-term contracts and annual agreements will be combined with 'spot' purchasing. In most cases buyers will adopt a multiple sourcing strategy. Buying at a minimum price while maintaining the required quality level and continuity of supply will take priority here. Small savings (small in terms of percentages) represent a large sum of money. This justifies an active market scanning through continuous market and supply research. Regularly, outsiders will be introduced so as to avoid price arrangements between the present suppliers.

  Buying of leverage products justifies a corporate or co-ordinated approach where corporate agreements with so-called preferred suppliers are negotiated which can be used by individual business units. Price changes caused by, for example, demand and supply changes, are monitored closely in order to estimate the effect on the cost price.

- Securing continuity of supply. The purchasing policy concerning bottleneck products should focus on securing continuity of supply, if necessary at additional cost. At the same time activities are conducted aimed at reducing the dependence on these suppliers. This is done by developing alternative products and looking for alternative suppliers. However, the costs involved in these actions (for example tests in laboratories) often exceed the cost savings obtained, which is why management often has difficulty in approving this type of action.

  A risk analysis to determine the most important bottleneck items in the short-, middle- and long-term supply is necessary. Based on this analysis contingency plans are made. With contingency planning, measures are prepared in case one of the established risks actually occurs. Examples of measures are consigned stock agreements aimed at keeping stock of the materials concerned at the supplier's or the company's own premises, preparing alternative modes of transportation and actively investigating product alternatives.

- **Category management** and e-procurement solutions. For reasons mentioned earlier, routine, MRO-products require a purchasing strategy which is aimed at reducing administrative and logistic complexity. Buyers will have to work out simple but efficient ordering and administrative routines with the suppliers in the form of electronic catalogues through which employees can order directly from the preselected supplier. A few aspects relevant to the policy for these products are standardizing the product assortment (article catalogue), reducing the number of suppliers, pursuing systems contracts for categories of MRO items (office supplies, technical maintenance products, cleaning products, catering, etc.), working with electronic catalogues, ordering through Internet technology, electronic payment or using the purchasing card and reverse billing. A final example is to contract out the purchasing of these articles to specialized purchasing offices or trading houses.

The use of the purchasing portfolio leads to a differentiated purchasing strategy. It points out that suppliers represent a different interest for a company. The different supplier strategies that have been discussed are summarized in Figure 9.6.

In Chapter 10, we will discuss how to develop a sourcing strategy, based on the position of a product in the purchasing portfolio. Memo 9.2 describes how the purchasing portfolio may be applied. In some European countries the portfolio methods is very popular. Some researchers have reported that 60% of industrial suppliers and manufacturers may use this approach in their purchasing organizations.

Quality system
The collection of methods and procedures used for quality management is called the quality system, which is usually recorded in a quality handbook.

Category management
Supports the first three initiatives of ECR discussed above. It can be defined as 'an interactive business process whereby retailers and manufacturers work together in mutual co-operation to manage categories as strategic business units within each store'.

MEMO 9.2 OUTSOURCING PISTONS AT CUMMINS

The decision to outsource a strategic component is one of the most wrenching for any company. However, it is precisely this willingness to lose a battle in order to win the war that separates industry leaders from the followers. Managers at Cummins were faced with just such a choice in the mid-1980s. Confronted with a need to develop much more advanced piston designs to meet emissions legislation, they discovered the need to make enormous investments in order to upgrade capabilities. The financial payback appeared dubious since Cummins could buy pistons from several suppliers. On the other hand, pistons were the very 'guts' of an engine, and there was an understandable reluctance to relinquish control of this component to a supplier.

An emotional debate raged for over three years. Should Cummins strive to rebuild its piston capability or turn to the best worldwide sources for piston technology? To quell the debate, senior management commissioned a team with representatives from engineering, manufacturing and purchasing to develop and implement an appropriate piston strategy. Engineers first identified the key technologies and capabilities that would be required to specify, design and manufacture pistons. The team visited the four leading piston suppliers and benchmarked internal capabilities relative to these suppliers.

The team discovered that Cummins's internal design and manufacturing capabilities lagged behind those of two suppliers who were world-class technologists. Moreover, these two companies were aggressive innovators.

Their scale allowed them to invest more than 20 times as much as Cummins did in product and process research and development. In fact, both suppliers had their own machine-tool divisions and foundries and developed highly specialized machines and metallurgical processes. Cumulative volumes that were many times larger than Cummins's allowed them to ride down the experience curve much faster.

Thus not only was Cummins's piston design and manufacturing capability low in relation to the suppliers; but so also was its relative rate of learning. In light of this disparity, it was unlikely that Cummins had any chance of matching the capabilities of these suppliers without substantial investments that were difficult to justify. This objective fact-finding mission confirmed that the right decision was for Cummins to outsource pistons.

Source: Venkatesan (1992)

'Dutch windmill'
Combination of buyer's purchasing portfolio and supplier's customer portfolio, leading to 16 different business-to-business relationships, each of which call for a different sourcing strategy.

To conclude this part, we should discuss the limitations of using the purchasing portfolio. From practice, we have observed that this approach may have an important shortcoming. If a product is positioned for the buyer in the strategic segment of his purchasing portfolio, this does not necessarily imply that this product is also of strategic relevance to the supplier involved. In order to develop effective collaboration, a good fit between the position of the product into the buyer's purchasing portfolio and the position of the product in the supplier's customer portfolio is necessary. Detailed knowledge and a good understanding of the dependence of both parties and vice versa may prevent disappointment. This is the reason why some companies have introduced the **'Dutch windmill'** as an extension to their purchasing portfolio analysis (see Figure 9.8). This portfolio approach allows the buyer to mirror his view to the one used by the supplier. In general, combining both the buyer's portfolio approach and be supplier's customers portfolio approach, leads to more realistic expectations and plans with regard to future buyer–seller collaboration. Based upon the Dutch windmill, 16 buyer–seller relationships are possible, out of which one probably is suitable for long-term collaboration. In most cases the position of the buyer versus the seller will be different. In most business-to-business relationships, either the buyer or the seller will be dominant.

FIGURE 9.6 Basic characteristics of the four supplier strategies

Strategies / Characteristics	Partnership	Competitive bidding	Secure supply	Category management and e-procurement solutions
• Objective	• Create mutual commitment in long-term relationship	• Obtain 'best deal' for short term	• Secure short- and long-term supply • Reduce supply risk	• Reduce logistic complexity • Improve operational efficiency • Reduce number of suppliers
• Suitable for	• Strategic products (gearboxes, axles, optics, engines)	• Leverage products (commodities, steelplate, wire)	• Bottleneck products (natural flavors, vitamins, pigments)	• Routine products (consumables, supplies)
• Activities	• Accurate forecast of future requirements • Supply-risk analysis • Careful supplier selection • 'Should cost' analysis • Rolling materials schedules • Effective change-order procedure • Vendor rating	• Improve product/market knowledge • Search for alternative products/suppliers • Reallocate purchasing volumes over suppliers • Optimize order quantities • 'Target-pricing'	• Accurate forecast of future requirements • Supply-risk analysis • Determine ranking in supplier's client list • Develop preventative measures (buffer stock, consigned stock, transportation) • Search for alternative products/suppliers	• Subcontract per product group/product family • Standardize product assortment • Design effective internal order delivery and invoicing procedures • Delegate order handling to internal user
• Decision level	• Board level • Cross-functional approach	• Board level • Purchasing	• Purchasing • Cross-functional approach	• Purchasing • Cross-functional approach

FIGURE 9.7 Siemens purchasing portfolio

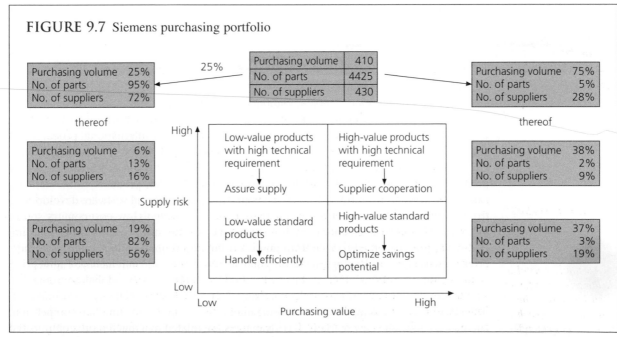

Source: Copyright © Siemens, Kowalski (1993) revised

FIGURE 9.8 'Dutch windmill': analysing buyer–seller interdependence

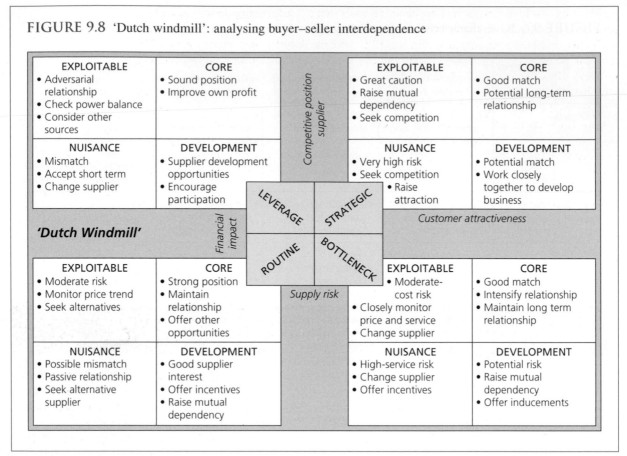

Source: *Purspective*, 2002

GLOBAL SOURCING

This chapter would not be complete without discussing global sourcing. Global sourcing is a term used to describe strategic sourcing in today's global setting (Monczka *et al.*, 2005). Most companies include global sourcing as part of their international procurement strategy. Its objective is to exploit global efficiencies in the delivery of a product or service. Examples of products and services that are globally sourced are labour-intensive manufactured components from China, furniture and wooden products from Vietnam, call centre services from English speaking countries, like India and software development from Eastern European countries. While these examples relate to low-cost country sourcing, global sourcing needs not to be limited to low-cost countries only. Global sourcing is defined as 'proactively integrating and co-ordinating common items and materials, processes, designs, technologies and suppliers across worldwide purchasing, engineering and operating locations' (Monczka *et al.*, 2005, p. 304). Clearly, global sourcing has advantages and disadvantages for the company. Advantages may relate to lower unit cost, benchmarking current suppliers, developing alternative suppliers to stimulate competition, and getting access to new markets. Disadvantages are related to a much more complicated distribution and logistics, increasing handling costs due to customs regulations and other formalities, problems that may occur due to dealing with different cultures, contractual problems, and higher uncertainty with regard to on-time delivery and quality. A specific factor to be considered in dealing with low-cost countries is the often rapidly changing political circumstances, which may affect the relationship with the supplier. Dealing with the specific problems related to global sourcing, forced large companies to set up International Procurement Offices (IPOs) in order to create a local presence in important supply markets. Besides getting a better idea of the supply opportunities which these markets may represent, these IPOs also may provide technical support to local suppliers in order to improve their product quality and service reliability. Apart from procurement experts, therefore these IPOs in many cases also employ experienced **quality assurance** specialists.

Quality assurance Related to keeping up the methods and procedures of quality management, i.e. systematically checking that they are efficient, that they lead to the desired objective and that they are applied correctly.

The practice of global sourcing has been subject of several studies. Memo 9.3 provides an overview of the research, which was conducted by Monczka *et al.* (2005) among US producers. As the study shows, global sourcing today is an important element of the sourcing strategies of large international companies and growing rapidly in importance.

MEMO 9.3   EFFECTIVE GLOBAL SOURCING AND SUPPLY FOR SUPERIOR RESULTS

The research showed that the magnitude of global sourcing is increasing. In 2000, firms in this study sourced between 21 and 30% of their total annual spend on a worldwide basis. In 2005, total non-domestic spend increased to between 31 and 40%. It is projected that in 2010 the total dollar amount of purchased items obtained from nondomestic sources will be between 41 and 50%.

The primary reasons for sourcing globally are cost related. On average, respondents achieved cost reductions of 19% and a total cost of ownership reduction of 12%.

The research revealed that the primary problems encountered when sourcing globally include the following: lengthened materials and service lead times, supplier delivery and quality problems, difficulty of locating and evaluating qualified suppliers, and lack of qualified business unit personnel to support the worldwide sourcing process.

However, these and other potential issues were at most considered a moderate problem. None of the issues were considered major. Overall, it appears that issues can be overcome with focus and resources. The research determined that for the most critical factors affecting global sourcing and supply, implementation at responding firms was at best only partial. These factors are as follows: (1) information availability, (2) personnel with required worldwide knowledge and skills, (3) knowledge of suppliers available worldwide, (4) time to develop worldwide strategies, (5) use of cross-functional teams, (6) effective logistics planning and execution, (7) availability of suppliers with worldwide capabilities.

The research determined that eight factors positively and statistically related to global sourcing performance outcomes. These eight factors were the following: (1) a defined global sourcing process, (2) centrally co-ordinated/centrally led decision-making, (3) site based control of operational activities, (4) information sharing with suppliers, (5) real-time communication tools, (6) availability of critical resources, (7) global sourcing and contracting systems and (8) international purchasing office support.

Global sourcing and supply effectiveness will reflect how well these factors, in the aggregate, are implemented with continuous improvement. Finally, the research revealed that organizations are and will be further integrating and co-ordinating global sourcing strategies across functions and locations to achieve superior performance.

Source: Monczka *et al.* (2005)

SUMMARY

One of the reasons why purchasing and supply management is getting a more prominent position in business strategy is closely connected with the strategic reorientation that many companies are involved in. After the diversification strategy of the 1970s, today's motto seems to be 'concentrate on your core business'. The advantages are self-evident: many activities can be carried out at lower cost by specialized suppliers, the company gains flexibility, and management's attention can focus on its 'core business'. These considerations are the reason why purchasing activity is receiving more attention from top management circles now than it did a few years ago. As companies have outsourced more of their activities, they have become more dependent on the competitiveness of their supply base. Purchasing's strategic role therefore is to develop a worldwide competitive supply base and to integrate these suppliers effectively in the company's business processes.

The purchasing strategy that is to be developed cannot be separated from the corporate policy or from competitive strategy. As we have seen the extremes of the strategic continuum are cost leadership and differentiation. These strategies cannot be pursued simultaneously, as their organizational requirements are completely different.

Whatever business strategy is developed, it needs to position the company against its three major groups of stakeholders, i.e. its customers, competitors and suppliers. Over the past decade there has been a large interest from managers and academics for customer and marketing management and competitive strategy. The interest for purchasing and supply (chain) management as a prime concern for top management is fairly recent. However, it is growing fast.

In the discussion on how to develop leverage in purchasing and supply management, the author has followed the ideas as developed by Monczka *et al.* (2005). They suggested a framework consisting of strategic management processes on hand, and enabling processes on the other hand. Strategic management processes are aimed at deciding what activities would be core or non-core, what commodity strategies should be developed, how the company could create procurement leverage among different business units, and how to integrate suppliers effectively in the company's business processes. Ideally, a company would need to go through eight different steps. However, this will not be necessary for all purchased products and commodities. Key to the suggested framework is to develop a supplier base which is 'world class' and to actively manage this supplier base. The six enabling processes that have been discussed allow for building the necessary infrastructure in terms of organization, team structures, information systems, performance measures and reporting. Both strategic management processes and enabling processes should be developed simultaneously.

When developing specific supplier strategies Kraljic's purchasing product portfolio may be very helpful (Kraljic, 1983). It recognizes that different products require different supplier strategies. It starts with a thorough analysis of both product groups and the supplier base based on two criteria: (1) purchasing's impact on company profitability and (2) the degree of supply risk associated with the purchase of a specific item. An analysis of these aspects provides the first clue for the purchasing strategy that has to be developed. The second step is to further analyse the four product categories: (1) strategic products, (2) leverage products, (3) bottleneck products and (4) routine products. For each of these products different supplier strategies can be developed. The value of this approach is that it explains that partnership and competitive bidding should be seen as complementary strategies rather than mutually exclusive. It also shows that the four basic supplier strategies serve different objectives. Global sourcing today is an essential element of the modern sourcing portfolio. Although initiated for cost reasons, global sourcing represents significant supply risk to companies. Which is why most large organizations have set up International Purchasing Offices in order to have local representation in their supply markets.

ASSIGNMENTS

9.1   At the beginning of this chapter the industry life cycle was introduced. Explain the characteristics of the purchasing strategy that would be most appropriate for each of the four stages that were identified. What focus would each purchasing strategy have in each stage?

9.2   Consider a manufacturer of food products (pasta products, dry soups and sauces). Analyse the purchasing portfolio based on Kraljic's portfolio analysis. Indicate which products can be characterized as strategic products, leverage products, bottleneck products and routine products.

9.3   Global sourcing has become more popular among manufacturing companies. For what segments of the purchasing portfolio would you recommend a global sourcing strategy? Discuss the advantages and disadvantages of global sourcing.

9.4   Many large manufacturers have tried to develop partnership relationships with their key vendors. How would you define a partnership relationship? Do you think a true partnership approach is feasible in the manufacturing industry? What conditions would buyers and sellers need to meet in order to be able to develop effective partnership relationships?

9.5   Monczka's Purchasing Excellence framework serves as a guideline for professionalizing purchasing within organizations. Discuss the weaknesses of this framework for purchasing managers. For what kind of companies would you consider this framework to be most useful?

REFERENCES

Fisher, M.L. (1997) 'What is the right supply chain for your product?', *Harvard Business Review*, March–April:105–16.

Kotler, P. and Keller, K.L. (2006) *Marketing Management*, Upper Saddle River, NJ: Pearson Prentice Hall.

Kraljic, P. (1983) 'Purchasing must become supply management', *Harvard Business Review*, September–October:109–17.

Lamming, R. (1993) *Beyond Partnership, Strategies for Innovation and Lean Supply*, Hampstead: Prentice-Hall.

Monczka, R.M. and Trent, R.J. (1991) Global sourcing: a development approach, *International Journal of Purchasing and Materials Management*, 27(2):2–8.

Monczka, R.M. and Trent, R.J. (1992) Worldwide sourcing: assessment and execution, *International Journal of Purchasing Materials and Management*, 28(4):9–19.

Monczka, R.M., Trent, R., and Handfield, R. (2005) *Purchasing and Supply Management*, 3rd edn, London: Thomson.

Porter, M.A. (1980) *Competitive Strategy, Techniques for Analyzing Industries and Competitors*, New York: The Free Press.

Venkatesan, R. (1992) 'Strategic sourcing: to make or not to make', *Harvard Business Review*, November–December: 98–107.

Womack, J.P., Jones, D.T.J., and Roos, D. (1990) *The Machine that Changed the World*, New York: Macmillan Collier.

CATEGORY SOURCING: GETTING BETTER PERFORMANCE FROM SUPPLIERS

LEARNING OBJECTIVES

After reading this chapter you should be able to do the following:

- Understand why in most deals with suppliers there is room for cost savings.
- What it takes to develop a sourcing strategy.
- Identify the different elements of a category sourcing plan.
- How to assemble a cross functional sourcing team.
- Identify key success factors for successful implementation of sourcing strategies.

INTRODUCTION

Category sourcing is at the heart of any professional purchasing organisation these days. As the following case study of HP illustrates, HP decided after the merger with Compaq to heavily centralize its purchasing activities. Sourcing strategies for all major, strategic commodities are today driven from the corporate centre in close cooperation with the divisions and business units. Rather than setting up a heavily staffed corporate purchasing organization, HP relies on the purchasing expertise and experience that is present in the different parts of the huge HP organization. Sourcing strategies are developed and implemented by carefully selected sourcing teams that consist of specialists of different disciplines, representing different parts of the HP organization. The activities of these teams are supervised by a Purchasing Council, which consists of the purchasing directors of the different divisions and business units and which is headed by HP's Corporate Purchasing Officer (CPO). Products and services that are specific to Business Units are purchased non-centrally.

The model that HP has chosen to organize its worldwide purchasing activities is exemplary of all major international companies these days. Why have these companies adopted this model? What do they want to accomplish with this structure? What role do these sourcing teams play in their international purchasing strategies and policies? What is their task? What is a sourcing strategy and what does it take to develop and implement these?

CASE STUDY HP SOURCES GLOBALLY TO CUT COSTS

When a company spends $43 billion per year on production materials, it wants to make sure it is getting the best price, the highest quality and the best support possible from suppliers. That's why Hewlett-Packard over the last . . . years has launched initiatives to exercise greater control of its spend, consolidate its purchases where possible and identify and develop emerging sources of supply in China, Eastern Europe and India.

Such an undertaking is no easy task for a company as big and diverse as Hewlett-Packard, which had $73 billion in sales in 2003, and is perhaps best known as a computer company. However, it is also a leading supplier of copiers, printers, networking equipment and storage systems. Its business units often have different supply requirements. HP believes it has found a way to satisfy all of its business units' supply and procurement requirements while still reducing cost and taking advantage of emerging markets.

Having revamped its approach to supplier management since its 2001 merger with Compaq Computer Corp., HP has centralized purchasing of key commodities, such as microprocessors, memory ICs and disk drives that are used by many of HP's four business units. For commodities that are unique to business units, such as chassis and power cords, it has a decentralized approach.

To support both corporate purchasing and purchasing at business units, HP has its Global Procurement Services group, which serves as an international procurement organization (IPO) and a buying arm for the company. HP uses its Purchasing Council to help develop purchasing strategies used throughout the company. It also has 'core' teams which work in new product development, and commodity teams which manage parts purchased for multiple HP business units.

HP's current procurement organization is the result of the work of 'clean teams' which were formed after the merger. The teams analyzed the procurement processes of both HP and Compaq and identified the best practices for each.

The teams found that Compaq's purchasing was very centralized, while HP's was decentralized because of its many business units.

'What we have now is a hybrid approach,' says Greg Shoemaker, vice president of procurement for HP. 'We have a certain number of commodities that are centralized and commodities that are pan HP – products such as microprocessors, disk drives and software,' he says. Corporate purchasing is responsible for those commodities.

Corporate purchasing combines the volumes of all its business units for those commodities to leverage its spend with suppliers.

'Then we have commodities that are business specific. Chassis would be an example. Not too many chassis are exactly alike. A desktop chassis is different than a storage rack chassis,' says Shoemaker. Business units are responsible for managing those commodities.

To help leverage commodity purchases, HP has established a Procurement Council comprised of the purchasing directors of business units and headed by Shoemaker. Those units include customer solutions, imaging and printing, technology solutions and personal systems.

The council meets monthly and, besides leveraging HP's purchasing power, the group focuses on professional development, IT toolsets and practices, and processes that can be used throughout the company. The idea is to share information about practices being used in individual business units to determine if they could be employed throughout HP.

Core teams, comprised of members of procurement, marketing and development are employed to help set supply strategies at HP.

The teams work with new product development and look at what products are going to be introduced and what parts will need to be purchased. The core teams then determine which of HP's sourcing strategies need to be in place for the parts used in the new product.

Core teams work closely with HP's strategic suppliers because HP needs the technical expertise of suppliers in its new products.

Source: *Purchasing*, 17th June 2004

This chapter addresses these questions. It will become clear that, when adopted properly, companies can realize substantial cost savings. Also, these sourcing strategies may result in much more constructive relationships with suppliers leading to new solutions and products and greater supply chain efficiencies.

REASONS UNDERLYING COST SAVINGS POTENTIAL IN PURCHASING

The cost-down programmes that have been set up over the past few years by many large companies have resulted, almost without exception, in large purchasing cost savings. Impressive savings have not only been reported in the area of production related buying, but most certainly also in the area of non-production related buying (see also Chapter 4 for a detailed discussion of this subject); this notwithstanding the often long-established and highly valued relationships with the suppliers that were involved. How were these cost savings realized? What activities have generated these? What reasons may explain the slack that apparently exists in the prices paid for the purchased materials and services? In general most manufacturers and suppliers are reluctant to share this type of information with the outside world. Based on our experience with numerous cost-down programmes the following are reasons why slack in materials costs and prices may exist:

- Traditional purchasing. In many companies, purchasing is managed in a traditional way. This means that buyers are only involved late, if at all, in the purchasing decision-making process and the company actually deals with a fixed group of familiar suppliers. Specific policies on purchasing or on how to deal with suppliers are hardly developed. If available, purchasing plans usually are not very ambitious. It might be that products are purchased for years without any knowledge of the underlying cost structure of the suppliers involved. Supplier representatives have free access to the company. In such a situation, where an appropriate governance on purchasing is lacking, much benefit can be gained from adopting a more professional way of working with suppliers.

- Continuous and relentless competitive bidding amongst a fixed group of suppliers. In many cases purchasers regularly sound out competition amongst their often known suppliers by playing them off against each other. The procedure here is that out of five bids, the buyer takes the lowest one, just to start a negotiation with this supplier to reduce the price even more. Then, the buyer will go with the lower price to the next supplier and also negotiates, etc. When applied regularly, it is clear that suppliers will anticipate this opportunistic buyer behaviour. First, they probably will refuse to offer in their quotations their lowest possible price, since they will keep some leeway in the 'game' of give and take, which will follow. These ritual dances between purchaser and supplier usually deliver limited results. Moreover, this process consumes valuable time. Second, when applied among a small group of suppliers, it promotes silent agreements among them and the forming of cartels. This type of purchasing behaviour is in some European countries widespread in the construction industry. It explains why relationships in this industry usually are at 'arm's length' and why collaboration between construction firms and their suppliers often is ill developed.

- Overspecification. In many cases technical specifications for purchased products are defined by R&D and technical departments only, without any input from purchasing specialists or suppliers. In most cases this leads to **'overspecification'**. In this situation technical requirements are imposed on suppliers, which are not necessary for the functionality of the product. An example is the corrugated carton boxes for food products, as used by a large food manufacturer, with full four-colour print, which

Overspecifying
A situation in which technical requirements are imposed on suppliers which are not necessary for the functionality of the product.

only served for transportation to the retailer's distribution centre. In general, the more specific the requirements for a given product, the fewer suppliers can be found for delivery. In some cases it may even lead to monopolistic supply situations (i.e. single sources), where manufacturers are very dependent on one specific supplier. The disadvantages of overspecification are obvious. Products may become unnecessarily expensive. Supplier knowledge for improving or simplifying product design is not used. It limits opportunities for competitive bidding amongst suppliers. These examples illustrate the need to work with cross-functional teams in dealings with suppliers. However, this often requires a drastic change in the company's organizational culture:

- Price increases in general are automatically passed on to the next in line. This phenomenon is referred to as the 'French Fries Principle' (see Memo 10.1). According to this principle suppliers will pass on cost increases to their customers, who in turn pass these increases in costs on to their final consumers. This happens not only with materials cost increases. Also increases in salaries, social insurance and other labour costs ultimately will be passed on to the customer next in line. As recent examples in the automotive and consumer electronics industry have shown, this practice cannot go on forever. In some cases this practice has led to customer prices that simply were no longer accepted by consumers, resulting in lost sales and significant financial losses by the companies concerned.

  Some visionary purchasing and supply directors have emphasized that manufacturers and suppliers in fact share one common goal: serving the final consumer in the best way possible. The more products are sold by the manufacturer, the more business will be generated from suppliers. This premise underlies the Total Customer Satisfaction Programme of Motorola (manufacturer of microchips and telecom equipment), where suppliers are working in integrated Customer Teams to improve customer satisfaction. In their view cost increases need to be prevented. Rather, both manufacturer and suppliers should consistently work to improve their joint value proposition to the end user.

- Supplier cartels in (international) supply markets. In spite of the agreements made on EC level and the EC competition laws, cartels in most European economies are very common. In many industries like the paper industry, the packaging industry, some construction materials (concrete, bricks), the pharmaceutical industry and some food ingredients (like sugar and some fragrances) concentration is very high. There are only a very limited number of players around, which makes it easier to make some silent agreements on pricing behaviour and division of markets. Usually, such a situation results in product prices which are not in any way related to the underlying cost structure of the manufacturers. Breaking up a cartel or finding ways to go around a cartel, may in those cases result in impressive cost savings.

- Suppliers' customer relationship programmes. Many suppliers avoid the discussion to improve their value proposition to their clients. Rather, they spend time and money on 'customer management programmes' trying to influence the preferences of decision-makers in their favour. The activities related to such programmes are abundant! Tactics vary from invitations for golf tournaments (IT companies), in-company seminars (banks), product presentations (car manufacturers), research funds (pharmaceutical) and personal gifts and presents, to straightforward bribes (all industries). All these activities aim to influence personal preferences of decision-makers on 'soft' aspects and to avoid an objective client testing the products and services. Given the often aggressive and personalized marketing and sales policies of many suppliers, most companies would benefit from a company-wide policy on business ethics and integrity.

MEMO 10.1   THE 'FRENCH FRIES PRINCIPLE' IN PURCHASING

The passing on of cost increases can best be described by the price developments of potatoes. A bad potato harvest has direct consequences for the price of a bag of chips. A good harvest has hardly any consequences.

If the harvest of potatoes in a given year is bad, supply will decrease. However, demand usually stays the same. As a result of the stable demand and shortages of supply, the price per kilo will increase. The prices per portion of french fries at the cafeteria will also increase.

What happens in the case of an abundant harvest of potatoes the next year? Then supply of course will increase, whilst demand remains the same. As a result the price for potatoes per kilo will decrease. One would expect that this in turn will result in a price reduction for a portion of french fries. However, in real life this is rarely the case! The idea of this principle is that cost increases, which have been incurred by suppliers, immediately are passed on to the customer. However, materials prices reductions and productivity gains are to be kept from the customer in order to improve supplier profitability. In most European economies this phenomenon is very visible as can be seen from the tariffs charged for gas, oil and energy, or for paper and corrugated board, petrol and gasoline, etc.

These points explain why in most cases suppliers have considerable slack in their price setting. The first points are related to the way purchasing processes are internally organized. The last points relate to characteristics of the supply market and the sales and marketing activities as applied by suppliers. The next section deals with the issue of how to identify slack in supplier prices and how to capture this cost reduction potential.

HOW TO IDENTIFY COST SAVINGS POTENTIAL

Any cost savings programme in purchasing starts with a thorough analysis of the company's purchasing spend by means of a spend cube. Based on this detailed spend data a category tree is set up (see Figure 10.1), which identifies the company's most important direct and indirect spend categories. A spend category is defined as 'a group of coherent products or services, bought from the supply market that are used in our company to satisfy internal or external customer demands'. Examples are connectors, IT, catering, gas, packaging materials, cleaning materials, etc. Before assigning cross-functional teams to each of these categories, the categories need to be prioritized on the basis of their cost savings potential and their ease of implementation using the Purchasing Prioritization Matrix (see Figure 10.2). According to this matrix projects can be grouped into different 'waves', allowing purchasing managers to set up short-term savings projects initially, in order to build credibility and support within the organization for this kind of initiative. After the first 'Quick Wins' have been gained, the more difficult projects can be conducted.

Category prioritization matrix
Matrix used to classify category cost-savings projects based upon two criteria, i.e. cost-savings potential and ease of implementation.

In assessing the cost savings potential of a certain spend category, purchasing managers may use different criteria. Cost savings potential may be dependent on the following factors:

- Customized versus standard (off-the-shelf) specification. If the company can replace a customized solution through a readily available, standard solution, this can result in considerable savings.

- Modular versus component buying. Savings may accrue from buying a total solution from a supplier rather than buying all individual components and putting them together internally.

- Buyer–supplier dependence. When a buyer is very dependent on a specific supplier and is held captive by a supplier, this may have very negative effects on pricing. Such risks

FIGURE 10.1 Category tree non-production related purchasing spend (example)

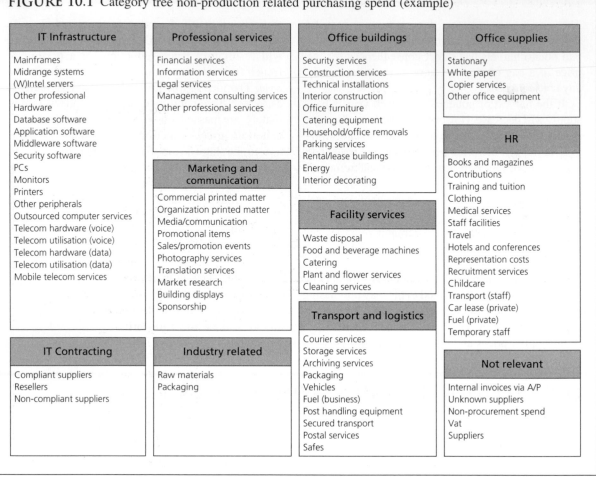

IT Infrastructure
Mainframes
Midrange systems
(W)Intel servers
Other professional
Hardware
Database software
Application software
Middleware software
Security software
PCs
Monitors
Printers
Other peripherals
Outsourced computer services
Telecom hardware (voice)
Telecom utilisation (voice)
Telecom hardware (data)
Telecom utilisation (data)
Mobile telecom services

Professional services
Financial services
Information services
Legal services
Management consulting services
Other professional services

Marketing and communication
Commercial printed matter
Organization printed matter
Media/communication
Promotional items
Sales/promotion events
Photography services
Translation services
Market research
Building displays
Sponsorship

Office buildings
Security services
Construction services
Technical installations
Interior construction
Office furniture
Catering equipment
Household/office removals
Parking services
Rental/lease buildings
Energy
Interior decorating

Facility services
Waste disposal
Food and beverage machines
Catering
Plant and flower services
Cleaning services

Transport and logistics
Courier services
Storage services
Archiving services
Packaging
Vehicles
Fuel (business)
Post handling equipment
Secured transport
Postal services
Safes

Office supplies
Stationary
White paper
Copier services
Other office equipment

HR
Books and magazines
Contributions
Training and tuition
Clothing
Medical services
Staff facilities
Travel
Hotels and conferences
Representation costs
Recruitment services
Childcare
Transport (staff)
Car lease (private)
Fuel (private)
Temporary staff

Not relevant
Internal invoices via A/P
Unknown suppliers
Non-procurement spend
Vat
Suppliers

IT Contracting
Compliant suppliers
Resellers
Non-compliant suppliers

Industry related
Raw materials
Packaging

may be present in a single source situation. This is why Philips Electronics as a principle holds that products preferably should not be single sourced.

- Number of suppliers involved in last tender. If only a limited number of suppliers had been involved the last time a tender was conducted, expanding the number of potential suppliers may lead to favourable price results.

- Scope of last tender. It may be worthwhile to occasionally expand the scope of the tender procedure beyond the suppliers that are currently known to the company. Including international and even global suppliers in a tender may lead to very favourable pricing.

- Type of contract and age of contract. When contracts have not been renewed for years, doing so may lead to better conditions. Changing the agreement from a pure price and bonus agreement to a more performance based contract may provide significant benefits.

- Market price versus cost price differential. Most cost analyses, when conducted for the first time, indicate a wide gap between the supplier's cost price and the price charged to the customer.

- Level of purchasing involvement. When professional buyers have never been involved in a supplier contract, doing so may lead to lower prices due to better specifications, a professional supplier selection and better contracts.

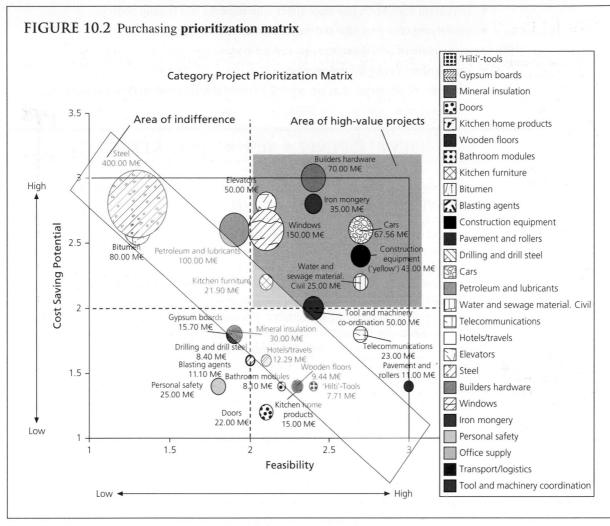

FIGURE 10.2 Purchasing **prioritization matrix**

Source: Skanska

Ease of implementation may be decided by totally different factors. One factor is the degree of resistance that can be expected internally when changing specifications or suppliers. The other is the internal technical expertise that is present within the company related to the spend category. A third is the supply market and contracting expertise that is available.

Usually, prior to deciding to develop a sourcing strategy for a certain spend category, all spend categories are analysed on both factors, i.e. cost savings potential and ease of implementation through a feasibility study or prestudy. This study allows the purchasing manager to indicate potential savings that may be generated in the future and the efforts and investments that will be needed in order to realize them. Based upon this cost–benefit analysis the priorities for handling each spend category can be decided.

The following is a list of the activities that are required when conducting a feasibility study:

- definition of category and sub-categories
- overview of current and future purchasing spend
- most important stakeholders and actors involved
- analysis of current supply base
- definition of future company requirements and needs
- functional and technical specification of purchased products

Category sourcing plan
Identifies the sourcing strategy for a certain category.

- important legislation that may affect requirements and buying process
- underlying cost structure and major cost drivers ownership
- assessment of initial savings that can be made
- assessment of ease if implementation
- overview of resources that are needed to build detailed **category sourcing plan**.

DEVELOPING A SOURCING STRATEGY

Based upon a thorough analysis of the company's future requirements and the company's current supply base, the future sourcing strategy needs to be decided for every spend category. Here, important questions are whether the supply base needs to be reduced or expanded and where suppliers should come from. Another question is what type of relationship the company would need to pursue with suppliers. A final aspect is what type of contract the company would like to put in place in its dealings with suppliers.

In addressing these questions, conducting the purchasing portfolio analysis (see Chapter 10) can be a first step. Over the past few years many companies have focused their sourcing strategy on reducing the number of suppliers. However, obviously this cannot go on forever. Reducing the number of suppliers should never be considered as a goal in itself. Rather, it should be seen as a vehicle to reduce costs or complexity.

Issues that should be addressed by a category sourcing strategy are the following:

- Single vs. multiple sourcing (see Memo 10.2). Does the company wish to purchase the product at one supplier or are several suppliers required for that same product? If the company purchases the product at one supplier, the company becomes dependent on that supplier. Supply risk is usually less when the same product is or can be sourced from more than one supplier. However, in that case transaction costs obviously will be higher.

- Global vs. local sourcing. Is an international, global supplier orientation required for this product or can a local, national orientation suffice? The answer depends on the type of product and the supply market structure. Factors in favour of local sourcing are when it concerns a high-tech product for which the product specification often changes, when a high flexibility and precision is required in terms of delivery, and when intensive personal communication is required in the relationship. Factors in favour of global sourcing are when it concerns bulk products or standardized products, when large price differences among suppliers exist for the same commodities in different parts of the world, when products can be bought in large quantities in order to benefit from transport economies, etc. These examples show that decisions on global versus local sourcing should always be based on considering the total cost of ownership.

- Partnership or competitive relationship. Does the company wish to buy the product from a supplier with whom a partnership relation is preferred, or is the supplier to be kept at a distance (at arm's length) and its relationship managed by regularly sounding out competition? Entering a partnership relationship has far-reaching consequences for the ways of working of the companies involved, the openness and willingness to share sensitive information and the type of contractual arrangements. These aspects will be discussed later in this chapter. Competitive tendering implies putting out a 'tender' regularly amongst a number of previously approved suppliers. Depending on the suppliers' propositions, the total volume is spread over the most attractive suppliers. In such a situation, for the individual supplier the allocated volume may differ from year to year. This tactic is mostly used when commodities are purchased, when the products are purchased in large volumes and when many suppliers are available.

MEMO 10.2   SINGLE SOURCING

E-procurement systems enable users within organizations to order directly from an electronic catalogue without interference from a purchasing department. Orders are acknowledged automatically by the supplier.

The user can verify the order status online, when desired (When will the order be delivered? What terms and conditions apply?). There is no need to contact the purchasing department with these kind of questions.

Many suppliers nowadays offer detailed tracking and tracing facilities which enable their customers to monitor order follow-up and delivery real-time. Besides this, e-procurement systems enable electronic invoicing, invoice matching and payment. As a result the traditional purchasing cycle is reduced and simplified considerably (see Figure 10.4).

Implementing e-procurement systems allows companies to reap significant benefits in terms of both lower materials prices and lower organizational costs. E-procurement systems represent an important productivity tool for both purchasing managers and departments, since these will lead to a significant reduction of administrative workload. At the same time customer service levels will improve since internal customers now will have responsibility and authority for ordering the materials they need through pre-arranged and efficient order routines. Finally, savings may result from the fact that common material requirements are grouped in homogeneous product families, which are ordered from electronic catalogues from far fewer suppliers.

Concentration of a larger volume among fewer suppliers, again may lead to better prices. However, implementation of e-procurement systems is a far from simple matter. It requires a high level of purchasing professionalism, clearly spelled out purchasing procedures and a seamless integration with the general ledger system and other systems within the company. Next, these systems need to match with the administrative systems of suppliers, which in many cases is a big problem!

Depending on the sourcing strategy, the contract strategy needs to be decided. Developing a contract strategy requires decisions on the following aspects:

- Buying on contract or buying on spot basis. Is the total volume of purchased products to be covered by a contract or is part of the volume to be bought on a spot basis (at the current market prices)? The advantage of buying under contract is that the volume is bought at a previously agreed price. The buyer is also certain of delivery. The disadvantage of covering the total volume under a contract is that the company loses its contact with the market. The suppliers who dropped out are aware that the company has secured the delivery of the products and therefore they will not continue to inform the company about the latest developments on the market. In case of expected price increases, a contract covering the greater part of the total purchasing volume is preferred. In case of expected price decreases, the opposite applies. As a rule, most companies choose a combination of both contract and spot buying.

- Price agreement vs. performance agreement. What kind of a contract is preferred? How detailed should it be? Should it be confined to a price agreement only? This may be sufficient when buying fabrics with certain standard qualities. Or is a detailed service level agreement (SLA) with specific arrangements on time of delivery, tests, maintenance, guarantees, etc. to be preferred? This is appropriate when contracting for specific process equipment or other investment goods. When buying services, SLAs have become increasingly popular. Another development can be found in the automotive industry. Most automotive companies use a 'life of type' contract for their suppliers of components which states that the prices have to decline a certain percentage every year as accumulated volumes go up and that the supplier should be able to deliver the specific component during the entire economic life span of the car.

These issues have to be well considered before searching the (international) supply market.

CATEGORY SOURCING PLANNING

As has been explained earlier, the spend cube (see Chapter 1) analyses the company's purchasing spend per type of purchase, per supplier and per budget holder. This analysis allows the company to set up a category tree, indicating the companies most important spend categories or spend segments (an illustration of spend analysis per category can be found in Figure 4.5).

A category has been defined as a group of products or services, which are purchased from the supply market and which are used as an element of the value proposition that our company offers to its customers or which are to be used in the internal company's operation. Therefore a category sourcing plan is a formal plan for a certain product category that explains how the company is going to deal with certain supply markets and its key supplier relationships. Category sourcing as a concept includes in fact three stages i.e.: Category Planning, Category Sourcing and Category Implementation. In the remainder of this chapter we will discuss the first two subject in more detail.

Figure 10.3 provides an overview of the content elements of a category sourcing plan.

Category sourcing plans need to have a strong link to the overall business goals and strategies. These serve as a point of departure for all planning activities. Understanding the company's customer markets and competitive priorities is important since these will reveal the company's competitive priorities. Next, it is important to understand who are the most important stakeholders in order to be able to involve these effectively and in a timely manner in the category planning process. As the stakeholders are identified during the pre-study the category planning process starts with assembling a cross-functional (and in many cases) cross-business category team, that will be responsible for all planning activities. Normally, this team will directly report to the board of directors. The team starts its activities based upon a thorough briefing based upon the results of the feasibility study. The analysis of the company's current and future spend is reviewed and where needed expanded. The same goes for the data reported on the company's supply base. A topic of particular interest is the definition of the company's present and future product and service requirements. These requirements are described in the broadest sense, recognizing future volumes, delivery and quality specifications, safety, environmental and legal conditions that should be reckoned with, etc.

All these data provide the background for defining the targets and objectives that should be realized. These in many cases relate to financial issues, such as material cost reduction and cash flow improvement, but may also relate to logistics issues as lead-time reduction and inventory reduction. New product innovation may also be a particular topic of concern to many sourcing teams as might mitigating supply chain risks that have been identified. When the deliverables of the sourcing strategy are clear, the different elements need to be discussed. Here, obvious concerns are what number of suppliers to deal with in the future, what type of relationship to pursue in order to be able to realize the sourcing objectives and targets. Also, the type of contract to pursue in the relationship with the supplier needs to be discussed as does the duration of the contract. When the contract type is decided, detailed draft contracts are prepared in order to include these in the bid packages that will be sent to the supplier later on. At that stage the team will also have discussed the most important key performance indicators (KPIs) that will be used to monitor contract compliance and supplier performance at contract execution.

During these activities the category sourcing team will frequently present its findings to the board of directors to check whether their plans are still attuned to the expectations of senior management. Approval from senior management for the intended sourcing strategy is required before entering into the next stage of the planning process.

FIGURE 10.3 Contents of a category sourcing plan

- Business strategy and business issues:
  - Business goals and issues
  - Current and future business requirements
  - Business priorities
  - Important stakeholders
  - Infrastructure and other organizational conditions.
- Analysis of historical data:
  - Historical usage and supplier performance reports
  - Functional, technical, quality, logistics and environmental specifications
  - Supply market analysis and supplier analysis
  - Current suppliers
  - Appraisal and ranking of suppliers
  - Price and cost analysis, important cost drivers
  - Legal and environmental conditions.
- Customer requirements and purchasing process
- Objectives sourcing strategy: statement of measurable results that need to be obtained in terms of:
  - Cost reduction
  - Quality improvement
  - Lead-time reduction
  - Inventory reduction
  - Reduction transaction cost
  - Reduction working capital.
- Commodity sourcing strategy:
  - Targeted number of suppliers
  - Supplier performance requirements
  - Location/geographic spread of suppliers
  - Type of preferred supplier relationship
  - Type of preferred contract
  - Supplier performance measures (KPIs).
- Planning of activities:
  - Briefing and team preparation
  - Spend and supply market analysis
  - Target setting and activity programming
  - Commodity strategy development
  - Sending out RFIs and RFPs
  - Sending out RFQs
  - Bid comparison and negotiations
  - Contract negotiations and contract signing
  - Communication and contract reviews.
- Organization and team composition
- Summary of expected net results

After such approval the team may start with the execution of the sourcing process itself (see Chapter 2). First, the team will put together the supplier long list, having sent out initial Requests for Information (RFIs) or Requests for Proposal (RFPs). The idea here is to check the qualifications of potential suppliers and to find out their interest in obtaining the company's business. Therefore, apart from collecting general company information (such as annual and financial reports), data with regard to the supplier's product range, its services and customer references is generated. The most promising suppliers, that meet the company's general list of supplier qualifications, are put on the supplier short list. The bid package, consisting of the buyer's purchasing requirements, a timetable and (sometimes) draft contract, is sent to these suppliers with the request to submit a competitive bid before a predefined target date. Special instructions about how to submit the bid (electronically or through a sealed envelope) are also part of the bid package. Having received all bids, the team starts to systematically analyse these and to compare the supplier proposals with the preset purchase requirements. Here, the team may decide to rank the different bids in a specific order to identify the two best suppliers. Next, the commercial negotiations may start between the parties involved. Non-competitive suppliers are informed about not being selected.

When sourcing teams arrive at this stage, it is important that they have sufficient mandate from the senior management for closing a deal on behalf of the company. Lack of mandate may lead to a lack of credibility in the discussions with suppliers and may slow down negotiations unnecessarily. Before finalizing the negotiations and closing the contract, senior management probably needs to be briefed again to gain their final approval for closing the deals with the supplier.

This process may seem simple and straightforward. However, it must be realized that category teams within multinational companies in most cases serve the interest of many business units, who all need to be represented at certain stages in the process. This makes the negotiations within the company often more difficult and time consuming than the ones that take place with the external suppliers. After the commercial negotiations the negotiations on the contract details will commence, which often requires intervention from legal specialists. In practice, these discussions may take much longer than those that were required for the commercial negotiations. When the appropriate signatures are put under the contract, most category managers consider their job to be done. However, in fact the work internally starts from the moment when the many internal stakeholders need to be informed about the scope and details of the contract. They should be urged to use the contracts in their dealings with suppliers. Having communicated the contracts, an important task of the category manager is to monitor contract compliance per business unit to secure that the company in total lives up to the agreements made with the suppliers. Another topic, that warrants efforts from the category manager, is to monitor supplier performance based upon the KPIs, that were agreed upon earlier in the contract. This information may be used in periodic supplier review meetings, where problems that have arisen in the relationship with the company are discussed and solved.

GETTING BETTER RESULTS FROM SUPPLIERS

Is it always necessary to work through this systematic category sourcing planning cycle? Is there a more simple way for companies that do not have sufficient employees to staff these category sourcing teams? Indeed, there is! Here is a way of working that has proven to be very effective in smaller organizations to drive down purchasing expenditure. The first step is to check the contracts that currently are in place with suppliers (if these are available at all), and to make sure that these are updated in close cooperation with the internal user. The second step is, now the company knows what contract to look for, to find the best possible supplier for its needs. The third step, finally, consists of developing the best possible solution for the company's needs in close collaboration with the selected, best in class supplier. Each of these steps will lead to significant benefits and savings. Each step is described in more detail below:

- Put the best possible legal contract in place. This step concerns a thorough analysis of current contract arrangements with existing suppliers. In many companies contract review results in considerable search activities, since it appears that contracts are difficult to find and have not been accurately documented. This is mostly true for contracts which have been closed without the involvement of the purchasing department. Often the supplier has to be contacted to provide a copy of the contract. The contract documents are analysed at this stage and checked for completeness and functionality. The main objective is to determine which price agreements have been made, whether the actual performance and satisfaction with the supplier have been documented and to assess the risks and responsibilities involved. Usually, such an analysis leads to a new, up-to-date and complete contract outlining the product and service performance required from the supplier. The objective of this step is to conclude a performance-based contract. Experiences have shown that this activity alone can lead to substantial savings (5–10%). An example is a food company where such analysis revealed a maintenance contract which was still being paid for while the machines had been sold and scrapped years ago!

- Select the best possible supplier. This step builds on the previous one. Having a sound legal contract in place, the question now arises as to whether the contracted partner is the best the company could get. This step, therefore, focuses on analysing the (international) supply market and sounding out international competition. The objective here is to get a competitive bid from a large number of new suppliers. An important element is that the number of possible suppliers is not limited to well-known companies. Before the supply market research, the company must decide which requirements the suppliers have to meet (supplier prequalification criteria). Then a shortlist is made of all the suppliers who conform to this profile. Based upon a thorough request for quotation the prequalified suppliers (5–15) are asked to present their proposals; a few international suppliers are deliberately included. Formal tendering procedures such as e-auctions may be used here to organise and speed up the process (see Chapter 2).

   Some companies do not use a tender or an e-auction and nevertheless are able to arrive at very competitive prices in their dealings with suppliers. After suppliers have been preselected, they are invited to come up with their proposals in a first round. Next, the three most promising suppliers are invited for a number of creative sessions together with the specialists from the customer. During these sessions the participants are challenged to come up with creative ideas for cost reduction, improvement of the product design and quality improvement. At a later stage, the customer team will visit the supplier in order to determine possible means of improving the product process, using a detailed process audit. The ideas that grew out of this workshop are presented to the management of the supplier at the end of the workshop. Honda of America developed a 'Best Practice Programme' for this purpose (see Memo 10.3). After these ideas have been processed in a final purchasing order specification, the suppliers are invited during a second round to present their final quotations. The final choice for a supplier is based on these quotations. The objective of this step is to identify the 'best-in-class supplier' for the required product or service, on a performance-based contract. Given the effort that this approach requires, it is only applied when buying key commodities and major investment goods. In most cases this step results again in considerable purchasing savings.

- Get the best possible solution from the best possible supplier. After the previous steps the company now has a performance-based contract with the 'best-in-class supplier'. From now on, the focus is on continuous improvement within the supplier relationship.

The assumption here is that there is a balance of power in the buyer–seller relationship, or that the balance of power is at the advantage of the buyer. At this stage concrete objectives and targets on price and cost reduction, quality improvement, lead-time reduction and improvement of customer service are settled. These objectives and targets are often prepared by the category sourcing teams. A major objective is to exchange ideas for improvement activities on both sides. Both parties exchange sensitive technical information and cost information. Often, buyers find out that the greater part of the homework has to be done on their side! Working this way leads to a situation where the supplier becomes gradually integrated in the customer's business processes. This is the reason why Chrysler in the 1990s introduced their 'Extended Enterprise Programme' (Dyer, 1996). At that time Chrysler saw their suppliers as an extension of their own company[1], that needed to be equally, or even better, managed than their internal operations. This approach can result in the early involvement of suppliers in the development of new products. During that period of time, specialists of the supplier are actually working within the organization of the buyer (residential engineering). Vice versa, engineers of the contractor can be present in the organization of the supplier when the first trial production runs take place, supporting them in solving start-up problems. This subject will be further discussed in Chapter 11. At this stage, some seasoned category managers will analyse the entire supply chain with help from their suppliers. The instrument used is Value Chain Mapping: per component, the source of origin of every part is determined. Then, per subcomponent the purchasing contracts are analysed and possible simplifications for purchasing or logistics are identified. In many cases, this results in the buyer helping the supplier improve his contracts with the next tier of suppliers. This approach is used at Japanese and some American manufacturers. In Europe this approach is still in its infancy. Characteristic for this stage is that the improvement activities are initiated and managed by the contractor and followed through progress meetings. Detailed vendor rating schedules showing the achievements of suppliers are discussed in these meetings. The result: continuous material cost savings, reduction of working capital and reductions of transaction costs.

MEMO 10.3   WORKING ON SUPPLIER QUALITY AT HONDA OF AMERICA

Honda of America deals with suppliers. The cooperation with suppliers is characterized by simplicity. Dave Nelson, vice-president purchasing says: *'When we receive a promising quotation from a new, unfamiliar supplier, we invite him to come and explain his proposal. At this meeting, a team of Honda specialists is present. If this meeting passes satisfactorily, one of Honda's younger engineers will visit the supplier's factory. The task of this engineer is to organize the working space of the supplier. He will start cleaning the machines and the tooling warehouse. Moulds and dies are inspected, cleaned and categorized so people will not have to search for them anymore. Then the factory is whitewashed to make it spotless. At first the engineer works alone, but after a while a few employees of the supplier cannot bear to see him working alone and will give him a hand. And that is precisely the intended plan. Eventually, we want to create a situation in which the supplier incorporates our management philosophy, which is based on respect for the individual and the full utilization of the creativity of employees. If that is accomplished, we are both working with common views, and barriers between the supplier and us automatically fade away.'* Honda of America work with their 'best practice programme', which stands for 'best practice', 'best price' and 'best process'. The purpose of this programme is to show suppliers how to eliminate the seven wastes in their production organization: standstill of machinery, moving materials, defects and failures, production disturbance, over-production, lead time and stocks.

[1]Chrysler's purchasing and supplier strategies changed dramatically after it was taken over by Daimler during the 1990s.

The major objective underlying this way of working is to develop and optimize the operational relationship with the best-in-class supplier and to integrate it into the new product development processes and projects. In this way suppliers are systematically challenged and mobilized to support the company's overall business strategies and to secure business success!

THE MYTH OF PARTNERSHIP

This chapter would be incomplete if it didn't discuss the issue of 'supplier partnership'. In recent years, large international manufacturers have spent a lot of time and money in the development of supplier partnership programmes. One of the first companies in Europe which focused on partnership was Philips Electronics, which introduced the term 'co-makership' aimed at 'building long-term relationships with a limited number of suppliers based on mutual trust'.

A major objective underlying this type of co-operation is to achieve significant improvements in:

- Logistics. By giving the suppliers insight into the supply needs and materials schedules for the coming months, they can anticipate much better the future requirements, which will lead to a higher level of service and lower logistics costs for both parties.
- Quality. Early mutual agreement on quality requirements enables zero defects deliveries, which in turn result in a reduction of quality costs for the contractor.
- Product and supply chain cost. By having a detailed understanding of the supplier's and the industry cost structure, targets are set to jointly reduce the supplier's underlying materials, labour and process costs.
- Product development. By introducing product and process engineering knowledge and experience of the supplier early into the development process, the time-to-market and start-up costs may be reduced.

The subject of partnership has been widely covered by academic research. In recent years, many concepts have been developed. Interesting views come originally from the early research done by Ellram and Hendrick (1993). In their investigations these authors used the following definition of partnership: 'A "partner" is defined as a firm with whom your company has an ongoing buyer–seller relationship, involving a commitment over an extended time-period, a mutual sharing of information and a sharing of risks and rewards resulting from the relationship.'

Based on this definition, the researchers concluded that, within the examined companies, less than 1% of the total of supplier relations could be defined as partnership relationships. These suppliers, however, were responsible for as much as 12% of the total purchasing volume of the examined companies.

Another interesting study on partnership was conducted during the 1990s in the British automobile industry (DTI, 1994). This study showed that the mutual trust between supplier and contractor is still out of reach. This research reports of 'many years of broken promises, abuse of trust, and conflicts', which made close collaboration in general and partnership between (car) manufacturers and their suppliers impossible. The researchers concluded: 'In developing new working agreements with their suppliers most vehicle manufacturers still appear to deal more in rhetoric than reality' (p. 5).

Reviewing the current practice of purchasing, these results do not come as a surprise. Co-operation with suppliers requires internal teamwork between all the disciplines involved. The functional structure in many companies interferes with an effective internal

FIGURE 10.4 How buyer–supplier relationships may change over time

Aspects	Supplier	Preferred supplier	Supply partner	Design partner
Relationship characteristics	• Operational	• Operational	• Tactical	• Strategic
Time horizon	• From order to order	• 1 Year	• 1–3 Years	• 1–5 Years
Quality	• As requested by producer • Qualitity control by producer	• As requested by producer • Quality control by producer and supplier	• 'Sign-off' by supplier • Quality assessment by supplier (process quality)	• 'Sign-off' by supplier • Early supplier involvement in design • Quality assessment by supplier (design quality)
Logistics	• Orders	• Annual agreements + call-off orders	• Periodical scheduling of materials requirement by producer	• Electronic document interchange
Contract	• From order to order	• Annual agreement (1 year)	• Annual agreement (>1 year) • Quality agreement	• Design contract • Life of type responsibility (product liability supply)
Price/cost	• Price	• Price + rebate	• Price + cost-reduction targets	• Price based on open calculation • Continuous improvement (design, quality, cycle time)

co-operation and as a consequence interferes with a close and effective co-operation with suppliers. Of course, there are some examples of successful partnership relationships available. However, it must be acknowledged that these were the result of many years of muddling through, disappointments and perseverance. Developing partnership relationships with suppliers takes time. This is illustrated in Figure 10.4. It shows the large differences in the relationships with a supplier and design partner.

We consider partnership to be the result of the contractors' continuous effort to improve results in the relationship with suppliers, rather than a technique which can be adapted and applied in a short time. This probably explains the small number of really successful partnership relationships in practice.

SUMMARY

Effective supplier management is another cornerstone for a successful business strategy. The way this policy is executed in organizations increasingly determines its shareholder value. Companies like AT&T, Ford, General Motors, Motorola and Volkswagen use purchasing and supply strategies as an integrated part of their company strategies. They are proof of the huge savings and significant improvements in operational processes that can be made through dedicated, effective supplier management.

The international competitive arena forces manufacturers to look continuously for ways to improve their value propositions to customers. Product costs need to be maintained at a competitive level. At the same time, manufacturers have to work continuously on product and process innovation. Suppliers are able to, and should, contribute to both objectives. The author's view is that this cannot be done automatically. In this chapter it has been explained why most suppliers do not automatically think in their clients' interest. Reasons are due to both the buyer's organization and the supplier's marketing and sales policies. It is fair to say that if contractors are not able to manage their suppliers, the suppliers without doubt will manage their customers. Successful companies tie their purchasing and supplier strategies to their overall business strategies. Suppliers basically should support their customers' business strategies in the best way possible. If their customers do well in terms of growth and volume, so will the suppliers. Successful buyers will try to overcome conflicting interests in the relationship with their suppliers, which may have developed over the years. This is done by developing carefully designed category sourcing programmes which focus on where to go for single sourcing, global sourcing or partnership. These category sourcing programmes always result in detailed action programmes which will highlight contract review, competitive bidding and co-operation with suppliers at the same time.

The foundation of any category sourcing plan is a sound spend analysis. The purchasing spend is categorized in homogeneous product categories though a category tree, that allows for segmenting categories based upon cost savings potential and ease of implementation. Next, the most promising product categories are subjected to a feasibility study that outlines what cost savings potential exists for a certain product category and what investments will be needed to capture these. In case of a positive return a category team is assigned the task to prepare for a detailed category sourcing plan, that will include detailed actions on how to arrive at a proper purchasing specification, a sound supplier selection and a legal arrangement with the best suppliers selected.

Smaller companies, that do not have the human resources needed for this approach, can embark on another, often more pragmatic route towards capturing purchasing cost savings.

The road to partnership is long and difficult. There are no easy ways or short cuts to success. Supplier strategies should be supported by senior management. Activities are to take place in cross-functional teams from both sides. This often requires a complete change of view on traditional purchasing practices. Purchasing needs to become more and more integrated into line management and the major business processes. The buyer, then, becomes just one of the team players. Firm rules on ethics and on how to deal with suppliers are needed in order to limit the effects of their often aggressive marketing and sales programmes.

ASSIGNMENTS

10.1 What is a sourcing strategy? What major questions need a sourcing strategy to address?

10.2 Consider the Product Life Cycle concept that you probably know from your marketing classes. Do you see any relationship between the different stages of the Product Life Cycle and the type of sourcing strategies that companies would need to follow?

10.3 What are the primary tasks of a category sourcing manager?

10.4 Why would companies in general benefit from reducing their supply base? Explain.

10.5 What sourcing strategies would help a company to build a dominant position in its supply chain? Give at least four examples of such sourcing strategies.

REFERENCES

DTI (1994) 'A review of the relationships between vehicle manufacturers and suppliers'. Report of the DTI/SMMT Automotive Components Supplier Initiative Stage Two, p. 28.

Dyer, J. (1996) How Chrysler created an American Keiretsu, *Harvard Business Review*, July–August:42–91.

Ellram, L. and Hendrick, Th. (1993) *Strategic Supplier Partnering: an International Study*, Phoenix, AZ: Center for Advanced Purchasing.

PURCHASING, INNOVATION AND QUALITY MANAGEMENT

LEARNING OBJECTIVES

After studying this chapter you should understand the following:

- Why large companies pursue 'open innovation' in their external relationships.
- The challenges of integrating purchasing in technical design and new product development processes.
- What it takes to involve suppliers early in new product development.
- The most important concepts concerning purchasing and quality management.
- Purchasing's role in and contribution to quality management.
- How to set up a Supplier Quality Assurance (SQA) programme.
- How to improve supplier performance.

INTRODUCTION

The following Pluriel case reflects several issues. First of all, it demonstrates that to be able to compete, PSA must pay considerable attention to reducing the 'time-to-market' of new car models. This is the time period between the moment the development of a product is started and the moment that it is introduced to the market. Japanese companies need considerably less time for this than European companies. Also, this situation, unfortunately, is not limited to the automotive industry. Secondly, this case description illustrates the importance of a supplier's contribution to new product development. Today, suppliers are a major source of innovation to companies: working closely together instead of at arm's length in new product development not only leads to considerable lead-time reduction, but also to important cost benefits. For if suppliers are involved in the product design at an early stage, they can provide their suggestions about simplification of the design and substitution of materials with components that are easier to process for them, etc.

This chapter addresses the role and significance of new product development in companies. The role assigned to purchasing in this context will be described and the

CASE STUDY SUPPLIERS AS A SOURCE OF INNOVATION: PSA'S PLURIEL PROJECT

PSA started the development of the Citroen C3 Pluriel in the beginning of 1999. The Pluriel was positioned as a fun car for youngsters, offering a stylish design based upon the C3. The Pluriel would feature a flexible roof system: drivers could instantaneously transform the car from a small sedan with an open roof, into a cabriolet or even into a roadster. When the concept was shown at the IAA 1999 auto fair in Frankfurt, the reactions were overwhelming. Shortly after that PSA decided to bring the car out in the market. Given the positive reaction of the market, a fast track development project was required. It was decided to start production mid-2002. An incredible time to market! As the basic design of the C3 body was available, the design and construction of the roof system posed most challenges. PSA knew that for its development, they had to rely on one of the larger roof systems manufacturers. At first, they considered the two market leaders: Meritor and Webasto. Given its unique features, Webasto had the impression that they were the only feasible supplier for this one-off roof system. The price proposal they made was marked by PSA purchasing specialist as not realistic. In the mean time, Inalfa, a Dutch specialist supplier of roof systems with manufacturing facilities in many countries, through it's newly established office in Paris, had heard about the Citroen C3 Pluriel and was desperate to make an offer to PSA for this unique project. Inalfa's management team decided to bring in a business case and submit a challenging price proposal. PSA's engineering team was impressed by Inalfa's thorough preparation; after a careful review of Inalfa's technical capabilities it was decided to award the order to them.

Different stakeholders were involved in the project. In order to work out the design, Italdesign was selected by PSA as lead designer and engineer. Italdesign is an Italian company that designs and builds prototypes and niche-models for large car manufacturers.

In their Milan headquarters, Italdesign set up a concurrent, highly international, engineering team, consisting of about 60 engineers from different organizations (25 from PSA, 25 from Italdesign, and 10 from various suppliers). PSA staff from Spain were involved since the new car was to be produced in the Spanish assembly plant. The idea from the outset was that the Citroen C3 and the special C3 Pluriel were to be produced on the same production line. Inalfa was one of the suppliers that was represented in the project team. Other suppliers were Wagon for the arches, Hutchinson for the seals, and Gestamp for stamped parts.

The Pluriel project was a far more complex project than the projects Inalfa had carried out previously. Several functionalities, like the folding roof, the electrical release, the full-size rear window, and the back door, had to be integrated. Tight time schedules challenged Inalfa to find new ways of working. Intensive collaboration with several development partners was necessary. Furthermore, extensive theoretical validation and computer simulations with the emphasis on kinematics and strength preceded practical verification. In this way, Inalfa was able to solve important engineering challenges and time constraints in an early phase of the project. Through endurance and functional tests the folding roof system was further verified and improved. Early supplier involvement was considered a necessity for several suppliers, especially for the sealing system that would be used. For this system, Inalfa involved a German supplier, Saargummi. For the other parts four or five main suppliers were selected. In a later phase the concept turned out to be more complex than anticipated, which forced Inalfa to initiate a collaboration with yet another supplier for the rotation frame.

A major challenge in the project has been managing the efforts of all parties involved. Especially with so many nationalities involved, communication became a major issue. Communication took place in five languages: Dutch, French, German, English, and Italian. Differences in working styles between the companies involved posed another challenge. Italdesign has a more practical approach in contrast to the much more theoretical approach of PSA, leaving Inalfa in between on many occasions. In addition, PSA used some unique design methodologies, like Failure Mode and Effect Analysis (FMEA) analysis, that had to be used in the integrated development process. Eventually, Inalfa hired some French expertise in this field to master the technique.

Finally, at the beginning of 2003, the manufacturing ramp-up took place from 30 to 350 products per day. In May 2003 the Citroen Pluriel was produced at full capacity.

The price for the roof system was initially based upon 220 parts. Eventually, the design turned out to consist of 480 parts, of which 80% were new to Inalfa. Notwithstanding the increased complexity of the product the price per unit remained close to the initial offer. Due to this innovation PSA has entered a new niche-market. The Pluriel was received very well by the market and contributes to PSA's reputation of building cars of extraordinary design.

Source: author interviews

contribution that purchasing can or should make to the company's quality policy will be discussed extensively. It will become clear that the implementation of total quality management generally has far-reaching consequences for the purchasing organization.

PURCHASING AND INNOVATION

Today, companies innovate in a totally different way than two decades ago. An example is Philips Electronics with its NatLab. This world famous research and development centre, which is located in Eindhoven, The Netherlands, stood for many years at the basis of many new Philips products, such as the incandescent lamp and its Philishave shaver. These products were created by internal experts and engineers who would use their creativity and experience to develop products and production processes. For reasons of security and confidentiality, their activities were protected against external curiosity. Which is why the access to these facilities for visitors was extremely difficult. Visitors had to face stringent security regulations and would not be able to enter the facilities without special permits. Of the many inventions, only a small number made it to market introduction. The rest was carefully archived and protected by patents against competition.

Today, visitors to the Philips High Tech Campus will experience a totally different scene. The NatLab is surrounded by a large number of high-tech companies, knowledge institutes and research centres, as well as suppliers, who set up shop to work together with Philips on new product innovations. Foldable LCD-screens and ambient technology have been the result of this. Ambient technology is embedded in new home lighting systems which automatically adapt to the personal preferences of the house owner. It is also applied in television screens that automatically reflect the colours of television programmes, providing a totally new experience for the viewer. Today, all the patents that have been obtained over many years are exploited through the Philips Alliance Office. The task of this Alliance Office, which reports directly to the Executive Board, is to exploit and commercialize the patents that are not core to Philips business, through new business projects in close collaboration with external technology partners. There are rumours that Philips Electronics generates more money through this activity than through all of its other activities together. The example of Philips has been followed by other industries. An example is the Chemelot Campus which was initiated by DSM, a leading chemical company in The Netherlands. These initiatives illustrate that innovation today cannot be executed effectively without close collaboration with external partners.

In academic literature these developments have been referred to as 'open innovation'. This term was introduced by Chesbrough (2003). This author compared **open innovation** with **closed innovation**. These terms reflect different paradigms on how to innovate. Closed innovation implies that companies try to develop new products and processes on

Innovation, open
The purpose of open innovation is to create close collaboration on research and development, new product design and development and market introduction with parties that would share the company's business interests in such collaboration.

Innovation, closed
Closed innovation implies that companies try to develop new products and processes based on the idea that the company itself has the best possible knowledge and resources for innovation.

the idea that the company itself has the best possible knowledge and resources for innovation. Basically, the concept is that technical knowledge and new product ideas should not be shared with external parties, because the knowledge and ideas could be abused by business partners. The problem with new product innovation, of course, is that only a few new product ideas make it to the market. Therefore, the company should generate as many ideas as possible. The innovation process should secure a careful screening of the most promising ideas at an early stage of development. By eliminating unsuccessful ideas at an early stage, unnecessary development costs may be prevented. This is the reason why many large companies have developed so-called stage gate processes for innovation. New ideas are developed according to a formal procedure, which identifies different stages in the new product development process, marked by so-called 'toll gates'. Each stage results in a decision document, which is reported to and discussed by a high-level innovation steering committee. This committee decides whether or not the project should be continued and what resources will be made available for it. This explains why innovation takes so much time and effort in companies. Since the company's resources are only limited, choices need to be made. It is impossible to continue all projects. As a result of the limited number of projects that can be funded, the number of new products introduced on the market is limited. Another problem is that the internal culture of companies represents a major barrier to breakthrough ideas. As a result the company may miss important market opportunities. The conservative IBM culture at the beginning of the 1980s stood in the way of developing the PC. IBM engineers, who were experts in developing mainframe computers and minicomputers, were of the opinion that IBM should have little to do with developing a small type of computers that only had small processing capacity. To overcome these cultural problems, it was decided to develop the PC on a remote location in high secrecy. This example illustrates just a few of the problems that companies may come across when they try to innovate on the basis of 'closed innovation' paradigm.

The knowledge and expertise that is needed for new product development today is so vast and varied, that this can hardly be found within one corporation anymore. The mobile telephone serves as an example. In only a few years this product developed from a telephone to a computerized personal assistant (PDA). Developing and manufacturing this type of device requires knowledge and expertise that need to be obtained from many external partners and experts. Another challenge that must be faced when developing this type of product effectively, is the massive investments required. These investments can barely be incurred by just one company. This is also true for the pharmaceutical industry. Today, it requires an investment of US$800 million on average to develop, test, register and market a new pharmaceutical product. In general, the average economic lifetime of these products becomes less and less. This implies that the massive investments in new product development need to be depreciated in a far shorter period of time. This is why even large pharmaceutical companies look for opportunities to share these investments with external business partners on a gain and risk-sharing basis. Innovation leads to totally new forms of collaboration among firms, which may result in new business ventures, technology alliances and spin-outs. They may also result in totally new forms of collaboration with suppliers, who more than ever are involved early in new product development. Such collaboration is characteristic of the open innovation paradigm. Its purpose is to create close collaboration on research and development, new product design and development and market introduction with parties that would share the business interests. The collaboration between Inalfa and PSA with regard to the Pluriel project is an illustration. It resulted for both companies in a new value proposition to their end markets. PSA was able to enter a new niche market successfully and reposition its brand. Inalfa was able to connect to other large automotive manufacturers and to offer them innovative, attractive roof solutions for the next generation of car models.

Figure 11.1 illustrates the differences between closed and open innovation.

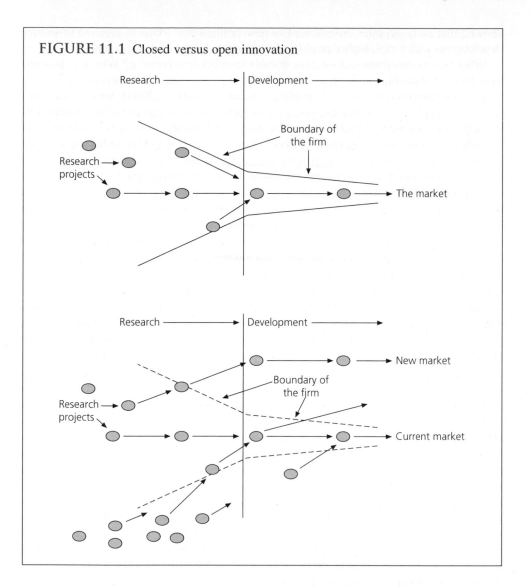

FIGURE 11.1 Closed versus open innovation

THE ROLE OF SUPPLIERS IN NEW PRODUCT DEVELOPMENT: EARLY SUPPLIER INVOLVEMENT

In many industries innovations are generated not so much by manufacturers as by their suppliers. Increasingly, suppliers are an important source of innovation. The automotive industry may serve as an illustration. Innovations in fuel injection (Bosch), sun protection and security glass (Saint Gobain), retractable roofs (Inalfa), car seats (Lear), tyre pressure sensors (Michelin), and airbags (Autoliv) came from suppliers. Therefore, the issue of how to mobilize the innovation potential of suppliers is of crucial importance for large manufacturers. These companies need to involve their suppliers closer to products and process innovation. This, however, is far from simple and it will not always, as academic research has demonstrated, lead to success. The results, reported from academic research on early supplier involvement, are controversial. The study reported by Ragatz *et al.* (1997) indeed showed that early supplier involvement in new product development resulted in shorter development lead times, higher product quality and a shorter time to market.

What factors determine the success of early supplier involvement? Why are, in some industries, relationships with suppliers in new product innovation troublesome?

Based on our own research (Wynstra, 1998 and van Echtelt, 2004), we conclude that involving suppliers early in new product development is a far from simple matter. The conditions for successful technological exchange and collaboration are not always met by the partners involved. Technological collaboration itself may lead to large resistance among the staff involved from both parties. A prerequisite for the customer organization is a good collaboration between research and development, product development, production, and purchasing. The idea is that companies are only able to collaborate successfully with suppliers if the relevant disciplines involved internally are able to collaborate. This type of cross-functional collaboration within companies is not always present. Other conditions to be met are that professional project management should be in place. Systems compatibility should be secured to be able to exchange technical information quickly and efficiently. Inter-systems operability is often underestimated by both partners and a source of significant problems in operations and communication. Internal R&D specialists often resist co-operating closely with external suppliers, simply because they fear for their jobs. If future development work is to be done by suppliers, what will remain for these engineers? Conflicts around intellectual property (IP) may further impede the intended collaboration. These name just a few of the problems that we encountered.

The supplier side may underestimate the research and development potential that is needed to support the customer's new product development processes. An efficient producer is not always a professional developer of products. In many cases a lot of knowledge and expertise need to be transferred from the customer to the supplier, which takes time and effort. Another challenge is the question of how to reward the supplier for its development efforts. We have witnessed many times the situation where a specific supplier has made great efforts to support their counterpart with their ideas and activities, even to the step of providing the prospective customer with a prototype of the new components, based on their own cost. Then, a buyer arrives on the scene who asks for different bids from different competitors. When this happens, the incumbent supplier would, of course, feel betrayed because he had done all the work and did not get paid for it. Such practices do not particularly help in fostering trustful long-term relationships with technology suppliers.

When discussing the benefits of early supplier involvement the distinction needs to be made between short-term and long-term benefits (van Echtelt, 2004). Short-term benefits may relate to better product quality, lower product cost, shorter development time, and lower development cost. These benefits may be generated from applying specialist product and technology knowledge, which is provided by the supplier. Long-term benefits may result from joint research programmes on new technologies, aligning technology strategies and roadmaps, and the ability to work with these technology suppliers on a gain and risk-sharing basis. When companies are able to do so totally new product concepts may emerge. As an illustration, here, we refer to the Senseo Crema (see Memo 11.1), that represented a completely new solution in the Dutch coffee market. This example has been followed by other companies.

The Senseo project is a good example of a technology breakthrough that would not have been possible without successful collaboration with an external specialist partner. Obviously the relationship between Sara Lee and Philips goes far beyond the traditional buyer–seller relationship. Both companies profited from the revenues that were made possible by jointly introducing this new coffee concept.

MEMO 11.1   OPEN INNOVATION IN CONSUMER ELECTRONICS: SENSEO CREMA

The Senseo coffee machine resulted from collaborative development by Sara Lee and Philips Electronics. Since the coffee market is saturated in many European countries, Sara Lee was looking for a new product. The company was looking for a concept which was more contemporary and would fit the need of the European consumer for a high quality coffee experience. The Italian espresso machines met these needs but they were laborious, expensive, and troublesome to work with. The new concept should overcome these problems, should be more efficient and affordable, easy to operate and should offer the consumer much better convenience. Since Sara Lee did not have any expertise and experience with the design and manufacturing of coffee machines, its product managers turned to Philips. The idea was to develop a coffee machine that was able to process the innovative Sara Lee coffee pads. These coffee pads, like tea bags, were easy to remove and should be available in different flavours. Having produced different prototypes, Philips was able to come up with a reliable design. The machine was introduced to the Dutch market in 2002 and was immediately a great success. Having solved some small technical problems, the concept has now been introduced to other European markets. With a similar success! Introduction to the US market is now contemplated.

Based upon the above, according to van Echtelt (2004) producers need to conduct three different types of activities in parallel:

- Strategic management processes. These processes are focused on providing the necessary infrastructure for future technological collaboration with suppliers. The result is that the company has decided about what core activities to focus on. Those technologies for which the company wants to rely on suppliers, the most important key technology partners are identified. Hence, the company has a clear picture of which suppliers to involve in new product development projects per technology area. Strategic management processes are aimed at:
  - Answering make-or-buy questions at the strategic level
  - Selection of potential future technology partners
  - Standardization and modularization of product designs
  - Evaluating supplier development capabilities and performance.
- Operational management processes. These processes relate to the management of individual development projects. Operational management processes help to decide which suppliers to address for what type of technological questions for a specific project, what suppliers to involve early and late in the project and what contracts to use in the relationship with the suppliers. Hence, operational management processes are aimed at:
  - Answering make-or-buy questions at the project level
  - Investigating alternative technological solutions for a project and deciding about the best technological option
  - Screening and selection of project partners (which are taken from the preferred supplier list)
  - Deciding when a supplier will be involved when in the project
  - Making project specific arrangements with the supplier
  - Evaluating supplier proposals and ways of working.

■ Collaboration processes. These processes are aimed at how to foster and implement technological collaboration with external partners. These processes may be particularly aimed at:

○ How to work with suppliers in new product development (e.g. based on target costing, time-to-market targets)

○ How to communicate with suppliers at the different management levels between both companies involved

○ How to assess intersystems compatibility and operability

○ How to evaluate product designs; how to test them based upon functional specifications

○ What contractual agreements to use in technological collaboration. Alternatives here are:

● **Time and materials contracts:** the supplier is paid for all work hours taken and materials spent

● Amortization of development cost: supplier development costs are amortized over the production series which will be produced later

● Gain and risk sharing: the supplier is rewarded with a percentage based on the sales made by the customer after the market introduction.

○ How to evaluate and measure the supplier development performance, and how to communicate with the supplier to improve performance.

Contract, time and materials
Contract in which the buyer agrees to pay the supplier all materials costs and employee hours against predetermined hourly rates and margins for services rendered (identical to cost reimbursable contract).

For a detailed discussion on the subject we refer to the specialized literature (van Echtelt *et al.*, 2008 and van Echtelt, 2004). Only when companies have implemented these three types of processes, sufficient conditions will be present for successful exchange with suppliers in new product development.

Our discussion explains why technological collaboration is so difficult and troublesome. It also explains the contradictory findings of academic research in this area. Figure 11.2 provides a schematic picture of our discussion. Now we will turn to the question of what role buyers may have in the different stages of new product development process.

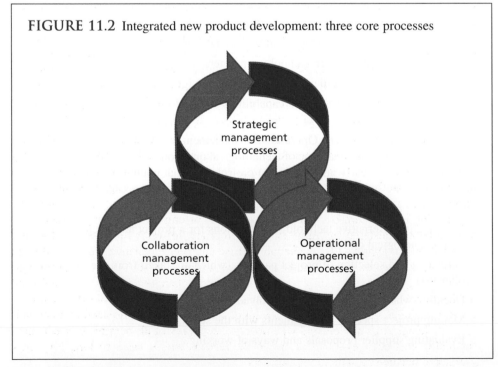

FIGURE 11.2 Integrated new product development: three core processes

Source: van Echtelt, 2004

PURCHASING AND NEW PRODUCT DEVELOPMENT

Depending on the nature of the product and the type of company, the development process, starting with conceptualization and ending with introduction on the market, will pass through the following stages:

- Idea generation. In this phase as many new product ideas are generated as possible. New ideas may emerge from customer contacts related to problems that customers experience in using the company's current products. These may also emerge from trends and developments that salesmen perceive in changing customer preferences. Finally, new product ideas may emerge from new technologies that, when applied to the current products, may result in new features that allow for more customer convenience.

- Concept study stage. At this stage the new product idea is translated in a first conceptual design. This conceptual design describes what functionality the product should offer to the intended target market. This stage may be subdivided into several activities, i.e. functional design, prestudy, feasibility study.

- Definition stage. The conceptual design is now translated into a technical design. Here, decisions are made about what materials to use, what physical requirements the product needs to meet, the technology that will be used to manufacture the product, etc. At this stage different product designs may be made, that are tested among prospective customers, in different working conditions. The testing programmes enable the marketeers to decide what the product is going to look like.

- Product development. In this phase the product design is translated into a number of prototypes or laboratory models. These models are extensively tested to obtain information about their durability, safety and functionality in different working conditions.

- Preproduction planning. The manufacturability of the product has already been considered during the product design stage. At this stage the production requirements are taken into account. After the prototype has been approved, preparation for production can be started. If it concerns a technically complex product, this phase may take a lot of time, since it may be necessary to purchase new production equipment. The capacity requirements of this new equipment will have to be determined based on (among other things) the market and sales forecasts, which have been prepared by the marketing department. Preproduction planning frequently results in a number of preproduction series.

- Pilot production. At this stage several preproduction series are manufactured. All products are subject to a thorough investigation and quality inspection. Also products may again be subjected to intensive usage tests to test the durability and sustainability of the new product. In this stage several engineering changes may be suggested in order to improve the robustness of the product design or allow for more consistent quality. All engineering changes are documented in technical or engineering change orders, that need to be administered carefully and, if appropriate, forwarded to suppliers for their approval. When approved by the supplier, these engineering change orders need to be signed off both by the supplier and the company's project leader. At this stage configuration management (i.e. keeping track of all technical changes and making sure that all parties work according to the latest versions of technical drawings) is of extreme importance. Of course, this stage represents a lot of work for buyers who need to communicate all changes to suppliers and who need to keep track of all possible consequences (including cost changes). This is one of the reasons why it takes so long for a new product to become available for customers.

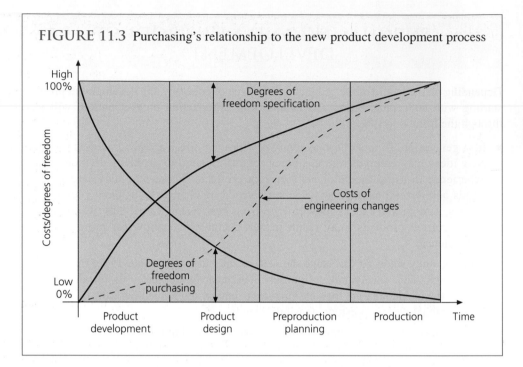

FIGURE 11.3 Purchasing's relationship to the new product development process

■ Start of regular production. After all the problems have been taken care of, actual production can commence and market introduction will follow. Initially all products are inspected. Later, when no quality defects have been observed, products produced are inspected on a sample base.

It goes without saying that it is possible to refine this sequence of steps depending on the nature of the product and the type of company. As the product development process advances, the specifications become more rigid and it becomes more difficult to introduce changes. The consequence for purchasing is that its latitude decreases and the costs of technical changes introduced at a later stage in the process become higher (see Figure 11.3).

Many engineers and developers usually play it safe: their primary interest is in materials and components that solve the technical problem they are faced with. Once a suitable material or construction technique has been found, tested and approved, the willingness to consider any alternatives (in the form of a different material, component or a substitute product from another supplier) will be limited. This is because each alternative ingredient or component will have to be tested and approved again, which implies not only a lot of work for the engineers involved, but also risks. This attitude of the engineer, to reduce technical risk, may result in certain components being specified in the direction of one particular supplier because of positive past experiences (see Memo 11.2). This puts the buyer in a difficult situation since it is very difficult to negotiate with such a supplier, if one can speak of negotiating at all. On the basis of job perception, a buyer will always attempt to have more than one supplier to fall back on. So, for the buyer to be able to go out into the market, the product must preferably be described in terms of functional specifications (rather than in terms of supplier or brand specifications). There exists, therefore, a kind of natural conflict in the way designers and buyers operate (Figure 11.4), which can only be solved by means of cross-functional development teams.

Involving buyers and suppliers early in new product development may result in considerable savings and at the same time more robust product designs. This is why some large manufacturers have initiated co-design relationships with their technology suppliers.

MEMO 11.2   THE VALUE OF SUPPLIER CATALOGUES

Some suppliers cleverly take advantage of the uncertainty that engineers experience in their design activities.

They make it easy for them by providing a catalog with all the information about the product assortment they carry. Examples are European distributors of technical components who provide electronic catalogs to their clients which list all their products. These concern small articles, such as switches, condensers, resistors, fasteners, etc. The most important technical data are presented for all these articles, together with the article number which can be used to order them. To specify the technical description of these articles is, of course, a very labor intensive task and, for the sake of convenience, many designers just list the article number from the catalog on their design. The result is that the articles, described in that way, can only be ordered from that specific distributor.

Through this practice some distributors have been able to build captive customer relationships against handsome margins. Electronic catalogs prove to be very successful. They often go with handy terminals, from which orders for materials can be placed directly at the distributor. Obviously, this type of relationship and ordering procedure is facilitated by Internet technology.

How do large manufacturers communicate with their first tier suppliers in product development projects? Possibilities are:

- Purchasing engineering. A **purchasing engineer** is a specialist function in the liaison between the engineering departments and the purchasing department. Purchasing engineers are members of the design teams, where they will evaluate designs against purchasing-specific criteria. It is their task to bring in specific supply market knowledge and new suppliers at an early stage of design, resulting in a design to target cost approach.

- Early supplier involvement (ESI). Those suppliers, who have proved in the past to be 'best-in-class', are invited to participate in the company's development projects at an early stage. In this way they are able to criticize future designs, suggest alternative materials, come up with ideas for more efficient manufacturing, etc., at a stage where engineering changes can be made without severe cost consequences.

- Residential engineering. A next step is to co-locate engineers from the supplier on a more or less permanent basis within the organization, in order to work on design or manufacturing problems which appear during the successive stages of development. Residential

Purchasing engineer
A purchasing engineer is a specialist function in the liaison between the engineering departments and the purchasing department.

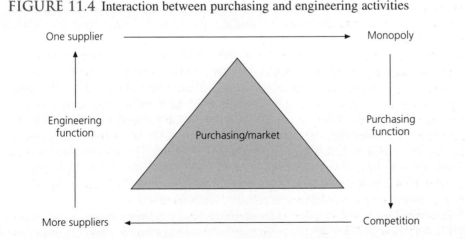

FIGURE 11.4 Interaction between purchasing and engineering activities

One supplier ⟶ Monopoly

Engineering function

Purchasing/market

Purchasing function

More suppliers ⟵ Competition

FIGURE 11.5 Early supplier involvement may lead to significant cost reductions

Product design stage	Degree of design complexity		
	Low (%)	Average (%)	High (%)
Initial design	2–5	10–25	30–50
Changing existing design	1–3	3–15	15–25
Redesign to improve quality	10	15–30	40–60

engineering also relates to a situation where a large OEM has placed its own engineering specialists at the supplier's premises in order to resolve a variety of technical problems (sometimes referred to as supplier support teams). This is quite common at some large car manufacturers like Honda and Toyota (see, for instance Liker and Choi, 2004).

Buyers are important scouts for any organization when it comes to spotting new technical developments; in their professional capacity they come into contact with suppliers, products and technologies much more frequently than engineers and developers. Buyers are generalists, while engineers are specialists. Involving buyers in development processes at an early stage can result in the contribution of new knowledge and a better understanding of construction, suitable materials, suppliers, and also the early introduction of supplier knowledge. Practice has shown that early supplier involvement can result in considerable cost reductions and product improvements (see Figure 11.5) This is the reason why, for example, Philips Electronics speaks of co-design in addition to co-makership.

Development projects require careful project management. Targets on design-to-cost and time-to-market need to be carefully translated in detailed action plans and cost-budgets. Ideally, the project planning for a new product development project will identify at what time suppliers will be involved in the project. Memo 11.3 shows how Océ, one of the major

MEMO 11.3 EARLY SUPPLIER INVOLVEMENT AT OCÉ

Océ's range of products contains copying, printing, plotter and document handling systems. Océ develops and produces the main part of these products by itself (see also Case Study at beginning of Chapter 9). The company is heavily research-oriented: annually about 7 per cent of the turnover is invested in research and development. For its new line of copiers Océ has started a technological cooperation with KMWE Precisie Eindhoven and Nedal Aluminum in order to develop a new photocarrier cylinder. This part is one of the hightech, key components of any copier.

Nedal Aluminum is the supplier of the basic aluminum and KMWE shapes this into the cylinder with high precision. KMWE has been a supplier for

Océ for many years, but this new product has many new and much higher technical requirements. For this reason KMWE was selected after a thorough and careful selection process.

For the supplier selection Océ has developed a special questionnaire: the Questionnaire for Preventive Supplier Evaluation. Through this the engineering capacity and capabilities of potential suppliers are assessed and documented. The questionnaire covers the following subjects:

Identification details: relates to subjects like ownership and shareholders of the company, organizational structure, major clients, breakdown of turnover, investments made recently and major suppliers.

Technical competence: relates to the production process, type of machinery and equipment available, transportation equipment and type of manufacturing systems in place, type of materials requirements planning systems used.

Financial situation: here Océ want the supplier to provide detailed financial figures and records.

Quality control: questions here relate to the quality control systems in place, quality certificates, organization of quality function, manuals which are available, method of evaluating suppliers.

Price information: here questions are asked on method of cost price calculation, allocation of overhead costs, and the willingness to cooperate based on open calculations.

Océ has a very clear strategy on product development and the involvement of suppliers in the new product development process. Prior to actually developing a new product, all parts, key components and subassemblies are plotted down into a matrix (see Figure 11.3). The technical aspects and costs of every part are analyzed. Furthermore the supply risk and the availability of each specific component is assessed. Based on this analysis, four quadrants usually apply:

Strategic products. In this quadrant Océ pursues a relationship with prospective suppliers based upon codevelopment.

The example of the photocarrier cylinder fits into this category. Suppliers for this type of components are selected at a very early stage in order to be able to let them participate in the development teams as early as possible. Part of the development and design work is done by the suppliers.

Leverage products. Here Océ pursues a relationship with the supplier based upon early supplier involvement. Actual development of the component is done by Océ itself. The suppliers involved are contacted in the engineering phase, before starting pre-production. At this stage suppliers bring in their ideas on how to manufacture the parts involved in the most efficient way. This may lead to some minor technical changes in the original design of the parts. Next, suppliers will provide prototypes which will be tested by Research and Development.

Routine products. Suppliers of routine products are involved when all design and development work and engineering activities have been finished. In fact they need to submit their proposals based on detailed designs and specifications, as provided to them by Océ. Relationships with suppliers here can be characterized as jobbers or routine suppliers.

Bottleneck products. This type of component normally causes a lot of trouble given the large dependence on the supplier. When identified early during the design and development process it is assured that sufficient alternatives are considered.

FIGURE 11.6 Development portfolio as used by Océ

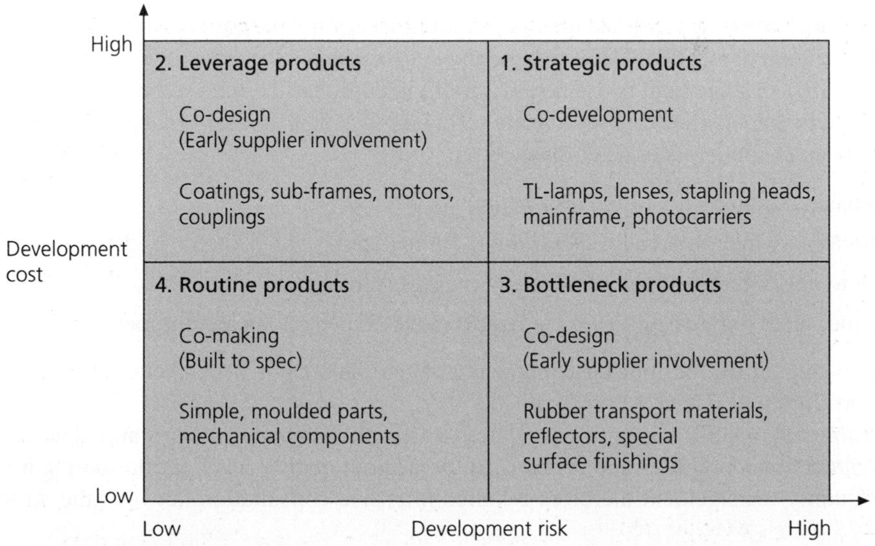

international document handling companies, has solved this problem: this company differentiates between four possible relationships with their supplier during the design and development process. A distinction is made between co-design (where a supplier engages in developing specifications), co-development (joint development of a prototype that meets the specifications) and co-making (manufacturing the product according to specifications and production schedule). In this case the term early supplier involvement relates only to the first two situations.

PURCHASING AND QUALITY MANAGEMENT

Definition of terms: quality and quality assurance

After the product specifications have been released the purchasing department must assure that they will be met by the supplier. The products that are to be manufactured must remain within these specifications. In addition, the purchasing department has to ensure that the suppliers will honour their agreements on other points, such as delivery time, quantity ordered and price. In this way buyers need to reflect total quality management approaches in their ways of working.

What exactly is quality? The literature on the subject contains almost as many definitions as there are authors who have written about it. A distinction is made between concepts such as 'functional quality', 'physical quality', 'fitness-for-use', etc. One common definition of quality is: 'The total of features and characteristics of a product or service that bear on its ability to satisfy a given need' (American National Standards Institute).' Without wanting to do any injustice to this definition, we favour IBM's simple definition of quality:

> *Quality is the degree in which customer requirements are met. We speak of a quality product or quality service when both supplier and customer agree on requirements and these requirements are met.*

The requirements mentioned in this definition can relate to the technical properties of a product or service. However, they can also relate to user-friendliness, ease of maintenance, delivery agreements and packaging instructions. Here, we propose to take a broad view in that the quality concept is related to more than just the physical properties of the product.

Most large companies initiate quality programmes for the purpose of effecting a change in attitude towards quality. These programmes also address the issue of quality management. Quality management is defined as: 'Making sure that the requirements are met and being able to demonstrate this objectively'. This implies that for every transaction between customer and supplier, they need to agree on:

- the basic requirements of the transaction
- the way in which the requirements are to be realized
- how to check that the requirements are (being) fulfilled
- the measures to be taken when the requirements/expectations are not met.

These steps form the four basic elements of the Plan–Do–Check–Act cycle, which is shown in Figure 11.7.

In summary, quality management relates to all activities and decisions aimed at taking the organization's products and services to the desired quality level and to maintain that level. Quality management therefore requires intensive consultation between the various

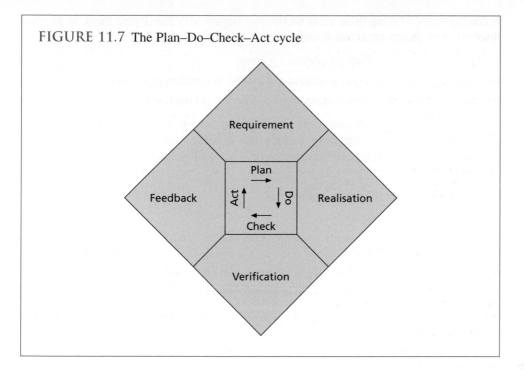

FIGURE 11.7 The Plan–Do–Check–Act cycle

departments in the organization and with outside suppliers and customers. After the desired quality level has been established, the complete production process must be organized in such a way that this level of quality is reached and maintained in a controllable manner. To accomplish this, quality management has at its disposal four interrelated functions: setting standards, assessment, control, and assurance. This last function will now be addressed in more detail.

Quality assurance is an important criterion for supplier selection. What guarantees can the supplier give with regard to design and technical specifications? According to what quality standards is it proposed to operate?

Quality assurance concerns keeping up the methods and procedures of quality management, i.e. systematically checking that they are efficient, that they lead to the desired objective, and that they are applied correctly. Internal company assessment of these issues is often called auditing; external assessment is referred to as verification. An external assessment establishes the degree to which the methods and procedures used satisfy the conditions that have been recorded in national and international standards. The best known are the ISO-9000 standards, which are accepted in many European countries. These will be discussed later.

The collection of methods and procedures used for quality management is called the quality system, which is usually recorded in a quality handbook. This handbook should be the (formal) reflection of the way in which quality management, including quality assurance, actually functions in practice.

THE COSTS OF QUALITY

Crosby (1984) pointed out that it is not so much quality, as the lack of it that costs money. The concept of quality costs can be used to initiate quality improvement initiatives. In many companies a considerable number of work hours are spent on the inspection of incoming goods and on solving acute quality problems (troubleshooting). The costs involved are often invisible and many companies have absolutely no idea what the lack of quality is costing them. Making these costs transparent begins with classifying them. In practice three types of quality costs are distinguished:

- prevention costs: the costs of preventing errors
- assessment costs: the costs related to the timely recognition of errors
- correction costs: the costs that result from (rectifying) mistakes.

Prevention costs are all costs that are related to actions aimed at preventing quality errors. Prevention costs therefore include the expenses related to the development, implementation and control of the system of total quality management. This concerns matters such as:

- conducting systematic product inspections
- executing process controls
- ensuring that product inspections and process control (auditing) are conducted systematically and periodically
- investigations to uncover the causes of errors and mistakes
- setting up the internal organization of quality management
- drawing up specifications, procedures, instructions and regulations for the total quality management system
- the development of special testing and measuring equipment and other tools in support of quality assessment
- education, training and motivation of personnel on quality management.

Assessment costs are incurred to minimize the consequences of errors. Examples are:

- incoming or acceptance inspection of purchased goods
- inspection of intermediate and semi-manufactured products
- sorting the goods produced (100% inspection) to track down faulty products and to separate them from good products
- final inspection of products and quality assessment of finished products
- registration and processing of and reporting on the measuring data.

Quality can be present in various degrees. This must be taken into account during the inspection procedure of a product series. Some of the rejected items may be made suitable for the client's production process by minimal rework. However, these corrections come with a price tag. The so-called error costs are usually divided into internal and external categories. Internal error costs (including wastes and losses) emerge as a result of mistakes which are noticed in time, i.e. before the product is delivered to the customer. These include:

- the costs of corrective measures
- losses due to product downgrading
- losses due to a reduced speed or even standstill of production, to the extent that they are caused by quality deviations in materials or components.

External error costs are a result of flaws identified by the customer. This group includes:

- the costs of processing complaints
- costs made for settling customer claims and disputes
- costs of processing return shipments from customers
- loss of 'goodwill'.

FIGURE 11.8 The quality costs model

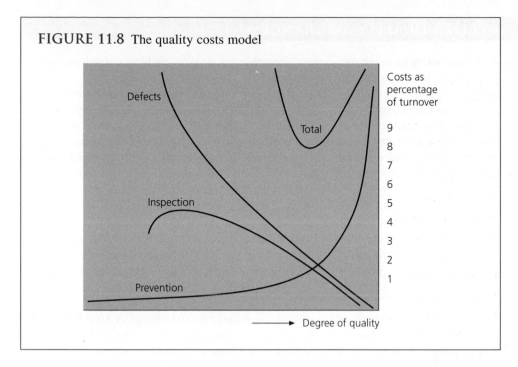

For many years the emphasis has shifted from correction to prevention. In an attempt to reduce the total quality costs, preventive quality management has been enhanced. This is illustrated by Figure 11.18 which shows the quality costs model.

SUPPLIER QUALITY ASSURANCE (SQA)

An important role in the implementation of total quality management is reserved for the purchasing department. This is because the quality of the finished product is determined to a large extent by the quality of the raw materials and components. Working on improving the quality offered by the suppliers is therefore a main task for buyers. For this reason many large manufacturers in Europe have initiated **supplier quality assurance** (SQA) programmes (see Memo 11.4).

To improve the quality of their products, many companies opt for an approach based on prevention. Co-operation is required from every department in the company, and this also applies to the purchasing department. With regard to purchasing, the objective of prevention is to maintain or improve the quality of goods and services to be purchased. This is based on selecting the supplier who can guarantee a sufficient level of quality. It is important that the supplier can also guarantee this quality level for the future. The preventive approach is expressed by the following measures:

■ Preparing the purchase order specification. Sound preparation is half the battle. Many problems can be prevented if there is an up-to-date, complete purchase order specification and it goes without saying that this specification contains a technical description, supplemented with the engineering designs and technical drawings. It will also contain an estimate of the materials requirements for the short and middle term, and additional logistic requirements such as packaging and transportation needs. At this stage clear sign-off procedures are important. The release of designs to suppliers cannot take place without the purchasing department's approval. This procedure also includes a description in how to deal with future engineering changes.

Supplier quality assurance (SQA)
Supplier quality assurance is all activities conducted by a company to arrive at a zero defects quality performance in its relationship with suppliers.

MEMO 11.4   SUPPLIER QUALITY ASSURANCE AT IBM

Large companies devote a lot of attention to improving cooperation across business functions. In this context IBM started developing a program to achieve 'zero defects' in cooperation with Philip Crosby. Top managers in all IBM branches took quality courses. These managers developed zero-defects programs in every production plant. The first initiatives were aimed at shifting attention from the detection and correction of errors to the prevention of errors.

The suppliers were invited to participate in the seminars, for the purpose of acquainting them with IBM's objective of zero defects, and to convince them of the importance of this objective. The role of the suppliers in all this was strongly emphasized. The supplier's employees were the next link that had to be made aware of the quality message.

Potential suppliers were selected on the basis of a checklist. The total quality performances of the supplier were considered: conformance, quality of production, the supplier's attitude towards quality and response to quality problems, facilities and personnel.

The quality performance (in a broad sense) of existing suppliers is evaluated continuously. One important parameter is the so-called quality-conformance of the supplier. Conformance in percentages is the ratio of the number of accepted deliveries divided by the total number of deliveries in one month. A delivery is accepted when inspected samples meet the standards. The suppliers are audited periodically. In addition, delivery reliability is measured and assessed, as are the price and cost behaviour and the administrative accuracy of the supplier!

Most production plants inform their suppliers about their performance on the subjects mentioned on a monthly basis. Every year the best supplier receives an award (the IBM Supplier Award). All of these measures are aimed at one objective: motivating suppliers towards continuous product and process improvements.

- Preliminary qualification of (potential) suppliers. Here the distinction between potential and existing suppliers must be made. Potential suppliers are sent a questionnaire before they can qualify for an order. The purpose of this questionnaire is to gain insight into the delivery possibilities of these suppliers. After a positive evaluation of the responses, a second round takes place. A team consisting of a buyer, a quality expert and a production manager visits the supplier and subjects the quality system in particular to an investigation (quality audit). A statement is then made about a possible order. As a rule, manufacturers document the results of their investigation and report on these to the supplier's management. Weaknesses found in the supplier (quality) organization and process are discussed. Corrective measures are suggested and agreed upon. These are to be written down by the supplier in a quality improvement programme. The activities recorded in this programme are checked in periodical progress meetings. Based on the observed progress it is determined whether a supplier qualifies for orders related to new (development) projects or if it can only supply for existing projects. Of course there is a third possibility: that the relationship will eventually be terminated.

- Sample inspection procedure. The next step on the road to acceptance of a new supplier is the sample inspection procedure. The supplier is requested to manufacture a sample product in co-operation with the engineering department. This product will then be assessed on its conformance with the requirements as agreed beforehand. Suggestions to achieve improvement of the product can be elaborated by the supplier as well as by the development team. This type of co-operation results in a certain degree of co-design. A number of large manufacturers use the number of times that the sample has to be offered for final approval (the initial sampling reject rate) as a measure for the supplier's design capability. The most important objective at this stage is to establish the degree to which the tools (moulds, templates) that will be used to produce the products will meet the requirements.

- Delivery of first and subsequent preproduction series. The next step is to have the prospective supplier manufacture a preproduction series. Specialists from the customer company will be present during production to audit the process. Attention is paid specifically to the degree of process control and the functioning of the quality management organization. Afterwards, the strong and the weak points of the process are analysed and agreements are made about adjusting the process. In the end this co-operation can result in a partnership agreement.

- Manufacture of the first production series. This is the moment of truth. Has the supplier lived up to its agreements? Is it capable of really meeting the zero-defects requirement? The customer checks the process completely: all products are inspected for quality (100% inspection). If everything is satisfactory, then the level of inspection is reduced. The ultimate goal is to reach a situation of direct acceptance of delivered products, i.e. without prior inspection. In this way the customer avoids the incoming inspection, which is a major source of costs.

- Quality agreement and certification. As a rule, a quality agreement is closed when the objective of zero-defects has been reached. This agreement determines that the supplier will manufacture the products involved in the way agreed upon with the manufacturer. It also describes the change procedures, which are so very important: in what way should the manufacturer and the supplier act if it is necessary to change the design or specifications. The quality agreement usually involves one product (article code). The supplier who proves able to supply, without any defects or mistakes, all deliveries of all products which are purchased from it is awarded a certificate by the manufacturer. The certified supplier is placed on the final list of preferred suppliers which means it is also eligible for new, future projects. If there are no problems, these suppliers' deliveries are subjected to inspection only a few times each year.

- Periodic verification. The instructions to the supplier with regards to what process improvement to implement must be checked periodically. Should it turn out that the targets were set too high, adjustments can be made. If the targets are met, then this results in new targets being formulated. In this way the concept of continuous quality improvement (or *kaizen*) in the relationship with the supplier is given substance. At this stage many large manufacturers work with computer-supported supplier rating systems, which are used to record and report on the suppliers' performances on several points (see Memo 11.5).

A few closing remarks in conclusion of this section now follow:

- Supplier selection. Selection of new suppliers is a cross-functional issue. Ideally, the following functions should be involved: purchasing, design, quality, production, production planning. Increasingly, environmental and sustainability criteria play a role in supplier selection. The idea is to preselect a limited number of qualified suppliers.

  At Ford Motor Company, for example, the cross-functional product development teams request two or three qualified suppliers to make a proposal for the design of new components. Following analysis, the buyer negotiates with the supplier. If this negotiation leads to acceptance of the proposal, this supplier usually remains solely responsible for the delivery during the life cycle of the product ('life-of-type responsibility').

- Functional design. Industrial customers must enable their suppliers to study the design of the complete subassembly beforehand. This is in line with the growing trend of drawing up only functional specifications. Based on these specifications, the supplier can submit a design proposal. The customer's designers should concentrate on the design of essential parts and not on designing, for instance, valves and switches. Here, standard components should be used rather than customer-specific components.

MEMO 11.5   SUPPLIER RATING AT ALCATEL BELL ANTWERP

'Alcatel Bell only buys from sources which have been selected on the basis of their ability to meet requirements' (ISO 9001, par. 4.6.2.). These sources are registered in the Procurement Management Systems Database as 'approved', 'potential', or 'discontinued'. Any buyer can purchase from the approved sources.

Purchase from suppliers with the status of 'potential' or 'discontinued' are subjected to the approval of senior buyers.

The quantity and identity of purchased goods is always verified at the receiving gate. Whether or not additionele incoming inspection is performed depends on the nature of the purchased materials and the confidence Bell Alcatel has in the supplier; this confidence is indicated by the Incoming Inspection Category (IIC) which once again features in the Procurement Management System Database.

The IIC ranges from 0 to 9. The IIC provides us with a steering mechanism enabling us to optimize the incoming inspection resources. We judge quality performance of a supplier by comparison with others who supply similar components. This comparison is based on two indices:

1 The IIC, which is a measure of the amount of incoming inspection we still have to perform and which consists of an average of the evaluated IICs.

2 The Quality Index (QI) based on the quality of actual deliveries. This QI takes into account the percentage of deliveries with a problem and the percentage of delivered products with a problem. For each percentage point, 5 points are deducted from a level arbitrarily set at 1000. Based on this score, suppliers are at present considered to be:

very good QI > 990
good 990 > QI > 950
poor 950 > QI > 900
bad QI < 900.

Source: Bell Alcatel, *Quality On Time Magazine*, 1st Quarter, 1991

- Feedback and recognition. Feedback and recognition are prerequisites to motivate suppliers towards a better performance. Looking at a company such as Hewlett-Packard, it is seen that they assess their suppliers every 3 months, every 6 months and every 12 months, depending on the nature of the delivered components. In the assessment they judge technology, quality, response time, reliability and costs. In addition there are consultations between members of the Hewlett-Packard purchasing teams and the major suppliers, in which the results and possibilities for improvement are discussed in detail. Just as for IBM (see Memo 11.4) and other large manufacturers, Hewlett-Packard provides an annual award to the best-performing supplier.

- Dependency. Raising quality requirements leads to a reduction of the number of suppliers. For many buyers, this development has resulted in the fear that suppliers might be gaining a more powerful position *vis-à-vis* the buyers. This fear is not completely justified because, as a result of the new co-operative relationships, many suppliers are also becoming more dependent on large manufacturers. Companies that start to function as 'single source' suppliers get involved in a product policy they have no control over, and as such they have no guarantees that the life cycle of the product is long enough for them to recover the investments they make. Large manufacturers must not lose sight of the fact that it is of vital importance to the suppliers that they keep making profits. Both parties would suffer if the supplier's financial resources were insufficient to invest in R&D, process innovation, training, etc.

- Testing relationships. To uncover the suppliers' needs, Ford Supplier Relations conducts a confidential survey annually. Several suppliers are asked to describe in detail how they experience their co-operation with Ford. The information gathered in this way is passed on to all management levels of the departments of Quality management, Design, Production Control and Purchasing. To motivate suppliers towards just-in-time deliveries, Ford also organizes regular seminars in areas such as statistical process control and total quality management.

ASSESSING SUPPLIER QUALITY: DIAGNOSTIC METHODS

Several methods are available for the evaluation or assessment of suppliers' quality policies. Earlier, a distinction was made between internal and external assessment. As a rule, the following methods for assessing a supplier's resources are at the buyer's disposal:

- **product audit**
- **process audit**
- **systems audit.**

The product audit provides an image of the degree to which a company succeeds in making everything run perfectly, i.e. according to the standards and demands established by the company itself. The product is judged and every flaw is registered, the cause located and removed. Frequently, the observed deviations are awarded defect points in terms of reject rates. The total score provides, to some extent, an image of the quality level of the entire production process.

The process audit is a systematic investigation of the extent to which the (technical) processes are capable of meeting the established standards in a predictable way. It is also checked whether the raw materials, semi-manufactured materials, etc. are satisfactory, and whether the job instructions and process instructions are complete and clear. In short, the process audit investigates whether the process operators have at their disposal all the facilities (including expertise) to ensure sound and controlled production. This is also sometimes called a 4M audit (man, materials, machines, methods).

The systems audit compares the quality system to external standards. A standard, or norm, is used which is a generally accepted guideline. Standards can be either general standards or company-specific standards. Examples of general standards are the Allied Quality Assurance Publications (AQAP), originating from the military, and the European NEN-ISO standards. The latter are presented in Table 11.1.

One major company-specific system standard that is used for auditing suppliers is the Ford Q101 procedure. The supplier is required to answer questions related to some 20 subjects. Questions are answered by means of awarding a score between 0 and 10. The total score gives an indication of the quality of the production process. Volvo employs a systems audit which is based on the Ford Q101 system. Table 11.2 shows the subjects that are addressed in such an audit.

Audit, product
The product audit provides an image of the degree to which a company succeeds in making everything run perfectly, i.e. according to the standards and requirements established by the company itself.

Audit, process
The process audit is a systematic investigation of the extent to which the (technical) processes are capable of meeting the established standards in a predictable way.

TABLE 11.1 The ISO 9000 series of quality assurance standards

Standard	Title
ISO 9000	Guidelines for selection and application of ISO 9000 through 9004
ISO 9001	Requirements concerning quality control in purchasing, development, production and sales (equivalent to AQAP 1)
ISO 9002	Requirements concerning quality control in purchasing, production and sales (equivalent to AQAP 4)
ISO 9003	Requirements concerning quality control of final inspection and testing (equivalent to AQAP 9)
ISO 9004	Guidelines for the organization of a quality system
ISO 8402	Terminology and definitions

TABLE 11.2 Structure of systems audit by automobile manufacturers

		Action plan					
No.	Subject	Jan Feb	Mar Apr	May Jun	July Aug	Sept Oct	Nov Dec
1.	Organization						
2.	Planning						
3.	Documentation and management of technical changes						
4.	Manufacturing equipment control						
5.	Production – procedures – instructions						
6.	Inspection – procedures – instructions						
7.	Standards						
8.	Means of inspection						
9.	Quality assurance purchased components						
10.	Process parameters						
11.	In-process inspection						
12.	Final inspection						
13.	Sampling instructions						
14.	Non-conformance						
15.	Quality and inspection status						
16.	Materials handling						
17.	Training personnel						
18.	Documentation and registration						
19.	Corrective measures						
20.	Volvo inspections at suppliers						

Classification		Required points
A1	Qualified	825–855
A2	Qualified, with comments	755–820
B1	Acceptable	645–750
B2	Acceptable, with reservation	535–640
C	Not acceptable	

MEMO 11.6 STRUCTURE OF A SYSTEMS AUDIT (AUTOMOBILE MANUFACTURER)

External verification contributes to the assurance of the quality system or, as the case may be, to keeping up the quality system, and also demonstrates that the system meets the standards.

Many suppliers strive to live up to the standards, especially the NEN-ISO standards. A supplier who meets the standards becomes eligible for certification. Whether or not the candidate-supplier possesses one or more certificates plays a major role in purchasing's decision to use this particular supplier.

Many companies have their organization assessed by an independent body in the context of a quality certifying programme. In most European countries Certification Councils have been founded during the last 10 years. These councils are the central (national)

institutions that confer competence on certifying organizations to give out NEN-ISO 9001, 9002 or 9003 certificates to the organizations that meet the relevant standards. Such a certificate is evidence of the company's capability with regard to the quality of the system, at least for the period of its validity.

Not all manufacturers attach the same value to these general standards and accompanying certificates. Some continue to use their own company-specific standards, which suppliers must meet to qualify for co-operation. Examples are the military AQAP standards[1] and the Ford Q101 standards mentioned earlier. Even during a long-term agreement between supplier and manufacturer, periodical checking (especially of the system, the process and the product) against the standards, is necessary. Based on the results of the audits, the decision is made to either continue the agreement or to start looking for an alternative supplier.

[1]AQAP stands for Allied Quality Assurance Publications, which were developed by the Ministry of Defense in the USA. The AQAP standards were the basis for the first quality systems standards for American industry. After World War II the AQAP standards applied to all suppliers to NATO.

IMPLEMENTING SUPPLIER QUALITY ASSURANCE: CONSEQUENCES FOR PURCHASING

As a rule, the implementation of total quality management requires considerable adjustments in terms of structure, systems and patterns of communication. The same applies to the purchasing department that wants to pursue a specific policy with regard to supplier quality assurance. Some of the most important changes that will have to be prepared for are now discussed:

- Clear task descriptions. There is not much point in formulating a general policy without formulating clear and unambiguous tasks. Therefore, it should be clear who is responsible for SQA within the firm. Next, it must be very clear what supplier quality assurance is expected to yield in terms of, for example:
  - maximum rejection percentages per article code or per supplier
  - the average term in which rejection reports must be dealt with (per buyer)
  - number of quality agreements closed with suppliers
  - number of certified suppliers, etc.
- Clarity concerning supplier selection. As the demands made on suppliers increase, there are also higher demands on the manufacturer's entire organization, and on the purchasing department in particular. It must be clear who within the company is competent to enter into relationships with suppliers. In particular it must be clear who is responsible for the ultimate selection of suppliers. Requirements must be communicated to the suppliers from one central point so as to prevent misunderstandings.
- Quality first. Taking responsibility for quality also means being accountable and being judged on it. If the ultimate selection of suppliers is made by the purchasing department, then it must also be possible to call this department to account on the quality these suppliers deliver. This means that rejection percentages, the number of quality agreements, etc. are becoming part of the buyer's annual assessment.
- To measure is to know. It is essential that suppliers receive feedback on their performance. This is done in the form of a report on the findings of the audit which has been carried out, but is also needed in the form of a supplier rating score on rejection rates,

too late or too early deliveries, administrative errors, etc. This requires the appropriate administrative procedures, which should be computerized where necessary. Producing such data is not necessarily a simple matter, because the basic information is often stored in different systems and in various locations within the company.

The implementation of quality management in organizations is frequently a process of trial and error, with many ups and downs. The same goes for introducing a supplier policy based on quality principles. The extent to which problems occur regarding these aspects provides an indication of the extent to which suppliers are really seen, or experienced, as an essential link in the business chain.

SUMMARY

In this chapter, the interfaces between purchasing, new product innovation and quality assurance have been shown. As the competitive environment of organizations become more turbulent, issues such as time-to-market, flexibility and product and service quality become more important. In those circumstances it is crucial to do things right the first time, because every error leads to time loss and extra costs.

Increasing competition forces companies to speed up their innovation processes. Traditionally, new product innovation was conducted using primarily internal resources. As a result new product innovation was slow and led to only a few market introductions a year. In order to speed up innovation and in order to share the massive investments that go with new product innovation, large corporations today have embraced the open innovation paradigm. Innovation today cannot be confined to the traditional boundaries of organizations anymore. Open innovation fosters early supplier involvement in new product development. This happens because suppliers increasingly are an important source of innovation. The challenge, however, is how to mobilize a supplier's innovation potential. This challenge is not without problems since it poses clear demands in terms of professionalism of all parties involved. When going for early supplier involvement, the buying company needs to consider three types of processes: strategic management processes, operational management processes and collaboration management processes.

A question to consider is what supplier to involve at what stage of the new product development process. The new product development portfolio may serve as a vehicle to support effective decision-making on this matter. As the product development process advances, the product specifications become more and more fixed, and it therefore becomes more difficult to introduce product changes. Furthermore, changes made at a later stage will make the costs rise exponentially.

Buyers are important scouts when it comes to spotting new technological developments that occur in the supplier market. Buyers are generalists, while designers and engineers are predominantly specialists. To them, the technical solution is often more important than supply. To prevent technical problems in the future, designers will tend to operate as specifically as possible and to record their designs in detail. This may go against the buyer's interests: it would like to see the product design drawn up in functional terms, so it can use different sources of supply in the future.

The product design is the basis for product quality. The term 'quality' has been taken in a broad sense, i.e. as 'the degree to which the requirements are met'. It has been seen that this concept entails more than just the technical properties. Quality management contains all activities and decisions whose purpose is to bring the organization's product to the desired quality level and to keep it there. These terms were central in the discussion of supplier quality assurance. The purpose of supplier quality assurance is improvement of supplier quality in the broadest sense, including environmental and sustainability aspects. Some elements involved in a quality approach towards suppliers are:

- preparation of the purchase order specification
- preliminary qualification of (potential) suppliers
- sample inspection procedure
- inspection of first and following preproduction series
- inspection of first and following production series
- conclude a quality agreement and certification
- periodic verification.

Several methods used by manufacturers to assess the qualities of their suppliers were considered and the distinction between the product audit, the process audit and the system audit was explored. With regard to the latter it is general practice to follow the ISO standards. The most widely known and followed systems audit developed by manufacturers is Ford's Q101.

ASSIGNMENTS

11.1 What kinds of risks are related to involving suppliers early in new product development projects? Answer this question from the perspective of (a) the buyer and (b) the new product development engineer.

11.2 What kinds of benefits would you as a manager of a company require in order to make up for the risks that were mentioned when answering the previous question?

11.3 What will it take from a buyer to develop innovative, collaborative relationships with suppliers?

11.4 What activities would be required from a buyer in order to get to zero defects deliveries from suppliers?

11.5 Which types of quality costs can be distinguished? Provide at least two examples of every type. To what extent can the purchasing department contribute to a reduction of the quality costs?

REFERENCES

Chesbrough (2003) Open Innovation: the New Imperative for Creating and Profiting from New Technology, Boston: Harvard Business Press.

Crosby, P.B. (1984) *Quality without Tears*, New York: McGraw-Hill.

Liker, J.K. and Choi, Th.Y (2004) Building deep supplier relationships, *Harvard Business Review*, December: 2–10

Ragatz, G.L., Handfield, R.B. and Scannell, T.V. (1997), 'Success factors for integrating suppliers into product development', *Journal of Product Innovation Management*, 14(3):190–20.

van Echtelt, F.E.A. (2004) New product development: shifting suppliers into gear, PhD dissertation, Eindhoven Center for Innovation Studies (ECIS), Eindhoven University of Technology, p. 370.

van Echtelt, F.E.A., Wynstra, J.Y.F., van Weele, A.J. and Duysters, G. (2008) Managing Supplier Involvement in New Product Development: a Mulitple-Case Study, *Journal of Product Innovation Management*, (25):180–201.

Wynstra, J.Y.F. (1998) Purchasing involvement in new product development, PhD dissertation, Eindhoven Center for Innovation Studies (ECIS), Eindhoven University of Technology.

PURCHASING, LOGISTICS AND SUPPLY CHAIN MANAGEMENT

LEARNING OBJECTIVES

After studying this chapter you should understand the following:

- The definition of supply chain management and the basic supply chain concepts
- The most important steps in the materials planning cycle
- How supply chain activities can be structured within organizations
- Characteristics of just-in-time scheduling and purchasing
- The most important elements of a purchasing information system.

INTRODUCTION

This chapter addresses the relationship between purchasing and supply chain management. In this context the focus is on several important concepts and developments in the field. The materials planning cycle is described, which will make clear how materials planning processes affect the purchasing order cycle and the incoming materials flow. In discussing this subject the chapter will differentiate between the varieties of supply structures that can be encountered in industry. Hence a distinction will be made between order-based materials processes and forecast-based materials processes. Given its importance there will be ample discussion of the subject of just-in-time manufacturing, lean supply and the impact of these concepts on purchasing and supplier relationships. Finally, this chapter discusses the major elements and principles in designing effective purchasing information systems.

PURCHASING, LOGISTICS AND SUPPLY CHAIN MANAGEMENT: DEFINITIONS AND CONCEPTS

Today companies use the term supply chain management to denote the way in which supply processes are managed and structured. Supply chain management relates to the way in which materials processes are managed within the company. However, the term also relates to the way in which the external materials processes are managed. Here, we can

CASE STUDY LI & FUNG

The impact and significance of integrated purchasing and supply chain management can be illustrated through Li & Fung, the fast growing supply chain integrator from Hong Kong.

Li & Fung started in 1906 as a traditional purchasing agent. Initially, simple, low cost consumer goods were purchased at a provision rate for customers in the USA and Europe. Production orders were allocated by Li & Fung among suppliers from the Chinese mainland on the basis of competitive tenders.

Today, the company has over 70 purchasing offices in over 40 countries, most of which are situated in Southeast Asia. Based upon the specifications of the Western customer (predominantly American and European department stores and DIY chains) Li & Fung designers may develop a range of products under the customer's private label. After approval of the design by the customer, the best manufacturer for the production order is selected within the network of manufacturers in Southeast Asia. Given their volume, Li & Fung works with a large number of carefully selected manufacturers. The company always makes sure to have about 50% of the turnover of a specific supplier in order to ensure that it is always treated by its suppliers as a preferred customer. A dedicated quality inspector will be on site to supervise the production order and to ensure that the products meet the agreed specifications and to monitor social and environmental requirements. The purchasing offices of Li & Fung supply all necessary raw and other materials (textiles, yarn, buttons, zips, packaging) to the manufacturer. Due to its scale, Li & Fung can stipulate far better conditions and qualities for their raw materials and components than can the individual manufacturers. After production, Li & Fung takes care of the shipment and transportation. The advantage lies in the consolidation of deliveries: different shipments for different customers may be consolidated into one

container so that transport costs for the customer are as low as possible. Here, too, the company profits from its expertise and scale. Li & Fung make no secret of their network. If required, the customer can visit the production facilities and orient itself. Li & Fung's integrated way of working allows them to work at 40% lower costs, compared with when departments stores would take care of their business themselves. Li & Fung's success is reflected in their financial figures: over the past decade the company produced double digit growth figures annually.

Li & Fung is an example of a new generation of supply chain integrators, which we expect to see many more of in the coming years. These supply chain integrators will turn the traditional supply chains upside down. Companies will arise that own nothing and nevertheless control everything. They will not be very capital intensive and have few assets. They will, however, have superior logistics and financial information systems, and will work with a great deal of discipline. They will have broad supplier networks at their disposal with which to maintain long-lasting relations that they continue to develop. What is essential to their business model is to create the position of chain director – a position that has to be carefully developed and strengthened.

This example demonstrates the key factors to success for effective and successful supply chain management: a strong position in the customer–supplier network, supported by advanced information technology and creative entrepreneurship. The key element is not the price that Li & Fung offers its customers, but rather the integrated value proposition for the design, purchasing, and logistics for a complete line of products. It is an example of an enterprise that is capable of successfully linking customer networks directly to its supplier networks.

Source: Arjan van Weele (2003)

differentiate between the outgoing materials flow and the incoming materials flow. The former relates to the way in which finished products are distributed by the company to its customers. This activity is commonly denoted as physical distribution. The incoming materials flow, obviously, covers all activities needed to optimize the goods flows up from suppliers to the point of consumption within the company itself. This activity used to be referred to as materials management. In many cases, the scope of supply chain management goes one step further in that it also relates to optimizing the materials flows from the supplier's suppliers to the company. As we will see later, supply chain management has matured due to the fact that advanced information systems have become available, which are able to trace and track complex materials flows in great detail.

Supply chain thinking started several decades ago with **logistics management**. The term 'logistics' originally stems from military organization and was already in use in the days of Louis XIV of France. Even then it was clear that the effectiveness of any military organization or operation did not depend solely on the weapons, the power and the fighting spirit of the soldiers. It was also affected by the possibilities of transportation and the efficient supply of ammunition and food. The rationalized consideration of the transportation and supply of materials, food and ammunition was called logistics. The French military successes of that time were mainly due to the importance that was given to logistics.

Logistics and flexibility go hand in hand. Flexibility is getting a lot of attention in many companies today where functional thinking still dominates. In a functional organization individual departments such as sales, production, product development, administration, purchasing and personnel, essentially are managed as separate activities. In most cases the managers responsible for each of these activity areas report directly to the executive board. Each department has very specific tasks that are to be realized through limited resources, which are agreed in annual departmental budgets. Realization of these budgetary targets is an important factor in the assessment of departmental managers. They, therefore, often strive to realize their own budget targets, even at the expense of other departments.

This practice can easily lead to departments operating fairly autonomously so that coordination of the whole is left to the interplay of forces between the departments themselves.

Logistics and supply chain management aim to counterbalance the shortcomings of the functional organization, by focussing on those processes through which customers can be better served. Logistics and supply chain management favour a process approach rather than a functional approach. All processes are aligned in order to meet specific customer needs and focussed on creating maximum customer satisfaction. Superior customer service, efficient customer complaint handling, and customer driven product development and innovation are important cornerstones of logistics and supply chain management.

Logistics management is related to all materials flows, from the flows of purchased materials into a facility, through the manufacturing process, and out to the customer. The starting point for any logistics process is the short-term sales plan and the related product plan. The total logistics function therefore includes short-term materials planning, the supply of raw materials and other purchased goods, internal transportation, storage and physical distribution. It may also include in some companies reverse logistics, i.e. recycling packaging materials and surplus materials.

Creating superior customer service and flexibility demand very close co-operation between all materials-related functions. Logistics management therefore applies to a very broad area of activities and is sometimes also referred to as materials management or integrated business logistics. Figure 12.1 illustrates the relationship between these and other materials concepts.

The following features are relevant to an understanding of the importance of co-ordinating the company's internal and external supply chain processes:

- Design, engineering and product development activities can strongly affect logistics processes, for these activities determine the structure of the (future) manufactured products. The tolerances and specifications of products and the components they are made up of can be defined in such detail that they can only be obtained from a few suppliers. One question in the context of the design activities is to what extent one strives for standardization of components. If new components are specified for each new end product being developed, then this irrevocably leads to a very extensive article assortment. This will have considerable consequences for logistics complexity and therefore the degree of sophistication of the materials, planning and control systems.

Logistics management
Logistics management includes the management of materials planning, the supply of raw materials and other purchased goods, internal transportation, storage and physical distribution. It may also include, in some companies, reverse logistics, i.e. recycling packaging materials and surplus materials.

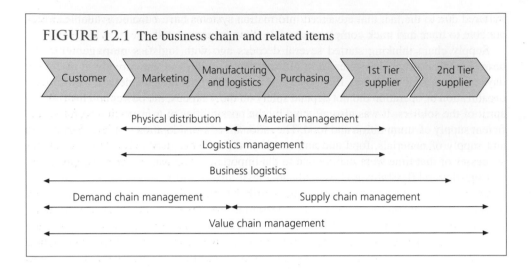

FIGURE 12.1 The business chain and related items

- The production department also determines the effectiveness and efficiency of the logistics function to a large extent. The production department will usually aim for a high-capacity utilization of its assets. Disruptions of the production process as a result of rejection and shortages of materials due to failing supplier deliveries are undesirable. A production manager will take certain measures to prevent such disruptions, for example by building up buffer stock. Although these measures may reduce the threat of production stops, the cause of the problem remains. In other words, these 'solutions' (which used to be applied in many companies) are an example of sub-optimization – although the measure is a solution for one department, it is not for the entire organization.

- Logistics management starts with the customer. If the sales organization, for the sake of landing an order, promises a delivery time within the internal production lead times, planning problems are likely to occur! This frequently results in 'rush work' in production planning, production, and purchasing. It leads to a situation in which purchasing must exert considerable pressure on suppliers to get the required materials earlier and often at considerable extra costs!

Some authors describe logistics management as the management (i.e. the planning, execution and control) of all factors that affect the materials flow, the financial flows related to it and the related information flows, seen from the perspective of customer requirements, in such a way that the highest delivery reliability, the best order fulfilment and the shortest delivery time are realised. Based upon this description we can differentiate between logistics management and supply chain management. This latter term is interesting, because the relationship between the company and its suppliers as well as its customers is included in this concept. Suppliers can make important contributions to the improvement of customer service levels. This was illustrated when a manufacturer of cleaning materials and detergents decided to analyse its low customer service levels. The supply organisation repeatedly was not able to meet promised delivery dates in the relationship with some major customers. The analysis revealed that 75% of the reasons were related to the bad deliveries of their suppliers! The analysis came to the conclusion that, where the company had to meet stringent delivery schedules as imposed by its customers and was evaluated on its customer service levels, the suppliers to the manufacturing organization were not monitored and evaluated at all on this key performance indicator. Based upon this finding the company started to put the same performance measures in place as those that were used by their customers. This immediately led to an improvement of the suppliers' delivery performance, and, next, to an improvement of the company's customer service levels.

Apart from suppliers, customers may also have considerable influence on the effectiveness of a company's supply chain. If customers are willing to give up or adjust certain requirements (for instance with regard to packaging and minimum delivery quantities) considerable savings due to the simplification of supply processes can be the result. When customers are willing to share important planning information with their suppliers, this will enable them to anticipate much more effectively future customer orders. Since both customers and suppliers can exert considerable influence on supply processes, we favour an expanded view on business logistics. Therefore, we will use the term supply chain management throughout this book.

Over the past decade more and more attention has been given to the concept of supply chain management (SCM). Stevens (1989) looks at the supply chain as the connected series of activities which is concerned with planning, co-ordinating and controlling materials, parts and finished goods from the company's suppliers up to its customers. This author extends the concept of business logistics to other tiers in the supply chain. This is also recognized by Cooper and Ellram (1993) who present supply chain management as an integrative philosophy to manage the total flow of a distribution channel from suppliers to the final consumer. Like vertical marketing systems SCM represents a systems approach to viewing the supply chain as an integrated entity rather than as a set of fragmented parts. SCM differs from traditional approaches to inventory control and focuses on the management of inventory control through the entire supply chain. Successful SCM relies on forming strategic partnerships with trading partners along the supply chain, with one partner playing a key role in coordinating and overseeing the whole supply chain . . . (*ibid.*, p. 3). However, effective supply chain management requires suppliers that are able to meet the demands of the company's operational processes. Therefore, supply base management needs to precede SCM.

This description shows that SCM can be considered as a logical extension of earlier logistics concepts. It says that in order to be able to manage cost throughout the supply chain, effective and co-operative supplier relationships are required. Hence, purchasing and supply management (including supplier management) can be seen as an integrated part of SCM. In fact, the latter concept encompasses both the logistics and the purchasing and supply function. Now that we have provided some definitions, let's have a closer look at how materials processes in organisations can be structured and managed.

MATERIALS REQUIREMENTS PLANNING

Materials requirements planning (MRP) starts in the sales department with the drawing up of a sales plan. This plan provides an estimate of the volume that management thinks can be sold in the following months or the year to come. Data are presented both at product-group level and at the product/article level. Comparison of the sales plan with the available finished product stock yields the volumes to be produced. This information is the input for the manufacturing planning and control system (see Figure 12.2) in which the following elements can be distinguished:

- Master planning. In the master plan the manufacturing plans at the level of the product families (product groups) are established in consultation between the departments of sales, product development, manufacturing, finance and administration and logistics. In the master plan the customer orders, the sales plan, the planned stocks of finished products and the production and purchasing plans are linked together.

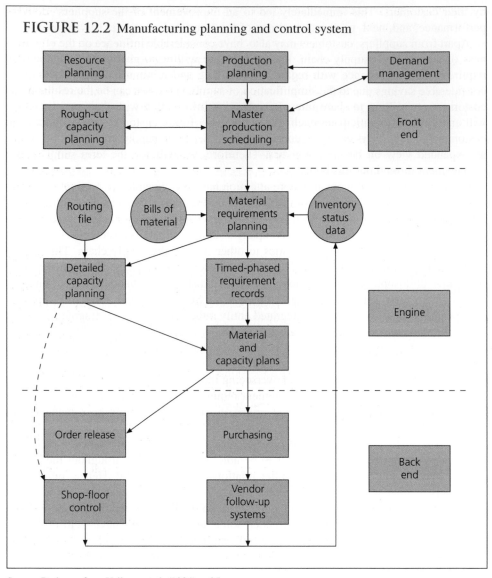

FIGURE 12.2 Manufacturing planning and control system

Source: Redrawn from Vollman et al. (1984) p. 25

- Manufacturing resources planning (MRP-II). The resources needed to realize the master plan are recorded in the manufacturing resources plan, from which the required composition of manufacturing resources is derived. In the process it may become clear that particular production series are not feasible because of limited production capacity. This then, will require an adjustment of the master planning or adjustment of the manufacturing capacity. In the latter case an investment plan needs to be prepared for adding additional production capacity.

- Master production scheduling (MPS). The MPS translates the master plan into specific materials requirements. The MPS is also the basis for computing the quantities of materials, semi-manufactured products and components which must be manufactured. In this way the MPS provides the input for calculating the net materials requirements.

- General capacity testing. The MPS must also be tested for capacity limitations. This should be done for all potential bottleneck capacities. Such a check may reveal that the internal capacity is insufficient to produce certain components. If that is the case, the possibilities of contracting out the production of these components, or buying them, must be investigated.

- Materials requirements planning (MRP). The materials requirements planning 'explodes' the requirements of the MPS level, step-by-step, in accordance with the bill of materials (BOM). It determines the materials requirements at the different levels of product structure and, finally, at the materials (item) level. If at some level identical requirements emerge from different MPS items, then these are grouped and added up per period. These needs are called the gross requirements and are converted into net requirements per period. This is accomplished by deducting the stock in hand from the gross requirements and subsequently deducting the manufacturing orders and purchasing order volumes that have already been placed. The net requirements are then plotted, taking into account the ordering procedures that have been developed. In this way the materials requisitions are built up. These requisitions must be available in time, to be ordered from the supplier or to be manufactured by the company's own manufacturing departments.

- Capacity requirements planning. Capacity requirements planning is conceptually comparable with materials requirement planning. The current and planned manufacturing orders from the materials requirements planning provide the input for the detailed production line planning. The required capacity is compared with the available capacity per production line (machine). The capacity requirements planning spots, at an early stage, where and when utilization problems will occur, so that preventive/alternative measures may be taken. If it is impossible to solve these problems, then the MPS must be adjusted.

- Order release. Order releases change the status of the manufacturing orders and purchase orders from 'planned' to 'released'. The decision to release is based on the availability of the required materials and capacity. If a manufacturing order is released by a planner, the information system automatically allocates the required materials to this order. This prevents these materials being allocated to another process or manufacturing order. The system generates documentation for issuing the materials and components required to feed the manufacturing orders; in case stock is insufficient it generates materials requisitions for purchasing (i.e. purchasing requisitions).

- Priority management. The priorities are derived directly from the master production schedule. Each unit receives a priority sheet which lists all manufacturing orders for that production line or machine centre. Orders with the highest priority should be given preference; regular 'overdue' reports indicate which manufacturing orders and purchasing requisitions will not be executed on time.

- Capacity management. The issue of managing lead times, work-in-progress (WIP) and capacity is a complex one. To prevent under-utilization, manufacturing always tends to take on more work. However, when the expected workload (the input) exceeds the available capacity, long waiting periods ensue. The various manufacturing orders will be waiting longer, the lead times increase, the amounts of work in progress grow and delivery reliability decreases. This is why it is of the utmost importance that the waiting times per processing group are controlled. Input/output reports have an important function here; to compare the realized output for a production unit against its planned output.

The literature makes a distinction between MRP-I and MRP-II. MRP-I stands for materials requirement planning; this type of management system aims at releasing manufacturing orders and purchasing requisitions and at managing them. MRP-II stands for manufacturing resources planning and entails more than MRP-I. It is an integral system that controls relevant materials flows and production capacity, while also taking into account the relationship between these materials flows and the required capacity.

BASIC LOGISTICS STRUCTURES

Customer order decoupling point (CODP)

The point in the supply chain where a production order becomes customer specific. Downstream of this point activities are planned based upon customer order and further downstream activities are planned based upon forecast.

Logistics structure, making and sending to stock (MSS)

Products are manufactured and distributed to various distribution points which are dispersed and located close to the customer. Manufacturing is based upon forecasts and on the expected stock turnover at the points of distribution.

The systems described above are characterized by the fact that they are forecast-based. The more accurate the sales forecasts, the more accurately production planning and materials requirements can be determined. It will be clear that in practice the unpredictability of sales orders is the stumbling block in the application of these systems. Furthermore, industrial manufacturing and logistics practice often shows much more variation than we have outlined here. Many companies have order-based production (as in the shipbuilding industry) instead of a forecast-based production (as is the practice in the petrochemical and processing industry). In customer-order-controlled manufacturing companies, production and materials planning are derived directly from the customer order. Every order is customer specific and therefore requires individual handling. Each sales order in fact represents a unique project. The customer's requirements tend to become known only at the last moment, which results in high time pressure. In such a situation the project approach to production is much more effective than an approach based on the MRP method. In other words, the application of MRP systems is limited to (small and large) series and process production.

In practice there are numerous hybrids between those production companies managed solely on the basis of customer orders and those based on forecast alone. Most manufacturing companies, unfortunately, have to deal with both types of manufacturing and goods flows. The order **decoupling point** (or order penetration point) concept is of major importance when organizing for efficient manufacturing and logistics. The order decoupling point indicates how deeply the customer order penetrates the firm's materials flow.[1] It defines from what moment on a production order becomes customer specific. Downstream from this point all activities are customer order driven; upstream of this point activities are forecast based. The order decoupling point separates the activities based on order information from the forecast-based activities. This is important because these two types of activity require totally different planning techniques. In general, the following situations can be distinguished:

- Making and sending to stock (MSS). Products are manufactured and distributed to various distribution points which are dispersed and located close to the customer. Manufacturing is based upon forecasts and on the expected stock turnover at the points of distribution. Examples are the manufacture of sweets, foods and beverages.

- Making to stock (central stock) (MTS). Finished products are kept in stock at the end of the production process and from there are shipped directly to many geographically dispersed customers, as in the manufacture of many consumer electronics products (such as dishwashers and refrigerators).

Logistics structure, making to order (MTO)

Only raw materials and components are kept in stock. Every customer order is a specific project. Examples are the manufacture of cans, basic construction materials.

- Assembly to order (ATO). Only systems elements or subassemblies are in stock at the manufacturing centre and final assembly takes place based on a specific customer order. In other words, manufacture of components takes place based on forecasts and final assembly takes place based on customer orders. Examples are the manufacture of cars, computers and materials handling equipment.

- Making to order (MTO). Only raw materials and components are kept in stock. Every customer order is a specific project. Examples are the manufacture of cans, basic construction materials.

---

[1]This discussion was originally based upon Hoekstra and Romme (1985), who did pioneering research in supply chains and customer order decoupling points.

- Engineering and making to order (ETO). In this situation there is no stock at all. The purchase and order of materials takes place on the basis of the specific customer order and the entire project is carried out for this one specific client. As a result this type of production structure results in long lead times. Examples are construction companies and shipyards. Figure 12.3 presents these situations in diagrammatic form.

The question of where the order decoupling point should be located in the company's primary processes is a major issue when designing the manufacturing and logistics organization. The answer to this question also determines where in the process inventories should be located and in what quantities. The role and position of the purchasing function will differ in each of the situations described above. In the first situation the planning of the quantities to be purchased per period is fairly predictable. Based on expected volumes, annual (bulk) agreements can be negotiated with suppliers or price agreements with a long period of operation can be made. Based on the production planning, delivery schedules can be drawn up and periodically communicated to the supplier.

In the last situation purchasing strongly resembles project purchasing. Every project is new – new suppliers have to be found for every production order, the products that are to

Logistics structure, (ETO)
In this situation there is no stock at all. The purchase and order of materials takes place on the basis of the specific customer order and the entire project is carried out for this one specific client. As a result this type of production structure results in long lead times.

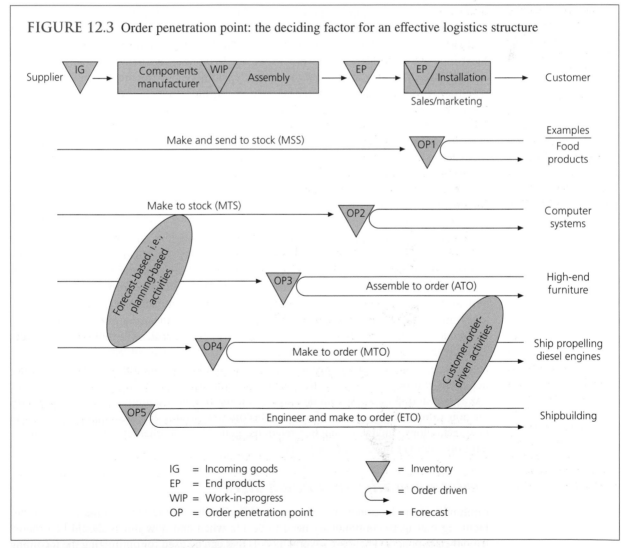

FIGURE 12.3 Order penetration point: the deciding factor for an effective logistics structure

Source: Redrawn from Hoekstra and Romme (1985)

be manufactured must be discussed in detail with suppliers, and intensive consultation between the design and engineering department is necessary. On-time delivery and quality are more important than price! Purchasing must be able to respond to changes in design and project planning quickly.

JUST-IN-TIME MANAGEMENT

Characteristics of just-in-time management

Just-in-time management (JIT)
All materials and products become available at the very moment when they are needed in the production process, not sooner and not later, but exactly on time and in exactly the right quantity.

The principle of **just-in-time management** (JIT) means that all materials and products become available at the very moment when they are needed in the production process, not sooner and not later, but exactly on time and in exactly the right quantity. The major objective underlying this approach is to continuously tackle and solve manufacturing bottlenecks within, and interface problems between, consecutive steps in the supply chain processes. Incoming inspection, buffer stock, and extensive quality control procedures on incoming materials are primarily considered as 'waste'. The basic idea is to strive continuously to reduce and eliminate these often 'hidden' costs in the factory.

JIT implies that nothing is produced if there is no demand. The production process is 'pulled' by customer orders. The 'customer' is in fact the organizational entity which is 'next-in-line'. This concept, therefore, may relate to other departments within the company itself. However, it may also relate to external customers, outside the organization. When no customer orders have been received, manufacturing activities will come to an end and the spare time is used to do minor repairs/maintenance, housekeeping or prepare for materials planning. The spare time may also be used to discuss how to improve on the work currently being conducted within the organizational entity ('small group activities'). No production, therefore, does not imply that the time is used unproductively.

Because they contract out a considerable amount of work, many large Japanese producers work closely with a limited number of suppliers (which are sometimes organized in supplier networks or supplier associations). The bulk of the materials requirements are sourced from these suppliers. It is not uncommon that one manufacturer is responsible for more than 50% of a supplier's turnover. At the same time this same supplier may deliver 80% of the manufacturer's specific materials requirements. This leads, in contrast to many European manufacturers, to a large interdependence between manufacturers and suppliers. As a result Japanese manufacturers are able to benefit much more from the supplier's expertise and capabilities. Another aspect is that Japanese manufacturers in general focus on assembly only. All component manufacturing is outsourced to specialized suppliers. Since the producer frequently represents a large share of the supplier's turnover, a maximum effort by the supplier is ensured. Obviously, there is some risk involved for suppliers when engaging in this type of relationship: if there is no market demand for the customer's product, there will be less work for the supplier. In this way part of the business's economic risk is transferred to the suppliers. However, if the producer can guarantee a certain production volume for a number of years, it becomes appealing for the supplier to invest in new technology. Japanese supplier relations, generally, are characterized by their long-term orientation (3 to 5-year contracts).

Order quantities and batch sizes

Continuity in production demands a constant availability of the required materials. Manufacturing managers continuously need to decide when and how much should be ordered from their suppliers. There are several models that can be used for optimizing the incoming materials flow. One very well-known model is **Camp's formula**. The variables used in this inventory model are:

S	fixed usage per period
t	delivery period
Q	order quantity
C_o	costs per order
C_i	inventory carrying costs for one unit during one time unit.

The economic order quantity is where the sum of inventory costs and ordering costs per unit is lowest. Ordering large quantities from suppliers has the advantage that the ordering costs (fixed costs) can be spread out over a larger number of products. Hence, large order quantities will lead to a lower order cost per unit. The disadvantage of ordering large quantities, however, is that larger quantities of the product must be kept in stock for a longer period of time, which naturally implies higher inventory carrying costs per product.

Starting with the order quantity Q and a usage rate per period S means that in a given period S/Q orders are required. The order costs for that specific period therefore will amount to $S/Q \times C_o$.

The average inventory level, measured over one period, is $1/2\ Q$ and the total inventory costs for the considered period are $1/2\ Q \times C_i$.

The total ordering and inventory costs will be

$$\frac{S}{Q} \times C_o + \frac{1}{2} Q \times C_i$$

The economic order quantity can now be calculated (Camp's formula) as

$$Q_o = \sqrt{\frac{2S \times C_o}{C_i}}$$

Although this formula has received significant interest from practitioners, it is only of significance under the following conditions:

- the consumption of the component at hand is fairly stable
- the consumption of the component is evenly spread over the course of time
- the delivery time of the product is fixed and not due to fluctuation
- the ordering costs per order are fixed
- the inventory carrying costs do not depend on the ordered quantity, etc.

The JIT approach basically challenges each of these assumptions. For example, order-related costs are analysed in terms of costs related to:

- negotiations with the supplier
- administrative processing
- follow-up and expediting of orders
- incoming and quality inspections.

Suppliers are now classified into categories, depending on the degree to which they represent work for the buyer. Suppliers who comply with the stringent JIT conditions require no more investigation. This saves costs on the four items mentioned above. By systematically considering how savings can be accomplished for each separate cost item, the buyer succeeds in reducing the optimal order quantity. A graphic representation is provided in Figure 12.4.

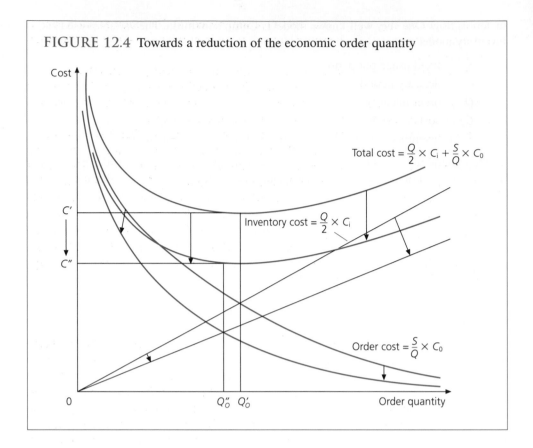

FIGURE 12.4 Towards a reduction of the economic order quantity

The reasoning used for determining the economic order quantity can also be applied to determining the (optimal) batch size in production. This issue arises when one production line is used to produce different products or product varieties. Changing production from one product to another means that the production line needs to be reset, a process which usually costs time and money. In general, four steps in the process of setting up a production line may be identified:

- Preparation. This includes gathering tools, moulds, spare parts, work instructions, etc. and transporting them to the machine or production line concerned.
- Conversion. This is the dismantling and rebuilding of the machine or production line, mounting the appropriate tools and moulds, and, if necessary, cleaning.
- Setting up. This refers to setting the machine in such a way that the desired quality and speed is achieved; a trial run may be necessary.
- Finishing. Finishing may consist of removing, cleaning and storing the used tools and spares, and removing the finished product.

While the machines are being reset nothing is produced. Many companies therefore regard setting up production lines as a necessary evil. In practice the easy solution is frequently chosen: the production line is used to make the same product for a longer period of time, so that less frequent resetting is required. In other words, the batch size is enlarged to benefit from economies of scale achieved as the result of a lower set-up cost per unit produced. Moreover, this practice leads to a much better capacity utilization in production (yield). Clearly, one disadvantage of this way of working is that the size of the stocks related to semi-manufactured products and finished products and the associated inventory carrying costs increase. The decision about the optimization of batch sizes must therefore be based on balancing set-up costs against inventory costs. The optimal batch size is achieved when the sum of the inventory costs of work in process and set-up costs per unit produced is lowest.

Thinking based upon economies-of-scale and production yields, which still can be observed in many manufacturing organizations, limits production flexibility and fast response to customer requirements. This poses a problem for manufacturers when customers demand short lead times, which happens in many markets nowadays.

By systematically striving for reducing set-up times, the optimal batch size can be reduced considerably as well. Often, when calculating the optimal batch size, the set-up costs of the production machinery, among other things, are considered fixed. These costs can be very high. Japanese production thinking has continuously focused on the question of whether these fixed costs can be made variable. Japanese producers have constantly looked for ways to minimize their set-up costs and set-up times. Much has been achieved by means of organizational measures, and new machines have been redesigned that are easier to handle and set up. As a result, optimal batch sizes have been reduced considerably, enabling Japanese producers to benefit from low costs per unit together with a high product mix flexibility in their production.

Quality and zero defects

Another characteristic of the JIT principle is related to quality awareness. Smaller batch sizes make it necessary to detect quality defects at an early stage. In most Japanese companies every employee is responsible for the quality of their work. If a production employee notices that a particular part does not meet the specifications, they immediately notify the colleague in the previous link of the production process. It may be that the conveyor belt has to be stopped. The advantage of this procedure is the fast response time – corrective action is taken immediately following a complaint. This situation is in sharp contrast with the practice of some European companies, where defective material is first put aside, then handed over to the quality department, which in turn contacts the production department in question in order to solve the problem.

It is clear that the JIT approach, in order to be successful must be supported by all functions within the company. Top management should actively support foremen and shop floor workers in providing the resources necessary to improve manufacturing operations. Adopting a JIT approach will take considerable time; it took Toyota 15 years to implement its famous **kanban** philosophy. There is considerable attention to quality in Japan because there is almost no slack in the production process. This means that any defective product may threaten the continuity of the entire production process.

Traditional quality control procedures were often based on inspection after a series of parts had been manufactured. The rejected parts were dismantled and, when appropriate, repaired. JIT management requires that everything goes right the first time. In Chapter 11, this principle is referred to as the 'zero defects' principle. It will be clear that JIT production and scheduling cannot be successfully implemented without a 'zero defects' philosophy.

Having discussed the major characteristics of JIT management, the question of what its introduction means for the purchasing department and for the performance of suppliers is now addressed.

JIT and the purchasing function

The JIT concept cannot be limited to production only. It must be supported and implemented in every functional area in the organization. Applied to purchasing, JIT is a philosophy that aims to make exactly the required materials and products available at exactly

Kanban
Form of jit scheduling based upon fixed volume lot delivery. When a lot is used, the kanban (card) will be sent to the supplier as a signal to replenish for that lot.

TABLE 12.1 Differences between the traditional approach and the JIT approach in purchasing

Purchasing activity	Traditional approach	JIT approach
Supplier selection	Minimum of two suppliers; price is central	Often one local supplier; frequent deliveries
Placing the order	Order specifies delivery time and quality	Annual order; deliveries called off as needed
Change of orders	Delivery time and quality often changed at the last moment	Delivery time and quality fixed, quantities are adjusted within predetermined margins if necessary
Follow-up of orders	Many phone calls to solve delivery problems	Few delivery problems thanks to sound agreements; quality and delivery problems are not tolerated
Incoming inspection	Inspection of quality and quantities of nearly every delivered order	Initial sample inspections; later, no inspections necessary
Supplier assessment	Qualitative assessment; delivery deviations of sometimes up to 10% are tolerated	Deviations are not accepted; price is fixed based on open calculation
Invoicing	Payment per order	Invoices are collected and settled on a monthly basis

the time they are needed, so that value is added only to the product which is to be manufactured, and indirect costs are avoided.

What does the introduction of JIT mean for the purchasing function? JIT has a major impact on both the quality and the quantity of the materials to be purchased. Table 12.1 lists the main differences between the traditional purchasing approach and the JIT approach.

The JIT approach is characterized by regular but flexible supply. Ordered materials are delivered frequently (sometimes, in an assembly environment, several times a day) in different quantities. To facilitate this, the supplier is informed of the production planning and the related purchasing requirements on a daily, weekly and monthly basis through delivery schedules which are available online. In this way the supplier is able to anticipate his customer's future requirements and will be able to plan production and materials requirements more effectively. Apart from this, there are some other definite advantages of working with suppliers in this way. The producer uses in general long-term contracts, against which periodic call-off orders are placed. Once (or more) a year the conditions are renegotiated with the supplier. Targets for productivity improvement and cost reduction, as required by the producer, are also part of these negotiations. Agreements on these issues are documented and communicated to the supplier. In essence, they are the standards against which the future performance of the supplier is going to be monitored and measured.

As far as quality is concerned, the guiding principle is zero defects. Imposing quality targets upon suppliers may represent large savings to the producer, both in terms of a reduction of the number of incoming quality inspections and a reduction of buffer stock. In this way the supplier is educated towards a better quality performance.

The practices described above are still different from the traditional purchasing practices of many European companies. Traditionally these are aimed at creating optimal competition between suppliers. Relations with suppliers are, in this approach, mostly focused on the short term; dependency on a single supplier is considered to be fundamentally wrong. Traditional purchasing theory prescribes multi-sourcing, i.e. obtaining materials from various suppliers. The underlying idea is that a company must not become too dependent on one single supplier. Therefore, many manufacturers prefer multiple sourcing in their supplier relationships. Where possible, single sourcing (see also Chapter 10 on this subject) should be prevented.

Looking at the characteristics of JIT it is clear that traditional buyers must alter their views and policies radically in two important aspects, in order to adopt this approach, They should be willing to consider single sourcing as an appropriate strategy and they should be willing to arrange longer term contracts instead of 'one-shot' deals.

The criteria used to select and assess suppliers must also be adjusted. The demands made by JIT on suppliers are different and (generally) considerably higher. These refer to both flawless product and process quality (zero defects) and delivery reliability (JIT). The purchase price, traditionally a prime issue in the negotiations, usually will get a lower ranking within the selection criteria used.

The JIT approach was initially introduced to the USA and Europe by subsidiaries of Japanese companies (see Memo 12.1). Nowadays, many European companies have followed their example. Philips Electronics and NedCar were among the first companies to introduce the JIT approach in their European plants in the relationships with their suppliers.

MEMO 12.1 SUPPLY-SIDE JIT

Since JIT got its start in the auto industry, it's not surprising that auto parts makers and assemblers have been among the first suppliers to implement JIT at their own plants. One early adopter, Johnson Controls Inc. (JCI), a $3-billion producer of seat assemblies, headliners, and instrument panels, has been using JIT manufacturing techniques since 1982.

John Rog, purchasing manager of supplier manufacturing development for JCI's Automotive Systems Group, says a JIT manufacturing environment has become a necessity for remaining a competitive tier-one automotive supplier.

'Minimizing inventories has always been our goal,' says Rog. 'However, with our customers' demanding that deliveries be on time or significant penalties would ensue, we found JIT a necessary means for maintaining business.'

Today, the Plymouth, Michigan-based seat supplier has 97 JIT manufacturing facilities located near customer operations in more than 17 countries. Rog says each plant has a local management team and slightly different supply bases, business demands, and practices. However, JCI has made certain that the JIT processes in use at its seat component plant in Linden, Tennessee, are the same as those at its seat assembly plant in Milton, Ontario, or any other facility around the globe.

'The goal,' says Rog, 'is to be able to walk into any JCI plant worldwide and see the same JIT setup and procedures and know exactly what's going on.'

Indeed, process standardization is key to JCI's JIT programme, which closely resembles the Toyota Production System that caused such a stir nearly two decades ago. According to Rog, all JCI facilities rely heavily on such Toyota-inspired techniques as visual management, Kanban, and Poka-Yoke. JCI has also embraced the Japanese concept of the 'five S's' – sort, stabilize, shine, standardize, and sustain – which aim to bring order and conformity to the plant floor.

By adhering to such core JIT concepts – and allowing enough flexibility for local variations – JCI has put its manufacturing operations on a course for continuous improvement, which is the key objective of the JIT process. One example: JCI's Lexington, Tennessee, plant, which produces a variety of automotive power-seat adjusters, power recliners, fineblanking, and broached products, achieved 100% on-time delivery for three consecutive years through the use of the core JIT principles mentioned above. Over the same period, the site's sales grew 55%.

Such results have earned JCI recognition as one of the nation's best implementers of JIT. In fact, JCI is the leading recipient of the National Association of Manufacturers' coveted Shingo Prize – named for the late Shigeo Shingo, who, along with Taiichi Ohno, created the Toyota Production System – which recognizes manufacturers for continuous improvements in productivity, quality, efficiency and customer service.

Source: 'JIT moves up the supply chain', *Purchasing*, 9th January 1998

Advantages and disadvantages for the supplier

The JIT concept has some specific advantages and disadvantages for suppliers. Let's start with discussing the advantages.

With the JIT approach the supplier is regularly informed about the quantities to be delivered. The supplier is able to plan his future production volume much better because of this information. The same holds for the planning of materials. As a result the pipeline inventory may be reduced. This advantage will be even larger when the supplier succeeds in implementing JIT principles in the relationship with his own suppliers.

JIT can, besides better planning, lead to administrative savings for the supplier. All handling of transaction documents is done electronically. Suppliers are able to connect their production and materials planning systems with those of their customers. This requires, of course, some sophistication of the computer systems which are available on both sides – this is why some large manufacturers shun those suppliers from their business, who do not have sufficient EDI capabilities. When the supplier is notified in case of quality defects, it immediately should take corrective action. Claims and bills will be avoided.

The constant communication between supplier and manufacturer on quality and cost improvements can lead to product and process innovations. These innovations can be very profitable for the supplier in other markets.

A final advantage for the supplier is the investment policy. JIT contracts are signed for a long period of time. A certain volume and turnover are guaranteed. This makes it easier to decide whether and when to invest in new production technology and equipment.

However, engaging in JIT relationships with a manufacturer obviously also has some disadvantages for the supplier. These types of relationships have affected in Japan not only supplier relationships, but also the industrial structure of this nation. In many industrial sectors a hierarchy can be observed in the different links of supply chains. In general the large manufacturers, at the top of the supplier pyramid (see Figure 12.5) have imposed their demands and requirements rather ruthlessly on the often much smaller suppliers. Given the high dependence on these large manufacturers, suppliers had to comply with these demands, at the risk of losing their entire business.

In general, it may take some time for a supplier to deliver at zero defects, or to produce zero defects. In the beginning the supplier has to conduct many quality checks and many products will fail the test. To deliver JIT with zero defects takes great effort and therefore initially requires high investments. These investments are not being paid for by the large manufacturers; they come at the expense of the supplier.

Another disadvantage is that the supplier can become very dependent on only one manufacturer. If the supplier focuses too much on the business of one or two manufacturers, this can become a threat to its continuity. After a long-term contract has ended, circumstances could have changed, which can result in the end of the relationship. Given its large dependence on that one manufacturer, the supplier will go to great lengths in order to get a new contract. Obviously, when a supplier is not able to keep up with competition and has missed the contract, it will not be easy to regain the lost territory.

In Japan JIT-management resulted in a pyramid-shaped supply structure. In this structure original equipment manufacturers (OEMs) work closely with system suppliers, responsible for the development and delivery of complete modules (dashboard units, transmission systems). These system suppliers buy their own materials from a second tier of suppliers. These suppliers, in their turn, do business with smaller suppliers who work on components. At the bottom of the pyramid are the often large and powerful suppliers of basic, raw materials.

This structure is criticized in both Japan and Europe. OEMs often make extreme demands of their system suppliers who shift these demands to their own suppliers and so

FIGURE 12.5 The supplier pyramid

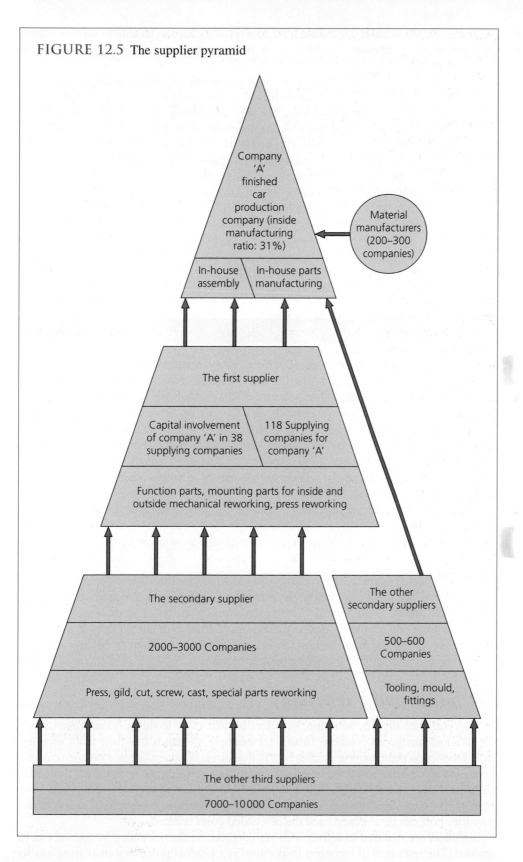

Vendor managed inventory

Is a continuous replenishment programme that uses the exchange of information between the retailer and the supplier to allow the supplier to manage and replenish product at the store or warehouse level. In this programme, the retailer supplies the vendor with the information necessary to maintain just enough products to meet customer demand.

on. In the end the smaller companies have to work very hard to be able to survive (therefore the smaller suppliers at the bottom of the pyramid often are referred to as 'sweatshops').

The system suppliers are in many cases strong, specialized and international companies who collaborate closely with their customers. In some cases this co-operation means not only delivering systems or components, but also assembling these into the end product. The system supplier is made responsible for the planning of delivery and the logistics involved. This principle is also referred to as JIT II (see Memo 12.2). Another principle, which is applied in dealings with those systems supplies, is 'pay for production'. The equivalent of this principle is 'pay for consumption'. The manufacturer only pays the supplier for the components which have actually been consumed during the production of a given day or batch. At Whirlpool and Xerox suppliers of key-components and packaging are no longer paid for the products they deliver, but for the products that actually have been consumed in a day at a certain production line. Through EDI a supplier can monitor every day which components have been consumed at the production lines of the manufacturer. At the end of the day the balance is made and the amount due paid electronically. Pay for production is closely related to JIT.

MEMO 12.2   JIT II

JIT II is a concept pioneered by the Bose Corporation. In Sales, Purchasing and Material Planning applications, the customer planner, buyer and supplier salesman are replaced by an 'in-plant' supplier employee who is empowered to place customer purchase orders on his company. Supplier access and linkage to customer computers is also utilized. The in-plant supplier also performs concurrent engineering with customer engineering departments from within the customer company. **'Vendor managed inventory'** and 'automatic material replenishment' are features of JIT II.

JIT II has been featured in front-page articles in the US and European *Wall Street Journal, Harvard Business Review* and other worldwide business periodicals. US corporations such as IBM, Intel, AT&T, Honeywell and many other major corporations have implemented JIT II nationally in scores of supplier relationships. *Business Week* named Bose one of the 'world class champs' in supplier management. Many corporations have adopted JIT II as a part of their sales and customer support programme.

Manufacturing organizations in Europe do not wish to follow the example of the Japanese industry. The main objection to the Japanese situation is the dependence on too few suppliers. In Japan, exclusiveness is demanded from suppliers: a supplier may deliver a product only to one company. Most organizations in Europe do not encourage too large a dependency of the supplier. Philips for example wishes suppliers to be dependent on Philips for less than 25% of their turnover.

JIT and supplier selection

In the context of supplier selection, suppliers located close to the customer organization are in an advantageous position. Toyota, for example, demands that their main suppliers have production plants within a radius of 30 kilometres. Business is based on open calculations, and agreements about the supplier's quality and delivery performance are reached in advance. If there are no suppliers in the immediate vicinity, then the company will try to do business with suppliers who are concentrated in particular geographical areas. In that way transport can be combined and the associated costs reduced.

Suppliers are required to deliver with zero defects, so that incoming inspection can be omitted. The reduction of incoming inspections is a gradual process of increasing quality and reliability, which takes time. The right products must be delivered at the right quantities at exactly the right moment. Quality and 'on time' are the two main criteria on which suppliers are assessed when applying JIT-purchasing and the following classification of suppliers is used often:

on-time delivery	A = excellent	B = good	C = inadequate
quality delivery	1 = excellent	2 = good	3 = inadequate

These scores are a simple way to rate the supplier's performance. A C1 supplier, for example, provides high quality, but does not always deliver on time. At worst this can cause interruptions in the manufacturing process. An A3 supplier, however, delivers on time, but the quality of products is poor. This means that incoming inspection remains a necessity, which is in conflict with the JIT concept.

In their discussions with their suppliers, buyers consistently emphasize that, preferably, all suppliers have to get into the A1 category, and remain there. A problem can occur if the buyer occupies a weak negotiating position (*vis-à-vis* the supplier). It will be very hard for a small producer, for example, to induce large suppliers to provide JIT deliveries. In that situation, the producer should try to find more accommodating suppliers, even if this means a higher purchase price.

In conclusion, it is argued that the implementation of JIT principles automatically leads to (more) single sourcing, closing long-term contracts and engaging local suppliers. The central issue affecting supplier selection is not so much the purchase price, as the level of the total costs, i.e. the costs including the 'waste' that results from poor supplier performance, safety stocks, quality and incoming inspections and (possibly) production standstills. Hence, this kind of supplier relationships should be embedded in agreements based on total cost of ownership (TCO).

ELEMENTS OF THE PURCHASING INFORMATION SYSTEM

The administrative complexity in purchasing can be very high. In a study conducted among 48 medium-sized industrial companies, we found that these companies had on average 16 600 different article items or stock keeping units (SKUs), which were obtained from 1155 suppliers. On average 19 980 purchasing requisitions had to be processed, which resulted in 18 900 orders. The deliveries had to be made payable by processing 26 980 purchasing invoices. These numbers show that a solid and efficient administrative organization is a prerequisite for the functioning of any purchasing organization, if it is to focus on its tactical and strategic tasks.

Figure 12.6 shows the most important elements of a purchasing information system. These are now briefly described:

- Requisitioning and ordering. By means of purchasing requisitions the internal users within the company express their requirements regarding goods or services to be purchased. These requisitions can be generated directly by the materials planning system, but they can also be generated manually. This is often the case for non-recurring purchases (for example investment goods). The purchasing requisition lists the article code (SKU number), provides a general description of the item, the quantities required, the desired delivery date and the data necessary for finance and administration (budget number, account number, etc.)
- Product, contract and supplier database. The data on the purchasing requisition then are transferred by purchasing to a purchase order document. Here, specific supplier and

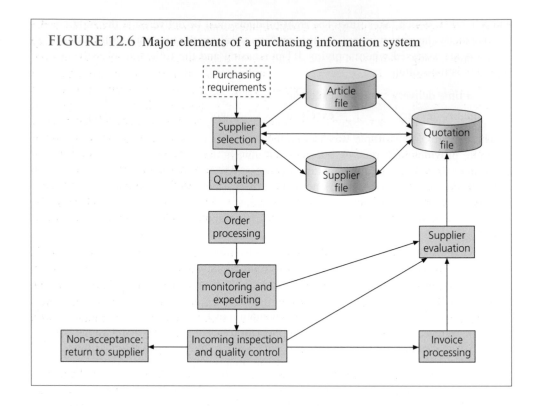

FIGURE 12.6 Major elements of a purchasing information system

product data are added, such as the price per unit and the address where the order should be delivered. In case of a frame agreement the purchase order also mentions the contract number. All purchase orders get a unique purchase order number, which should be used by suppliers in all future correspondence and documents. The purchase order is the basis for delivery. Without it, a supplier should neither deliver, nor get paid. Some manufacturers require their suppliers to confirm their orders prior to delivery (by means of an order confirmation).

- Order follow-up. Subsequently the order must be monitored (order follow-up or expediting). Delivery of the goods by the supplier in accordance with the agreement must be checked. To ensure effective monitoring, the buyer uses numerous exception reports. One of the most important of these is the delivery overdue list, which lists the purchase orders that should be delivered by a certain date but which have not been delivered yet. Another important list here is the incoming inspection report, which lists the purchase orders which at delivery have been rejected by Quality Control. Of course, in these cases the buyer will need to take immediate corrective action (this activity is referred to as 'trouble shooting'). Some advanced purchasing systems allow the buyer to assign a code to purchase orders, strategic materials and unreliable suppliers. This code is used for generating several signalling reports, through which the buyer can take preventive action: those suppliers usually are requested through fax or e-mail to confirm and restate that they will meet the required delivery dates (this enables a differentiated approach to order-expediting as described in Chapter 2). In case of delivery of complex investment goods it may be necessary to visit the supplier several times during production and assembly. This type of expediting is referred to as field expediting. This way of working is common in the defence and aircraft industries.

- Delivery. Normally, the supplier will deliver the goods which have been ordered at the right time and at the right quantity. At delivery the supplier will produce a delivery document (freight bill), which needs to be signed by personnel of incoming inspection. They will check the delivered goods against the (electronic) order copy. Both quantity and quality are inspected. When approved, a copy of the delivery document is sent to finance and administration. At the same time the goods are released and shipped to warehousing or the user. When the shipment by the supplier does not match the original order, a complaint form is filled in. Complaints may relate to quality, delivered quantity or packaging. These data are, again put into the system. These are the basis of the vendor rating system, which records the performance of a supplier in a given period. Complaint reports are sent to purchasing who will discuss the problems with the supplier to prevent them being repeated in the future. When handled by purchasing, the form will be sent back to the quality control department, which will authorize the report and file it.

- Invoice handling and payment. Some time after the delivery the supplier will send an invoice. Normally, the invoice will be sent to finance and administration who will match it with the original order and the delivery document. When matching is possible, the invoice will be paid to the supplier according to the agreed payment terms. Sometimes matching is not possible. In that case the invoice is sent for approval to purchasing, who will investigate why the invoice does not match with the order. After the differences are cleared, the invoice will be sent to finance and administration for final handling.

In recent years various computer systems have become available to buyers and purchasing managers which can support the activities described above. Examples are SAP, Baan Triton, JD Edwards, MAPICS and MFG-PRO. These systems have been found appropriate for supporting purchasing transactional processes. However, in many cases they are still not capable of producing the required purchasing management information. Most systems have difficulty in providing overviews of spend figures ranked by product, supplier, purchaser, country or currency. Furthermore, they lack facilities to support advanced vendor rating. A final aspect is that they do not provide sufficient opportunities to provide management reports on the performance of the purchasing department. Obviously, in this area there is still a lot of work to be done by the large **enterprise resource planning (ERP)** systems providers.

In many smaller and medium-sized companies automation in purchasing is limited to the administrative processing of the purchasing requisitions. Many purchasing systems are isolated and not linked to materials planning systems. This implies that the ordering data must be entered manually into the purchasing system, and this increases the risk of mistakes. It also makes the work of buyers very laborious and time-consuming. Therefore, introducing advanced purchasing systems and electronic procurement solutions (see Memo 12.3) into an organization is a prerequisite for improving both efficiency and its professionalism.

Consultants and suppliers of these solutions have great expectations of the possible profits resulting from these solutions. They claim that by using electronic catalogue systems, more purchasing transactions can be contracted so that the percentage of maverick buying[2] can be drastically reduced. This would result in considerable savings. Also, the transaction costs can be reduced (from a mere hundred to just tens of euros per transaction) by using this kind of integrated procurement solutions. Hence, e-procurement systems represent an important productivity tool for both purchasing managers and internal departments, since these will lead to a significant reduction of administrative workload. At the same time customer service levels will improve since internal customers will now have

Enterprise resource planning (ERP) system.
Refers to a company-wide information system for managing the company's operational and support processes, its administrative processes, its human resources, its materials resources and financial resources.

---

[2]This refers to the share of the purchasing volume that is bought without a contract (often a considerable share of the total purchasing expenditure).

MEMO 12.3   WHAT PROBLEMS ARE SOLVED BY E-PROCUREMENT SYSTEMS?

E-procurement systems[3] enable users within organizations to order directly from an electronic catalogue without interference of a purchasing department. Orders are acknowledged automatically by the supplier. The user can verify the order status on line, when desired ('When will the order be delivered? What terms and conditions apply?'). There is no need to relate to the purchasing department for this kind of question. Many suppliers nowadays offer detailed tracking and tracing facilities which enable their customers to monitor order follow-up and delivery in real-time. Besides this, e-procurement systems enable electronic invoicing, invoice matching and payment. As a result the traditional purchasing cycle is reduced and simplified considerably (see Figure 12.7).

FIGURE 12.7 E-procurement systems result in a significant reduction of the traditional purchasing cycle

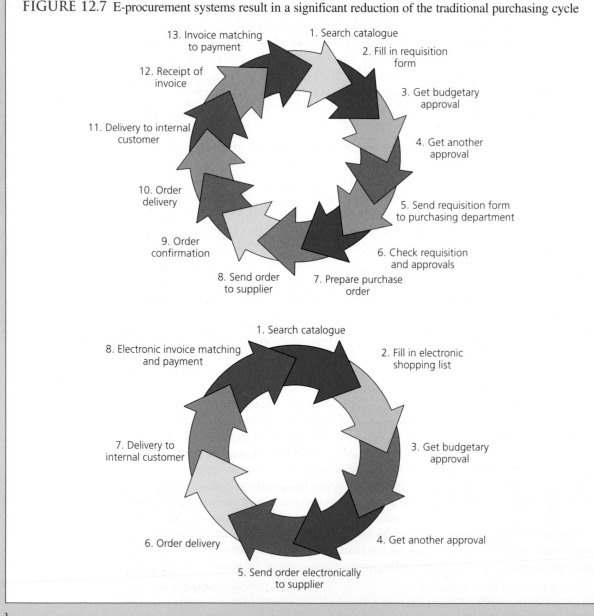

13. Invoice matching to payment
1. Search catalogue
2. Fill in requisition form
12. Receipt of invoice
3. Get budgetary approval
11. Delivery to internal customer
4. Get another approval
10. Order delivery
5. Send requisition form to purchasing department
9. Order confirmation
6. Check requisition and approvals
8. Send order to supplier
7. Prepare purchase order

1. Search catalogue
8. Electronic invoice matching and payment
2. Fill in electronic shopping list
7. Delivery to internal customer
3. Get budgetary approval
6. Order delivery
4. Get another approval
5. Send order electronically to supplier

[3]Here the term is used in the narrow sense. See also Kalakota and Robinson (2001), Chapter 10, for a detailed discussion.

responsibility and authority for ordering the materials they need directly through pre-arranged and efficient order routines. Due to a much better administrative control, savings may result from the fact that common material requirements are grouped in homogeneous product families, i.e. categories, which are ordered through electronic catalogues from far fewer suppliers. Concentration of a larger volume among fewer suppliers, again, may lead to better prices.

Implementation of e-procurement systems is a far from simple matter. It requires a high level of purchasing professionalism, clearly spelled out purchasing procedures and a seamless integration with the general ledger system and other administrative systems within the company. Next, these systems need to match with the administrative systems of suppliers, which in many cases raises quite some challenges.

CO-ORDINATION PROBLEMS BETWEEN PURCHASING AND LOGISTICS

This chapter has made clear that production planning and materials planning in most companies are far from simple matters. The large amount of data to be processed, the huge differences in the demand structure of products and the related differences in predictability of expenditure, render these subjects extremely complicated in practice. It is therefore not at all surprising that, in practice, many problems are encountered. Some typical problem situations are discussed below:

- Lack of well-defined specifications. Specifications are sometimes described ambiguously and bills of materials can be incomplete. In a recent investigation of a manufacturer of food products, it was found that specification sheets were absent or incomplete for 50% of the raw materials that were being purchased. This made it very difficult if not impossible to purchase materials at the right quality (because actually it was not clear what the right quality was); each stakeholder in the discussion (production, laboratory, quality control, supplier) appeared to use its own definition. The result was a very high reject rate on incoming raw materials and a lot of useless discussions among the persons involved.

- Lack of standardization. Needlessly complex specifications are sometimes used where standard products would suffice. These limit the buyer's latitude and lead to an expansion of the article assortment. The result is an increasing administrative and logistic complexity and often an excessive dependence on one supplier.

- Frequent changes in materials planning. Frequent changes in the materials planning due to changes in the production planning disrupt the delivery schedules with suppliers. The consequence is that delivery agreements have to be cancelled or that deliveries have to take place before the agreed delivery dates. This increases the number of rush orders and the cost of non-quality to an unacceptable level.

- Unreliable planning information. MRP systems must be provided with sound information. Keeping basic but fundamental logistics information up-to-date is an important task. Working with incorrect stock and delivery information causes (unnecessary) orders to be placed, too frequently, and inside the suppliers' lead times, which generates extra work and raises transportation costs.

- Insufficient integration of purchasing in materials management. When it is decided to automate the production and logistics systems, purchasing often lags behind. The problems which result often become clear when logistics managers want to add a purchasing control module to their electronic materials planning systems. For then it turns out that descriptions of materials and articles must, for example, be available in four languages, that the units in which purchases are made (for instance in metres, kilograms) differ from the units which are invoiced (units, volume), etc. Implementation of purchasing systems may then take years instead of months.

These problems show that co-ordination of logistics and purchasing systems is a far from simple matter. It may take years to develop a systems solution that is satisfactory to both logistics and purchasing managers. Co-ordination of systems may be facilitated when purchasing and logistics activities are reporting to one overall supply chain executive. Which explains the growing popularity of this function.

SUMMARY

In this chapter, the relationship between purchasing, materials planning and logistics has been discussed. The co-operation between these functions should result in an efficient and uninterrupted flow of products. This requires an integrated approach to managing materials planning processes. Apart from materials management and physical distribution, we have described the role and importance of logistics and supply chain management. Logistics management aims at optimizing the total flow of goods, up from customer demands to the supplier. Supply chain management looks at how to optimize materials processes throughout the whole supply chain. These are no simple matters, since in reality customer demands seldom fit exactly to the capabilities of the firm. Therefore many advanced materials planning methods have been developed, the most important being materials requirements planning and manufacturing resources planning. Both systems are basically forecast driven and require the use of advanced computer-supported planning systems. Apart from forecast-based planning systems, companies may use order-based planning systems. JIT scheduling is a third type of planning system. Basically, it is forecast based; however, it is aimed at continuously reducing cycle times and lead times, so that planning horizons may be shortened. Suppliers play a vital role in implementing JIT. They need to be challenged constantly to look for ways to improve their operational processes. In the end this may result in a situation where suppliers are requested to fully integrate their activities with those of their customers. This principle has been referred to as JIT II.

This chapter has also presented five different structures which may underlie a company's production and logistics activities. Consecutively we discussed: make and send to stock (MSS), **make to stock (MTS)**, **assemble to order (ATO)**, make to order (MTO) and engineer and make to order (ETO). A central element in the discussion has been the order penetration point. Downstream from this point all activities are customer order driven; upstream of this point activities are forecast-based. Understanding this principle is necessary to understand how purchasing processes may vary in an organization.

Managing suppliers as described in this chapter requires lots of very detailed logistics data and management information. Therefore, the most important elements of a purchasing information system have been discussed. The conclusion is that most available ERP systems are capable of supporting the operational, transactional purchasing activities. However, they do not sufficiently support the needs of generating management information and reports. E-procurement solutions, i.e electronic catalogues, in general will allow for a better control of purchasing spend and lower transaction costs. The actual ordering of goods and services is delegated to the user, who can order what they need directly from the supplier. This results in much better convenience and shorter purchasing administrative lead times.

Logistics structure, making to stock (central stock) (MTS) Finished products are kept in stock at the end of the production process and from there shipped directly to many geographically dispersed customers, as in the manufacture of many consumer electronics products (such as dishwashers and refrigerators).

Logistics structure, assembly to order (ATO) Only systems elements or subassemblies are in stock at the manufacturing centre and final assembly takes place based on a specific customer order. In other words, manufacture of components takes place based on forecasts and final assembly takes place based on customer orders.

ASSIGNMENTS

12.1 Supply chain management is about managing the materials flows, information flows and financial flows throughout the supply chain. Discuss how Li & Fung in the introductory case study of this chapter keeps control of each of these flows.

12.2 What would you consider to be the main difference between supply chain management and value chain management?

12.3 Supply chain management assumes that the companies involved in the supply chain are willing to work closely together and are willing to develop partnership relationships. How valid is this assumption in your opinion? Under what circumstances are companies willing to develop partnership relationships?

12.4 Some critics argue that the supply chain concept is a too narrow view of the reality that can be observed in many industries today. Rather, they favour a network approach since they feel this reflects much better the interdependencies that may exist between customers and suppliers in several sectors. What is meant by this statement? When optimizing supplier relationships, what view do you favour? Discuss.

12.5 What logistics concepts can be used to optimize the logistics flows between a manufacturer and a supplier? What can both parties do to take costs out of the supply chain? Investigate and discuss.

REFERENCES

Cooper, M.C. and Ellram, L.M. (1993) 'Characteristics of supply chain management and the implications for purchasing and logistics strategy', *The International Journal of Logistics Management*, 4(2):13–24.

Hoekstra, Sj. and Romme, J.H.J.M. (eds) (1985) *Op weg naar integrale logistieke strucuren*, Deventer: Kluwer (Dutch text).

Kalakota, R. and Robinson, M. (2001) *E-Business 2.0, Roadmap for success*, Reading, MA: Addison Wesley.

Stevens, G.C. (1989) 'Integrating the supply chain', *International Journal of Physical Distribution and Materials Management*, 19(8):3–8.

ORGANIZATION AND STRUCTURE OF PURCHASING

LEARNING OBJECTIVES

After studying this chapter you should understand the following:

- The structure of the purchasing function within organizations
- The underlying factors that determine the role, position and organizational structure of purchasing
- The major tasks, responsibilities and competences of purchasing and how to organize these
- How to get organized for purchasing in single-unit companies
- How to get organized for purchasing in multi-unit companies
- Which criteria to use in deciding on centralized versus decentralized purchasing
- The most important job profiles in purchasing.

INTRODUCTION

As the following case shows, the fierce competition in the construction industry caused Skanska Sweden to turn around its purchasing organization. Key decision-making on strategic commodities was centralized, and at the same time framework agreements for key commodities were negotiated. The more strategic role of purchasing within Skanska led to some drastic changes in the way project managers needed to operate. Instead of everyone dealing with purchases on a project-by-project basis, they now have to accept the idea of using the framework agreements that were prepared by Skanska's procurement experts. Skanska buyers needed to move away from their operational and transactional tasks into more strategic tasks. In order to be able to perform these tasks effectively, higher demands were imposed onto them in terms of communication with the project managers and senior management. New tools, such as electronic sourcing and electronic procurement systems, supported this major change initiative.

This chapter discusses the major changes which companies are experiencing nowadays in restructuring their purchasing and supply organizations. Also discussed is how to get organized for purchasing and supply management. In particular, the question of how to

CASE STUDY BUILDING BLOCKS OF CHANGE

For the construction industry, the message is clear. While other industries have continuously reduced prices for products and services while maintaining margins, the construction industry has been increasing prices without any corresponding improvement in profitability. At Skanska, transforming and developing supply chains is at the heart of a long-term strategic initiative that reveals huge potential.

With 3000 construction projects per year and a spend volume of about two and half billion Euro in Sweden alone, you would expect Skanska to leverage purchasing volumes as a matter of course. This is being done today, but 5 years ago no systematic efforts were made to improve and develop purchasing practices.

The reason for this lack of focus lies in the nature of the industry. A building project, be it a road, a bridge or a building is essentially a local undertaking where the project manager on the spot and his team make all the decisions.

Realizing the potential of leveraging volumes, Skanska Sweden launched a major supply chain initiative in 2004. Part of the initiative is a five-step plan to introduce electronic procurement, collaborative commerce with subcontractors, electronic sourcing, logistics and order/invoice matching throughout the company. The plan was first introduced in Sweden.

But any initiative implying change will meet resistance, also in the very traditional construction industry. 'When we started, our first challenge was to convince stakeholders that this initiative really was of strategic importance, that it wasn't just another new scheme from head office,' says the purchasing manager Mikael Sjölund.

His own reaction at being offered a job within purchasing is a typical example. At Skanska I worked first as a production manager then as a construction project manager. In 2001, I was asked if I wanted to work with purchasing. I thought 'No, that is non-core, it is something I might do later in my career. A year later I was asked again and I accepted, because the management team made it clear that purchasing transformation was a strategic necessity. It was such a challenge and had such potential that I really wanted to be part of it,' he says.

His colleague, purchasing development manager Sandra Petersson, also recalls the excitement of discovering the huge potential savings to be made from procurement transformation.

'Wherever we looked we saw possibilities. There were practically no common processes or tools in place, so we had an open field,' she says. For instance, quality issues or delivery issues were difficult to resolve with suppliers because Skanska had no computerized systems in place to measure performance. 'We would get information from a number of construction projects that there were such issues but had no statistics or easily accessible data on earlier supplier performance. That lack of information puts you at a severe disadvantage when it is time to negotiate new service-level agreements or prices,' Sandra Petersson points out.

Changing procurement processes and introducing new tools also means creating a new organization. The procurement function at Skanska Sweden has gone from 15 to 100 people in 5 years, recruited both from within the company and from the outside.

'In the first wave, we hired 40 people. It was a case of profound belief in the value of transformation. You do not get the go-ahead for this kind of investment from management if they are not 100% committed,' says Petersson.

'Commitment from management is all very well, but you would not come very far if people in the construction projects do not feel concerned by what you are doing,' she warns. 'You absolutely must involve all stakeholders. This takes time, sometimes much more time than you had planned for. That is the struggle: keeping up a long-term effort.'

'You just cannot shove new practices down people's throats, you must involve them in the new practices. That is why any change process will take time,' Petersson reflects.

'For instance, some project managers fear that they might lose touch with market conditions if they rely on the frame agreement suggested by the head office commodity specialists. Therefore, you have to build trust by demonstrating that end-user feedback is taken seriously,' says Sjölund.

Skanska Sweden has a yearly turnover of some €3 billion, of which 70% is cost of purchased goods and services.

'In 4 years we have gone from 15 to 30% of spend under management, defined as a purchase regulated by a frame agreement and processed through our electronic procurement system . . . Compared to other industries this might not seem very impressive, but the sums involved are huge and the savings have been considerable,' says Petersson.

The next target is to have 50% of spend under management by 2010 . . .

Source: *Efficient Purchasing*, No. 7, 2008, pp. 28–36

define primary purchasing tasks, responsibilities and competences in the relationship with other departments will be addressed. Furthermore, this chapter will describe how to organize for purchasing and supply management in a single and multi-unit environment. In this respect the relationship between purchasing and internal users on the one hand, and logistics management on the other, are discussed. Next, some time is spent on the issue of centralization/decentralization in purchasing and supply management, and the issue of purchasing coordination. Finally, some important job profiles in purchasing and supply management are presented.

PURCHASING ORGANIZATION STRUCTURE

The location and structure of purchasing is very much dependent on business characteristics and situational factors. For example, the buying of raw materials in chemical industries is often executed by a small group of specialists which reports directly to the board of directors. Some very large companies, such as Dow Chemicals, have created a separate department or even a separate business unit for this purpose. In small- and medium-sized enterprises, however, this could be the exclusive responsibility of the general manager. The same pattern can be seen for the buying of investment goods. Small- and medium-sized companies may buy these goods with only marginal interference by the purchasing department.

However, in large companies (such as AKZO Nobel, Heineken or Procter & Gamble), these types of buying decisions are prepared by a corporate purchasing department. It is not uncommon to find the purchasing of raw materials, commodities and production-related materials on the one hand, and technical equipment and spare parts on the other, to be organizationally separated. The organization of purchasing, therefore, is highly dependent on the characteristics of the company, the type of industry and the characteristics of the products purchased.

The survey conducted by Johnson and Leenders (2004) in the USA and Canada provided some relevant data on how purchasing is organized. This survey was based on an in-depth analysis of international purchasing practices at 284 large multinational industrial and service companies. The results of this survey were compared with similar surveys conducted in 1988 and 1995 (see Table 13.1). The surveys showed that the **hybrid** structure (including centralized hybrid, hybrid and decentralized hybrid) remained the most popular organizational mode, accounting for 67% of respondents. However, 66% 'leaned' towards centralization (centralized and centralized hybrid) and 24% 'leaned' towards decentralization (decentralized and hybrid decentralized). Respondents from the services sector favoured centralization (31%) more frequently than respondents from the manufacturing sector (Johnson and Leenders, 2004, p. 136). Since 1987, when hybrid structures accounted for 59%, there has been an increase in hybrid's popularity, to 67% in 2003. Based on these figures, it is fair to conclude that purchasing activities in international companies among business units have become more and more coordinated. Similar research in Europe has not been conducted and so we cannot compare the situation of European companies with their American and Canadian counterparts. However, based upon our experience we expect the trends and developments to be identical.

Table 13.2 shows the reporting lines of purchasing executives within larger organizations. It can be observed that there has been a steady increase in the percentage of respondent

Purchasing organization, hybrid
A hybrid structure represents a combination of the centralized and the decentralized structure. The terms 'hybrid', 'pooling' and 'co-ordination' are used interchangeably.

TABLE 13.1 Supply organizational structure for 1987, 1995 and 2003

| | 2003 | | 1995 | | 1987 | |
| | Total | | Total | | Total | |
Organizational Structure	#	%	#	%	#	%
Centralized	72	25.35%	69	22.85%	83	28.04%
Centralized hybrid	116	40.85%	—	—	—	—
Hybrid	28	9.86%	196	64.90%	175	59.12%
Decentralized hybrid	46	16.20%	—	—	—	—
Decentralized	22	7.75%	37	12.25%	38	12.84%
Total	284	100.00%	302	100.00%	296	100.00%

Source: Johnson and Leenders, 2004, p. 26

corporate purchasing executives (CPOs) to one of the top five executive positions. For 2003, 70% reported to a top five executive category (president/corporate executive officer (CEO), corporate operations officer (COO), executive vice president, senior vice president/group vice president, and chief financial officer (CFO)/vice president finance), while 66% did so in 1995 and 44% in 1987 (the COO category was not included in 1995 or 1987 surveys). The CFO/vice president finance reporting line has shown steady increase, with 16% of CPOs reporting to this position in 2003, compared with 11% in 1995 and 7% in 1987. A greater percentage of CPOs reported to the top five executive position categories in the manufacturing sector (73%) compared with the services sector (66%), and a greater

TABLE 13.2 CPO reporting line for 1987, 1993 and 2003

| | 2003 | | 1995 | | 1987 | |
CPO Reporting Line	#	%	#	%	#	%
Senior VP/Group VP	48	16.90%	57	18.75%	6	2.06%
VP Financial /CFO	46	16.20%	34	11.18%	21	7.22%
Executive VP	43	15.14%	47	15.46%	54	18.56%
President/CEO	41	14.44%	48	15.79%	47	16.15%
COO	21	7.39%	—	—	—	—
VP Administration	21	7.39%	26	8.55%	40	13.75%
VP Manufacturing/ Production/Operations	19	6.69%	48	15.79%	71	24.40%
Other	19	6.69%	18	5.92%	23	7.90%
VP Corporate/Shared Services VP	17	5.99%	2	0.66%	—	—
VP Materials/Logistics	5	1.76%	22	7.24%	25	8.59%
VP Engineering	4	1.41%	2	0.66%	4	1.37%
Total	284	100.00%	304	100.00%	291	100.00%

Source: Johnson and Leenders, 2004, p. 31

percentage of respondents from the services sector reported to the vice president finance/ CFO (19 versus 14%). All of these figures show that over the past decades purchasing has become much more visible at the top floor of large corporations.

FACTORS INFLUENCING THE LOCATION OF PURCHASING IN THE ORGANIZATION

The organizational location of purchasing is very much dependent on the view management holds towards the purchasing function. When management considers the purchasing function mainly as an operational activity, this will result in a position of the purchasing department relatively low in the organizational hierarchy. If management considers purchasing to be an important competitive factor, however, and of strategic importance to the organization, then the purchasing manager might very well be reporting to or even be part of the board of directors. Management's view of purchasing is, to a large extent, related to the following factors:

- Purchasing's share in the end-product's cost-price. The higher the purchasing content, the more strategic the purchasing function is considered by management.
- The financial position of the company. In times of severe financial losses, management will become more demanding on its purchasing operations and purchasing-related costs, resulting in a greater accountability being demanded.
- The extent to which the company is depending on the suppliers' market. Supply markets with high concentration ratios usually get more attention from management.

The implementation of materials requirements planning or JIT principles leads to a greater need for integrating purchasing and supply management with logistics management. As a result the purchasing manager in those companies will often report to the logistics manager.

In technically oriented companies, however, which are confronted with rapid changes in product or process technology, the purchasing manager may report to the production manager. Table 13.3 shows how some of these factors may influence the reporting relationships of purchasing managers.

TABLE 13.3 Factors influencing purchasing's reporting relationships

	Purchasing reports to			
	General management	Production management	Logistics management	Financial management
Purchasing turnover ratio				
High	x			x
Low		x	x	
Technical complexity				
High		x	x	
Low	x			x
Logistics complexity				
High		x	x	
Low	x			x
Strategic impact				
High	x			x
Low		x	x	

LEVELS OF TASKS, RESPONSIBILITIES AND AUTHORITY

With regard to the allocation of purchasing tasks, responsibilities and authority, three different levels may be differentiated: the strategic level, the tactical level, and the operational level.

Strategic level

The strategic level covers those purchase decisions that influence the market position of the company in the long run. These decisions primarily reside under the responsibility of top management. Examples of purchase decisions at this level are:

- The development and issuing of operational guidelines, procedures and task descriptions, which provide authority to the purchasing department.
- The development and implementation of auditing and review programmes in order to monitor and improve purchasing operations and performance.
- Decisions to outsource activities, which currently have been executed by the company to outside suppliers.
- Establishing long-term contracts and contacts with certified or preferred suppliers (for example long-term purchasing agreements, license agreements, partnership agreements, co-design agreements).
- Decisions related to supplier and sourcing strategies based on multi- versus single sourcing.
- Major investment decisions (in buildings, equipment, computers).
- Decisions with regard to backward integration, i.e. decisions to participate financially in supplier organizations in order to safeguard future supply of critical materials.
- Decisions related to policies concerning transfer-pricing and inter-company supplies.
- Decisions related to policies on reciprocal arrangements, countertrade and barter-deals.

This list illustrates the long-term, strategic impact that purchasing and supply decisions may have on the company's competitive position.

Tactical level

The tactical level encompasses the involvement of the purchasing function affecting product, process and supplier selection. Examples of purchasing decisions at this level are:

- Agreement on corporate or annual supplier framework agreements.
- Preparing and developing value analysis programmes, programmes aimed at design-review and product standardization.
- Adopting and conducting certification programmes (including audits) for suppliers in order to improve the quality of incoming goods and materials.
- Selection and contracting of suppliers in general and programmes aimed at supply-base reduction in particular.

Decisions on these issues often have a medium-term impact (1 to 3 years). They are cross-functional in the sense that dealing with them effectively, requires the co-ordination and co-operation of other disciplines within the company (including engineering, manufacturing, logistics, quality assurance). Earlier, in Chapter 1, these activities were referred to as 'initial purchasing'.

TABLE 13.4 Relationship between the three managerial levels of purchasing and some management positions

Task	Managerial level				
	Top management	Logistics management	Purchasing management	Senior buyer	Buying assistant/ materials planner
Strategic level	x	x	x		
Tactical level		x	x	x	
Operations level				x	x

Operational level

The operational level addresses all activities related to the ordering and expediting function. This level of activities incorporates the ordering of materials, monitoring the deliveries and settling quality disputes on incoming materials. More specifically the operational activities of the purchasing function include:

- The ordering process (including release of orders corresponding to already concluded agreements with suppliers).
- All expediting activities related to released orders.
- Troubleshooting: solving daily problems on quality, supply and payment in the relationship with the supplier.
- The monitoring and evaluation of supplier performance.

Table 13.4 presents the relationships between the three defined task levels and a number of purchasing activities.

ORGANIZATIONAL STRUCTURES WITHIN PURCHASING

This section describes some alternative structures on which to organize the purchasing function within companies. For this purpose the discussion differentiates between multi-unit companies and single-unit companies.

Structure of purchasing in multi-unit companies

For the organization of purchasing in multi-unit companies a number of alternatives are available:

- decentralized purchasing structure
- centralized purchasing structure
- hybrid structure
- cross-functional sourcing teams.

Decentralized purchasing structure

This structure can be found in companies with a business-unit structure. A major characteristic is that every business-unit manager is responsible for his own financial results (see

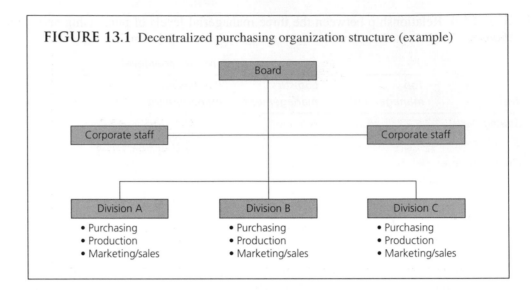

FIGURE 13.1 Decentralized purchasing organization structure (example)

Purchasing structure, decentralized

A major characteristic is that all business-unit-managers are responsible for their own financial results. Hence, the management of the business unit is fully responsible for all its purchasing activities.

Figure 13.1).[1] Hence, the management of the business unit is fully responsible for all its purchasing activities. One of the disadvantages of this structure is that different business units, belonging tot the same corporation, may negotiate with the same supplier for the same products, and as a result arrive at different purchase prices and conditions. When supplier capacity is tight, business units can operate as real competitors to each other, who are fighting for the same supplier capacity.

This structure is particularly attractive to conglomerates that have a business-unit structure, and where each business-unit purchases products that are unique and markedly different from those of the other units. In this case bundling of common purchasing requirements would provide only limited advantages or savings.

Centralized purchasing structure

In this situation at the corporate level, a central purchasing department can be found where corporate contracting specialists operate at the strategic and tactical level (see Figure 13.2). Decisions on product specifications are made centrally (often in close co-operation with a central engineering or R&D organization), and the same goes for supplier selection decisions; contracts with suppliers are prepared and negotiated centrally. These contracts are often multi-year agreements with pre-selected suppliers stating the general and specific purchase conditions. The operational purchase activities are conducted by the operating companies.

Purchasing organization, centralized

In this situation at the corporate level, a central purchasing department can be found where corporate contracting specialists operate at the strategic and tactical level.

General Motors Europe and Volkswagen may serve as examples of companies which have centralized their strategic and tactical purchasing operations to a high degree. Other examples are Xerox and Ford Motor Company. Also this structure may be found in large retail companies. The main advantage of this structure is that, through co-ordination of purchasing, better conditions (both in terms of prices and costs and in terms of service and quality) from suppliers can be achieved. Another advantage is that it will facilitate efforts towards product and supplier standardization.

The disadvantages are also obvious: the management of the individual business unit has only limited responsibility for decisions on purchasing. Often the problem is that the

---

[1]The term 'business unit' is used here as equivalent to operating unit or operating company. With this term the author refers to a situation where the unit management is profit responsible and operates with a large degree of autonomy.

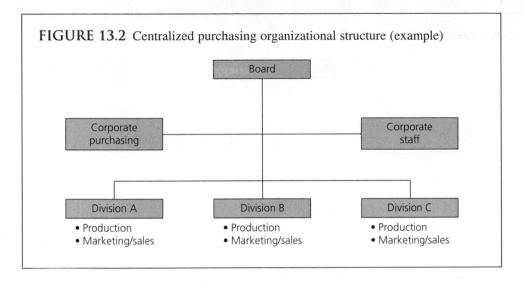

FIGURE 13.2 Centralized purchasing organizational structure (example)

business-unit managers are convinced that they are able to reach better conditions on their own, and will act individually; in this way they will gradually undermine the position of the corporate purchasing department.

This structure is appropriate in cases where several business units buy the same products, which at the same time are of strategic importance to them.

Line/staff organization[2]

In some major manufacturing companies a corporate purchasing department exists at a corporate level, while individual business units also conduct strategic and tactical purchasing activities. In this case a corporate purchasing department usually deals with the design of procedures and guidelines for purchasing. Furthermore, it may conduct audits when requested to do so by the management of the business units (see Figure 13.3).

Often, the central department also conducts detailed supply market studies on strategic commodities, the results of which are made available to the purchasing departments of the business units through periodical brochures, bulletins or intranet. Furthermore, this corporate purchasing department may serve as a vehicle to facilitate or solve co-ordination issues between divisions or business units. However, no tactical purchase activities are conducted. These all reside within the divisional purchasing organizations or the purchasing organizations at the business units. Finally, the corporate purchasing department in this structure may be responsible for human resource management in purchasing and supply.

From this description it follows that this type of structure is in general limited to very large international companies.

Hybrid structure

As explained earlier, a hybrid structure represents a combination of the previous two organizational structures. The terms 'hybrid', 'pooling' and 'co-ordination' are used interchangeably. Both concepts relate to efforts aimed at combining common materials requirements among two or more operating units with the objective to improve the leverage of the company in order to reduce overall materials costs or to improve the service obtained from outside suppliers. However, a lot of variety still exists in practice—depending on the type of commodity, co-ordination in purchasing may be forced upon the business units or may

[2]Sometimes referred to as a hybrid structure or line-staff structure.

FIGURE 13.3 Centralized/decentralized purchasing organizational structure (example)

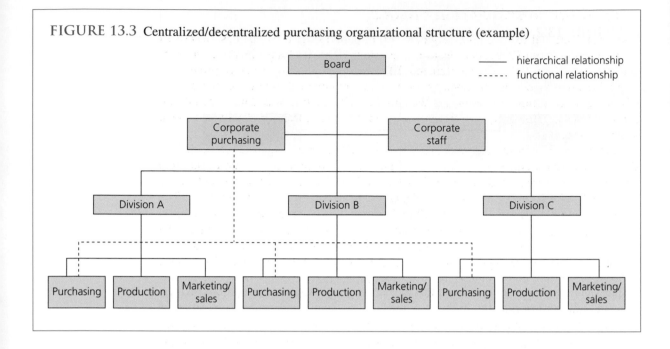

have a more voluntary character. In order to illustrate the major characteristics of this structure, some examples of pooling structures are now described:

- Voluntary coordination. In this case a considerable exchange of information takes place between the purchasing departments of the operating companies. Based on this data every business unit is free to decide whether to take part in a (corporate) contract or to operate individually. Contracts are prepared by purchasing coordination committees (or commodity teams), in which the largest users are represented.

- Lead buyership. In this case the business unit that has the greatest volume for a specific type of commodity is made responsible for negotiating a corporate agreement with the supplier involved. This business unit collects all relevant data from all other units and negotiates with the supplier. Each individual business unit periodically releases orders directly to the supplier referring to the appropriate contract conditions.

- Lead design concept. The guiding principle underlying this form of co-ordination is co-design—the operating unit or division, which is responsible for the design of the specific product or component (the 'lead-house') is also responsible for contracting all materials and components from suppliers. An example would be a division of a major automotive company responsible for developing a new fuel-injection system. After approval of the new technology, the technology is offered to the other divisions which may incorporate it in their new models. Materials and components, however, are obtained from suppliers which have been approved and contracted by the 'lead-house' division. Suppliers are involved in discussions on development and design at an early stage, so that the assembler may benefit optimally from the supplier's technical knowledge.

Co-ordination may occur at different levels of aggregation, i.e. at article level, at supplier level, at business-unit level, at division level and at regional level.

As mentioned earlier purchasing organizational structures are influenced by a large number of variables, which makes companies difficult to compare. As the research conducted by Johnson and Leenders (2004) has shown, most companies have opted for a hybrid structure to organize their international purchasing activities.

Cross-functional sourcing teams

This organizational form is relatively new within purchasing. It can be best described by an example from IBM. As a result of enormous financial losses in 1992, the purchasing function at IBM was reorganized. IBM's new purchasing structure provided a consolidation of needs on components for the entire company through one single point of contact (the commodity team) for the supplier. Contracting was done centrally on corporate level. However, in all cases the operational purchasing activities were decentralized.

Purchasing components and other production-related goods are organized through divisional global procurement executives (see Figure 13.4). These managers are responsible for purchasing, sourcing and supplier policy for a well-defined group of components. They report to the chief purchasing officer (CPO) and to their own business-unit manager. The business-unit managers meet with the CPO through various corporate business councils where purchasing and supplier issues are discussed and decisions are being made. The CPO communicates with every business-unit manager separately in order to match the corporate purchasing strategy with the needs of the individual divisions and business units. This guarantees a thorough integration of the purchasing and supplier policy in the organization. In this way IBM was able to use its enormous purchasing power in combination with maximum flexibility.

Corporate commodity plans are submitted to the CPO and, next, to the procurement executive council. They are prepared by cross-functional commodity teams. These teams consist of professionals in product development, research and development, marketing, production, distribution and finance, together with purchasing professionals. The leader of this team is a commodity manager, who does not necessarily need to be a procurement professional. The structure of the team is virtual because most professionals may work all over the world. They communicate through e-mail, fax and video conferencing. These commodity teams have the authority to select suppliers and contract them for a specific commodity.

For purchasing of production-related materials IBM pursues uniform purchasing procedures and ways of working all over the world. Defining purchasing requirements, how to prequalify suppliers, how to select suppliers and what contract templates to use should be done following corporate rules and guidelines. Focus is on selecting suppliers which offer products and services at a world-class level and which have global presence. This leads to lower price and cost levels, higher quality, better service delivery and lower inventories. It also results in fewer suppliers and a growing commitment from these suppliers because the purchasing turnover is spread over fewer suppliers. Therefore more attention can be given to the relationship with an individual supplier in the value chain and a relationship based on continuous performance improvement can be developed.

Key factors to realize and improve a global sourcing process are strong leadership, active involvement of management, formalized supplier management, corporate commodity plans, cross-functional teams and standardization of logistics and delivery processes.

Centralized versus decentralized purchasing: some criteria to consider

The question as to what extent to centralize or decentralize purchasing cannot be easily answered. Most companies balance between the two extremes: at one moment they will have a centralized purchasing organization, whereas some years later they may opt for a more decentralized purchasing organization. In recent years many automotive companies have decided to centralize their purchasing operations. The same goes for some major office

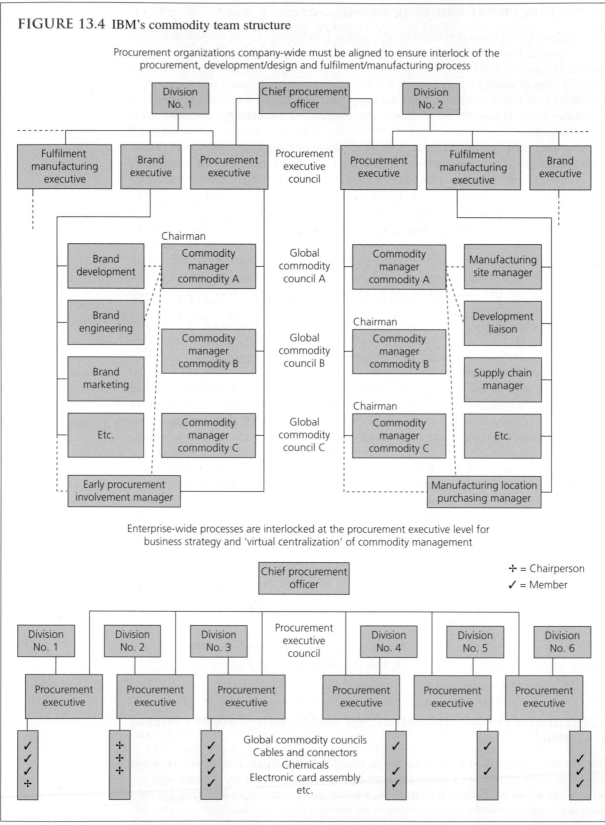

FIGURE 13.4 IBM's commodity team structure

Source: van Weele and Rozemeijer, (1996) , p. 142

equipment manufacturers (such as Xerox) while other companies, such as Air France-KLM, have changed from a functional to a divisional structure. As a result the central purchasing department was split up into a number of decentralized purchasing departments within each of the divisions and business units.

The following factors or criteria are commonly used when deciding to opt for centralization or decentralization in purchasing:

- Commonality of purchase requirements. The greater the commonality of the purchased products and services required by the business units, the more benefits can be obtained from a centralized or co-ordinated approach. This is why the buying of raw materials and packaging materials in large companies is often concentrated at one (corporate) location.

- Geographic location. When business units are situated in different countries or regions this may hamper co-ordination efforts considerably. In practice there appear to be significant differences in trading and business practices between Europe and the USA. Even within a European context significant cultural differences exist and some large companies have changed their co-ordination strategy from a global to a regional approach.

- Supply market structure. Sometimes the company is confronted in some of its supply markets with one or a limited number of very large supplier organizations. In such a situation the power balance is definitely to the advantage of the supplier and, then, it makes sense to adopt a co-ordinated purchasing approach in order to arrange for a better negotiating position *vis-à-vis* these powerful business partners.

- Savings potential. Prices of some types of raw materials are very sensitive to volume: in such circumstances buying higher volumes may immediately lead to cost savings. This is true both for standard commodities and high-tech components.

- Expertise required. Sometimes, very specific expertise is required for effective buying, as in the purchase of high-tech semiconductors and microchips. Besides technology, prices are also strongly related to the laws of supply and demand. As a result most manufacturers of electronics goods have centralized the buying of these products. The same goes for the buying of software and hardware.

- Price fluctuations. If commodity (e.g. fruit juices, wheat, coffee) prices are highly sensitive to the political and economic climate, a centralized purchasing approach is favoured.

- Customer demands. Sometimes customers may dictate to the manufacturer which products it has to purchase. This is typical for the aircraft industry. These conditions are agreed upon with the business unit that is responsible for manufacturing the product. This practice will clearly obstruct any efforts aimed at purchasing co-ordination.

In practice these considerations appear to be decisive when deciding on buying products centrally or otherwise.

In summarizing this section, the advantages and disadvantages of decentralization are shown in Figure 13.5. For centralization, the inverse of the arguments may be used.

Over the past years, the topic of how to foster purchasing synergies in a corporate environment has received much attention. Recent research reveals that the way in which corporations should leverage their purchasing and supplier strategies is dependent on two factors, i.e. purchasing maturity and corporate cohesion. Differences in how companies deal with purchasing co-ordination may be explained by these two variables (see Memo 13.1).

FIGURE 13.5 Some advantages and disadvantages related to decentralized purchasing

Advantages	Disadvantages
• Direct responsibility for profit centres	• Dispersed purchasing power, lack of economies of scale
• Stronger customer orientation towards internal user	• No uniform attitude towards suppliers
• Less bureaucratic purchasing procedures	• Scattered market research
• Less need for internal coordination	• Limited possibilities for building up specific expertise on purchasing and materials
• Direct communication with suppliers	• Probably different commercial purchase conditions for different business units

MEMO 13.1   CREATING CORPORATE ADVANTAGE IN PURCHASING

The results from the survey suggest that corporate purchasing initiatives should be congruent with the overall level of corporate coherence and the level of maturity of the purchasing function. Corporate coherence is related to the extent to which the different parts of the corporation operate and are managed as one entity. Major differences across business units in, management style, vision, strategy, culture and structure reflect a low corporate coherence. When differences in culture and structure exist across business units, the integration of the purchasing function will be a significant challenge. Purchasing maturity is related (amongst others) to the level of professionalism in the purchasing function as expressed in the status of the function, the role and organizational status of the purchasing departments, availability of purchasing information systems, quality of the people involved in purchasing, and the level of collaboration with suppliers. Our research suggests that when the purchasing function is highly mature, companies will use a different and more advanced approach to manage corporate purchasing synergy, than in the situation where one is dealing with low purchasing maturity (see Figure 13.6). In cases were

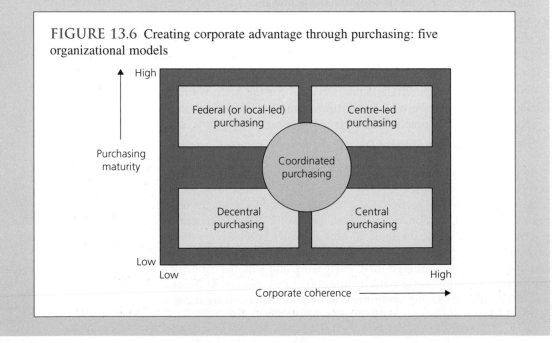

FIGURE 13.6 Creating corporate advantage through purchasing: five organizational models

both purchasing maturity and corporate coherence are low, decentralized purchasing is most likely to be found. In such a situation central coordination efforts will be hardly sustainable. In this situation, we expect little homogeneity in specifications across business units. However, there are opportunities to realize purchasing synergy through exchanging information of supply markets, suppliers and prices, by using voluntary working groups. In cases where both constructs are high, a centre-led structure has good chances to succeed. In such a structure cross-functional/cross-business teams conduct co-ordination activities with active support of the business units, whilst strongly managed by a corporate purchasing staff. If both parameters have a medium value, a hybrid structure, with both central purchasing and voluntary purchasing co-ordination activities are most likely to be found. Federal (or local-led) purchasing consists of a small corporate purchasing staff supporting a number of autonomous decentralized purchasing units in their voluntary efforts to exploit potential synergies. The central purchasing model represents a situation in which most strategic commodities are contracted from a corporate purchasing department. The latter appears to be only feasible in organizations where purchasing at the operating company

level is hardly developed and corporate coherence is high.

In our view, top managers do not add value by choosing a certain approach to create corporate advantage in purchasing as such. They add value by creating a fit between the approach used to create corporate advantage in purchasing, and the level of corporate coherence and purchasing maturity. In practice, this is not very often the case. Our research revealed a number of initiatives that were not aimed at creating long-term corporate advantage, but at short-term cost reductions. In many of those cases external consultants were hired to drive corporate purchasing cost reduction initiatives. Often, however, after the consultants had left, the companies gradually returned to their former and less co-operative ways of working, not using the momentum to establish formal organizational mechanisms, or other measures, to create sustainable corporate advantage in purchasing. In our view, this is related to the fact that the approach used by the consultants was not congruent with the level of corporate coherence and purchasing maturity of these companies.

Source: Rozemeijer and van Weele, 2003, pp. 10–11

Purchasing organization in single-unit companies

In a single-unit organization the issue of centralized versus decentralized purchasing relates to the question as to what extent purchases need to be made through the purchasing department. This refers directly to what authority should be assigned to the purchasing department and, in general, depends on the following variables:

- Management's view towards purchasing. This clearly affects the tasks, responsibilities and authority assigned to the purchasing department (see Chapter 5).

- Information technology. This directly affects the possibilities for co-ordination of all materials-related activities within the company. Generally, implementation of contemporary ERP systems will alter the traditional ways of working within purchasing. In general, it will require better discipline and more systematic communication from purchasing operations. As a result purchasing procedures need to be changed and adapted and changes within the materials organization may even be necessary. Information systems also enable better management information and reports. As a result of a greater transparency of purchasing operations, its reporting relationships may need to be reviewed.

- Personal relationships. As in any organizational issue, personal relationships often play an overriding role in discussions on how to structure reporting relationships.

If the purchasing manager is to report to the logistics manager, it is important that the latter shows some affinity with the purchasing job. Otherwise, conflicts may occur.

■ Total cost approach. A better understanding of some important logistics parameters, such as inventory turnover, supplier delivery reliability, the supplier reject rate, etc. will avoid a too dominant price orientation. As a result purchasing decisions will become more cost oriented instead of price oriented, which has been the tradition in many companies. Knowledge of these additional 'performance indicators' often leads to a less autonomously operating purchasing department and to a better integration with the logistics function.

Based on these variables purchasing's reporting relationships in a single unit organization may take different forms, as is highlighted in the structures given below[3]:

■ The fully integrated logistics structure. Here, purchasing reports directly to the logistics manager at the same level as production planning and physical distribution (see Figure 13.7).

■ The partially integrated logistics structure. In this structure purchasing, production planning and physical distribution report to the logistics manager in various ways. Figure 13.8 shows three possible configurations.

In the preceding chapters, some important changes have been discussed which affect the role and position of the purchasing organization. These changes can be divided into external and internal changes. External changes are related to changes outside the company. They are not to be influenced by the company. Internal changes are related to changes inside the company. In most cases they result from rethinking the value chain, i.e. the company's primary processes and its relationships with suppliers.

It may be clear, that all of these changes influence the tasks, responsibilities and authority of the purchasing function and, hence, they will affect and change the structure of the purchasing organization (see Figure 13.9).

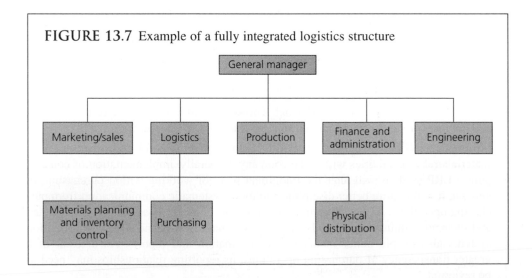

FIGURE 13.7 Example of a fully integrated logistics structure

---

[3]This discussion was originally based upon the contribution by Miller and Gilmour (1979).

FIGURE 13.8 Example of a partially integrated logistics structure

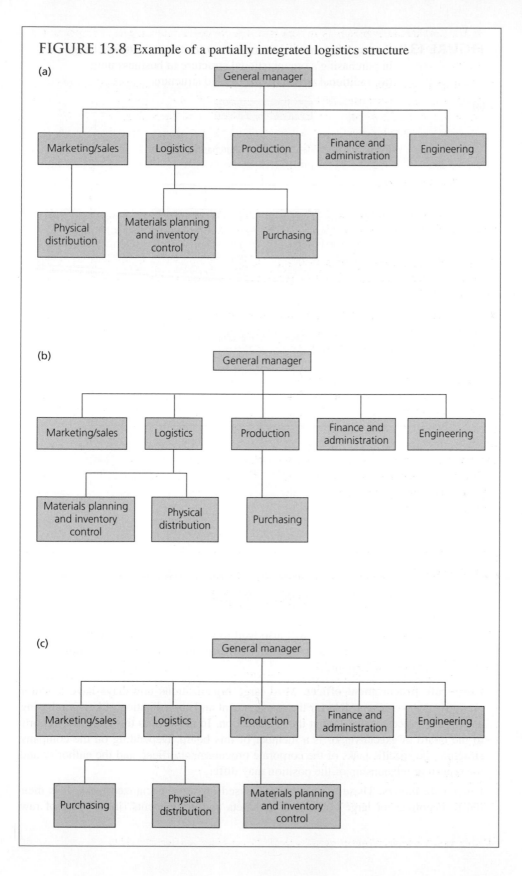

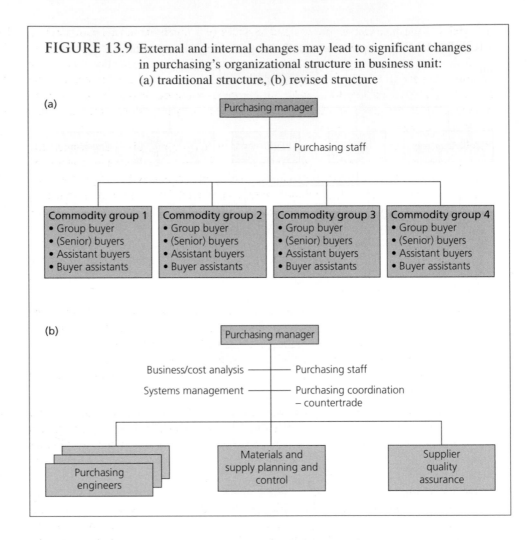

FIGURE 13.9 External and internal changes may lead to significant changes in purchasing's organizational structure in business unit: (a) traditional structure, (b) revised structure

PURCHASING JOB PROFILES

The developments described above will also lead to significant changes in the necessary skills and abilities required by the purchasing department. In most large companies the following positions can be found:

Corporate procurement officer (CPO) Senior executive, who is responsible for the management and co-ordination of key purchasing and supply processes throughout the corporate organization.

- **Corporate procurement officer.** Most large organizations nowadays have a senior executive, who is responsible for the management and co-ordination of key purchasing and supply processes throughout the organization. In most cases this executive reports to the board of executives or is a member of this board. Depending on the company structure the specific tasks of the corporate procurement officer, and the authority and the reporting relationship of the position may differ.

- **Corporate buyers.** These are generally focused on very specialized tasks. It is their job to negotiate for large volumes of products and components (in the case of raw materials), large investment projects and services (e.g. in the case of manufacturing equipment and computer hardware and software). Their counterparts at the supplier are often account managers, who are highly educated and experienced. For this reason corporate buyers preferably have a similar educational background, often at university level. They are responsible for developing corporate sourcing strategies for key commodities, which are prepared with the product specialists who reside in different parts of the corporation.

- **Purchasing engineers.** These buyers, often working at a decentralized level, normally have a shorter planning horizon and a more operational task. As they have to meet and converse frequently with engineers and other technical specialists they require an adequate technical background, combined with commercial skills. In fact, purchasing engineers are the liaison between the engineering and purchasing departments in new product development programmes. Most of their time is spent discussing specifications, both internally and externally, conducting supply market research, selection of suppliers, and preparing and conducting contract negotiations with suppliers. As soon as the product has been introduced to the market, their product, supplier and contract files are passed on to the category buyer.

- **Project buyers.** The tasks of the project buyers are somewhat similar to those of the purchasing engineer. However, the purchasing engineer deals with production materials, whereas the project purchaser deals primarily with investment goods. For this job a technical background of university level is required. Since these decisions always require a team approach, project buyers should have excellent communication and presentation skills.

- **Materials planners.** Materials planners are responsible for materials planning and ordering. In companies with a high degree of computerization within the materials area, both tasks are often combined in one function. Here, the materials planner focuses on calling off the materials required against the prearranged framework agreements. Furthermore they monitor and control suppliers on their quality and delivery performance. For this job a secondary educational level will be sufficient. Most important here are personal abilities, such as stress-resistance, service orientation and the ability to organize the work effectively. Apart from this, this job provides a good opportunity for future buyers to become acquainted with the work as a first step.

- **NPR buyers.** These buyers are responsible for buying not-product-related goods and services. For an NPR buyer a general, polytechnic education will suffice. With regard to the purchasing of spare parts, the delivery of these items in general will be covered in the original contract for the investment good. The NPR assortment is generally very large and it is the task of the NPR buyer to manage these assortments effectively, rather than striving to optimize the price performance for each individual item. Therefore, a good understanding of logistics management and techniques (of inventory management and order management specifically), catalogue solutions and e-procurement applications would be basic to this type of buyer.

Table 13.5 summarizes the most important skills and abilities of the functions described above. Memo 13.2 describes how the purchasing job has changed over time and how recognition by senior management is growing. Although taken from a survey among US companies, we feel the trends and developments in Europe to be similar.

Corporate buyers
Buyers operating at the corporate level with global sourcing responsibilities for key commodities. It is their job to negotiate for large volumes of products and components (in the case of raw materials) and large investment projects and services.

Materials planners
Materials planners are responsible for materials planning and ordering. Materials planners focus on calling off the materials required against the prearranged framework agreements. Furthermore, they monitor and control suppliers on their quality and delivery performance.

NPR buyers
These buyers are responsible for buying and non-product-related goods and services.

TABLE 13.5 Buyer profiles and their most important responsibilities and skills

Function	Responsibilities	Skills required
Chief procurement officer	Developing corporate sourcing strategies, systems and reporting	General management skills Leadership Communication skills
Corporate buyer	Strategic commodities	Commercial skills Long-term planning horizon Broad business orientation Communication skills
Category buyer	New materials and components New suppliers	All-around technical education Medium planning horizon Commercial skills Communication skills
Project buyer	Investment goods and maintenance goods and services	Project management skills Technical education
NPR-buyer	General and facility goods and services	Generalist Business administration Communication skills
Operational buyer/ materials planner	Materials planning Order handling Troubleshooting Vendor rating	All-around Pragmatic Customer driven Stress resistant

MEMO 13.2   HOW BUYERS ARE CHANGING

Today's purchasing professional is a little older, has been on the job slightly longer, and is responsible for spending a lot more dollars than a comparable buying pro of 10 years ago. Today's purchasing professional is much more likely to be a woman than 10 years ago—or even 5 years ago. They are more likely to have chosen purchasing as a career than in the past. Their dollar volume responsibility is twice as high as it was in 1997 and three times higher than in 1992. Paperwork and transaction processing continues to be the bane of many of these procurement professionals—despite quantum improvements being made in automating the buying process. They are negotiating more long-term agreements with selected suppliers. Looking out on a global market scape, today's purchasing professional is negotiating outsourcing agreements with suppliers around the world and a vast majority of these buying

executives continue to pare away at costs and the size of their supply bases.

These are some of the findings of *Purchasing* magazine's latest survey of procurement officers and supply chain executives. A close examination of this latest picture of the purchasing executive shows a pro who regularly handles huge sums of money, takes part in corporate-wide profitability decisions, is responsible for performance of a number of non-purchasing functions, works closely with top management and is constantly on the lookout for new approaches and techniques to cut costs and improve supply chain efficiency.

What follows is a best effort summary and anatomy of the purchasing professional in 2003:

■ Ten years ago men dominated the purchasing profession—holding down 82% of all the jobs.

Today male dominance is still considerable, but falling. Just over 68% of the jobs in purchasing are now held by men . . .

- Today 67.4% of all purchasing executives boast a 4-year college degree. This compares with 61.2% in 1992%. In addition, nearly 13% of all purchasing execs are working for degrees or advanced degrees . . .

- Business is the degree of preference with 61% of all degrees held by purchasing executives. Liberal arts degrees are in second place with 17%, followed by science/engineering (15%) and other (mostly assorted technical specialties) at 5%.

- Certification has grown slowly since it came on the scene in 1987. Today 21% of purchasing execs polled hold either C.P.M. or C.P.I.M. (American Inventory Control Society) certification.

- The average respondent to this survey has been in purchasing 9.8 years.

- What is the total value of the purchases the individual purchasing pro controls/supervises? Answers to this question vary all over the lot—from less than $1 million to $526 million. The average purchasing responsibility is $31.3 million. In 1992 it was a little more than $11 million.

- More than 81% of purchasing professionals say they are responsible for maintaining inventory levels. This is up from 77% 5-years ago. Inventory is a shared responsibility for 40% of the respondents—mainly with a sales manager or plant manager. And for 37% of those purchasing officers with inventory responsibility, it's an unshared responsibility.

- 56% of respondents say they have systems for rating supplier performance. Of the companies with performance measurement systems, 32% are formal systems.

- Among those purchasing executives involved in product development a rough estimate of time devoted to these activities was 14% . . .

- Purchasing departments across the land have experienced serious downsizing efforts in the past two years (82.1%). Much of the downsizing can be traced to the introduction of serious e-sourcing tools in purchasing. Also playing a major role are the introduction of supply chain management techniques to purchasing organizations and increased attention to staffing structures.

- A large plurality of respondents (31%) feel as Ralph Richardson, manager of purchasing and stores at EPB, Chattanooga, does that there is great satisfaction in 'negotiating long-term deals with suppliers' and potential suppliers . . . Other areas of job satisfaction listed by survey participants include maximizing sourcing development, reducing costs and problem solving.

Source: J. Morgan, How buyers are changing: profile of a purchasing professional, *Purchasing*, 14th August, 2003, pp. 33–36)

SUMMARY

In this chapter, issues related to purchasing organizations have been discussed. Purchasing structures appear to vary to a great extent among companies. This is due to the different views which top managers hold towards purchasing and supply. Apart from this some company-specific characteristics may define purchasing's reporting relationships. Among these, purchasing's share in the end products' costs, the financial position of the company and the company's dependency on the supplier market seem to be the most important.

When analysing the scope, tasks, responsibilities and authority of the purchasing function, we differentiated between the strategic level, the tactical level and the operational level. When redesigning purchasing structures managers should make sure that each of the task levels is given sufficient attention. The outcome of such a process will probably be different for multi-unit companies and single-unit companies. In a multi-unit environment it should be decided to what extent the purchasing function should be decentralized. In this respect four types of organizational structures have been discussed: the centralized structure, the decentralized structure, the hybrid structure and cross-functional sourcing teams. The last two are the most complicated; however, their popularity is growing rapidly. Hybrid structures may have different forms. They may be structured based upon voluntary co-ordination, the lead buyer concept and the lead design concept. The decision whether to centralize or decentralize and what co-ordination form would be the best, would depend on a limited number of parameters. Here, we discussed purchasing maturity and corporate cohesion as important factors. It is fair to conclude that there is no single best way to get organized for purchasing in a corporate, multi-unit environment.

Purchasing structures appear to be highly volatile: a period of centralized purchasing is often followed by a change to the other way around. Due to increasing international competition and the maturing of many end-user markets, the present trend is towards co-ordination and more participative, process approaches. Many companies try to reap the benefits of co-ordinated purchasing of common materials requirements, whilst preserving the advantage of entrepreneurship, residing low in the organization.

When designing purchasing structures in a single-unit environment a number of parameters need to be considered. As computerization in the materials-related functions progresses, purchasing activities become more integrated with logistics management. In this respect various options are open to managers. They may choose a totally integrated logistics organizational model or decide on a partially integrated model.

Major organizational changes are reflected in future profiles of purchasing positions. For this reason we discussed the profile of the chief procurement officer, the corporate buyer, the purchasing engineer, the project buyer, the materials planner and the NPR buyer. From this discussion it became clear that the purchasing and supply arena provides significant challenges to those with an engineering and MBA background.

ASSIGNMENTS

13.1 When discussing the opportunity to foster synergies in the area of purchasing, some top managers stated that 'purchasing in our company is too important to leave it only to buyers!'. Would you agree with this? How would you see the buyer's role in creating corporate, leveraged purchasing strategies?

13.2 In this chapter it was argued that most large companies have opted for a hybrid structure to organize their purchasing activities. What is meant by this? Why would companies choose such a structure?

13.3 When applying for a new job in medium sized company a prospective purchasing manager was asked to whom he would prefer to report: (1) the financial manager, (2) the production manager and (3) the logistics manager. Each of these managers reports at the same hierarchical level. What would you consider to be the most important advantages and disadvantages of each option? What option would you prefer?

13.4 Some complaints that can be heard from chief procurement officers in companies is that their carefully negotiated corporate agreements are barely used by the decentralized business companies. These contracts suffer from a high degree of 'maverick buying'. What could be the reason for this phenomenon?

13.5 How would you explain the growing popularity of cross-functional sourcing teams when co-ordinating purchasing at the corporate level? What would you consider to be the critical success factors of such teams?

13.6 Cross-functional teams would prepare corporate sourcing plans for strategic commodities. How would such a commodity plan look like? What elements need to be taken into account in such a plan?

REFERENCES

Johnson, P.F. and Leenders, M.R. (2004), 'Supply's role and responsibilities', Arizona: Center for Advanced Purchasing Studies.

Miller, J.G. and Gilmour, P. (1979) 'Materials managers: who needs them?', *Harvard Business Review*, July–August:143–53.

Rozemeijer, F.A. and van Weele, A.J. (2003) 'Creating corporate advantage through purchasing: a contingency model', *The Journal of Supply Chain Management*, (Winter), pp. 4–13.

PERFORMANCE MEASUREMENT AND GOVERNANCE IN PURCHASING

LEARNING OBJECTIVES

After studying this chapter you should understand the following:

- The factors that influence the way performance measurement is executed and evaluated.
- The key areas that should be considered when measuring and evaluating purchasing performance.
- The methods, techniques and performance measures that can be used.
- How to conduct a purchasing audit as a tool to improve purchasing performance.
- The value of benchmarking in purchasing.
- The role and importance of governance rules in purchasing.

INTRODUCTION

The following case study illustrates the fact that measuring and evaluating purchasing performance is a fuzzy issue, yet it is one of major concern for many companies. The question of how to measure and evaluate purchasing performance is not easily answered. A major problem is that to date no single, practical approach that produces consistent results for different types of companies has been found. It is highly uncertain whether such a yardstick, or method of universal application, could be developed. This chapter will explain why. The consequence is that purchasing managers typically need to rely on their own insight and experience when establishing procedures and systems to monitor the effectiveness and efficiency of their purchasing organizations.

The intention of this chapter is to develop a consistent approach to the subject; specific questions to be addressed are:

- Why should purchasing performance be measured and evaluated? What are the major benefits to be derived from such an activity?
- What problems are involved in assessing purchasing performance?
- What should be measured and evaluated?

CASE STUDY THE INTRODUCTION OF A QUALITY PROGRAMME BY AN INDUSTRIAL COMPONENTS MANUFACTURER

The strategy of a large manufacturer of industrial components is to become a quality leader in the field. According to management's view, quality improvement is the only way to survive in the highly competitive environment. Management is aware of the direct relationship between product quality and process quality and that high quality components can only be manufactured if the manufacturing processes are in full control. Therefore, it was decided to comply to ISO 9001 standards and a quality manager was appointed to help the organization make the necessary transitions.

The task of the quality manager was, more specifically, to support the company's departments into developing their own quality programmes. Furthermore, they had to ensure that the targets, as agreed by the departmental managers, were realized.

The purchasing department was actively involved in the company's quality programme and, like their colleagues, the purchasing manager came up with a quality programme for their department. However, as time went by, the programme met with little enthusiasm from its buyers to support the plan.

Gradually the purchasing manager got the feeling that their staff would regard the implementation of the quality plan to be primarily a responsibility of the quality manager. Later, through complaints from production, they discovered that their buyers in their contracts with suppliers primarily discussed price, rather than quality. When discussing this matter with the quality manager it became clear that targets concerning quality improvement were translated insufficiently into individual buyer targets. It was not clear to the quality manager how each individual buyer would contribute to the overall quality objectives of the company. On the other hand, objectives with regard to price reduction were readily available and specified per buyer in a fair degree of detail. Every month individual buyers were assessed on their budget results at which time actual prices were compared with budgeted prices. Variance reports were prepared on each buyer's activity and discussed in the monthly meeting of the purchasing team. The purchasing manager eventually found out that their buyers primarily responded to what they are evaluated on, not on what they were expected to do. Clearly, the present situation could not continue. They started to think about how to change the situation . . .

- What measures and techniques exist in order to perform such an evaluation?
- How could an evaluation system be implemented?
- How to benchmark purchasing processes?

FACTORS INFLUENCING PURCHASING PERFORMANCE MEASUREMENT

One of the most important factors that influences the way in which purchasing results are measured, is how management looks upon the role and the importance of the purchasing function. In general management may hold one of the following views towards purchasing:

- Operational, administrative activity. In this case management evaluates purchasing operations primarily on parameters such as order backlog, purchasing administrative lead time, number of orders issued, number of requests for quotations issued, adherence to existing procedures, number of complaints, etc.
- Commercial activity. In this situation management is aware of the savings potential which purchasing may represent. Targets are agreed upon annually with the purchasing department on price or cost reduction. Purchasing should issue competitive bids to suppliers in order to keep them sharp. Parameters being used here are the total savings

reported by purchasing (per product group and per buyer), number of quotations issued, variance reports, inflation reports, etc.

■ Part of integrated logistics. Management becomes aware that price hunting has its drawbacks and may lead to sub-optimization. Putting too much pressure on prices may seduce buyers to buy 'penny wise and pound foolish'. Demands on lower prices appear always to be met by suppliers to the detriment of quality and delivery reliability. At this stage management introduces, besides cost reduction targets, targets to buyers on quality improvement, inventory reduction, improving payment terms, lead time reduction and improving supplier delivery reliability.

■ Strategic business area. Here, purchasing is actively involved in deciding on the company's future business strategy and how to strengthen the company's competitive position. It is actively engaged in make-or-buy studies leading to the outsourcing decisions. Local suppliers are consistently put to the test of international competition. Here, management evaluates purchasing on a number of aspects including supply base reduction, the number of new (international) suppliers being contracted, its contribution to the bottom line in terms of savings realized and its contribution to the top line in terms of new business revenues generated through suppliers.

Depending on the prevailing view, the position of the purchasing department within the organizational structure will differ, and the measures used for purchasing performance measurement and evaluation will differ significantly. As shown in Figure 14.1, when purchasing is seen as an operational function, performance measures are largely quantitative and administrative in character. On the other hand, when purchasing is considered to be a strategic business area, performance measures are also qualitative and strategic. In this case, a complex framework of procedures and guidelines typically is used to monitor progress against specific plans to improve **purchasing effectiveness**.

Which factors determine the prevailing purchasing mode? Firms that consider purchasing as a strategic business area are frequently forced to do so by external factors, such as strong pressure on prices and margins, loss of market share, the need for severe cost

Purchasing effectiveness Is defined as the extent to which, by choosing a certain course of action, a previously established goal or standard is being met.

FIGURE 14.1 How management may look at purchasing

Alternative viewpoints	Hierarchical position of purchasing	Performance measures
Purchasing as an operational administrative function	Low in organization	Number of orders, order backlog, purchasing administration lead time, authorization, procedures, etc.
Purchasing as a commercial function	Reporting to management	Savings, price reduction, ROI-measures, inflation reports, variance reports
Purchasing as a part of integrated logistics management	Purchasing integrated with other materials-related functions	Savings, cost reduction, supplier delivery reliability, reject rates, lead-time reduction
Purchasing as a strategic business function	Purchasing represented in top management	'Should cost' analysis, early supplier involvement, make-or-buy, supply-base reduction source: Adapted from van Weele (1984a), p. 17

reduction on incoming materials, and severe price fluctuations in their supply markets. These issues often force managers to focus attention on the need for high-level purchasing performance. In addition, internal factors may also affect or change the view that management holds towards purchasing. Among these are factors such as management style, the extent to which supply chain management has been implemented within the company, the degree to which modern quality concepts have been introduced and applied, the degree of computerization in the materials area, etc.

In summary, it can be said that the way purchasing activities are measured and judged will be different for every company; this makes it almost impossible to develop one uniform yardstick, methodology or system for performance measurement in purchasing.

WHY MEASURE PURCHASING PERFORMANCE?

What benefits can be derived from a systematic performance evaluation? Many purchasing managers were asked this question during one of our surveys and their answers are summarized in the following statements:

- Purchasing performance evaluation will lead to better decision-making since it identifies variances from planned results; these variances can be analysed to determine their causes and action can be taken to prevent their occurrence in the future.
- It may lead to better communication with other departments: e.g. analysing the number of invoices that cannot be matched with a purchasing order leads to better arrangements in payment procedures and improves mutual understanding between the purchasing department and the financial administration.
- It makes things visible: regular reporting of actual versus planned results enables a buyer to verify whether their expectations, i.e. targets, have been realized. This provides constructive feedback to the buyer and it also provides information to management about individual and group performance, and hence contributes to the recognition of the purchasing department.
- It may contribute to better motivation: properly designed, a performance evaluation system can meet the personal and motivational needs of the buyer. It can be used effectively for constructive goal setting, and motivational and personal development programmes in purchasing.

Collectively, these comments indicate that purchasing performance evaluation should result in a higher added value of the purchasing department to the firm. This added value might take the form of cost reductions, lower material prices, fewer rejects of incoming goods, better sourcing decisions, etc.

Purchasing performance should be evaluated regularly for two reasons. First, performance evaluation should be conducted to rate the individual buyer. In this sense, measurement is used primarily to serve the purposes of functional and individual performance assessment. Second, systematic performance assessment should serve the purpose of self-appraisal. In this sense, improvement of purchasing activities can be achieved most effectively by enabling each buyer to assess the results of their own purchasing activities. Hence, the evaluation activity is directed towards support of the individual buyer in doing a better professional job.

Some academics have argued that the purchasing department is one of the more difficult departments to evaluate. Based upon our own experience we would say that, certainly in comparison with other business areas, this is not necessarily true. Advanced business software packages (ERP-solutions) have improved possibilities to trace and track purchasing information considerably. However, there are some major problems that make it difficult to evaluate purchasing performance. One is the lack of definition. Although frequently used in practice as well as in theory, terms like purchasing performance, purchasing effectiveness, and **purchasing efficiency** have not been precisely defined. Some authors even use these concepts interchangeably. Another problem is the lack of formal objectives and performance standards. The objectives and strategies of the purchasing function in companies are often not clearly defined. When clear targets for purchasing activities are missing, it will be difficult to evaluate performance of purchasing in objective terms. A third problem is related to the accuracy with which purchasing performance actually can be measured. Purchasing is not an isolated function. Purchasing performance is a result of many activities which, due to their intangible character, are difficult to evaluate. In general, direct input–output relationships are difficult to identify. Just increasing the number of buyers in an organization, will not necessarily lead to better results. The lack of a straightforward input–output relationship in purchasing seriously limits the possibility of measuring and evaluating purchasing activities in an accurate and comprehensive way. Memo 14.1 illustrates this problem. A final problem is related to the difference in scope of purchasing. As was argued in the second section of this chapter, purchasing tasks and responsibilities differ greatly from one company to another, even within the same industry. This precludes the development of a uniform benchmarking and evaluation systems for purchasing.

Purchasing efficiency
Is related to the resources which are required to realize the previously established goals and objectives and their related activities. Essentially, it refers to the relationship between planned and actual costs.

MEMO 14.1   HOW TO MEASURE PURCHASING PERFORMANCE

A large, multinational company was looking for a young, ambitious purchasing manager. The candidate, when given to job, was required to accept the challenge to reduce purchasing costs by 5% within 1 year. When asked if he felt uncomfortable with this target, the appointee said: 'Not at all. Management still has to make up their mind how they are going to measure my performance.'

HOW TO ASSESS PURCHASING PERFORMANCE?

In order to decide what should be measured, it is necessary first to define purchasing performance. For the purpose of this chapter, purchasing performance is considered to be the outcome of two elements: purchasing effectiveness and purchasing efficiency.

Purchasing effectiveness is defined as the extent to which, by choosing a certain course of action, a previously established goal or standard is being met. It is important to recognize that effectiveness essentially refers to the relationship between actual and planned performance of any human activity. Purchasing effectiveness relates to the degree to which previously established goals and objectives have been met. A strategy or activity is either effective or not: a goal is reached or not. However, the goal can be expressed in terms of aspiration levels; the strategy or action that realizes a higher level may then be considered as more effective than another.

Purchasing efficiency is defined as the relationship between planned and actual sacrifices made in order to realize a goal previously agreed upon. Purchasing efficiency, then, is related to the resources which are required to realize the previously established goals and objectives and their related activities. Essentially it refers to the relationship between planned and actual costs.

Purchasing performance can thus be considered as the extent to which the purchasing function is able to realize its predetermined goals at the sacrifice of a minimum of the company's resources, i.e. costs.

This definition is very relevant. It assumes that any evaluation of purchasing activities would include both measures related to effectiveness and to efficiency. But this is not sufficient. Also, a differentiation needs to be made between purchasing's strategic and operational contribution (Carter and Mosconi 2005). The first is related to building superior relationships with best in class suppliers across the company's supply chain, which will help the company achieve superior supply chain performance. To be able to do so the purchasing function needs to provide for superior supply chain processes, systems and competencies. All these activities should result in a situation in which the company's supply chain performs better than the supply chains of its main competitors. Purchasing's strategic contribution should translate into superior operational performance. This performance relates to flawless purchasing and business processes that are operated at the lowest possible cost. Purchasing's operational performance is demonstrated by superior material cost control and production, superior supplier delivery performance, superior supplier delivery lead times and superior supplier product quality.

The relationship between these dimensions is illustrated by Figure 14.2 and discussed in detail in the following paragraph.

FIGURE 14.2 Key areas of purchasing performance measurement

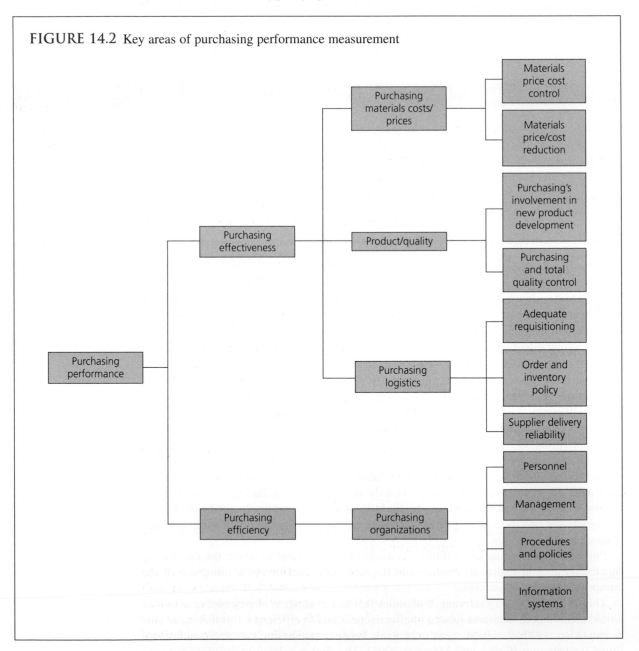

MEASURING PURCHASING PERFORMANCE: FOUR KEY AREAS

Purchasing effectiveness is thus related to the goals and objectives of the purchasing func- tion. The classical statement summarizing the overall objectives of the purchasing function is that it should obtain the right material, in the right quantity, from the right source, at the right time, at the right place and at the right price. Next, purchasing should contribute to product and process innovation and reduce the company's overall supply risk. Purchasing efficiency relates, as has been argued before, to the resources which are required in order to meet the objectives which have been set for the purchasing function. Therefore efficiency relates to the purchasing organization. More specifically it relates to the way purchasing is organized, systems are being used, procedures and guidelines that are in place, and the purchasing staff. In line with this discussion, four dimensions are suggested on which measurement and evaluation of purchasing activities can be based:

- a price/cost dimension
- a product/quality dimension
- a logistics dimension
- an organizational dimension.

Each of these dimensions is discussed in more detail below.

Purchasing price/cost dimension

This dimension refers to the relationship between standard and actual prices paid for materials and services. Here, a distinction is made between:

- Price/cost control, which refers to the continuous monitoring and evaluation of prices and price increases as they are charged by suppliers. Examples of reports and measures to be used are materials budgets, price inflation reports, variance reports, etc. The main objective here is to monitor purchasing prices in order to control them and to prevent them getting out of hand.

- Price/cost reduction, which relates to the continuous monitoring and evaluation of activities initiated to reduce costs in a structured way associated with purchased materi- als and services. Cost reduction may be the result of searches for new suppliers or substitute materials, value analysis or co-ordination of purchasing requirements among business units. The main objective here is to monitor those activities which have been initiated to structurally reduce materials costs.

Budgets are important instruments for performance planning and monitoring with regard to the price/cost dimension.

Purchasing product/quality dimension

Purchasing's responsibility with regard to the quality of purchased materials should not be defined too narrowly. Here we differentiate between:

- Purchasing's involvement in new product development. This relates to purchasing's contribution to product innovation. Obviously, it is important that the organization's new product plans in terms of target cost and time to market are being met by all disci- plines involved, including purchasing and suppliers. Measures to be used here are the number of personnel hours spent by purchasing on innovation projects, the number of engineering hours spent by suppliers, the project's overall lead time. Specific measures are the number of technical change orders and the initial sampling reject rate. The former relates to the number of engineering changes that have to be communicated to suppliers. The latter relates to the number of times a sample or prototype of a component for a new product needs to be presented by the supplier to have it approved by engineering. Measures of these activities will indicate why new product development projects are getting out of control both in terms of costs and time-to-market.

- Purchasing's contribution to total quality control. After product specifications have been released by engineering it is purchasing's job to ensure that goods ordered are delivered according to the company's specifications. Here, parameters are being used such as reject rates on incoming goods, line reject rates, number of approved suppliers, number of certified suppliers, number of reject reports, number of supplier quality agreements, number of ISO certified suppliers, etc. These measures indicate to what extent the company is able to secure a flawless incoming materials flow from suppliers.

Purchasing logistics dimension

A third key performance area is purchasing's role in contributing to an efficient incoming flow of purchased materials and services. This area includes the following major activities:

- Control of the timely and accurate handling of purchasing requisitions. Measures used here are average purchasing administrative lead time, number of orders issued, order backlog. Important measures to improve performance in this area are electronic ordering systems, introducing e-commerce solutions to internal customers and suppliers, and EDI.
- Control of timely delivery by suppliers. Measures which can be used here are supplier delivery reliability, materials shortages, over/under delivery, number of JIT-deliveries. These measures indicate the level of control over the incoming materials flow.
- Control of quantities delivered. In some cases, purchasing has the responsibility for determination and control of inventory levels. Measures used here are inventory turnover ratio, number of over/under deliveries, average order size, pipeline inventory, etc.

Supplier evaluation and vendor rating are techniques used to monitor and improve supplier performance in terms of quality and delivery reliability. Many of the performance indicators, which have been mentioned here, will be part of the company's supplier rating system.

Purchasing's organizational dimension

This dimension includes the major resources that are used to achieve the goals and objectives of the purchasing function, namely:

- Purchasing staff. This relates to background, level, training and development and competencies of purchasing personnel and its costs.
- Purchasing management. This refers to the way the purchasing department is managed. It encompasses the quality and availability of purchasing strategies, action plans and reporting procedures. It also relates to management style and communications structure.
- Purchasing procedures and guidelines. This refers to the availability of procedures and working instructions for purchasing staff and suppliers in order to make sure that work is done in the most efficient manner.
- Purchasing information systems. This subject relates to the efforts made to improve the information systems which are required to support purchasing staff and other employees in their daily activities and to generate necessary management information on purchasing activities and performance.

Table 14.1 provides an overview of the key areas of purchasing performance evaluation and some examples of performance parameters which can be used per key area. A comprehensive assessment of any purchasing organization should cover each of these areas, individually and collectively. Hence, it follows that a comprehensive performance measurement system in purchasing should monitor effectiveness as well as efficiency and therefore should include, preferably, measures of each key-performance area.

Interrelationships exist among all four dimensions. For example, if purchasing pushes too hard for lower prices, this action may ultimately affect material quality negatively. The reverse may also be true: the requirement of a zero-defects quality level may ultimately result in higher material prices. However, the result may be less unplanned downtime in production and, hence, a lower total cost of ownership.

Finally, each of the four dimensions can be measured and evaluated at different levels of aggregation, i.e. per line-item level, per individual supplier level, per individual buyer, at departmental level, at the overall company level. It is therefore clear that performance measurement systems in purchasing will show a large degree of variation. Purchasing performance measures and reporting systems need to be tailored to the specific needs of the company.

The next paragraph deals with some important control instruments for purchasing. The following are described: different types of purchasing budgets, definition of purchasing savings and how to measure them and performance measures and ratios with regard to quality and delivery logistics.

TABLE 14.1 Examples of purchasing performance indicators

Area	Measurement aimed at	Continuous/ incidental	Examples
Purchased materials prices and costs	Purchased materials cost control	C	Materials budgets, variance reports, price inflation, reports, purchasing turnover
	Purchased materials cost reduction	C	Purchasing cost saving and avoidances, impact on return and investment
Product/quality of purchased materials	Early purchasing involvement in design and development	I	Time spent by purchasing on design and engineering projects, initial sampling reject rate (%)
	Incoming inspection quality control and assurance	C	Reject rate (%), line reject rate (%), quality costs per supplier
Purchasing logistics and supply	Monitoring requisitioning	I/C	Purchasing administrative lead times, order backlog (per buyer)
	Delivery reliability (quality and quantity)		Rush orders, delivery reliability index per supplier, materials shortages, inventory turnover ratio, JIT deliveries
Purchasing staff and organization	Training and motivation of purchasing staff	I	Time and workload analysis of purchasing department, purchasing budget, purchasing and supply audit
	Purchasing management quality		
	Purchasing systems and procedures		
	Purchasing research		

Source: van Weele (1991)

PURCHASING BUDGETS, PURCHASING SAVINGS AND OTHER PERFORMANCE MEASURES

The planning cycle within a company starts with setting up the company's annual sales plan. The input comes from next year's sales estimates and new product introduction plans. The sales plan is an important input for the other plans of the company including the production, materials investment, personnel and also the purchasing plan. The purchasing plan usually breaks down into five different sub plans including the purchased materials budget, the purchasing budget indirect materials, the investment budget, the supplier tooling budget and the purchasing departmental budget.

A budget is the reflection of the resources in quantitative terms related to the personnel, materials and services that are needed for the company's business processes in its broadest sense for a certain period. A budget serves as a vehicle for delegating activities and responsibilities to lower management levels in the organization. When approved by senior management, budget holders may operate rather autonomously as long as they stay within their financial budget.

Purchasing materials budget
Reflects, often per product item, the volume which is expected to be purchased for the next planning period, usually a year, and the expected price level for that specific product.

Purchasing materials budget

The purchasing materials budget reflects, often per product item, the volume which is expected to be purchased for the next planning period, usually a year, and the expected price level for that specific product. The volume estimate is from the production and materials requirements plan. The estimate for the price that is expected to be paid has to come from the buyer. Often the final budget estimate is decided after a thorough discussion between the buyer or purchasing manager in order to make sure that price targets are set at a challenging level.

Sometimes the price targets are dictated by senior management. Many manufacturing companies nowadays are being confronted with severe cost competition. This results in a strong focus on materials cost reductions. In the automotive industry annual cost reductions of 5% are no exception. In this type of company, purchasing may account for 80% of the total cost price of a car. In such a case, the target imposed by management on purchasing will then amount to 4%. Based upon this overall target, every buyer should submit detailed action plans to meet the overall goals of the purchasing department.

Deciding about the purchasing materials budget is a far from simple matter. In customer markets, that strongly fluctuate, exact production and materials volumes are hard to predict. In such a situation it will be difficult to provide a reliable volume forecast to suppliers. If suppliers do not know what volume will come their way, they will not be able to submit a reliable and solid price for the components that they will supply. Budgeting in purchasing, therefore, requires a lot of guesswork. Nevertheless, this guesswork is very important. A price estimate that at a later stage appears to have been too high, may lead to an end product cost and sales price that has been too high. As a result of this a company might have lost important business to competitors. If the buyer's estimate has been, in hindsight, too low, the company might have sold its products at a too low sales price. As a result the company's profitability might have suffered. The more volatile a market is, the more frequent monitoring of budget performance and adjustment of budgeted targets will be required.

The actual performance against the initial budget is closely monitored through monthly variance reports, which indicate, per buyer and component, deviations from the agreed targets. Variance reports are therefore an important tool when it comes to evaluating the performance of individual buyers.

Purchasing budget indirect materials

Budgeting for indirect materials usually is conducted per department per spend category. As the budgets for individual departments have been approved by senior management, the relevant spend for indirect materials (and investments) is aggregated and put down into a coherent spend budget for indirect materials. Usually, this task is conducted by the purchasing department. Departmental budgets for indirect materials are usually based upon historic usage and consumption. The budget for next year is based upon the one from last year, and adapted on the basis of some kind of index (e.g. consumer price index). As was discussed earlier, these budgets cover a wide variety of products and services, ranging from marketing expenditure to IT products and services, facilities goods and services, insurance and temporary labour. Purchase orders for indirect materials may be very different in terms of spend volume and order frequency. All of these characteristics make these product categories hard to manage (see also Chapter 4 of this book).

In some cases, for instance in the case of maintenance goods and services, specific planning techniques may be used, allowing for a better control of indirect purchasing spend. Technical maintenance can be based on corrective or preventive maintenance. In the latter case, maintenance is systematically planned for each type of equipment, allowing the purchasing department to inform its suppliers in time and allowing an efficient planning of the ordering and deliveries for the components and services involved.

The investment and tooling budget

The investment budget and the tooling budget are not specifically purchasing budgets. However, in many cases buyers are involved when these budgets are executed. Based upon sales forecasts, production planning will provide an estimate of how existing production capacity will be utilized. If the capacity available does not match the required capacity, it needs to be expanded. Investments into additional production capacity then need to be made by the company. An alternative may be to contract the required additional capacity from a specialist subcontractor. In both cases investments must be made. In the first case additional production equipment needs to be acquired. In the second, investments probably need to be made in specific supplier tooling. This is required, for example, when buying plastic shampoo bottles that require specific moulds to be provided to the supplier by the shampoo manufacturer. In manufacturing companies, therefore, a distinction is made between the investment budget and the supplier tooling budget. The latter relates to planned investments in supplier specific tools. In the automotive industry investments in tooling can be substantial. The actual planning for these budgets normally happens outside the purchasing department.

Purchasing departmental budget

Based upon the overall purchasing activity plan and the purchasing materials budget, the purchasing staff and resources required can be budgeted. The purchasing departmental budget (mostly around 1–2% of the total company's payroll) covers all expenses related to the salaries paid to buyers, social security and taxes, travel cost, telephone cost, office cost, systems costs and other organizational cost. It will not come as a surprise that this type of budget is among the most used in purchasing. In most cases the size of the purchasing staff will not fluctuate strongly from year-to-year. Therefore this budget is fairly simple to administer.

Purchasing cost savings: definitions and measures

Purchasing cost savings are among the most popular when it comes to evaluating purchasing and individual buyer performance. These measures are also the hardest to measure. The problem is how to define them. There seems to be no general consensus on how to do this.

Cost avoidance
Cost avoidance is a variance between the historical and the actual purchase price paid per unit. A cost avoidance is not considered to be sustainable.

In general a distinction is made between **cost avoidances** and cost reductions. A cost avoidance is a variance between the historical and the actual purchase price paid per unit. A cost avoidance is not considered to be sustainable. Cost avoidances may be the result of putting extra pressure on a supplier during contract negotiations, playing off suppliers against each other, ordering larger quantities than before resulting in quantity discounts, accepting one time promotional actions offered by a specific supplier, etc. In contrast, cost reductions are sustainable in character. These may be the result of a change of the specification, a change of supplier, or omitting unnecessary product quality requirements (e.g. using a general specification rather than a supplier or product brand name).

Since every purchasing activity essentially is cross-functional, it is extremely difficult to attribute purchasing savings to the purchasing department only. If a purchasing manager is going to claim all the savings that have been generated on his account, this will not make him particularly popular among his fellow managers. Purchasing savings therefore need to be reported at the company level rather then at the purchasing departmental level. Cost savings reports that only reflect price effects, may lead to wrong judgments. Figure 14.3 illustrates how purchasing savings can be classified.

When setting up a company-wide purchasing cost reduction programme, the following suggestions may be helpful. First, clear savings targets need to be agreed upon upfront that may guide the programme. These targets are not to be compromised during the execution of the programme. Second, external factors that cannot be influenced by the buyers, need to be left out of the reporting. This is, for example, the case when market prices go down. In this case, it is not fair to attribute the cost savings to buyer action. Buyers only need to be evaluated on factors that are within their range of influence. Third, a distinction needs to be made between theoretical and actual cost savings. Theoretical cost savings can be calculated as the difference between the historical price paid less the contract price paid, multiplied by the contracted volume on a 12-months basis. Actual savings may differ greatly from these theoretical savings ('money in the pocket' versus 'money in the air'). Actual savings are calculated by the difference between the actual price paid and the historical price paid, multiplied by the actual volumes ordered against the contract.

FIGURE 14.3 Classification of purchase savings

1. Competitive bidding. Supplier selection based on competitive bidding. Purchasing cost savings realized through lower prices at present suppliers or introduction of new suppliers, after having used competitive bidding or electronic auctions.

2. Negotiation. Savings generated by negotiating a better deal compared to the supplier's initial bid i.e. quotation.

3. Distribution. Purchase cost savings realized by negotiating on transportation cost, inventory reduction, materials handling cost or other distribution cost

4. Purchasing policy. Purchasing cost savings realized by increasing the number of annual (bonus) agreements for existing goods and services.

5. Purchasing ordering and logistics. Purchasing cost savings realized by a better co-ordination between purchasing and other departments resulted in a optimized incoming materials flow and lower transaction and logistics cost.

6. Value analysis, substitution and standardization. Purchasing cost savings realized through value analysis, substitution and standardization, initiated by purchasing. Cost savings as a result of changing specifications, lower cost substitutes and standard specifications. Purchasing cost savings obtained by detailed supplier and supply chain cost analysis.

7. Make-or-buy. Purchase cost savings realized by outsourcing activities that were originally internally executed.

Theoretical cost savings are '*ex ante*'; actual cost savings are '*ex post*'. The difference between the two concepts is referred to as 'contract leakage'. This is an important indicator for measuring contract compliance and 'maverick buying'. Fourth, for reasons of credibility purchasing cost savings cannot be reported by purchasing managers. Rather, they should be part of general management reporting and be reported by business controlling.

Why are these specific guidelines on how to define and report purchasing savings needed? Why do companies have so many definitions on purchasing cost savings? One of the reasons is that corporate purchasing agreements are not always followed in organizations. One of the problems that need to be overcome is the phenomenon of 'maverick buying'. Maverick buying implies that managers in the organization do not automatically follow corporate agreements with contracted suppliers but for some reason stick to their traditional suppliers. If this happens, the expected savings that have been indicated and reported by the purchasing manager, will not materialize, simply because the contracted volumes will not be made in the relationship with the contract suppliers. As a result the company misses out on purchasing cost savings and end-of-year bonuses.

This is not a theoretical problem. During the beginning of this decade Ahold, the international supermarket chain with headquarters in The Netherlands, had to report disappointing financial figures to the financial world. One of Ahold's divisions in the USA, i.e. US Foodservices, had negotiated corporate agreements with key suppliers for most of its food products and beverages. Part of the deal were large bonuses to be paid at the end of the year when the contracted volumes would be made with the suppliers involved. At the end of 2002 most of these volumes appeared not to have been made. In many cases, local managers decided to stick to their incumbent suppliers for a number of reasons. As a consequence the contract suppliers did not pay the promised bonuses to Ahold, resulting in a much lower profit for the company amounting to hundreds of millions of dollars. As a result of this failure and some other irregularities, Ahold's chairman and chief financial officer had to leave the company. Other companies suffer from similar problems.

This is why many purchasing managers today keep a sharp eye on purchasing cost savings and especially their compliance rate. This is the percentage of the volume that has been ordered from contracted suppliers versus the total contract spend. A low contract compliance means a lack of discipline within the company to live up to the agreements made with suppliers. It also, in general, means having missed out on a huge potential for cost savings!

Ratios and key performance indicators

Performance ratios can be classified in different ways. Carter and Mosconi (2005) differentiate between ratios related to price/cost, revenue, inventory, availability, technology/innovation/new product introduction, workforce, supplier performance, operations and customer satisfaction. For practical reasons we limit our discussion to measures related to quality and purchasing logistics.

When measuring the quality of incoming goods and services, in principle the following key performance measures are available:

- percentage rejected deliveries related to the number of total deliveries made
- percentage rejected, but repaired goods
- cost related to repair of incoming goods and services
- line reject rate, due to inferior quality of components
- cost related to quality inspection and auditing of incoming goods
- number of credit notes to suppliers and the cost related to non-quality deliveries
- number of quality claims to suppliers and amounts involved.

MEMO 14.2   SUPPLIER QUALITY INDEX: EXAMPLE

This index is based on the frequency and the gravity of the defects related to a specific supplier's deliveries. More serious defects will result in a higher score.

Examples of criteria and weight factors:

Decision with regard to delivery	Weight factor	Action
Return	15	Return to supplier, credit note to supplier
Rejected, but process to avoid production problems	15	Credit note to supplier for repair work
Acceptable, but slight quality defects	8	Charge inspection cost to supplier
Functionally acceptable, not exactly in line with specification	5	Inform supplier
In line with our specifications	0	No action required

Suppose a supplier makes 20 shipments in a certain time period. In this time period three shipments are returned, five shipments are found to be acceptable and the rest of the shipments are in line with specifications. Hence, the supplier quality index can be calculated as follows:

$$\text{Supplier quality index} = 100 - [(15 \times 3) + (8 \times 5)]/20 = 95.75$$

Using this index allows the purchasing manager to compare the quality performance of suppliers. However, she should be careful since not all products have the same technical complexity. For more complex, technical products 100% quality may be very difficult to realize. For standardized commodities a 100% quality level may be very easy to realize. Quality indexes therefore should not be used to compare suppliers of different components and products. Rather, they should be used to monitor the quality performance of a specific supplier over time. It is fairly easy to computerize this type of information.

Sometimes supplier quality performance is expressed by means of an index (see Memo 14.2).

Apart from indexes and the ratios, surveys and special reports can be used with regard to assessing purchasing quality. Surveys can be internally as well as externally oriented. Internally they are aimed at assessing internal customer satisfaction with regard to how the purchasing department performs in its relationship with its internal customers. Externally, surveys can be used to assess how suppliers think about doing business with the company. How attractive is the company to its suppliers and how does the company relate to a specific supplier compared with other customers? The information obtained through these surveys can be used by the purchasing manager to improve the organization.

With regard to assessing purchasing logistics performance the following critical performance measures are available:

Ordering

- purchasing administrative lead time
- purchasing order backlog per month
- number of requisitions processed per month
- number of supplier quotations obtained per month
- number of orders issued per month
- number of rush orders per month.

On-time delivery

- number of on-time deliveries
- number of late deliveries
- number of deliveries made too early
- number of incomplete deliveries
- premium transportation cost due to rush orders.

Payment

- average payment term versus standard payment term
- number of invoices processed
- number of non-matching invoices
- average invoice value
- number of invoices per supplier.

Supply chain efficiency

- percentage non-moving inventory
- material shortages per month
- number of partial deliveries
- number of all rush orders
- inventory turnover ratio per month
- inventory value per month
- number of outstanding orders (quantity and volume) per month.

When using this type of ratio and performance indicators, the purchasing manager should be aware that only part of the logistics problems can be attributed to the supplier. In many cases they result from insufficient materials planning and requisitioning by their own company. Purchase orders can be changed repeatedly which makes timely and flawless delivery for the supplier a nightmare. Purchase requisitions, issued by internal departments, can be made not respecting the suppliers lead time, leading to a high number rush orders and unnecessary distribution cost. For this reason we recommend purchasing managers differentiate between internal and external performance indicators. Every company gets the supplier that it deserves!

In most cases it is not realistic to keep track of the performance of all suppliers. Therefore, one needs to decide for what products and suppliers such monitoring is required. Here, a distinction can be made between products that are obtained from problematic suppliers, and those that are crucial for the continuity of the company's business processes. Products can be crucial because they cannot be kept in stock. Products can also be crucial because they are on the critical path of project planning.

Another distinction is that between critical and non-critical deliveries. Critical deliveries are those that are beyond their delivery date as a result of which the continuity of the company's business processes is in immediate danger. Non-critical deliveries are orders that are past their delivery date without immediate damage to the company.

Figure 14.4 provides an example of how a supplier reliability index can be calculated. The example shows that a sound, computerized purchasing information system is a must. The input necessary for calculating these kinds of indicators cannot be created economically without such an information system. Actual vendor rating scores can be translated into vendor ranking scores (A, B or C-suppliers). Such a classification allows the buyer to focus its efforts on those suppliers that need most attention.

Earlier we argued that one of the problems related to purchasing performance measurement is the lack of a direct input–output relationship between the resources that are used

FIGURE 14.4 How to calculate a supplier delivery index (example)

Supplier	Too early in weeks			On time		Too late in weeks			Too many/few		
	>8	8 to 5	4 to 3	2	1	1	2	3	>4		
Weight factor	0	0	1	1	1	1.0	0.9	0.6	0.2	0.0	0.5
PO number											
123456											
234561											
345612											
etc.											

The following example may serve as an illustration

	Supplier X				Delivery time		Quantity	
PO number	Delivery in week	Received in week	Ordered quantity	Quantity received	Weight factor	Score	Weight factor	Score
123456	35	38	120	120	0.2 × 100	20		0
234561	35	32	120	120	0.6 × 100	60		0
345612	35	35	120	120	1 × 100	100		0
456123	35	35	120	130	1 × 100	100	0.5 × (130 − 120)	−5
561234	35	35	120	110	1 × 100	100	0.5 × (120 − 110)	−5
Total						380		−10
Supplier delivery index	(actual score/maximum score) × 100% = 370/500 × 100% = 74%							

in purchasing and the results that are obtained from these. As a consequence purchasing as a business function is less measurable than for example production activities where a direct relationship between input and output is much more present. This again implies that purchasing managers should need both purchasing effectiveness and efficiency and should use measures covering each of the four dimensions of purchasing performance. The relationship between these concepts can be assessed using a periodic purchasing audit. The subject is discussed in one of the next paragraphs.

The ratios and performance measures that have been described in this paragraph are sufficient to create a picture of the operational purchasing performance. Purchasing's strategic contribution ratios and measures are much harder to obtain. Here a lot of development work is still necessary. CAPS Research publishes regularly about purchasing performance in different types of industry. Their benchmark reports per industry are very insightful and useful for purchasing managers to get an idea of how they perform relative to their colleagues in the same industry. See Memo 14.3 for an illustration.

MEMO 14.3   CAPS RESEARCH BENCHMARK REPORT

The Center for Advanced Purchasing Studies (CAPS) in the USA (www.capsresearch.org) reports periodically on specific purchasing performance measures in different types of industry. Data are collected using quantitative surveys that are filled in by a score of companies. Data only relate to companies in the USA.

FIGURE 14.5 CAPS Research Benchmark report 2008

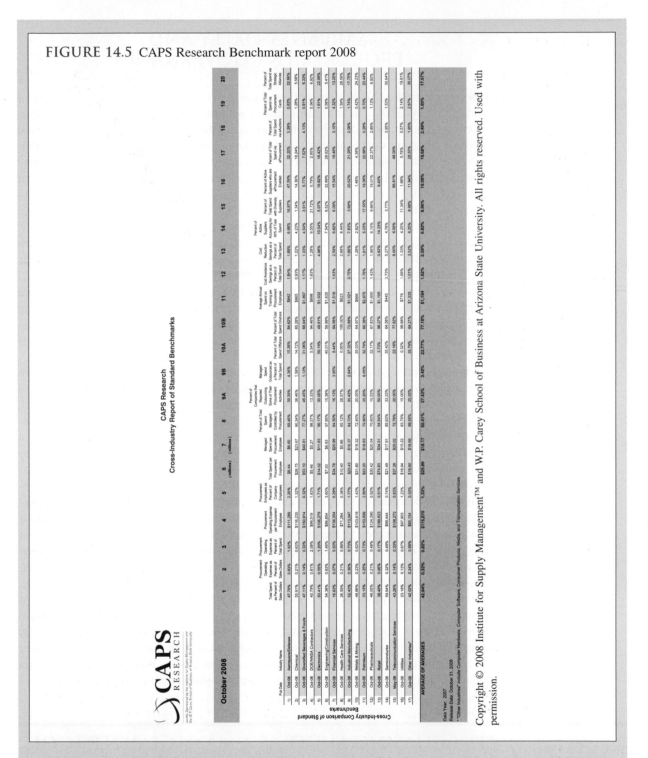

This type of report can be helpful in identifying whether a purchasing department in a specific company is developing in the right direction. Inter-company comparison on just one criterion seems less useful. However, analysing the position of the purchasing department on the basis of all performance measures will provide a picture of the company's position relative to its competitors.

Source: www.capsresearch.org

SARBANES–OXLEY AND PROCUREMENT GOVERNANCE

Corporate governance has become a prime concern to large companies, due to the financial scandals of early 2000. The discussion started with the fraud at Enron, where the leadership engaged in a number of malversations to secure their end-of-year bonuses. As a result of this the company went bankrupt. It also meant the bankruptcy of its accountant, Arthur Andersen. Another examples was WorldCom, a company that also went bankrupt because of mismanagement. In all cases the supervision and control that was conducted was found to be negligent. Of course, political action in the USA followed, led by the senators Sarbanes and Oxley. These senators proposed strict rules and guidelines for the control and financial reporting of large international companies, quoted at the stock exchange. Today, companies and chartered accountants are required to demonstrate that all company financial and administrative processes, including procurement processes, are in control. The same is requested for all information systems that are used within the company.

Also in Europe similar cases were reported. In The Netherlands Ahold was prosecuted for fraud. In Italy Parmalat went down due to company fraud and in Germany the top management of Siemens AG had to appear before court to explain massive bribes to customers. As a consequence, European legislation on corporate governance has been significantly strengthened.

Within corporate governance, the discussion on how to secure control of procurement processes has received increasing interest. Procurement governance includes 'the coherent set of rules and guidelines within a company that arrange for the ownership, management, accountability, reporting, penalties and incentives of all activities related to external providers who conduct activities for the company on the basis of a commercial contract'. Not surprisingly, purchasing processes appear to be extremely sensitive to fraud. This is why many companies today have reinforced the control on these processes. One popular measure has been to nominate a chief procurement officer (CPO), who is put in charge of orchestrating and organizing all purchasing processes, procedures and systems throughout the company. However, business unit managers and line managers are kept responsible for implementing and deploying these processes, procedures and systems in their domain of responsibility. Together, these managers are responsible for executing procurement governance. An element of procurement governance is that no invoices are paid by the company without reference to a purchase order number. Another element is that ordering, inspection of delivery and payment cannot be done by one and the same person. Part of procurement governance is also that business is awarded to suppliers using competitive bidding among at least three to five suppliers and that corporate agreements are actually going to be used by business unit managers. Such a set of rules and guidelines is necessary to achieve full control of the company's purchasing processes. Whoever keeps an eye on the daily financial press, is aware that a lot of improvement can still be made!

PURCHASING AUDIT AS A MANAGEMENT TOOL

Through a purchasing audit, management may assess the extent to which goals and objectives of the purchasing department are balanced with its resources. The latter relate to the elements of the organizational dimension. The purchasing audit is a form of action research, the effectiveness of which depends on the expertise with which it is conducted. More important, however, are the actions which are derived from it at a later stage. The audit must therefore be conducted in such a way that people do not feel threatened, and in a way which builds trust and generates professionalism.

Audits can be preventive or corrective in nature. Preventive audits are to be compared with periodical check-ups – with the aid of a limited number of standard check lists, the department is checked to see whether it meets the expectations of its most important stakeholders. Another objective is to see where the purchasing processes are conducted in line with the company's overall financial procedures and guidelines. Corrective audits focus on acute problems apparent in the functioning of the department – the situation can be sufficiently grave that immediate treatment is imperative. Based on a quick scan, the (internal) auditor identifies the problems and proposes some alternative solutions, which are then to be carried out with priority. This is known in management consulting as turn around management. After such an operation, the purchasing organization often will go through a substantial metamorphosis. Purchasing management and personnel are changed, new managers are recruited, the product assortment and supply base are reorganized and so on. Audits for turn around situations should be conducted by experts.

Figure 14.6 shows the points of reference which must be included in a purchasing audit. This figure shows that final purchasing performance is affected by several factors:

- **The requirements that the corporate system lays down for the purchasing function.** Purchasing policy must be in line with overall company policy; changes in the business system will affect purchasing objectives or the required performance of the department.

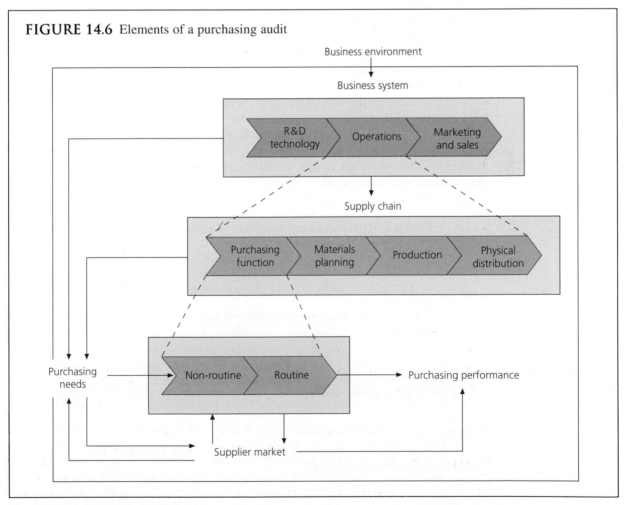

FIGURE 14.6 Elements of a purchasing audit

Source: redrawn from van Weele (1991), p.131

- Changes in the company's supply chain. The purchasing function must respond optimally to the requirements of its internal customers. Changes in the supply chain manifest themselves in changing materials requirements. The purchasing department will have to react to these changes or anticipate them flexibly.

- The opportunities provided by the supplier market to fulfil the materials requirements, as defined. Changes in the supplier's technology or in the supplier market can strongly affect materials availability and prices. As we have seen earlier, suppliers determine, to a large extent, internal customer satisfaction and company performance.

The purchasing audit will map the major requirements that the stakeholders lay down to the purchasing department, as well as the changes which occur to these requirements. This implies that the audit must pay attention to the quality of the interfaces between purchasing and other departments. Regarding the internal performance of the purchasing department, a distinction can be made between the tactical, non-routine purchasing activities (defining specifications, supply market research, supplier selection, etc.) and the operational, routine purchasing activities (e.g. order processing, expediting, invoice handling, supplier rating, etc.).

The starting point is the intake interview, in which the auditor clarifies the goals and structure of the audit. This is done in a meeting with the purchasing manager and their superior. The auditor explains what can be expected of the audit as well as the methods to be used. Ideally this is followed by an introduction to the purchasing department, during which the purchasing manager explains the functioning of the department. The rest of the organization is informed about the audit and the auditors will set to work. First of all, they will gather factual information concerning the purchasing department, with the aid of a structured checklist; Figure 14.6 shows several subjects on which data could be gathered. A selection is then made of the key personnel to be interviewed; confidentiality towards the respondents must be guaranteed, a factor that frequently constitutes a reason for using external consultants in this kind of research. Figure 14.7 shows some questions which may serve as terms of reference for the investigation.

Based on the information gathered the auditor will prepare a report, the initial findings of which are first checked with the purchasing manager. This provides the opportunity to find out to what extent the results are recognized. Also at this stage some ideas about improvement measures can be exchanged. A meeting with top management will then

---

FIGURE 14.7 Examples of key data relating to the purchasing function

- *Commercial data:* sales turnover, cost of materials, ratio of materials cost to sales turnover
- *Personnel and organization:* total number of employees, number of purchasing employees (classified according to educational level, functioning level, years of experience), ratio of purchasing employees to total employees
- *Purchasing's place in the organization* (organizational diagram)
- *Reporting relationships:* top management, materials management, etc.
- *Job description:* primary tasks, authority and responsibilities of the purchasing department
- *Purchasing data:* number of articles (production related, non-production related), number of suppliers, number of purchasing requisitions, number of requests for quotations, number of orders, number of purchasing invoices, Pareto analyses of purchasing turnover according to article, order quantities, supplier, country of origin, etc. Purchasing department budget, divided according to nature of costs
- *Relationships with other departments*
- *Action plans:* in the areas of cost reduction, quality improvement, automation, etc.
- *Purchasing procedures and systems.*

FIGURE 14.8 Aspects to be considered in a purchasing audit

Goals and objectives

Goal orientation

- What are the purchasing department's goals?
- What are the purchasing department's responsibilities?
- To what extent are the purchasing department's tasks stated in objective and verifiable terms?

Client orientation

- Does the purchasing department communicate efficiently with its internal customers?
- Is there adequate reaction to the requirements and wants of the internal customers?
- Is the purchasing department sufficiently aware of new internal developments and changes in the supplier market?

Risk

- What are the major risks with regard to price behavior of high-value items and availability of critical materials?
- Is purchasing sufficiently aware of these risks and what measures have been taken in order to cope with them?
- In general, is continuity of supply and purchasing operations sufficiently guaranteed?

Resources

Results and resources

- To what extent does purchasing meet its tasks and objectives?
- Is the purchasing department adequately equipped in terms of people and systems to be able to meet expectations?
- What measures are taken in order to improve on results on the one hand and systems and human resources on the other?

Flexibility

- Does purchasing adequately react to changing materials requirements and internal customer needs?
- Is purchasing sufficiently interested in pursuing new technology?
- What important changes have taken place in the service and organization of the purchasing department?

Management

- Is teamwork within the purchasing department sufficiently developed?
- Is the purchasing department a well-respected partner for discussion of internal customer problems?
- What measures have been taken in order to keep the quality of human resources up to date?

---

follow, after which a final report is drawn up containing recommendations in the form of a policy plan or action programme. An important part of the final report is taken up by the documentation of performance indicators, which will serve in the future as a means to monitor progress.

SUMMARY

Performance measurement in purchasing cannot be considered in isolation. Rather, it is a crucial part of the purchasing management process. Planning and control go hand in hand. If the purchasing function lacks a clear vision, when purchasing strategies and action plans are ill developed and management reporting is absent, systematic performance measurement and evaluation will be difficult if not impossible. Without it, a procurement organization and purchasing cannot be in control.

This chapter has shown that the degree of sophistication in measuring purchasing performance differs among companies. A major factor influencing the parameters used to assess purchasing is the view which management holds towards purchasing. When purchasing is considered primarily as an administrative function, this will be reflected in administrative parameters that are used. If purchasing is considered as a strategic business function, which is deeply rooted in the overall business strategy and processes, this will result in an extensive management reporting.

Purchasing performance measurement is important since it will lead to a greater visibility and recognition by all other business functions. When applied effectively, it may lead to better communication with other disciplines, better decision-making, a higher motivation of staff involved and a greater transparency of the company's dealings with suppliers.

Objective performance measurement is, however, in many cases a difficult matter since, in practice, it is hampered by poor definitions and poor reporting. Moreover, information systems may not sufficiently support the data gathering and reporting structures required.

When measuring purchasing performance, it is suggested to focus both on purchasing effectiveness and efficiency. Purchasing effectiveness relates to the extent to which previously agreed goals and objectives have been met by the purchasing department, and is covered by three key areas, i.e. purchasing prices/costs, purchasing quality and purchasing logistics. Purchasing efficiency is related to the resources which are needed to realize predetermined targets and plans. It relates to the actual costs incurred against the budgeted costs for managing the purchasing function. Therefore, it encompasses the costs related to purchasing organization, i.e. purchasing staff, management, procedures and guidelines and information systems. For each of these key areas a number of tools, monitoring reports, ratios and performance indicators can be selected, which enable a holistic view on how purchasing actually has performed. During the past years, external data have become available that can be used to assess purchasing performance. For example, the industry benchmark reports that are published by CAPS Research in the USA allow purchasing managers to get insight into their relative position compared with their major competitors.

The purchasing audit can be used to thoroughly analyse the purchasing organization. Conducting such an audit in general meets with resistance from the organization, which is why it needs to be carefully prepared and introduced to the organization.

Performance measurement is part of procurement governance. Procurement governance relates to the set of rules and guidelines within a company that arrange for the ownership, management, accountability, reporting, penalties and incentives of all activities related to external providers who conduct activities for the company on the basis of a commercial contract. Without effective procurement governance it will be impossible to get control of purchasing processes.

ASSIGNMENTS

14.1 How would you define purchasing performance for an industrial company? What performance measures would you suggest to use for a purchasing department of a company producing medical equipment?

14.2 How would you define purchasing savings for direct and indirect purchasing spend?

14.3 As a purchasing manager you want to measure purchasing cost savings in terms of total cost of ownership rather than purchasing price. How would you proceed?

14.4 What five indicators would you use to compare your company's purchasing performance with that of your main competitors? When answering this question, make use of the industry benchmark reports published by CAPS Research (www.capsresearch.org)

14.5 What are the main differences between supplier evaluation and supplier rating?

14.6 How would your balance scorecard look for a purchasing depart and a manufacturer of automobiles?

REFERENCE

Carter, P. and Mosconi, T. (2005) *Strategic Performance Measurement for Purchasing and Supply*, Phoenix, AZ: CAPS Research.

INTEGRATIVE CASE 14.1

INTERNATIONAL
LAUSANNE – SWITZERLAND

THOMAS MEDICAL SYSTEMS' OUTSOURCING POLICY

It was mid-summer 1997. Sylvia Rittmeyer, development manager in the cardiovascular division of Thomas Medical Systems (TMS), and Hans Schmitz, the purchasing manager, were talking about the company's latest entry into the cardiac imaging market: the Apollo B® (the development of which the company called the 'Tannhauser Project'). The Apollo B® had come in on time and within target, and was well received by the marketplace. In spite of these positive outcomes, however, the members of the project team were not happy with their performance on the Tannhauser project. Both Schmitz and Rittmeyer were concerned about some of the problems that had arisen during Tannhauser. Rittmeyer remarked:

> We were fortunate that things turned out as well as they did! A lot of our time and resources were wasted, causing the final costs to be higher than we had hoped to achieve. In hindsight, we were developing in parallel both a new product and a new way of working, creating many additional problems.

Schmitz agreed with her and added:

> When we started the Tannhauser project, we knew we wanted to move towards purchasing more assemblies, as opposed to individual parts for assembly in-house. The problem was that we had developed no clear policy to guide us. We need to take the time now to document the experience while it is fresh in our minds, so that we can learn from it and use that new knowledge on future projects.

▶

Background on Thomas Medical Systems

Thomas Medical Systems (TMS) is a leading supplier of diagnostic imaging systems that use X-ray, magnetic resonance and ultrasound technologies. Among the top companies producing these types of systems for the healthcare sector, TMS is part of Thomas Electronics, with headquarters in Berlin, Germany.

The product: the Apollo B® Series for cardiology

The Apollo B® Series is the newest addition to the cardiology family and includes many innovative features pioneered by TMS (Exhibit 1). The Apollo B® is a digital cardiac imaging system that produces high-quality digital images using X-rays combined with exclusive sensor technology. The exclusive sensor technology allows the stand to move quickly and precisely while minimizing the safety concerns associated with conventional high-speed motorized stands. This new Apollo series also incorporates Thomas' comprehensive approach to X-ray dose management, which provides the tools necessary for cardiologists to optimize the image quality while minimizing the dose applied to the patient.

The Apollo B® also provides several possible configurations that adapt to the localized needs of the user. Depending on both the space constraints

EXHIBIT 1 The Apollo B®

Source: Thomas Medical Systems

and other systems the hospital wants to use in parallel, two configurations are available (Figure 1):

- Floor mounted, for dedicated cardio work. This system utilizes a base assembly for supporting the C-Arc.

- Ceiling mounted, adding full body coverage. This version utilizes an L-Arm longitudinal carriage assembly to support the C-Arc.

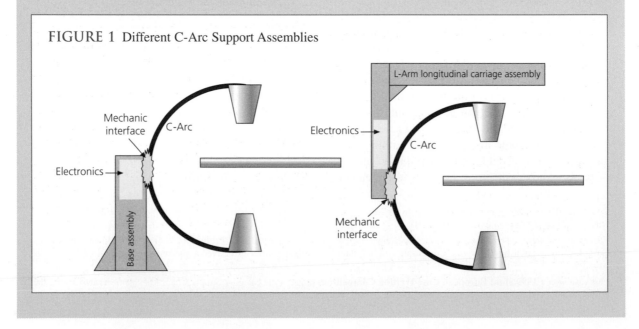

FIGURE 1 Different C-Arc Support Assemblies

All the systems are based on TMS' new compact, open-stand design, which minimizes the space requirements and maximizes the doctor's access to the patient.

The drive for greater cost effectiveness in healthcare is redefining the industry; the traditional approach for managing hospitals is being replaced by a more businesslike approach. For mature products such as those sold by TMS, there is price erosion as well as pressures to enhance the value/cost ratio delivered in the overall bundle of goods and services they provide. One major 'enhancement' comes from the need for the healthcare providers to upgrade their approaches to information management. Hospitals hold large volumes of information in their databases, information that needs to be shared by different providers to improve the quality of healthcare. With over one thousand different standards currently in use by hospitals, the Apollo B® feature of interoperability in multi-vendor information environments and networks has made it a cost-effective approach to the management of digital images and information in the hospital.

The Tannhauser project

Traditionally, TMS developed all the detailed components and assembled this kind of unit in-house. But in the Tannhauser project, the company expected to do some detailing and engineering in consultation with the suppliers.

At the beginning of 1995, TMS decided to move away from the purchase of individual or 'monoparts', which it would assemble, towards what the company called 'higher level purchasing'. Higher level purchasing embodied management's goal of purchasing assemblies in order to reduce the quantity of parts to be purchased. Sub-contracted assembly was expected to be cheaper than assembling the parts in-house at TMS. The fundamental objective was to change fixed cost into variable cost. At the time of this decision, the criterion for choosing between suppliers was simple: TMS reviewed the different sub-assemblies, and the supplier with the highest-value parts was considered the best choice for assembly (TMS assumed this supplier would have the internal competency to maximize the added value to its parts). Overall, the Tannhauser project had five main suppliers, one of which was Wolfsberg Machine Werks. The first two assemblies to be outsourced

were the base assembly and the L-Arm longitudinal carriage assembly. The base assembly is used in the floor-mounted configuration, and the L-Arm longitudinal carriage is used in the ceiling-mounted configuration. The electronics and the interfaces between the units and the C-Arc were identical (Figure 1).

The same supplier – Wolfsberg Machine Werks – was used to produce both assemblies. Work on the project started at the supplier's plant in April 1995. Of the five main suppliers, Wolfsberg was responsible for the largest outsourced subassemblies of the overall product.

Initially, TMS asked Wolfsberg to produce on the basis of 'duplication' – TMS defined all assembly and part specifications, which are called technical product documentation (TPD). The supplier was expected to make the parts and assemble them according to these specifications. At the end of 1995, the decision was made to hand over the ownership of the TPD (and therefore the responsibility for maintaining it) to the supplier after the prototype phase. By giving Wolfsberg the TPD of the base assembly as well as providing detailed knowledge of the other modules that would interface with the base assembly, Thomas expected that Wolfsberg would be able to identify potential design improvements. Although the decision was made at the end of 1995, Wolfsberg did not receive the TPDs until July 1996. At that time, participation by the supplier went a step further, with TMS asking Wolfsberg to participate more directly in the detailed product design of the L-Arm. Shortly thereafter, TMS provided Wolfsberg with the basic specifications for both the packaging and hoisting units (devices for shipping and installing the units at the user sites), which Wolfsberg was allowed to modify within certain parameters. Since Wolfsberg Machine Werks now had the responsibility for the TPDs for the base and L-Arm assemblies, it also now had the task of preparing these documents in such a way that they could be passed back to TMS for official release of the products. Wolfsberg handed over the completed TPD for the base assembly to TMS in April 1997; the TPD for the L-Arm longitudinal carriage assembly followed in September 1997.

Technical issues

The decision to transfer final development of the TPDs to Wolfsberg Machine Werks proved to be an extremely time-consuming exercise because of the incompatibility between the respective computer systems. Not only were the CAD/CAM systems used by TMS and Wolfsberg Machine Werks incompatible, but there were also incompatibilities between divisions of Wolfsberg Machine Werks. The result was that, from the beginning of July 1996 until the end of the year, Ulrich Neubauer, a mechanical engineer from TMS, spent 50% of their time working on-site at Wolfsberg to co-ordinate work on the L-Arm assembly. Neubauer spent about half this time at Wolfsberg Machine Werks reworking the TPDs to produce a complete drawing at the supplier's site. The necessity of passing the TPDs back to TMS for official release at the end of the development phase, made their work doubly difficult. TMS paid additional development costs to Wolfsberg Machine Werks to cover the expenses incurred with the TPD transfer. Additionally, TMS and Wolfsberg Machine Werks agreed (on a fifty-fifty basis) to develop special software to perform the transfer of TPDs between Autocad and Microstation files. Another problem involved the level of detail on the drawings. Wolfsberg Machine Werks was not in the habit of maintaining or producing the very detailed TPDs that TMS required. This difference became apparent during the summer of 1996, after TMS transferred some of the detailed design work to Wolfsberg.

These difficulties in working with suppliers to jointly develop the detailed specifications took much more time than the team from TMS had anticipated. In the end, one of the team members summed up the experience like this:

Our easiest supplier to work with on the Tannhauser project was the one that refused to accept the TPD!

Underwriters Laboratories (UL) certification[1]

At the beginning of July 1996, TMS asked Wolfsberg Machine Werks if they had UL certification. Wolfsberg was not UL certified. Numerous questions and difficulties arose related to meeting the requirements for UL certification. TMS assigned one of their staff to review Wolfsberg's systems and to come up with a list of points that Wolfsberg would

need to address to meet TMS' internal purchasing specifications. The difficulties were compounded by the debate between the two companies over who should be responsible for certifying of large outsourced assemblies. The final decision was to have the entire system UL certified at TMS. Preparing and applying for the certification took roughly 1 year.

Purchasing Issues As stated previously, early in the development stage the TMS management decided to implement higher level purchasing (HLP) with the goal of reducing the quantities of part-numbers purchased. Cost reduction was the desired end result. (An overview of TMS' development process is presented in Exhibit 2.) Traditionally, TMS selected suppliers at the transition point at the end of phase 3, when detailed technical specifications have been defined down to the component level. In the new way of working, TMS wished to involve the suppliers early in phase 3, and eventually in phase 2. Purchasing implemented HLP, outsourcing certain sub-assemblies to several main suppliers. When it began negotiating with the suppliers, purchasing did not have target costs for the various outsourced sub-assemblies. Its approach to setting a target price was called material and direct labour costs (MLC) plus 10%. Additionally, it took 6 months for TMS to decide exactly what it wanted Wolfsberg Machine Werks to deliver. Wolfsberg found it difficult to provide a meaningful price estimate because of the very abstract nature of the work TMS expected it to perform. TMS provided all the suppliers, including the five main ones, with identical contracts. Based on a verbal agreement from TMS, Wolfsberg Machine Werks actually began work on five prototypes in January 1996. TMS assigned two buyers to Wolfsberg, one for the base assembly, the second for the L-Arm assembly. The two buyers used different cost systems in their negotiations with Wolfsberg. There were also instances where the supplier of a mono-part delivered the same part to both TMS and Wolfsberg, with separate invoices, based on orders originating from both. At first, this seemed like unnecessary duplication, but in reality the purchasing systems at TMS did not allow for delivery to be specified in two places. Moreover,

[1] UL is the leading third-party certification organization in the USA and the largest in North America. As a not-for-profit product safety testing and certification organization, UL has been evaluating products in the interest of public safety since 1894. Source UL homepage: http://www.ul.com/about/index.html.

EXHIBIT 2 The Phases in the TMS Product Development Process with Outputs

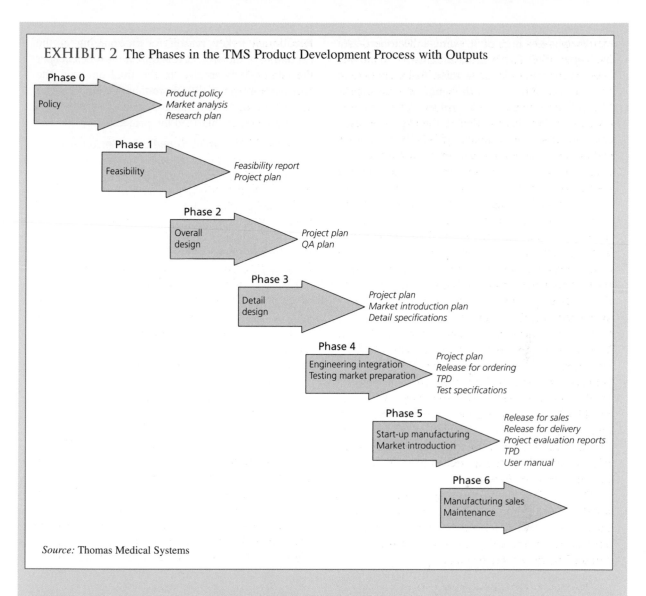

Phase 0
Policy

Product policy
Market analysis
Research plan

Phase 1
Feasibility

Feasibility report
Project plan

Phase 2
Overall
design

Project plan
QA plan

Phase 3
Detail
design

Project plan
Market introduction plan
Detail specifications

Phase 4
Engineering integration
Testing market preparation

Project plan
Release for ordering
TPD
Test specifications

Phase 5
Start-up manufacturing
Market introduction

Release for sales
Release for delivery
Project evaluation reports
TPD
User manual

Phase 6
Manufacturing sales
Maintenance

Source: Thomas Medical Systems

TMS did not wish to do the detailed ordering and coordination for the parts needed by its suppliers.

Supplier issues From the beginning of the project, the suppliers were very keen to develop a closer alliance with TMS. Unfortunately, both TMS and the suppliers severely underestimated the amount of work that goes into developing a successful partnership. Adding to the complexity was the fact that, throughout the duration of the project, TMS kept redefining its expectations. In the space of 2 years, for example, Wolfsberg Machine Werks moved from being a supplier of a mono-part, to doing some assembly in-house, to designing some modules in the final sub-assembly. To support this transition,

Wolfsberg expanded its engineering department by adding a chief design engineer, an electronic designer and a research assistant.

Both TMS and the suppliers took a long time to formalize a project plan. This resulted in a lack of clear focus for the project. The suppliers were forced to deal with high levels of uncertainty related to TMS' technical and capacity expectations. The expected annual demand in 1998 for the base assembly and the L-Arm varied continuously. In February 1996 the expected demand for the base assemblies stood at 250 units, by June of the same year that number had dropped to 120 units, and by November 1996 the number had risen to 420 units. The expected demand for the L-Arm also fluctuated, from a low of 140 units to a high of 300 units in October 1996. In January 1997 TMS started an initiative to provide better market knowledge to their main suppliers in order to help them deal with volume fluctuations.

Another communication problem between TMS and its suppliers had to do with the implicit knowledge housed in the heads of the TMS employees. TMS had traditionally done the assembly, and did not recognize that the supplier companies did not have the assembly skills. Interestingly, it was not until a problem arose that it became apparent that the suppliers worked to different standards or norms. When a problem did come up, the first question was, what implicit knowledge do we have? The second was, what do we need to communicate to the suppliers to prevent these types of problems?

Results to date

The Apollo B® went on the market in September 1997 meeting all regulatory requirements. As of May 1998 some 500 systems had been sold. Of this number, 300 have the L-Arm configuration; the remaining 200 systems have the base-mounted configuration.

While the overall system came in on target, the two sub-assemblies – the base assembly and the L-Arm assembly – came in above their target costs.

Recall that a key reason for outsourcing at the beginning of the project was this: it must be cheaper than doing it internally. In the final analysis, the base assembly cost 13% more than it would have to assemble it internally; the L-Arm cost 15% more.

Rittmeyer summarized the project:

In spite of the problems and delays encountered, we are satisfied with the end result (the Apollo B®) and the learning effect. This is, however, accompanied by a feeling of insecurity in terms of where we are heading in the future and what the effect of this will be on development activities.

Schmitz agreed, and added:

We need to crystallize the learning we have achieved on the Tannhauser project, and formulate a new policy for purchasing in this context. We also need to make this policy clear throughout the organization. There is a wide spread belief that the only reason for outsourcing is to replace Thomas work hours with ones done by cheaper sub-contractors. The use of MLC to evaluate the project only reinforces this opinion.

What has been the Thomas Medical Systems experience in outsourcing? In what ways has it been successful? Not successful?

TELCO: DEVELOPING A SOURCING STRATEGY FOR MARKETING AND CALL CENTRE SERVICES

BY ARJAN VAN WEELE

Memorandum

To	: Sean Lim, Category Manager Marketing and Call Centre Services
From	: Janet da Silva, Corporate Procurement Officer
c.c.	: Peter Brewster, Business Controller
Concerns	: Outcome Audit Trail Marketing and Call Centre Services
Date	: Singapore, June 2nd, 2009

Dear Sean,

Let me first of all express my congratulations to you for having accepted this challenging job as TELCO's Category Manager Marketing and Call Centre Services. Obviously, we have selected you as a seasoned TELCO professional to professionalize our purchasing strategies for this important spend category. We are full of confidence that you will be able to tackle this important business area.

As promised last week I hereby share our preliminary findings on this category. Coincidentally, these were gathered recently by one of our young trainees from Business Controlling, Peter Ho, to whom you are referred to for further information.

Peter Brewster and I have read these findings with obvious concerns. We feel TELCO could and should benefit significantly from a more professional purchasing approach. Given the serious concerns we would like to give priority to an action plan. Therefore we invite you to present your Business Case in our management meeting next week. Based upon your own findings we would like you to report on the most important problems that need to be tackled. Moreover, we like to have your advice on what should be done to solve the problems that you have identified.

We realize that our briefing may be rather concise; in case important information is missing we would like you to report on this and we invite you to present how you think to gather this missing information.

There is no need to write a detailed project plan. Please, for the sake of brevity, present your business case in the form of a PowerPoint Presentation. Time available to you is half an hour.

We look forward to a challenging proposal. Good luck!

Janet da Silva, Corporate Procurement Manager

Attachment: 1

This case describes the problems of a European Telecom Company related to developing a sourcing strategy for marketing and call centre services. The case has been based on practical experiences by the author related to sourcing for indirect services. Any similarities to an actual situation will be purely coincidental.

Attachment

Memorandum

To	: Janet da Silva, Corporate Procurement Officer
	Peter Brewster, Business Controller
From	: Peter Ho, Trainee Business Controlling
Concerns	: Audit Trail Marketing and Call Centre Services
Date	: Singapore, May 25th, 2009

Dear Ms. da Silva, Mr Brewster,

As part of my management traineeship at TELCO as assistant controller I have conducted, at your request, an operational audit with regard to the purchasing processes related to Marketing and Call Centre Services expenses. Your request was to identify the total purchasing spend, analyse the current supply base and the level of control with regards to the purchasing to pay cycle.

Hereby I submit my major observations and findings. This report consists of the following sections:

- General findings with regard to TELCO-supplier relationships.
- Contract information and contractual relationships.
- Specific findings with regard to order to pay cycle.

Basic purchasing facts are provided in Exhibit 1.

EXHIBIT 1: General overview of TELCO purchasing spend marketing and call centre services (2008; number in millions Singapore Dollars)

Products and Services	Spend	Number of suppliers
Advertising above the line[1]	$40	45
Advertising below the line	$60	213
Events and promotions	$12	238
Market Research	$11	42
Media	$96	76
Print	$19	198
Trade fairs and shop furniture	$5	53
Sponsoring	$3	56
Total TELCO spend	$246	921

- 10% of the suppliers is responsible for 80% of the total spend
- Spend covered in framework agreements (FWAs) is 90%.

---

[1]In business, 'below the line' is an advertising technique. It uses less conventional methods than the usual specific channels of advertising to promote products, services, etc., 'above the line' advertising strategy; these may include activities such as direct mail, public relations and sales promotion for which a fee is agreed upon and charged up front. Below the line advertising typically focuses on direct means of communication, most commonly direct mail and e-mail, often using highly targeted lists of names to maximize response rates.

My conclusion is that there is an apparent lack of control with regard to this type of purchases. Vice versa there are many opportunities for improvement. However, the way in which the process of improvement should be designed is beyond my level of knowledge and experience. Therefore, I suggest that these findings are forwarded to the purchasing professionals within TELCO in order to get a better control of this important type of expenditure.

All in all this exercise has been very interesting and rewarding to me since it gave me the opportunity to relate to many persons in the organization. I want to thank you for having provided this challenging assignment to me and look forward to new challenges.

General findings with regard to TELCO–supplier relationships:

- Briefings for Advertising Agencies are often revised, in one occasion even 17 times.
- It is not unusual for suppliers to send their proposals by email. Internal customers often directly reply on these emails for approval.
- Every month new suppliers are introduced. The total number of suppliers amounts to 921 (2008)
- We could not find evidence that suppliers are selected according to a structured approach (i.e. no RFQ, no supplier selection criteria, no market research, etc.). Further research indicates that internal customers prefer to do business with the suppliers they know best.

Contract information and contractual relationships:

- A confrontation between invoices and contracts (the contracts we could find . . .), indicates that a large number of invoices are not in line with the contract (e.g. higher fees than agreed upon, additional costs for travel and administration, . . .).
- Supplier performance is evaluated through quarterly *Quality Perception Surveys* among internal customers. However, this standard procedures is followed only for a small part of the category.
- KPIs and bonus/malus agreements are negotiated with the large agencies. KPIs are measured by using *Supplier Scorecards* (Monthly). These scorecards are often subject of disputes with the suppliers (e.g. when their bonus is lower than expected).
- In one case, there was a budget for supplier bonuses of $600 000 which was only used for $100 000 at the end of the year because of poor supplier performance.

Specific findings with regard to order to pay cycle:

- Purchase order numbers are not always available on incoming invoices ('guestimate': 30%).
- Purchase order confirmations by suppliers are often lacking ('guestimate': 50%).
- Analysis of *Accounts Payable* shows a large number of invoices. Also, the average amount on these invoices is relatively low (16 989 invoices below $5000 in 2008).
- The *Cognos Procurement information System* indicates an increase in the number of invoices from 15. 826 (2006) to 25 084 (2008).
- In-depth analysis shows a large number of invoices that do not belong in this category.
- Several suppliers send interest invoices to TELCO, with the argument that TELCO does not pay on time.
- *Miracle* (Procurement system of TELCO Mobile) showed a lack of formal service delivery acceptance, consequently invoices are not paid and suppliers send interest invoices to TELCO.
- TELCO's strict authorization rules result in large delays. In one occasion it took 4 months before the Commercial Director signed the request. The strict procurement authorization rules explain why in most cases suppliers are paid late, resulting in extra interest notes.

ABC BANK: SOURCING FOR TEMPORARY LABOUR

BY ARJAN VAN WEELE

Part One

Introduction

Hans De Wit, vice president strategic sourcing and Geert Zandstra, vice president HRM, both working for ABC Bank, peered somberly over the outskirts of a rainy Amsterdam from the eighth floor of the bank's headquarters. Both men were aware of the tremendous changes the bank was going through in these years and the pressure that it posed upon managers and employees. Under the energetic leadership of the current CEO, Mr Derk Vandervoort, offspring of a successful banking family and a relentless driver of innovation, the bank had changed in a couple of years from a traditional, product-oriented financial services provider into an innovative and entrepreneurial company, which had endorsed modern marketing and promotion concepts. This change was apparent in the many branch offices of the bank where traditional offices have made room for smaller 'bank-shops' that provide only necessary services to customers, linked to the leading edge, web-based financial systems of the bank providing easy access to all services and products and enabling much more flexibility and speed.

Although the focus of the top management for obvious reasons had been on the bank's prime business and customer contacts, over the past years their attention has shifted to the bank's back office activities. The general view was that staff had grown too fast, indirect labour productivity was too low, and the bank's massive purchasing expenditure was spent ineffectively and inefficiently. Last week, Mr Vandervoort had met with Hans De Wit and Gerard Zandstra to discuss what could be done to reduce the spend on all personnel related services.

He had provided his opinion on this subject friendly but firmly. 'Gentlemen,' he said:

Times are changing. It is now time to address the productivity of our back offices and our massive purchasing spend in a number of areas. Mr. Frank de Graaff, our CFO, informed me yesterday about the tremendous amount of suppliers we are dealing with. The purchasing spend that is involved just with buying personnel services is spiralling out of control. Our workers council has asked questions about why we have put so much pressure on our own people, whilst leaving our many temps untouched. Personally, I feel sympathy for their point of view. My request to you is to submit your plans on how to deal with personnel services providers in the future. I am particularly interested in temporary labour, where I have observed that in many cases there are differences in income between our own employees and the temps that we hire. Obviously, gentlemen, given the new EC compliance rules on labour, we cannot accept this situation anymore. Moreover, I think we can get better value for money here. I would like you to dive into this subject as well. I would appreciate if we could discuss your plans, say, within two weeks.

Having exchanged some niceties, the meeting was closed and both men went to the Board's Executive Secretary to set an appointment a fortnight away. That was yesterday; now both men pondered on how they would satisfy Mr Vandervoort's interests. 'Geert, this is going to require quite some time from us for the coming days, I am afraid,' Hans said. 'I'd better cancel my participation in the Heineken golf tournament tomorrow.' 'Yes,' Geert replied, 'And probably you can cancel your private appointments for the weekend too. It will be a hell of a challenge, knowing our internal culture and the deep-rooted relationships of some suppliers with our organization, to squeeze out some real money in this area. If it was a simple task, we would not have had this

This case describes the challenges related to the complex sourcing process of services. Its content was based on a real life situation. The case study has been written for educational purposes. For reasons of confidentiality, the authentic figures and numbers have been replaced with artificial, yet realistic figures and numbers. ABC Bank is a leading European banking conglomerate with its headquarters in The Netherlands.

discussion.' 'We'd better get started,' Hans replied, 'Let's first make a list of the information we need, where we can get it, and who we would need to involve in this initiative. We certainly need to get some extra help over here. Setting up a sourcing strategy for this category will be far from simple.'

Both men sipped their coffees and started to plan their activities. There was little time to lose.

Part Two

ABC Bank: Background and mission ABC Bank is the leading bank in The Netherlands. It was founded in the early 1990s when two major Dutch banks merged into the present company. Although the culture of both organizations was quite different, over the years the company developed into an integrated structure with a strong brand image. Thanks to the entrepreneurial drive of the Executive Board, which was presided by Mr Vandervoort, the bank was able to catch up with competition quickly. Today, thanks to the major investments that were made in information technology, the bank is a leading edge provider of differentiated financial services both to consumers and business customers.

The group strategy consists, according to the Bank's brochure, of five key areas:

- Creating value for the bank's clients by offering high quality financial solutions which best meet their current needs and long-term goals.

- Focus on:
  - ○ Consumer and commercial clients in home markets (The Netherlands, US Midwest and Brazil) and selected growth markets around the world
  - ○ Selected wholesale clients with an emphasis on Europe and financial institutions
  - ○ Private clients.

- Leveraging our advantages in products and people to benefit all of our clients.

- Sharing expertise and operational excellence across the Group.

- Creating 'fuel for growth' by allocating capital and talent according to the principle of managing for value, our value-based model.

Early 2005 ABC Bank Group adopted one global tag line, i.e. 'Customer Always Come First' for all their major subsidiaries sharing the red and blue shield logo since the Group's rebranding project in 2003. The idea to have one global tagline was in line with this rebranding.The tagline communicated the ABC Bank Group's focus on sustainability, creating synergies among its business units and its business principles. In this way the bank wanted to build and reinforce its shared values and corporate identity. 'Making the impossible possible,' therefore, plays a role beyond advertising. It supports the corporate strategy, concisely summing up all of what the brand stands for in a way that's understood by all stakeholders.

Exhibit 1 provides a picture of ABC Bank's major customer segments.

From its base in The Netherlands, the company has expanded significantly in other countries. Thanks to an aggressive takeover policy, the company today enjoys strong market positions in the UK, USA and Brazil. In the latter country it took the third position in terms of privately owned banks. Plans to strengthen the bank's position in major European markets lie ahead. In 2005 its plans to take over a major bank in Italy roused great rumours in that country where banking until that time was limited to Italian banks only. Apart from Italy, the

EXHIBIT 1 ABC Bank's major customer segments

Customer segments	Consumer	Commercial
• Top end clients	• Top private clients	• Multinational companies
• Mid market clients	• Private clients/ mass affluent clients	• Mid market/ financial institutions
• Mass market clients	• Mass retail	• Small businesses

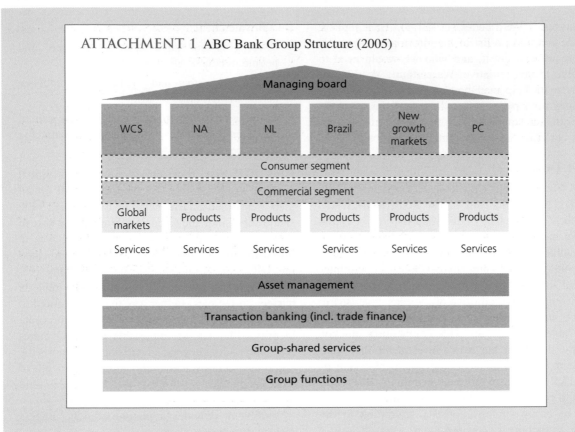

ATTACHMENT 1 ABC Bank Group Structure (2005)

company plans to expand its activities in rapid growth areas such as India and China.

Attachment 1 provides a picture of how ABC Bank's activities are structured. Currently activities are structured around three major customers segments including: (1) wholesale clients (WSC) which include business accounts, (2) consumer clients (CC) that are included in mass retail and (3) private clients (PC) that are served through investment banking. These segments can be found in every local country structure, where products and services, tailored to each of these segments, are provided. All core activities are supported by four major back-office activities, that are grouped into: (1) asset management, (2) transaction banking, (3) group shared services and (4) group staff functions.

All activities are grouped regionally into four major business units (BUs) including: The Netherlands, UK, USA and rest of world (ROW).

Management reporting and financial accounts are conducted individually to each of these four BUs.

Global Procurement within ABC Bank Global procurement activities reside within ABC Bank's newly formed group shared services entity (GSS). Here all activities can be found related to: information technology (IT)[1], HR services, operations (including worldwide payment services and money and credit card transport), finance and facilities. Concentrating these activities into one global service centre allowed ABC Bank to benefit from economies of scale, leverage and focus.

Although managed from a corporate centre, global procurement activities physically reside within the BUs. Therefore purchasing organizations can be found in The Netherlands, UK, USA and Brazil. Organizationally, the purchasing organizations of Amsterdam and London report to one senior purchasing executive. The matrix organization is

[1]In 2005 ABC Bank decided to outsource a major part of the IT activities to a consortium consisting of IBM and a number of IT-providers in India.

organized around two axes: (1) a regional axis, where purchasing activities within a region i.e. BUs report to one regional head and (2) a category axis, where for each major spend category, all purchasing activities are managed by one dedicated global category manager. Through this structure, ABC Bank could benefit from both corporate leverage and local purchasing expertise.

In this way, ABC Bank tried to get control of its impressive purchasing spend, which in 2004 amounted to approximately €5 billion. The purchasing spend within the BU The Netherlands (BU NL) was €889 million. As can be seen from Exhibit 2 the most important spend categories included facilities management, HR services and information technology.

Exhibit 3 provides a breakdown of the purchasing spend of HR Services of the BU NL. As can be

concluded from this picture, temporary labour and training and education represent about two-thirds of this spend category.

Temporary labour: demand, legal environment and market characteristics Having done his initial homework, Hans De Wit thought about assembling his team for this project. He recruited two assistant HR-managers from different divisions. Next, he put a labour law specialist at his side. The team was completed with one of the promising young graduates of the procurement organization. As the team convened for the first time, it was decided to gather all data necessary before embarking on the preparation of a sound sourcing strategy. First, all spend data were analysed. In all BUs temporary labour appeared to

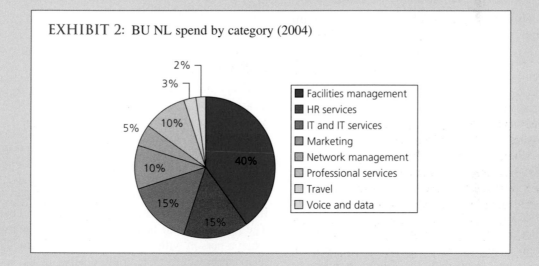

EXHIBIT 2: BU NL spend by category (2004)

- Facilities management
- HR services
- IT and IT services
- Marketing
- Network management
- Professional services
- Travel
- Voice and data

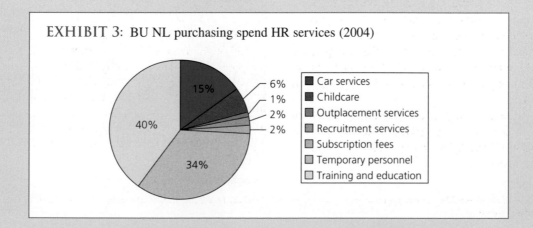

EXHIBIT 3: BU NL purchasing spend HR services (2004)

- Car services
- Childcare
- Outplacement services
- Recruitment services
- Subscription fees
- Temporary personnel
- Training and education

represent a large part of the total spend on HR Services. Next, opportunities were investigated to arrive at a corporate, ABC Bank wide agreement for temps. However, this possibility was discarded quickly for several reasons. First, legal and governmental rules appeared to be different among the countries and regions involved. Second, there were no providers available that could serve ABC Bank's demand on a global scale. Third, the number of stakeholders that need to be consulted was too large in order to be able to handle this efficiently. Hence, it was decided that every BU would go on its own. Given the amount of money involved, Hans De Wit decided to start with BU NL first. He pondered about what type of data he would need for a thorough analysis of this important purchasing category in order to come up with a convincing business case.

Part Three: Preparing the Business Case on Temps

External and internal analysis   Hans De Wit and his team started to work on the business case. Hans thought it useful to differentiate his team's activities. Two team members spent their time on conducting the external analysis. The other two members were given the task to conduct the internal analysis.

External analysis
Internal demand. One of the first things that was done was to identify ABC Bank's demand. More specifically a clear view needed to be established the roles and functions that were hired by the bank. The demand analysis showed that 80% of the spend on temps was related to the following functions (or 'roles'):

- administrative clerk
- call centre agent
- data entry operator
- mailroom clerk
- secretary
- executive secretary
- support officer
- sales manager
- cashier.

Each of these roles was described in terms of tasks to be performed and qualifications that were required. This represented a significant amount of work from the team. Based upon their enquiries, the team found that the demand for temps would decrease in the near future for BU NL. The analysis confirmed that deals were locally negotiated and that the global buying power of ABC Bank was neither used nor could be used in the future. Temps were seen as non-business critical. Business managers expressed a clear wish to have better transparency and comparable compensation; the latter meaning that staff doing a similar job, would receive similar payment, regardless of whether they were paid by ABC Bank or a temp agency.

Pricing structure. In all BUs pricing appeared to be based on the 'cost plus % margin model', that fitted the regional or local market. Pricing was made up of the following elements:

- gross hourly salary of the temp
- associated costs (e.g. social benefits and insurance)
- % margin for the temp's agency
- VAT (19%).

These elements together added up to the 'direct costs' of a temp. It appeared that ABC Bank did not have any influence on the salary that was paid to a temp by the agency. An agency clearly would benefit from sending temps with a higher salary to the bank: the bank would pay for all direct costs. The agency would benefit from a higher margin when a person with a higher salary was sent. The team discovered that, traditionally, deals with temp agencies were based on discussions about the agency margin. Hans and his team clearly saw the backside of this type of deal, but did not have a solution readily available. It appeared that this type of contracting was common in the temp market. Also social insurance and other associated cost were outside the reach of customers that hired temp.

Attachment 2 provides some more details on the various elements of the total cost per employee hour of a temp.

Attachment 2

ATTACHMENT 2 Cost model of temp

	1 Month to end contract		2 Weeks to end contract	
Gross salaray	%	100		100
Compensation waiting days	0.80	100.80	0.80	100.80
Vacation	12.00		12.00	
Bank holidays	2.50		2.50	
Illness (short)	1.00		1.00	
	15.50	116.30	15.50	116.30
Vacation allowance	10.00	126.30	10.00	126.30
Social security allowance	6.50		6.50	
Unemployment allowance	1.00		1.00	
Disablement allowance	9.00		9.00	
Health insurance	8.00		8.00	
Pension allowance	2.10		2.10	
Training allowance	1.00		1.00	
	27.60	153.90	27.60	153.90
Illness (long term)	8.00		8.00	
Other direct costs	8.00		12.00	
	16.00	**169.90**	20.00	**173.90**

Supply market. The temps market is highly competitive due to the large number of suppliers and due to the fact that temps are seen by many HR-managers as a commodity. The supply market is very fragmented: the top six suppliers in The Netherlands only account for 17% of the total market of about €250 billion (see Exhibit 4).

EXHIBIT 4 Top six temps agencies worldwide (2003)

Top 6 temps agencies worldwide (2003, × billion euro)

Position	Company	Country	Sales	Marketshare %
1	Adecco	Swi	13.5	5.5
2	Manpower	US	10.8	4.4
3	Vedior	NL	6.0	2.5
4	Randstad	NL	5.3	2.2
5	Kelly services	US	3.8	1.6
6	Spherion	US	1.8	0.8
	Total		41.2	17.0

In order to get out of the price war that is going on in the temps market, the large providers try to move up in the value chain by providing value-adding services to their customers, such as insourcing labour intensive services of customers (e.g. processing mailrooms), insourcing HR-management roles of the client (including recruitment, payrolling consultancy) and insourcing personnel planning of units that are regularly using flex workers (for example, call centres). Next, some agencies experimented with performance-based contracts. These were used for instance for sales staff. These people were in that case not paid per work hour but on the basis of the number of products sold. Hans De Wit and his staff concluded, however, that these value-added strategies would not be sufficient for most agencies to survive. They expected that a shake-out would occur in this market in the near future. The Dutch market appeared to be highly regulated due to the collective labour agreements for temporary labour that applied to all companies. ABC Bank appeared to be among the top five customers for temporary staff. Currently, the bank worked with two preferred suppliers, Randstad and Vedior, who

▶

both made up 62% of total spend in this category. A quick comparison with other large companies showed that most opted for a two-vendor stategy.

Labour law. In order to be able to run a temporary labour agency, providers need to have a special permit from the government indicating that they have proven to adhere to local rules and labour laws. During the past months the regulations changed on one important point.

Until recently, customers could pay the salaries as indicated by the temps providers during a maximum period of 6 months, even if these salaries deviated from the salaries that customers would pay their own staff. This, however, is no longer possible.

Internal analysis
Apart from the external analysis, Hans De Wit and his team analysed how temps were actually acquired by the bank. The process was time consuming, complicated and consisted in general of the following steps:

- The manager of the department where temporary support was required would contact his local HR manager indicating his requirements.
- The HR manager would contact the manager of the local temp agency.
- The local temp agency would send a number of CVs to the HR manager; CVs would relate to persons who have been thoroughly screened by the agency.
- CVs would be sent to the functional manager concerned.
- The functional manager would discuss the profiles with the HR manager and would select persons for an interview.
- Interviews would be held and thereafter the preferred person would be selected.
- The HR manager would confirm the choice to the agency.
- The agency would call the person involved and contract them.
- The person selected would start their job at the bank. Every day the number of working hours would be registered and signed for approval by the functional manager.
- The weekly hours notes would be handed over to the agency.

- The agency would prepare an invoice on a weekly basis.
- Temps would be paid at the end of the month.
- The invoice would be checked with the functional manager and approved.
- Payment would be made to the agency respecting the agreed payment terms.

Additional issues
Having conducted the external and internal analysis, Hans De Wit and his team sat back and tried to arrive at some important conclusions and learning points. After a thorough brainstorm session they came to the following observations:

- The bank did not have sufficient control of its expenditure on temps, due to the current margin-based arrangement with agencies. The current model stimulated agencies to send expensive temps to ABC Bank. The challenge was to find another contracting model which would stimulate agencies to find more cost effective solutions. This issue needed to be solved.
- Although the bank had a dual vendor strategy for temps (i.e. Randstad and Vedior), records showed that in many cases other vendors were used to hire temps. Interviews showed that this was due to personal preferences of HR managers or local managers, good experiences in the past with some providers, lack of knowledge about the contracts that ABC Bank had with Randstad and Vedior, sheer dissatisfaction with the services of these two providers, etc. These were reasons why in many cases rates superseded those charged by the two prime vendors.
- Administration and payment processes appeared to be extremely complex and time-consuming. Due to all checks and balances that were incorporated in the bank's administrative system, the bank could barely meet its standard payment terms of 60 days net. Shorter payment periods, in order to take advantage of payment discounts, were not possible. Next, the number of invoices received was overwhelming (over 125 000 per annum), requiring eight full-time staff in F&A to manage the administration. Recently, controlling had complained about the massive workload related to this activity. Their analysis showed that costs of handling of an invoice amounted to on average €50!

Hans De Wit and his staff saw great opportunities for P-Card applications in this area in order to reduce transaction costs. Another solution was to outsource this activity in the near future to one of the global IT-providers. However, this solution needed to be worked out in more detail.

- Due to the lack of sophisticated computer systems, agencies were not able to provide the bank with up-to-date information about the number of temps working for ABC Bank, nor the costs involved. There appeared to be a sheer lack of management information on this important spend category, which is why proper control of this spend was not possible. Clearly, the bank needed to come up with its own solution here.

- Intermediaries entering the market. A recently new phenomenon was that specialist consultants were contacting large companies for managing their relationships with temps agencies. Usually, these consultancies were started by former temp agency employees, who saw attractive new business in providing their clients with lots of ideas on how to reduce costs on temps. Some large temps providers also had suggested to act as a one-stop-shopping-centre for their clients by orchestrating all their contacts with other temps agencies.

- Reciprocal relationships were an issue to be considered. All large temps providers were large customers of the bank and the marketing and account executives were extremely sensitive not to put the commercial relationship with these providers in jeopardy. Therefore, they monitored the activities of Hans and his team with great interest, keeping the Executive Board informed about their impressions and opinions. Hans had to find a way to keep both his commercial colleagues on the sales side satisfied, whilst improving the value for money of temps for the bank!

Apart from these observations it was clear that the issue of professionalizing the buying of temps held low priority with most managers. Most of them were busy with other issues; in many cases the requests for information by Hans and his team had raised some eyebrows. Why were they keeping people from their work? There were other important matters and business issues to turn to. Hans and this team pondered on how they would get the business owners and HR managers more on their side. It was impor-tant to get a clear picture on who actually would own the contracts that were to be prepared by his team.

The sourcing challenge on temporary labour

Having made their analyses, the team needed to decide on the sourcing strategy for temps. First, they needed to decide upon what supplier strategy to follow. In designing an appropriate strategy, the team decided to use the purchasing portfolio analysis. Next, they needed to decide upon a single, dual or multiple vendor strategy. Thirdly, they should decide upon the contracting period and the type of contract to pursue in their dealings with the suppliers. This contract should not any longer be based on the traditional margin-percentage model, that had been used. Having developed a broad outline of the sourcing strategy, preparations needed to be made for the next step: developing a detailed request for proposal (RFP) for the vendors to be invited. Here, the question was what elements to include in the RFP in order to make sure that the selected vendors would come up with comparable proposals.

The technicalities were all to be solved, in Hans's opinion. A matter of greater concern to him was how to get the buy-in from the managers within the organization. After giving it a lot of thought, he took up the phone and dialled Geert Zandstra. Perhaps he could help him out. 'Geert, this is Hans calling . . . Remember the project we embarked on? Tomorrow we need to report to Vandervoort as you know. On most topics we have found a way out, however, there is one thing that puzzles me a lot, which is our corporate culture. How are we going to make sure that when we have landed a competitive contract with our vendors, that it actually is going to be used within our organization?' Geert replied: 'Yeah, our culture is a real issue . . . I have thought about it too . . . why don't you come over for a cup of coffee and listen to my ideas?'

Discussion

Q1 What would you consider to be the most important problems within ABC Bank related to contracting for temps in the present situation?

Q2 What are the most important issues that need to be addressed in order to deal more effectively in the future in contracting for temps?

Q3 Suppose that the scope of the project is going to be limited to the Dutch Business Unit: what sourcing strategy would you propose for the contracting of temps within ABC Bank? What elements would you include in the discussion with providers?

Q4 What roadblocks would you foresee in effectively implementing a corporate agreement on temps related to the internal organization of ABC Bank?

INTEGRATIVE CASE 14.4

INTERNATIONAL FOODS INDUSTRIES: HEADING TOWARDS PURCHASING SYNERGY

IFI: Heading towards purchasing synergy

Group structure International Foods Industries (IFI) is an international company that operates in the European foods market. The company has operating companies in The Netherlands (5), Belgium (2) and Germany (1). Its headquarters are located at Arnhem, The Netherlands. The operating companies are responsible for marketing and sales, product development, production and logistics and sales. They all operate in the area of foods: soups and sauces, dried pasta products, soft drinks and fruit juices, sports drinks, snacks and diet products. The sports drinks and diet products are growing especially rapidly. Two companies operate in the business-to-business market and produce premixes and food ingredients for the food industry. These pre mixes and food ingredients are also delivered to other parts of the IFI group. These two manufacturing companies are accommodated within the Industrial Products Division. The other operating companies together form the consumer products division. The operating companies vary considerably in size: from 100 to 750 employees.

With a view to a decentralized management philosophy, the holding is of limited size. The following departments are housed at the head office: human resources, management development, public relations, group finance and controlling and information systems. needless to say, the board of management is based here, too.

See Appendix 1 for an overview of the group structure.

Decentralized entrepreneurship Responsibility for results implies that the operating companies are responsible for their own commercial policy. Market and sales policies are drawn up for each operating company. The personnel policy is also determined locally within the general guidelines set by the head office (regarding the remuneration, function profiles of personnel). As previously mentioned, each operating company has its own production operations. The companies primarily produce a wide range of foods for the consumer market. These are sold via the retail trade (supermarket chains and franchise organisations). A limited proportion of the turnover is obtained from exports (approximately 30%).

Market situation The retail trade has been characterized for many years by heavy competition. As a result of increasing concentration, retailers are in a position to exert tremendous pressure on the producers, which results in decreasing margins and falling returns. Producers therefore constantly have to seek ways of producing more efficiently and in a more client-oriented manner. In other words: the costs per unit of product must constantly be reduced.

Purchasing policy
Purchasing takes place within the operating company itself. At group level there is no co-ordination

This case describes the problems relating to the achievement of purchasing synergy in an internationally operating manufacturing company with various operating companies and sales organisations. Its content was based on various practical situations. International Foods Industries Ltd. is a fictional company that produces and sells dry foodstuffs. Any similarities with existing companies are purely coincidental.

in this area. That is a pity, as many operating companies sometimes do business with the same (large) suppliers, purchasing the same products from them. Examples in the production area include packaging, labels, aroma and flavourings, filling equipment. Examples in the indirect area include computer equipment and software, cleaning services, car leasing, maintenance items. A recent comparative study showed that suppliers often charge different prices for the same products and services.

The group management has placed question marks alongside the current purchasing structure. The generally held view is that there must be much more collaboration between the companies in the purchasing area in order to benefit from, as they put it, the 'potential purchasing synergy within IFI'. This intention is coming up against some resistance among the management boards of the operating companies who feel that this is interference from the head office in internal matters. They feel that purchasing is a matter for the companies themselves. They want to remain closely involved with the purchasing initiatives. They are very much afraid that a decision will be made to set up a group-wide purchasing department, which will lay down the law to the operating companies. Two companies, which were recently taken over by IFI, had poor experiences with this approach in their previous situation. The collaboration between group purchasing staff and the local purchasing departments came up against problems. This resulted in those departments being closed down, but without much discussion. These experiences are still fresh in the memories of the managers involved!

Purchasing co-ordination under the motto: everything decentralized, unless . . .

The executive board recently met with the general managers of the operating companies. The meeting's input was formed by an overview of purchasing expenditure per operating company, ordered by size and article group. Examples were also given of highly varied prices being paid by the relevant operating companies to a single supplier for the same articles. A painful example was the flexible foils, for which – assuming that they are of the same quality – there were price differences of 30% from the same supplier! Some managers raised the

point that some competitors of IFI had better conditions with the same suppliers, despite ordering a lower volume. This drew the comment from one of the directors present that the IFI's buyers evidently were not up to the job. Surely it is extremely important for IFI to get away from the image of being a 'soft touch' in the purchasing area? The idea was put forward of bringing together the purchasing managers of the operating companies involved in the form of a group purchasing committee (GPC). There was a discussion about who would chair such a committee. Ideas varied from the purchasing manager of the biggest operating company to a director from the group staff (the name of the director of group finance was mentioned; he would have the greatest affinity with finance and costs).

Despite the close involvement of all those that were party to the discussion, no decision was made. All of the directors felt that it was worth combining forces in the purchasing area, but were reluctant to relinquish their current autonomy. Most of the directors were themselves actively involved in closing the most important deals with suppliers; they knew the suppliers personally and were very attached to those contacts. If they relinquished their autonomy, they ran the risk of being saddled with a supplier and a product that they did not know. They were also worried about the existence of a central purchasing department at group level which would lay down the law to the operating companies. It was generally acknowledged that the departments of this nature are not very effective. A final comment related to the quality of the purchasing departments and buyers in most of the operating companies. Generally speaking, purchasing departments had little status and authority within the companies. When it came to reducing the number of product variants and suppliers, this would undoubtedly come up against strong resistance from product developers and production departments.

The dilemma that those involved felt they were faced with was the question of how they could benefit from the potential buying power of IFI without that being achieved at the expense of the operational effectiveness and decisiveness within the operating companies.

The management meeting did not arrive at a decision. Those present were advised to go away and think again. The pros and cons of central versus decentralized purchasing would have to be compared at the next meeting. An indication of which article groups lent themselves best to a more co-ordinated approach would also have to be given. Clarity will also have to be provided regarding the question of whether the synergy initiatives should be limited to production goods rather than also taken action in the area of non-production goods. Finally, it could be worth holding a brainstorming session on the possible alternatives that could be aimed for in order to achieve more synergy in the purchasing area. The idea of creating a GPC will have to be discussed in more detail.

IFI Case – Appendix 1 Organigram

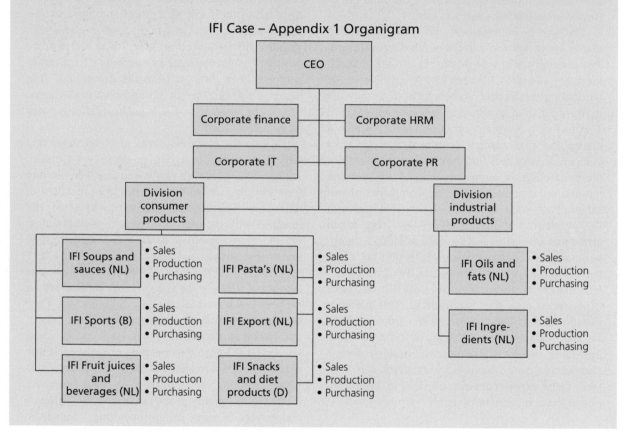

IMPLEMENTATION

PREPARING FOR PARTNERSHIP WITH SUPPLIERS: COST APPROACHES AND TECHNIQUES

LEARNING OBJECTIVES

After studying this chapter you should understand the following:

- How prices are set by suppliers.
- How to use the learning curve technique as a basis for price negotiations.
- Supplier evaluation and vendor rating techniques.
- How to evaluate the financial position of suppliers.
- What it takes to develop suppliers.

INTRODUCTION

As has been argued earlier, purchased materials and services make up a large part of the cost price of industrial end products, and decisions relating to the purchasing price determine the cost price of the end product to a high degree. The importance of purchasing as a function increases if rises in materials prices cannot be automatically passed on to the customer. Price is therefore one of the most important elements in the purchasing decision.

Industrial salesmen will always attempt to hide their prices and cost structures as much as possible. It is in their interest that the pricing method remains obscure to the buyer. However, it is the buyer's task to unveil its suppliers' pricing methods and cost structures and, if this cannot be done directly, it should try more indirect methods. The buyer must constantly and systematically gather information that will yield some insight into the seller's pricing methods and cost structures.

Cost-analysis techniques provide tools to check whether price increases announced by the supplier are justified. Insight into the cost price, and comparison of this cost price with those of the supplier's competitors may help the buyer decide whether or not to agree to the suppliers' request to accept a price increase. The buyer often works with several suppliers, so it can compare the most effective manufacturing techniques, track down inefficiencies in the production process of a specific supplier, provide the latter with suggestions for

CASE STUDY BUILDING A NEW HEADQUARTERS

The management of an international company is considering building a new headquarters. As this is a major project, management approaches several architects and, based on the submitted provisional designs, a choice is made. Only then does the real work start, beginning with the basic specifications. The structural design is prepared meticulously: the foundation of the building is specified in detail, the strength of the structure is calculated based on the various types of materials that are going to be used. Once the basic design is complete, quotations are solicited from a few selected contractors.

Naturally, management will have indicated the available budget at an early stage. Based on empirical data and price information, the design department prepares a cost estimate of the project. At this stage, without detailed specifications being available, the estimate is only approximate. As the design is elaborated, it becomes possible to estimate the costs at a more detailed level. However, the final price will depend to a large extent on the buoyancy of the construction industry. If there is a need for work, the sum contracted for will be related directly to the estimated costs. If the contractors' order books are filled, however, the price will be influenced considerably by the supply and demand situation. An intimate knowledge of the local market, an insight into the order positions of individual contractors, and an idea of the expected building costs, are therefore of crucial importance in preparing for the negotiations with the contractor.

improvement, and therefore get better prices. In dealing with suppliers, the following questions should be asked:

- Does a particular supplier belong to the 'best-in-class' companies?
- What is the supplier's ratio of direct to indirect costs?
- What is the supplier's cost breakdown in terms of overheads, energy, labour and materials?
- Does the supplier experience learning curve effects in its production or service operational processes?
- What are the costs of non-quality for this particular supplier?

The answers will indicate whether a particular supplier is among the most advanced and respected companies in a particular industry.

Pricing and cost-price information are of course insufficient to answer all of these questions. It is also essential that the buyer knows how to use financial-economic analysis techniques. From annual reports and additional financial information, a complete picture of the supplier's financial situation can be built up. This chapter will discuss several costing methods and in this context will also address the learning curve, particularly from the buyer's perspective. It will also touch upon a few analytical techniques used in the area of financial auditing.

HOW IS THE PURCHASE PRICE DETERMINED?

Basically, the price ultimately paid for materials and services is the result of environmental factors – both internal and external. Figure 15.1 shows the relationship between these factors.

Internal factors can bring about a change in the materials cost before the finished product is introduced on the market. These factors may be logistical, technical or organizational in character; examples are changes in delivery time, quality, or product specifications.

External factors are those factors that may affect the short-term and long-term availability of a product in a given market and they can be divided into economic, socio-political, and technological developments. Examples are changes in general economic conditions,

FIGURE 15.1 The influence of internal and external factors on purchase price

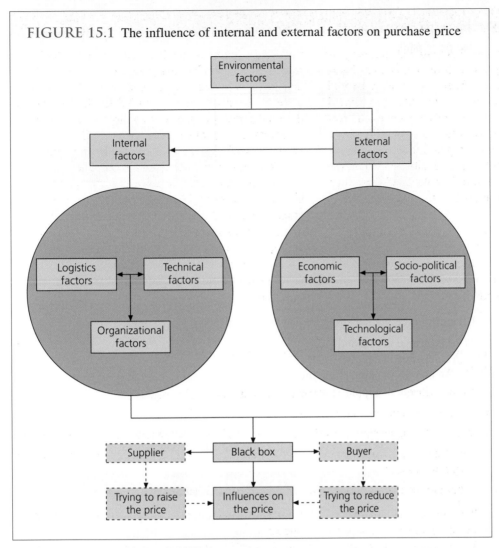

Source: Redrawn from van Eck *et al.* (1982)

changes in the structure of the supply market, legislation, product technology, etc. External factors in general influence internal factors, although the reverse never occurs. The price of a product can be influenced by external factors in two ways (see Figure 15.2), due to direct changes in the cost structure of a particular product or, indirectly, due to changes in market structure and shifts in supply/demand relationships.

If the change in cost factors is identified by the symbol $f(c)$, and the change in market factors by the symbol $f(m)$, with f as a weighting factor, then the formula is

$$\sum[f(c) + f(m)] = 100\% \text{ of the price}$$

According to this formula, a change in the price paid is to be considered as the sum of the changes in the cost factors or changes in the market factors. Changes in cost factors can stem from

$f(c1)$: change in labour costs
$f(c2)$: change in materials costs
$f(c3)$: change in energy costs
$f(c4)$: labour productivity
$f(cn)$: etc.

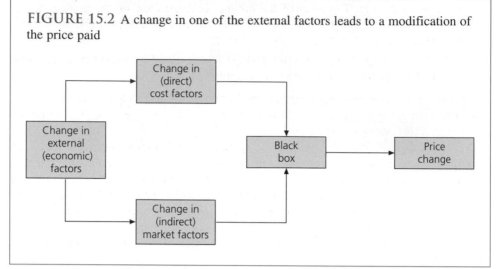

FIGURE 15.2 A change in one of the external factors leads to a modification of the price paid

Source: Redrawn from Van Eck *et al.* (1982)

Pricing, cost-based
The supplier's sales price is derived directly from its cost price; what most systems boil down to is that a particular profit margin is added to all costs, including the costs of sales (mark-up pricing).

Changes in the market structure can stem from

f (m1): change in demand
f (m2): change in supply
f (m3): change in supply side inventory
f (m4): change in supply side capacity utilization
f (mn): etc.

Some products react almost entirely to changes in cost factors, others to changes in market factors. Still others react to changes in both cost and market factors; see Memo 15.1.

MEMO 15.1   VARIATIONS IN DETERMINING PURCHASE PRICE

For plastic components, $\sum f(c)$ is nearly 100. In other words, the price modification can be attributed almost exclusively to a change in the cost factors. For example, an increase in labor costs will cause the price of these components to increase in proportion with the share of labor costs in the product's price.

For copper, $\sum f(m)$ is almost 100, but only in the short term. In other words, the price paid for copper is almost completely determined by the market situation, and cannot be influenced by the individual buyer. For instance, if economic activity declines, market circumstances will change and the price will

fall. Clearly, the purchase price for derivative products is strongly related to the market price for the raw material.

For petrochemical raw materials, the sum of the cost factors is about the same as the sum of the market factors, i.e $\sum f(c) = \sum f(m)$. In other words, the ultimate market price is determined both by cost elements and by general market conditions. Relative to time, the price level will tend to move, both upward and downward, at a given distance from the predictable cost line. In this case, the purchase price is neither determined entirely by the market price nor by the cost price.

Pricing, mark-up
The most common way of setting a price is by adding a fixed percentage mark-up to the cost price (cost-based pricing).

The classification described here agrees to some extent with the concepts discussed by Corey (1978), who considers prices to be based essentially on three different models:

- Cost-based pricing. In this case the supplier's offering price is derived directly from his cost price; what most systems boil down to is that a particular profit margin is added to all costs, including the costs of sales (**mark-up pricing).**

- Market-based pricing. The price of the product is determined on the market, and is generated exclusively by market circumstances such as demand, supply, stock positions, the economic situation and political factors.

- Competitive bidding. The price of the product is influenced by market factors as well as cost factors. This situation is the most common.

Raw materials and semi-manufactured products are traded mainly in a relatively free market in large quantities. The purchase price paid at a given moment strongly depends on market conditions at a given point in time.

As far as technical components are concerned, one must differentiate between components made to the supplier's specification (standard), and those made to the customer's specification (non-standard). In the latter case, the buyer will know precisely the cost of the material to be purchased; in the first case, the buyer can only obtain a rough indication of the product's cost by means of market research. For this reason, prices for non-standard components are typically determined on the basis of competitive bids or negotiation.

What has just been said about non-standard components also applies, for the most part, to finished products.

MRO products comprise such a heterogeneous group of materials that no general statement can be made about the methodology utilized in setting prices. Their prices are determined neither by market circumstances alone, nor on the basis of cost factors only.

The most heterogeneous group, however, is that consisting of the services. The price for services can usually be based on cost, assuming that the activities to be performed have been specified with precision and that the hours and hourly rates have been previously agreed upon. For services such as software design and implementation, however, the price typically is based on market factors. In this case, the cost structure is so difficult to determine and the demand so large, that usually the price quoted by the firm must be paid.

Table 15.1 reflects the relationship between the pricing methods and the various purchasing product groups.

Pricing, market-based
The price of the product is determined on the market, and is generated exclusively by market circumstances such as demand, supply, stock positions, the economic situation and political factors.

TABLE 15.1 Relationship between various purchase product groups and methods of price setting

Purchase product group	Method of 'price setting'				
	Primarily based on cost factors	Based both on market and cost factors			Primarily based on market factors
		With the emphasis on cost factors	50/50	With the emphasis on market factors	
Raw materials				x	x
Semi-manufactured goods			x	x	
Components					
Standard		x	x	x	
Non-standard	x	x	x		
Finished products	x	x	x		
MRO		x	x	x	
Services	x	x	x	x	x

Source: van Eck, de Weerd and van Weele (1982)

PRICING METHODS

Fixing the selling price is no simple matter. The supplier has to take into account many factors, a few of which are listed below:

- The expected demand for its product – if demand is high, the supplier will normally set the price a little higher than when demand is low. In such cases it will not be willing to make price concessions easily.

- The number of competitors in the market – the monopolist's situation is, of course, ideal. Buyers have to go to it for a specific product. It therefore has a high degree of freedom in determining the selling price. This situation is rare in practice. As a rule, suppliers will look to their competitors' prices when setting their own prices.

- The expected development of the cost price per product unit – large-scale production makes low prices possible. If the supplier expects its production volume to increase in the future, it will take this into account. It will anticipate its cost development based on potential learning-curve effects (see next part).

- The customer's order volume – suppliers are often willing to make price concessions in exchange for the promise of 'more business' in the future. This principle is often recognized in pricing methods, usually by awarding extra discounts for larger purchased quantities. Many suppliers employ a sliding scale to indicate which price or discount applies to which quantities.

- The importance of the customer to the supplier – from a commercial point of view the supplier's position may be strengthened by good references. For this reason it will be eager to do business with certain large, well-reputed companies. In order to gain access to this type of customer, suppliers often charge 'special prices'. However, after some time has passed they will try to re-establish the price at 'normal' levels.

- The value of the product to the customer – some products (for example spare parts for manufacturing equipment) have a value to the customer that bears no relationship to their manufacturing cost. In some circumstances supply of spare parts is critical for continuity of production. It is not uncommon for suppliers to charge prices for critical spare parts, which are a multiple of the original cost price.

All of these factors affect the selling or purchasing price. In practice, the following pricing methods can be distinguished (Kotler and Keller, 2006, pp. 444–448):

- Mark-up pricing. The most common way of setting a price is by adding a fixed percentage mark-up to the cost price. If the cost price of a product is €100, and a mark-up of 50% is used, then the selling price will be €150. This method of pricing does not take competitors' prices into account, nor does it acknowledge developments in the demand for the product. Nevertheless, this method is frequently used in practice because of its simplicity. Another important reason is that it is often difficult for the seller to estimate the demand for the product. But it does know the cost price, so why not take this as a starting point for its sales price?

Pricing, target return
In this situation the price is based on the amount of profit that should be realized. Based on the fixed and variable costs and the expected selling price, the required sales volume is calculated.

- Target-return pricing. In this situation the price is determined based on the amount of profit that should be realized. Based on the fixed and variable costs and the expected selling price, the required sales volume is calculated. This is done in two steps. First, the break-even volume is determined through a break-even analysis. Then, based on the profit that is to be made, the required extra volume is determined. Finally, a check is made as to whether this required sales volume can be realized at the estimated price. If this is not the case, then the calculation is repeated based on a lower price. In this situation, it is essential that the buyer finds out the potential total volume of sales of the product involved, as well as the supplier's sales target. If the sales representative has realized his goal, chances are that he will probably honour extra pressure on the price in negotiations. He will be less willing to do so if he hasn't made his profit and sales targets yet.

- Perceived value pricing. A general rule in marketing is that you do not base your selling price on the cost price of the product, but rather on what the market can bear. In this reasoning the price that the buyer is willing to pay is related primarily to the value he attaches to the product. This pricing method is often used for consumer products (well-known branded articles), and also for industrial products. As has been explained earlier, the prices of spare parts for production machinery are often not directly related to the costs of the product. They are usually related to what they are worth to the buyer in particular emergency situations.

- Value pricing. Here, the company tries to win customers by charging them fairly low prices for high-quality offerings. An example is IKEA, a company known for the value for money that it offers to consumers. Value pricing is not a matter of simply setting lower prices. It is a matter of re-engineering the company's operations to become a low-cost producer without sacrificing quality, and lowering prices significantly to attract a large number of value conscious customers. Wal-Mart is another example of a company which attracts large masses of consumers through its every day low pricing (EDLP) strategy. As a consequence, suppliers and food manufacturers are consistently challenged to reduce their operational cost and transfer the benefits to Wal-Mart and its consumers.

- Going rate pricing. In going rate pricing, the firm bases its price largely on competitor prices. The firm might charge the same amount more, or less than major competitors. In such cases companies may follow the market leader in setting their prices. Some oligopolistic markets are characterized by price leadership. Smaller companies follow the market leader's pricing behaviour, often at some distance. Fuel prices in many European countries are examples of this pricing method.

- Auction type pricing. Due to the increasing popularity of the Internet, reverse auctions have become more popular among buyers. Professional buyers today may use a large number of marketplaces, which allow for organizing buying processes through electronic auctions. Suppliers may use auctions to dispose of excess inventories or used goods. Auctions are used when buyers decide to go for a straight tendering process. Such a tender may be selective or public. In the last case, all suppliers that qualify may participate in the tender. Tendering is quite common in public procurement and some industries (such as the petrochemical, construction and defence industries). Based on a request for quotation from the principal, contractors are invited to submit bids for a specific job. These bids are handed over in a sealed envelope to the principal by all bidders simultaneously (sealed bidding). The job is awarded to the contractor who submits the lowest bid. The bidding process, today, may be facilitated by using electronic sourcing technology (see Chapter 2).

One special characteristic of pricing policies for industrial products is the discount policy which is applied. Some authors differentiate between the following discount practices:

- Cash discount. This discount usually depends on the industry (e.g. 2% discount with 10 days payment). The advantages are, among other things, acceleration of payments, advantages from quick payment for buyers and reduction of the amounts of accounts receivable for suppliers.

- Quantity discounts. Small orders often require the same amount of work, in terms of production and administrative and physical processing, as large orders. This means that small orders have a higher cost per product. To stimulate larger quantity orders, many suppliers use quantity discounts in which the advantage for the buyer is that it can

Pricing, perceived value
A general rule in marketing is that you do not base your selling price on the cost price of the product, but rather on what the market can bear. In this reasoning, the price that the buyer is willing to pay is related primarily to the value it attaches to the product. This pricing method is often used for consumer products (well-known branded articles).

Pricing, value
Here, the company tries to win customers by charging them fairly low prices for high-quality offerings. Value pricing is not a matter of simply setting lower prices. It is a matter of re-engineering the company's operations to become a low-cost producer without sacrificing quality, and lowering prices significantly to attract a large number of value-conscious customers.

Pricing, going rate
In going rate pricing, the firm bases its price largely on competitor prices.

Discounts, cash
Is offered by the supplier if the buyers pays within a certain, pre-specified period. This discount usually depends on the industry (e.g. 2% discount with 10 days payment).

realize a lower price per unit. However, this price advantage must be considered against the extra costs resulting from longer storage and the risk of obsolescence.

- Volume bonus. The bonus is linked to the amounts purchased from a specific supplier for a specific period (usually 1 year). The supplier often employs a sliding scale, in which the bonus percentage increases in proportion to the turnover. The advantage of a volume bonus for the supplier is that it reinforces customer loyalty. Bonuses are paid to the buyer at the end of the year based upon the total order volume, that actually has been made.

- Geographical discount. This discount is given to customers who are located close to the supplier's factory or distribution centre, making the transportation costs much lower than average: part of the cost benefit is passed on to the buyer. In this way a local supplier can keep more distant suppliers away.

- Seasonal discount. This discount is applied to improve manufacturing capacity utilization in periods when sales are low. If the buyer orders out of season, it will get a lower price. Special offerings during the winter season among bicycle manufacturers, for example, stimulate dealers to place their orders in the winter (when consumer sales are rather low due to weather conditions), after which delivery takes place in spring. In this way cycle manufacturers are able to spread their production volumes more evenly throughout the year.

- Promotional discount. This discount is provided to temporarily stimulate the sale of a product, or, if it concerns a new product, to lower the entry barrier (special offer discount).

It is not easy for the buyer to track down the pricing method used by the supplier, and the discount policy makes this matter even more difficult. To get a grip on the prices used by the supplier, a distinction should be made – in line with what has been discussed before – between the cost price analysis and the pricing method. When conducting an analysis of the supplier's cost structure buyers should create detailed knowledge about: (1) the supplier's materials costs (to be itemized according to the major components), (2) direct labour costs (information about labour costs can often be obtained by consulting the collective labour agreements for that particular industry), (3) energy consumption and CO_2 emission rights, (4) transportation and distribution costs and (5) indirect costs, to be divided into general management overhead and sales costs.

As a general rule, the higher the share of the fixed costs in the cost price of the end product, the greater the supplier's **price elasticity**. By expanding the order volume to the supplier, the buyer will be able to create a decrease in the fixed costs per unit, and this should result in lower price per unit.

When product prices are mainly determined by variable costs, variances in underlying materials cost will directly affect the sales price, i.e. purchase price. In such a situation, the actual pricing dynamics going on in the supplier's supply markets, must be closely monitored to prevent the supplier communicating unjustified price increases.

THE LEARNING CURVE

The learning curve is an important instrument in the development of purchasing strategies. The learning curve was originally developed in the American aircraft industry. It was discovered that the cost price per aeroplane decreased at a fixed percentage as experience, i.e. the cumulative production volume of a particular type of aircraft, increased. This decrease of costs per unit had nothing to do with effects of scale; the result was to be attributed to the learning effect. The learning effect in general results from the following factors:

- reduced supervision as experience with production of a particular product grows
- increased profits, from improved efficiency through streamlining the production process

- reduced defects and line reject rates during the production process
- (as a rule) increased batch size, which means that less time is spent on resetting machines; the result is reduced production downtime
- (after a while) improved production equipment
- improved process control: reduced loss of time as a result of emergency measures
- reduced engineering changes (initially required to deal with unforeseen manufacturing problems).

The basic principle of the learning curve is that 'each time the cumulative production volume of a particular item doubles, the average time required to produce that item is approximately $x\%$ of the initially required time'. An 80% learning curve means that if the cumulative number of produced goods is doubled, only 80% of the original amount of hours is needed for producing one unit (see Table 15.2).

These data can also be reproduced graphically; regular graph paper yields a curve (see Figure 15.3), while log–log paper produces a straight line (see Figure 15.4).

TABLE 15.2 Learning effect results in cost price reduction (example)

Cumulative amount produced	Required time in hours per unit
1000	20.0
2000	16.0
4000	12.8
8000	10.24
1 6000	8.2

FIGURE 15.3 80% Learning curve on ordinary graph paper

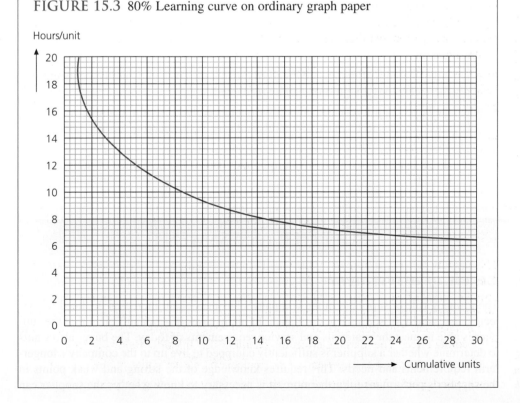

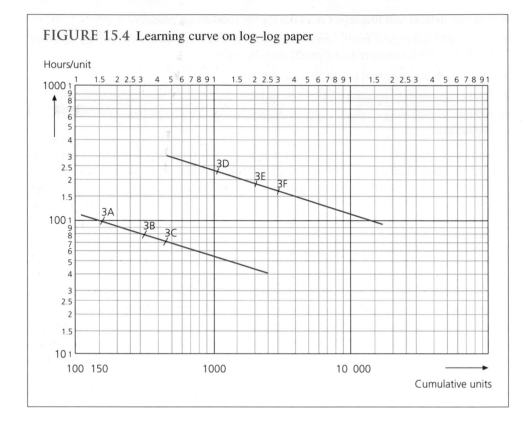

FIGURE 15.4 Learning curve on log–log paper

This knowledge is clearly of vital importance to the buyer. Anticipating the supplier's learning experience, he can negotiate price reductions in the future. The learning curve is preferably used in the following situations:

- when it concerns customized components, manufactured by a supplier to the customer's specification

- when large amounts of money are involved (so that the costs which must be incurred to apply the technology in question can be recovered)

- when the buyer cannot request competitive quotations because, for example, a considerable investment has to be made in moulds and specific production tooling, which leads the buyer to single sourcing

- when direct labour costs make up an important part of the cost price of the product to be produced.

SUPPLIER ASSESSMENT

Supplier assessment, levels

Supplier assessment may take place at four different levels of abstraction, i.e. product level, process level, quality assurance system level and company level.

Levels of assessment

The growing role of suppliers in the company's business chain increases the need for objective assessment of supplier performance. In many cases it is not sufficient that the supplier is able to meet the materials and service requirements of today. The buyer also wants to determine whether a supplier is sufficiently equipped to live up to the company's longer-term requirements and needs. This requires knowledge of the strong and weak points in the supplier's performance. Furthermore, it is necessary to know whether the supplier can

guarantee sustained continuity of supply. The systematic gathering of supplier performance data enables the buyer to negotiate strict agreements about improving reject rates,
reducing total lead time and contributing to cost reduction.

Supplier assessment may take place at four different levels of abstraction:

- Product level. This level focuses on establishing and improving the supplier's product quality; incoming inspections and quality inspections are conducted, which result in establishing the degree of quality conformance of incoming materials.

- Process level. Here it is not the product which is the subject of inspection, it is the supplier's production process that is closely investigated. The underlying idea is that the quality of the product strongly relates to the supplier's manufacturing process. If this process is under control through consistent application of quality procedures, this will result in a product which conforms to the expressed quality standards and specifications. In this approach the state of the supplier's machinery and the quality control system are subjected to in-depth auditing.

- Quality assurance system level. Quality assurance means checking the way in which procedures regarding quality inspection are developed, kept up-to-date/maintained and refined. In other words, not only the procedures and guidelines are investigated, but the entire quality organization is the subject of investigation by the customer.

- Company level. This is the highest level of investigation. In this approach auditors not only focus on quality aspects; they also take financial aspects into consideration. And finally, they want to get an idea of the quality of the management. In this way the customer tries to establish how competitive that particular supplier will be in the near future.

Most supplier evaluation is limited to the first two levels.

Supplier assessment methods

The methods used to assess supplier performance may vary from company to company
(see also Chapter 14); two types may be differentiated. Subjective methods are used when
companies evaluate suppliers through personal judgements, for example by combining
various departments' experiences with the supplier; objective methods attempt to quantify
the supplier's performance. In general the following tools and techniques can be used for
supplier assessment:

Supplier assessment, methods
These include spread-sheets, qualitative assessments, vendor rating, supplier audits and cost modelling.

- Spreadsheets. These are used to systematically compare and assess quotations obtained from the suppliers. The most important criteria for evaluation are listed on one axis, the supplier quotations on the other. This gives a matrix with fields that can be filled in. Applying this very simple, but often extremely illuminating method is made easier when the suppliers have drawn up their quotations in a similar way. For this reason buyers are advised to use well-structured requests for quotations, which provide clear guidelines to suppliers on how to submit their quotations.

- Qualitative assessment. This method is used for those suppliers with whom close business relationships exist. Various specialists, who have experience with this supplier (e.g. quality control, engineering, manufacturing, production planning, purchasing), are asked to 'rate' it according to a previously agreed checklist.

- Vendor rating. This is limited to quantitative data only. It entails measuring the aspects of price, quality and delivery reliability per supplier. The supplier's price history is investigated and compared with the development of its competitors. Quality is measured in terms of the rejection percentage or the number of production line stops as a result of faulty materials. Delivery reliability is measured by means of registration of the number of late (or early) deliveries. This may appear simple, but such systems are very difficult to establish, due to the enormous amounts of administrative data which need to be extracted from internal company records. To do this economically, an integrated computerized materials planning system should be in place.

- Supplier audit. This method entails that the supplier is periodically visited by specialists from the customer. They subject its production process and quality organization to a thorough investigation. Faults and weaknesses are reported and discussed with the supplier. Measures for improvement are negotiated and established. During a subsequent visit it is checked to see to what extent progress against targets has been made.

- Cost modelling. This is a very detailed approach. Specialists at the buying company estimate the supplier's unit cost by means of shadow calculation, based on the production technology, which currently is being used by the supplier. A detailed analysis is made of the supplier's direct and indirect costs: materials consumption, materials prices, storage costs, waste, personnel costs, costs of supervising, overheads, etc. Usually this analysis leads to some interesting insights, which then can be discussed with the supplier. Based upon this information, some professional buyers go one step further and conduct a should-cost analysis. Based upon what they consider to be the most advanced state-of-the-art production technology and structure, what the supplier's cost price of a particular component really should be is calculated. The difference between the two then becomes, of course, the subject of discussion between buyer and supplier. There is an intensive exchange of ideas on how the should-cost position might be achieved. These discussions frequently result in the supplier having to invest in the existing manufacturing equipment. To compensate, the client is often prepared to offer long-term purchasing contracts. The use of cost models and should-cost techniques usually deepens the relationship between both parties. These cannot, however, be implemented overnight since the supplier needs to develop trust in the other party. The supplier should be convinced that the buyer is not after a next round of cutting into its margin but that both parties equally will benefit from the efficiency improvements gained. The issue of developing trust in buyer–seller relationships actually takes a lot of time!

Memo 15.2 illustrates how to proceed when developing a cost model for purchasing.

MEMO 15.2 DEVELOPING COST MODELS FOR PURCHASING

Cost models should provide a clear picture of the total cost of ownership of a purchased component. Since these models require a lot of analysis and many data, these still are not widely used. As experience shows, only some leading-edge companies are applying this technique. However, its popularity will increase steadily for years to come.

In developing cost models a few principles can be used. First it is important to build cost models not only on cost elements (such as labour, materials) but also around the actual cost drivers. Capturing the cost drivers produces a model that answers the question 'what if?' instead of 'what is?' (Laseter, 1998, p. 37). Examples are production lot sizes, set-up times, labour rates.

Cost models should expose at least three elements: materials purchase prices, the actual acquisition costs that the company incurs in buying the

materials, and the cost of use. Taking copying equipment as an example, it is seen that the purchase price of this type of equipment in general only represents a small part of the total usage cost. Building a cost model for copying machines would then require a detailed breakdown of (a) the actual supplier cost price of the equipment, (b) the company's acquisition costs and (c) the cost related to accessories, maintenance and other services, costs and supply of spare parts, etc. Building a cost model for an aluminum die casted product would require a breakdown of the following cost elements: tooling, quality, logistics, purchasing administration, scrap, supplier inventory, supplier overheads, supplier indirect and direct labour, energy consumption and materials costs. In each of these cases these cost elements should be related to the actual cost drivers.

TABLE 15.3 Identifying cost drivers

Category	Description	Examples
Design	Costs attributable to product design trade-offs	Materials specifications Product line complexity
Facility	Costs related to the size of the facility, equipment and process technology employed	Facility scale Degree of vertical integration Use of automation
Geography	Costs associated with the location of the facility relative to the customer	Location related wage rate difference Transportation costs to customer
Operations	Costs that differentiate a well run facility from a poorly run facility	Labour productivity Facility utilization Rejection rates

Source: Laseter (1998), p. 51

Laseter (1998, p. 51) provides an interesting framework that may help buyers identify the most important cost drivers for their commodities (see Table 15.3).

The techniques mentioned above cannot be applied in all circumstances. Naturally, the costs and the benefits must be weighed. The last two methods are extremely labour intensive and will only be used with 'strategic' suppliers and products. Application of all methods requires co-operation between specialists in the areas of engineering, manufacturing, calculation, quality control and purchasing.

The first three methods, being less time consuming, are more broadly applicable. Table 15.4 indicates the major differences between supplier auditing and vendor rating. Vendor rating will be used to judge existing suppliers. It has a more quantitative focus than auditing techniques.

Financial assessment

The financial assessment of suppliers is carried out on the basis of annual financial reports. These can be obtained from the supplier. In most European countries legislation requires companies to file a summary of their financial reports at the local chamber of commerce where the supplier is registered. Dun & Bradstreet, Graydon and other information brokers provide on the WorldWideWeb detailed electronic databases nowadays

TABLE 15.4 Major differences between supplier auditing and vendor rating

Aspect	Supplier auditing	Vendor rating
Orientation	Focus on future	Based on historical data
Application	New and current suppliers	Current suppliers
Nature	Mainly qualitative	Mainly quantitative
Scope	Broad, many aspects	Limited, few aspects
Work	Time-consuming	Standard data
Data processing	Subjective, manually	Factual, computerized
Relation with suppliers	Co-operation required	Based on internal administrative data

FIGURE 15.5 Some financial indicators for assessing a supplier's financial position

Profitability

- earnings before tax and depreciation/net capital employed
- operational profit/net capital employed
- operational profit/production value
- earnings before tax and depreciation/equity.

Equity/debt relationship

- interest coverage rate
- cash flow/investments
- long-term debt/fixed assets
- equity/total assets.

Cash management

- turnover ratio of net capital employed
- average payment terms debtors
- average payment terms creditors
- inventory turnover ratio
- inventory/sales turnover.

from which up-to-date financial and other information can be obtained (see for example www.dnb.com). Based on these financial reports the supplier's financial performance can be evaluated. When conducting this analysis, one should keep in mind that this analysis is based on historical data. However, quite often it is possible, using financial forecasting techniques, to judge the potential future opportunities and threats based on these data. That makes the financial analysis an interesting instrument to the buyer. A financial analysis can only be carried out if one has access to the supplier's annual reports. The results give a first impression of the quality of the supplier's management. Such an analysis enables the buyer to visit the supplier well-prepared, and to ask pointed questions.

A financial analysis provides insight into the development of the quality of the supplier's results. If information is available about other companies (either directly, or indirectly in the shape of the industrial statistics of the Central Statistical Office), comparison with competitors becomes possible. This knowledge can be used in discussions with the supplier to achieve improvements in his organization.

Figure 15.5 provides an overview of the financial indicators that can be used to assess a supplier's financial position.

SUPPLIER DEVELOPMENT

Supplier assessment and developing cost models do not provide a purpose in themselves. They are aimed at improving the performance of suppliers in their relationship with the buying organization. As we have argued before, due to outsourcing companies becoming increasingly dependent on their suppliers, in many cases suppliers do not only determine a company's overall cost position, but also its innovative capabilities and customer service.

For this reason many large companies have developed specific programmes, which are aimed at improving supplier performance in a consistent way. Of course, it is not necessary to develop deep, collaborative relationships with all suppliers, which a company does business with. Sourcing strategies usually are different for different categories.

In order to develop differentiated supplier strategies, companies have segmented their suppliers into distinct **supplier segments**. An example is BASF, a German producer of base and specialty chemicals, who differentiates between (1) strategic partnerships, (2) performance partnerships, (3) preferred suppliers and (4) competitive suppliers. Based on this segmentation, BASF has developed different relationships with different suppliers. Such differentiation, which leads to differences in the way of working with suppliers, is necessary because most suppliers put their best people, technologies, and ideas with their best customers. In general, suppliers have become quite sophisticated in developing tailored marketing and customer strategies, which are built based on specific marketing and customer portfolio techniques. The best customers and customers with the best development potential get most of the attention and most of the supplier's resources. This is why it is necessary for buyers to position their company as a '**customer of choice**' to their supplier markets. The idea here is to promote the company to strategic suppliers as an attractive business partner. In doing so, several actions are required. First, purchasing professionals need to provide their suppliers consistently with honest and clear feedback on their performance. Supplier performance reports need to be communicated and discussed regularly in order to develop the right measures to improve on this. When buyers engage in this type of discussion, it will appear that a lot of improvement measures will relate to their own organization. Second, it will be needed to check how satisfied a supplier is with its relationship with the customer company. This is why a limited number of companies have started to conduct periodic **supplier satisfaction surveys**. This seems logical, since effective business-to-business collaboration requires the best efforts of both the seller and the buyer organization involved. Based upon specific supplier feedback, the company may need to improve its internal operations and new product development processes. Suppliers may represent an important source of information since they probably deal also with the company's competitors and therefore they are able to make a fair comparison between the

Supplier segments
Suppliers may be classified into different segments, depending on the value and risk which they represent to the company. Segments may include: (1) strategic partners, (2) performance partners, (3) preferred suppliers and (4) competitive suppliers.

'Customer of choice'
For such a customer, suppliers are prepared to invest in the relationship resulting in a better product and service, allowing the customer company to make a difference in its end user and customer markets, irrespective of the business cycle.

Supplier satisfaction survey
Periodically, the buyer invites suppliers through a standardized survey to suggest ideas which may improve business relationships.

purchasing practices involved. Today, supplier performance measurement is in some indus-trial and service sectors still not widely spread. Even rarer are the companies that measure supplier satisfaction. Here, the theory is clearly ahead of practice.

The subject of building closer, collaborative and deeper supplier relationships has been discussed by many authors (see, for example, Dyer, 2000 and Liker and Choi 2004). Re-peatedly, some large Japanese manufacturing companies are described as the role models for taking a more collaborative view on supplier relationships. However, one must not be mistaken, since these Japanese companies (including Toyota and Honda) belong to the most demanding companies which a supplier can work for. What makes these companies stand out *vis-à-vis* their Western competitors, is that they take supplier development very seriously. Which is shown by the fact that all of these companies have specific supplier support and supplier engineers departments, who provide technical assistance to a supplier, when needed.

What does a purchasing professional need to do in order to develop this suppliers, i.e. to take supplier performance to a higher level? In general, he or she can initiate three types of actions:

Supplier suggestion programme
Here the buyer actively solicits ideas for improvement from sup-pliers. These ideas may relate to new product design, cur-rent product designs, operational processes, quality assurance, logistics activities, inventory and distribu-tion activities and transactional processes.

- Supplier suggestion programme. Here the buyer actively solicits ideas for improve-ment from suppliers. These ideas may relate to new product design, current product designs, operational processes, quality assurance, logistics activities, inventory and distribution activities, transactional processes. Ideas may be solicited in a formal or informal way.

- Supplier development. One of the Western companies, which generated great results during the 1990s, was Chrysler. Its SCORE program (Supplier COst REduction) resulted in suggestions from suppliers, which delivered hundreds of millions of dollars in cost savings. Characteristic of this programme was that Chrysler shared the benefits gained from all supplier improvement activities with its suppliers, rather than taking it all itself. If suppliers performed better than target, they were allowed to keep the benefits. Ideas for improvement in the relationship were gathered by asking questions like:
  o What is going right in our relationship?
  o What needs or should be improved?
  o What will be needed to make these improvements?
  o How do we measure progress and follow-up?

- Supplier satisfaction survey. Developing a close, collaborative relationship between business partners requires that expectations between all stakeholders involved are made explicit. Next, the actual experiences from both partners in doing business together need to be assessed. Part of this can be done by setting up advanced supplier perfor-mance reports. The other part needs to come from suppliers, who should be invited to express their concerns and ideas as well. Ideas for improving future collaboration could be exchanged by asking the following questions:
  o why are both parties in business together?
  o how do they value the relationship during the past years?
  o how do they value the current relationship?
  o what would they expect from their future business relationship?

Answering these questions requires a multilevel communication structure, ranging from top management meetings up to more operational meetings among the staff operating on the shop floor.

Dyer (2000) and Liker and Choi (2004) argue that building up collaborative relation-ships takes many years and a lot of effort. Starting from the beginning, business partners

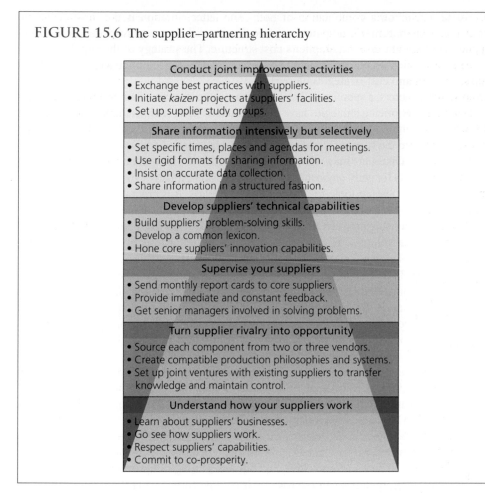

FIGURE 15.6 The supplier–partnering hierarchy

Conduct joint improvement activities
• Exchange best practices with suppliers.
• Initiate *kaizen* projects at suppliers' facilities.
• Set up supplier study groups.

Share information intensively but selectively
• Set specific times, places and agendas for meetings.
• Use rigid formats for sharing information.
• Insist on accurate data collection.
• Share information in a structured fashion.

Develop suppliers' technical capabilities
• Build suppliers' problem-solving skills.
• Develop a common lexicon.
• Hone core suppliers' innovation capabilities.

Supervise your suppliers
• Send monthly report cards to core suppliers.
• Provide immediate and constant feedback.
• Get senior managers involved in solving problems.

Turn supplier rivalry into opportunity
• Source each component from two or three vendors.
• Create compatible production philosophies and systems.
• Set up joint ventures with existing suppliers to transfer knowledge and maintain control.

Understand how your suppliers work
• Learn about suppliers' businesses.
• Go see how suppliers work.
• Respect suppliers' capabilities.
• Commit to co-prosperity.

Source: Liker *et al.*, 2004, p. 4

will go through several consecutive stages to develop from a traditional, arm's length relationship to a more collaborative relationship. Figure 15.6 illustrates what it takes from both partners to go down this route.

These initiatives should enable the buying company to acquire a position of 'customer of choice'. For such a customer, suppliers prepared to invest in the relationship resulting in a better product and service, allowing the customer company to make a difference in its end user and customer markets, irrespective of the business cycle. Acquiring such a status requires purchasing professionals to look at their own company and activities through their suppliers' eyes. An exercise, which generally is not a line with the nature and character of the buying job and for which in many cases insufficient time is made available.

SUMMARY

This chapter has dealt with supplier pricing and cost structures. Pricing and cost structures are always interrelated, but the effect they have on one another is not always clear. Pricing policies of industrial products and services are subjected to both external market factors and internal cost factors. The prices of goods and services can be based on market factors, on cost factors or on a combination of both. The latter situation is the most common. Effective cost management and purchasing requires that a buyer or purchasing professional has a detailed insight into the supplier's cost structure. The strategy of the supplier is usually to prevent such a detailed insight. This explains why the supplier will always try to keep its pricing and cost strategies blurred.

Besides cost factors, a supplier will consider many other factors when deciding on its pricing policy. Several pricing strategies have been presented here, such as market pricing, target return pricing, perceived value pricing, value pricing, going rate pricing, and auction type pricing. Apart from the supplier's pricing strategy, the buyer should be aware of the supplier's discount strategy. Discounts may relate to volume discounts, promotional discounts, seasonal discounts, discounts for early payment, etc. This discussion explains why the suppliers pricing usually is such an obscure topic to deal with. Nevertheless, it is crucial to buyers to have a thorough understanding of the suppliers costing and pricing policy. Especially, it needs to be aware of the relationship between fixed and variable costs. High fixed cost can be influenced by changing order volumes. High variable cost can be influenced by having an in-depth knowledge of the suppliers' materials cost. The buyer can achieve this by closely monitoring the developments in the supply and demand situation in his supply markets.

Next, when doing business with a supplier, it is important that the buyer is aware of his financial performance. Such knowledge is important to avoid unpleasant surprises in a situation of an economic downturn. Assessing the financial performance of a supplier requires insight into the supplier's profitability, its equity/debt ratio and its cash position.

In order to improve supplier performance, such performance need to be measured both in a qualitative and quantitative way. Supplier audits are an example of a qualitative approach to supplier performance improvement. Supplier performance indicators are examples of a quantitative approach. Both types of approaches are complementary to each other and need to be used in combination.

Supplier cost analysis and performance measurement are needed to improve supplier performance. This is necessary since suppliers today determine for many companies their cost position as well as their innovative capabilities. Through improving the performance of their suppliers, companies can improve their own performance in the relationship with their customers. Therefore, it is needed to develop differentiated strategies for different supplier segments. Suppliers can be differentiated in to strategic suppliers, preferred suppliers and competitive suppliers. For each type of suppliers different strategies are put in place. However, suppliers pursue different strategies towards their customers. Usually, the best ideas and resources are made available to the best customers. Therefore, buyers need to position their company through their purchasing strategies as a customer of choice *vis-à-vis* their most strategic suppliers. To achieve such a position purchasing managers can actively solicit ideas for improvement from their suppliers, provide technical support to their suppliers and conduct periodic supplier satisfaction surveys. The information which is derived from these kinds of activities will enable the buyer to build more collaborative and constructive relationships with its key suppliers.

ASSIGNMENTS

15.1 To be able to build long-term collaborative relationships with the supplier, the supplier needs to have a sound financial position. Apart from financial reports, what weak signals would indicate that things are going wrong with the supplier and that its continuity may be at stake? Give a few examples.

15.2 A supplier of components announces that it has to raise its prices by 10%, because it has lost a major customer. It states that it is now forced to spread its fixed cost across a smaller production volume. What costing method does this supplier use? Assuming that this supplier is important to you, how would you deal with the supplier's request? What steps would you take?

15.3 In this chapter vendor rating was named as one of the methods that can be used to measure supplier performance. Delivery reliability and quality performance of the supplier are two aspects of vendor rating. How can a supplier's delivery reliability and quality performance be measured in a practical way? What KPIs would you suggest?

15.4 Last year you purchased 100 units of product X from a supplier at €50.00 each. You estimate that you will purchase 300 units of this product from the same supplier this year. You are now preparing for the price discussion with the supplier. What price are you willing to pay, assuming that an 80% learning curve applies to this product?

15.5 Name examples of products for which the price is set by means of cost-based pricing, market-based pricing and competitive bidding. Which arguments will the buyer use in each of these cases to obtain the lowest possible purchase price?

REFERENCES

Corey, E.R. (1978) *Procurement Management: Strategy, Organization and Decision-making*, Boston: CBI Publishing Company.

Dyer, J.H. (2000) *Collaborative Advantage, Winning Through Extended Enterprise Supplier Networks*, New York: Oxford University Press.

Kotler, Ph. and Keller, K.L. (2006) *Marketing Management*, 12th edn, New York: Prentice-Hall.

Laseter, T.M. (1998) *Balanced Sourcing: Cooperation and Competition in Supplier Relationships*, San Francisco: Jossey-Bass Publishers.

Liker, J.K. and Choi, Th.Y (2004) 'Building deep supplier relationships', *Harvard Business Review*, December: 2–11.

BUYING AND SUPPLY MANAGEMENT IN RETAIL

LEARNING OBJECTIVES

After studying this chapter you should understand the following:

- The main characteristics and importance of buying and supply in trade and retail companies.
- The most important developments in the buying policies of trade and retail companies.
- The way in which the buying function can be organized in trade and retail companies.
- The profile of the trade and retail buyer.

INTRODUCTION

Welcome to the world of retail! As the following case study demonstrates, buying for retail is much more than just buying products. Due to the thin margins, retail buyers have to take cost out of their supply chains where they can. This is one reason why retail buyers have adopted advanced supply chain management concepts and techniques. Through intricate and real time logistics systems they are able to trace and track their materials flows from minute to minute. Of course, their activities are based upon sound category management. Based upon a thorough analysis of consumer-buying patterns, retail formats and product assortments are constantly adapted and changed. Since retail buyers usually deal with large and strong manufacturers of branded products, they have adopted new methods and tools in order to stimulate competition among them. Electronic auctions and marketplaces belong nowadays to the standard toolbox of retail buying.

The buying function in trade and retail companies is much closer to sales. Although the term 'buying' is used in other chapters, in this chapter 'buying' and 'category management' are used since these terms are much more familiar to retail buyers. As will be seen in this chapter, the sales, buying and logistics functions over the years have become highly integrated in these companies. In retail, buyers are responsible for

CASE STUDY AHOLD

Ahold is one of the leading supermarket chains in Europe and the USA. With sales of over €28 billion, it operates about 1100 stores in Europe and the USA. Apart from retail Ahold wants to increase its 'share-of-stomach' in the countries where it operates through building up a strong position in food-service. One of its major supermarket chains in The Netherlands is Albert Heijn. This operating company is leading edge in applying new concepts in retail and supply chain management.

Modern retail thinking within Albert Heijn centres on the term ECR: **efficient consumer response**. ECR means that the consumer is the trigger for the logistics process within the food chain. Cash register scanning (using RFID or bar code technology) immediately shows how much has been sold of a particular product on a particular day. If the shelf stock drops beneath a certain level, then an order is automatically generated for the supplier. The supplier is expected to restock within a certain, previously agreed time period (often limited to a couple of hours), either through direct delivery to the store (fresh products) or to the distribution centre of the retailer. In the view of Albert Heijn, ECR is a situation in which the manufacturer/supplier is no longer paid for the products that have been delivered. Preferably, payment is based on the volume that actually has been sold within a given period. In essence the manufacturer/supplier becomes the logistics manager and distributor to the retailer. The supplier performs most of the logistics tasks. Based upon real time sales information, the manufacturer is supposed to determine the volume which is to be replenished the next day. In case full truckloads are preferred by the manufacturer (for reasons of transport economies), the surplus volume can be stocked in the distribution centre; however, the square

metres that are being used for this purpose are to be paid for by the manufacturer. Replenishment generally takes place on the basis of the principle of cross-docking. Deliveries to the distribution centre are cross-loaded to waiting trucks, which transport the goods directly to the stores (instead of leaving them to be stored at the distribution centre).

Retail buyers (now often referred to as category managers) increasingly focus on refining retail concepts and improving category management. In this way the traditional retail buyer in many supermarket chains has evolved rapidly from a deal maker into a sophisticated retail entrepreneur. Customer loyalty cards form the basis for in-depth studies about consumer behaviour. Using customer loyalty programs, retailers try to attract and retain customers with tailor-made offers. Using intricate logistics systems, the logistics goods flow can be tracked and traced. As a result, store personnel can check on the status of orders and deliveries independently. Order processing and payment take place electronically using EDI or some other electronic buying solution. Advanced shelf allocation systems (e.g. SpaceMan) allow for detailed yield analyses per article, per article group, or per supplier.

In order to make sure manufacturers meet world market standards, Ahold started the World Wide Retail Exchange (WWRE) in 1998 aimed at facilitating global sourcing. Through Internet-enabled reverse auctions suppliers are challenged to provide their best offer to the Ahold companies. Web supported transaction processing furthermore allows the company to drastically reduce transaction costs and speed up the process of ordering, shipment, delivery and payment. Next, the WWRE is used to monitor tracing and tracking of products, inventories and goods flows within Ahold's global supply networks.

Efficient consumer response (ECR)

Is a grocery industry supply chain management strategy aimed at eliminating inefficiencies, and excessive or non-value-added costs within the supply chain, thus delivering better value to grocery consumers.

decisions related to running a whole product assortment. Sales and buying decisions are weighed against each other so that an optimal financial return can be achieved. It goes without saying that in order to be able to do this, buyers in trade companies need to have a broad business orientation, in which price is only one of the elements of the decision-making process.

Trade and retail companies in most European countries account for a considerable share of the total number of transactions. The buying-to-sales content is rather high, since these companies do not add significant value to their products. A buying-to-sales ratio of more than 80% is not uncommon. This means that functions such as buying, logistics and sales are core activities. Buying for trade companies means 'bottom line' thinking. Margins on products (especially in the retail business) are usually very small.

This means that the buyer must take into consideration all the costs that are made in the trajectory from manufacturer to end customer. Effective cost control is a prerequisite for the continued existence of trade companies. Costs related to materials handling, transportation and storage cannot be ignored. This concept is at the root of the development of strategic cost management techniques (such as **direct product cost** and **direct product profitability**) and shelf or display simulation systems, which will be explained later in this chapter. These information systems are nowadays important management tools for the modern retail buyer.

This chapter describes the role and importance of the buying function in trade and retail companies. In doing so the issue of how to organize for buying in these kinds of company will be addressed. The chapter will also discuss the major developments and changes taking place in the sourcing and supply management strategies of retailers and their relationships with suppliers; however, definitions of some important concepts are discussed first.

Direct product cost (DPC)
DPC relates to all costs that can be allocated directly to the product (including the costs of materials handling, taking in return packaging, pricing, etc.).

DEFINITIONS

Trade companies are characterized by the absence of a production process. There is no transformation in the technical sense. At most there are some packaging or 'bulk-breaking' activities. The value added in trade and retail companies, when compared with manufacturing companies, is therefore rather low. The mere existence of the trade company is based primarily on the exchange of value, i.e. products between different parties in the market. Essentially the **trade function** can be described as 'bridging time, place, quantity, assortment and knowledge'. The products, that are sold, must travel the road from manufacturer to the final consumer. The primary process of the trade company takes care of this. The buying function, together with (inbound) logistics, is of major importance. In addition, outbound logistics (physical distribution) is a major activity in trade companies. Due to the lack of a production function, the time which elapses between the purchase and the actual sale is very short. This is one reason why in some retail companies buying and selling are integrated into one function, since buying decisions may, to a large extent, determine the sales potential for a specific product (and vice versa). Where this occurs, this integrated commercial function is often referred to as category management.

Trade companies can be divided into two different levels, the **wholesale** level and the retail level. Companies that operate on the wholesale level deliver their products to other companies. Their customers are the retail, industrial and service companies, which in their turn may deliver directly to the final consumer (see Figure 16.1).

Direct product profitability (DPP)
Based upon sales price and direct product cost, the retail buyer determines the direct (net) profit margin per product (DPP).

Trade function
Activity aimed at bridging time, place, quantity, assortment and knowledge between a buyer and a seller.

Wholesale
Trading firms who deliver their products to other companies. Their customers are the retail, industrial and service companies, which in their turn may deliver directly to the final consumer.

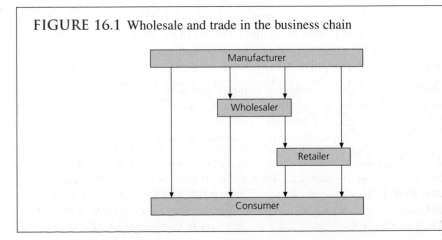

FIGURE 16.1 Wholesale and trade in the business chain

Wholesale companies differ from retailers in several ways. As a rule they spend less effort on promotion, shop layout and selection of location since their contacts are mostly other industrial companies or retailers, rather than final consumers. Furthermore, wholesalers often make large transactions with a limited number of (retail) companies. The retailer, however, derives its income primarily from small purchases from a large number of consumers.

ROLE AND IMPORTANCE OF BUYING IN TRADE AND RETAIL COMPANIES

Trade companies fulfil the function of intermediary between producer and end user. They are able to execute several activities more efficiently than the manufacturers. Their added value, and therefore the rationale of their existence, lies in the following activities:

- Sales and promotion. Trade companies can reach many small customers at relatively low costs. Through their marketing and advertising activities, which are often considerable, they can create a brand image that is experienced as more positive than the image of the (for the consumer, often distant) producer.

- Buying and building up a product assortment. Trade companies select products and build up an assortment based on the needs of a specific target group. In this way they make the market offer transparent and more easily accessible for the customer.

- Bulk breaking. By buying products in large quantities and then selling them in smaller units, the trade companies reduce costs for the producer and improve the accessibility of his products for the public.

- Storage. By maintaining stocks they reduce the costs for both manufacturer and end user. At the same time they realize a high degree of availability for the end user.

- Transportation. There is also added value of trade companies in the fact that they take over the transportation function from the manufacturer. As a result of a higher loading level they are often able to execute this function more efficiently.

- Carrying the risk. Some products are perishable or carry a high risk in terms of pilferage, damage and obsolescence. Trade companies take over part of these risks from the producer.

- Market information. Thanks to the continuous advances of information technology (e.g. customer loyalty cards), many trade companies have an excellent picture of the characteristics of their target groups and of the sales opportunities and problems with regard to the assortment they carry. This aspect is becoming more and more important in the relationship with producers who can use this information to improve existing or develop new products.

- Management and marketing services. Intensive interaction between trade and manufacturers results increasingly in new ideas and concepts in the area of shop layout, shelf layout, displays and the improvement of inventory management systems. Quite often trade companies take the initiative here.

Trade companies may handle an extensive range of products. In the wholesale business these products can vary from raw materials for numerous manufacturing companies and bulk food products for the catering industry to office supplies for government institutions. With regard to the retail trade, various types of stores can be distinguished in the area of consumer products, such as:

- speciality store
- department store
- supermarket

- convenience store
- combination store, superstore and hypermarket
- service business.

The wide variety of enterprises in the trade sector, and their widely different modes of operation, make it impossible to generalize on their buying policies and the 'ideal' structure of the buying organization. The scope of this book necessitates a decision on this issue, so for the remainder of this chapter the focus will be on the buying function in retail organizations.

STRUCTURE AND ORGANIZATION OF THE BUYING PROCESS

As has been seen, the buying and sales and marketing functions are closely interrelated in trade companies. This is especially true in the case of products with short life cycles, such as perishables (which usually have a shelf life of some hours/days) and fashionable clothing and particular leisure goods (where the shelf life is a couple of weeks or months). Some perishables (such as vegetables, fresh fruit) may even find their final destination on the same day that they were purchased by the retailer. As a result the effectiveness of buying decision-making is easy to assess. In the words of the buying manager of a retail chain store: 'We know on Friday whether Monday's purchases were good or not.'

The following stages in the buying–selling cycle can be distinguished:

- Estimating the demand for a particular item. In this stage the sales opportunities of the product concerned are estimated based on either market research or market intuition. These sales opportunities are translated into sales forecasts and budgets for the coming period, preferably detailed at a monthly or weekly level. This information provides the basis for the next stage.
- Determining product assortment policy and distribution strategy. The next step is to determine the product's assortment policy. Important decisions here are to decide how deep (number of product items per product line) and how broad (number of product lines per product group) the assortment needs to be. With regard to the distribution policy, important elements are to decide which products will be kept in stock, for which products consigned stocks will be used, which products are to be delivered through the company's own distribution centre, and which products are to be delivered directly from the manufacturer to the store or even to the customer.
- Selection of the most suitable supplier. Based on the information indicated above, a list of potential suppliers can be drawn up. In general the circle of (potential) suppliers is limited. Quite often the ideas for new products are presented to the retail buyer by the manufacturers. In that situation the buyer will have to judge whether the new product fits into the assortment policy, or whether the latter must be adjusted. If the buyer has personally developed a viable product idea, they will have to start looking for a supplier. The procedure that can be followed in this case is identical to the procedure described in Chapter 2. That risks are also run by retailers during this stage of the buying process is demonstrated in Memo 16.1.
- Contractual agreements. When the most suitable supplier has been selected, a contract is drawn up. This contract records all rights and obligations of both parties, as well as terms and conditions related to, among other things, price, method of packing, order size, payment, delivery and quality. Other important issues are product safety and environmental issues. Especially when the trade company has its own brand (private label), making

MEMO 16.1   PROBLEMS SURROUNDING THE PURCHASE OF NEW SOFT DRINK BOTTLES

Soft drinks suppliers in the Benelux countries have standardized their arrangements about bottles (contents and material), crates, deposits and prices. One of the results of this agreement has been that one manufacturer can take in the bottles of another. The following case concerns plastic soft drink bottles.

A large retail organization in food products wanted to expand its assortment with a low-cost soft drink, and intended to sell it under a private label. The retail buyer asked for quotations from several bottling companies with the result that all suppliers quoted almost the same price. The buyer, however, also requested an outsider in another European country to prepare a bid. This supplier was an affiliate of a large conglomerate located in Southern Europe. Negotiations were started and it soon turned out that this supplier could provide the required quantities at a much more favourable price. However, the bottles were different from those normally used in the Benelux countries. The crates were also different and were covered with the Southern European company's name. Another problem was the deposit. The

retailer had to invest a considerable sum of money in deposits, the money being returned by the bottling company only when the bottles and crates had been received. Before signing the contract, the retailer had requested a bank guarantee from the Southern European company's bank. This guarantee did not arrive in time, and the buyer decided to go ahead without waiting for the bank guarantee.

Sale of the company's new soft drink (under its own private label) started. The turnover was high. However, a year after signing the contract, the retailer learned that the bottling company had gone bankrupt. This was a setback, because at least €750 000 worth of crates and bottles were in the pipeline from distribution centres to consumers. These crates differed from the other crates on the market, so the retail organization had no way to reuse them. None of the money could be recovered through the lawyers or the trustee from the Southern European firm.

The problem was later solved when a new supplier of soft drinks proved willing to fill the empty bottles and sell them to the Middle East.

specific arrangements on these topics in a contract can prevent many problems. In the food industry some products are bought on committed volumes: based on a thorough forecast the buyer is obliged to purchase a certain volume of the product and the seller is obliged to supply. This is often the case with so-called harvest products (canned and pickled products), of which the buyer wants to secure a particular quantity. Other products often have no firm agreements about quantities. The buyer only provides an estimate of the amounts to be purchased, based on historical information and sales forecasts. Based on this information the parties try to arrive at a price. In general, negotiations between retailers and suppliers have become more complex over the years, as more and more requirements, apart from quality and price, are being put forward (see Memo 16.2).

- Ordering. The ordering process is kept as simple as possible in view of the philosophy that the stores should focus primarily on selling products. Because the retail outlets often have limited space for storage and materials handling, frequent delivery is required, which is why most retail companies have developed sophisticated ordering techniques: with the aid of a pen that reads the bar codes of the various products (order entry) and a portable computer, orders are placed directly at the distribution centres, which subsequently make the delivery. In most retail companies nowadays, all products are scanned at the cash register; at that moment the product is reduced from the store inventory. Next, after the store inventory has been reduced beyond a certain minimum level, an order signal is automatically triggered to the distribution centre. The distribution centres are responsible for maintaining their stocks at the desired level. Their ordering systems are directly coupled to the receiving orders systems of the suppliers (often through EDI). Invoicing takes place at the central level. For some products, such as fresh foods, central

MEMO 16.2   MORE SUBSTANTIAL NEGOTIATIONS IN RETAIL TRADE

At present, negotiations between buyers for super-market chains and their suppliers are very tough, not only because of the buyers' increased power, but also due to the pressure on their profits. The suppliers have to prove themselves repeatedly, and the outcome of negotiations is less predictable than it used to be.

Typical characteristics of modern discussions about terms and conditions include the following:

Element of marketing mix	Topics
Product mix	assortment portfolio-analysis (performance in terms of turnover and DPP)
	market research data (concerning consumer behavior, brand performance, competition)
	exclusivity in sales and new products
	arrangements on returnable items (slow movers, new product introductions, seasonal products)
	shelf filling packaging (in order to use shelf space to the maximum)
	uniform article codes (to optimize product scanning)
Price mix	price and delivery conditions (a classic area of negotiation)
	recommended selling prices (in order to provide retailer with terms of reference)
	pre-pricing of products (to reduce handling in stores)
Presentation mix	detailed shelf layouts and displays
	cost-saving materials and packaging (ready for sale packaging and displays, etc.)
	optimal use of transport packaging (in line with shelf systems)
Personnel mix	effective use of supplier sales staff for in-store activities, commercial advice and training
	rack jobbing for difficult and labor intensive categories (improved operations)
	training and development (providing knowledge to sales personnel and other staff)
Promotion mix	incentives for in-store personnel (turnover and display contests).

order handling is not suitable. These products, then, are ordered by the retail outlets directly from the supplier, who also delivers the order directly. A new development is that bar coding technology is replaced by radio frequency identification (RFID) technology, which allows retail companies to manage their transaction and operational processes without human interference. Through a small microchip each product can be traced using radio technology wherever it resides in the retailer's supply chain.

■ Advanced information systems have enabled 'automatic replenishment'. Based upon cash-register scanning retailers now know what has been sold on a specific day. This information is transferred to suppliers through electronic linkages, who are requested to ship exactly these volumes of the products to the retailer's distribution centre during the night. Early in the morning the stores are replenished with the requested volumes. This practice is often referred to as 'quick response logistics'. In fact, suppliers are able to monitor on a daily basis what has been sold by their customers. Through these advanced information systems, logistics (planning) tasks are increasingly shifted to the (food-) manufacturers and their suppliers.

■ Expediting and evaluation. As has been discussed, the ordered goods are delivered by the supplier either directly to the retail outlets, or to the distribution centres. Monitoring the delivered quantity and quality and time of delivery takes place where the goods are delivered. The delivered quantities are also entered into the inventory control system. Some large retailers have sophisticated vendor-rating systems in place in order to monitor and improve the overall supplier performance.

Based on this description the following additional observations are worth making.

The process as has been described here, illustrates that the function of the retail buyer gradually has evolved from straight buying to commodity or category management, where cross-functional category teams are responsible for managing all aspects of a category in order to generate a maximum return for the retail company. Ordering and buying are often separate activities within the retail company. Buying and category management are conducted centrally within the organization, whereas ordering is carried out, as much as possible, decentrally (by the stores and the distribution centres). Decentralized ordering has become possible thanks to sophisticated, computerized ordering and inventory control systems. Where automatic replenishment has been implemented, planning tasks are shifted to the supplier who is kept fully responsible for the timely delivery of products in the exact quantity needed.

Given the scope and importance of the buying function it makes sense to have it report high in the organizational hierarchy. As a rule, the buying director reports directly to general management. With regard to the organization of buying it is possible to differentiate between a functional buying structure and a cross-functional structure.

In a functional buying structure the buying department predominantly acts as a separate organizational entity, which operates more or less autonomously from physical distribution and sales and store management. Based on sales forecasts retail buyers prepare their category plans.

In the cross-functional structure the buying function, styling, visual merchandizing and physical distribution (apart from store operations) operate in one organizational entity. As has been mentioned before, this often is referred to as 'category management'. Category managers are responsible for assortment policy, product policy, buying and supplier management, and distribution policy. Store operations mostly reside outside their area of responsibility.

DEVELOPMENTS IN TRADE AND RETAIL COMPANIES

The buying function in trade companies is subject to significant change. Some important changes are now described:

- Changing consumer behaviour. Changes in consumer behaviour have a major impact on the retailer's product-market strategies. It is the retail buyer's job to identify these changes in time and to translate them into new product concepts and design new shelf displays and shop layouts. The following are typical of changes that confront retail organizations in European countries:
  - ○ ageing population, ongoing individualization, more men shopping
  - ○ increasing income gap between population groups, more one- and two-person households (in large urban areas)
  - ○ growing number of earning couples (two incomes, no children)
  - ○ increased integration of ethnic minorities, exposure to other cultures through tourism, adopting other cultural consumption patterns
  - ○ increased concern for the environment, manifested in the cry for biodegradable containers and packaging
  - ○ increased attention to healthier living, expressed in a strong growth of the number of health food and diet products.

This means that the commodity manager or retail buyer must constantly tailor their product assortment to ever more specific, and often smaller, target groups. This results in a wider variety of products and an increased complexity with regard to managing the incoming and outgoing goods flow:

- Concentration. Especially in retail and food manufacturing globalization of competition and concentration through mergers and acquisitions are characteristic developments. For manufacturers this concentration means that there will be more mono-production, which makes it possible to achieve better economies of scale. It is expected that there will be fewer and fewer suppliers of food products in the near future and, as a result, retail companies will be dealing primarily with a few very large manufacturers. The trend towards globalization of business and economies of scale will also affect the scale of retail businesses. As a result many large retailers have become very active in mergers and acquisitions over the past decade.

- International co-operation. Due to the concentration of power on the suppliers' side, many trade companies are diligently searching for possibilities with which to counterbalance this development. Internationalization is an option seen by many. It can be difficult to realize internationalization of retail organizations. In Europe, for example, the market often turns out to be culturally determined or dependent on the country. There is only a limited number of products that can be sold internationally with the same marketing formula. Packaging is also culturally related; e.g. the French consumers will not accept canned soup. Another aspect is, when it comes to packaging, that product labels always should be stated in the language of the country in question. These realities limit the possibilities of achieving further economies of scale. International buying combinations have great difficulty getting off the ground. The Dutch Ahold group of companies has entered into collaboration with six other large retailers in Sweden, France, Great Britain, Finland and Denmark. By buying products jointly, price advantages are being realized. This does not function optimally, however, because there are few 'euro-products' and because (large) suppliers like Unilever, Coca-Cola and Nestlé prefer, for obvious reasons, to sell their products to each country separately.

- Private labels. More and more retail companies have embraced private labels or company brands. Private labels support retailer identity and their (quality) image. By buying products, giving them a company label and taking over the promotion, the retailer will have the advantage of a higher margin. Carrying their own private label implies that product liability lies with the retailer. As the product carries the trade company's brand, this company presents itself as the producer of the product. The buyer must be aware of this and should include it in the contract with the supplier. In case of any problems about the quality of the product or customer complaints the retailer then may be able to recover the costs from the producer.

- Space management. Since shelf-space is limited, the extensive product lines offered by manufacturers force the retail buyer to make a selection. In this context computerized space-management systems may support him. They enable the simulation of several display layouts (for a different number of facings) based on detailed cost information, to decide on the most profitable layout. Important concepts, underlying space management systems, are direct product cost (DPC) and direct product profitability (DPP). DPC relates to all costs that can be allocated directly to the product (including the costs of materials handling, taking in return packaging, pricing, etc.). The retail buyer tries to trace these costs in detail: she compares these to the sales price, and is then able to determine the direct profit margin per product (DPP).

- 'Green' issues. Ecological considerations are growing in importance. This started initially with the replacement of artificial flavourings and odours by natural products. At

Space management *Computer-supported simulation systems used by retail buyers to optimize their income per square metre of shelf space. These systems enable the simulation of several display layouts (for a different number of facings) based on detailed cost information, to decide on the most profitable layout. Important concepts, underlying space management systems, are direct product cost (DPC) and direct product profitability (DPP).*

present the emphasis is on biodegradable packing materials, PVC-less packaging and a minimum of blister packs. There are some problems, such as the soft drink bottle, that should be solved by the industry in question so that standardization can be achieved (see Memo 16.1). International suppliers bring extra problems, for instance manufacturers of toothpaste have been obliged to eliminate their carton boxes, which they used as a packaging for their end products, due to environmental legislation. Recently, the government in Germany decided to put a refund on tins and cans in order to discourage the use of one-way packaging in the drink industry.

■ Information. Information technology is an important asset for the retail buyer. Some developments in information technology have an immediate impact on the consumer. They are manifest in, for instance, electronic banking, bar coding, RFID and teleshopping. There are also developments that are far less visible to the consumer.

These developments generally relate to the retail trade, wholesale trade and manufacturing companies. Let's see what is happening to the sourcing and supply chain strategies of these companies.

SOURCING AND SUPPLY CHAIN STRATEGY TRENDS

Collaborative planning, forecasting and replenishment (CPFR)
This concept allows co-operation across the supply chain, using a set of processes and technology models. Its goal is to provide dynamic information sharing that is integrating both 'demand' and 'supply' side processes (and thus linking manufacturers, retailers and carriers), and effectively planning, forecasting and replenishing customer needs through the total supply chain.

Continuous replenishment is defined as the practice of partnering among distribution channel members that changes the traditional replenishment process from distributor-generated purchase order to one based on actual or forecast consumer demand.

Supply chain management is at the heart of successful modern retail. Wal-Mart is widely recognized for their landmark performance in this area. Their philosophy on 'everyday low prices' is founded on the belief that taking cost out of the supply chain is the only way to remain competitive. The idea is that a more efficient supply chain allows them to pass on cost economies to the final consumer, who given the price difference compared to competitors, would therefore be seduced to buy from Wal-Mart. Here, we will discuss some important concept on which modern supply chain management in retail is based. We will consecutively deal with vendor managed inventory (VMI), efficient consumer response (ECR), **collaborative planning, forecasting and replenishment** (CPFR), electronic marketplaces, and RFID.

Vendor managed inventory

VMI is now a widely practiced initiative in the retail industry. Also known as **continuous replenishment** or supplier-managed inventory, it was popularized in the late 1980s by Wal-Mart and Procter & Gamble. Successful VMI initiatives have been trumpeted by other companies in the USA, including Campbell Soup, Kraft Foods, and Johnson & Johnson and by some European firms. VMI is a continuous replenishment programme that uses the exchange of information between the retailer and the supplier to allow the supplier to manage and replenish product at the store or warehouse level. In this programme, the retailer supplies the vendor with the information necessary to maintain just enough products to meet customer demand. This enables the supplier to better plan and anticipate the amount of product it needs to produce or supply. Through the use of electronic transfer of information VMI gives visibility across the supply chain pipeline. With information available at a more detailed level it allows the manufacturer to be more customer-specific in its planning. With the ability of supply chain applications to manage inventories at retailer locations, VMI concepts are being used at both the distribution centre-level and the store-level of retail companies.

In the fulfilment process using VMI, typically the activities of forecasting, scheduling, requisitioning and ordering are performed by the supplier and no longer by the retailer.

Electronic data interchange (EDI) is an integral part of VMI process and takes a vital role in the process of data communication. The retailer sends the sales and inventory data to the vendor via EDI and the supplier creates the purchase orders based on the established inventory levels and fill rates. In the VMI process, the retailer is free of forecasting and creating the orders as the vendor generates the orders. The vendor is responsible for creating and maintaining the stock plan for the retailer. The vendor sends the shipment notices before shipping the product to the retailer's store or warehouse. Soon after this, the vendor sends the invoice to the retailer. Upon receiving the product, the retailer does the invoice matching and handles payment through their account payable systems.

> *Electronic data interchange (EDI)*
> *Can be defined as an inter organizational exchange of business documentation in a structured, machine-processable form.*

Trading partners who focus on changing business relationships definitely maximize their bottom lines by using VMI. Benefits of implementing VMI also include reduced shipping costs and lead times, fewer human errors and improved service levels. Perhaps the most important benefit of engaging in a strategic VMI alliance is the possibility to build a strong and lasting relationship between the vendor and the customer, which in the long run can bring rich rewards to both. Another attractive feature of VMI is changing of the retailer focus from buying to selling. Under VMI, manufacturers, retailers and distributors can focus on the same issue – how to sell more products to the end consumer more efficiently.

VMI has its drawbacks when not implemented properly. Some possible drawbacks of VMI might include: EDI problems, employee acceptance, lack of trust among supply chain partners. EDI sometimes creates a challenge due to the many different standards in use. This makes it difficult to communicate and translate information between companies. If manufacturers are to assume stock-keeping responsibility, they must be able to communicate in real time with their (retail) partners in a uniform way. With VMI, all employees involved in the process must fully understand and accept this new way of doing business. All employees who are involved must be willing participants.

VMI can also fail when setting up rules for how the relationship should work. For example, the supplier and the customer must agree on how to deal with overstocks, ordering errors and obsolete stock. Finally, both parties must understand that this is a learning process that takes time. Equally as important as time is trust. Many retailers and consumer goods firms are naturally reluctant to share information in advance, fearing that the information will somehow fall into the hands of competitors or they will lose control in some way.

VMI represents a powerful tool to take cost out of the supply chain. Developed in the early 1980s, this approach to inventory and order fulfilment is still used by many companies and also acts as an underlying concept for more recent trends, such as ECR and CPFR, which share the same idea of supply chain integration through information sharing and employ the same technological principles (see Claassen *et al.* (2008) for a detailed discussion on VMI).

Efficient consumer response

ECR is a grocery industry supply chain management strategy aimed at eliminating inefficiencies and excessive or non-value-added costs within the supply chain, thus delivering better value to grocery consumers. It is designed to re-engineer the grocery supply chain away from a 'push system', in which manufacturers 'push' products into stores, towards a 'pull system', in which products are 'pulled' down the supply chain into the store by consumer-demand information captured at the point of sale.

The ultimate goal of ECR is to produce a responsive, consumer-driven supply chain which allows distributors and suppliers to work together in order to maximize consumer satisfaction and minimize cost. The technologies, which are primarily electronic commerce (e-commerce) components, are used to automate these efficient business processes, as well as to enhance the communication and relationships between companies. ECR is thus an application of e-commerce within the grocery supply chain.

One of the most celebrated examples of an ECR in the UK is that achieved by Tesco and Birds Eye Walls (BEW) (McKinnon, 1996). This resulted in delivery lead times dropping from 7 days in 1986 to 2 days in 1993. Over this period both firms dramatically reduced their inventory levels: Tesco's stock of BEW products fell by 71% and BEW's stocks by 50%. There are similar examples of ECR success in other countries such as Albert Heijn & Heineken in The Netherlands and Wal-Mart and Proctor & Gamble in the USA.

ECR attempts to eliminate inefficiencies within the grocery industry supply chain by introducing strategic initiatives in four areas:

- Efficient store assortment. This initiative is aimed at optimizing the productivity of inventory and shelf management at the consumer interface – the store level.

- Efficient product introduction. The objective of this initiative is to maximize the effectiveness of new product development and introduction activities, in order to reduce costs and failure rates in introducing new products.

- Efficient promotion. This initiative aims at maximizing the total system efficiency of trade and consumer promotions. This can be achieved by introducing better alternative trade and consumer promotions, such as pay for consumption and every day low price policies.

- Efficient product replenishment. The objective of this initiative is to optimize time and cost in the replenishment system by the provision of the right product to the right place at the right time in the right quantity and in the most efficient manner possible.

These strategies are supported by two programmes and five enabling technologies as shown in Figure 16.2.

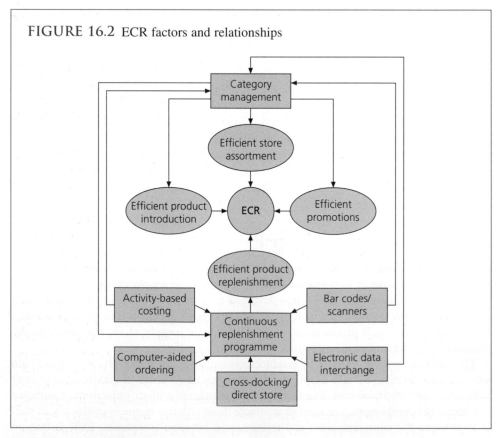

FIGURE 16.2 ECR factors and relationships

Source: Kurnia *et al.*, 2002

Programmes that companies need to have in place are:

- Category management. Category management supports the first three initiatives of ECR discussed above. It can be defined as an interactive business process whereby retailers and manufacturers work together in mutual co-operation to manage categories as strategic business units within each store. A category is a group of products which can be substituted for one another by a consumer and examples include cereals, bakery, household products, body care and so on. The types of categories to be included in a store have to be determined correctly to meet consumer demand and at the same time, to maximize profit. Category management employs EDI, bar codes and scanners to accurately capture information on customer demand on each category and to share the information between trading partners.

- Continuous replenishment programme (CRP). This programme supports the efficient product replenishment initiative. CRP is defined as the practice of partnering among distribution channel members that changes the traditional replenishment process from distributor-generated purchase order to one based on actual or forecast consumer demand. CRP transfers responsibility for inventory replenishment from retailers/distributors to suppliers and, thus, the approach is also known as VMI (see above). With CRP, orders are transmitted electronically and are made more frequently and in smaller quantities. CRP is also supported by the category management programme, which forms the shelf management strategy to track the inventory and demand for each individual category.

Category management and continuous replenishment need to be supported by some critical technologies and concepts:

- Bar codes/scanners. The use of bar codes and scanners is a fundamental element for ECR implementation in the grocery industry as it allows accurate and faster information capture to be obtained, which in turn can be shared with trading partners.

- Electronic data interchange (EDI). EDI can be defined as an 'inter organizational exchange of business documentation in a structured, machine-processable form'. Besides purchase orders and invoices, another common business document exchanged electronically in the grocery industry is the advance shipping notice (ASN), the EDI message which precedes the arrival of pallets at their destination.

- Computer-aided ordering (CAO). CAO is a retail-based system that automatically generates orders for replenishment when the inventory level drops below a predetermined reorder level. The system keeps track of the inventory levels of all items in the store and makes necessary adjustments when sales or replenishments occur.

- Cross-docking/direct store delivery. **Cross-docking or flow-through distribution** is a direct flow of merchandise/product from receiving to shipping, thus eliminating additional handling and storage steps in the distribution cycle. The idea of cross-docking is analogous to 'direct store delivery', in which manufacturers deliver products directly to the retailer, bypassing the wholesaler to eliminate warehouse handling.

- Activity-based costing (ABC). ABC is a costing method that identifies activities in an organization and assigns the cost of each activity's resources to all products and services that actually consume these resources. In this way an organization can more accurately establish the true cost of its individual products and services for the purposes of identifying and eliminating those which are unprofitable and lower the prices of those which are overpriced. Essentially, the ABC methodology assigns an organization's resource costs through activities to the products and services provided to its customers. It is generally used as a tool for understanding product and customer cost and profitability. As such, ABC has predominantly been used to support strategic decisions such as pricing, outsourcing and identification and measurement of process improvement initiatives.

Computer-aided ordering (CAO)
Is 'a retail-based system that automatically generates orders for replenishment when the inventory level drops below a pre determined reorder level'.

Cross-docking or flow-through distribution
Is a direct flow of merchandise/product from receiving to shipping, thus eliminating additional handling and storage steps in the distribution cycle.

The main obstacle to ECR is not technical but managerial, with many managers reluctant to transform their traditional, often adversarial, trading relationships into the open partnership that ECR requires. The ideal state envisioned by ECR cannot be reached through individual self-interested activity of the participants. ECR adoption requires co-operation and trust between trading partners, which are unlikely to happen unless costs, benefits and risks of ECR implementation can be mutually shared.

Collaborative planning, forecasting and replenishment

Another concept that is based on joint decision-making through information deployment is CPFR. This concept allows cooperation across the supply chain, using a set of processes and technology models. Its goal is to provide dynamic information sharing that is integrating both 'demand' and 'supply' side processes (and thus linking manufacturers, retailers and carriers), and effectively planning, forecasting and replenishing customer needs through the total supply chain.

This concept was introduced in 1996, and since then it has been embraced by several retailers such as Target, Best Buy, Wal-Mart, Tesco as well as some of the world's largest consumer good suppliers (Procter & Gamble, Henkel, Colgate-Palmolive, Johnson & Johnson). Although it has been reported that the concept's wide spread adoption is rather slow and not too many companies have employed it successfully [Nannery (2002)].

The essence of CPFR is in utilizing technology/information capabilities to support trading partner interaction and joint decision-making. A great deal of time and effort is needed up-front to negotiate specific items such as goals and objectives, frequency of updates to the sales and supply plans, exception criteria, and key measures. The result is a published document defining relevant issues that has been jointly developed and agreed to.

Foote and Krishnamurthi (2001) provide a case example of CPFR employment between Wal-Mart and Warner Lambert. The company started its road towards complete supply chain collaboration by integration of their own data from all the stores and warehouses into one single data warehouse. This was triggered by their need to obtain detailed information at a store level to be able to meet the needs of customers who come to a specific Wal-Mart store. The next step was establishing CPFR with their key suppliers.

The forecasting process begins with a data warehouse, which is designed for CPFR. The retail link system extracts the data relevant to Warner-Lambert products sales. The data are then sorted in a CPFR server. Wal-Mart buying agents use a spreadsheet (CPFR workbench) to make a preliminary forecast. A copy of this forecast appears on Warner-Lambert's CPFR server, so Warner-Lambert's planners can add comments and suggest revisions, which is viewed by Wal-Mart's planners. After a few iterations, an agreed-upon forecast is made for each product. This is used as a guide for production planning at Warner-Lambert (using SAP applications) and the inventory management at Wal-Mart. The communication between Wal-Mart and Warner-Lambert is done electronically.

IT tools that are used for CPFR come from a very broad arena. They rank from tailor-made applications from large IT vendors to simple tools based on a combination of non-proprietary processes and technology models. In general these models should be (1) open, yet allowing secure communications, (2) flexible across the industry, (3) extensible to all supply chain processes and (4) supporting a broad set of requirements (new data types, interoperability with different databases, etc.).

According to McCarthy et al. there are several barriers for CPFR implementation. These mainly relate the provision of adequate technology and software, difficulties of real-time co-ordination of information exchange, substantial investment of time and personnel for set-up, the process-intensive nature of maintaining the efforts across several suppliers and products, lack of scalability from the pilot stage, and the required synchronous changes in corporate culture for both firms in the collaborative relationship.

The advantages of CPFR are many, yet the authors who are publishing in this field differ in their importance. According to McCarthy and Golicic (2002) the advantages can be summarized as follows: increased responsiveness, product availability assurance, optimized inventory and associated costs, increased revenues and earnings. Other researchers claim that the main opportunities for retailers are reducing inventory levels and associated costs, increasing inventory turns, reducing or eliminating out-of-stock situations, maximizing the profitability of the product mix and buying at the lowest cost, saving on invoice processing, resolving exceptions, and transaction costs. For example, in the apparel industry, Sara Lee and Wal-Mart have reported a reduction of inventories through CPFR by 12% while increasing service levels by 2.7% for 23 branded underwear items. Furthermore Procter & Gamble anticipates savings over 1.5 billion dollars using the streamlined CPFR initiative by 2005. Most participants see as the main advantage of CPFR improved relationships with their trading partners.

One of the biggest impediments to mass adoption of CPFR seems to be the issue of trust. Many retailers, competitive by nature, continue to be reluctant to do the kind of data sharing that CPFR requires as they fear that giving away too much forecast or inventory data will damage their negotiating position. Furthermore the fact that technology for many-to-many CPFR has not yet been developed prevents widespread adoption. The tough part is collaborative replenishment that requires constant sharing of point-of-sales data and is especially tough to gauge during a promotion.

E-marketplaces and supply chain management

A more and more widespread application in retail is the business-to-business electronic marketplace (e-marketplace). A distinction can be made between open exchanges (accessible for everyone) and private exchanges. Some of the open exchanges are founded by retailers and could therefore be viewed as retailer oriented: worldwide retail exchange (WWRE) and GlobalNetExchange. Also, some large retailers develop their own private marketplaces because of safety reasons and because in this way the retailers are able to tie their suppliers closer to the company. Two examples of retailers who developed their own private marketplace are Tesco (Tesco Information Exchange) and Sainsbury's (Sainsbury's Information Direct).

An e-marketplace using a shared Internet-based structure can provide companies with a platform for:

- Core commerce transactions which can automate and streamline the entire requisition-to-payment process online (including procurement, customer management and selling).
- A collaborative network for production design, supply chain planning, optimization and fulfilment process.
- Industry-wide product information that is aggregated into a common classification and catalogue structure.
- An environment in which sourcing, negotiations and other trading processes such as auctions can take place real-time (online).
- An online community for publishing and exchanging industry news, information and events.

These functions allow the traditional supply chain process to reduce costs and increase speed to respond to supply and demand needs. With regard to buying function, it can reduce buying costs and achieve higher volume contract terms with preferred suppliers by accumulating buying across divisions and companies. It provides a single point of contact, minimizes off-contract buying and lowers selection cost through multiple suppliers.

MEMO 16.3 ELECTRONIC MARKET PLACES IN RETAIL: THE TESCO INFORMATION EXCHANGE

One of the examples of a private marketplace is the Tesco Information Exchange (TIE). It is a collaboration between Tesco and Global eXchange Services (GXS). More than 450 suppliers of Tesco are currently using this system. Via a web browser, TIE allows suppliers to view daily electronic point of sale (EPOS) data, which enables them to respond more quickly to variations in customer demand and ensure that the optimal stock is available at Tesco shelves at all times. Notoriously complex, the promotional process requires significant interaction between retailer and supplier. The promotion Management feature of TIE enables Tesco and its suppliers to jointly plan, execute, track and evaluate promotions by sharing common data through a structured online process. Other features that TIE provides to Tesco's suppliers are:

- collects real-time sales data and make them available for suppliers
- enables trading partners to track service levels performance at different points in the supply chain
- handles new product introduction and
- puts store directories and manuals online.

A lot of advantages were obtained using this system. It enhanced customer satisfaction, improved product availability, reduced waste, streamlined business process, reduced 33% of the lost sales on promotions and reduced 30% of the promotion overhead and waste!

Source: Case study obtained from www.gxs.com (2005)

In general e-marketplaces in retail seem to contribute to greater efficiency in the supply chain (Eng, 2003). The perceived contributions of e-marketplaces to supply chain management are unit cost reduction, increased efficiency and streamlined operations. The main process which contributed to these advantages was the electronic auction.

While the e-marketplace may provide many benefits for supply chain management, firms must not overlook the time-consuming process of relationship development. Companies always have to weigh the costs and benefits associated with the implementation of the e-marketplace system.

E-marketplaces offer companies a real-time web-based solution that can be used to increase efficiency of sourcing, buying and negotiating. They can streamline the supply chain, reduce costs and speed up the response time to supply and demand needs. Of course, before the advantage can be obtained some barriers have to be overcome. Companies have to have a sufficient amount of trust before they share 'valuable and confidential' information with outside parties. Also, technologically, it is very important to be able to guarantee the security of the system, which is fairly difficult when it concerns a web application. These are the two main barriers to adopt/use e-marketplaces. Some other obstacles that have to be challenged are employee acceptance and (initial) costs of entering and using the system.

Radio frequency identification

The next step in total co-operation between the partners in the retail industry is creating an open global network that can identify anything, anywhere, automatically. This dream-like solution is currently under development by the Auto-ID Centre (a collaboration of several universities, i.e. MIT, University of Cambridge, Keio University) and gets a lot of attention and sponsorship from industries (among others: Ahold, Coca-Cola, Accenture, Sun, Gillette, Home Depot, Johnson & Johnson, Kraft, Lowes, Metro, Pepsico, Pfizer, Procter & Gamble, Sara Lee, Target, Tesco, Unilever, UPS, Wal-Mart).

The Auto-ID Centre is designing, building, testing and deploying a global infrastructure – a layer on top of the Internet – that will make it possible for computers to identify any object anywhere in the world instantly. This network will not just provide the means to feed reliable, accurate, real-time information into existing business applications; it will usher in a whole new era of innovation and opportunity. It seeks to give companies near-perfect supply chain visibility. That is, companies will be able to know exactly where every item in their supply chain is at any time. The system, if widely adopted, could eliminate human error from data collection, reduce inventories, keep product in-stock, reduce loss and waste, free up staff to perform more value-added functions, and improve safety and security. The possibilities seem endless.

The technology behind this is RFID. RFID is a generic term for technologies that use radio waves to automatically identify individual items. There are several methods of identifying objects using RFID, but the most common is to store a serial number that identifies a product, and perhaps other information, on a microchip that is attached to an antenna. The antenna enables the chip to transmit the identification information to a reader. The reader converts the radio waves returned from the RFID tag into a form that can then be passed on to computers that can make use of it.

Although the described network of things might seam a bit like science fiction, it receives quite some support from big companies. Wal-Mart has already demanded their top suppliers to ship products with auto-ID tags, and Tesco has opened an RFID-enabled warehouse for high volume items. Also business researchers have started giving this development appropriate concern, arguing already about its commercial profitability. It can be concluded that this field will continue to receive a lot of attention in the coming years, and it is recommendable to set it as a possible direction for future research.

These four major developments show how the landscape of the traditional retail buyer has changed and will change in the near future. Electronic payment systems and customer loyalty cards, which are providing insight into buying frequency, composition of the consumer's daily shopping basket, and the customer's address, are at the heart of the retailers' planning and logistics systems. These systems will allow them to carefully optimize their supply chain operations. Scanning gives the retail buyers an immediate insight into the actual sales in their stores and the stock situation in the distribution centres. Space management enables them to simulate display layouts, based on detailed cost information, so that the optimal return can be realized. The concepts that have been described here show that the future competition in retail will no longer be among individual companies. Rather it will be among clusters of companies, with the retail firm at the heart surrounded by a limited number of large manufacturers who are highly integrated through intricate information and logistics networks which are tied to the retailers operations. As research evidence shows, the development towards this kind of highly integrated supply networks is long and troublesome due to the fact that inter-firm collaboration requires trust between the partners, a long-term commitment and a balanced sharing of risks and rewards from the relationship. These are conditions which in practice are seldom met.

SUMMARY

This chapter shows that the buying function plays a very important role in trade companies. We have discussed this role both for wholesale and retail companies. The basic difference between these two types of trade is in the type of customer: the wholesaler sells to other companies and institutions, whereas the retailer sells to the final consumer. Trade companies fulfil the role of intermediary between manufacturer and end user. The buyer's basic task is to translate the customers' demands into a suitable offer of products and services and make the product offerings available to them in the most cost-efficient way.

Several differences exist in the area of buying when comparing retail companies with industrial companies. In retail companies buying policy is much more integrated with sales and marketing policy, and company policy is primarily focused on improving turnover and margin whilst reducing working capital. As a result of the fierce competition, most retailers and wholesalers over the years have adopted a strong bottom line orientation. Thanks to modern information technology important progress has been made in terms of integrated logistics, distribution, transportation and store operations.

The buying–selling cycle usually begins with an estimate of the demand for a particular item. Based on this estimate the assortment and the distribution strategy will be determined. Then the investigation of what to contract for and whom to contract with can be started. At the same time preparations can be made for renegotiating contracts with existing suppliers. In most retail companies the initial buying activities are co-ordinated centrally. Ordering, expediting and evaluation often take place decentrally in the stores and the distribution centres. Thanks to computerized order entry systems, the number of administrative actions can be kept to a minimum.

Retail today is a truly international business. Both the retail market and the market for fast-moving consumer goods are characterised by a high degree of concentration. In order to improve their negotiating position retailers increasingly turn to private labels. Space management systems allow them to have detailed insight into direct cost and direct profitability of the products that are sold to them by manufacturers. These data are used in the relationship with suppliers to challenge them to continuously improve their logistics and quality performance. Advanced information systems are at the heart of the modern retail organization, allowing for the application of new logistics concepts and tools such as VMI, ECR, CPFR and electronic marketplaces. Implementing these concepts and using these tools in practice, however, requires that all partners commit to these initiatives for a long period of time and share the same vision and beliefs. The more advanced the concepts, the higher the commitment and requirements in terms of trust and cultural fit. It is here where most concepts suffer from the lack of willingness to share information and gains and risks resulting from the relationship.

ASSIGNMENTS

16.1 The criticism often made of retail buyers is that they are too price and margin-oriented. Rather, they should look into total cost of ownership in their dealings with suppliers. How would you explain such a critique? What tools would you suggest retail buyers to use to be able to negotiate more effectively on the basis of total cost of ownership?

16.2 ECR is sometimes referred to as a concept in which suppliers are not paid any more for the products that they have delivered? Explain. What are the necessary conditions that should be present to make ECR work in a relationship with a supplier?

16.3 What are main differences between retail buying and category management? What tasks does a category manager fulfil?

16.4 What does it take from a retailer and a manufacturer to implement vendor managed inventory (VMI)? Discuss implications for strategy, organization, processes, information systems and communication between both parties.

16.5 What functionality do electronic marketplaces offer to retail buyers. Answer this question by comparing at least three such marketplaces. To what extent are they successful? Why?

REFERENCES

Claassen, M.J.T., van Weele, A.J. and van Raaij, E.M. (2008) 'Performance outcomes and success factors of vendor managed inventory (VMI)', *Supply Chain Management: an International Journal*, 13(6):406–14.

Eng, T.Y. (2003) 'The role of e-marketplaces in Supply Chain Management', *Industrial Marketing Management*, 5567:1–9.

Foote, P.S. and Krishnamurthi, M. (2001) 'Forecasting using data warehousing model: Wal-Mart's experience', *The Journal of Business Forecasting Methods & Systems*, 20(3):13.

McCarthy, T.M. and Golicic, S.L. (2002) 'Implementing collaborative forecasting to improve supply chain performance', *International Journal of Physical Distribution & Logistics Management*, 32(6):431–54.

McKinnon, A.C. (1996) *The Development of Retail Logistics in the UK*, Heriot–Watt University: School of Management.

Nannery, M. (2002) 'Dropping the 'R'', *Chain Store Age*, 78(5):162.

Kurnia, S., Swatman, P.M.C., and Schauder, D. (2002) 'Efficient consumer response: a preliminary comparison of U.S. and European experiences', paper given at 11th International Conference on Electronic Commerce, Bled, Slovenia, June 8–10:126–43.

PURCHASING, CORPORATE SOCIAL RESPONSIBILITY AND ETHICS

LEARNING OBJECTIVES

After studying this chapter you should understand the following:

- The importance of corporate social responsibility to large international companies.
- Purchasing's contribution to 'People, Planet, Profit'.
- How corporate responsible purchasing can be embedded in a company's culture.
- The importance of integrity codes within purchasing.
- How companies can act responsibly in their relationships with their suppliers.

INTRODUCTION

Today, global sourcing in the business world is widely developed. Most consumer products in Europe are coming from foreign manufacturers. International toy manufacturers in many cases do not sell products that come from their own factories. Increasingly, these products come from so-called contract manufacturers, who manufacture their products based on the requirements of their European customers. Ever increasing competitive pressures force toy manufacturers like Mattel, reseller of the famous Barbie dolls, to continuously look for cheaper sources of supply. China, Thailand, Malaysia but also Indonesia and Vietnam, because of their low costs, are, for many buyers, interesting destinations for international trade. However, doing business successfully in these countries requires careful preparation. Local laws on how to protect the environment and labour conditions are not widely developed, and where present not enforced. Child labour, long labour hours (a 12-hour working day, 6 days a week is no exception) and horrible labour conditions are frequently encountered in these countries. When Western companies do business with these countries, obviously international, humanitarian laws should be respected. But there is another reason why Western companies need to operate carefully in these regions. Most Western consumers do not accept companies which do business with suppliers, where these circumstances prevail. As a result, consumers boycott the products of the manufacturers involved. Unethical sourcing practices, therefore, can do major harm to the reputation of companies in Western markets and may result in major financial damage and losses.

386 SECTION 3 IMPLEMENTATION

CASE STUDY WHY MATTEL APOLOGIZED TO CHINA

So are toys from China safe or not? If you think you're confused, it looks as if even Mattel, the largest toymaker in the USA, doesn't know.

On Friday, Mattel's executive vice president for worldwide operations, Thomas Debrowski, met with the Chinese product safety chief Li Changjiang, to apologize for the company's own weak safety controls. 'Our reputation has been damaged lately by these recalls,' Mr. Debrowski told Li. 'And Mattel takes full responsibility for these recalls and apologizes personally to you, the Chinese people, and all of our customers who received the toys.'

It's a stunning reversal. In August, after the company announced its recalls of several toys because they were made using lead paint, reporters grilled Mattel CEO Bob Eckert about how lead paint, which is banned for use on children's toys in the USA, ended up on its 'Sarge' toy cars. Surprisingly, he had answers . . . He blamed it on a subcontractor who violated Mattel's policies and 'utilized paint from a non-authorized third-party supplier.' . . . By pointing out specifically where things broke down and then spelling out what he would do to fix it – testing every batch of toys before it leaves China, rather than relying on testing raw materials – the CEO reassured American consumers that he understood the problem and would back up his apology with action.

Eckert is now paying the price for his candor. Mattel needs China just as much as China needs Mattel, and it cannot afford to jeopardize its relationship with the country that produces 65% of its toys. In a global public relations campaign, Chinese officials have emphasized that the country does have strong safety standards, and that problems at a few companies shouldn't be used to paint the whole country's products as unsafe.

So Mattel found a face-saving way of taking back the blame that it had previously placed so squarely on its Chinese partners, the source of all the toys it recalled this year. 'The vast majority of those products that were recalled were the result of a design flaw in Mattel's design, not through a manufacturing flaw in China's manufacturers,' Debrowski said. 'We understand and appreciate deeply the issues that this has caused for the reputation of Chinese manufacturers.'

Technically, Mattel's analysis is correct. Of the 19.6 million toys that it has recalled this year globally, 2.2 million were due to lead paint; the remaining 17.4 million (11.7 million in the USA) were toys recalled not because of lead paint but because they were made with super-strong magnets. If they come loose and are swallowed in multiples, those magnets can come together with force enough to tear through the intestines of a young child. (Mattel's announcement noted three such serious injuries that required surgery.) The magnet recall was unusually large because it includes toys sold as far back as 2002, before Mattel changed its design to encase the magnets in plastic to make them more secure.

Perhaps it was convenient for Mattel to issue the magnet recall at the same time as its much smaller lead-paint recalls. Or perhaps the company was using an abundance of caution in recalling any toy that might pose a potential hazard. Either way, lead paint in toys from China is not an issue Mattel can correct overnight. That isn't a happy situation for anyone, from families in the USA to workers in Chinese factories who face a daily risk of lead poisoning. It will take much more than yet another apology from Mattel to fix that.

Source: *Time*, Friday, 21st September 2007

The case of Mattel may serve as an illustration. In September 2007, this company had to recall products from its markets three times. In total, 21 million toys needed to be taken back from the market, leading to major financial losses for the company. There is little doubt that Mattel, like many Western manufacturers, has become much more critical with respect to the way in which purchases are made. Today, all Far Eastern suppliers are thoroughly screened on sustainability issues and labour conditions, and production orders are monitored and supervised accurately by quality inspectors on site.

This chapter deals with the subject of how procurement managers can contribute to corporate social responsibility. Corporate social responsibility is about how to contribute to a better world, a better environment and better labour conditions. Socially responsible purchasing needs to be based on the general business principles that are used to guide the whole company. Responsible procurement cannot be looked upon in isolation. For this reason we start this chapter with a discussion of this subject. We will also discuss the importance of purchasing ethics in supplier relationships.

BUSINESS PRINCIPLES AND PROCUREMENT

Imagine the following situation. You are a project buyer employed by Shell in Brunei, and assigned with the important task of buying the materials and equipment for one of Shell's many exploration projects conducted in the Indonesian archipelago. For the drilling work, the company needs many miles of steel piping, that need to be imported from the West. The project planning is critical. If a drilling project comes to a halt due to material shortages this will result in a financial loss of tens of thousands of dollars per day. Being a buyer, it is better to avoid these kind of tricky situations! Your supplier informs you that the piping that you ordered has been shipped to the port of destination. However, they still need to pass through the port's customs. Customs is busy. At your request to process the approval of your order quickly, the customs officials let you know that they suffer from a heavy workload. As a result of this, processing your cargo probably will take several weeks. Things may be speeded up if Shell is willing to pay the officer for the extra work involved . . .

What would you do in such a situation? Would you engage in a discussion with the customs and pay a little amount of money to make sure that the drilling work can be continued?

Shell is of the opinion that such a situation cannot be decided upon by individual buyers or local managers. The answer to this and similar situations is to be found in Shell's business principles that apply to every Shell employee worldwide. Shell shall never pay in this type of situation. Illegal customs practices will be prosecuted before court. As a consequence Shell will accept the loss that the company will incur as a result of the delay incurred at customs. Memo 17.1 provides an overview of the subjects that are discussed in the Shell business principles. Every Shell employee is supposed to be familiar with these principles. These principles provide the context and foundation for every manager to guide their daily decision-making.

MEMO 17.1   SHELL GENERAL BUSINESS PRINCIPLES

The Shell business principles include the following:

- Our values
- Sustainable development and
- Responsibilities
  - to shareholders
  - to customers
  - to employees
  - to whom we do business with
  - to society.
- Principle 1: Economic
- Principle 2: Competition

- Principle 3: Business integrity
- Principle 4: Political activities
- Principle 5: Health, safety, security and the environment
- Principle 6: Local communities
- Principle 7: Communication and engagement
- Principle 8: Compliance
- Living by our principles.

Source: www.shell.com

As the principles show, each Shell employee should respect under every circumstance local and international laws including humanitarian laws. The company does not allow competition to be limited in whatever form whatsoever. Honesty, integrity and transparency are keystones in the way the company is managed. Accepting or providing bribes is considered illegal. The company will not provide financial support to local political parties, neither will it interfere in local political activity. This does not exclude, however, financial support that Shell may provide to local municipalities in order to improve living conditions for its local workers.

Other large companies have similar regulations and arrangements. One reason for these regulations can be explained by the increasing globalization of business. As a consequence international companies get into contact with more and different cultures. Another important reason is the fact that if a company wants to impose higher demands on is external business partners it should, of course, be able to meet these requirements itself. 'Improve the world, but start with yourself' is the motto for corporate social responsibility. Business integrity is, as we will see later, an important part of this.

TOWARDS A SUSTAINABLE ENVIRONMENT: 'PEOPLE, PLANET, PROFIT'

Corporate social responsibility today is a prime topic on the agenda of many top managers. In 2007 the Dutch minister of Healthcare and Environmental Policy announced that all purchases made by the government from 2010 need to meet sustainable and environmental requirements. The intention is clear, but a major question is how to define sustainable purchasing. What does the government actually mean when they refer to corporate social responsibility and responsible purchasing?

Sustainability seems to be used as a general, container concept. It clearly has different aspects. Most of the time it is referred to as corporate social responsibility (CSR). Sometimes it is referred to as sustainability. The idea is to develop business solutions in such a way that requirements of the current world population are met without doing harm to the needs of future generations. This is a far from simple issue. Sustainable development is aimed at developing a better world. Sustainable purchasing, therefore, is about buying for a better future world. These concepts today are widely adopted by the Western world. As a consequence, companies just going for their economic benefits only are not accepted by the general public any more. The traditional *shareholder* focus had made way for a *stakeholder* focus which has a much wider scope. Sustainable profitability can only be achieved if the company is able to balance the interests of customers, employees, the environment, and its shareholders, i.e. serving the needs of 'People, Planet, Profit'. This idea was expressed by Carroll (1991) in his famous sustainability pyramid (see Figure 17.1)

For this reason large companies pay a lot of attention to sustainability. A company like DSM, for example, articulated some years ago as a major objective developing a top position in chemical industry on the issue of sustainability. This can be understood, if one considers the environmental damage that is usually caused by this type of company. As these chemical companies have now become very visible to the general public, they need to pay attention to environmental concerns. In their corporate social responsibility policies they pay interest to three major stakeholders: 'People, Planet, Profit'.

The 'People' aspect includes all activities that are focused on providing good labour conditions to employees and a labour climate in which individual employees are able to develop their skills and competencies. This explains the great interest today for safety, health, and environment (SHE) within companies and suppliers. The 'Planet' aspect includes all activities that are focused on an efficient use of natural sources of energy, raw materials and of other natural resources. Waste disposal, reuse of scrap and surplus materials, and reverse logistics are part of the 'Planet' aspect. The 'Profit' aspect provides guidelines for sustainable financial

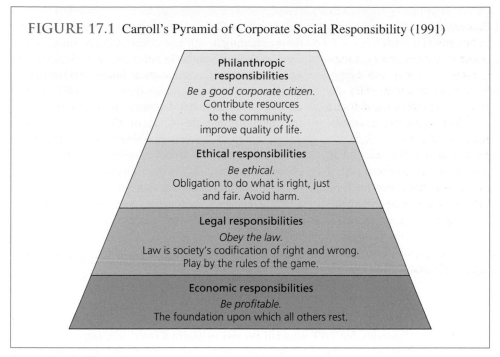

FIGURE 17.1   Carroll's Pyramid of Corporate Social Responsibility (1991)

Source: Carroll, 1991

development of a company, measured over a longer period of time. When improving profitability, the idea is that the company keeps a good eye on the interests of all stakeholders concerned, like customers, shareholders, employees and suppliers. For a bank like Treodos Bank, this may imply that investments are only made in companies that offer sustainable solutions to the environment. Investing in heavy polluting industries, or companies that manufacture weapons for the defence industry may not be in line with the bank's sustainability principles.

The basic idea is that business decisions are continuously tested against these three principles. Another company which has paid attention to sustainability is TNT Post (see memo 17.2). In 2006 this company started to operate two new Boeing 747 airplanes, to allow for a weekly transport schedule between the Far East and Europe. As a result of this decision, the fuel consumption of the company almost doubled! How do you explain this to your stakeholders? How do you communicate this message to your employees? Peter Bakker, the CEO of TNT, is of the opinion that there is only one option: you need to demonstrate that TNT acts responsibly in its operations by showing that the company pursues the best possible efficiency in its business operations with regard to the use of fossil fuels and energy. As the memo shows, TNT actively takes responsibility for managing its supply chain and imposing sustainability requirements on its suppliers and other business partners.

MEMO 17.2   TNT: MANAGING RESPONSIBILITY

We participate actively in initiatives such as the Logistics and Transport Sustainability Group of the World Economic Forum (WEF) and base our report on the G3 and the GRI sector supplement to improve transparency in performance. In addition to initiatives related specifically to social responsibility (SR), we are also involved actively in initiatives such as the European Express Association (EEA), the Global Express Association (GEA), CAPEC and the International Postal Corporation . . .

Guidance is given by the TNT Business Principles, which deal with topics such as compliance with the law, accurate and timely disclosure, transparency, equal opportunities, fair treatment, conflicts of interests, corruption, fair competition and social responsibility. The TNT Business Principles are aligned with the UN Global Compact and with the Partnering Against Corruption Initiative principles . . .

At TNT, we acknowledge the significant ecological and social impact that we have in our supply chain and on our suppliers' local communities. As such, we are committed to raising our social and ecological standards as well as those of our suppliers and subcontractors.

TNT has a large number of suppliers located all around the world. In 2007 we focused on that part of the supply chain in which we purchase goods for TNT. Within TNT, local entities are responsible for procuring the goods and services needed for their business.

Due to this diversity, we are developing a company-wide Code of Conduct for suppliers and contractors based on the TNT Business Principles and our SR

policies. This Code of Conduct defines our expectations regarding health and safety of the products and services, labour standards, adherence to national law and human rights, prohibition of bribery and traceability of all business transactions with TNT. The divisional procurement departments are responsible for implementing the Code of Conduct in close co-operation with the divisional SR directors and operational managers which indicates further integration of social responsibility in our functional areas.

We have developed a supplier risk assessment aimed at managing the social responsibility risks in our supply chain and will assess our suppliers in 2008.

Source: TNT Social Responsibility Report, 2007 (edited by the author)

The memo illustrates that TNT wants to comply to external standards. Important indicators for sustainability are the Dow Jones Sustainability Index and the Global Reporting Initiative. In their reporting, these institution use a wide range of indicators. The list of indicators is just as impressive. The manner in which the company is managed, i.e. its corporate governance, risk and crisis management, ethical codes that are present within the organization, the way in which the company tries to improve eco-efficiency and reduce without proper care and carbon footprint (CO_2), fuel efficiency, labour conditions and social reporting, are just a few of these indicators.

The relationship with suppliers is an important issue. This seems logical when one realizes that companies today employ more people outside their company than inside their company. This is why we pay attention to what companies must do to improve sustainability in their supply chains.

SUSTAINABLE PURCHASING: TOWARDS SUSTAINABLE SUPPLY CHAINS

As we have seen earlier, suppliers are an important source for competitive advantage to companies. However, as the example of Mattel at the beginning of this chapter showed, suppliers can also be an important source of unforeseen problems. The company's reputation can be severely damaged if suppliers are selected without proper precaution. How do you put principles in place with regard to people, planet and profit? How do you convince suppliers to promote sustainability principles in the operational processes? Companies, that have an answer to these questions are still rare. Some companies are leading the way. In answering these questions we follow the purchasing practices of Philips Electronics.

In 2002 Philips started with a worldwide sustainability programme for its global procurement organization. For this purpose in 2003 a standard was developed with regards to the requirements that suppliers should meet in the area of sustainability. The standard was implemented in 2004. This is no small thing, if one realizes that more than 50 000 suppliers worldwide were involved in this programme. All suppliers were invited to participate in the programme through a formal letter sent by Philips' Chair of the Executive Board. The letter encouraged suppliers to conduct a 'self assessment' (see Figure 17.2) and to report the

FIGURE 17.2 Self assessment supplier sustainability

		Answer options yes/no/ NA	Score on Performance/ Implementation 1: Failures do exist; Implementation: beginner stage/just started 2: Failures potentially exist; Implementation: work in progress, >50% completed
9.1 GENERAL			
9.1.1	Has the top management of your company laid down and signed-off policies covering at least Environment, Health and Safety, Child Labour, Forced Labour, Discrimination, Compensation and Work Hours and which are in compliance with all applicable local laws and regulations?		
9.1.2	Does your company make sure that these policies are communicated to and understood by every employee?		
9.1.3	Does your company make sure in a structural way that these rules are known and respected by its own supply base and subcontractors?		
9.2 ENVIRONMENT			
	Does your company have an environmental strategy/policy in place?		
9.2.1	Is your company ISO 14001 certified?		
	If no, does your company have an Environmental Management System equivalent to ISO 14001?		
9.2.2	Does your company hold and comply with all necessary environmental licences?		
9.2.3	Does your company produce an annual environmental report and is a copy provided to their customers?		
	Does your company currently do business with a Philips Product Division?		
	If yes, does your company fully comply with the environmental banned and relevant substance lists appropriate to the Philips Product Division you supply?		
	Does your company consider reduction of environmental impact during the product creation process?		
9.2.4	Does your company request evidence from your subcontractors of conduct relevant testing on all relevant incoming material (e.g. dyes, plasticizer, solder, packaging, . . .) to assure compliance with environmental requirements?		

FIGURE 17.2 (*Continued*)

		Answer options yes/no/ NA	Score on Performance/ Implementation 1: Failures do exist; Implementation: beginner stage/just started 2: Failures potentially exist; Implementation: work in progress, >50% completed
9.2.5	If banned substances are detected, are all affected articles taken back from the customers including the relevant supply chain? Are they disposed of properly according to (local) regulations (with evidence/report)?		
9.2.6	Does your company and sub-suppliers have a system in place to monitor the traceability of incoming substances and materials throughout the whole supply chain and the manufacturing processes?		
9.3 HEALTH AND SAFETY			
9.3.1.	Is there a written safety and health policy available signed-off by Top Management and communicated, in which is laid down how to protect the health and safety of the employees and contract labour and minimize any adverse effect on the environment?		
9.3.2	Does your company provide appropriate training to ensure that employees and managers are aware of their own responsibility for the health and safety of themselves and others and that they have adequate competence on occupational health, safety and environmental matters?		
9.3.3	Are working stations, hygiene-relevant places, housing facilities and any place subject to employee presence, in a maintenance condition that makes them free from any risk to personal health and safety, from contamination risk, electrical hazard, and provide adequate level of cleanliness, air circulation and filtering, lighting and temperature?		
9.3.4	Is a fire prevention system in place that is compliant with local applicable regulations and company insurance clauses. Does the system cover the whole company and its annexes, tested and is in perfect working conditions?		
9.4 CHILD LABOUR			
9.4.1	Are written policies and procedures in place to prevent the use of child labour and to implement programmes and procedures to the transition of any child found to be performing child labour?		

9.4.2	Does the youngest age of workers comply with legal requirements and according to convention 138 of the International Labour Organisation?		
9.4.3	Is your company prepared to take immediate remedial action by taking into account ILO 138 and with a clear time-phased corrective action?		
9.5 FORCED LABOUR			
9.5.1	Are written policies and procedures in place to prevent forced and compulsory labour and are these in compliance when applicable?		
9.5.2	Is a system in place that totally and effectively bans any use of any physical force or verbal aggression towards workers?		
9.5.3	Is voluntary presence of employees fully respected and not forced in any way and at any moment against their own will?		
9.6 COLLECTIVE BARGAINING AND RIGHT TO ORGANIZE			
9.6.1	Does your company respect the right of all personnel to form and join trade unions of their choice?		
9.6.2	Does your company acknowledge unions in discussions of labour conditions?		
9.6.3	Does your company, in those situations in which the right to freedom of association and collective bargaining are restricted under law, facilitate the development of parallel means of independent and free association and bargaining for all personnel?		
9.7 DISCRIMINATION			
9.7.1	Are written policies and procedures in place to ensure equal opportunities or eliminate/avoid discrimination (e.g. gender, race, religion, ethnic minority, sexual orientation or disability)?		
9.7.2	Does your company make sure that each employee receives and understands all applicable rules with respect to non-discrimination (e.g. race, colour, sex, age, language, religion, political or other opinion, national or social origin, property, birth or other status)?		

Source: www.philips.com

outcome of this self-assessment to Philips. Next, Philips would conduct a similar audit by its own internal experts. For this programme all of Philips' more than 400 associates were trained and educated. Next, the results of the Philips' audit were compared with the results from the supplier self assessments.

Variances between both audits were discussed and suppliers were invited to come up with an action plan to take corrective measures, which were periodically followed up by Philips' procurement organization. In its audits Philips focuses on sustainability and the way in which suppliers deal with issues like environmental protection, labour conditions, safety, child labour, discrimination and diversity, the number of labour hours and the compliance with local labour laws. Apart from this the auditors focus on the presence of banned substances. Also attention is paid to the suppliers relationships with unions. Apparently, asking suppliers to sign a declaration in which they declare to comply with Philips environmental policies, like in the past, was not enough any more. Many suppliers were, with the eye on future business, very much willing to put their signature without hesitation. For Philips' Executive Board this was no longer sufficient. The company wanted to secure that suppliers were meeting its CSR-requirements. Suppliers that did not meet these requirements were dropped from Philips suppliers list. As a result, the number of suppliers worldwide was reduced from 50 000 to about 30 000, most of them are now in line with Philips environmental policies.

Is the approach sufficient for the future? The answer, clearly, is 'no'. Phillips at this moment has aligned its first-tier suppliers with its environmental policies. What is now important, is that these suppliers transfer the Philips' policies to their (second-tier) suppliers and raw materials producers. In this area the company still has a long way to go. It is still a long way from integrated, sustainable supply chains. The efforts to improve sustainability in suppliers relationships will be a challenge for a long time for Philips' purchasing professionals.

TRUST, BUSINESS INTEGRITY AND ETHICS

During the past decade there have been many debates over the issue of integrity and trust in business-to-business relationships. As companies become more dependent on each other, trust becomes more important. Some academics have advocated that future competition will not be among individual companies anymore, rather competition will occur between integrated supply chains. Supply chain integration, however, will require a long-term orientation towards the relationship, a willingness to mutually share information and active collaboration among the parties involved. As research evidence has shown partnership in business-to-business relationships is still poorly developed. In a research project that was conducted in the 1990s by the Center of Advanced Purchasing Studies (CAPS) in the USA, it was found that real partnerships among the over 300 companies that were investigated were less than 1% of the total number of supplier relationships. We therefore conclude that trust is a topic that usually meets a lot of interest, both in academia as among business practitioners; however, apparently it is extremely difficult in practice to build trustful relationships. Of course, the question is: why is this the case? And why this interest for trust in business-to-business relationships?

The answer may come from insights that were developed originally at Motorola some years ago. Motorola considers trust basically to be the result of two factors: trustworthiness, i.e. the situation in which trust is granted to you by other parties, and competence. Obviously, trust cannot be asked for by a person or requested; it is the other party who decides whether it is willing to grant trust to you or not. In order to make the other party willing to do so, companies need to work both on competence and trustworthiness (see Figure 17.3). Building competence is about developing people's skills, experience and creativity. Companies that have skilled staff available, who have great expertise in what they do, generate more confidence and trust in their clients than companies that do not have competent staff. Having a skilled labour force is a necessary but not a sufficient condition for building trust in business-to-business relationships as is shown. In order to be able to generate trustworthiness companies also need to have strict ethical principles and procedures. Trust can only be generated if company staff act in a consistent and reliable manner. Sales staff should be able to live up to their word; if sales staff are replaced, customers should be able to trust that agreements made are met by the new person. The same is true for changes at the management level. These observations apply for the organization of both the seller and the buyer. Trustworthiness, as

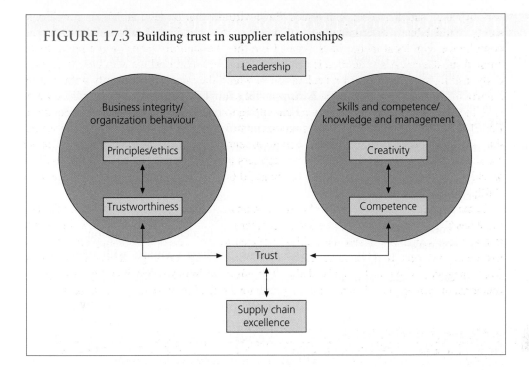

FIGURE 17.3 Building trust in supplier relationships

we see it, primarily stems from ethical and consistent organizational behaviour. Traditionally, most companies have made great efforts and continue to do so in improving the skills and competences of their labour force. This may be one explanation why topics such as 'competence management' and 'knowledge management' have generated so much interest over the past decade. However, only very few companies have explicit policies and corporate programmes on 'business integrity and ethics'. The fact that a few large multinational companies have got into large financial problems due to unethical behaviour is changing this picture dramatically, as we have seen in this chapter.

It is in the interest of the company that purchasing negotiations achieve the best possible results by using means and tactics that are proper and responsible in terms of ethics. A buyer is exposed to many temptations. These vary from Christmas presents sent by the supplier to their home address at the end of the year, to vacations, which are offered disguised as a business trip to an overseas conference. In the international sales arena lots of activities are undertaken to put the customer in the most positive frame of mind about a possible purchase. The question of course is what can and what cannot be accepted from the supplier. In business, this question is not easily answered. Questions can also be raised on the side of the buyer as to how far one should go in a relationship with a supplier. In this context the following questions may occur:

- How should confidential supplier (price) information be handled?
- How to deal with quotations: should we only use quotations if we are seriously considering requesting a firm bid from a supplier, or do we only use them to check our current supplier's prices?
- What is the maximum share we as customers want to have in the supplier's turnover, in order to prevent excessive dependency on us?
- Do we always strive to have at least two suppliers (dual sourcing) or are single sources allowed in particular circumstances?
- How far do we go in negotiations with suppliers? Are we willing to buy at prices we know for a fact aren't sufficient to cover the supplier's cost price?

MEMO 17.3   NEVI'S[1] PROFESSIONAL CODE OF CONDUCT

The basic rules set out below are vital for a responsible performance of purchase activities. In certain cases, they are inextricably linked. Each individual assumption is worked out in separate policies against which purchasing professionals can test their own actions.

1. Loyalty to the company

When undertaking purchase activities, purchasers must follow the interests of the company (rather than their personal interests or feelings). Serving the interests of the company means serving the interests of all customers who buy products and services from the company.

1.1 The purchaser must, of his own accord, report to his supervisor any personal interests that may conflict with business interests.

1.2 The purchaser may not request or accept money, loans or credits from existing or potential suppliers. He must refuse to accept gifts, business entertainment, favours or courtesies and always avoid even the appearance of impressionability.

1.3 All resources and information available to the purchaser in the context of his employment relationship with the company must be used exclusively in the interests of the company.

1.4 The purchaser may only be involved in accepting or stipulating price discounts in relation to goods and services provided by suppliers for the personal and private benefit of employees if the company consents.

2. Proper dealing with suppliers

The purchaser must maintain good relations with suppliers and take the interests of the supplier into account.

2.1 The purchaser must provide suppliers with accurate information that cannot be construed in any way as misleading.

2.2 The purchaser may not pressurize suppliers into disclosing information on competitors.

2.3 The purchaser must make the supplier aware of the potential consequences if a situation arises where the supplier's turnover depends excessively on orders placed by the purchasing company.

3. Supporting fair competition

The suppliers concerned must be offered an equal opportunity to compete for orders.

3.1 Any information on prices, products and processes, obtained from suppliers in the performance of purchase duties, must be treated confidentially.

3.2 The purchaser must provide all potential suppliers with identical information.

3.3 Pairing purchase contracts with sales contracts (reciprocity) must be avoided if it restricts competition.

3.4 Suppliers must be selected primarily on the grounds of objective criteria, not on the basis of personal preference.

4. Upholding the profession's reputation

Maintaining the image of reliability is essential for a proper performance of duties by the purchaser.

4.1 The purchaser must always strive to achieve the optimum level of professional skills.

4.2 Agreements and understandings must be duly observed.

4.3 The purchaser must contribute, where possible, to promoting the quality and reputation of the professional purchasing community.

Conduct of suppliers The conduct of suppliers also has an impact on the reputation of purchasers, the purchasing company and the purchasing profession. Due to this influence on the purchaser's reputation and social responsibilities, suppliers must also be judged by their actions. For instance, if a supplier employs children in his production process or pollutes the environment to cut production costs, the purchasing company will have to assume its own share of the responsibility. The purchaser must, therefore, guard against practices which are considered unacceptable to the company and the purchasing profession.

[1]NEVI is the Dutch Association of Purchasing Management

Source: www.nevi.nl (edited by author)

To increase uniformity in behaviour towards the business community, a number of large companies have become explicit on their policies with regard to 'business integrity' explaining their company's business values and regulations on matters such as conflict of interest. As a part of these policies they have urged their purchasing managers to draw up and subscribe to several rules of conduct for their dealings with suppliers. Rules of conduct have also been drawn up by the International Federation of Purchasing and Materials Management (see Memo 17.3), which may serve as a guidance to purchasing managers that want to set up specific policies on this topic for their company.

SUMMARY

Corporate social responsibility (CSR) clearly has increased in importance during the past years. It now resides as a high priority item on the management agenda of today's international corporations. One reason for this is the fact that raw materials have become scarcer. Another reason is global warming. These environmental changes necessitate companies to use natural resources in a more prudent way. A third reason may be the fact that business today is global and global business, due to the international media, has become more transparent. An environmental or social scandal may quickly ruin a company reputation that took years to develop. As a result large companies feel the need to deal with social and environmental issues in a uniform way. Since suppliers are an important part of the company's value chain today, supplier relationships have become an important focus area of sustainability programmes.

The basic idea behind CSR is to meet the needs of current generations without sacrificing the resource needs to meet the requirements of future generations. The case of Mattel at the beginning of the chapter shows what may happen if a company is not careful in selecting its first tier and second-tier suppliers. Because of the lead-containing paint used by one of its subcontractors, Mattel needed to recall millions of products from its end-user markets and had to pay millions to do this. Even worse, its company reputation was badly damaged. This situation could have been prevented, if Mattel had had an explicit policy with regard to 'People, Planet, Profit', the three pillars of CSR. Sustainable development focuses on creating economic growth while respecting local laws, environmental regulations and labour conditions. Just having a policy on these matters is not sufficient. Operational processes of suppliers need to be controlled and monitored for compliance. For this reason procurement managers of large companies, including Philips electronics, conduct sustainability audits of their suppliers. Suppliers first are invited to conduct a self-assessment, the outcomes of which are later compared with the audits conducted by Philips' auditors. Large manufacturers require that the first tier suppliers will transfer their environmental policies to their second tier suppliers. In this way, large manufacturers intend to reach sustainable supply chains in the end.

As companies become more dependent on their suppliers, supply chain integration becomes more of a challenge to them. Supply chain integration can only be built upon constructive, long-term supplier relationships. To be able to do so requires a fair degree of trust among the parties involved. Developing trust in business-to-business relationships requires competent and experienced staff. Next it requires consistency and reliability in the way the company staff and managers operate and behave towards external partners and the way in which commitments that have been agreed upon are met. This explains why issues such as 'business integrity' and 'purchasing ethics' have met great interest over the past years. We hypothesize that this topic will even gain more relevance in the near future. For purchasing professionals this will imply that they need to work according to the highest professional and ethical standards, that have been laid down in explicit procedures and guidelines. The ethical code of the International Federation of Purchasing and Materials Management can serve as a guideline here.

ASSIGNMENTS

17.1 What are the reasons underlying corporate social responsibility programmes of companies these days? What do companies mean by responsible purchasing?

17.2 What would you consider to be the most important elements of a socially responsible purchasing programme?

17.3 What is the value of a statement made by a supplier that its organization is sustainable?

17.4 Under what circumstances would you feel that the following is allowed in purchasing: (1) accepting gifts from a supplier, (2) accepting invitations for a dinner, (3) engaging in a personal friendship with a supplier sales representative, (4) extending the deadline for a competitive bid to one of your suppliers and (5) giving the 'right of first refusal' to your current supplier?

17.5 Would you feel that integrity codes as used by some companies have the same relevance for procurement managers as for sales managers? Discuss.

REFERENCE

Carroll, A.B. (1991) 'The pyramid of corporate social responsibility: toward the moral management of organizational stakeholders', *Business Horizons* 34(4):39–48.

INTEGRATIVE CASE 17.1

SERVING THE CUSTOMER AT JOYCIES PRODUCTS LTD: TOWARDS INTEGRATED SUPPLY CHAIN MANAGEMENT

BY ARJAN VAN WEELE

Introduction

The management of Joycies Products Limited (hereafter referred to as Joycies) faces some difficult problems. Being a successful marketer and producer of deli-food products, the firm is confronted with rapidly changing and ever increasing demands from its customers. Of course every manager at Joycies had witnessed the concentration tendencies going on in the retail sector with some concern. Now that the dust has settled after the merger of two large customers, the combined firm (Big Food Store; BFS) confronted them with seemingly impossible demands. In order to safeguard future business the account team recently was told, Joycies should meet the following demands: 8-hour delivery of products ordered to BFS' warehouses throughout the country enabling cross-docking and direct supply. Moreover Joycies should take back all packaging materials. Finally, the food giant requested a quality guarantee implying that Joycies would officially be kept responsible for all claims and cost related to bad quality and health

This case describes the problems of a medium sized food company that needs to meet the increasing demands of a large retailer. In order to meet the stringent delivery requirements of retail the company needs to revise its traditional commercial activities, its production and logistics activities and its purchasing activities and supplier relationships.

problems related to their products from BFS' consumers. It wanted that all artificial ingredients were replaced by natural products within a year in order to meet BFS' 'Top Fit' branded product range.

Sharon Fitzgerald, Commercial Director at Joycies, reported her findings to the management team. She peered out of the window and sighed: 'This really was a cold shower, we have got over there. This new Supply Chain Manager really is stirring up things. I am afraid this will not go over, however. On the contrary, this example will be followed by a score of other customers, who carefully watch Big Food Store's steps. Being in this business for over 20 years now, I never have seen such outrageous targets. And I do not know how we are going to meet these.'

The other persons in the executive room remained silent: everyone was aware of the average lead time of 3 days, which Joycies barely could meet, and the many logistics problems, that were reported. It was clear that the problem could not be solved just by working harder or by putting pressure on the production organization or logistics department. George Lim, general manager, pondered about the situation. 'OK, this will not be a simple issue. Let us think about it for a while and discuss it during our next management meeting.' What should be done?

Joycies' history

Joycies is a successful marketer and manufacturer of bakery and food products. It was started in 1962 by a creative baker, William Sutch, at Springfield, Illinois, USA, whose speciality was the manufacture of traditional, but very tasty cookies and bakeries. In 1966 the company was so reputed that people would come all the way from Chicago to Springfield just to buy these cookies. Given the wide acceptance of his products Sutch started to open up new bakery outlets. In 1969 he managed 20 shops where the homemade products were shipped twice a day. Of course, at that time the bakery's manufacturing facilities were expanded for the third time. Given his ever-increasing workload, the management of the shops, including the hiring of sales personnel was delegated to his wife (Joyce), to whom he renamed the company (Joycies Food Products). Being a true craftsman, Sutch concentrated on the development of new products and varieties and he experimented with new ingredients. This added to the range of products, which after some careful

consideration he decided to sell as well through other bakery stores and retail outlets.

Through his personal zeal and zest and feel for quality, his love for his work and thanks to his wonderful wife, he was able to build a company, which in 1980 had more than 400 employees.

At that time he decided to separate the sales organization and the manufacturing site (the latter was moved out of central Springfield in 1975 when local residents consistently complained about the constant smell of baked products in the air and the noise of the ever stronger ventilators and other equipment). Both activities were brought into a separate limited unit; both companies reported to a holding.

Friendly takeover by Silo's Consumer Products

Sutch was getting older, and so was his wife. Since they did not have children a successor was not easy to find. In 1999 he was contacted by Silo's Consumer Products (SCP), who wanted to expand its foothold in Illinois and who was looking for a healthy takeover target. The deal was closed and Joyce stayed on board for three consecutive years in order to help the new owner to learn how to manage this type of business. New management came in and steered the company into another growth scenario. Since it decided to focus on the development, marketing, distribution and manufacturing of top quality bakery products, it decided to sell all shops to a retail chain who was primarily interested in the A-one locations on which the Joycies bakery shops were located. No shop survived as a speciality bakery outlet.

The cash flow generated by this decision was invested in new production equipment and new product lines. In 2000 the company manufactured not only a broad range of cookies and chocolate products, it also developed a successful range of snacks and diet products. These products were manufactured on two major product lines. Most of the equipment was specialized to manufacture large runs. This enabled Joycies in the past to produce a limited number of end products efficiently. Since 2000, however, when a new marketing manager was appointed, product variety has increased considerably. Not only two new product lines (diet products and snacks) were introduced on the market; also the variety in Joycies traditional product range (cookies and chocolate products) increased considerably.

Moreover, batch sizes tended to decrease, which led to increasing pressure on the manufacturing department, where more and more time was spent on cleaning machines and setting them up for the production of the next batch of new products.

Serving the market: facing concentration in the retail market

In 2000 Joycies had over 550 employees; 350 were employed in manufacturing. The rest were employed in research and development, marketing, distribution (Joycies worked together with a provider of specialist logistics services, Food Logistics Specialists, who operated a warehouse at the other side of the street where the manufacturing plant was located, planning, administration and other staff activities.

The company was structured in a straightforward, though rather hierarchical way (see appendix). Insiders would say that marketing was dominant in the company; through its creative though aggressive marketing campaigns Joycies holds a strong brand image in at least three of the four product ranges. Marketing campaigns could not be copied easily, although some competitors tried sometimes. Products were mainly sold to large retailer organizations and franchised bakery shops: 60% of the sales turnover was realized in the USA, the rest was made primarily in Canada and nascent export sales to the UK and other parts of Western Europe. Apart from marketing Joycies had a strong sales organization, where account managers (since 2000) dealt with large customer accounts. On a regular basis they discussed advertising campaigns, promotional actions (often tailored per retail chain), sales premiums and promotional support. Tailored actions were required in order to maintain or even expand shelf space.

Since 2000 new information systems were adopted by most retail chains, enabling them to trace and track products from suppliers and manufacturers, through the warehouses/distribution centres to the retail stores. Through these detailed systems retail buyers were able to compare their suppliers on direct product cost (DPC) and direct product profit (DPP) per product per square metre. As a result buyers shifted their focus from price and (gross) margin to total cost and net revenue. Detailed records were kept of supplier performance: some retailers sent their records on a monthly basis to their manufacturers now, indicating transport efficiency, delivery reliability, quality problems, packaging problems, administrative efficiency, etc.

Sharon Fitzgerald, acting as account manager for BFS since 2000, was often surprised about what customers knew about her organization. BFS required Joycies to link into its logistics planning systems in 2004, when it was agreed that Joycies would be responsible for the materials planning, scheduling and distribution. Based on min-max inventories Joycies would check these every day and replenish each warehouse two or three times a week, based on the actual volume needed. This situation lasted until 2004 when BSF, during its '2005 Supplier Conference', explained that it wanted to reduce inventories considerably, suppliers needed to support this initiative and they were 'invited' to deliver in 8 hours throughout the country. If storage was necessary, BFS would provide space, but would charge this back to the manufacturer. It was also said on that occasion that BFS was studying the possibilities for direct supply by its suppliers . . .

Logistics management and physical distribution at Joycies

Early 2000 Joycies set up an advanced logistics planning department. Its major tasks were to monitor volume usage at the distribution centres of the so-called key accounts (through EDI computer linkages), to check incoming orders from small accounts, to translate the product volume into a detailed production planning, to plan for production capacity, calculate the gross materials requirements and to match these with the current inventories of raw materials and packaging, after which materials requisitions were sent out to the purchasing department. The purchasing department would then place the orders for materials to their suppliers. Given the bulk character of most materials and components, orders were placed once or twice a month; products were, however, delivered daily or several times a week by most suppliers. For storage of raw materials Joycies had large tanks and silos available which served as a buffer stock.

Incoming orders from different customers were grouped until an economic lot-size was reached for production. Then a production order and a corresponding production plan were made. The company now worked with two major product lines (one for cookies and chocolate products and one for diet products and low-fat snacks).

The rapidly growing product variety during the early 1990s made line planning and materials planning a difficult issue. Although the company tried several planning systems, it could not maintain the production yield it had experienced during the previous years. Changing production equipment and setting them up for another new batch happened almost daily. Production worked with three shifts; introduction of a four-shift system was considered now, in order to meet the ever changing and growing customer demand.

After production, products would be packed and directly moved to the warehouse of Farmers Logistics Specialist (FLS) at the other side of the street. Joycies planning department then would issue a transport and routing schedule to FLS, providing information on where to and when to ship the products.

Early 2005 it was clear that this structure was not working effectively. Logistics planning and production could often not meet the min-max arrangements made for the key accounts, leading to discussion with the respective account managers who increasingly lost confidence in the manufacturing organisation. The increasing number of orders from small accounts often could not be made within the promised lead times. Although it was logistics' basic principle to 'freeze' the production schedule for the coming three days, changes in mix and volume had become quite normal. This of course had a detrimental effect on production and logistics efficiency. It happened more than once that half full FLS-trucks were sent out, just in order to make sure that the customer got its products in time. In many of those cases customers would complain that they had only received a partial delivery . . .

Purchasing and supplier relationships

Purchasing reported to the production manager. It was responsible for supplier selection, conducting negotiations on annual agreements and other contracts, placing and monitoring orders and troubleshooting. Raw materials, components, pre-mixes and other ingredients as well as packaging were bought from over 300 suppliers, most of whom had been around for many years. Some of these suppliers were large conglomerates for whom Joycies only represented an 'interesting' customer. For other suppliers

(such as the pre mixes and some flavours) Joycies belonged to the top five customers.

Materials were delivered based on purchase orders; most voluminous items were called off on a daily basis in line with the production schedule. Most products were bought in a traditional way from known suppliers. Some ingredients could be supplier specific: in those cases Joycies would not have a detailed product description (just a listing of the major ingredients would do in order to satisfy local regulations on food safety and health). For most new end products no detailed specifications of ingredients were available. This often led to problems when incoming materials (based on a sample test by the laboratory) were rejected. More than once production had felt that materials could still be used when the laboratory and the quality department had ordered purchasing to send the materials back to the supplier.

Given the fact that production schedules were changing at a daily rate, the purchasing department had to change materials delivery schedules constantly. This meant cancelling orders one day, and chasing orders and placing rush orders the other day. In order to be able to get some stability in this process, it was decided 3-years ago to build extra storage capacity for buffer stock. This had eased the pressure somewhat. However, now there was that excessive demand of BSF to change to natural ingredients within 1 year. This beyond doubt would imply considerable work for purchasing, since new suppliers should be found for these ingredients, while at the same time agreements with existing suppliers needed to be ended.

Meeting the challenge of the future

Driving home, Kevin O'Driscoll thought about the situation. Meeting the challenges posed by BFS would be an enormous task and would probably not be done without some breakthrough decisions. He doubted whether the present, hierarchical and functional structure, on which Joycies success traditionally had been based, would be sufficient for the future. More teamwork within his organization would be required and probably also the reduction of the number of management layers. Marketing, planning, production, logistics and purchasing probably needed to operate in a much more integrated way. But how? He decided to focus his thoughts on the changes that would be required in marketing, logistics and purchasing first. Based on these outcomes he would consider the changes that would be required in organizational structure, systems and personnel skills.

He kicked the accelerator of his car. He wanted to get home early now. There was no time to lose!

Questions

1 What do you regard as the most important problems in this case? Make a distinction between problems related to the following topics: (1) marketing and sales, (2) production and logistics and (3) purchasing and supplier relationships.

2 Which measures for improvement would you want to put forward per topic?

3 Where would you position the customer order decoupling point? What supply chain configuration should you go for? Why?

As a presentation team you are asked to set out your findings in a punchy and well-designed PowerPoint presentation. You are also asked to summarize the results in the form of a concise paper (maximum 8–10 pages, not including appendices).

When making your proposals, make use of the theory described in chapters 11, 12 and 16 of this textbook. You should also add at least two articles (not more than 5-years-old) from scientific trade literature, with a link to the problem described in this case.

The other teams are asked to prepare a paper of 4–5 pages based on the problem definition. You must at least discuss the content of chapters 11, 12 and 16 of the textbook in your paper.

The way in which you link scientific insights to practical solutions is an important point of assessment for your paper and presentation.

It is possible that not all answers can be found in the textbook. In that case, you will have to rely on your own creativity. Or better still: you are expected to consult scientific literature with a link to the relevant subject. Include at least two recent articles from international scientific journals, not older than 5 years.

GLOSSARY

Acceptance test This is a technical test performed at either the supplier's site, the buyer's site or both, to check whether the equipment that is bought by the buyer meets their functional and technical requirements.

Auction, electronic (e-auction) Electronic auction (e-auction) is a tool used by the buyer to invite suppliers to bid simultaneously based on a predetermined purchasing specification using web technology.

Auction, forward An e-auction which is used by suppliers to enforce bidding among a number of prospective buyers based on a starting price that is increased during the auction.

Auction, reverse An e-auction which is used by buyers to enforce competitive bidding among a limited number of prequalified suppliers based on a starting price that is lowered during the auction.

Audit, process The process audit is a systematic investigation of the extent to which the (technical) processes are capable of meeting the established standards in a predictable way.

Audit, product The product audit provides an image of the degree to which a company succeeds in making everything run perfectly, i.e. according to the standards and requirements established by the company itself.

Bidders' long list Includes those suppliers that meet the buyer's prequalification criteria and that will be requested to submit a first proposal.

Bidders' short list Includes those suppliers that meet the buyer's prequalification criteria and who will be requested to submit a detailed bid.

Budget A budget serves as a vehicle for delegating activities and responsibilities to lower management levels in the organization.

Budget authority Allows a manager to spend money and resources of the company for company purposes.

Buying centre Relates to all those individuals and groups who participate in the purchasing decision-making process, who share some common goals and the risks arising from the decisions (identical to decision-making unit).

Buying processes Includes determining the purchasing needs, selecting the supplier, arriving at a proper price, specifying terms and conditions, issuing the contract or order, and following up to ensure proper delivery and payment.

Camp's formula Mathematical formula based upon inventory costs and ordering costs to decide about optimal economic order quantity (EOQ).

Cartel Price can be set by a market or price-leader, or arranged through some form of price arrangements (cartels).

Category A group of products which can be substituted for one another by a consumer; examples include cereals, bakery, household products, body care and so on.

Category tree Product classification based upon product or supply market characteristics. Basis for category sourcing strategies.

Category management Supports the first three initiatives of ECR discussed above. It can be defined as 'an interactive business process whereby retailers and manufacturers work together in mutual co-operation to manage categories as strategic business units within each store'.

Category prioritization matrix Matrix used to classify category cost-savings projects based upon two criteria, i.e. cost-savings potential and ease of implementation.

Category sourcing plan Identifies the sourcing strategy for a certain category.

Cost avoidance Cost avoidance is a variance between the historical and the actual purchase price paid per unit. A cost avoidance is not considered to be sustainable.

Cost reductions Purchasing cost reductions are sustainable in character. These may be the result from a change of the specification, a change of supplier, or omitting an unnecessary product quality requirement.

Corporate buyers Buyers operating at the corporate level with a global sourcing responsibilities for key commodities. It is their job to negotiate for large volumes of products and components (in the case of raw materials), large investment projects and services.

Corporate procurement officer (CPO) Senior executive, who is responsible for the management and co-ordination of key purchasing and supply processes throughout the corporate organization.

Cross-docking or flow-through distribution Is a direct flow of merchandise/product from receiving to shipping, thus eliminating additional handling and storage steps in the distribution cycle.

Continuous replenishment Is defined as the practice of partnering among distribution channel members that changes the traditional replenishment process from distributor-generated purchase order to one based on actual or forecast consumer demand.

Computer-aided ordering (CAO) 'Is a retail-based system that automatically generates orders for replenishment when the inventory level drops below a predetermined reorder level'.

Collaborative planning, forecasting and replenishment (CPFR) This concept allows co-operation across the supply chain, using a set of processes and technology models. Its goal is to provide dynamic information sharing that is integrating both 'demand' and 'supply' side processes (and thus linking manufacturers, retailers and carriers), and effectively planning, forecasting and replenishing customer needs through the total supply chain.

Competitive bidding Situation where a buyer asks for bids from different suppliers, creating a level playing field (identical to tender).

Components Components are manufactured goods which will not undergo additional physical changes, but which will be incorporated into a system with which there is a functional relationship by joining it with other components.

Contract, lump sum Contract is based upon a fixed price (per period) for executing the project or a certain activity.

Contract, reimbursable Contract in which the buyer agrees to pay the supplier all materials costs and employee hours against predetermined hourly rates and margins for services rendered (identical to time and materials contract).

Contract, time and materials Contract in which the buyer agrees to pay the supplier all materials costs and employee hours against predetermined hourly rates and margins for services rendered (identical to cost reimbursable contract).

Contract, unit rate Rates are agreed for regular, routine activities, the size of which cannot be anticipated. Rates are defined per square metre of paintwork, metre of cable to be installed, etc. Payments are made based upon the actual number of units produced during the completion of the work.

Core competences, approach The core competence approach is based on the assumption that, in order to create a sustainable competitive advantage, a company should concentrate its resources on a set of core competencies where it can achieve definable pre-eminence and provide a unique value for the customer. Therefore, it should outsource all other activities.

Corporate social responsibility How to contribute to a better world, a better environment and better labour conditions. The idea is to develop business solutions in such a way that requirements of the current world population are met without doing harm to the needs of future generations. Companies need to balance the interests of customers, employees, the environment and its shareholders, i.e. serving the needs of 'People, Planet, Profit'.

Cross-functional buying teams Specialists from user departments and buyers are put together in teams to develop specific sourcing and commodity strategies and plans.

Customer order decoupling point (CODP) The point in the supply chain where a production order becomes customer-specific. Downstream of this point activities are planned based upon customer order and further downstream activities are planned based on forecast.

'Customer of choice' For such a customer, suppliers are prepared to invest in the relationship resulting in a better product and service, allowing the customer company to make a difference in its end user and customer markets, irrespective of the business cycle.

Decision-making unit (DMU) Relates to all those individuals and groups who participate in the purchasing decision-making process, who share some common goals and the risks arising from the decisions (identical to buying centre).

Derived demand Most companies sell to other companies. Few manufacturing companies deliver directly to the end user. For this reason developments in industrial markets are often influenced by changes which occur in the end-user markets.

Direct materials All purchased materials and services that become part of the company's value proposition. These include raw materials, semi-manufactured goods or half fabricates, components and modules.

Direct product cost (DPC) DPC relates to all costs that can be allocated directly to the product (including the costs of materials handling, taking in return packaging, pricing, etc.)

Direct product profitability (DPP) Based upon sales price and direct product cost, the retail buyer determines the direct (net) profit margin per product (DPP).

Discounts, cash Is offered by the supplier if the buyer pays within a certain, prespecified period. This discount usually depends on the industry (e.g. 2% discount with 10 days payment).

Discount, geographical This discount is given to customers who are located close to the supplier's factory or distribution centre, making the transportation costs much lower than average. In this way, a local supplier can keep more distant suppliers away.

Discount, promotional This discount is provided to temporarily stimulate the sale of a product, or, if it concerns a new product, to lower the entry barrier (special offer discount).

Discount, quantity To stimulate larger quantity orders, many suppliers use quantity discounts in which the advantage for the buyer is that it can realize a lower price per unit.

Discount, seasonal This discount is applied to improve manufacturing capacity utilization in periods when sales are low. Buyers ordering out of season get a lower price.

DuPont analysis Financial diagnostic tool to calculate the company's return on investment based upon sales margin and capital turnover ratio. Used to assess the effect of a 2% purchasing saving on the company's return on investment (ROI).

'Dutch windmill' Combination of buyer's purchasing portfolio and supplier's customer portfolio, leading to 16 different business-to-business relationships, each of which call for a different sourcing strategy.

Early supplier involvement (ESI) Situation where the supplier is involved by the buyer in an early stage of the new product development process.

Electronic data interchange (EDI) Can be defined as an interorganizational exchange of business documentation in a structured, machine-processable form.

Efficient consumer response (ECR) Is a grocery industry supply chain management strategy aimed at eliminating inefficiencies, and excessive or non-value-added costs within the supply chain, thus delivering better value to grocery consumers.

Electronic catalogues and ordering systems Are used for more efficient order handling, improved logistics and improved and better-controlled payments. May be integrated with the company's ERP-system.

Electronic marketplace Is a marketplace on the Internet where, with the support of Internet technology, transactions between business-to-business partners can be made.

E-procurement solutions Relate to all web enabled solutions aimed at supporting the purchasing process and all electronic data exchange that is needed for efficient transaction processing. E-procurement solutions can be divided into three types, i.e. electronic marketplaces, electronic auctions (e-auctions) and electronic catalogues and order and payment solutions (order to pay solutions).

Enterprise resource planning (ERP) system Refers to a company-wide information system for managing the company's operational and support processes, its administrative processes, its human resources, its materials resources and financial resources.

Escalation clause Price is linked to a price adjustment formula (index), which is based on external factors such as material costs or changes in labour costs.

Expediting Following up on a purchase order to make sure that the supplier is going to perform as it has confirmed through the purchase order confirmation. There are three types of expediting, i.e. routine status check, advanced status check and field expediting.

External structure External structure consists of a number of links (companies, institutions) that are connected via markets.

External factors Are those which determine the degree of availability of a certain product and which cannot be influenced by individual companies.

Facilities Relate to all the physical conditions that enable an organization to conduct its primary activities.

Facilities management Relates to the management (planning, execution and control), and the realization of housing and accommodation, the services related to these, and other means in order to enable the organization to realize its mission.

Finished products These encompass all products which are purchased to be sold, after negligible added value, either together with other finished products or manufactured products (identical to trade items).

Framework agreement A framework agreement is an agreement between one or more contracting entities and one or more suppliers, the purpose of which is to establish the terms governing contracts to be awarded during a given period, in particular with regard to price and, where appropriate, the quantities envisaged.

Functional specification Describes the functionality which the product must have for the user.

Global sourcing (i) Products are increasingly sourced from foreign, low-cost countries. Global sourcing may come in different forms (low-cost country sourcing, regional sourcing and offshoring).

Global sourcing (ii) Proactively integrating and co-ordinating common items and materials, processes, designs, technologies and suppliers across worldwide purchasing, engineering and operating locations.

Indirect materials All purchased materials and services that do not become part of the company's value proposition. May be classified into MRO-supplies, investment goods (also referred to as capital expenditure, or CAPEX) and services (identical to non-BOM-materials or non-production materials).

Industrial branch Is defined as the horizontal relationship of organizations that experience each other as effective competitors (for example, the leather and footwear industry and the electronics industry).

Industrial buying behaviour Set of internal and external variables and model that explain how organizations make buying decisions.

Industrial column Is defined as a series of companies (links) in which the consecutive stages of production of an economic product take place – from primary producer to consumer.

Innovation, closed Closed innovation implies that companies try to develop new products and processes based on the idea that the company itself has the best possible knowledge and resources for innovation.

Innovation, open The purpose of open innovation is to create close collaboration on research and development, new product design and development and market introduction with parties that would share the company's business interests in such collaboration.

Investment goods or capital equipment Products which are not consumed immediately, but whose purchasing value is depreciated during its economic life cycle.

Just-in-time management (JIT) All materials and products become available at the very moment when they are needed in the production process, not sooner and not later, but exactly on time and in exactly the right quantity.

Kanban Form of just-in-time scheduling based upon fixed volume lot delivery. When a lot is used, the *kanban* (card) will be sent to the supplier as a signal to replenish for that lot.

Kraljic portfolio See 'purchasing portfolio'.

Lean management Lean management is a philosophy concerning how to run a manufacturing organization. It covers all aspects of the business system in general, including design, and manufacturing and supply management in particular. Fundamental to lean management is that it transfers the maximum number of tasks and responsibilities to those workers actually adding value to the car on the line, and it has in place a system for detecting defects that quickly traces every problem, once discovered, to its ultimate cause.

Learning curve The learning curve was originally developed in the American aircraft industry. It was discovered that the cost price per airplane decreased at a fixed percentage as experience, i.e. the cumulative production volume of a particular type of aircraft, doubled.

Logistics management Logistics management includes the management of materials planning, the supply of raw materials and other purchased goods, internal transportation, storage and physical distribution. It may also include, in some companies, reverse logistics, i.e. recycling packaging materials and surplus materials.

Logistics structure, making and sending to stock (MSS) Products are manufactured and distributed to various distribution points which are dispersed and located close to the customer. Manufacturing is based upon forecasts and on the expected stock turnover at the points of distribution.

Logistics structure, making to stock (central stock) (MTS) Finished products are kept in stock at the end of the production process and from there shipped directly to many geographically dispersed customers, as in the manufacture of many consumer electronics products (such as dishwashers and refrigerators).

Logistics structure, assembly to order (ATO) Only systems elements or subassemblies are in stock at the manufacturing centre and final assembly takes place based on a specific customer order. In other words, manufacture of components takes place based on forecasts and final assembly takes place based on customer orders.

Logistics structure, making to order (MTO) Only raw materials and components are kept in stock. Every customer order is a specific project. Examples are the manufacture of cans and basic construction materials.

Logistics structure, engineering and making to order (ETO) In this situation there is no stock at all. The purchase and order of materials takes place on the basis of the specific customer order and the entire project is carried out for this one specific client. As a result this type of production structure results in long lead times.

Macroeconomic research This refers to the general economic and business environment. It focuses on factors that can influence the future balance between supply and demand.

Maintenance, repair and operating materials (MRO items) These products, sometimes referred to as indirect materials or consumable items, represent materials, which are necessary for keeping the organization running in general, and for the support activities in particular.

Make to order (MTO) Only raw materials and components are kept in stock. Every customer order is a specific project. Examples are the manufacture of cans and basic construction materials.

Materials planners Materials planners are responsible for materials planning and ordering. Materials planners focus on calling off the materials required against the prearranged framework agreements. Furthermore, they monitor and control suppliers on their quality and delivery performance.

Mesoeconomic research Research which focuses on specific sectors of industry.

Microeconomic research Research which focuses on assessing strengths and weaknesses of individual suppliers and products.

Market structure Is defined in this book as the total set of conditions in which a company sells its products, with special attention to the number of parties in the market and the nature of the product being traded.

Modified rebuy Relates to a situation when the organization wants to purchase a new product from a known supplier, or an existing product from a new supplier.

Monopoly Is characterized by the presence of only one supplier of the product in question.

Monopolistic competition This market structure is similar to many actual markets and is characterized by a high degree of product differentiation.

Monopsony In this situation there is only one buyer of the product versus a large number of suppliers.

New-task situation Situation when the organization decides to buy a completely new product, supplied by an unknown supplier.

Non-task variables Variables that are related to the personalities of the persons involved in the purchase decision-making process.

NPR buyers These buyers are responsible for buying and non-product-related goods and services.

Offshoring Offshoring relates to the commissioning of work, which was previously done in-house, to a provider in a low-cost country. In many cases, offshoring is concerned with outsourcing of services.

Oligopoly An oligopoly is a market type characterized by a limited number of suppliers and a limited product differentiation.

Oligopsony This is the oligopoly situation in reverse: there are only a few buyers and a large number of suppliers.

Ordering Ordering refers to the placing of purchase orders at a supplier against previously arranged conditions or when orders are placed directly at the supplier, without questioning the supplier's conditions.

Output Relates to the functionality of the service instead of the activity itself.

Outsourcing Outsourcing means that the company divests itself of the resources to fulfil a particular activity to another company, to focus more effectively on its own competence. The difference with subcontracting is the divestment of assets, infrastructure, people and competencies.

Outsourcing, partial Partial outsourcing refers to the case in which only a part of an integrated function is outsourced. The co-ordination of the function and activities still lies with the client (the buyer).

Outsourcing, process The outsourcing process can be structured around essentially three distinct phases: a strategic phase (why, what, who?), a transition phase (how?) and an operation phase (how to manage?).

Outsourcing, turnkey Turnkey outsourcing applies when the responsibility for the execution of the entire outsourced function (or set of outsourced activities) lies with the external provider. This includes not only the execution of the activities, but also the co-ordination of these activities.

Overspecifying A situation in which technical requirements are imposed on suppliers which are not necessary for the functionality of the product.

Partner A (supplier) partner is defined as a firm with whom your company has an ongoing buyer–seller relationship, involving a commitment over an extended period, a mutual sharing of information and a sharing of risks and rewards resulting from the relationship.

Payment terms Payment terms relate to what, how and when the buyer will pay for the products and services delivered by the supplier.

Penalty clause That part of the contract which will stipulate what will happen if a supplier does not meet its obligations.

Price elasticity Extent to which price per unit changes with the volume that is purchased.

Pricing, competitive The price paid for a product is based upon competitive tendering among a number of preselected suppliers. E-auctions or other formal tendering vehicles may be used.

Pricing, cost-based The supplier's sales price is derived directly from its cost price; what most systems boil down to is that a particular profit margin is added to all costs, including the costs of sales (mark-up pricing).

Pricing, going rate In going rate pricing, the firm bases its price largely on competitor prices.

Pricing, market-based The price of the product is determined on the market, and is generated exclusively by market circumstances such as demand, supply, stock positions, the economic situation and political factors.

Pricing, mark-up The most common way of setting a price is by adding a fixed percentage mark-up to the cost price (cost-based pricing).

Pricing, perceived value A general rule in marketing is that you do not base your selling price on the cost price of the product, but rather on what the market can bear. In this reasoning, the price that the buyer is willing to pay is related primarily to the value it attaches to the product. This pricing method is often used for consumer products (well-known branded articles).

Pricing, target return In this situation the price is based on the amount of profit that should be realized. Based on the fixed and variable costs and the expected selling price, the required sales volume is calculated.

Pricing, value Here, the company tries to win customers by charging them fairly low prices for high-quality offerings. Value pricing is not a matter of simply setting lower prices. It is a matter of re-engineering the company's operations to become a low-cost producer without sacrificing quality, and lowering prices significantly to attract a large number of value-conscious customers.

Primary activities Primary activities are those activities that are required to offer the company's value proposition to its customers. They consist of inbound logistics, operations, outbound logistics, marketing and sales and customer service activities.

Principal Provides the assignment to the supplier or service provider. Principal is equivalent to customer or buyer.

Procurement Includes all activities required in order to get the product from the supplier to its final destination. It encompasses the purchasing function, stores, traffic and transportation, incoming inspection and quality control and assurance, allowing companies to make supplier selection decisions based on total cost of ownership (TCO), rather than price. Procurement is used when relating to buying based upon total cost of ownership in a project environment.

Products, bottleneck These items represent a relatively limited value in terms of money but they are vulnerable with regard to their supply. They can only be obtained from one supplier.

Products, leverage In general, these are the products that can be obtained from various suppliers at standard quality grades. They represent a relatively large share of the end product's cost price and are bought at large volumes.

Products, routine These products produce few technical or commercial problems from a purchasing point of view. They usually have a small value per item and there are many alternative suppliers.

Products, strategic These are high-tech, high-volume products, which are often supplied at customer specification.

Public procurement, design contest The design contest is a procedure that is used to obtain a plan or a design based on competition among expert parties. The design is to be judged by a professional jury.

Public procurement, law Public procurement law prescribes in a formal way how to go about government contracts, i.e. how to deal with suppliers and how to award public contracts. Major constituents of public procurement law are the European Public Procurement Directives 2004/17 for the public utilities sector and 2004/18 for the classical government.

Public procurement, negotiation procedure Here, the contracting authority can negotiate face-to-face with market parties about the contents, execution and costs related to the contract. The negotiation procedure can be used with or without (pre)announcement.

Public procurement, principles Four major principles underlie each of the procurement directives. These are nondiscrimination, equality, transparency and proportionality.

Public procurement, procedures Public procurement procedures relate to the procedures that public institutions need to adhere to when making purchasing decisions. Different procedures are: (1) open procedure, (2) restricted procedure, (3) competitive dialogue, (4) negotiated procedure with prior publication of a contract notice (5) negotiated procedure without prior publication of a contract notice and (6) design contest.

Public procurement, restricted procedure This procedure acknowledges two distinct stages: the stage of selecting suppliers that are interested, and the stage in which the preselected suppliers are invited for tender. This procedure is also referred to as the procedure with pre-selection.

Public procurement, open procedure The open procedure implies that every market party within the EU should be able to subscribe to a governmental tender.

Public procurement, scope The European directives apply to all governmental institutions, including the State, regional or local authorities and bodies governed by public law.

Public procurement, threshold values Threshold values represent the purchasing volumes beyond which public institutions are obliged to follow European legislation when making their purchase decisions. There are different threshold values for work, supplies and services.

Purchase order A purchase order is the legal document from a buyer to a supplier requesting delivery. It includes the following entities: a contract number, an order number, a concise description of the product, unit price, number of units required, expected delivery time or date, delivery address and invoicing address. A purchase order may contain several order lines that describe different products that must be delivered.

Purchase order confirmation A document that is used by the supplier in which they agree to perform according to the buyer's purchase order.

Purchasing The management of the company's external resources in such a way that the supply of all goods, services, capabilities and knowledge which are necessary for running, maintaining and managing the company's primary and support activities is secured under the most favourable conditions.

Purchasing and supply development model This model identifies six stages of development over time, indicating how purchasing and supply may develop in terms of professionalism within a company. These six stages are: transaction orientation, commercial orientation, co-ordination orientation, internal integration, external integration and value chain integration.

Purchasing authority Allows a manager to legally bind their company to an external partner.

Purchasing function Covers activities aimed at determining the purchasing specifications based upon 'fitness for use', selecting the best possible supplier and developing procedures and routines to be able to do so, preparing and conducting negotiations with the supplier in order to establish an agreement and to write up the legal contract, placing the order with the selected supplier or to develop efficient purchase order and handling routines, monitoring and control of the order in order to secure supply (expediting), follow-up and evaluation (settling claims, keeping product and supplier files up-to-date, supplier rating and supplier ranking).

Purchasing effectiveness Is defined as the extent to which, by choosing a certain course of action, a previously established goal or standard is being met.

Purchasing efficiency Is related to the resources which are required to realize the previously established goals and objectives and their related activities. Essentially, it refers to the relationship between planned and actual costs.

Purchasing engineer A purchasing engineer is a specialist function in the liaison between the engineering departments and the purchasing department.

Purchasing excellence, model Explains how to professionalize purchasing, making use of two types of processes, i.e. strategic management processes and enabling processes.

Purchasing management Relates to all activities necessary to manage supplier relationships in such a way that their activities are aligned with the company's overall business strategies and interests.

Purchasing market research The systematic gathering, classification and analysis of data considering all relevant factors that influence the procurement of goods and services for the purpose of meeting present and future company requirements.

Purchasing materials budget Reflects, often per product item, the volume which is expected to be purchased for the next planning period, usually a year, and the expected price level for that specific product.

Purchasing performance The extent to which the purchasing function is able to realize its predetermined goals at the sacrifice of a minimum of the company's resources, i.e. costs.

Purchasing performance measurement Four dimensions are suggested on which measurement and evaluation of purchasing activities can be based: (1) a price/cost dimension, (2) a product/quality dimension, (3) a logistics dimension and (4) an organizational dimension.

Purchase (order) specification Relates to all specifications needed to select the right supplier including quality specifications, logistics specifications, maintenance specifications, legal and environmental requirements and a target budget.

Purchasing structure, decentralized A major characteristic is that all business-unit managers are responsible for their own financial results. Hence, the management of the business unit is fully responsible for all its purchasing activities.

Purchasing organization, centralized In this situation at the corporate level, a central purchasing department can be found where corporate contracting specialists operate at the strategic and tactical level.

Purchasing organization, hybrid A hybrid structure represents a combination of the centralized and the decentralized structure. The terms 'hybrid', 'pooling' and 'co-ordination' are used interchangeably. The idea is to combine common materials requirements among two or more business units or companies with the objective to improve purchasing leverage in order to reduce overall materials costs or to improve the service obtained from outside suppliers through a more powerful negotiation position.

Purchasing portfolio, approach (identical to Kraljic portfolio) Portfolio consisting of four quadrants (i.e. leverage products, strategic products, routine products and bottleneck products) based upon two criteria: financial impact and supply risk. Serves to develop four differentiated supplier strategies.

Pure competition Characteristic of this market structure is that neither the supplier nor the buyer can influence the price of the product.

Quality Quality refers to the total of features and characteristics of a product or service that bear on its ability to satisfy a given need (American National Standards Institute). Quality is meeting an (internal or external) customer's requirements that have been formally agreed between a customer and a supplier.

Quality assurance Related to keeping up the methods and procedures of quality management, i.e. systematically checking that they are efficient, that they lead to the desired objective and that they are applied correctly.

Quality costs Relate to three types of costs, i.e. prevention costs (the costs of preventing errors), assessment costs (the costs related to the timely recognition of errors), correction costs (the costs that result from correcting mistakes).

Quality system The collection of methods and procedures used for quality management is called the quality system, which is usually recorded in a quality handbook.

Raw materials Materials which have undergone no transformation or a minimal transformation, and they serve as the basis materials for a production process.

Request for information (RFI) Suppliers are invited to submit general information that may help them to qualify for a potential tender.

Request for proposal (RFP) Suppliers are invited to submit a first proposal prior to the buyer's invitation to tender which meets the requirements as laid down in the request for quotation.

Request for quotation (RFQ) Suppliers are invited to submit a detailed bid which meets the requirements as laid down in the request for quotation against the lowest possible price (identical to request for tender).

Request for tender Suppliers are invited to submit a detailed bid which meets the requirements as laid down in the request for quotation against the lowest possible price (identical to request for quotation).

Residential engineering Situation where engineers from the supplier on a more or less permanent basis are co-located at the buyer's organization, in order to work on design or manufacturing problems which appear during the successive stages of development. Residential engineering also relates to a situation where a large OEM has placed its own engineering specialists at the supplier's premises in order to resolve a variety of technical problems.

Risk, commercial Commercial risk is related to the uncertainty with regard to the price we will pay and the costs that we will incur when having outsourced our activities to the supplier.

Risk, matrix Risks are assessed based on two criteria: (1) the negative impact on the company's financial performance or operations and (2) the likelihood with which the risk factor probably would occur.

Risk, performance These risks relate to the chance that the supplier is not capable of doing the job it was hired for.

Risk, technical This kind of risk is related to the extent to which the provider is able to provide the desired functionality and performance.

Routine buy Relates to the acquisition of a known product from a known supplier (identical to straight rebuy).

Semi-manufactured products These products have already been processed once or more, and they will be processed further at a later stage.

Services (i) Differentiated from goods through four basic characteristics, i.e. intangibility, perishability, heterogeneity and simultaneity. Basically, four types of services can be identified: (1) component services, that are passed on unaltered to the final customers of the buying organization (e.g. luggage handling at the airport for an airline company), (2) semi-manufactured services, that are being integrated into the buying organization's value proposition to its customers (e.g. in-flight catering services contracted for by an airline), (3) instrumental services, that are used by the buying organization to change their primary processes (i.e. management consultancy to professionalize the airline's operational processes) and (4) consumption services, that are used in different support processes within the buying organization (e.g. cleaning services for offices of the same airline company).

Services (ii) Relate to a series of more or less tangible activities, that normally take place in the interaction between customer and supplier employees, and/or physical resources and systems, that are offered as an integrated solution to customer problems.

Service level agreements The functionality of the service is emphasized, i.e. keeping the machine running instead, rather than focusing on how well the maintenance activities were conducted by the supplier.

Service level agreement (SLA) A service level agreement describes the performance which needs to be delivered by the supplier. Key performance indicators (in terms of cost, service and quality levels) are agreed by both parties. Payment to suppliers is based upon specific rates plus a bonus or minus based upon actual performance versus targeted performance.

Sourcing Finding, selecting, contracting and managing the best possible source of supply on a worldwide basis.

Sourcing, global Global sourcing is defined as proactively integrating and coordinating common items and materials, processes, designs, technologies and suppliers across worldwide purchasing, engineering and operating locations.

Sourcing, multiple Situation in which a company within a certain category buys from more than one supplier.

Sourcing, single Situation in which a company within a certain category with clear intent buys from just one supplier.

Sourcing, sole Situation in which a company within a certain category buys, due to external circumstances, from one, monopolist supplier.

Sourcing strategy Identifies for a certain category from how many suppliers to buy, what type of relationship to pursue, contract duration, type of contract to negotiate for, and whether to source locally, regionally or globally.

Space management Computer-supported simulation systems used by retail buyers to optimize their income per square metre of shelf space. These systems enable the simulation of several display layouts (for a different number of facings) based on detailed cost information, to decide on the most profitable layout. Important concepts, underlying space management systems, are direct product cost (DPC) and direct product profitability (DPP).

Straight rebuy Relates to the acquisition of a known product from a known supplier (identical to routine buy).

Strategic triangle Explains how a company positions itself against its three main stakeholders, i.e. customers, competitors and suppliers.

Strategy, cost leadership The main focus of this strategy is to continually work at reducing the cost price of the end product. If a company succeeds in marketing products at a lower cost price than its competitors, it will achieve a satisfactory return.

Strategy, differentiation This strategy aims at marketing products which are perceived by the customer as being unique. Product individuality can be in the design (Swatch watches), the logo (Lacoste), the technology (Apple), service (American Express) and many other dimensions.

Strategy, focus This strategy aims to serve a specific, clearly-defined group of customers in an optimal way. A focus strategy means that the company studies the activities of the customer group, becomes familiar with their operational requirements and provides specific solutions.

Supplementary materials These are materials which are not absorbed physically in the end product; they are used or consumed during the production process.

Supplier assessment, levels Supplier assessment may take place at four different levels of abstraction, i.e. product level, process level, quality assurance system level and company level.

Supplier assessment, methods These include spreadsheets, qualitative assessments, vendor rating, supplier audits and cost modelling.

Supplier development Characteristic for this type of programme is that the buying company shares the benefits gained from all supplier improvement activities that are generated from its suppliers, rather than taking it all itself.

Supplier satisfaction survey Periodically, the buyer invites suppliers through a standardized survey to suggest ideas which may improve business relationships.

Supplier selection Supplier selection relates to all activities, which are required to select the best possible supplier and includes determining the method of subcontracting, preliminary qualification of suppliers and drawing up the 'bidders list', preparation of the request for quotation and analysis of the bids received and selection of the supplier.

Supplier quality assurance (SQA) Supplier quality assurance is all activities conducted by a company to arrive at a zero defects quality performance in its relationship with suppliers.

Supplier segments Suppliers may be classified into different segments, depending on the value and risk which they represent to the company. Segments may include: (1) strategic partners, (2) performance partners, (3) preferred suppliers and (4) competitive suppliers.

Supplier suggestion programme Here the buyer actively solicits ideas for improvement from suppliers. These ideas may relate to new product design, current product designs, operational processes, quality assurance, logistics activities, inventory and distribution activities and transactional processes.

Supply Includes at least purchasing, materials management, incoming inspection and receiving. Supply is used when relating to buying based upon total cost of ownership in a manufacturing environment.

Supply chain A series of companies (links) in which the consecutive stages of production of an economic product take place, from primary producer to final consumer.

Supply chain management The management of all activities, information, knowledge and financial resources associated with the flow and transformation of goods and services up from the raw materials suppliers, component suppliers and other suppliers in such a way that the expectations of the end users of the company are met or surpassed.

Supply market research Defined as the systematic gathering, classification and analysis of data considering all relevant factors that influence the procurement of goods and services for the purpose of meeting present and future company requirements.

Support activities Those value activities that are required to support the company's primary activities. These include procurement, technology development, human resources management and facilities management (i.e. those activities aimed at maintaining the firm's infrastructure).

Task variables Are those variables that are related to the tasks, responsibilities and competences assigned by the organization to the persons involved in the purchase decision-making process.

Technical specification Describes the technical properties and characteristics of the product as well as the activities to be performed by the supplier.

Tender Situation where a buyer asks for bids from different suppliers, creating a level playing field (identical to competitive bidding).

Total cost of ownership (TCO) Relates to the total costs that the company will incur over the lifetime of the product that is purchased.

Trade function Activity aimed at bridging time, place, quantity, assortment and knowledge between a buyer and a seller.

Trade products These encompass all products which are purchased to be sold, after negligible added value, either together with other finished products or manufactured products (identical to finished products).

Transaction costs The costs that are associated with an exchange between two parties. The level of the transaction costs depends upon three important factors: the frequency of the transaction, the level of the transaction-specific investments and the external and internal uncertainty.

Transaction cost approach The transaction cost approach is based on the idea of finding a governance structure to arrive at the lowest cost possible for each transaction and comparing whether to perform an activity internally or outsource the activity in the market.

Value chain Composed of value activities and a margin which is achieved by these activities. Value activities can be divided into primary activities and support activities. The margin represents the value that customers want to pay extra for the company's efforts compared with the costs that were required for these.

Value chain management All stakeholders belonging to the same value chain are challenged to improve the (buying) company's value proposition to its final end customers i.e. consumers.

Vendor managed inventory Is a continuous replenishment programme that uses the exchange of information between the retailer and the supplier to allow the supplier to manage and replenish product at the store or warehouse level. In this programme, the retailer supplies the vendor with the information necessary to maintain just enough products to meet customer demand.

Wholesale Trading firms who deliver their products to other companies. Their customers are the retail, industrial and service companies, which in their turn may deliver directly to the final consumer.

INDEX